The Jew in Medieval Iberia

1100-1500

Jews in Space and Time

ACADEMIC
STUDIES
PRESS

THE JEW IN MEDIEVAL IBERIA

1100-1500

Edited by Jonathan Ray

Boston
2013

Library of Congress Cataloging-in-Publication Data:
A bibliographic record for this title is available from the Library of Congress.

Copyright ©2012 Academic Studies Press
All rights reserved
ISBN 978-1-936235-66-7 (cloth)
ISBN 978-1-61811-292-7 (paper)

Book design by Ivan Grave

On the cover and p. 158: Christ among the Doctors, 1400-1429. Tempera and gold on wood, 44 x 30 in. (111.8 x 76.2 cm). The Friedsam Collection, Bequest of Michael Friedsam, 1931 (32.100.123).
Catalan School.

Illustrations:
p. 142: Panels with scenes from the Life of Christ. 13th century. Spanish. Tempera on wood, Overall (a): 41 3/8 x 15 5/8 x 13/16 in. (105.1 x 39.7 x 2.1 cm) Overall (b): 41 1/2 x 16 3/8 x 13/16 in. (105.4 x 41.6 x 2.1 cm).
The Cloisters Collection (55.62a,b, 1977.94)

p. 144: Scenes from the Life of Saint Andrew. Altarpiece, late 14th century. Spanish, Made in Spain, Castile. Tempera on wood, gold ground. Overall: 78 1/4 x 39 3/4 in. (198.8 x 101 cm). Front View.
The Cloisters Collection, 1925 (25.120.257)

p. 157: Domingo Ram (a. 1464-1507), "Annunciation to Zacharias," Altarpiece of Saint John the Baptist, 1480. Spanish. Tempera on wood, gold ground, 37 1/2 x 27 1/4 in. (95.3 x 69.2 cm) Entire Retable: 139 x 100 in. (353.1 x 254 cm).
The Cloisters Collection (25.120.929).

Images copyright © The Metropolitan Museum of Art.
Images source: Art Resource, NY

Published by Academic Studies Press in 2012, paperback edition 2013.

28 Montfern Avenue
Brighton, MA 02135, USA
press@academicstudiespress.com
www.academicstudiespress.com

Table of Contents

LIST OF ILLUSTRATIONS

Hispano-Jewish Society: An Introduction

Jonathan Ray

The rich history of Iberian Jewry has been a powerful muse for scholars of Jewish and medieval studies for over a century. For many, the subject conjures up images of a Golden Age of Jewish civilization characterized by great material success and an outpouring of religious and intellectual works. For others, this alluring image of Jewish achievement is juxtaposed with, and often overshadowed by, a much darker legacy of marginalization and persecution that culminated in the eventual expulsion of Spanish Jewry in 1492. *The Jew in Medieval Iberia* attempts to embrace this complexity and present a portrait of Jewish life in Christian Iberia that emphasizes both the internal diversity of this community and the variety of ways it interacted with its host society. During the high and late Middle Ages, Iberian Jews fulfilled a number of distinct roles, acting as economic catalysts, diplomats, physicians and transmitters of culture. At the same time, the propagation of Jewish intellectual culture advanced along a variety of different pathways. In the hands of rabbis and Jewish courtiers, this intellectual culture also became linked to the general identity and the social and political fortunes of the average Jew. The essays collected in this volume introduce readers to some of the leading figures and social groups of Hispano-Jewish society, and explore the way in which they responded to the opportunities and challenges of their times.

Historical Overview

In many ways, Jewish life in medieval Iberia was characterized by patterns that were established prior to their settlement in Christian "Spain." Jews had formed an important segment of Iberian society since Roman times, but were subject to erratic and often coercive policies under Visigothic rule. During the period of Muslim dominance in the Peninsula (eighth-eleventh centuries), the Jews created a society whose general prosperity and depth and range of intellectual culture rivaled that of any time or place in Jewish history. Andalusi-Jewish merchants formed part of the trade networks that traversed the medieval Mediterranean, and continued to thrive even after the collapse of Umayyad Córdoba in the early eleventh century. As the Caliphate gave way to independent city-states known as *taifas*, the proliferation of princely courts expanded opportunities for Jewish advisors, tax collectors and other civil servants. These and other wealthy Jews were patrons of religious and literary creativity. Andalusi academies (*yeshivot*) became major centers for exegetical study and the codification of Jewish law. Jewish poets wrote songs of praise for God and Zion, even as they extolled the worldly pleasures of al-Andalus. The general affluence and intellectual dynamism of Jewish life in Muslim Iberia succeeded in attracting Jewish settlers, students and merchants from throughout the medieval Jewish world.[1]

The twelfth century brought with it a protracted period of instability and persecution under the Almoravid and Almohad dynasties that succeeded in driving the majority of Jews out of al-Andalus. Yet, just as Jews were being pushed out of Muslim Iberia, they were simultaneously being pulled into the lands controlled by Christian lords. Between the conquest of Toledo in 1085 to the fall of Seville in 1248, the balance of power in the Peninsula permanently shifted to the Christian kingdoms of Portugal, Castile-Leon and the Crown of Aragon. The dynamic frontier society created by the steady expansion of Christian power in the Peninsula was one in which the Jews would once again thrive as artisans, merchants and

---

[1] Raymond Scheindlin, "Merchants and Intellectuals, Rabbis and Poets: Judeo-Arabic Culture in the Golden Age of Islam," in *Cultures of the Jews: A New History*, ed. David Biale (New York: Schocken, 2002), 313-86.

courtiers. The Arabized Jews came to settle among a native Jewish population that had inhabited the Christian cities of the north for centuries. Together they formed communities that were highly prized by Christian lords as catalysts for economic development, and which were granted a host of privileges in order to secure their permanent settlement in the towns or cities that had recently come under Christian rule.

The relocation of the vast majority of Iberian Jews from Muslim to Christian territories also brought them more firmly within the cultural orbit of medieval Europe. This turn toward Christian Europe resulted in more intimate contact with the Jewish centers of Provence, northern France and the Rhine Valley. During the later Middle Ages, the Jewish communities of Christian Iberia became the site of an important fusion of Andalusi and northern European intellectual traditions. During the twelfth century, Andalusi-born scholars and translators settled north of the Pyrenees, introducing Greco-Arabic science and philosophy to new audiences of Christian and Jewish intellectuals. In the thirteenth century, this earlier wave of refugees was followed by Jewish students from Christian Iberia who traveled northward to study at Ashkenazi *yeshivot*, and who returned home with new insights into Jewish texts. Finally, when political instability wracked the Jewish communities of France and Germany, the flow of Jewish scholars and ideas came full circle. As the Jews were expelled from one region after another, leading Ashkenazi scholars found safe haven among the Jews of Iberia, bringing with them the abundance of their legal and exegetical traditions.[2]

These contacts helped to usher in a new period of mystical speculation throughout Iberia, with distinct centers in northern Castile and Catalonia. The popularity of kabbalah formed part of an expanded curriculum for Hispano-Jewish intellectuals, together with the study of Hebrew grammar, legal codes, and the various fields of science and philosophy.

---

[2] Avraham Grossman, "Relations between Spanish and Ashkenazi Jewry in the Middle Ages," in *Moreshet Sepharad: The Sephardi Legacy*, ed. Haim Beinart, 2 vols. (Jerusalem: Magnes Press, 1992), 1:220-39; and Ephraim Kanarfogel, "Between Ashkenaz and Sepharad: Tosafist Teachings in the Talmudic Commentaries of Ritva," in *Between Rashi and Maimonides: Themes in Medieval Jewish Thought, Literature and Exegesis*, ed. Ephraim Kanarfogel and Moshe Sokolow (New York: Yeshiva University Press, 2010), 237-73.

This amalgamation of religious and intellectual traditions was often contentious. In addition to engaging Christian scholars through public disputations and polemical treatises, leading rabbinic authorities and intellectuals also participated in heated debates among themselves over a wide range of topics. Factions formed among the Jewish intelligentsia that championed various philosophical, legal or mystical schools of thought. In promoting their own methodology for the interpretation of sacred texts, these factions came to challenge the veracity and even the very permissibility of other approaches. Impassioned disputes between Jewish intellectuals raged across northern Iberia and Provence over which of these subjects deserved greater attention, and which posed threats to proper religious observance. Some rabbis went so far as to lobby for the institution of bans against the study of kabbalah or philosophy. Yet despite the intensity of these quarrels, no one faction emerged victorious. Throughout the Middle Ages, and indeed long afterward, the heterogeneity of Hispano-Jewish intellectual culture remained one of its enduring hallmarks.[3]

The relationship between Iberian Jews and the surrounding Christian society was equally varied. Throughout the Middle Ages, the negative images of the Jews as religious outsiders and unwanted economic competitors were mitigated by a number of factors. From the point of view of religion, Jews were seen as guardians of the "Old Law," a fact that brought them a measure of respect among Christian theologians and stimulated hope for their conversion.[4] Economically, the association of Jews with banking and trade led Europe's barons and bishops to prize them as economic catalysts and valuable civil servants. Indeed, in most of medieval Europe, Jewish settlements were the result of efforts on the part of Christian lords to attract Jews as a means to stimulate trade. In addition to these factors, the daily contact between Christians and Jews that took place in towns

---

[3] Idit Dobbs Weinstein, "The Maimonidean Controversy," in *History of Jewish Philosophy*, ed. Daniel H. Frank and Oliver Leaman (London: Routledge, 1997), 331-49; and Bernard Septimus, *Hispano-Jewish Culture in Transition: The Career and Controversies of Ramah* (Cambridge, MA: Harvard University Press, 1982).

[4] Jeremy Cohen, *Living letters of the Law: Ideas of the Jew in Medieval Christianity* (Berkeley, CA: University of California Press, 1999).

and cities all over Iberia also helped to foster amicable ties between members of the two groups.[5]

Religious and social animosities challenged these interfaith relationships. Persistent theological opposition to the practice of lending money at interest generally, and the outright prohibition of such activity among Christians, cast such financial activity in a negative light. The figure of the Jewish money lender was lampooned in Spanish literary and artistic classics such as the epic poem *El Cantar de Mio Cid*, and the great compendium of illustrated songs the *Cantigas de Santa Maria*.[6] Nonetheless, such efforts to disparage both the general practice of money lending and Jewish association with it in particular did little to decrease Christian society's dependence upon such transactions. By the twelfth century, credit had already become firmly established within European economy, and was an essential feature of urban life.[7]

Indeed, it was Hispano-Christian society's steady acceptance of banking, not its demonization, that had the greatest impact on the Jews. As elsewhere in medieval Europe, the expansion of Christian involvement in banking and commerce together with the formation of organized artisan guilds led to decreased dependence upon the Jews, and eventually to their exclusion from these activities in many cities.

The growth of towns in Christian Iberia produced an increasingly large and active cohort of Christian merchants, bankers and artisans. As these groups developed, they viewed the Jews as unwanted competitors, and sought to exclude them from various sectors of the economy. The Jews fought back against this economic marginalization as best they could, petitioning the crown for defense of their rights, and making accommodations with their Christian

---

[5] Jonathan Ray, "Jew in the Text: What Christian Charters Tell us about Medieval Jewish Society," *Medieval Encounters* 16 (2010): 243-67.

[6] Dwayne E. Carpenter, "The Portrayal of the Jew in Alfonso the Learned's 'Cantigas de Santa Maria,'" in *In Iberia and Beyond*, ed. Bernard Dov Cooperman (Newark, DE: University of Delaware Press, 1998), 15-42; and Louise Mirrer, "Representing "Other" Men: Muslims, Jews and Masculine Ideals in Medieval Castilian Epic and Ballad," in *Medieval Masculinities: Regarding Men in the Middle Ages*, ed. Clare A. Lees (Minneapolis, MN: University of Minnesota Press, 1994), 169-86.

[7] Kenneth R. Stow, "Papal and Royal Attitudes toward Jewish Lending in the 13th century," *AJS Review* 6 (1981): 161-84.

neighbors whenever possible. Jews remained active in banking and commerce, lending money and acting as investors or silent partners with Christians involved in long-distance trade. However, as Christian influence in these areas continued to grow over the course of the fourteenth and fifteenth century, the economic balance of power shifted decisively away from the Jews.

During the period of Jewish resettlement in Christian lands (roughly the eleventh to thirteenth centuries), life in the Iberian Peninsula had been dominated by warfare between Muslim and Christian lords. During this period of nearly constant religious and political conflict, the region's Jews benefited from their position as non-combatants. They played the role of economic and cultural intermediaries between Muslim and Christian society and held positions as diplomats, translators, and trusted advisors. However, after the mid-thirteenth century, a series of transformations within Hispano-Christian society came to have a deleterious effect on the status of Iberian Jewry.

Perhaps the most significant development was the suspension of Christian participation in the so-called *Reconquista* by the end of the thirteenth century. As royal energies shifted from conquest of the Peninsula's remaining Muslim territory to political, social and economic consolidation of lands already won, Christian society began to evolve from one organized for war to one characterized by an interest in commerce, legal administration, and the establishment of artisans' guilds. These developments dramatically reduced Christian society's need for the Jews. At the same time, the Jews' special status as a royally protected minority whose taxes benefited the crown rather than the local municipalities or the Church began to foster popular resentment among the other sectors of Christian society. This negative association between the Jews and the crown was further exacerbated by the latter's growing power. Over the course of the thirteenth and fourteenth centuries, the Church, the nobility and the towns of the Spanish kingdoms all began to chafe under the expanding authority of the various peninsular monarchies. As resentment of this political centralization of power increased, one of the easiest ways to lash out against it was to attack the status of the protected minorities: Jews and Muslims.

In the domain of religion, the spirit of reform that began to sweep through Hispano-Christian society during the thirteenth century[8] also had a critical impact on the Jews in their midst. Missionary efforts to enhance Christian religious devotion and practice also led to an associated interest in converting the Peninsula's Jewish and Muslim communities. Jews were subjected to sermons by Christian preachers and forced to participate in public disputations. Christian interest in religious reform and the concerted push to convert the Jews galvanized the religious leadership within Iberia's Jewish *aljamas*. As rabbinical authorities became increasingly concerned with the corrosive effects of this new missionary activity, they too took up the question of reform. Perennial themes of Jewish moralists and religious leaders, such as the irreverent attitudes of Jewish courtiers, the study of "foreign" (non-rabbinic) literature among Jewish intellectuals, and the general question of popular piety and religious observance, now garnered new attention. The intensification of Jewish spirituality also found expression in various confraternal organizations. Groups of Jews came together to form private fellowships (*havurot*) or *Talmud Torah* societies that engaged in pious acts ranging from extraordinary sessions of prayer and penitence to providing for the education and material wellbeing of the Jewish poor.[9]

As threats to Jewish status and security developed along a number of fronts, the Jews became increasingly dependent upon the efficacy of royal protection. The deterioration of both the will and the ability of the various peninsular monarchs to defend their Jewish subjects was, perhaps, the most troubling change that took place during the fourteenth century. To be sure, the actual implementation of anti-Jewish policies was erratic. Most kings continued to show little interest in enforcing regulations such as the prohibition of Jews from serving as courtiers and the requirement that they wear a distinguishing mark on their outer garments. Nonetheless, their recognition of

---

[8] Jonathan Ray, *The Sephardic Frontier: The Reconquista and the Jewish Community in Medieval Iberia* (Ithaca, NY: Cornell University Press, 2006).

[9] Yom Tov Assis, "Welfare and Mutual Aid in Spanish-Jewish Communities," in *Moreshet Sepharad: The Sephardi Legacy*, ed. Haim Beinart, 2 vols. (Jerusalem: Magnes Press, 1992), 1:318-45; and Judah Galinsky, "Jewish Charitable Bequests and the Hekdesh Trust in Thirteenth-Century Spain," *Journal of Interdisciplinary History* 35 (2004): 423-40.

the popular and ecclesiastical hostility toward the Jews represented an ominous development. Where the kings of Castile and Aragon had previously been staunch defenders of Jewish rights, those who came to power in the mid- to late fourteenth century began to show an increased willingness to curtail Jewish rights in order to mollify their critics and win popular support. With the outbreak of Civil War in Castile in the 1360s, Count Henry de Trastamara played on popular animosity against the Jews to help win support for his bid for the throne. Once in power, the newly crowned Henry II quickly reverted to the longstanding policy of using Jews as royal advisors and administrators.

This cynical manipulation of anti-Jewish sentiment also characterized the career of the influential cleric from Seville, Ferrant Martinez, who used his sermons to incite mobs to attack and forcibly convert Jews. The crown, the nobility and the Church all officially censured such attacks, but proved relatively powerless to prevent them. In the Crown of Aragon, the itinerant Dominican preacher Vicente Ferrer represented a very different approach to the new Christian mission to the Jews. Ferrer was genuinely motivated by theological concerns, and his successful conversion of prominent rabbis such as Solomon Halevi and Joshua Halorki suggest a more intellectual methodology than that of his Castilian counterpart. In any event, both tactics proved disastrous for Iberian Jewry.[10]

The combination of political opportunism and popular religious zeal came to a head in the spring and summer of 1391, setting off a wave of destruction and conversion that swept across much of the Peninsula. The mass conversions prompted by these riots devastated many of the Jewish communities, and were followed by decades of continued missionary fervor. Although the ecclesiastical intention of converting the remainder of Iberian Jewry was never fully realized, the creation of a *converso* society succeeded in adding yet another dimension to the complex framework of the Hispano-Jewish community during its final century on Iberian soil.

Medieval rabbinic authorities were fairly uniform in their categorization of the conversos as *"anusim"* or "forced converts,"

---

[10] Benjamin R. Gampel, "A Letter to a Wayward Teacher: Transformation of Sephardic Culture in Christian Iberia," in *Cultures of the Jews: A New History,* ed. David Biale (New York: Schocken, 2002), 389-447.

and thus still Jews.[11] However, popular Jewish opinion with regard to the conversos was far more complex. While many Jews showed deep sympathy for the plight of the conversos, others questioned their allegiance to Judaism, even accusing the converts and their offspring of being opportunists who readily embraced the social and economic benefits of Christian identity. The disparity in Jewish attitudes regarding converso society was often bound up with the particulars of each situation. Family ties, personal misfortunes, and petty-jealousies determined how Jews thought about their former coreligionists as much as did the pronouncements of their rabbinic leaders.

Among the conversos, too, there existed a variety of responses to their sudden change in religious status. Many came to accommodate themselves to their new religion, a trend that increased among later generations that had no personal memory of professing Judaism. Some conversos even emerged as leading Christian theologians. Others remained steadfast to their ancestral religion, and maintained close ties to their Jewish friends and relatives who aided them in their secret efforts to observe a form of "crypto-Judaism."

By the late fifteenth century, the uncertainty over their religious allegiances was sufficiently widespread and enduring that it prompted King Ferdinand and Queen Isabella to search for a permanent solution. After years of attempting to enforce the separation of the Jewish and converso communities and quiet rumors of crypto-Judaism among the latter, the Catholic Monarchs established a new office of the Inquisition under their direct control in order to ascertain the true religious character of the new Christians. This kingdom-wide Castilian Inquisition (later to be known as the Spanish Inquisition) began to operate in 1480, and soon reported back to the crown that the single greatest impediment to the true Christianization of the conversos was their ongoing relationship with their Jewish neighbors. The crown ordered the expulsion of the Jews from the province of Andalucía in 1483, and from Zaragoza and Albarracín in 1486. Neither proved effective, but the monarchs remained committed to resolving the problem of converso religiosity

---

[11] Benzion Netanyahu, *The Marranos of Spain: From the Late 14th to the Early 16th Century, According to Contemporary Hebrew Sources* (Ithaca, NY: Cornell University Press, 1999), 5-76.

through the physical removal of the Jews. This policy culminated in the expulsion of all Jews from Spanish territories in 1492.[12]

The Diversity of Hispano-Jewish Society

The preceding narrative is offered as a basic description of Jewish history in medieval Iberia. However, while the triumphs and tragedies of Hispano-Jewish civilization were undeniably significant, it would be misleading to imagine this society as a collection of pious intellectuals and unfortunate victims. Indeed, both the outstanding cultural achievements of Iberian Jewry and their eventual social and economic marginalization threaten to overshadow the community's remarkable diversity. Any attempt at understanding the way in which the Jews experienced life in medieval Iberia must take into consideration the multifaceted nature of Jewish society.

For medieval Jews, daily life was shaped by personal wealth, power, gender, profession, and geographical location as well as by their religious traditions. The highly localized character of Hispano-Jewish society reflected the general structure of medieval Iberia. Between 1000 and 1500, the borders of Christian Iberia were in a state of flux as Christian princes battled Muslim armies and each other. The region of Murcia passed between the crowns of Castile and Aragon, while Mallorca and Provence moved between Aragon and independence. A politically unified Spain did not begin to coalesce until the very end of the Middle Ages, and even then there existed little in the way of a national culture or ideology. Indeed, despite the best efforts of Iberian monarchs to centralize political authority in their realms, regional political and cultural identities remained strong throughout the Middle Ages. This regionalism also colored the attitudes and identities of Iberian Jews.

Even the impact of 1391 and the conversionary pressure that came in its wake varied significantly from one region to another. In Catalonia, the Jewish population was decimated, while the Jewish communities of other regions, such as the Kingdom of Portugal,

---

[12] For a concise overview of the Jews' final century in Spain, see Eleazar Gutwirth, "Towards Expulsion: 1391-1492," in *Spain and the Jews: The Sephardi Experience, 1492 and After*, ed. Elie Kedourie (London: Thames and Hudson, 1992), 51-73.

emerged intact. In cities such as Valencia, Toledo, and Seville, the riots created a complex situation in which significant numbers of Jews and conversos were left to share the same neighborhoods. The mixed legacy of 1391 also meant that the triangular relationship between Jews, conversos, and "Old" Christians would continue to follow different paths over the course of the fifteenth century. The anti-converso legislation and popular violence that took place in Toledo in 1449 strongly linked the Jews to the deteriorating position of the New Christians, while in other towns the three groups established a working relationship that functioned to their mutual benefit.[13]

Within a given city, the daily experience of different sectors of Jewish society differed from one another. The independent municipal *aljama*, which was the standard structure of Jewish political organization in medieval Iberia, was essentially a loose association of extended families, intellectual circles and other social groups. Internal divisions posed perennial challenges to Jewish communal authority that were as great as or greater than those from the external Christian world. Religious identity distinguished Jews from their Christian and Muslim neighbors, but fell short of producing a truly unified community. For most Jews, respect for the Jewish legal traditions and for the authorities responsible for their implementation remained strong. However, such respect did not preclude them from bending Jewish law and challenging or ignoring communal authorities when it suited them to do so. The ability of prominent Jews to circumvent their communal councils through direct appeals to the crown had a particularly destabilizing effect. Moreover, the special rights and privileges granted to well-connected merchants and courtiers often came at the expense of other sectors of Jewish society. Success in obtaining royal exemptions from taxes transferred the tax burden to other members of the community. Similarly, the increased centralization of royal power in the various peninsular kingdoms might have strengthened the position of Jewish courtiers, but the latter often used their newfound power

---

[13] See the contrasting situation in Castile and Valencia in Angus MacKay, "Popular Movements and Pogroms in Fifteenth-Century Castile," *Past and Present* 55 (1972): 33-67; and Mark D. Meyerson, *A Jewish Renaissance in Fifteenth-Century Spain* (Princeton, NJ: Princeton University Press, 2004), chapter 6.

to undermine the governing councils of local Jewish *aljamas*. In turn, the leaders of these communities fiercely defended their right to religious and political autonomy, but were frequently unable to exercise control over their communities without the support or intervention of Christian authorities.[14]

The Jew in Medieval Iberia examines the composition and contributions of Hispano-Jewish society through a collection of studies of the various roles played by different sectors of the Jewish community. In so doing, it endeavors to provide a fresh look at the ways in which medieval Jews conceived of themselves and their communities, as well as their relationship to the surrounding society. The essays presented here offer an important corrective to a once dominant view that portrayed Jewish life in Christian Spain as a period of steady cultural decline, and underscore the remarkable resilience of Iberian Jews. They transcend older stereotypes of Christian persecution and Jewish piety to reveal complex and vibrant Jewish communities of merchants and scholars, townsmen and -women, cultural intermediaries and guardians of religious tradition. The portrait that is painted by these collected studies is offered as a learned and wide-ranging introduction to Jewish life in Christian Iberia.

While the participation of medieval Jews in fields such as medicine, philosophy, and commerce is generally recognized as an important feature of medieval society, it is far less common to consider Jewish physicians, intellectuals and merchants of medieval Iberia as distinct social types. The essays by Yom Tov Assis, Gregory Milton and Maud Kozodoy help to contextualize the function of Jewish merchants, financiers and physicians within both Jewish and general medieval society. These authors look at the way in which the experience of these groups differed from others within the Jewish community, as well as the way in which their activities shaped the relationship between Jewish and Christian society.

In addition to these more familiar figures, the medieval Jewish community also included groups that have heretofore commanded relatively little scholarly attention. The chapters by Renée Levine Melammed and Vivian Mann discuss the experience of two

---

[14] Ray, *Sephardic Frontier,* chapters 5-6.

segments of Hispano-Jewish society: Jewish women and artists, whose contributions to the representation and practice of Judaism greatly amplify our notion of Jewish-Christian relations in the Middle Ages. Levine Melammed's study argues that the experience of Jewish women was not always the same as that of Jewish men, and reminds us that gender is as important a category as profession or religious school of thought to understanding the course of Jewish history in medieval Iberia. Far from being the passive-but-pious two-dimensional figures that we encounter in more traditional histories of medieval Jewish life, women in Hispano-Jewish and converso communities were often skillful, independent-minded Jews who were actively engaged in a broad range of social and economic activities, as well as in the propagation of Judaism.

Leadership of this multifaceted Jewish community required talents that were equally wide-ranging and diverse. Jewish courtiers and rabbis were figures who straddled the divide between social and intellectual history. They could be venal and excessively combative, yet as communal leaders they often succeeded in rising to meet the social and intellectual challenges of the day, especially in the tumultuous period after 1391. They sought to hold together an assortment of competing Jewish factions and ideologies, while at the same time responding to the shifting demands of Christian political and religious culture. Jonathan Decter, Eric Lawee and Ram Ben Shalom offer three different takes on the nature of Jewish communal leadership in Medieval Iberia. Each of their studies shows that the course of Hispano-Jewish history was often determined by the efforts and personal characteristics of particular individuals. Their essays also emphasize the multifaceted nature of the Hispano-Jewish religious landscape, complicating the notion of Sephardic Judaism. Hartley Lachter's discussion of Castilian Jews as keepers of a secret esoteric tradition provides further evidence of the breadth and complexity of Judaism in Christian Iberia.

Many of these essays also demonstrate the interrelation between Jewish intellectual and social life. The role of the Jew as cultural intermediary is a central theme of Mariano Gomez-Aranda's study of Jewish scientists and philosophers and Jane Gerber's chapter on the Samuel Halevi synagogue in Toledo. Both authors, along with several others in this volume, highlight the continued importance of Andalusi intellectual traditions to the social and cultural identity of the Jews in Christian lands. They also note that the persistence of certain elements of the Andalusi intellectual curriculum was as controversial as it was enduring, a theme of Hispano-Jewish society that is taken up by Esperanza Alfonso in the book's final essay. Alfonso's analysis of a single rabbinic commentary reveals that the heirs to the cultural legacy of Iberian Jewry continued to fight among themselves for the recognition of their own particular version of this legacy. Her essay takes our narrative past the great expulsion of 1492, and regards the history of Iberian Jewry from the vantage point of the Sephardic Diaspora. In it, she demonstrates how Jewish scholars continued to promote certain aspects of the region's intellectual heritage as more authentic and correct. In so doing, they often emphasized the importance of their own familial and scholarly genealogies. Members of these great clans saw themselves as the protectors of particular cultural traditions as much as they did defenders of the Jewish heritage, broadly construed.

In sum, the following essays identify the major trends and defining characteristics of Hispano-Jewish life. They shed new light on the place of the Jew in medieval Iberian history, illuminating the contributions of both the famous and the anonymous. They suggest the need to consider Jewish society from a variety of different vantage points in order to better understand it. Furthermore, they assert the importance of this society to the development of both medieval and Jewish history. Rather than view the Jews of Christian Spain merely as tragic figures, victims of a persecuting society and intellectually inferior to their Andalusi predecessors, they present them as part of a vital nexus in the long continuum of Jewish history. The culture produced by these Jews combined and amplified the intellectual heritages of Andalusi and Franco-German Jewry, and became the bedrock of post-expulsion Sephardic religious life.

Works Cited

Assis, Yom Tov. "Welfare and Mutual Aid in Spanish-Jewish Communities." In *Moreshet Sepharad: The Sephardi Legacy*, edited by Haim Beinart, 2 vols., 1:318-45. Jerusalem: Magnes Press, 1992.

Carpenter, Dwayne E. "The Portrayal of the Jew in Alfonso the Learned's 'Cantigas de Santa Maria.'" In *In Iberia and Beyond*, edited by Bernard Dov Cooperman, 15-42. Newark, DE: University of Delaware Press, 1998.

Cohen, Jeremy. *Living letters of the Law: Ideas of the Jew in Medieval Christianity*. Berkeley, CA: University of California Press, 1999.

Dobbs Weinstein, Idit. "The Maimonidean Controversy." In *History of Jewish Philosophy*, edited by Daniel H. Frank and Oliver Leaman, 331-49. London: Routledge, 1997.

Galinsky, Judah. "Jewish Charitable Bequests and the Hekdesh Trust in Thirteenth-Century Spain." *Journal of Interdisciplinary History* 35 (2004): 423-40.

Gampel, Benjamin R. "A Letter to a Wayward Teacher: Transformation of Sephardic Culture in Christian Iberia," in *Cultures of the Jews: A New History*, edited by David Biale, 389-47. New York, NY: Schocken, 2002.

Grossman, Avraham. "Relations between Spanish and Ashkenazi Jewry in the Middle Ages," in *Moreshet Sepharad: The Sephardi Legacy*, edited by Haim Beinart, 2 vols., 1:220-39. Jerusalem: Magnes Press, 1992.

Gutwirth, Eleazar. "Towards Expulsion: 1391-1492." In *Spain and the Jews: The Sephardi Experience, 1492 and After*, edited by Elie Kedourie, 51-73. London: Thames and Hudson, 1992.

Kanarfogel, Ephraim. "Between Ashkenaz and Sepharad: Tosafist Teachings in the Talmudic Commentaries of Ritva." In *Between Rashi and Maimonides: Themes in Medieval Jewish Thought, Literature and Exegesis*, edited by Ephraim Kanarfogel and Moshe Sokolow, 237-73. New York: Yeshiva University Press, 2010.

MacKay, Angus. "Popular Movements and Pogroms in Fifteenth-Century Castile." *Past and Present* 55 (1972): 33-67.

Meyerson, Mark D. *A Jewish Renaissance in Fifteenth-Century Spain.* Princeton, NJ: Princeton University Press, 2004.

Mirrer, Louise. "Representing "Other" Men: Muslims, Jews and Masculine Ideals in Medieval Castilian Epic and Ballad." In *Medieval Masculinities: Regarding Men in the Middle Ages,* edited by Clare A. Lees, Minneapolis, 169-86. MN: University of Minnesota Press, 1994.

Ray, Jonathan. *The Sephardic Frontier: The Reconquista and the Jewish Community in Medieval Iberia.* Ithaca, NY: Cornell University Press, 2006.

------. "The Jew in the Text: What Christian Charters Tell Us about Medieval Jewish Society." *Medieval Encounters* 16 (2010): 243-67.

Scheindlin, Raymond. "Merchants and Intellectuals, Rabbis and Poets: Judeo-Arabic Culture in the Golden Age of Islam." In *Cultures of the Jews: A New History,* edited by David Biale, 313-86. New York: Schocken, 2002.

Septimus, Bernard. *Hispano-Jewish Culture in Transition: The Career and Controversies of Ramah.* Cambridge, MA: Harvard University Press, 1982.

Stow, Kenneth R. "Papal and Royal Attitudes toward Jewish Lending in the 13th century." *AJS Review* 6 (1981): 161-84.

Before Caliphs and Kings: Jewish Courtiers in Medieval Iberia

....   Jonathan P. Decter

Jewish men were a common presence in the courts of medieval Iberian rulers, from the times of the caliphs at Córdoba down through the era of the Catholic Monarchs who expelled the Jews. For the founders of the academic field of Jewish studies in nineteenth-century Germany, Iberian court Jews were a subject of fascination, for their existence seemed to augur the Jewish entry into European history and to validate the aspirations of an emancipation-oriented Jewry. Heinrich Graetz, a nineteenth-century pioneer in the field of Jewish history, described Hasdai ibn Shaprut, the first Jewish courtier of note in al-Andalus, as:

> quite modern in his character, entirely different from the type of his predecessors. His easy, pliant, and genial nature was free both from the heaviness of the Orientals and the gloomy earnestness of the Jews. His actions and expressions make us look upon him as a European, and through him, so to speak, Jewish history receives a European character.[1]

For this seminal figure of Jewish historical studies, the Arabic-speaking Jewish courtier was neither Arab nor (typically) Jewish but

---

[1] Heinrich Graetz, *History of the Jews: From the Earliest Times to the Present Day*, partially translated by Bella Löwy (London: David Nutt, 1892), 3:220-21.

1

was most essentially *European*, an identity that would have been entirely foreign to Ibn Shaprut and that would not emerge in earnest for centuries. At the same time, Graetz did not view Ibn Shaprut's aspiration for power in opportunistic terms but rather cast the leader as one who safeguarded the needs of his community, "[Ibn Shaprut] inspired a favorable opinion of his co-religionists amongst the Andalusian Moslems, and was able, through his personal intercourse with the Caliphs, to shield them from misrepresentation."[2]

A fuller treatment of court Jews (though not dealing with medieval Iberia for the most part) was undertaken in the twentieth century by Selma Stern, whose book *The Court Jew* (1950) became a classic.[3] For Stern, the Jews who inhabited the halls of kings were the "forerunners of the emancipation;" the court Jew "attempted to achieve a synthesis between the two worlds [i.e., Jewish and gentile] without surrendering his identity."[4] Stern's book was sharply critiqued by the German-Jewish political theorist Hannah Arendt, who attributed to Stern's study "remnants of apologetics" and described Stern as being "haunted by the question of collective Jewish responsibility for certain activities of court Jews, which have turned out to be so obviously destructive to the general population."[5] Arendt was writing soon after the Holocaust and judged pre-modern court Jews not as harbingers of the Emancipation but rather as "dictators in their communities" who foreshadowed those Jews who were appointed by the Nazis to control the ghetto populations. She was troubled by the faith Jews had historically invested in what has been termed the "myth of the royal alliance"—the belief that a tacit reciprocal contract existed by which Jews who committed their loyalty to rulers would enjoy protection and favor.[6]

---

[2] Graetz, *History of the Jews*, 3:222.

[3] Selma Stern, *The Court Jew: A Contribution to the History of the Period of Absolutism in Central Europe*, trans. Ralph Weiman (Philadelphia: Jewish Publication Society, 1950). The book was first written in German, though the earliest published version was this English translation.

[4] Marina Sassenberg, "The Face of Janus: The Historian Selma Stern (1890-1981) and Her Portrait of the Court Jew," *European Judaism* 33 (2000): 72-79, here 73-74.

[5] The review appeared in *Jewish Social Studies* 14 (1957): 176-8.

[6] This is only hinted at in the review of Stern. For the phrase "dictators in their communities," see Hannah Arendt, *The Origins of Totalitarianism* (New York: Harcourt, Brace, 1951), ix and elsewhere. See also the discussion in the review essay by Elliot Horowitz, "The Court Jews and the Jewish Question," *Jewish History* 12 (1998): 113-36. For the "myth of the royal alliance," see Yosef Hayim Yerushalmi, *The Lisbon Massacre of 1506 and the Royal Image in the* Shebet Yehudah (Cincinnati: Hebrew Union College, 1976).

To ask whether the Jews of the medieval Iberian courts were the predecessors either of prominent Jewish citizens of modern states or sinister accomplices of the Nazis is, of course, not fair. The question is not a simple "either/or," nor is it the only one we might ask about these figures, who cannot be collapsed into a single category or be understood apart from their immediate contexts.[7] Why should we hold Jewish courtiers to a higher standard of ethical conduct than Muslim or Christian courtiers in their respective kingdoms? Like most figures of power in a variety of political structures, Jewish courtiers in medieval Iberia felt pressure from rulers and from the ruled, and struck (different) balances between bolstering their own positions and securing the interests of those beneath them. And like other political figures, they had their share of triumphs, foibles, moral shortcomings, and scandals.

The question I wish to address in this essay deals less with the courtiers' loyalty to their coreligionists—though data will be reviewed on this question as well—than with the function(s) Jewish courtiers held for the non-Jewish rulers they served. This question will be pursued with an eye directed toward local and changing Iberian contexts. To understand the place of Jewish courtiers in medieval Iberia, it is perhaps best to take a broad view of the subject, looking at Muslim and Christian contexts from the tenth through the fifteenth centuries, though a singular vector of continuity should not be presumed. Thus the essay will focus on three individuals from different moments in Iberian history: 1) Hasdai ibn Shaprut (ca. 915-970), who served the Caliph 'Abd al-Rahmān III during the period of Umayyad rule in al-Andalus; 2) Abraham ibn al-Fakhār (d. ca. 1239), who served Alfonso VIII of Castile at the height of the so-called Reconquista; and 3) Isaac Abravanel (1437-1508), who was born in

---

[7] This question has been foremost in much scholarly literature concerning Iberian court Jews. In addition to the sources above in note 6, see Haim Beinart, "*Demutah shel ha-hazranut ha-yehudit bi-Sefarad*," in *Qevusot 'elit ve-shikhvot manhigot be-toledot Yisra'el u-ve-toledot ha-'amim* (Jerusalem: Ha-hevrah ha-historit ha-Yisra'elit, 1966), 55-71. Some other questions are posed by David Wasserstein regarding the social roles of Jewish elites in al-Andalus, particularly their connections with Muslim elites, etc.; Wasserstein is rather pessimistic about answering these questions, given the paucity of sources. Still, the questions are valuable. See David Wasserstein, "Jewish Elites in al-Andalus," in *The Jews of Medieval Islam: Community, Society, and Identity*, ed. Daniel Frank (Leiden: Brill, 1992), 101-10, here 103.

Portugal, where he served King Afonso V before fleeing to Castile, where he became a significant figure at the court of Ferdinand and Isabella during the final decade leading up to the Expulsion of 1492 (after which he settled in Naples and later Venice, where he died). Each figure will be contextualized within his historical moment, and other courtier personalities will be discussed as well. This structure will not only show the high visibility of Jews within the courts of Muslim and Christian rulers but also highlight continuities and discontinuities in their functions as well as the extent and limit of their authority and influence.

At the Court of 'Abd al-Rahman III: Hasdai Ibn Shaprut in al-Andalus[8]

The rise of Jewish courtiers in Islamic Iberia must be seen as part of a broader phenomenon within the Islamic world. Before Hasdai ibn Shaprut rose to power in Umayyad al-Andalus, Joseph Ben Pinhas and Aaron Ben Amram were powerful bankers in 'Abbasid Baghdad.[9] Contemporary with Ibn Shaprut was Jacob ibn Qillis, who held powerful positions at Fatimid outposts and ultimately converted to Islam, which enhanced his power further still.[10] Despite theoretical restrictions in Islamic legal literature limiting Jews and Christians from wielding power over Muslims, and protestations from jurists that such restrictions were not being followed, caliphs of various dynasties found it advantageous to employ religious minorities within their ranks, most often as bankers, physicians, and astronomers/astrologers, more rarely as diplomats, scribes (*kātibs*) and viziers (*wazīrs*). Partly a result of the relative tolerance Islam extended toward non-Muslim minorities, the position of *dhimma* courtiers should also be viewed as a strategic means of cultivating

---

[8] The biographical sketch is based on a judicious reading of the chapter on Ibn Shaprut in Eliahu Ashtor, *The Jews of Moslem Spain* (Philadelphia: Jewish Publication Society, 1992), 1:155-227, and a revisiting of many of the sources therein. See also other sources below.

[9] Walter Fischel, *Jews in the Economic and Political Life of Mediaeval Islam* (London: The Royal Asiatic Society, 1937).

[10] Mark Cohen and Sasson Somekh, "In the Court of Ya'qūb Ibn Killis: A Fragment from the Cairo Genizah," *Jewish Quarterly Review* 80 (1990): 283-314.

and securing the loyalty of minority communities and their (sometimes wealthy) leaders, an interest that had to be balanced with preserving the Islamic character of the state.

It is generally unclear what enabled particular Jews access to Muslim courts. Some hailed from prominent families, though courtier positions only seldom passed from father to son. Many held simultaneous positions as heads of Jewish communities, though it is difficult to tell whether this was the cause or the effect of their prominence at court. Some possessed resources or specific skills (in medicine, finance, or epistle writing), and we might presume that Jewish diplomats possessed the skills for which diplomats are traditionally known— cultural adaptability, social grace, and eloquence. But again, it is generally unclear how these skills translated into actual positions.

It is thus not surprising that a cloud of fog surrounds the rise to prominence of Hasdai ibn Shaprut, the aforementioned courtier romanticized by Graetz and whose mystique has been recalled in publications down to the present.[11] Ibn Shaprut served 'Abd al-Rahmān III (891-961), the first Umayyad ruler to declare himself Caliph, thereby challenging the legitimacy of the 'Abbasid empire whose capital was Baghdad. 'Abd al-Rahmān's royal entourage included a mixture of Andalusi ethnic (Arab, Berber, Hispano-Muslim) and religious (Muslim, Christian, Jewish) groups as well as non-Andalusi Muslims, and had a bureaucratic structure that was likely designed to create unity out of the cacophony of political, ethnic, religious, and ideological divisions that had generated conflict on the Peninsula.

---

[11] As late as the 1960s, in Israel rather than Europe, Ibn Shaprut was the subject of significant romanticization. Ashtor wrote regarding Ibn Shaprut (*The Jews of Moslem Spain*, 159), "In the 940s there rose into the ascendant in the skies of Andalusia the star of a court Jew." On the question of the balance of Ibn Shaprut's self-interest versus his imperative to protect his fellow Jews, Ashtor was mixed. At one point (160), he wrote, "He was not concerned about the welfare of the masses, but rather sought for himself happiness, success, and wealth. Hasdai believed in himself, in his ability, and in his future." Elsewhere (183), he wrote, "No matter how wrapped up he was in the governmental affairs of the kingdom of 'Abdarrahmān III, Hasdai Ibn Shaprut never forgot his origin. On the contrary, he endeavored with all his power to exploit the opportunities given him to do good for his people wherever they were.... Hasdai—and other Jewish courtiers who came later resembled him in this respect—did not sever himself from his people but was always with them, at least in spirit." Ibn Shaprut continues to be the subject of many articles, particularly in European languages.

The prestigious position afforded non-Muslims in the Umayyad government proved to be a source of both strength and weakness, since it procured the loyalty of minority religious communities even as it fomented opposition among some Muslims, the judicial class in particular.

As far as can be discerned, Ibn Shaprut was never granted an official title such as *wazīr* (vizier) or *kātib* (scribe) within ʿAbd al-Rahmān's court.[12] It is generally presumed that his entre into court life was possible due to his knowledge of pharmacology and medicine, though this is not certain. Ibn Shaprut is credited by the Muslim historian of medicine Ibn Abi Uṣaybiʿa with rediscovering the correct blend of herbs for theriaca, an elixir whose precise compound had proved elusive since the days of the ancient Romans. Ibn Shaprut was already well-established at court when he collaborated on the translation from Greek into Arabic of the pharmacological treatise *De Materia Medica* by Dioscorides, which had been sent as a gift to ʿAbd al-Rahmān by the emperor of Byzantium, a kingdom with which the Caliph pursued an alliance to secure his position against the Fatimids, a Shiʿīte dynasty that was gaining power in the Maghrib (and that would ultimately conquer Egypt). Sāʿid al-Andalusī included an entry on Ibn Shaprut in his history of science organized according to the contributions of various nations, the final chapter dealing with the "Children of Israel:" "[Ibn Shaprut] was skilled in the practice of medicine, very learned in the legal science of the Jews,[13] and he was the first to open up for those of them who were in al-Andalus their legal and historical and other sciences."[14]

[12] Jacob Mann refers to him as a "treasurer" because he was able to alleviate the Jews' burdensome taxes. Jacob Mann, *Texts and Studies in Jewish History and Literature* (Cincinnati: Hebrew Union College, 1931-35), 1:4. This need not make him a treasurer, per se. Ashtor also calls him a "director of customs."

[13] It is striking that Ibn Shaprut's "expertise" in Jewish law is noted mainly by Muslim authors and that a work such as Abraham Ibn Daud's *Book of Tradition*, which does not fail to recount figures' knowledge of Jewish law, makes no such assertion in the case of Ibn Shaprut. Nor does Moses Ibn Ezra's Judeo-Arabic *Book of Conversations and Discussions*, which only specifies that Hasdai was a patron of Jewish legal scholars and others. *The Book of Tradition* says relatively little about Hasdai in general, probably in order to make the appearance of Samuel ha-Nagid, a new social type, all the more dramatic. See Gerson D. Cohen, *Sefer ha-Qabbalah: The Book of Tradition by Abraham Ibn Daud* (Philadelphia: Jewish Publication Society, 1967), 271-72. See also note 18 below.

[14] Translated in an article by David Wasserstein, "The Muslims and the Golden Age of the Jews in al-Andalus," *Israel Oriental Studies* 17 (1997): 179-96; here 189.

Relative to the attention given Ibn Shaprut by Muslim authors on the history of science, Muslim sources are relatively reticent about his diplomatic activities, perhaps because the presence of the Jew at court roused some consternation. Over a century after Ibn Shaprut's death, the renowned philosopher Ibn Rushd (Averroes) was able to cite a verse that had been uttered by a jurist in order to persuade 'Abd al-Rahmān to turn against "Hasdai the Jew:" "Regarding the prophet, for whose sake alone you are honored, this [Jew] says that he is a liar."[15] Still, Ibn Shaprut's role in at least two diplomatic missions can be reconstructed with some accuracy. He worked toward defusing a sensitive situation involving a missive sent to 'Abd al-Rahmān by the German King Otto I (r. 936 - 973) that contained deprecations against Islam. Ibn Shaprut worked closely with Otto's envoy, the monk Johannes of Gorze, who led the mission to Córdoba and in whose biography the events are recorded.[16]

The second instance of Ibn Shaprut's diplomacy requires some background. When King Ordoño III of the Hispano-Christian kingdom of Leon died in 956, he was succeeded by his half-brother Sancho I, son of the princess of Navarre and the grandson of Queen Toda. After a period of truce, Sancho renewed attacks against al-Andalus, which led to a Muslim counterattack. Meanwhile, the nobles of Leon conspired against Sancho and forced his dethronement in 958, rousing the ire of Sancho's progenitors in Navarre, especially Queen Toda. 'Abd al-Rahmān seized this opportunity to build an alliance with Leon and brought Sancho and Queen Toda to Córdoba, where they were received amid much pomp. The spectacle signaled the Christian monarchs' reliance upon the Caliph and the latter's power and grandeur. The Muslim and Christian rulers plotted a simultaneous attack on Castile and Leon and succeeded in reinstating Sancho, who remained indebted to 'Abd al-Rahmān III. According to a Hebrew poem by Dunash ibn Labrat, it was Hasdai ibn Shaprut who lured Sancho and Toda to Córdoba "with the strength of his wisdom and the might of his cunning, his many devices and smooth

---

[15] S.M. Stern, "*Shetei yedi'ot hadashot 'al Hasdai Ibn Shaprut,*" *Zion* 11 (1946): 141-46; here 141. Ibn Rushd cited the verse in his commentary on Aristotle's poetics. The same verse is cited in another work in connection with a Christian courtier.

[16] Ashtor, *The Jews of Moslem Spain*, 169-76.

speech."[17] We do not know of Ibn Shaprut's involvement from any source apart from this poem. Even if his role were fairly minor, it was sufficiently important for the Hebrew poet to lavish praise upon him.

It is interesting to note that Ibn Shaprut's diplomatic missions were to Christian kingdoms only. Perhaps the Caliph's sending a Jew was a way of signaling to the Christian monarch that the Umayyad Caliphate exercised a policy of tolerance toward religious minorities. Employing a Jewish emissary in a dispute with another Muslim dynasty may have conveyed that the Caliph was taking the matter lightly or could have exposed the Caliph to charges of illegitimacy for veering from a strict application of Islamic law.

Ibn Shaprut enjoyed prestige among Jews as a leader beyond the borders of al-Andalus within the Mediterranean more broadly. Although there is a tendency to view Ibn Shaprut as the initiator of an independent Andalusi Jewry that paralleled the emergence of 'Abd al-Rahmān III's breakaway Caliphate, the title by which he is referred to in the aforementioned poem by Dunash Ibn Labrat is *Rosh Kallah;* this title could only be bestowed by a Gaon (dean of the academy in Baghdad) and speaks to Ibn Shaprut's place within the Iraqi academy's hierarchy.[18] He corresponded with Jews in southern France, Sicily, Palestine, and Iraq, petitioned the rulers of Byzantium for the betterment of its Jewish populace, and, most famously, sent an epistle to King Joseph of Khazaria, a Jewish kingdom near the Caspian Sea that captured the imagination of Andalusi Jewry and many others for centuries to come.[19]

---

[17] Hebrew text in Jefim Schirmann, *Ha-shirah ha-'ivrit bi-sefarad u-ve-provans* (Tel Aviv: Dvir; Jerusalem: Mosad Bialik, 1954-60), 1:38 (ll. 49-50).

[18] The title was often given to individuals who were particularly learned in Jewish law, though it was also bestowed upon certain powerful figures. In later works produced by Iberian authors, Ibn Shaprut was referred to by the title *Nasi,* "prince," but not by the title *Rosh Kallah.* The omission of the latter might reflect a tendency to recast the figure as the progenitor of the Andalusi social and intellectual revolution, which would necessarily require downplaying his lesser role within the Babylonian hierarchy.

[19] Ashtor cites the various sources, but see especially those in Jacob Mann, *Texts and Studies,* 1:3-33. For the letter from Sicily, see Alexander Scheiber and Zvi Malachi, "Letter from Sicily to Ḥasdai Ibn Shaprut," *Proceedings of the American Academy for Jewish Research* 41/42 (1973-1974): 207-218. The letter to the king of Khazaria is available in English: Franz Kobler, *A Treasury of Jewish Letters: Letters from the Famous and the Humble* (Philadelphia: Jewish Publication Society, 1953), 97-99.

Ibn Shaprut must have been fully conversant in the cultural and political idiom of the Caliphal court and it seems that he recreated courtly practices on a smaller scale within Jewish circles. Just as the Caliph patronized Muslim learning and surrounded himself with scholars, scribes, and eulogizing poets, so Ibn Shaprut sponsored Jewish learning, maintained scribes for Hebrew correspondence, and received the praise of Hebrew poets. Over a century after his death, Ibn Shaprut's activities were remembered by Moses ibn Ezra when recounting the literary history of the Jews of al-Andalus:

> .... In [Ibn Shaprut's] days, men of the highest rank competed to make known the knowledge with which God had entrusted them and the learning He had bestowed upon them. They composed lofty works and assembled eminent collections. They roused his [Ibn Shaprut's] emotions with their wondrous poems and marvelous eloquent orations. Therefore their status was elevated with him and he awarded them the utmost of their requests and the extreme of their desires.[20]

Ibn Shaprut lent particular support to two competing grammarian-poets: Menahem Ben Saruq, a native of al-Andalus who penned poems and Hebrew epistles for Ibn Shaprut as well as an early dictionary of biblical Hebrew; and Dunash Ibn Labrat, a Maghrib-born, Baghdad-educated émigré who wrote a treatise exposing the deficiencies of Menahem's dictionary and who introduced a synthetic innovation into Hebrew poetry so that it could adopt the meter of Arabic poetry.[21] Both poets wrote panegyrics for Ibn Shaprut that recall the social function of the Arabic court panegyric: to express or negotiate the bond between poet and patron and to create a legitimizing image of the leader for public consumption.

Romanticization aside, the career of Ibn Shaprut in many ways foreshadowed (but did not necessarily cause) the careers of other Jews who attained stations in Andalusi Muslim courts. Jacob ibn Jau was appointed by the Umayyad Caliph Hishām II (976-1009) over

---

[20] Moses Ibn Ezra, *Kitāb al-muḥāḍara wa'l-mudhākara*, ed. A.S. Halkin (Jerusalem: Mekize Nirdamim, 1975), 56.

[21] Just as Dunash was more open to Arabization in Hebrew verse, his approach to Hebrew grammar was likewise open to close comparison with Arabic (and Aramaic) cognates whereas Menahem's approach to lexicography was contextual only. Their students also carried on the grammatical debates they initiated.

the Jews of his region "to adjudicate their litigations ... to appoint over them whomsoever he wished and to extract from them any tax or payment to which they might be subject."[22] We also know of several Jewish courtiers during the period of the Muslim Taifa (Party) kings (1031-1090), after the Umayyad Caliphate collapsed and al-Andalus was divided into numerous warring states. It is likely that the multiplicity of states and the existence of parallel bureaucratic structures created broader opportunities for talented men of the religious minorities. It is also possible that Taifa kings believed that appointing Jewish courtiers might attract the loyalty of Jews living under rival Muslim dynasties. Isaac ibn Albalia, who authored a commentary on difficult passages of the Talmud, a work on the Jewish calendar, and Hebrew poetry, was appointed as an astrologer in the court of al-Mu'tamid ibn 'Abbād (1040-95) of Seville. Abraham ibn al-Muhājir, learned in Talmud and astronomy and a patron of the Hebrew poet Moses ibn Ezra, also served al-Mu'tamid and was given the title *wazīr*.

Jewish *wazīrs* are also known from Almeria and Saragossa during the Taifa period. Yet no Jewish figure of the Taifa period was as illustrious as one of the earliest, Isma'īl ibn Naghrīla (a.k.a. Samuel ibn Naghrela, or Samuel ha-Nagid, 993-1055/56), who rose to fame as an Arabic court scribe (*kātib*) under the Zirids of Granada and also earned the title *wazīr*. Although we must read with a grain of salt the account of Ibn Naghrila's meteoric ascent as described by the Jewish chronicler Abraham ibn Daud—according to which the Jew kept himself in modest circumstances until his scribal brilliance was almost accidentally discovered by an associate of the Zirid court—attestations by Muslim biographers of his mastery of Arabic epistle writing, down to the details of particular Muslim formulations, should be taken as accurate.[23] Like Ibn Shaprut, he assumed the leadership of the Jewish community, lent support to Jewish intellectuals, and was lauded by Hebrew poets. Yet unlike Ibn Shaprut, he was a master of Hebrew poetic composition in his own right and also authored a work on Jewish law. Some of his verse comprises

---

[22] Cohen, *Book of Tradition*, 69, according to which Ibn Jau was also imprisoned when he failed to produce expected funds.

[23] For the story of his rise, see Cohen, *The Book of Tradition*, 71-73.

aphorisms regarding courtly conduct and reflects familiarity with Arabic "Mirrors for Princes" literature.

According to his own Hebrew poetry, Ibn Naghrīla served in many battles on behalf of the Zirid state against its Andalusi rivals. He consistently presents his military involvement as benefitting the Jewish people broadly, though this seems difficult to accept since Jewish populations also resided within the rival states, whose kings also maintained Jewish courtiers. Contemporary Jewish critiques of Ibn Naghrīla's role are hinted at even within his own poetry, in which he defends himself against one who "quarrels with me for associating with kings."[24] After Ibn Naghrīla's death, he was succeeded in his capacities within the court and the Jewish community by his son Joseph. According to Jewish and Muslim sources, Joseph failed to conduct himself with modesty, precipitating an attack against him and the Jewish community of Granada during which some four thousand Jews, including Joseph, were massacred.[25]

Even beyond Jews who held actual administrative posts, there emerged in al-Andalus an intellectual elite of Jewish men who pursued mastery of Jewish and Arabic subjects, who authored works that synthesized these areas of knowledge, and who cultivated a lifestyle modeled after that of the Muslim elite. They, along with courtiers proper, have been referred to with different emphases on their intellectual and social roles as "courtier rabbis," "Arabized Jews," and "Jewish elites."[26] Their values are captured most richly in the hundreds of poems they wrote for one another. These poems idealize a life of wealth and sophistication, of social wine drinking in palatine-garden settings, of nature's revival in springtime, of friendship and

---

[24] Schirmann, *Ha-shirah ha-'ivrit*, 1:109 [31], l. 7.

[25] Ibn Naghrīla, and all that he signified, was discussed for centuries after his death in Muslim works of literary history, historical chronicle, heresiography, and polemical literature. The representations range from admiring portrayals of an intelligent and well-integrated courtier to rancorous denouncements of a seditious heretic who ridiculed Islamic tenets. Further, see Ross Brann, *Power in the Portrayal: Representations of Jews and Muslims in Eleventh- and Twelfth-Century Islamic Spain* (Princeton: Princeton University Press, 2002).

[26] Cohen, *The Book of Tradition*, 269-76; Wasserstein, "Jewish Elites in al-Andalus"; Ross Brann, "The Arabized Jews," in *The Literature of al-Andalus*, ed. María Rosa Menocal, Raymond P. Scheindlin, and Michael Sells (Cambridge: Cambridge University Press, 2000), 435-54.

sexual passion.[27] Although it is, of course, difficult to reconstruct the full reality of their world from poetic sources, their courtly predilections were sufficiently concrete, at least, to merit contemporary critique.[28]

In the Court of Alfonso VIII: Abraham Ibn al-Fakhār in Castile[29]

To Abraham ibn Daud, writing from Christian Toledo in 1161 after being displaced from Córdoba by the Almohad invasion (1147), the hopes of restoring the Jewish glory of the Andalusi Jewish past on Christian soil seemed quite reasonable, even destined. According to his Hebrew *Book of Tradition*, God caused King Alfonso the *Emperador* to appoint Judah ibn Ezra—a descendant of "the leaders of Granada, holders of high office and men of power"—ruler over Calatrava, a city of refuge for the exiles, "and to place all royal provisions in his charge."[30] Ibn Daud's text creates the impression of continuity between the Jewish courtiers of al-Andalus and the recent courtiers of Castile such that the switch from serving Muslims to Christians was almost immaterial.

Although it seems unlikely that the Christian rulers of Castile were concerned with the precise lineage of potential Jewish appointees, the intellectual, administrative, and cultural knowledge possessed by Jews in cities such as Toledo—still highly Arabized at least through the thirteenth century—made them of particular value during the age of Christian territorial expansion and consolidation of royal power. As Yosef Kaplan points out, "The conquering kings

---

[27] Joseph Weiss, "*Tarbut hasranit ve-shirah hasranit.*" *World Congress of Jewish Studies* 1 (1947): 396-402.

[28] Bezalel Safran, "Bahya Ibn Paquda's Attitude Toward the Courtier Class," in *Studies in Medieval Jewish History and Literature*, vol. 1, ed. Isadore Twersky (Cambridge, MA: Harvard University Press, 1979), 154-96.

[29] The information on al-Fakhār is based on my forthcoming article, "May God Curse Them Both: Ibrāhīm Ibn al-Fakhār al-Yahūdi Between Castile and the Maghrib," in *Beyond Religious Borders: Interaction and Intellectual Exchange in the Medieval Islamic World*, ed. David M. Freidenreich and Miriam Goldstein (Philadelphia: University of Pennsylvania Press, forthcoming in 2012). See this article for detailed bibliographic information.

[30] Cohen, *The Book of Tradition*, 97.

found the Jews necessary and useful in consolidating their regimes, in establishing administrative infrastructure, for colonization following the expansion of their borders, and for the development of commerce in newly conquered urban centers."[31] Jonathan Ray has demonstrated that Jewish courtiers played key functions in establishing Castilian settlements along the Christian-Muslim frontier, where Jewish tax collectors and advisors were granted lands, including one area collectively known as the "Village of the Jews," which was distinct from the communal property set aside for the local Jewish *aljamas* (municipal corporate bodies).[32] Finally, Castilian kings, most famously Alfonso X (r. 1252-1284), sometimes employed Jews within their courts to collaborate on intellectual projects such as translations and Castilian synthetic works. These factors, along with legislation restricting the placement of Jews in administrative offices promulgated by the Fourth Lateran Council (1215), might explain why the Jewish courtier phenomenon was so common in Christian Iberia but relatively rare elsewhere in medieval Christendom.[33]

The status of Jewish courtiers could rouse the resentment of Christians and Jews alike. As in the Muslim environment, Christian rulers had to balance their alliance with the Jews with other state interests, such as retaining the support of the Christian nobility. In the Crown of Aragon under Pedro III (c. 1239-85), for example, the Christian nobility refused to send forces during the king's campaign against the French unless he dismissed his Jewish officials. The king partially capitulated and promised that no Jew would be appointed to the position of *baile* (bailiff), though he did retain Jews in the areas of medicine and finance.[34] Many Jews served as tax farmers (*almoxarifes*), not exactly the most popular office amongst taxpayers, whether Christian or Jewish. The second half of the thirteenth century also witnessed the emergence of the office of "Crown Rabbi,"

---

[31] Yosef Kaplan, "Court Jews before the 'Hofjuden,'" *From Court Jews to the Rothschilds: Art, Patronage, and Power, 1600-1800*, ed. Vivian B. Mann and Richard I. Cohen (New York: Jewish Museum, 1996), 11-25; here 15.

[32] Jonathan Ray, *The Sephardic Frontier: The Reconquista and the Jewish Community in Medieval Iberia* (Ithaca, NY: Cornell University Press, 2006), 20 and elsewhere.

[33] For a few examples of Jewish courtiers in Christendom outside of Iberia, see Yosef Kaplan, "Court Jews before the 'Hofjuden,'" 15.

[34] Yom Tov Assis, *The Golden Age of Aragonese Jewry* (Oxford: The Littman Library of Jewish Civilization, 1997), 13-15.

an appointed judicial (and often tax farming) position within the Jewish community that allowed Christian rulers to extend their influence into the individual Jewish communities, or *aljamas*, an administrative development consistent with broader bureaucratic reforms of the period. Sometimes appointed for their political connections rather than their accomplishments in Jewish legal thought, Crown Rabbis could find their appointments sharply contested by the *aljamas*.[35] Struggles between the Jewish courtier class and the lower classes of Jewish society are well documented in Aragon. While the community often benefited from the courtiers' access to court, the special privileges bestowed upon them by the Crown widened the gap between the powerful families of the oligarchic establishment and the poor.[36] Critiques of the courtier class often took aim at their sumptuous lifestyle, the reality of which is attested to (in Castile) in the poetry of Todros Halevi Abulafia, a courtier in the orbit of Alfonso X.[37] Similarly, there existed perennial tensions among the elite clans of Jewish Iberia over which family would enjoy royal favor and the associated wealth and prestige it brought.

Most of the career of Abraham al-Fakhār was spent in the service of King Alfonso VIII of Castile, who supported other Jewish courtiers including the *almoxarife* (tax farmer) Joseph ibn Shoshan, whose possession of a royally granted estate and various privileges are attested to in notarial records. Alfonso's reign from 1158 until 1214 was as monumental as it was long. He was king during a crucial

---

[35] Jonathan Ray, "Royal Authority and the Jewish Community: the Crown Rabbi in Medieval Spain and Portugal," in *Jewish Religious Leadership: Image and Reality*, ed. Jack Wertheimer (New York: Jewish Theological Seminary, 2004), 1:307-31.

[36] Bernard Septimus notes the rise of an anti-aristocratic class that characterized the ruling elite in Catalonia as lax in religious observance, corrupt in leadership, and immoral in sexual behavior. From the aristocratic camp, we hear voices of rebuke directed toward "slaves who have revolted against their kings and rebelled against their masters." Bernard Septimus, "Piety and Power in Thirteenth-Century Catalonia." *Studies in Medieval Jewish History and Literature* vol. 1, ed. Isadore Twersky (Cambridge, MA: Harvard University Press, 1979), 197-230. See also Jonathan Decter, *Iberian Jewish Literature: Between al-Andalus and Christian Europe* (Bloomington: Indiana University Press, 2007), chapter six.

[37] Aviva Doron, *Meshorer be-hasar ha-melekh: Todros Halevi Abulafiah, shirah 'ivrit bi-sefarad ha-nosrit* (Tel Aviv: Dvir, 1989). In the fourteenth century, Menahem Ben Zerah composed the Hebrew *Provisions for the Road* as a legal guide especially for "those who walk in the court of the king" since they often failed to follow Jewish law properly (concerning such subjects as prayer, blessings, prohibited foods, observing the Sabbath, relations with women, etc.). See Beinart, "*Demutah shel ha-hazranut ha-yehudit bi-Sefarad*," 65.

period of the Reconquista when the balance of power tipped in favor of Castile and against the Muslim Almohad dynasty that ruled in North Africa and al-Andalus. Both at times of Castile's strength and weakness, al-Fakhār served as a diplomat on behalf of Castile. He was of particular value in this role because of his deep knowledge of the Arabic language and culture despite his loyalty to his Christian sovereign.

Alfonso VIII's rule coincided with that of the most powerful Almohad caliphs, all of whom proved formidable military opponents. The early years of Alfonso's reign were marked by disorder and the loss of territory to neighboring kingdoms, both Almohad and Christian. In particular, the Battle of Alarcos (known as al-Arak in Arabic sources) in 1195 is recalled as a crushing defeat for Alfonso at the hands of the Almohads. However, in 1212, near the end of his reign, Alfonso attained victory at the Battle of Las Navas de Tolosa (known in Arabic as al-'Iqāb), which forever shifted the balance of Muslim/Christian power in Iberia. Al-Nāsir, the last of the great Almohad caliphs, was squarely defeated and died one year later; he was succeeded by the youth Abū Ya'qūb Yūsuf al-Mustansir (1213-1224), who was compelled to sign truces with Castile (and Aragon). Alfonso died in 1214, leaving the crown to his young son Enrique I.

Al-Fakhār was active as a diplomat at both the nadir and the apogee of Alfonso's power. According to the Muslim historian Ibn 'Idhārī (d. c. 1295), al-Fakhār first came to Marrakech as a diplomat in 1203, eight years after Alfonso's defeat at Alarcos, when Alfonso sent him to negotiate the deferment of paying tribute and a new truce. This was followed by several years of peace between Muslims and Christians. We next hear of al-Fakhār in 1214, two years after Alfonso's victory at Las Navas de Tolosa and after the death of al-Nāsir when al-Mustansir became Caliph. Sent by Alfonso, al-Fakhār traveled to Marrakech to begin negotiations for a definitive peace between Castile and the Almohads; Alfonso died on October 6, 1214 without seeing the truce completed, though al-Fakhār continued the negotiation after his death under the direction of Doña Berenguela, guardian of the minor Enrique I.

In many ways, al-Fakhār's intellectual values, which were essential to his place in the Jewish community and at court, represented a continuation of those possessed by the Arabized Jews of al-Andalus. Al-Fakhār was learned in several areas, knew multiple languages, composed (Arabic) poetry, and was able to assume different modes of cultural discourse. He spoke Arabic in Marrakech (and probably in Toledo as well), undoubtedly spoke Castilian in the court of Alfonso VIII, and had a command of Hebrew that allowed at least for the appreciation of Hebrew literary works. A number of al-Fakhār's Arabic poems have been preserved by Muslim anthologists. Such Arabic literary collections, along with some historical accounts, relate the most detailed records of al-Fakhār's activities, particularly in al-Andalus and the Maghrib.

Ibn Sa'īd al-Maghribī (1213-86) relates in his biographical dictionary of Arabic poets that he met al-Fakhār personally. He describes the Jew as a "doctor" who "was prevalent in Toledo and became an emissary from its Christian King Alfonso (Adhfunsh) to the nation of the Banū 'Abd al-Ma'amūn at the court of Marrakech. My father described him as a master of poetry, learning in ancient sciences and logic." Gaining elevated status within Alfonso's court was also expected to earn al-Fakhār respect in Muslim circles, as evidenced by an anecdote recounted by a Muslim anthologist in which al-Fakhār upbraids (in verse) a Muslim who failed to treat him with the dignity befitting a royal appointee.[38]

As a diplomat to the Maghrib, al-Fakhār relied upon his knowledge of Arabic and Islamic culture in order to navigate the world of the Almohad court. According to one anecdote, al-Fakhār was sent to Marrakech, to the court of al-Mustansir, on a diplomatic mission during the period of Almohad decline. As was common in Muslim courts, the Caliph was kept fairly inaccessible, such that one would have to pass through various sections of the palace and numerous guards before being granted audience. The story is related in al-Fakhār's voice:

> They brought me into the garden of the Caliph al-Mustansir, which I found to be of the utmost beauty as though it were Paradise. By its gate I saw a guard of the utmost hideousness. When the vizier asked me about my state of delight, I said, "I saw Paradise though I heard that Paradise would have Riḍwān by its gate but by this gate is Mālik.

---

[38] See my "May God Curse Them Both," appendix.

He laughed and informed the Caliph of what occurred. [The Caliph] said to [the vizier], "Tell him that we did this by design. Were Ridwan the guard by the gate, we would fear that he would turn away [the visitor] from [the garden] and say to him, 'You are not in the right place.' But since it is Mālik, he ushers [the visitor] into [the garden] since he does not realize what is behind him and imagines that it is Gehennum. [Al-Fakhār] said, "When the vizier informed me of this I said to him, 'God knows best how to carry out his mission.'"

According to Qur'ān 43:77, Mālik is the gatekeeper of Gehennum (Hell), while Islamic tradition associates Ridwan with Paradise. Hence al-Fakhār's joke that gained the attention of the Caliph was grounded in learning that was specifically Muslim. Indeed, when al-Fakhār responded at the end, "God knows best how to carry out his mission," he was quoting the Qur'an (6:124). Undoubtedly, being versed in Islamic culture was of great advantage for gaining access to and negotiating with Muslim figures of power. Al-Fakhār's quick and witty tongue might have lightened the mood of this encounter, whose political background likely disposed the Caliph negatively toward the diplomat. Such were the qualities that made al-Fakhār of value to the Castilian state.

Interestingly, al-Fakhār also evoked the Qur'ān when praising his Christian patron Alfonso VIII. He wrote in a couplet:

> The court of Alfonso is a wife still in her succulent days,
> Take off your shoes in honor of its soil for it is holy.

The Arabic phrasing of the second line closely mimics Qur'ān 20:11-12, which recounts Moses' appearance before the Burning Bush. The reference has the effect of likening appearing in Alfonso's court with holding audience before God Himself in a moment charged with religious significance. The effect is not lost in translation for a Christian or Jewish audience since the verse still evokes the biblical scene of Moses at the Burning Bush (Exod. 3:5), where he is also told to remove his shoes. Thus the verse evokes a point of overlap between Jewish/Christian and Muslim scriptures and resonates within multiple literary and cultural worlds. We do not know whether this couplet was recited in Toledo before Alfonso directly or whether it was used by al-Fakhār to spread an image of his king in

17

the Arabic speaking world only. Either way, it is clear that Arabic panegyric enjoyed some function within the machinery of the Castilian
state much as it did within Islamic political culture. It is possible that
Alfonso VIII fashioned himself as a political leader after the image
of the very caliphs with whom he competed.[39] The prominence of
Jewish courtiers with literary skills continued in Castile through the
fourteenth century with Santob de Carrión (a.k.a., Shem Tov ibn
Ardutiel), who dedicated his *Proverbios Morales* (Moral Proverbs)
to King Pedro IV, whom he also served as treasurer. [40]

Not surprisingly, al-Fakhār's activities within the Jewish community are best preserved in Hebrew sources, in which he appears as a
diplomat, a learned leader, and a tax collector. He served as a patron
for Hebrew writers such as Judah ibn Shabbetai, who dedicated his
Gift of Judah the Misogynist to al-Fakhār and featured the patron as
a character within the text. Ibn Shabbetai writes in his praise, noting
his eminent position among Muslims and Christians:

> The Lord established him to determine justice for his people. He
> bears sovereignty upon his shoulder. Whose greatness can compare
> with his? Tongues fail to declare his praise. Because of him lands are
> elevated even above the skies! Of him the prophets spoke. For his sake
> all creation was made. Muslim kings purify themselves in the waters
> of his wisdom, and Christian chiefs wage war at his command: 'They
> set out at his word and at his word they return' (Numbers 27:21).
> Before him they are dumbfounded and upon them falls his dread
> for they behold things never told before. He is the "father of many
> nations" (Genesis 17:4) and the master of Torah.[41]

---

[39] Maribel Fierro, "Alfonso the Wise: The Last Almohad Caliph?" *Medieval Encounters* 15
(2009): 175-198 argues that the more famous Alfonso X fashioned himself according to the
typology of the Almohad Caliphs (though she does not deal with panegyric specifically).
Earlier, in Norman Sicily, Arabic panegyrics were composed in honor of Roger II (1130-54).

[40] In the work, the poet lavishes praise upon the king and defends the work's value despite
its "lowly" origin: "For being born on the thorn bush, the rose is certainly not worth less,
nor is good wine if taken from the lesser branches of the vine... nor are good proverbs [of
less value] if spoken by a Jew." *The Moral Proverbs of Santob de Carrión: Jewish Wisdom in
Christian Spain*, trans. T.A. Perry (Princeton: Princeton University Press, 1987), 19-20 (ll.
169-89). Santob also authored works in Hebrew.

[41] For a partial English translation of the narrative by Raymond Scheindlin, see "The
Misogynist," in *Rabbinic Fantasies*, ed. David Stern and Mark Jay Mirsky (Philadelphia:
Jewish Publication Society, 1990), 269-94. The translation here is my own.

The phrase "father of many nations" evokes al-Fakhār's namesake, the biblical Abraham, yet here the moniker refers to the diplomat's status among contemporary religious communities. The passage from Numbers is also apposite in that it makes reference to the biblical Joshua, Moses' successor, precisely at the moment of his being invested with Moses' authority. Hence al-Fakhār is presented as a legitimate heir to Moses' leadership (though the troops referred to here seem to be Christian rather than Israelite). Here we have another parallel with the Jewish court culture of al-Andalus: al-Fakhār served (and praised) his monarch and in turn was praised by Hebrew authors who portrayed their patron as a ruler.

Whereas the Jewish courtiers of al-Andalus have virtually always been evoked by modern scholars in a celebratory manner, the Jewish courtiers of Christian Iberia were judged with ambivalence by Yitzhak Baer, the towering twentieth-century scholar of the Jews in Christian Iberia. Baer saw the courtiers' situation as exceedingly fragile and subject to "the whims and vagaries of the king's mind," here referring to the reversal of fate for Jewish tax collectors under Alfonso X of Castile from favored employment to imprisonment.[42] More importantly, Baer took issue with the moral laxity and philosophical preoccupations of the courtiers themselves and denounced those who "attained political power and high office in the administration" and "did not hesitate to trample upon the vital interests of their coreligionists."[43] Baer was an émigré from Germany who published his masterpiece *A History of the Jews in Christian Spain* (in Hebrew) in Jerusalem, 1945.[44] Like Hannah Arendt's perspective, Baer's was likely informed by the tragedy of the Holocaust and the complicit, even malevolent, role of Nazi Jewish appointees.[45] One focus of Baer's magnum opus was to determine why the Expulsion

---

[42] Yitzhak Baer, *A History of the Jews in Christian Spain*, trans. Louis Schiffman (Philadelphia: Jewish Publication Society, 1961-66), 1:129.

[43] *A History of the Jews in Christian Spain*, 1:241-2. Only a few courtiers merit praise in Baer's eyes, such as Todros Halevi Abulafia, about whom Baer notes, "as a mystic and an ascetic who practiced what he preached, he personified the very antithesis of the current tendency among Jewish courtiers to assimilate the ways of the Christian knighthood and the licentiousness of the royal court," 1:119. See also Elliot Horowitz, "The Court Jews and the Jewish Question," 116-18.

[44] After originally undertaking the project in German, Baer was convinced to publish in Hebrew as part as an expression of Zionism.

[45] Suggested also in Horowitz, "The Court Jews and the Jewish Question," 117.

occurred, and although blame was ultimately placed upon the Catholic Monarchs who issued the edict of Expulsion, an internal Jewish factor was identified in the decadence, intellectual pursuits, and moral turpitude of the courtier class.[46]

Toward the Expulsion: Isaac Abravanel at the Court of Ferdinand and Isabella

In hindsight, the period from 1391, when widespread attacks against Iberian Jewry left many dead and created a massive *converso* population, until the Expulsion of 1492 has seemed to some like an inexorable if not precipitous decline. Although the century was punctuated by numerous instances of restriction, exclusion, and even violence, one cannot allow the looming specter of the Expulsion to color the reading of earlier moments, even as late as the time just before the Expulsion.[47] Iberian Jewry, including its courtiers proximate to royalty, had little sense that expulsion was imminent.

In the century prior to the Expulsion, the place of the court Jew continued to be prominent even as Iberian society went through political and social transformations.[48] On the other hand, court Jews appear mostly as financiers and tax farmers (some of whom were also physicians) whereas astronomers, ambassadors, and advisors had become rare. Restricting Jewish functions at court was likely designed to appease a restless Christian nobility as it maneuvered to attain greater influence. We should not assign too much grandeur to the rank of tax farmer despite the fact that it was an extremely lucrative profession; such figures were often despised by Jews and

---

[46] See also the introductory essay by Benjamin Gampel to the reprint of the English edition, "Yitzhak Baer's *A History of the Jews in Christian Spain*," xv-lvi.

[47] See also the introductory remarks by Mark D. Meyerson, *A Jewish Renaissance in Fifteenth-Century Spain* (Princeton: Princeton University Press, 2004).

[48] The discussion below largely concerns Castile, where the courtier phenomenon was more common. On Aragon, see Yom Tov Assis, *The Golden Age of Aragonese Jewry* (Oxford: The Littman Library of Jewish Civilization, 1997); D. Romano, "Cortesanos judíos en la Corona de Aragón," *Destierros Aragoneses* 1 (1988): 25-37. The fifteenth century also saw the rise of *converso* courtiers, whose Christian status first afforded them mobility barred to Jews. *Converso* roles at court were ultimately restricted, however, and *conversos* were often suspected of religious recidivism.

Christians alike and occupied relatively low rank within what had become an extensive fiscal hierarchy.

The most prominent Jewish courtier in Castile during the first half of the fifteenth century was Abraham Benveniste (1406-54), a member of a well-established Sephardi family. He was appointed to a post in fiscal administration by a noble in the service of Juan I, worked as a tax farmer, and helped finance military campaigns. At the *aljamas'* request, he was appointed by the king to the position of "Crown Rabbi" with its dual functions in adjudication and the administration of taxes within the Jewish community. The enactments Benveniste supported within the Jewish community were directed toward tax equitability, communal reform, religious education, and the restriction of ostentatious dress and public behavior.[49] However, like many other rabbinic enactments, these do not seem to have been strictly enforced and thus reflect Benveniste's social ideals more than concrete social changes.

As the century progressed, circles of courtiers emerged in various centers, which need to be studied individually and on a local level. In Madrid, for example, during the period between 1450 and 1475, members of new families (including royal physicians) became the dominant voices within the *aljamas* and secured proximity with royalty. At one point in Madrid, the *aljamas* protested vociferously when a Christian was appointed to a post traditionally held by Jews, ultimately leading to the Christian's removal from office. The incident likely signifies a royal attempt to exert greater influence over the *aljamas* even as it demonstrates the *aljamas'* power to deflect encroachments upon its traditional authority.[50]

Abraham Señor, first documented in 1466 as a financier who loaned a significant sum to King Henry IV of Castile, emerged as a leading courtier during the second half of the fifteenth century. He attained positions in tax administration that were theoretically barred to Jews according to laws promulgated in 1465 in order to

---

[49] Baer, *A History of the Jews in Christian Spain*, 2:259-70. See also the brief article by Zvi Avineri, "Abraham Benveniste," in *Encyclopedia Judaica*, eds. Michael Berenbaum and Fred Skolnik, 2nd ed. (Detroit: Macmillan Reference USA, 2007), 3:382.

[50] Javier Castaño, "Social Networks in a Castilian Jewish Aljama and the Court Jews in the Fifteenth Century: A Preliminary Survey (Madrid 1440-75)," *En la España medieval* 20 (1997): 379-92.

assuage an aggrieved nobility. Like many Jewish courtiers, he was granted tax exemptions and land. Señor seems to have had certain tensions with the *aljamas,* though, as Eleazar Gutwirth argues, these were "political, fiscal, socio-economic issues rather than religious controversies."[51] A sixteenth-century Hebrew chronicle credits Señor with a role in arranging the marriage between the Catholic Monarchs Ferdinand and Isabella, though this is likely apocryphal. Still, Señor clearly aligned himself with Isabella in her battle of succession against her niece Juana la Beltraneja, and his career continued to flourish in the united kingdom of Castile and Aragon, where he promoted the centralizing fiscal policies of the Crown. Señor has been remembered foremost in Jewish history for converting to Catholicism in 1492 rather than accepting the yoke of expulsion, though this fact should not overshadow the significance of his career as a courtier.

The figure with which we will conclude this essay, Don Isaac Abravanel (1437-1508), was atypical as a courtier with respect to origins, versatility, intellectual prowess, and ultimate fate.[52] He was not born in the kingdom of Castile from which he was ultimately expelled but rather hailed from Portugal (he did, however, derive from a prominent Castilian family). His grandfather served under Castilian kings and ultimately converted to Christianity, though Isaac's own father, Judah, remained within the Jewish fold and attained wealth as a merchant and tax farmer in Lisbon, where he financed Prince Fernando in an expedition against Tangier. Isaac was also atypical among fifteenth-century Jewish courtiers in that the prolific writings he composed (mostly but not exclusively after the Expulsion)—in the areas of biblical exegesis, dogma, polemics, and commentaries on Maimonides' *Guide of the Perplexed,* the Passover *Haggadah,* and the *Ethics of the Fathers*—merited his place as one of the foremost intellectuals of late medieval Judaism. His peregri-

---

[51] Eleazar Gutwirth, "Abraham Seneor: Social Tensions and the Court-Jew," *Michael* 11 (1989): 169-229; here 228.

[52] His name appears in many variant spellings in medieval documents, usually Abravanel or Abarbanel. The biographical information below is largely based on Elias Lipiner, *Two Portuguese Exiles in Castile: Dom David Negro and Dom Isaac Abravanel* (Jerusalem: Magnes Press, 1997); Eric Lawee, *Isaac Abarbanel's Stance Toward Tradition* (Albany: SUNY Press, 2001); and Benzion Netanyahu, *Don Isaac Abravanel: Statesman and Philosopher* (Philadelphia: Jewish Publication Society, 1953).

nations and exceptional status allow us to conclude this essay on a poignant (if somewhat dramatic) note.

Despite the relatively stable Jewish-Christian relations characteristic of Portugal during the fifteenth century, the young Isaac Abravanel would have been witness, in 1449, during the reign of King Afonso V, to anti-Jewish riots in Lisbon that began with a limited assault by some Christian hoodlums but spun into an attack on the Jewish quarter.[53] Still, Jewish power seems not to have been shaken, with numerous Jewish families maintaining close connections to royalty. As a merchant, Abravanel supplied fine cloth to the king and others and accumulated great wealth. In a fifteenth-century document, Abravanel figures prominently along with other Jews in a list of contributors for expenses toward the Portuguese war against Castile.[54] Already in the 1460s, Abravanel appears in royal records as holding special privileges, including the right to carry weapons, to stay in Christian inns, and exemption from wearing the "Jewish badge." In the 1470s, King Afonso granted Abravanel, in exchange for services he had rendered the court, the right to settle outside the Jewish quarter and "all the honors and liberties enjoyed by the Christians."[55]

Abravanel's special privileges and riches spawned the resentment of some Christian notables. Still, Abravanel was well connected to the Portuguese Christian nobility. As with his predecessor, al-Fakhār, it is likely that his knowledge of scripture and theology, in addition to his acumen in matters economic and financial, smoothed his interactions at court. A condolence letter sent to the count of Faro in Portuguese attests not only to the social bond that existed between the Jewish author and his Christian addressee but also to the intellectual ground they shared.[56] Abravanel also maintained ties with leading Jewish intellectuals outside of Portugal.

In 1481, João II succeeded Afonso as king and, in 1483, a warrant for Abravanel's arrest was issued on the charge of conspiring against the king in cahoots with the duke of Bragança (the duke was

---

[53] For the events, see Lipiner, *Two Portuguese Exiles*, 78.

[54] Lipiner, *Two Portuguese Exiles*, 49.

[55] Lipiner, *Two Portuguese Exiles*, 51.

[56] On the letter, see Eleazar Gutwirth, "*Hercules furens* and War: On Abravanel's Courtly Context," *Jewish History* 23 (2009): 293-312.

ultimately executed). Abravanel fled for Castile and was sentenced to death in absentia (he was likely executed in effigy as well). While the reality behind the treason charge will never be known with certainty, Abravanel insisted upon his innocence in his autobiographical introduction to his commentary on the book of Joshua, which was written soon after his flight from Portugal.[57] His artful and dramatic prose is executed in a high biblical register that constantly evokes specific biblical verses:

> The king was angry with me too [Deuteronomy 1:37], although I never did any injustice [1 Chronicles 12:17] and no deceit was found in my mouth [Isaiah 53:9]. Only because from time immemorial [Isaiah 23:7] and from old good times I was an intimate friend of the persecuted noblemen and they asked for my counsel [Job 29:21], the man, the lord of the earth [the king], spoke roughly to me [Genesis 42:30] and attacked me with his mighty hand [Job 30:21]. He included me amongst the conspirators [2 Samuel 15:31], maintaining that these men would not do anything without first revealing their secret and all their intimate thoughts to me [Isaiah 3:20].[58]

Furthermore, Abravanel denounced treason against even a wanton king on theoretical grounds. In an extensive excursus on kingship in his commentary on Deuteronomy 17:14, Abravanel writes that the subject of dethroning a wicked king had been "studied by the wise men of the nations" and adds:

> I discussed this subject before kings and their wise men. I proved that [dethronement] is not proper since the people do not have the right to rebel against their king and remove his sovereignty and kingship, even if he acted wantonly through every transgression.[59]

Abravanel argues this on three principles: 1) because the people entered into a covenant with the king that cannot be transgressed

---

[57] On Abravanel's use of autobiographical style, see Cedric Cohen Skalli, "Abravanel's Commentary on the Former Prophets: Portraits, Self-Portraits, and Models of Leadership," *Jewish History* 23 (2009): 255-80. This entire volume of *Jewish History* is dedicated to Abravanel, commemorating 500 years since his death. On Abravanel's autobiographical mode in the context of fifteenth-century humanist writing, see also Eleazar Gutwirth, "Don Ishaq Abravanel and Vernacular Humanism in Fifteenth Century Iberia," *Bibliothèque d'Humanisme et Renaissance* 60 (1998): 641–671.

[58] Translated by Lipiner in *Two Portuguese Exiles*, 57.

[59] My translation.

irrespective of the king's acts; 2) because "the king in the land occupies the place of God in the universe," i.e., just as God can transgress the laws of nature for a given purpose (i.e., miracles), so the king is above the law to which others must adhere. Rebellion against a king is thus akin to rebellion against God; and 3) (a reason that is specific to the case of a king of Israel) because the king is not selected by the people but rather by God.[60] Monarchy was a preoccupation within Abravanel's thought and it seems obvious that his political theorizing in this case dovetails with his life experience.

In Castile, Abravanel was able to rebuild his wealth through tax farming and dealing in precious metals during the course of the 1480s. Given the establishment of an expanded arm of the Inquisition under royal control, the expulsion of the Jews from Andalusia in 1483, and the Expulsion of 1492, Benzion Netanyahu characterized Abravanel's Spain as a "Land of Persecution." "Yet," Eric Lawee notes, "if this characterization captures much that occurred to Jews and *conversos* during Abarbanel's Spanish sojourn, it does not reflect his own experience of Spain—not even as he himself recalled it after 1492."[61] Abravanel helped finance the Catholic Monarchs' campaign against Granada and, in 1484, officially entered into their service. Abravanel recounts his career under the monarchs in his commentary to I Kings,

> As I was about to begin the commentary of the book of Kings, I was called to come into the Court of the King [Esther 4:11], the King of Spain, the greatest king of earth [...] and I came to the court of the King's and Queen's house [Esther 5:1] and I was close to them [Genesis 45:10] for a long time, and the Lord gave me their favor and the favor of the nobles who see the King's face, and sat first in the kingdom [Esther 1:14][62]

Abravanel seems to have had every expectation that his service to the Catholic Monarchs would continue indefinitely. As late as 1491, the monarchs renewed their contract with Abravanel (and with Abraham Señor, by the way) as a tax farmer.

---

[60] The subject is also discussed elsewhere in his commentaries, e.g. I Samuel 24:7.

[61] Lawee, *Isaac Abravanel's Stance Toward Tradition*, 16, with reference to Netanyahu, *Don Isaac Abravanel*, 33.

[62] Translated by Cedric Cohen Skalli in "Abravanel's Commentary on the Former Prophets," 257.

Unlike most other Jewish courtiers at the time, we have no record of Abravanel's interaction with the *aljamas*, though it is difficult to imagine his not being involved with the Jewish community on some level or with other Jewish courtiers at the very least. While in Portugal, Abravanel had raised ransom money in order to free Jewish captives. In his biblical commentary, Abravanel represents himself as addressing the king with much bravado and assiduously petitioning Spanish nobles to revoke the Expulsion edict:

> And I was there in the inner court of the King's house [Esther 5:1], I was weary of pleading, my throat was dried [Psalm 69:4]. I spoke three times, I entreated him with my mouth [Job 19:16]: 'Help, my lord, O king!' [2 Kings 6:26], 'Why are you treating your servants this way [Exodus 5:15]. Ask us much dowry and gift [Genesis 34:2], gold and silver, all that a man will give for his country' [Job 2:4]. I called for my friends [Lamentations 1:19] who see the king's face [Esther 1:14], to make supplication unto my people [Esther 4:8], and nobles took counsel together [Psalm 2:2] to speak to the King with all the strength necessary in order to reverse the letter of anger and wrath and his intention to destroy the Jews [Esther 8:5]. He was like the deaf asp that stops his ear [Psalm 58:5] and he did not answer to any of the requests [Proverbs 30:30].[63]

Although we have no other source to confirm these events, it may well be that Abravanel's efforts partly explain the one-month lag between the edict's signing and its promulgation. Pragmatist that he was, Abravanel spent time in the months before departure collecting as many unpaid debts as possible. We also know that Abravanel's privileges continued even through the Expulsion as royal edicts exempted him from restrictions to which other Jews were subject regarding departure with currency and valuables.[64] Following the Expulsion, Abravanel settled in the kingdom of Naples, where again he established himself with much renown and became a trusted advisor to the king. He spent his final years in Venice.

What could Abravanel have meant to Ferdinand and Isabella, particularly in that his service was bookended by the local expulsion of Andalusian Jewry and the mass Expulsion of 1492? We need

---

[63] Trans. by Cedric Cohen Skalli in "Abravanel's Commentary on the Former Prophets," 280.

[64] Lawee, *Isaac Abravanel's Stance Toward Tradition*, 224, n. 68.

not attribute insidious motives in the case of these monarchs any more (or less) than we might in the case of other monarchs. Surely Abravanel's appointment had little to do with hopes of extending deeper control over the *aljamas*, since his connections there seem to have been limited. Perhaps it seemed wise to maintain Jews within the court precisely while the Inquisition was interrogating the *conversos* in order to encourage Jewish cooperation. Perhaps Abravanel was simply valued for his political and economic acumen, or at the very least his money. Ferdinand and Isabella may have seen in Abravanel strategic advantage not in his identity as a Jew but as a Portuguese political refugee, the stripped courtier of an enemy state with deep knowledge of its affairs. Even if we accept Abravanel's claims of innocence in the charge of conspiracy against João II, it is clear that his loyalty was for specific rulers and not for a specific state. It is also clear that his rulers' loyalty could be at least as capricious.

The fact that Jews were present in so many courtly contexts in medieval Iberia makes it tempting to imagine the continuity of a Sephardi courtier type. Certain parallels are present, especially among the Andalusi courts and the early Castilian courts, in which rulers fashioned court culture around bureaucratic reform and intellectual foment that required knowledge of multiple languages, administrative know-how, and specialized skills. The role of the Jewish courtier remained similar because court culture itself was somewhat continuous. Jews were functional not only because they often shared the political and intellectual commitments of the ruling culture but also because they could mediate between their home governments and foreign (including enemy) kingdoms. While some of these points remain true in later centuries, the political realities— both domestic and international—of the fifteenth century made the role of the Jewish courtier rather distinct. Throughout the Peninsula, monarchs had to contend with an increasingly powerful nobility while attempting to extend their power within the Jewish *aljamas.* As financiers, Jewish courtiers were appreciated as supporters of the state. As tax farmers, they were appreciated by rulers but often resented by the masses, which might also have been by design. One need not be a cynic to view the celebrated role of the Jewish courtier in pragmatic or utilitarian terms.

We must refrain from ascribing to the Jewish courtiers of medieval Iberia strict continuity, much less uniformity. The courtier phenomenon is best understood on a local level. In fact, it might be most wise to concentrate on those figures whose careers were less accomplished or dramatic than those of Ibn Shaprut, al-Fakhār, or Abravanel. Typical Jewish courtiers stirred little controversy and were not especially brilliant or memorable. They were, however, essential in different ways within the political cultures of medieval Iberia.

Works Cited:

Arendt, Hannah. *The Origins of Totalitarianism*. New York: Harcourt, Brace, 1951.

------. Review of Selma Stern, "*The Court Jew*," *Jewish Social Studies* 14 (1952): 176-8.

Ashtor, Eliahu. *The Jews of Moslem Spain*. Philadelphia: Jewish Publication Society, 1992.

Assis, Yom Tov. *The Golden Age of Aragonese Jewry*. Oxford: The Littman Library of Jewish Civilization, 1997.

Avineri, Zvi. "Abraham Benveniste." In *Encyclopedia Judaica, 2ⁿᵈ ed.*, edited by Michael Berenbaum and Fred Skolnik. Detroit: Macmillan Reference USA, 2007. 3: 382

Baer, Yitzhak. *A History of the Jews in Christian Spain*. Translated by Louis Schiffman. Philadelphia: Jewish Publication Society, 1961-66.

Beinart, Haim. "Demutah shel ha-hazranut ha-yehudit bi-Sefarad." *Qevusot 'elit ve-shikhvot manhigot be-toledot Yisra'el u-ve-toledot ha-'amim*. Jerusalem: Ha-hevrah ha-historit ha-Yisra'elit, 1966.

Brann, Ross. "The Arabized Jews." In *The Literature of al-Andalus*, edited by María Rosa Menocal, Raymond P. Scheindlin, and Michael Sells, 435-454. Cambridge: Cambridge University Press, 2000.

------. *Power in the Portrayal: Representations of Jews and Muslims in Eleventh- and Twelfth-Century Islamic Spain*. Princeton: Princeton University Press, 2002.

Castaño, Javier. "Social Networks in a Castilian Jewish Aljama and the Court Jews in the Fifteenth Century: A Preliminary Survey (Madrid 1440-75)." *En la España medieval* 20 (1997): 379-92.

Cohen, Gerson D. *Sefer ha-Qabbalah: The Book of Tradition by Abraham Ibn Daud*. Philadelphia: Jewish Publication Society, 1967.

Cohen, Mark and Sasson Somekh. "In the Court of Ya'qūb Ibn Killis: A Fragment from the Cairo Genizah." *Jewish Quarterly Review* 80 (1990): 283-314.

Decter, Jonathan. *Iberian Jewish Literature: Between al-Andalus and Christian Europe*. Bloomington: Indiana University Press, 2007.

------. "May God Curse Them Both: Ibrāhīm Ibn al-Fakhār al-Yahūdi Between Castile and the Maghrib." In *Beyond Religious Borders: Interaction and Intellectual Exchange in the Medieval Islamic World,* ed. David M. Freidenreich and Miriam Goldstein (Philadelphia: University of Pennsylvania Press, forthcoming in 2012.

Doron, Aviva. *Meshorer be-hasar ha-melekh: Todros Halevi Abulafiah, shirah 'ivrit bi-Sefarad ha-nosrit.* Tel Aviv: Dvir, 1989.

Fierro, Maribel. "Alfonso X 'The Wise': The Last Almohad Caliph?" *Medieval Encounters* 15 (2009): 175-198.

Fischel, Walter. *Jews in the Economic and Political Life of Mediaeval Islam.* London: The Royal Asiatic Society, 1937.

Graetz, Heinrich. *History of the Jews: From the Earliest Times to the Present Day.* Translated by Bella Löwy. London: David Nutt, 1892.

Gutwirth, Eleazar. "Abraham Seneor: Social Tensions and the Court-Jew." *Michael* 11 (1989): 169-229.

------. "Don Ishaq Abravanel and Vernacular Humanism in Fifteenth Century Iberia." *Bibliothèque d'Humanisme et Renaissance* 60 (1998): 641–671.

------. "Hercules furens and War: On Abravanel's Courtly Context." *Jewish History* 23 (2009): 293-312.

Horowitz, Elliot. "The Court Jews and the Jewish Question." *Jewish History* 12 (1998): 113-36.

Kaplan, Yosef. "Court Jews before the 'Hofjuden.'" In *From Court Jews to the Rothschilds: Art, Patronage, and Power, 1600-1800,* edited by Vivian B. Mann and Richard I. Cohen, 11-25. New York: Jewish Museum, 1996.

Kobler, Franz. *A Treasury of Jewish Letters: Letters from the Famous and the Humble.* Philadelphia: Jewish Publication Society, 1953.

Lawee, Eric. *Isaac Abarbanel's Stance Toward Tradition.* Albany: SUNY Press, 2001.

Lipiner, Elias. *Two Portuguese Exiles in Castile: Dom David Negro and Dom Isaac Abravanel.* Jerusalem: Magnes Press, 1997.

Mann, Jacob. *Texts and Studies in Jewish History and Literature.* Cincinnati: Hebrew Union College, 1931-35.

Meyerson, Mark D. *A Jewish Renaissance in Fifteenth-Century Spain.* Princeton: Princeton University Press, 2004.

Netanyahu, Benzion. *Don Isaac Abravanel: Statesman and Philosopher.* Philadelphia: Jewish Publication Society, 1953.

Perry, T.A. *The Moral Proverbs of Santob de Carrión: Jewish Wisdom in Christian Spain.* Princeton: Princeton University Press, 1987.

Ray, Jonathan. "Royal Authority and the Jewish Community: The Crown Rabbi in Medieval Spain and Portugal." In *Jewish Religious Leadership: Image and Reality,* edited by Jack Wertheimer, 307-331. New York: Jewish Theological Seminary, 2004.

------. *The Sephardic Frontier: The Reconquista and the Jewish Community in Medieval Iberia.* Ithaca: Cornell University Press, 2006.

Romano, David. "Cortesanos judíos en la Corona de Aragón." *Desíierros Aragoneses* 1 (1988): 25-37.

Safran, Bezalel. "Bahya Ibn Paquda's Attitude Toward the Courtier Class." In *Studies in Medieval Jewish History and Literature,* vol. 1, edited by Isadore Twersky, 154-196. Cambridge, MA: Harvard University Press, 1979.

Sassenberg, Marina. "The Face of Janus: The Historian Selma Stern (1890-1981) and Her Portrait of the Court Jew." *European Judaism* 33 (2000): 72-79.

Scheiber, Alexander and Zvi Malachi. "Letter from Sicily to Hasdai Ibn Shaprut." *Proceedings of the American Academy for Jewish Research* 41/42 (1973 – 1974): 207-218.

Schirmann, Jefim. *Ha-shirah ha-'ivrit bi-sefarad u-ve-provans.* Tel Aviv: Dvir, 1954-60.

Septimus, Bernard. "Piety and Power in Thirteenth-Century Catalonia." In *Studies in Medieval Jewish History and Literature,* edited by Isadore Twersky, 197-230. Cambridge, MA: Harvard University Press, 1979.

Skalli, Cedric Cohen. "Abravanel's Commentary on the Former Prophets: Portraits, Self-Portraits, and Models of Leadership." *Jewish History* 23 (2009): 255-80.

Stern, Selma. *The Court Jew: A Contribution to the History of the Period of Absolutism in Central Europe.* Translated by Ralph Weiman. Philadelphia: Jewish Publication Society, 1950.

Stern, S.M. "Shetei yedi'ot hadashot 'al Hasdai Ibn Shaprut." *Zion* 11 (1946): 141-46.

Wasserstein, David. "Jewish Elites in al-Andalus." In *The Jews of Medieval Islam: Community, Society, and Identity*, edited by Daniel Frank, 101-110. Leiden: Brill, 1992.

------. "The Muslims and the Golden Age of the Jews in al-Andalus." *Israel Oriental Studies* 17 (1997): 179-96.

Weiss, Joseph. "Tarbut hasranit ve-shirah hasranit." *World Congress of Jewish Studies* 1 (1947): 396-402.

Yerushalmi, Yosef Haim. *The Lisbon Massacre of 1506 and the Royal Image in the Shebet Yehudah.* Cincinnati: Hebrew Union College, 1976.

The World of Samuel Halevi: Testimony from the El Transito Synagogue of Toledo

.... Jane S. Gerber

The transplantation of the Jews from Muslim to Christian Spain as a result of the twelfth-century Almohad persecutions did not spell the end of the rich culture they had forged in Andalusia. Continuities with the past endured even as new challenges arose. As medieval Spain entered the cultural orbit of Northern Europe and retreated from the world of Islam, new formulations of Iberian Jewish civilization were expressed in the arts as well as in their halakhic formulations. While art historians have demonstrated repeatedly how the co-existence of cultures brought creative tension and originality to the arts of Christian Spain, rarely have the artifacts and monuments commissioned by the small elite of "Arabized Jews" of the courtier class been examined. Although few Jewish architectural monuments have survived the vicissitudes of medieval times, the few that have point to the persistence of Islamic cultural influences in the artistic realm.

Toledo contained the largest Jewish community in medieval Christian Spain. Geographically located at the juncture of the Iberian Muslim and Christian civilizations, Toledo's role as a cultural meeting ground also extended to its Jewish population. Jews were natural intermediaries in the cultural encounters on Toledan soil: they spoke several languages, straddled the many borders and geographic and linguistic frontiers of Iberia, and could instinctively adapt to both Muslim and Christian cultural milieus. With co-religionists dispersed in Muslim and Christian Spain, the Jews of Toledo crossed cultural as well as geographic borders with ease. From the vantage point of Sephardic Judaism, Toledo also served as a meeting ground for the Ashkenazic and Sephardic halakhic traditions.[1] Just as the Christian art of Toledo expressed the composite nature of Christian culture in the Kingdom of Castile, so the Jewish arts in Toledo experienced a melding of disparate elements into new syntheses. In some cases, the melding of cultures was deliberate: the retention and re-shaping of Muslim cultural motifs in Christian Spain went beyond the purely decorative and ornamental, on the one hand, or triumphalist or imitative, on the other. In the case of the Halevi synagogue and its architecture, other important messages were intended in the choice of its decorative visual vocabulary.

Toledo's place as a royal city of Spain goes back to Roman and Visigothic times. When the Arabs conquered Toledo in 711, the city had been largely abandoned by fleeing Christian inhabitants. The Jews, only recently forcibly converted to Christianity by the last Visigothic kings, began to come out of hiding as the Arabs approached the city. According to later Arabic chronicles, the conquerors assigned the Jews to serve as gatekeepers and patrols while their aggressive warriors continued their expansion northwards.[2] The Muslim invaders apparently recognized the local Jews as a dependable urban population, more interested in living peacefully than in forming bellicose alliances with the Christian powers to the North.

Under the expanding umbrella of Muslim rule the Jews of Toledo prospered. They were concentrated in their own quarter (*Rabd al-Yahud* or *Madinat al-Yahud*), nestled on a hill in the southwest corner

---

[1] See Bernard Septimus, *Hispano-Jewish Culture in Transition: The Career and Controversies of Ramah* (Cambridge: Harvard University Press, 1982) on the advent of Ashkenazic scholarship to Spain with the arrival of the Ramah (1165-1244).

[2] Norman Stillman, *The Jews of Muslim Lands* (Philadelphia: Jewish Publication Society, 1986), 156, and Norman Roth, "The Arab Conquest of Spain and the Jews," *Jewish Social Studies* 37 (1976): 135-158.

of the city. Their population concentration at one of the city gates was reflected in the naming of that gate *Bab el-Yahud* (the gate of the Jews.) Jewish residents could be found in several neighborhoods or *barrios* in early medieval times, where they lived among Muslims and Christians. A fortress in the southern city walls was inhabited by Jews and was known as "the citadel of the Jews." One of the city walls of Toledo formed the north side of the Jewish quarter. Settlement of the Jews in fortresses and fortified walls suggests that they were able to assume a trustworthy defensive role when necessary.

Toledo was the first major Muslim city to fall to the Christians in 1085 in their long struggle to uproot the Muslims, known as the reconquest *(Reconquista)*. Toledo's early reconquest by the Christians left the city in a unique position: for over one century it remained a Christian enclave in a predominantly Muslim region, poised strategically between the warring Christian and Muslim kingdoms. The geopolitical situation of Toledo played a crucial role in the shaping of its cultural identity. When the city surrendered, Muslims were initially permitted to remain. The Jews were induced to remain and continued to possess their homes and fields and orchards. Estimates of the medieval Jewish population in Christian Toledo vary widely. According to Yitzhak Baer, Jewish taxpayers (meaning heads of households) numbered 3,600 by the end of the thirteenth century. A more inflated estimate places the eleventh century total population of Toledo at around 37,000 with the Jews numbering perhaps as many as 12,000.[3] Perhaps one index of the size of the Jewish population in Toledo is the number of synagogues that the city contained. At least fourteen synagogues and schools are mentioned in fourteenth-century sources, many of them probably built in an earlier era. Their beauty was so striking that Judah al-Harizi was inspired to declare in his *Tahkemoni* "What beautiful palaces are in her that put to shame the luminaries with the splendor of their beauty and loveliness. And how many synagogues are in her whose beauty is incomparable." [4]

Only two of Toledo's medieval synagogues, the synagogue known as Santa Maria la Blanca and the synagogue known as the El

---

[3] This figure is mentioned by Abraham ben Samuel Zacuto, *Sefer Yuhasin ha-Shalem*, ed. H. Filipowski (London: [u. a.], 1857), Photo reprint (Jerusalem, 1963), fol. 221b.

[4] Judah al-Harizi, *Tahkemoni*, ed. J. Toporovsky (Tel Aviv, 1952), 345-346.

Transito Synagogue, remain standing today. Both synagogues were converted into churches in the fifteenth century and were declared Spanish national monuments in the nineteenth century. The other synagogues of medieval Toledo have long since disappeared, recalled for posterity in a mournful medieval elegy commemorating the pogrom in Toledo of August 1391 that was recited thereafter on the fast day of the Ninth of Ab.[5] Synagogue numbers can be a misleading index of population size since many were erected by wealthy Jewish individuals for their personal use in their own homes. Sources agree, however, that Toledo was the largest Jewish community in the Kingdom of Castile.

The Jewish culture of al-Andalus, born in Córdoba and Lucena, did not quickly die among the refugees who regrouped in Christian Spain. The initial hope of the intellectuals was to re-establish the old Andalusian culture on safer soil, to restore, as Ibn Daud declaimed, "the poetry and the philosophy, the sciences and the Torah that would display the same harmony on the shores of the Tagus as they had on the Guadalquivir." This hope was to prove illusory. The frontier between the two triumphalist faiths of Christianity and Islam was not merely a border but a perilous region of constant warfare in which the Jews would find themselves increasingly vulnerable. Christian Europe, moreover, had entered a new phase in which the proselytizing mission of the Church would bring little respite for Jews or Muslims in Spain.

During the changeover from Muslim to Christian rule, Jews were permitted to remain in their original quarters in Toledo. Their two extant medieval synagogues, Santa Maria la Blanca and the synagogue of courtier Samuel Halevi Abulafia, known as El Transito, date from the thirteenth and fourteenth centuries respectively. Most often, they are cited as evidence of and testimony to the medieval *"convivencia"* when Muslims, Christians and Jews lived side by side in the medieval capital of the Kingdom of Castile. The Samuel Halevi synagogue is the handiwork of the chief treasurer (*Tesoro mayor del rey*) to King Pedro I (1350-1369) of Castile, known in history as Pedro the Cruel. It was constructed to serve as Halevi's personal

---

[5] Cecil Roth, "A Hebrew Elegy on the Martyrs of Toledo, 1391," *Jewish Quarterly Review* 39 (1948): 135-50.

house of worship, easily accessible to his sumptuous home nearby. The monument can be understood on several levels. On the one hand, as a fourteenth century Jewish house of worship attached to the residence of an important government official, the structure mirrors the edifices built by nobles, high church officials, or princes. In this context, it reflects the tastes of the patron's time while also incorporating timeless features common to Jewish houses of worship everywhere. On the other hand, its decorative vocabulary and checkered history testify in stone and stucco to the complexity of its patron, Halevi, and his cultural identity. Situated within the Jewish quarter, El Transito also should be examined as a manifestation of Samuel, the court Jew, and his relationship to his co-religionists.

The construction of a new synagogue in fourteenth-century Toledo begs further explanation. New synagogue construction was probably not a regular occurrence in light of the restrictions placed on synagogues in general by this time. Its decorative details supply an alternative visual source to speak about the internalization of cultural elements of the surrounding society in ways that a written text might not necessarily express. While some of this information may be highly conjectural, historical reconstruction often combines the conjectural in the absence of the textual.

The objective data surrounding the history of the synagogue are fairly straightforward. The building, according to its dedicatory plaque, was dedicated in the year 5117 (1357). Its main sanctuary measures seventy-five feet in length, thirty-one feet in width, and thirty-nine feet in height. Its walls are richly decorated with stucco paneling, Castilian coats of arms (a fortress for Castile and a lion for Leon) and graceful interlacing vegetal motifs in a characteristic Islamic-inspired *mudéjar* style, a style generally characterized by stucco surface ornamentation of vegetal and arabesque motifs and architecturally-integrated inscriptions. The style was inspired by Islamic forms, but its use did not require a Muslim presence nor did it necessarily carry Islamic religious meaning.

The most noteworthy feature of the synagogue is the exceptionally beautiful set of Hebrew inscriptions that adorn its four walls in three bands of varying sizes encircling the entire main sanctuary. They are surely the most famous Hebrew inscriptions of the Middle

Ages. Most surprising and somewhat enigmatic is the presence of Arabic inscriptions, placed high up amidst the Hebrew inscriptions and barely visible from ground level. In contrast to the enormous richness, variety and clarity of the Hebrew inscriptions, the Arabic calligraphy is much smaller in size and barely legible, lacking diacritical marks and containing a few repetitious phrases or words. They are inconspicuously located under one of the rows of Hebrew inscriptions, in the carved wooden ceiling beams which form octagonal stars amidst interlocking squares, and tucked into several cartouches or medallions. Some of the Arabic inscriptions seem to float inconspicuously in and out of the vegetal frieze in which they are entwined. Given the placement of the Arabic inscriptions high up in the building and the absence of diacritical marks they were clearly not intended to be read by worshippers. Yet, their presence provides a neglected clue to understanding the persona of the Jewish courtier who commissioned the synagogue while also shedding light on the courtier's relationship to his king and to the culture of the society in which he moved.

In contrast to the absence of a tradition of scholarly discussion of the inconspicuous Arabic inscriptions, the Hebrew inscriptions in the Halevi synagogue have been the subject of considerable scholarly interest. They were first recorded in the eighteenth century. In 1905 the Spanish scholar Rodrigo Amador de los Rios published a full transcription and Spanish translation of them and also noted the presence of the Arabic inscriptions, identifying them as Quranic.[6] This identification has been generally accepted at face value without further comments, partially as a result of the stature of Amador in Spanish scholarship. Only recently has the question of the literal and symbolic meaning of the synagogue's Arabic inscriptions been raised. The inscriptions, like the ambiguous identity of their

---

[6] Rodrigo Amador de los Rios, *Monumentos arquitectónicos de España: Toledo* (Madrid: Izquierdo, 1905). On the Hebrew inscriptions see Francisco Cantera Burgos and J. M. Millás Vallicrosa, *Las Inscripciones hebraicas de España* (Madrid: Izquierdo, 1956); and Cecil Roth, "Las Inscripciones históricas en la Sinagoga Toledana de R. Samuel ha-Levi de Toledo," *Sefarad* 8 (1948): 3-22. A transcription of the Hebrew inscriptions can be found in Mordechai Omer, "The Samuel ha-Levi Synagogue," in *The Synagogue of Samuel ha-Levi*, trans. by G. Levin (Tel Aviv: Genia Scheiber University Gallery, 1992), 167-81.

patron, demand further explanation.[7] It has been suggested recently by Maria Menocal that the presence of Arabic inscriptions in the synagogue constituted an expression of "positive proof of Jewish gratitude of a culture of tolerance" i.e. Islam.[8] This politically charged contemporary explanation, however, obscures the role that Islamic-style art played in conveying other messages of cultural meaning in Christian Spain.

The construction of a new and beautifully decorated synagogue in fourteenth-century Spain raises immediate questions. Apparently, the injunctions against the construction of new synagogues promulgated at various Spanish regional councils during the fourteenth century were only sporadically enforced. It is possible that Samuel undertook his project at a propitious moment or that the prohibition against new synagogue construction was waived in the case of his synagogue as a result of his relationship with the king. It was not unusual for synagogue construction to proceed upon the payment of special fees or bribes or through the personal dispensation of the Crown. Or, perhaps, the prohibition did not apply in Castile to synagogues dedicated in private homes, a favored method in both Christian and Muslim territories to circumvent the ban against the erection of new synagogues. In the case of the Halevi synagogue, recently uncovered archeological evidence suggests that the synagogue may have been built on the ruins of a former synagogue dating back to Muslim times, thereby avoiding the ban

---

[7] Synagogue architectural historian Rachel Wischnitzer in *The Architecture of the European Synagogue* (Philadelphia: Jewish Publication Society, 1964) accepts the Quranic identification without comment. Jerrilynn Dodds also identifies the Arabic inscription as "texts from the Qur'an" in "Mudéjar Tradition and the Synagogues of Medieval Spain: Cultural Identity and Cultural Hegemony", in *Convivencia: Jews, Muslims, and Christians in Medieval Spain*, ed. Vivian Mann, Thomas F. Glick and Jerrilynn Dodds (New York: George Braziler, 1992), 113-32. Most recently, the mudéjar style of the synagogue and its Arabic inscriptions have been cited by Maria Rosa Menocal in *The Ornament of the World* (Boston: Little, Brown, 2002) as "positive proof of Jewish gratitude for the Islamic culture of tolerance." in what she calls "a palace of memory of a culture of tolerance." For an extensive and judicious discussion of the Arabic inscriptions, see Elise Anne Foster's M.A. thesis "The Writing on the Walls: The Presence of Arabic Inscriptions in the Synagogue El Transito" submitted to the Department of Art History, Southern Methodist University, 2004.

[8] See Maria Rosa Menocal "Culture in the Time of Tolerance: Al-Andalus as a Model for our Time," *Yale Law School Occasional Paper*, Second Series, No. 6. (N.D.)

on the construction of a new synagogue altogether.[9] Given the lavish encomia of the reigning monarch that Halevi included in his synagogue's dedicatory plaque, it is highly likely that the king was party to the erection of this private house of worship, perhaps even participating personally at its dedication.

The vicissitudes of the Samuel Halevi synagogue in Toledo mirror those of its patron and his community. The building is listed as *Beit Knesset Sar Shmuel Halevi, Nasi Yisrael* (The Synagogue of Samuel Halevi, Prince of Israel) among the ten synagogues and five schools (*Batei Midrash*) desecrated in Toledo in the devastating pogrom that swept through Spain in 1391. Its sacking is mournfully recalled in a special dirge that was recited by Sephardic Jews on Ninth of Ab.[10] It was abandoned when the Jews were expelled in 1492 and ceded to the military Order of the Knights of Calatrava two years later. The Knights of the Order used the building as a hospice and chapel for several generations. The burial sites of nineteen knights are located under the floor of its main sanctuary. With the decline of the military order in the seventeenth century the building was donated to the Jesuits and acquired the name "El Transito de nuestra Senora" or simply El Transito, the name that it bears until today. During the Napoleonic era the building was temporarily converted into a military barracks. Finally, in 1877 the building was declared a Spanish national monument. Renovation began soon thereafter and continues to the present. The Sephardic Museum of Toledo is currently housed in what was once the women's gallery of the synagogue.

The El Transito synagogue is a classic example of the *mudéjar* or Islamic-inspired style of art and architecture that was popular in medieval Spain, a style that has become synonymous with Spanish art. Toledo was the center of this style in the fourteenth century. A characteristic feature of *mudéjar* art is the inclusion of Arabic and pseudo-Arabic inscriptions, even when the building or object in question had a clearly Christian religious purpose. From the tenth century onwards Islamic buildings were characterized by

---

[9] Santiago Palomera Plaza, Ana María López Álvarez and Yasmina Álvarez Delgado, "Excavations around the Samuel Halevi Synagogue (El Tránsito) in Toledo," *Jewish Art* 18 (1992): 48-57.

[10] Cecil Roth, "A Hebrew Elegy on the Martyrs of Toledo, 1391," *op.cit.,n.5.*

decorative portals while the rest of the building was left relatively plain or decorated with individual panels, bands of inscriptions and rows of niches. Glazed tiles and painted stuccos combined with carved wooden elements in their building materials. The use of floral designs, arabesques, and foliated vines was characteristic of Islamic art whether in mosques, tombs, or on decorated boxes and the ornamental covers of Qurans. The most important and characteristic element in the art of the Islamic world is calligraphy. Its prominence is based upon the role of Arabic script as embodying the word of God in the Quran. Despite differences of scripts and styles throughout the Muslim world, calligraphy in architecture was an element that bound all the different styles together. Until today, it is difficult to find a building or an object of art in the Islamic world that does not have an inscription somewhere on its surface.

At first blush, the construction of a synagogue or church in the *mudéjar* style would appear anachronistic and puzzling. After all, the power of Islam had receded on most of the peninsula after the battle of Las Navas de Tolosa in 1212 and certainly by the time of the fall of Córdoba and Seville in 1236 and 1248 respectively. By the fourteenth century, Toledo was the seat of the most powerful Christian kingdom on the Iberian Peninsula. Despite the retreat of Islam as a political force in Iberia, its cultural influence did not disappear. The *mudéjar* style and its artistic vocabulary, including Arabic calligraphy, remained a favorite style, even on Christian religious buildings, suggesting to some observers either the re-cycling of formerly Muslim monuments or the handiwork of Muslims who served as stonemasons, plasterers, and carpenters of the buildings. These Muslim artisans, it is suggested, out of a sense of spite or as a mischievous prank, would covertly insert Quranic verses into their designs. Their Christian sponsors, unable to read the Arabic language and hence probably unaware of the presence of Arabic script, simply appreciated the shape of the lines as a decorative motif. Such reasoning is highly unlikely in the case of the El Transito synagogue. Its patron and owner, Samuel Halevi, was an exacting and demanding man of the world. He was an extremely efficient businessman who dealt extensively with the Muslim court in Granada and undoubtedly spoke Arabic. Given his temperament and attention to detail, it is highly unlikely that he left the building plans for his personal chapel to an underling or was not involved in every detail of its decoration. His closeness to the king of Granada probably included some cultural affinities including language. Like many educated Jews in Christian Spain, Halevi probably spoke Arabic even if he didn't read Arabic characters, and he would certainly have been able to recognize its script. In general, Arabic culture remained an essential ingredient of Sephardic Jewish culture even within the Latin and Romance environment of Christian Spain. Recognition of Arabic lettering, even without a reading knowledge of the language, was quite common among Jews in Toledo as late as the fourteenth century and even into the fifteenth century.[11] Jewish signatures from fifteenth-century documents attest to the continuing daily use of the language long after Muslims had ceased to play a major role economically or intellectually in Christian Spain. Additionally, Arabic remained the language of the communal ordinances of the Jewish community of Toledo. Knowledge of Arabic, especially on the part of courtiers, provided a valuable tool in administration and diplomacy. The quality of multi-lingualism which had served the Jews so well during the first stages of the Reconquest would remain an important Sephardic skill in their many lands of dispersion after the expulsion.

The use of Arabic inscriptions in medieval buildings, whether in synagogues, palaces, or churches, served several purposes that had little to do with religion. The most obvious is the primary function of providing information on the date of construction and the identity of the buildings patron and/or the ruling dynasty. Some inscriptions, such as the ones that appear repeatedly on the walls of the Alhambra Palace proclaiming "Power to our Lord Abu Abdallah" or even "There is no Victorious One but God" were more political than religious in intent. They cover the palace's walls in celebration of the ruler of the Nasrid Kingdom of Granada, Muhammed V (1354-1391), and his victory over the Christian armies at Algeciras. Another use of iconographic inscriptions is to emphasize the special purpose that a building serves or to make an association that is not

---

[11] Yom Tov Assis, "The Judeo-Arabic Tradition in Christian Spain" in *The Jews of Medieval Islam*, ed. Daniel Frank (New York: Brill, 1995), 115.

necessarily overt. Islamic art historian Oleg Grabar, in his important work on the Alhambra and in his masterful book *The Meditation of Ornament*, has argued that Arabic script was frequently monoptic, that is, that its form could immediately provide the viewer with a meaning outside of its text.[12] In light of the fact that Arabic script is frequently quite difficult to decipher, even in a purely Islamic context, it is important to emphasize that it is sometimes inserted in an object simply for the pleasure of the viewer. The very shape of the lettering of a word and the strictly formal qualities of words constitute an art form capable of conveying ideological meanings. In Grabar's view the Arabic script on the walls of the Alhambra fit this last function, constituting an extravagant statement of royal luxury intended to awe the spectator with the power of the Muslim king.

Samuel Halevi's use of Arabic inscriptions in his private synagogue should be considered in similar fashion. The presence of Arabic on the synagogue walls was probably neither accidental nor solely decorative. It contained several meanings. Viewed together with the Hebrew inscriptions, the use of Arabic defined Samuel Halevi, the quintessential courtier Jew. His synagogue was not simply an imitation of contemporary palatine structures but possessed its own language and messages for his co-religionists who might worship there. Who was Samuel Halevi and what meaning might he have attached to the decorative motifs of his private synagogue?

Samuel Halevi Abulafia was descended from the prominent Abulafia family whose members furnished several generations of financiers, poets, and doctors to the royal courts in Spain. A courtier from his youth, Samuel entered the royal service in the court of Alfonso XI (1312-1350) in 1344 as a protégé of Juan Alfonso de Albuquerque. Albuquerque acted as confidant and tutor to Alfonso's son Pedro I (1350-1369), later known as Pedro the Cruel. Samuel rose in official circles as a result of his friendship with Albuquerque and the success of young Pedro in the contested accession to the throne. Samuel's steadfast support of Pedro, despite the king's repeated marital and extramarital entanglements, earned the Jewish courtier numerous enemies among the nobility, especially the king's

---

[12] Oleg Grabar, *The Meditation of Ornament* (Princeton: Princeton University Press, 1992), 103.

illegitimate half-brothers Enrique and Fadrique de Trastamara. With the backing of Albuquerque Samuel was appointed to serve as chief treasurer (*Tesoro mayor del rey*) to King Pedro I. He also served as a diplomat in negotiations between the kingdoms of Castile and Portugal. As was commonplace, Samuel appointed several members of his family to political and financial posts during his tenure as chief treasurer.

Samuel Halevi functioned as a dynamic and aggressive administrator for Pedro from 1353-1360. As a result of his efficient tax farming and tax collecting he succeeded in collecting vast sums of money for the king in the form of tax arrears, effectively confiscating the estates of recalcitrant nobles. In addition to the courtier's ability to function in Arabic and his ability to extend credit to the king, his independence of the nobility and total dependence on the king were extremely valuable traits. All the while that Halevi rose in the king's esteem he advanced the cause of Don Pedro,[13] and while enriching the king he also enriched his own private purse. Wealth and royal service went hand in hand. Without a degree of personal wealth, a Jewish courtier was of little service to his monarch. Royal service apparently also offered the opportunity to share in both the profits and prerogatives of royal government. One index of Samuel's vast power is the fact that he was entrusted with the use of the official seal of Castile (a castle). This privilege was clear proof of Samuel's relationship of trust with King Pedro I and of his exercise of real as opposed to symbolic power. The seal would be a prominent decorative feature of his synagogue.

During his years of royal service Samuel built several synagogues for himself, notably in Seville and Toledo. This last was dedicated in 1357. Its stucco walls had scarcely dried when, in December 1360, Samuel was arrested on charges of corruption, imprisoned in Seville, and tortured to death.[14] It is not clear who denounced Samuel Halevi, accusing him of hiding a fortune that rightfully belonged to his monarch and possibly also implicating him in conspiratorial

---

[13] On the reign of Pedro I see Clara Estow, *Pedro the Cruel of Castile* (Leiden: Brill, 1995), especially chapter 7, "Ennobler of Jews and Moors," 155-179.

[14] See Benjamin F. Taggie, "Samuel ha-Levi Abulafia and the Hebraic Policy of Pedro I of Castile 1350-1369," *Fifteenth Century Studies* 5 (1972): 191-208, and especially Clara Estow, *Pedro the Cruel of Castile*. Halevi appears repeatedly in an unfavorable light in the partisan contemporary chronicle of Don Pedro López de Ayala.

activities against the Crown. Halevi's arrest, perhaps coincidentally, occurred four days following the arrest of the Archbishop of Toledo on charges of conspiracy against the king. Pedro's personal role in the betrayal and murder of his Jewish financier is uncertain, despite his reputation in Spanish history as King Pedro the Cruel. According to the (biased and anti-Jewish) chronicler of Pedro's reign, Don Pedro Lopez de Ayala, Halevi's confiscated fortune was enormous, consisting of 107,000 doubloons, 4,000 silver marks, 125 chests filled with gold, silver and precious textiles and 80 Muslim slaves. It is indeed doubtful whether even the most favored Jewish courtier would have been permitted to hold such a vast number of slaves, given both Jewish opposition to slaveholding and prevailing Christian legislation against Jewish slaveholding. The accusation is nonetheless significant in light of the repeated sermons that the rabbis of Spain delivered admonishing the courtier class and warning of the corrupting influence of slave-holding and its resulting concubinage among the rich and powerful. Samuel probably shared this practice of the rich in the community. His grim fate was sealed by his close association with a mercurial monarch and an unpopular dynasty. When civil war broke out between Pedro and his half-brothers in the 1360's, convulsing the country for almost a decade, the Jewish community of Toledo experienced enormous suffering. One accusation hurled against King Pedro by his rival half-brothers was that he was an "ennobler of Jews and Moors."[15]

The El Transito synagogue is a classic example of the *mudéjar* style of architecture. The term *mudéjar* has a dual meaning. *Mudéjares* was the term applied to those Spanish Muslims who lived under Christian rule (from the Arabic *mudajjan*-the ones who remained). It is used as well in reference to Islamic- or Arabic-style art and architecture. Although the term implies intercultural and interethnic relations in Iberia, it is rarely used by art historians in reference to Jewish architecture or art, even when the Jewish

---

[15] The term "ennobler" of the Jews appeared in a list of grievances against Pedro in 1366. Estow, 175, n. 58 from Luciano Serrano, *Cartulario del Infantado de Covarrubias* (Madrid: Del Amo, 1907), 217-219. See Pedro López de Ayala (1322-1407), *Crónica del rey don Pedro*, ed. Constance L. Wilkins and Heanon M. Wilkins (Madison: Hispanic Seminary of Medieval Studies, 1985). Ayala was extremely hostile to Pedro as well as to Halevi, but his chronicle nonetheless remains an invaluable source of information on the regime.

structures exhibited the same mélange of cultural influences as the Christian structures or objects of the same period and style. With the notable exception of Jerrilynn Dodds, most art historians do not include synagogues when discussing the *mudéjar* style. This omission is surprising since *mudéjar* was the architectural style of three of the four medieval synagogues that have survived in Spain (two in Toledo and one in Córdoba).

During the period of the Christian reconquest many of the churches that sprang up in the conquered territories were buildings transformed from their original purpose as mosques. It is therefore natural that these buildings would contain vestiges of Islamic decoration from their former function. Yet some of the most beautiful churches in Spain, built specifically to serve as churches, employed Islamic-style decorative motifs from their inception. In many instances these newly constructed *mudéjar* churches included Arabic inscriptions or inscriptions that had the appearance of Arabic but were actually pseudo-Arabic; these inscriptions were frequently devoid of meaning and *intended purely for decoration*. Although the script used to ornament the churches might be recognizable as Arabic, it was not Islamic in content. Its effect was meant to be fashionable and aesthetic. Just as it is quite illogical to assume that the use of Arabic script to decorate a church, especially one erected during the era of the *Reconquista* when enmity between Christianity and Islam was at its height, constituted "a tribute to the tolerance of Islam" or to the culture of the "other," the same logic applies in the case of the Arabic script found in the El Transito synagogue. It is highly probable that the presence of Arabic script in the synagogue was selected for its decorative qualities and with other purposes in mind and did not constitute an expression of gratitude to Islam and its policies of rule.

The *mudéjar* style, widely employed in Northern Spain during the great boom in church construction accompanying the reconquest, recalled the affluence and power of the previous Andalusian historical epoch. Art historians have suggested that it was widely understood as representing a Spanish national style, reminiscent of Iberian greatness under the Muslims, in opposition to the Romanesque and Gothic style of architecture so popular among the clerics, mendicants, and Northern European artists streaming into Spain from France.[16] In selecting the *mudéjar* style the Jewish courtier was embracing the popular Spanish national cultural idiom that surrounded him and reached a peak in popularity in fourteenth-century Castile.

The bonds of friendship between King Pedro and the King of Granada should also not be discounted. King Pedro, Halevi's patron, was raised in Andalusia and never lost his taste and affection for Andalusian tastes and styles. In renovating his royal complex, the Alcazar in Seville, Pedro retained and restored many of the decorative touches and inscriptions that had existed in the former Almohad fortress. The Alcazar was one of Pedro's favorite residences, one on which he lavished funds and attention. The dates of the palace's construction, 1353-1364, overlapped precisely with Halevi's synagogue building project. The same years also witnessed the construction of the majestic royal palace complex of the Alhambra in Granada under King Muhammed V. As a man of the world, Samuel Halevi was at ease in the palaces of the Muslim and Christian potentates of his day. The impressive and similar decorative motifs of the two exceptional royal residences that Samuel visited must have been etched in his mind since he replicated them down to several minute details on the walls of his own house of worship. Since the Castilian king and the Muslim king were personal friends and frequent allies, it was natural that they might share architects and artisans to embellish their reputations and their residences. Perhaps their masons and artists also offered advice (and their labors) to the self-confident Jewish courtier who shuttled back and forth between Seville, Granada and Toledo, collecting taxes and making loans, all the while concentrating on his personal project of building a private synagogue adjoining his house. As King Pedro's chief treasurer, Halevi probably also had to deal personally with the king's contractors and architects while they pored over construction budgets and building blueprints. Pedro had a peripatetic court and was often away from the palace on hunting expeditions or fighting

---

[16] See Jerrilynn Dodds, "Mudéjar Tradition in Architecture" and, "The Arts of al-Andalus" in *The Legacy of Muslim Spain* II, ed. S. Jayyusi (Leiden: Brill, 1992) 592-599-618, and Dodds, *Architecture and Ideology in Early Medieval Spain* (University Park: Pennsylvania State University, 1990).

his half-brothers. During Samuel's frequent official business visits to Seville or Granada in the course of the decade of the 1350s, it is likely that Halevi found himself alone on occasion in the Alcazar, with ample time on his hands to contemplate its exquisite architecture and tasteful Arabic inscriptions at leisure.

Even the most superficial comparison of the stucco decoration on the walls of the two famous palaces with the synagogue's reveals remarkable similarities in their poly-lobed arches and graceful Arabic inscriptions. The same scallop and diamond designs abound. A similar profusion of interlacing leaf and vine scrolls, the pronounced pinecones, and the prominent decorative role of inscriptions as decoration when viewed together suggest the hand of the same designer at work. The choice of the *mudéjar* style in all three edifices is not that surprising. Given the relationship of the three men, it is not inconceivable that the Castilian Christian king, the Grenadine Muslim king and the Jewish courtier shared a common artistic vocabulary and popular taste as they embarked upon their building projects. It was the preferred style of nobility. And Halevi considered himself Jewish nobility, a prince among princes of the tribe of Levi.

While the fact that Halevi emulated the royal style of the king of Castile and the king of Granada in selecting the design and interior decoration of his synagogue seems obvious, several other questions remain. Was there any specific role that the Arabic inscriptions may have played in the synagogue of Toledo beyond the merely decorative? Were the inscriptions in Arabic even intended to be read or were they merely aesthetic touches? And do they bear any relationship to the Hebrew inscriptions beyond the aesthetic effect of the juxtaposition of several scripts? What might the overall effect of the several scripts and inscriptions have been on the worshippers in attendance at the synagogue? In order to answer these questions it is necessary to examine the Arabic and Hebrew inscriptions more closely.

While the Arabic epigraphy in the Alhambra and the Alcazar is profuse, visible and also quite legible, appearing everywhere—in various public as well as private areas of the two official palaces— its position in the synagogue is starkly different. There it is barely noticeable and scarcely legible. It is significant that no Arabic is included on the eastern wall of the synagogue. This contrast between public art and private décor raises questions about the public role of Samuel Halevi. It is intriguing to speculate, lacking much evidence, on the place of Arabic in fourteenth-century Jewish life, in general, and in the cultural identity of the courtier Jew in particular. Why would Halevi commission Arabic inscriptions for his private synagogue if the comprehension of these inscriptions was not important? What might the Hebrew and Arabic inscriptions suggest about Halevi's relationship with King Pedro I and with his co-religionists?

Most of the Arabic inscriptions in the synagogue are quite decorative. While they appear to be Arabic they don't form actual words or phrases. In contrast to these long but apparently meaningless inscriptions, those that are legible are quite brief. A few inscriptions appear repeatedly containing a few staccato phrases or formularies: *Bi'l ni'mah wa-b'il salamah wa-bi'l quwah wa bo'l karamah*: "By (or in) grace, power, magnanimity (or, alternatively, generosity or happiness), salvation." [17] From a religious point of view these phrases are neutral and would certainly not have offended any Jew contemplating them as his eye wandered while he meditated during worship. Even in the two instances where the word "Allah" may have been inscribed, it is not necessary to assume that the word was intended as an Islamic religious term but could be construed simply as the Arabic word for God. Arabic-speaking Jews used the word Allah without compunctions in geniza documents to denote God. Significantly, the cursive script in one medallion declares that "Allah is the one and only" or "God is one." Even this slogan, so strikingly Islamic, could be employed comfortably in a synagogue: the declaration of the unity of God in the Hebrew prayer *Shema Yisrael* is a fundamental tenet of Judaism.

The placement of the Arabic epigraphy in the El Transito synagogue is subtle—in some places it is almost hidden from view— and the fact that it is devoid of diacritical marks suggests that it was probably not meant to be read. Significantly, Arabic inscriptions do not appear on the eastern wall of the synagogue, the most important focus of attention of the Jewish worshipper since it is the

---

[17] See Foster's summary of the possible Arabic translations in the Appendix to her thesis, "The Writing on the Wall", op. cit.

wall containing the niche for the ark housing the Torah scrolls. In contrast to the other walls of the synagogue, the eastern wall is also the site of important Hebrew dedicatory plaques and inscriptions containing personal data about Halevi, his royal mentor and the date of dedication of the building. The inscriptions on this wall, derived primarily from the Book of Psalms, are rich in Biblical allusions to the various parts of the Temple of Jerusalem. Past heroes of the Jewish people invoked in the wall's verses include King David and especially King Solomon, as well as the ancient courtier Mordechai and Samuel's biblical namesake, the Prophet Samuel. An implied comparison between the greatest kings of ancient Israel and Halevi is intended. In this spirit of grandiosity the Hebrew inscription on the right side of the ark summons the viewer to attention, proclaiming the likeness of the various parts of the Toledo synagogue—its lectern, Torah and lamps—to the ancient glories of the Temple of Solomon in Jerusalem:[18]

> See the sanctuary now consecrated in Israel
> And the house which was built by Samuel
> With a pulpit of wood for reading the law
> With its scrolls and its crowns all for God
> And its lavers and lamps to illuminate
> And its windows like the windows of Ariel

The inscription to the left of the Torah niche further details the parts of the Temple (and the synagogue), drawing attention once again to the parallels between Halevi's chapel in Toledo and the Temple of Jerusalem, melding the two sacred spaces into one image:

> And its courts for them that cherish the perfect law
> With a seat for each who sits in the shade of God
> And those who see it will almost say it appears
> Like a work that was wrought by Bezalel
> Go ye nations and enter into its gates
> And seek the Lord, for it is a house of God even as Bethel.

---

[18] See the Spanish translation of the Hebrew inscriptions in Francisco Cantera Burgos, *Sinagogas Espanolas: con especial studio de la Córdoba y la toledana de El Tránsito* (Madrid: Arias Montano, 1955); Amador de los Rios, *Monumentos arquitectónicos de España*. See Omer, "The Samuel Ha-Levi Synagogue," for the English translations by G. Levin. Omer's additions to the worn and incomplete inscriptions are in parentheses.

The Biblical verses under the stucco carpet pattern on the eastern wall lavishly praise Halevi as savior of Israel, "a noble of nobles" who stands before kings and seeks "the good of his people." In these laudatory phrases ancient heroes of Israel are intertwined with Samuel Halevi and King Pedro as skillfully as the delicately interlacing arabesques on the walls. It is as difficult to separate the heroes of old from the contemporary strongmen in Spain as it is to separate the strands connecting scrolls and vines in the decoration:

> Of the graces of the Lord let us sing and of the works of the Lord according to what he has bestowed on us and hath done great things with us...instituting judges and ministers to save his people from the hand of
>
> Enemies and oppressors. And there is no King in Israel, he hath not left us without a
>
> Redeemer. He is the bulwark of the tower, which since the day of the exile of Ariel.
>
> None like him has risen in Israel. From the line of high descent and a noble of nobles of The land...Of its exalted and great ones who stand (in the breach). The type of greatness.
>
> The foundation of position and stature. For the Name and the glory and the praise.
>
> Known is his name in Israel since the day he dwelt on his land and stood before Kings.
>
> To him who stands in the breach. And seeks the good of his people. Head of the exile of Ariel, The select of the leaders.
>
> The crown and the great man of the Jews. To him peoples come from the ends of the

Earth. ....He is the ruler of the land. The great tamarisk. Fort of strength and greatness.

He ascended in the degrees of greatness in accordance with his praise, and great and holy
Will he be called. The right pillar upon which the House of the Levite (Halevi) and the House of Israel are set. And who can count his praises? His virtues and his deeds.

Who can recount. And who will attain to complete praise. Diadem of rule
Prestige of dignity. He stands at the head of the order. Exalted among the exalted of the
Levites of God Samuel Ha-Levy.

The man raised on high. May God be with him and let him go up. He found grace and
Favor in the eyes of the great eagle, the great one, the man of war and the man of the middle The fear of whom has fallen on all the peoples. Great is his name among the nations. The great King, our shelter and our lord the King Don Pedro. May God aid him, And increase

His might and his glory. And guard him as the shepherd of his flock. The King has made
Him great and exalted him. And raised his throne above all the ministers.

..... And without him shall no man lift up his hand or his foot. And the nobles bowed

Themselves to him with their face to the
ground.

.... Through all the land is he known and
among
The peoples heard. His fame has been
heard through all the kingdoms, And
ha has been to Israel a savior.

The carpet panel continues below (to the left)with hyperbolic praises of Samuel Halevi:

He has saved (us) from (our) enemies- and
since the day of our exile not one of the
Children of Israel has attained to his
height...Tree with multiple roots.
The great compassionate and righteous
man the exalted among the exalted of
the Levites.

Rabbi Samuel Halevi Luminary of society,
great in observance-...
...The Law and those who learn it. Who
restores (crowns as in) the first
Days and an(cient) years- (as in the day) of
God's gift. A man (who)
Added to and increased all the(se) to build
a house of prayer for the Lord God of
Israel

.... And built the house and completed it
In the year GOOD (for the Jews) (=117) or
5117 1356/57

In these final Biblical passages the relationship of the courtier to his earthly sovereign is underscored. The escutcheon with the coat of arms of Castile and Leon, liberally interspersed amidst the verses, provides an additional visual reminder of Halevi's relationship with the Castilian dynasty. The private chapel is thus transformed into an assertion of the power of Halevi, the self-declared prince among the princes of the tribe of Levi. By placing Don Pedro's name boldly and prominently in the Torah niche's dedicatory plaque Halevi is simultaneously invoking the powerful presence of the temporal king. Association with royal power was the trademark of the courtier just as it constituted the key to his privileges within the Jewish community. Halevi might also be reminding his community of his nephew Yosef Halevi, also a courtier (*almoxarife*) in Seville.

Yet another layer of meaning that is not immediately apparent may be concealed in the multilayered texts on the synagogue walls. Perhaps the inscribed verses also allude to another powerful Samuel, one who was also a Levite, Samuel ibn Naghrela (993-1056), the most powerful Jewish statesman of medieval times. Ibn Naghrela, long familiar to medieval Jews in Spain, held high office in the Berber Zirid Kingdom of Granada for several decades during the eleventh century. His martial poetry excited generations of Spanish Jews. His poetic reconstruction of the medieval battle of Alfuente may have been as stirring to the Jews of his day as were the ballads recounting the exploits of El Cid to their Christian neighbors. Perhaps Ibn Naghrela's martial poem was even more thrilling since his were the only Hebrew poems chronicling Jewish military prowess since the heroic age of the Bible.

Halevi's allusions to and comparisons with Ibn Naghrela may not have been as veiled nor as hyperbolic as they appear today. Halevi was no stranger to Granada, the home of Ibn Naghrela. Accounts of Samuel ibn Naghrela's feats and defeats were incorporated in the eleventh century history of the Berber Zirid Kingdom in Granada and recalled by its Jews. The palace city of Alhambra, then in the process of reconstruction, allegedly incorporated remnants of the Ibn Naghrela family home that was probably previously located on the hilltop building site. As the old palace was being transformed, Halevi may have been privy to discussions about the identity and lore surrounding the earlier Samuel the courtier Jew. According to Ruggles, the Alhambra was erected on the site of the original villa of the Ibn Naghrela family. When Samuel died in 1056, his son Joseph inherited his father's government post as well as his opulent villa, embellishing it with fountains and statuary. The Alhambra's famed

Lion's Court incorporates these eleventh-century stone lions. A description of this statuary appears in one of Samuel ibn Naghrela's Hebrew poetic descriptions of a beautiful Andalusian garden setting. The lion statuary was presumably moved to the Alhambra and recycled when the Nasrid palace complex was reconstructed on the site of the former Ibn Naghrela villa. Architecture, by its nature, can create a persuasive setting that has the power to mine both history and myth.[19] If this was indeed the case, it is not surprising that the figure of Ibn Naghrela might come to mind quite naturally as a role model for a latter day Jewish courtier. Even if Halevi never saw the completed Alhambra prior to the dedication of his synagogue, he probably saw the plans that contained the Nasrid palace's various luxury features while they were on the drawing board. Moreover, Ibn Naghrela's sepulcher in Granada was famous for centuries and his poetry remained within the Jewish repertoire of medieval poetic accomplishment.

Other affinities between eleventh-century Samuel ibn Naghrela and fourteenth-century Samuel Halevi may also have entered the courtier's mind as he designed his synagogue. Both Samuels proudly proclaimed their Levitic descent, each using rhetorical flourishes and hyperbole to trumpet their genealogy and to project their earthly power and its legitimacy. Each manifested his colossal ego, Ibn Nagrela in his Hebrew verses and Halevi in the epigraphy on the walls of his palatine chapel. Both courtiers also brought widespread destruction upon their communities within a decade of their deaths, partially as a result of their positions of power, which exceeded the tolerable limits of what was permissible to a Jew. The vulnerability of both men was the product, in both cases, of their association

---

[19] According to Dodds, the opulence of the Alhambra was a gesture of defiance in the face of the rapidly eroding power of the Muslims in Spain. Perhaps Halevi's claims to power in his synagogue setting were no less audacious in the context of declining power of the Jews in fourteenth century Spain. See Dodds in S. Jayyusi, ed., *The Legacy of Muslim Spain*, 618. It should be noted that the portion of the Alhambra containing the *Patio de los Leones* was built after El Transito was completed. Even if Halevi never saw the finished product prior to the completion of his synagogue, he probably saw the plans while the palace's various luxury features were on the drawing board. Ibn Naghrela's sepulcher in Granada was famous for centuries and his poetry remained within the Jewish repertoire of medieval poetic accomplishment.

with an unpleasant and unpopular contender to the throne.[20] The Alhambra is an extraordinary palace celebrating a culture that was aged but still potent in the fourteenth century. Its countless Arabic inscriptions, forming a curtain of script on its walls, laud the military prowess of a Muslim dynasty that was then on the verge of collapse. The victory at Algeciras which the Alhambra celebrates was, in reality, little more than a small border skirmish constituting only a minor reversal in the long history of Muslim decline on the Iberian Peninsula. Muhammed V (1354-1359/1362-1391), like his Castilian friend King Pedro I, was a monarch of more bluster than substance.

An additional indication of Halevi's sense of self-importance can be discerned in a striking parallel between the synagogue and the royal palace of the Alcazar. Above the entrance to the Alcazar the following words are inscribed: "The exalted, the most powerful, by the Grace of God, King of Castile and Leon built this Alcazar, this palace, this entrance in 1364."[21] In similar fashion, pre-dating the Alcazar by only a few years, the following inscription grandly acknowledges Halevi on the eastern wall: "The exalted pious prince of princes of Levi...has exceeded in all deeds by building a house of prayer for the Lord God of Israel... and he commenced building this house in the year (1357)." While the Muslim and Christian kings had little cause to imitate Halevi, there is every reason to believe that Halevi was privy to their construction plans, his architectural masterpiece preceding their implementation simply because the construction of a private synagogue was a speedier undertaking. The entire Granada palace complex was completed in1369, the same year that King Pedro was murdered.

The proud courtier tradition inscribed on the walls of the El Transito synagogue with its allusions to the breathtaking grandeur and luxury of Muhammed V's palace of pleasure in Granada and Pedro I's royal residence in Seville offer vivid visual evidence of the continuing force of Islamic-inspired culture among the Jews

---

[20] See Ross Brann, *Power in the Portrayal* (Princeton: Princeton University Press, 2002), for a close textual reading of the literary campaign against Ibn Naghrela and his son that culminated in a pogrom. The Muslim outrage focused specifically on the exercise and manifestations of power on the part of the Jew. See Bernard Lewis "An Ode Against the Jews," in *Islam in History* (New York: Library Press, 1973), 158-165. See Estow, *Pedro the Cruel of Castile*, for details on the pogrom in Toledo spearheaded by Pedro's fraternal rivals.
[21] Albert F. Calvert, *Moorish Remains in Spain* (New York: J. Lane, 1960), 342.

of Christian Spain. Halevi's use of the *mudéjar* vocabulary was a clear reflection of royal luxury. Although it is difficult to assign past meanings to recycled motifs, especially when removed from their original context, the several layers of associations conjured up by the Hebrew and Arabic in the synagogue of El Transito provide a glimpse into the ambiguous identity of the Jewish courtier class. It is entirely possible that the subtle connections between Ibn Naghrela and Halevi also held special appeal for the Jews in Toledo. That the two medieval Levites were so powerful within their communities yet ultimately powerless vis a vis their royal patron carries no small measure of irony. The tensions between royal power and Jewish powerlessness undoubtedly resonated with the Jews of Halevi's day.

Perhaps Samuel Halevi had more noble aims in mind than a projection of his personal power when he carpeted the walls of his synagogue with lofty Biblical verse, subtle Arabic script and the escutcheon of the kingdom of Castile. Identification with the opulence of Islamic culture was perhaps less important than the allusions in verse to the triumphs of ancient Israel. Referencing the Temple of Jerusalem enhanced the status of this medieval building while simultaneously reminding the Jews of the divine promises for the Temple's restoration. Such expressions of the glory of Jerusalem would fill the Jewish worshippers with optimism and pride as well as with hope. The repetitious Arabic mantras "happiness, power, beneficence, prosperity" etched in the walls were the lifeblood of the courtier, embodying his most tenaciously held aspirations and values. They also echoed the aspirations of a declining and embattled community.

In the 1350s and again in 1366, the Jewish community of Toledo was sacked. Hundreds of Jews were killed and heavy fines were meted out to the survivors. Halevi's synagogue withstood these attacks. It even managed to survive the great pogrom of 1391. The El Transito synagogue of Samuel Halevi remains standing in Toledo, its name and its inscriptions testifying to the ambiguous and enigmatic history of the courtier Jew as well as his successful integration of Islamic and Jewish artistic motifs in one enduring structure.

Works Cited:

Assis, Yom Tov. "Synagogues in Medieval Spain." *Jewish Art* 18 (1992): 6-29.

------. "The Judeo-Arabic Tradition in Christian Spain." In *The Jews of Medieval Islam*, edited by Daniel Frank, 111-124. New York, 1995.

Cantera Burgos, Francisco. *Sinagogas españolas*. Madrid: Arias Montano, 1955.

Cantera Burgos, Francisco, and José María Millás Vallicrosa. *Inscripciones hebraicas de España*. Madrid: [s.n.], 1956.

Dodds, Jerrilynn D. *Archeology and Ideology in Early Medieval Spain*. University Park: Pennsylvania State University Press, 1990.

------, ed. *Al-Andalus: The Art of Islamic Spain*. New York: Metropolitan Museum, 1992.

------. "Mudejar Tradition in Architecture." In *The Legacy of Muslim Spain*, vol. 2, edited by S. Jayyusi, 592-98. Leiden: Brill, 1992.

------. "Mudejar Tradition and the Synagogues of Medieval Spain: Cultural Identity and Cultural Hegemony." In *Convivencia: Jews, Muslims, and Christians in Medieval Spain*, edited by Vivian Mann, Thomas F. Glick, and Jerrilynn D. Dodds. New York: George Braziller, 1992.

Dodds, Jerrilynn D., Maria Rosa Menocal and Abigail Krasner Balbale. *The Arts of Intimacy: Christians, Jews, and Muslims in the Making of Castilian Culture*. New Haven: Yale University Press, 2008.

Estow, Clara. *Pedro the Cruel of Castile 1350-1369*. Leiden: Brill, 1995.

Foster, Elise Anne. "The Writing on the Walls." M.A. thesis, Southern Methodist University, Department of Art, 2004.

Goldman, Esther W. "Samuel Halevi Abulafia's Synagogue (El Transito) in Toledo." *Jewish Art* 18 (1992): 59-69.

------. *The Meditation of Ornament*. Princeton: Princeton University Press, 1992.

Krinsky, Carol. *Synagogues of Europe: Architecture, History, Meaning*. Cambridge, MA: MIT Press, 1985.

López de Ayala, Pedro. *Crónica del rey don Pedro*. BAE. Vol. 66, 399-593. Madrid, 1953.

Menocal, Maria Rosa. "Culture in the Time of Tolerance: Al-Andalus as a Model for our Time." Yale Law School Occasional Paper, second series, No.6, [n.d].

------. *The Ornament of the World: How Muslims, Jews, and Christians Created a Culture of Tolerance in Medieval Spain*. New York: Little, Brown, 2002.

Ruggles, D. Fairchild. *Gardens, Landscape, and Vision in the Palaces of Islamic Spain*. University Park: Pennsylvania State University Press, 2000.

Ray, Jonathan. *The Sephardic Frontier: The Reconquista and the Jewish Community in Medieval Iberia*. Ithaca, NY: Cornell University Press, 2006.

Taggie, Benjamin. "Samuel ha-Levi Abulafia and the Hebraic Policy of Pedro I of Castile 1350-1369." *Fifteenth Century Studies* 5 (1982): 191-208.

Wischnitzer, Rachel. *The Architecture of the European Synagogue*. Philadelphia: Jewish Publication Society, 1964.

The Jew as Scientist and Philosopher in Medieval Iberia

·· Mariano Gómez Aranda

Cresques Abnarrabi, physician and astrologer of John II, king of Aragon (1458-1479), operated on the king to remove a cataract from his right eye with great success. The king then asked him to do the same in his left eye, and Cresques Abnarrabi responded with a letter written in 1468, in which he said the following:

> Your Highness,
>
> I have just received the letter from your Majesty in which you inform me that the vision of your right eye is now very good. I have to tell you that the reason that the cataract operation that I performed in your right eye was a success is that you chose the best possible day to have it done: September, 11th. If you want to have an operation in your left eye with absolute success, you have to wait twelve years until there is a conjunction of stars similar to that which took place when you had the operation in your right eye. In any case, if you do not want to wait for such a long time, I recommend October, 12th as the best day—or the least worst day—to have such an operation. Your choice in the case of your right eye was the best, and is a proof of your intelligence, as is written in the Bible, "inspired decisions are on the lips of a king; his mouth does not sin in judgement" (Prov. 16:10).[1]

---

[1] Vicente Vignau, "Carta dirigida á D. Juan II de Aragón, por su médico, fijándole día para operarle los ojos," *Revista de Archivos, Bibliotecas y Museos* 4 (1874): 135-137, 230-231.

This apparently simple anecdote may serve to illustrate some characteristics of Jewish science in the Middle Ages. Medicine, astronomy and astrology were the most important scientific disciplines studied by the Jews at those times. Astrology was very much connected to the practice of medicine, and physicians in the service of kings and rulers used to consult the position of stars before having an operation or being diagnosed. This anecdote also shows how close the Jewish scientific spirit was to the interpretation of the biblical text. In this case, a biblical verse is adduced to prove that the intelligence of the king in choosing the best day according to his astrological knowledge has a biblical foundation. The book of Proverbs demonstrates that kings are clever in making judgments; in this case, astrological judgments. It was common practice in the Middle Ages for Jewish scientific writers to quote biblical verses to provide a religious support for their secular scientific ideas, on the one hand, and for Jewish interpreters of the Bible to make use of scientific ideas to explain the meanings of difficult biblical passages, on the other hand. In medieval Iberia, science and religion interrelated one to another to give answers to the classical conflict between reason and faith. Likewise, Jewish philosophy in medieval Iberia is centered on the efforts of the Jews to reconcile rationalist thought and the Jewish religion.

The Iberian Peninsula in the Middle Ages was the setting for an intense Jewish involvement in the sciences. No other Jewish community ever took so much sustained and active interest in science as did the Jews of medieval Iberia. Science was held in high esteem in the Jewish communities. Scientific ideas penetrated into almost every branch of Jewish learning and provided themes for poetry and liturgy.[2]

The achievements of Jewish science are but one aspect of the flowering of Jewish culture as a result of its contact with Muslim-Arab culture. The Muslims appropriated the classical heritage through a

---

[2] For the most complete analysis of the contribution of the Iberian Jews to the development of science in the Middle Ages, see Y. Tzvi Langermann, "Science in the Jewish Communities of the Iberian Peninsula: An Interim Report," in his *The Jews and the Sciences in the Middle Ages* (Aldershot: Ashgate Variorum, 1999), 1-54. See also Mariano Gómez-Aranda, "The Contribution of the Jews of Spain to the Transmission of Science in the Middle Ages," *European Review* 16 (2008): 169-181.

process of translation of Greek writings into Arabic and of adaptation to Islamic conceptions and contemporary needs. A similar process of acquisition of Hellenistic, Arabic, and other foreign sciences, and of adaptation to Jewish conceptions and ideas, took place in the Jewish communities of medieval Iberia. Arabic, then, became the language of science, much as English is the language of computer science today. Only later—and due to a change of the historical circumstances, as we shall see later—Hebrew was used by the Jews for transmitting scientific knowledge. Latin was occasionally used in Jewish scientific writings.

Translations of scientific works from Greek into Arabic, and from Arabic into Hebrew and Latin, served as the most effective method of reception of Graeco-Arabic learning and its integration into Jewish culture. The Jews also composed, in Arabic, Hebrew, or Latin, original works on mathematics, astronomy, astrology, medicine and philosophy, in which the theories developed by the Greeks and the Muslims were adapted to the worldview of their own times. In this sense, medieval Jewish scientists can be considered more as transmitters than as true innovators of science; however, this does not imply that their scientific work lacks originality. What is new and original in medieval scientific works written by Jews is how they were able to apply and adapt the scientific theories of the time to the knowledge and practice of their own religion. Theories on the circular motion of the planets and the fixed stars around the earth were used to determine the Jewish calendar and fix the exact dates and times of Jewish feasts. The knowledge of the philosophical ideas of such Greek philosophers as Plato and Aristotle was very valuable in order to understand the scientific basis of the Jewish religious creed. Scientific theories also helped Jews to understand and explain the biblical text, and provided them with the rational arguments necessary to justify their own religion and traditions in the several controversies with Muslims and Christians.

In medieval Jewish communities, science was often regarded as something alien to Jewish culture. Religious authorities might have objected to the study of science as an unnecessary investment of precious time in non-sacral activities. As a consequence, Jewish scientists felt the need to legitimize the study of science in their writings by providing biblical support for their scientific ideas.

Some Jewish scholars from ancient times believed that science was not so "alien" to Judaism as some people might think. They defended the idea that their ancestors were truly engaged in science and that the Greeks had "stolen" philosophy from the Jews. Many Jewish intellectuals in medieval Iberia therefore assumed that by developing sciences of Greek or Arabic origin they were actually restoring their own brilliant scientific tradition.[3]

Science in the Middle Ages was also considered an element of power. Medieval kings, caliphs or sultans promoted the development of science in their own territories, for it contributed to their prestige and splendor, and was a way to express their superiority over their enemies. Jews soon realized that, by cooperating with Muslim or Christian powers in scientific and cultural matters, they were able to elevate their own social status. Jews participated in several major projects sponsored by non-Jews, and right up until the expulsion of 1492, Jews served at the courts of Christian and Muslim rulers as astronomers, astrologers, physicians, and translators.

The cooperation of Jews, Muslims and Christians in scientific projects was part of the legacy of the culture developed in the Iberian Peninsula in both Muslim and Christian Spain. The so-called "School of Translators of Toledo" during the reign of Alfonso X (thirteenth century) is a good example of how astronomy was usually regarded as a neutral meeting ground for scholars who were sharply divided on religious questions. In the case of this discipline, scholars of one faith had no problem borrowing ideas from scholars of another.[4]

In this chapter I will analyze the most important contributions of the Jews of medieval Iberia to the sciences of astronomy, astrology, physics and philosophy. Since an entire later chapter in this book is dedicated to medieval Jewish medicine, that field is excluded from this analysis.

---

[3] For a discussion of these ideas, see Norman Roth, "The 'Theft of Philosophy' by the Greeks from the Jews," *Classical Folia* 32 (1978): 53-67.

[4] On this topic concerning astronomy, see Bernard Goldstein, "Astronomy as a 'Neutral Zone': Interreligious Cooperation in Medieval Spain," *Medieval Encounters* 15 (2009): 159-174.

Solomon Ibn Gabirol and Jewish Neoplatonism

Medieval Neoplatonism—which was largely based on the writings of philosophers such as Plotinus and Proclus and complemented by elements stemming from Islamic religious traditions—provided the philosophical context for the thought of many cultivated Jews of the eleventh and twelfth centuries.[5]

Solomon ibn Gabirol, born in Malaga in 1021, is considered to be the most representative Jewish Neoplatonist in the Middle Ages. His philosophy was expounded in a lengthy work written in Arabic and later translated into Latin with the title *Fons Vitae* (The Fountain of Life). This is a work of pure philosophy in the sense of the philosophical works of the classical Greek philosophers. It contains no biblical quotations and not a single allusion to the Jewish religion. These characteristics made it possible for Christian authors in the Middle Ages, such as Albertus Magnus and Thomas Aquinas, to frequently cite *The Fountain of Life*, attributing it to an Arab philosopher called Avicebron or Avencebrol. Only in the middle of the nineteenth century was it proved that the author behind the name of Avicebron was actually a Jewish philosopher named Solomon ibn Gabirol.

The Fountain of Life is a good example of the non-confessional character of medieval philosophy, in which the philosophy in question is pure science and not exclusively the application of the scientific ideas to a specific revealed religion. It is written in the form of a dialogue, evidently in imitation of Plato's works. At the beginning of this work, Ibn Gabirol expresses the idea that knowledge is the supreme aim of human life and its reason for existing, a typical statement for the Neoplatonic treatises of that time.

> Since the knowing part being is the best of human beings, that which human beings must seek is knowledge. What they must especially seek to know is themselves, in order to arrive at the knowledge of the

---

[5] On medieval Jewish Neoplatonism, see Colette Sirat, *A History of Jewish Philosophy in the Middle Ages* (Paris-Cambridge: Editions de la Maison des Sciences de l'Homme-Cambridge University Press, 1985), 57-112, and Sarah Pessin, "Jewish Neoplatonism: Being Above Being and Divine Emanation in Solomon Ibn Gabirol and Isaac Israeli," in *The Cambridge Companion to Medieval Jewish Philosophy*, ed. D. H. Frank and O. Leaman (Cambridge: Cambridge University Press, 2003), 91-110.

other things that are not themselves; for their essence comprehends all the things and penetrates them, and all the things are subject to the power of human beings. As well as this, they must seek to know the final cause for which they were created, so that they may attain supreme felicity. For human being's existence has a final cause for which they were created, for everything is subject to the will of the one God.[6]

The concept that science is the ultimate goal of human life is rooted in medieval Neoplatonic thought. The theme that the knowledge of oneself comprises the knowledge of everything is connected with the concept of the human being as a microcosm, an idea that was developed by other medieval Jewish Neoplatonists, such as Isaac Israeli and Joseph ibn Zaddik. Another typical Neoplatonic idea found in Ibn Gabirol's text is that human beings can attain the supreme benefits intended for them by God only by knowing the Will of the Creator, on whom everything depends.

One of the most relevant ideas of *The Fountain of Life* is that everything that exists, except God, is composed of two elements: matter and form. These elements are universal and were created by the divine Will. The connection among these concepts is expressed by Ibn Gabirol as follows:

> There are only three things in being: matter and form, the first substance [God], and Will, which is the intermediary between the extremes. The reason that only these three things exist is that there cannot be an effect without a cause and there must be an intermediary between the two. The cause is the first substance; the effect is matter together with form; the intermediary between the two is the Will. Matter and form are like human beings' body and its shape, which is the composition of its members; Will is like the soul and the first substance is like the intellect.[7]

According to this exposition, human beings are able to apprehend God as the first substance, His Will, Matter and Form. This is only possible because human beings find in themselves the equivalents of these three things: the intelligence corresponds to the first substance, the human soul to the Will, and human matter and form

---

[6] Sirat, *History*, 71, slightly modified.
[7] Sirat, *History*, 73.

to the First Matter and the First Form. Human intelligence, as being the equivalent to God, is able to comprehend God by knowing His actions and everything that derives from Him. The entire universe, spiritual as well as material, is composed of matter and form and originates in God; in consequence, it is subject to our knowledge.

The *Fountain of Life* also deals with another idea commonly found in Neoplatonic treatises: the science of the soul. The knowledge that human beings have a soul leads them to the knowledge of the world and of the divine Will.

> When one knows the art of demonstration [logic], what one should study first of all, and what is the most useful study, is the essence of the soul, its faculties, its accidents and everything that inheres in it and adheres to it, for the soul is the substratum of the sciences and it perceives all things by its faculties, which penetrate everything. If you study the science of the soul, [...] you will then realize that you yourself encompass everything that you know of things that exist, and that the existing things that you know subsist in some way in yourself. [...] But you could not do this if the soul were not substance both subtle and strong, penetrating all things and being the dwelling of all things.[8]

According to Ibn Gabirol, the soul, being the equivalent of the divine Will, is pure and infinite; it penetrates the world and dwells in it. By knowing the soul, human beings are therefore able to comprehend the world and God's Will.

Ibn Gabirol also develops the Platonic idea that the human soul belongs to the spiritual soul and that during life, it is imprisoned in the body. In order to make the soul return to its former place, human beings should purify their soul from the imperfections of this world in two ways: by knowledge and by the practice of pious and moral works. Although Ibn Gabirol does not specify what he meant by the word 'practice,' we may assume that he is referring to the notion of a moral conduct based primarily on the practice of religious laws and commandments. As Ibn Gabirol states, the ultimate goal of all this process is the knowledge of God.

> The purpose of all this is to know the world of the Divinity, which is altogether great, while all that is here below, in comparison with Him,

---

[8] Sirat, *History*, 71.

is extremely small. This sublime knowledge is reached by a double road: first by knowledge of the Will, which comprehends matter and form, and secondly by the knowledge of that superior faculty when it is pure of all mixing of matter and form. But to arrive at the knowledge of this faculty, which is entirely distinct from matter and from form, you must attach yourself to the faculty which is commingled with matter and form, and by degrees ascend with this faculty, until you arrive at its origin and at its source.[9]

Ibn Gabirol summarizes in this paragraph the purpose of a human being's life. Apart from attaining to God by the knowledge of created things composed of matter and form, Ibn Gabirol proposes another more spiritual procedure. One should distance oneself from all the sensible things and concentrate on the spiritual soul. By separating themselves from everything that is composed of matter and form, human beings are able to purify the essence of their souls, come closer to God and reach eternal life.

Allegorical Interpretation of the Bible

Like other medieval Jewish philosophers, Ibn Gabirol also made an effort to reconcile philosophy and the Jewish religion. In his work entitled *Keter Malchut* (*The Kingly Crown*), Ibn Gabirol expresses the philosophical concepts developed in *The Fountain of Life* in a more religious and rabbinical style.

Ibn Gabirol also tried to make philosophy compatible with the Hebrew Bible by using the allegorical method of biblical interpretation. His explanations on the Garden of Eden have been preserved in Abraham ibn Ezra's first commentary on Gen. 3:21, in which Ibn Ezra quotes Ibn Gabirol's own words:

> I shall reveal to you the mystery of the garden and the flowers and the tunics, and I have not found this mystery in any of the great, but only in Rabbi Solomon ibn Gabirol, for he was profoundly versed in the knowledge of the soul. Eden is the superior world; the garden is full of angelic spirits which are its plants; the river is like a mother, that is, the universal matter of all the bodies; the four branches of the river are the four elements; man is the rational soul that gives names; Eve,

[9] Sirat, *History*, 78.

67

as is shown by her name, designates the animal soul, and the serpent the concupiscent soul.[10]

Abraham ibn Ezra continues by quoting other comparisons by Ibn Gabirol between philosophical concepts and other elements of the Garden of Eden. Ibn Gabirol tried to prove that several Neoplatonic ideas can be found in the biblical text itself, in an attempt to harmonize philosophy and the Jewish religion. Especially relevant is the identification of the Platonic and Aristotelian division of the three souls with the personages mentioned in Genesis: Adam is the rational soul, Eve the animal soul and the serpent the appetitive soul.

Other allegorical interpretations by Ibn Gabirol are found in Ibn Ezra's commentary on Jacob's dream of the ladder. According to Ibn Gabirol, Jacob's ladder is a symbol of the superior soul and the angels of God signify the thoughts of wisdom.

These allegorical interpretations repeated themes and ideas found in *The Fountain of Life*: the flow of matter from the superior towards the inferior world, and the soul that enjoys felicity through the knowledge of the superior world.

Ibn Gabirol's *Fountain of Life* was widely read by the Latin scholastics. It was influential, within important limits, and vigorously debated. Albertus Magnus and Thomas Aquinas used this work very frequently, although they showed their most strenuous opposition to Ibn Gabirol's arguments.[11]

Abraham bar Hiyya and the Legitimization of Science

With the arrival of the Almoravids and the Almohads in the Peninsula in the eleventh and twelfth century respectively, and their policy of intolerance toward Jews and Christians, many Jews emigrated to Christian territories in the Peninsula or to other lands far away from the danger of this policy. The Jewish scientists who emigrated carried with them the scientific knowledge they had acquired in al-Andalus and thus contributed to the spread of science

---

[10] Sirat, *History*, 79.

[11] On the influence of Ibn Gabirol on the scholastic philosophers, see Bernard McGinn, "Ibn Gabirol: The Sage Among the Schoolmen," in *Neoplatonism and Jewish Thought*, edited by L. E. Goodman , (New York: SUNY Press, 1992), 77-109.

in Western Europe. In this process, Jewish scholars progressively abandoned Arabic and adopted Hebrew and Latin as vehicles for expressing secular and scientific ideas.

Abraham bar Hiyya (ca. 1065-ca. 1140) created an entire Hebrew scientific literature, writing the first medieval Hebrew works on astronomy, astrology, and mathematics. He also wrote an encyclopedia, which is only partially extant, and a philosophical treatise.[12]

In his astronomical work *Surat ha-Ares* (The Shape of the Earth), Abraham bar Hiyya explained two of the most relevant astronomical theories of Claudius Ptolemy (second century CE) which had a great influence in the Middle Ages: the eccentric model of planetary motion and the theory of the epicycles of the planets.[13] According to the eccentric model, the terrestrial sphere is fixed in the center of the universe, and the Sun, the Moon, the other five planets—Mercury, Venus, Mars, Jupiter, and Saturn—, and the fixed stars all move around the earth. Observed from what was considered to be the fixed earth, the motions of the planets are extremely varied in speed and direction. From ancient times, astronomers had tried to discover a uniform circular motion of the planets. Claudius Ptolemy described the planetary motions by reducing them to their simplest components, that is, by discovering the real order underlying apparent disorder. Ptolemy affirmed that the center of the circle of the Sun around the earth does not coincide with the center of the earth itself; therefore, sometimes the Sun is closer to the earth and sometimes is farther to it. The eccentric model explains the variations of the seasons.

Regarding the five planets mentioned above, Ptolemy devised the theory of the epicycles of the planets. According to him, the planets move around the earth in two uniformly circular motions: first, the planets move around the earth in a big circle called the deferent; second, the planet moves around a small circle—called epicycle—with its center in the deferent. The planets move uniformly around the epicycle, and meanwhile the center of the epicycle moves uniformly around the deferent. The theory of the epicycles explains

---

[12] Langermann, "Science in the Jewish Communities," 10-16.

[13] On Ptolemy's theories, see David C. Lindberg, *The Beginnings of Western Science* (Chicago: University of Chicago Press, 1992), 98-105.

that, for a terrestrial observer, it seems that the planets are slow, or that they speed up, or delay or even retreat.[14]

In the introduction to his *Surat ha-Ares*, Bar Hiyya included an apology for studying the sciences. He cited some biblical verses to justify it, stating that, since science reveals to us secrets of creation, those who study the work of the earth and the heavens and understand the motions and dispositions of the planets would be able to comprehend the power, glory and wisdom of the Creator. We may assume that Bar Hiyya found it necessary to introduce such explanations in order to legitimate the knowledge of secular sciences for a religious Jewish audience.

Abraham bar Hiyya also composed the first Hebrew encyclopedia of sciences, entitled *Yesode ha-Tevuna u-Migdal ha-Emuna* (The Foundations of Understanding and the Tower of Faith).[15] He wrote it at the request of the Jews of France, who longed for translations of scientific works. In the introduction, the author explained his intent to conciliate science and faith: the "foundations of understanding" are all the scientific disciplines necessary on which to base a religious life and to study the holy Law; the "tower of faith" is a summary of religious knowledge. From this work, only the parts on geometry and arithmetic are extant.

In his work *Heshbon Mahlakhot ha-Kokhavim* (The Computation of the Motion of Stars), Bar Hiyya explained how to compute the course of the moving celestial bodies, and how to ascertain the positions of the stars and the planets, by using his astronomical tables.[16] His mathematical treatise, *Ḥibbur ha-Meshiḥa ve-ha-Tishboret* (Treatise on Measurement and Calculation) is concerned with

---

[14] Abraham bar Hiyya, *La obra Forma de la Tierra. Traducción del hebreo con prólogo y notas por J. M. Millás Vallicrosa* (Madrid-Barcelona: CSIC, 1956), 55-64.

[15] Abraham bar Hiyya, *La obra enciclopédica Yĕsodé ha-Tĕbuná u-Migdal ha-Ĕmuná.* Edición crítica con traducción, prólogo y notas por J. M. Millás Vallicrosa, Madrid-Barcelona: CSIC 1952. See also Mercedes Rubio, "The First Hebrew Encyclopedia of Science: Abraham bar Hiyya's *Yesodei ha-Tevunah u-Migdal ha-Emunah*," in *The Medieval Hebrew Encyclopedias of Science and Philosophy*, ed. Steven Harvey (Dordrecht: Kluwer Academic Publishers, 2000), 140-153.

[16] Abraham bar Hiyya, *La obra Séfer Hešbón mahlekot ha-kokabim: Edición crítica, con traducción, introducción y notas por J. M. Millás Vallicrosa* (Barcelona: CSIC, 1959). On Bar Hiyya's tables, see Bernard Goldstein, "Star Lists in Hebrew," *Centaurus* 28 (1985): 185-208.

practical geometry.[17] In it, Bar Hiyya explains how to use geometrical figures to calculate the measurements of fields and lands. Bar Hiyya also wrote a Hebrew work on the Jewish calendar entitled *Sefer ha-Ibbur* (The Book of Intercalation).[18]

Abraham bar Hiyya also dealt with astrological matters in his scientific treatises.[19] His work *Megillat ha-Megalleh* (The Scroll of the Revealer) was composed to foretell the exact date of the coming of the Messiah by using Scriptural data. Its fifth chapter was aimed at providing astrological speculations on several periods of the history of the world, such as the history of Israel until the destruction of the second Temple, the development of Christianity from its origins until the time of the First Crusade, and the future coming of the Messiah.[20]

Bar Hiyya also wrote a long, apologetic epistle addressed to Rabbi Judah Barzilai of Barcelona, in which he tried to justify the study and use of a specific kind of astrology: that which is attached to and dependent on astronomy. He considered that this type of astrology was sanctioned as admissible by the ancient sages:

> The first part of the science of the stars[21] consists of the investigation of the form of the earth and the heavens... it investigates the stars and calculates their motions. [...] The second part is dependent upon the first, and it consists of the knowledge of the sway and the power granted to the stars ... and of the knowledge of how this power changes when the stars change their motions. [...] And our forefathers, may

[17] Abraham bar Hiyya, *Chibur ha-Meschichta weha-Tischboret: Herausgegeben und mit Ammerkungen versehen von Dr. M. Guttmann* (Berlin: Mekitse Nirdamim, 1913). For an analysis of this work, see Tony Lévy, "Les débuts de la litterature mathématique hébraïque: La géométrie d'Abraham bar Hiyya (XIe-XIIe siècle)," *Micrologus* 9 (2001): 35-64, and Francisco Sánchez Faba, "Abraham bar Hiyya (1070-1136) y su *Libro de Geometría*," *Gaceta matemática* 32 (1982): 101-115.

[18] Abraham bar Hiyya, *Sefer ha-Ibbur*. Ed. H. Philipowski (London: Longman, Brown, Green and Longmans, 1851).

[19] Shlomo Sela, "Abraham Bar Hiyya's Astrological Work and Thought," *Jewish Studies Quarterly* 13 (2006): 128-158.

[20] Abraham bar Hiyya, *Sefer Megillat ha-Megalleh: Zum ersten Male herausgegeben von Dr. A. Poznanski. Revidiert und mit Einleitung versehen von Prof. Dr. J. Guttmann* (Berlin: Mekitse Nirdamim, 1924).

[21] The expression "science of the stars" is used by Bar Hiyya to refer to both astronomy and astrology.

their memory be blessed, praised both parts, and they dealt with their investigation and busied themselves with them.[22]

However, Bar Hiyya considered astrology inferior to astronomy, and labelled it as an art based on experience and observation that "does not belong to truly scientific knowledge." This opinion reflects the medieval mentality in which knowledge acquired by experience, with no theoretical basis, was reduced to a lower degree and labelled as art, whereas theoretical knowledge was considered truly science.[23]

In addressing a Jewish audience, Bar Hiyya found the need to provide a respectable image and full legitimization to the new scientific knowledge transmitted to them. Consequently, he tried to prove that astronomy and astrology were part of the Jewish tradition, and were considered permissible by the ancient sages.

Abraham ibn Ezra: Science and Biblical Interpretation

Abraham ibn Ezra was born in Muslim Tudela at the end of the eleventh century. He was a Jewish intellectual, imbued with Arabic culture, who left al-Andalus and travelled widely around Christian Europe. In his wanderings through Italy, France and England, Ibn Ezra spread the scientific and cultural learning that he acquired in his homeland.[24]

In his *Yesod Mor'ah* (The Foundation of Reverence), a book devoted to explain the rationale of the commandments of the Jewish religion, Ibn Ezra expressed his views on science. According to him, the Jewish scholar must combine and integrate all the available human scientific knowledge to elucidate the meaning of obscure biblical passages or Talmudic texts:

> Wisdom gives life to the one who acquires it. Now there are many categories of wisdom, each one of which is helpful. All of them are rungs in the ladder that leads to True Wisdom. Happy are they whose

---

[22] Shlomo Sela, "The Fuzzy Borders between Astronomy and Astrology in the Thought and Work of Three Twelfth-Century Jewish Intellectuals," *Aleph* 1 (2001): 59-100: 82-83.

[23] On this concept and the influence of Aristotle, see Sela, "Fuzzy Borders," 98-99.

[24] On the connections between Ibn Ezra's life and works, see Shlomo Sela and Gad Freudenthal, "Abraham ibn Ezra's Scholarly Writings: A Chronological Listing," *Aleph* 6 (2006): 13-55.

intelligence has been opened. At their end they will flow towards God and His goodness.[25]

The various branches of science—among which Ibn Ezra mentions linguistics, astronomy, astrology, arithmetic, geometry, natural science, psychology, and logic—are like gradual steps that lead to the understanding of Scripture and to the knowledge of God. In order to illustrate this statement, Ibn Ezra affirmed that it is impossible for an intelligent person to understand how to establish the correct times for festivals in the Jewish calendar, "unless he studies astronomy and learns the orbits of the Sun and the Moon."[26] Similarly, he stated that "an intelligent person who did not study psychology will not understand the five ways in which a human being's soul is similar to its Creator."[27]

In light of such a clear position, it is not surprising that Ibn Ezra dedicated his intellectual and literary efforts to the field of science. Abraham ibn Ezra is the author of a significant corpus of scientific treatises on what he called "the wisdom of stars," a term that embraced mathematics, astrology and astronomy.[28] As Shlomo Sela has pointed out, Ibn Ezra's scientific contribution can be considered as "the rise of medieval Hebrew science," a process in which Jewish scholars gradually abandoned the Arabic language and adopted Hebrew as a vehicle for the expression of secular and scientific ideas.[29]

Abraham ibn Ezra's *Sefer ha-Mispar* (Book of the Number) is an important contribution to the development of mathematics in Western Europe, and one of the fundamental texts for the historiography of mathematics in the Middle Ages.[30] It is a treatise

---

[25] Abraham ibn Ezra, *Yesod Mora ve-Sod Torah: The Foundation of Reverence and the Secret of the Torah: An Annotated Critical Edition*, second revised and enlarged edition by J. Cohen and U. Simon (Ramat Gan: Bar-Ilan University Press, 2007), 65. For an English translation, see Abraham ibn Ezra, *The Secret of the Torah*, Translated and Annotated by H. Norman Strickman (Northvale, New Jersey: Jason Aronson, 1995), 7-9.

[26] Abraham ibn Ezra, *Yesod Mora*, p. 79 and *The Secret*, 21.

[27] Abraham ibn Ezra, *Yesod Mora*, p. 80 and *The Secret*, 22.

[28] The best and most comprehensive analysis of Ibn Ezra's scientific works is Shlomo Sela, *Abraham ibn Ezra and the Rise of Medieval Hebrew Science* (Leiden: Brill, 2003).

[29] Sela, *The Rise*, 17.

[30] Abraham ibn Ezra, *Sefer Ha-Mispar: Das Buch der Zahl: Ein hebräisch-arithmetisches Werk des R. Abraham ibn Esra*. Zum ersten Male herausgegeben, ins Deutsche übersetzt und erläutert von Dr. M. Silberberg (Frankfurt A. M.: J. Kauffmann, 1895). For an analysis

on arithmetic in which Ibn Ezra explained, for the first time in Hebrew, the decimal place-value system of numeration invented by the Indians and transmitted to the Muslim world by al-Khwarizmi's *Treatise on Calculation with the Hindu Numerals*. He also explained the four basic operations of addition, subtraction, multiplication and division as well as the extraction of the square root. Ibn Ezra's treatise is one of the first to introduce Arab arithmetic to the Jews of Latin Europe, together with a presentation of the decimal positional system.[31].

As Ibn Ezra pointed out in his *Yesod Mor'ah* (The Foundation of Reverence), the knowledge of the precise movement of the stars was essential in order to determine the Jewish calendar and fix the accurate dates and times of feasts and Sabbaths. He wrote several treatises designed to teach the use of scientific tools and instruments, such as astronomical tables and the astrolabe, and to explain the astronomical foundations of the Jewish calendar. In his *Sefer ha-Ibbur* (The Book of Intercalation; as distinct from Bar Hiyya's book of the same name), he dealt with the controversial question of the length of the solar year, and presented the opinions of several astronomical schools in the matter.[32] According to Ibn Ezra, there were three schools of astronomers separated by the question of whether the exact length of the solar year is more or less than 365 days plus a quarter of a day. The first school was represented by those who added a small amount of time to the quarter of a day: approximately twelve minutes or twelve and a half minutes. This was the theory of the scholars of India and Persia and some Arabic astronomers such as al-Khwarizmi and Abu Mashar. The second school was represented by Claudius Ptolemy, who considered the length of a solar year to be

---

of this work, see Tony Levy, "Abraham ibn Ezra et les mathematiques: Remarques bibliographiques et historiques," in *Abraham ibn Ezra, savant universel*, ed. Peter J. Tomson (Brussels: Institutum Iudaicum, 2000), 60-75.

[31] Shlomo Sela, "Abraham ibn Ezra's Scientific Corpus: Basic Constituents and General Characterization," *Arabic Sciences and Philosophy* 11 (2001): 91-149, here 97, and *The Rise*,

[21] It is contemporary with another Latin version of al-Khwarizmi's mathematical treatise entitled *Liber Ysagogarum Alchorismi*. André Allard, "The Arabic Origins and Development of Latin Algorisms in the Twelfth Century," *Arabic Sciences and Philosophy* 1 (1991): 233-283.

[32] Abraham ibn Ezra, *Sefer ha-Ibbur*. Ed. L. Silbermann (Lyck: Mekitse Nirdamim, 1874). See also Sela, *The Rise*, 39-44 and 280-288.

365 days plus a quarter of a day minus the 300th part of a day, that is, around five minutes. The third school was represented by some Arabic astronomers who followed Ptolemy's principle of deducting a certain amount of time from the additional part of the day. In their opinion the length of a solar year is 365 days plus a quarter of a day minus the 106th part of a day, that is, thirteen and a half minutes. Ibn Ezra concluded that, since Greek and Arabic astronomers were unable to determine exactly the length of a year, the Jews "ought to rely, without any doubt, on what our sages have transmitted to us, since their words are correct, and if we act according to them, we fulfill our religious obligations." In other words, since the multiple solutions proposed by scientific research to fix the length of the solar year were of little use for the Jewish worshipper—who needs clear calendric instructions to perform his ritual obligations—the Jews should then rely on the opinions of the sages, which are based on tradition and are one of the foundations of Judaism. This is an example of how Ibn Ezra tried to harmonize the principles of the Jewish religion with the scientific theories of his time.

However, this attitude does not imply that Ibn Ezra totally rejected the scientific considerations on the length of the solar year. He remarked that "according to the calculation of the Jews and to their way of computing the holidays, the fraction which is less than a quarter of a day in the framework of a year is equivalent to the 320th part," which is very close to Ptolemy's reckoning. In Ibn Ezra's view, the decisions of the Talmudic sages regarding the Jewish calendar were of so much value because they were based on astronomical computations and were similar to those of Claudius Ptolemy.[33]

Reshit Hokhmah (The Beginning of Wisdom) is one of the most important astrological treatises by Ibn Ezra.[34] It is a textbook that explains the most basic principles of medieval astrology,[35] including descriptions of the fixed stars, the Zodiac constellations, and the conjunctions of the planets and all that they prognosticate for all creatures existing on the earth. It also explains the astrological characteristics of the twelve houses or divisions of the celestial sphere

---

[33] Sela, *The Rise*, 89.

[34] Abraham ibn Ezra, *The Beginning of Wisdom*. Edited by Raphael Levy and Francisco Cantera (Baltimore: Johns Hopkins Press, 1939).

[35] Sela, "Scientific Corpus," 120-121 and *The Rise*, 58-59.

into twelve parts, as well as the methods to calculate the positions of stars to make a horoscope.

In the introduction to this treatise, Ibn Ezra expounded in a few lines his views on the character of astral influences and how to be protected by them:

> "The fear of the Lord is the beginning of wisdom" (Ps. 111:10), that is, the foundation, for when a man refrains from following his eyes and his heart in their tendency to satisfy his desires, then "wisdom comes to rest in his heart" (Prov. 14:33); furthermore, the fear of the Lord protects him from the "ordinances of heaven and their dominion on the earth" (Job 38:33) all the days of his life, and after the soul takes leave of his body, he will inherit substance and will live for ever.[36]

This paragraph shows that Ibn Ezra was far from having a deterministic and fatalistic concept of astrology; on the contrary, he considered that human beings may be protected from the astral decrees—the so called "ordinances of heaven"—by a combination of faith and wisdom. Ibn Ezra used biblical verses to prove that when human beings "fear the Lord," on the one hand, and when "wisdom comes to rest in their heart," on the other hand, they are protected from the astral influences. Wisdom in this case comprises all the scientific knowledge—astronomy and astrology included— necessary to avoid such influences. However, the ultimate salvation from the stars can only be achieved after the human soul departs from its body and ascends to the upper world.[37]

This work was soon translated into French, English, Catalan and Latin. The French translation, undertaken by a Jew called Hagin in 1273, was a significant contribution to the development of a scientific vocabulary in medieval French, and is still a relevant text for the study of the French language from a historical perspective.[38]

Ibn Ezra wrote his *Sefer ha-Teʿamim* (Book of Reasons) in two versions in order to provide the rational explanations behind the

---

[36] Sela, *The Rise*, 196.

[37] On an analysis of this idea in Ibn Ezra's scientific treatises, see Sela, *The Rise*, 195-199.

[38] On the importance of this translation, see Raphael Levy, *The Astrological Works of Abraham ibn Ezra* (Baltimore: The Johns Hopkins Press, 1927), 19-32 and 68-153; see also Ibn Ezra, *The Beginning of Wisdom*, p. 15.

basic astrological concepts explained in his *Reshit Hokhmah*.[39] One of the most controversial subjects of this work is the question of the physical natures of the planets. According to the standard medieval astronomical doctrine, the Sun is intrinsically hot, the Moon is cold and moist, Mars is hot and burning, and the rest of the planets have similar intrinsic natures. Ibn Ezra rejected this doctrine:

> The truth is that there is neither a planet nor an upper star that is either cold or hot, because they are made of a fifth element, as Aristotle explained with incontrovertible proofs. However, because the body of the Sun is large, [...] it generates a warming force in the air by its motion. Although it is close to the Earth, the Moon generates moisture in the air because its body is smaller than the Earth's body and also because of its motion. [...] The general rule is that neither the planets nor the luminaries generate cold, but only heat, on account of their motion and the nature of the light emitted by them.[40]

Ibn Ezra here introduced the Aristotelian principle that celestial bodies are composed of a fifth element to conclude that all planets generate heat only as a consequence of their motion and of the nature of their light, but are neither hot nor cold by themselves.[41]

In his two versions of *Sefer ha-'Olam* (Book of the World), Ibn Ezra dealt with the branch of astrology concerned with the interpretation and prognostication of political, historical and religions events.[42] One of the most relevant doctrines in this work is the use of the cycles of the conjunctions of the superior planets, Jupiter and Saturn, for the prediction of human events or historical analysis. In a remarkable passage of the second version of this book, Ibn Ezra explained how the conjunctions of Jupiter and Saturn predicted the emergence of the three monotheistic religions. The births of Jesus Christ and Muhammad were foreshadowed by two Jupiter-Saturn conjunctions in Leo and Scorpio, the zodiacal signs of Christians and Muslims respectively. Regarding the Jews and their zodiacal sign, Aquarius, Ibn Ezra affirmed:

---

[39] Abraham ibn Ezra, *The Book of Reasons. A Parallel Hebrew-English Critical Edition of the Two Versions of the Text* by Shlomo Sela (Leiden: Brill, 2007).

[40] Abraham ibn Ezra, *Book of Reasons*, 35.

[41] See Sela's analysis of this idea in Abraham ibn Ezra, *Book of Reasons*, 17-18 and 119-120.

[42] Abraham ibn Ezra, *The Book of the World. A Parallel Hebrew-English Critical Edition of the Two Versions of the Text Edited, Translated and Annotated by Shlomo Sela* (Leiden: Brill, 2010). See also Sela, "Scientific Corpus," 129-131 and *The Rise*, 67-69.

Aquarius is the zodiacal sign of Israel, but know that our sages said that "There is no zodiacal sign for Israel" (Shabbat 156a, Nedarim 32a). This is true, because as long as they cleave to God no zodiacal sign exerts any influence on them, whether for good or for evil. Cleaving to God means knowing Him and observing His commandments. [...] But when Israel is not on the straight path, the zodiacal sign dominates them, and then they are regarded the same as all the other nations[43]

In this passage, Ibn Ezra tried to harmonize the standard astrological idea that Aquarius is the sign of Israel with the talmudic dictum that Israel is not under the influence of any zodiacal sign. According to Ibn Ezra's explanation, if the Jews observe the Law, they may escape collectively the decrees of the stars; however, if they do not keep the Law, then they are regarded as all the other nations, and Aquarius or the conjunction of Jupiter and Saturn in this sign determine their fate. In his view, the stars had decreed that Israel should remain in exile in Egypt; however, God saved them from this astral influence, and released the people of Israel so that they could receive his Torah.[44]

Abraham ibn Ezra's interest in astronomy and astrology is connected with the activity that made him famous in his own time and gave him an important place in the history of Jewish thought: the interpretation of the Bible. In his introduction to his commentaries on the Pentateuch, he stated that biblical exegesis should be based on rational principles, on the one hand, and on all branches of knowledge, on the other hand, for "reason is the foundation [of the Torah], because the Torah was not given to those who have no knowledge, and the angel [i.e. mediator] between a human being and God is his intelligence."[45]

In his commentary on Ecclesiastes, Ibn Ezra stated that this biblical book deals with the laws of nature, although these laws are not explained in the book in a clear and evident manner, because the purpose of its author was not to teach science. Consequently, the

---

[43] Abraham ibn Ezra, *The Book of the World*, 165.

[44] Abraham ibn Ezra, *The Book of the World*, 19-21 and 204-207.

[45] Uriel Simon, "Abraham ibn Ezra," in Magne Sæbø (ed.), *Hebrew Bible/Old Testament. The History of Its Interpretation*. Volume I: *From the Beginnings to the Middle Ages (Until 1300)*. Part 2: *The Middle Ages* (Göttingen: Vandenhoeck and Ruprecht, 2000), 377-387: 379.

purpose of the exegete is to uncover the scientific theories hidden in the biblical text and show that the knowledge provided by the Bible conforms to that provided by secular sciences. Ibn Ezra found in Ecclesiastes allusions to several theories of medieval scientific thought, such as the four elements that compose all created beings, the peculiarities of the movements of the sun and the other heavenly objects around the earth, the sublunar world as a model of the superior world, the dependence of time and space on the motions of stars, and the dependence of human beings' fate on the positions of stars and planets.[46]

Regarding the controversial verse "What advantage do people have from all the toil at which they toil under the sun?" (Eccles. 1:3), Ibn Ezra explained that Solomon[47] meant that every activity in this world—that is, "under the sun"—is useless, because everything depends on the influence of stars; however, this implies that there must be something worthwhile "above the sun." Ibn Ezra concluded that "one who toils to seek wisdom in order to cleanse his soul derives benefit, because the human soul is not under the sun." He drew on the Neoplatonic idea that the human soul comes from the upper world to prove that the only worthwhile activity in this world is the purification of the soul: since the soul is not "under the sun," it is not under the influence of stars, and therefore it can be purified through the development of wisdom.[48]

The idea that each day of the week is governed and under the influence of a certain planet was typical of medieval astrology. Saturn was believed to be the planet that rules on Saturday, and was considered the most malignant of the seven planets; it was associated with destructions, illnesses, exiles, poverty, fears, deaths, and other terrible things. In his commentary on Exod. 20:13, Ibn Ezra explained the reasons for the Ten Commandments. The fourth commandment says, "Remember the Sabbath day, and keep it holy,"

---

[46] Mariano Gómez Aranda, *El comentario de Abraham ibn Ezra al libro del Eclesiastés.* Introducción, traducción y edición crítica (Madrid: CSIC, 1994). On an analysis of Ibn Ezra's scientific exegesis on Ecclesiastes, see Mariano Gómez Aranda, "The Meaning of Qohelet According to Ibn Ezra's Scientific Explanations," *Aleph* 6 (2006): 339-370.

[47] According to the Jewish tradition, King Solomon was the author of the book of Ecclesiastes.

[48] Gómez Aranda, "Meaning of Qohelet," 355-356.

which, according to the Jewish tradition, means that one should not do any kind of work whatsoever on the Sabbath. In his explanation of this commandment, Ibn Ezra affirmed:

> The fourth statement [i.e., commandment], the statement about the Sabbath, corresponds to the sphere of Saturn. The astrologers tell us that each one of the planets has a certain day in the week in which its power is manifest. [...] They say that Saturn and Mars are harmful stars. Therefore harm befalls anyone who begins any work or sets out on a journey when one or the other dominates. [...] It is therefore unfit for one to occupy himself on Saturday with everyday matters. On the contrary, one should devote himself on this day to the fear of God.[49]

Ibn Ezra provided the rationale of the prohibition against working on Saturday by connecting this religious commandment with the medieval idea of the astrological influence of the planet Saturn: it is inappropriate to do any work on Saturday because Saturn's influence on this day will lead to terrible consequences.[50]

Other examples of Ibn Ezra's connections between astrology and biblical exegesis may be found in his commentary on Job.[51] As is well known, this biblical book deals with the controversial theme of the righteous man who suffers all kinds of misfortunes in spite of his fulfillment of God's commandments. Ibn Ezra attempted to solve this problem by explaining that the angels and Satan who presented themselves before God to receive their corresponding missions refer to the planets, stars and constellations, the causes of celestial decrees. He considered the angels to be the forces that move the stars, and through their movements astrological influences on earthly beings are set. Under the figure of Satan, the influence of wicked stars is hidden. Since he is a wicked angel who rebelled against God, he is responsible for the wicked influence of wicked stars on earth.

---

[49] Abraham ibn Ezra, *Commentary on the Pentateuch: Exodus (Shemot)*. Translated and Annotated by H. N. Strickman and A. M. Silver (New York: Menorah, 1996), 433-434.

[50] On Ibn Ezra's views on the planet Saturn, see Shlomo Sela, "Abraham ibn Ezra's Appropriation of Saturn," *Kabbalah: Journal for the Study of Jewish Mystical Texts* 10 (2004): 21-53.

[51] Mariano Gómez Aranda, *El Comentario de Abraham Ibn Ezra al Libro de Job. Edición crítica, traducción y estudio introductorio* (Madrid: CSIC, 2004). On an analysis of Ibn Ezra's scientific exegesis on the book of Job, see Mariano Gómez Aranda, "Aspectos científicos en el Comentario de Abraham ibn Ezra al libro de Job," *Henoch* 23 (2001): 81-96.

Therefore, according to Ibn Ezra, Job's misfortunes are the natural consequences of the wicked influence of stars. Job cursed the day that he was born, for Job was born under a bad sign.

Ibn Ezra's use of scientific themes in his explanation of biblical verses is the best example of how science was integrated and legitimized in the religious thought of Iberian Jewish intellectuals.

Maimonides and Jewish Aristotelianism

Since the beginning of the medieval period, the greater part of Aristotle's works had been translated into Arabic to further the knowledge of Muslim, Jewish and Christian philosophers. Aristotelian philosophy derived a great number of truly Aristotelian notions in a strict sense, but at the same time admitted several Neoplatonic ideas. This medieval Aristotle is sometimes quite different from the Aristotle of Antiquity, for he reached the medieval philosophers already accompanied by commentaries written by Greek authors, most of whom were Neoplatonists who developed their own positions within Aristotelian categories. In this sense, Neoplatonism and Aristotelianism are not two clearly distinct systems of thought in the Middle Ages.

Moses ben Maimon, also known as Rambam or Maimonides, is the most representative Jewish philosopher of medieval Aristotelianism. Born in Córdoba in 1138, he left the country when very young and travelled through al-Andalus, Morocco, where he lived for some years, and North Africa. He finally settled in Egypt, where he was a practitioner of medicine and became the physician of the Sultan. In Egypt, Maimonides completed his two major works, the *Mishneh Torah* in 1180 and the *Guide of the Perplexed* in 1190.

Maimonides' controversial position on the creation of the world is expounded in his *Guide of the Perplexed*. He presents three views: creation out of nothing (the biblical view according to his exegesis), creation from pre-existing matter (the Platonic view), and the Aristotelian view that is committed to the eternity of the world. His discussion on this issue is the best example in the Maimonidean corpus of the interaction between two traditions, the religious and the philosophical, using the philosophical arguments to explicate the religious tradition.[52]

Maimonides finds that both the Aristotelian and the Platonic positions have not been sufficiently demonstrated and are therefore inconclusive. Maimonides then presents a kind of transcendental argument on behalf of the biblical account: creation out of nothing. The existence of revelation, revealed law, presupposes the existence of a God who is free to do as He pleases, when He pleases. This idea paves the way for belief in creation out of nothing.

In his explanation of Gen. 1:1, Maimonides tries to prove that God created the world out of nothing together with time, and that time did not exist before creation. In this sense, Maimonides tries to link his idea of creation with the Aristotelian principle that time belongs only to created beings.

> The world has not been created in a temporal beginning, as we have explained, for time belongs to the created things. For this reason it says **In the beginning** [*bereshith*]. For the "be" has the meaning of "in." The true translation of this verse is: In the origin God created what is high and what is low. This is the translation that fits in with creation in time. On the other hand the statement, which you find formulated by some of the sages, that affirms that time existed before the creation of the world is very difficult. For that is the opinion of Aristotle, which I have explained to you: he holds that time cannot be conceived to have a beginning, which is incongruous. [...] I have already made it known to you that the foundation of the whole Law is the view that God has brought the world into being out of nothing without there having been a temporal beginning. For time is created, being consequent upon the motion of the sphere, which is created.[53]

Maimonides continues to explain that the process of creation described in the first chapter of Genesis is perfectly compatible with Aristotle's physics. After explaining that the name *earth* mentioned in the expression *In the beginning God created the heaven and the earth* (Gen. 1:1) refers to the entire lower world, Maimonides continues to prove that the four elements of nature—namely fire,

---

[52] Sirat, *History*, 188-192. See also D. H. Frank, "Maimonides and Medieval Jewish Aristotelianism," in *The Cambridge Companion*, 136-156.

[53] Maimonides, *The Guide of the Perplexed*. Translated and with an Introduction and Notes by Shlomo Pines (Chicago: University of Chicago Press, 1963), vol. 2, 349-50.

air, water and earth—are alluded to in subsequent verses of Genesis
1. The word *darkness* in the expression *darkness was upon the face
of the deep* (Gen. 1:2) is interpreted by Maimonides as alluding to
the elemental fire. In order to prove his statement, he quotes two
synonymous biblical expressions in which the words *fire* and *darkness*
are interchangeable: *You heard his words coming out of the fire* (Deut.
4:36) and *When you heard the voice out of the darkness* (Deut. 5:23).
He also refers to a verse in which two parallel expressions including
darkness and *fire* are employed with a similar meaning: *All darkness
is laid up for their treasures; a fire fanned by no one will devour them*
(Job 20:26). But Maimonides adds also a rational explanation to
sustain the identification of darkness with fire: "The elemental fire
was designated by this term, because it is not luminous, but only
transparent; for if the elemental fire had been luminous, we should
have seen at night the whole atmosphere in flame like fire."[54] The
expression *a wind from God swept over the face of the waters* (Gen.
1:2) proves that the elemental air is alluded to in the word *wind* (or
spirit), and the elemental water in the word *waters*. The elemental
earth is alluded to in the expression *And God called the dry land
earth* (Gen. 1:10).

Maimonides then arrives at the conclusion that "the elements
are mentioned according to their natural position: first the earth,
then the water that is above it, then the air that adheres to the water,
then the fire that is above the air."[55] In fact, according to Aristotle's
cosmology, the universe is an eternal sphere divided into an upper
and a lower region by the sphere of the moon. The sublunar region
is the world of generation, corruption and impermanence because
it is formed of the four elements of nature. These elements are
arranged in spheres. Because earth and water are heavy, it is their
nature to descend toward the center of the universe. Because of its
greater heaviness, earth would collect at the center, with water in
a concentrical sphere around the earth. Air and fire are light, fire
being the lighter of the two. They are both arranged in concentric
spheres around the earth. As we have seen, Maimonides accepted
Aristotle's physics in everything that concerns the lower world, the

---

[54] Maimonides, *Guide*, vol. 2, 351.
[55] Maimonides, *Guide*, vol. 2, 351.

sublunar world; however, he showed himself extremely dubious about Aristotle's celestial world.

Maimonides' views on prophecy are expressed in philosophical terminology. Maimonides defines prophecy as follows:

> Know that the true reality and quiddity of prophecy consist in its being an overflow overflowing from God, may He be cherished and honored, through the intermediation of the Active Intellect, toward the rational faculty in the first place and thereafter toward the imaginative faculty. This is the highest degree of human beings and the ultimate term of perfection for the imaginative faculty.[56]

According to Maimonides, prophecy is understood as the epitome of intellectual excellence. The ultimate cause of prophecy is God, and the immediate cause is the Active Intellect. The receiver is the rational faculty, which in its turn overflows into the imaginative.[57] But for Maimonides not all human beings are prepared to receive prophecy. Several conditions are necessary for this, such as the perfection of the bodily faculties, to which the imaginative faculty belongs. Prophets have to be morally perfect and entirely detached from all sensual desire and all vain ambition. Effort and merit are rewarded, and God makes prophets of those who by themselves have achieved the moral and intellectual capacity for it. For Maimonides, Moses is the prophet-philosopher *par excellence*. While the other biblical prophets heard God's words through the intermediary of an angel or through a dream of prophecy, Moses heard God speak directly to him, for he was very close to the Active Intellect.

Following certain Neoplatonic currents and some Muslim philosophers, Maimonides defends the so-called negative theology, which means that one can only assign negative attributes to God. Given that God is utterly transcendent, Maimonides defends the idea that human language about God cannot describe Him in any straightforward and direct manner. As a consequence, all predications about God—that He is one, eternal, and others—must be understood as denials of imperfections of Him.

---

[56] Maimonides, *Guide,* vol. 2, 369.
[57] Sirat, *History,* 192-198.

According to Maimonides, Moses—the most perfect knowledgeable human being—was able to know God not by knowing His essence, but by knowing His attributes, namely His actions.

> Know that the master of those who know, Moses our Master, peace be on him, made two requests and received an answer to both of them. One request consisted in his asking Him, may He be exalted, to let him know His essence and true reality. The second request, which he put first, was that He should let him know His attributes. The answer to the two requests that He, may He be exalted, gave him consisted in His promising him to let him know all His attributes, making it known to him that they are His actions, and teaching him that His essence cannot be grasped as it really is.[58]

Maimonides then explains that the request made by Moses to God, "Show me Your ways so that I may know you" (Exod. 33:13), indicates that God is known through His works. In consequence, to know God's works is to know the different branches of science that lead to metaphysics. The road leading towards God is scientific knowledge, the purpose for which human beings are created.[59]

Maimonides' high concept of the sciences is manifested in his use of several scientific doctrines in his biblical exegesis. Maimonides used his knowledge of medicine and other sciences to explain Jewish religious laws. In his *Mishneh Torah*, which is a rational explanation of the Jewish laws, he frequently made use of his medical theories to justify the divine precepts.[60] He affirmed that "When the body is healthy and sound one treads in the ways of the Lord,"[61] and considered Jewish religious precepts to be in accordance with the rules of hygiene.

Maimonides also dealt with medicine in the *Guide of the Perplexed*. In one of the chapters, he gave medical reasons for the prohibitions concerning food in Judaism, concentrating on the medical arguments for forbidding various kinds of food:

---

[58] Maimonides, *Guide*, vol. 1, 123.

[59] Maimonides' famous philosophical doctrine of the negative attributes of God was later criticized in Jewish philosophical circles by Gersonides and outside those circles by Thomas Aquinas. D. H. Frank, "Maimonides and Medieval Jewish Aristotelianism," 148.

[60] On this topic see Fred Rosner, *Medicine in the* Mishneh Torah *of Maimonides* (New York: Ktav, 1984).

[61] Rosner, *Medicine in the* Mishneh Torah, 81.

I say, then, that to eat any of the various kinds of food that the Law has forbidden us is blameworthy. Among all those forbidden to us, only pork and fat may be imagined not to be harmful. But this is not so, for pork is more humid than is proper and contains much superfluous matter. The major reason why the Law abhors it is its being very dirty and feeding on dirty things. [...] As for the prohibition against eating meat [boiled] in milk, it is in my opinion not improbable that-in addition to this being undoubtedly very gross food and very filling-idolatry had something to do with it.[62]

Maimonides tried to prove that all forbidden food is harmful to the body. Regarding pork, he affirmed that it is unhealthy for its excessive humidity[63] and the large quantity of superfluous matter that it contains, referring probably to its excessive fat. He also added the reason that pig-breeding is unhygienic. In the case of the Torah prohibition against cooking "a kid in the milk of its mother" (Exod. 23:19, 34:26; Deut. 16:31), Maimonides believed that it must have been an ancient pagan custom associated to idolatry. He also added a medical reason: it is a very gross food and very filling. Therefore, in *The Guide of the Perplexed*, Maimonides expressed his expertise as a physician regarding the unhealthy quality of prohibited food. His main purpose was to prove that his medical considerations on a healthy diet, as explained in his medical writings, agreed with the dietary prohibitions explicit in the Torah.[64]

Maimonides also showed his expertise in other scientific disciplines, and tried to fully integrate them in his own views of Judaism. In his treatise on the *Sanctification of the New Moon*, he recognized the value and importance of astronomy, especially with regard to establishing the Jewish calendar. However, he clearly rejected astrology for not being based on reason. He associated astronomy with mathematics and calendar regulation, and astrology with the practices of magicians and sorcerers.[65]

---

[62] Maimonides, *Guide*, vol. 2, 598-599. On this topic, see Jacob Levinger, "Maimonides' *Guide of the Perplexed* on Forbidden Food in the Light of His Own Medical Opinion," in *Perspectives on Maimonides: Philosophical and Historical Studies*, ed. Joel L. Kraemer (Oxford: Oxford University Press, 1991), 195-208.

[63] In the Middle Ages, an excess of humidity in food was considered bad for health.

[64] Levinger, "On Forbidden Food," 206.

[65] On Maimonides' opinions regarding astronomy and astrology, see Y. Tzvi Langermann, "Maimonides' Repudiation of Astrology," in *Maimonides and the Sciences*, ed. R. S. Cohen

Maimonides' medical writings and philosophical works had a great impact in the Middle Ages and the Renaissance and enjoyed considerable popularity. They were soon translated into Hebrew by members of the Ibn Tibbon family in the south of France. These translations contributed to the expansion of medicine and philosophy in the Jewish communities of Europe. They were also translated into Latin, thus influencing Christian scholars such as Thomas Aquinas. The Latin translations were printed several times in the fifteenth and sixteenth centuries.

The Transmission of Science in Medieval Jewish Encyclopedias

The medieval Hebrew encyclopedias of science and philosophy made their appearance in the twelfth and thirteenth centuries, at a time when Hebrew was replacing Arabic as the literary and scientific language of the Jews. These texts offered the non-Arabic-reading Jews of Spain, Provence and Italy their first direct contact with classical and contemporary scientific knowledge, and played an important role in the transmission of science and philosophy from the Arabic and Greek worlds.[66]

The *Midrash ha-Hokhmah* (The Interpretation of Wisdom) by Judah ben Solomon ha-Cohen is considered the oldest extant Hebrew encyclopedia of science. Born in Toledo around 1215, the author was a famous mathematician who joined the circle of scholars of the imperial court of Frederick II in Italy. His encyclopedia, originally written in Arabic, was later translated into Hebrew by the author himself.[67]

---

and H. Levine (Dordrecht-Boston-London: Kluwer Academic Publishers 2000), 131-157, and Sela, "Fuzzy Borders," 63-80.

[66] The best analysis on this topic is S. Harvey, ed., *The Medieval Hebrew Encyclopedias of Science and Philosophy*. See also Mariano Gómez Aranda, "Enciclopedias hebreas en la época medieval," in *Las Enciclopedias en España antes de l'Encyclopédie*, ed. A. Alvar Ezquerra (Madrid: CSIC, 2009), 105-124.

[67] On this encyclopedia, see Resianne Fontaine, "Judah ben Solomon ha-Cohen's *Midrash ha-Hokhmah*: Its Sources and Use of Sources," in *The Medieval Hebrew Encyclopedias*, 191-210.

Judah ha-Cohen gives a classification of the sciences following the Aristotelian tripartite division of sciences into natural, mathematical and divine science. He also explains that this structure reflects the threefold division of all created beings into three worlds: the world of generation and corruption, the world of the spheres and the divine world. Aristotle's writings—together with Averroes' commentaries on Aristotle's writings—are the sources for the philosophical part of this encyclopedia. Euclid's *Elements* is the source for the geometrical section, and Ptolemy's *Almagest* for the astronomical and astrological sections, complemented with al-Bitruji's *Principles of Astronomy*.

Judah ha-Cohen substitutes for the part corresponding to metaphysics in Aristotle's division some comments on Jewish religion and biblical exegesis. He expresses his own views on Aristotle's "theological" doctrines as follows:

> You have seen the doctrine of Aristotle and of his commentators, like Averroes and others, about the question of the demonstration of the existence of the Creator, Blessed be He, and of His unity, and of the fact that He is not a body [...] and that it is not possible that He is at rest first and then acting. But this is not Jacob's inheritance, because He is the Creator of the universe, as we will explain here below, in the commentary on some passages of the Bible.[68]

It seems that Judah ha-Cohen was not satisfied with the philosophical knowledge provided by Aristotle's *Metaphysics*, probably because it does not provide the same degree of certainty as revealed knowledge. In this sense, he felt the need to supplement his encyclopedia with a more religion-oriented knowledge closer to the Jewish tradition.

In fact, Judah ha-Cohen's intention in writing his encyclopedia was to provide Jews with the secular scientific knowledge necessary to respond to the intellectual challenges of his time. Given that not many philosophical texts had been translated into Hebrew by the time that Judah ha-Cohen composed the Hebrew version of his work, the encylopedic approach seemed to be the best possible option to provide such knowledge.[69]

---

[68] Mauro Zonta, "The Place of Aristotelian Metaphysics in the Thirteenth-Century Encyclopedias," in *The Medieval Hebrew Encyclopedias*, 414-426, here 421.

[69] Fontaine, "Judah ben Solomon ha-Cohen," 207-208.

Shem Tob ibn Falaquera, who lived in northern Spain or Provence in the thirteenth century, is the author of *De'ot ha Filosofim* (*The Opinions of the Philosophers*), the most representative work of the encyclopedic approach in medieval times. Ibn Falaquera states his intention in writing this encyclopedia as follows:

> I endeavored to translate these opinions [of the philosophers] from Arabic to Hebrew, and to compile them from the books that are scattered there, so that whoever wishes to grasp these opinions will find them in one book, and will not need to weary himself by reading all the books [on these subjects], for all the opinions [of the philosophers], general and particular, on natural science and divine science are included in this composition.[70]

Ibn Falaquera's intention was not to write something new and original, but to teach the Jewish intellectuals of his time the concepts and ideas of Aristotelian science and philosophy as transmitted by Alfarabi, Avicenna, Averroes, Maimonides, and other philosophers.

Athough Ibn Falaquera believed that natural science is supported by proofs and that few things in it are doubtful, his *De'ot ha Filosofim* shows the difficulties involved in integrating several of Aristotle's scientific ideas into Jewish thought. One of Aristotle's ideas discussed by medieval scientists was that the sublunar world is composed of the four elements, whereas the stars and planets are formed of a fifth element called *ether*. Since the Sun is not composed of the element of fire and consequently cannot emit heat by itself, Aristotle arrived at the conclusion that the heat of the Sun depends on its motion. The motion of the Sun around the earth produces generation and corruption because it is an eternal continuous motion.[71]

Ibn Falaquera was not satisfied with Aristotle's solution and, following Averroes, affirmed that the motion of the Sun is not the reason to explain the origin of heat, because all the stars and planets move around the earth, and not all of them emit heat. Ibn Falaquera continues his argument: since the heavenly bodies are not by them-

---

[70] Steven Harvey, "Shem-Tov Ibn Falaquera's *De'ot ha-Filosofim*: Its Sources and Use of Sources," in *The Medieval Hebrew Encyclopedias*, 211-237, here 216.

[71] Gad Freudenthal, "Providence, Astrology, and Celestial Influences on the Sublunar World in Shem-Tov Ibn Falaquera's *De'ot ha-Filosofim*," in *The Medieval Hebrew Encyclopedias*, 335-370.

selves warm, and since motion per se cannot account for heating, there must be something particular in the heavenly bodies that causes them to warm. Ibn Falaquera's conclusion, similar to that given by Averroes, is as follows: "The light as light, when its luminosity is reflected, warms the bodies down here by virtue of a divine force."[72] The notion of "divine force," by virtue of which reflected rays of light generate heat, gave Ibn Falaquera the opportunity to explain a natural phenomenon by a theological concept. The understanding of one of the most common natural phenomena could not be achieved through purely physical notions. The intervention of a divine element made it possible to connect natural philosophy with the divine science of theology.

The School of Translators of Toledo

In Christian Spain, there was a great deal of activity in translating scientific and philosophical texts from the twelfth century onward in the so-called "School of Translators of Toledo."[73] Under the patronage of archbishop Raimundo, Jewish scholars were invited to participate in the process of the transmission of science. Iohannes Avendeut Hispanus cooperated with the Christian Dominicus Gundissalinus in the translation of several philosophical works by Aristotle, Ibn Gabirol's *Fons Vitae*, and al-Ghazali's books on logic and philosophy, which became very influential among scholastic Christian theologians.

In the thirteenth century, the "School" received the support of Alfonso X of Castile, and engaged in a second wave of translations. The purpose of the king was to provide Castilian scholars engaged in studying the sciences with a working library, mainly in the Castilian

---

[72] Freudenthal, "Providence, Astrology, and Celestial Influences," 348.

[73] José S. Gil, *La escuela de traductores de Toledo y sus colaboradores judíos* (Toledo: Instituto Provincial de Investigaciones y Estudios Toledanos, 1985), Serafín Vegas González, "Significado histórico y significación filosófica en la revisión de los planteamientos concernientes a la Escuela de Traductores de Toledo," *Revista Española de Filosofía Medieval* 12 (2005): 109-134, and D. Romano, "The Jews' Contribution to Medicine, Science and General Learning," in *Moreshet Sepharad: The Sephardi Legacy*, ed. Haim Beinart (Jerusalem: Magnes Press, 1992), vol. 1, 240-260, here 256-57.

language.[74] Works on astronomical and astrological subjects, such as Abenragel's treatise on judicial astrology *Libro conplido en los iudizios de las estrellas* (The Complete Book of the Judgments of the Stars), were translated from Arabic into Castilian and Latin. These translations contributed to the creation and expansion of a new scientific vocabulary in Castilian.

In addition to translations, there was one particularly important original text composed at the court of Alfonso X, *The Alfonsine Tables of Toledo*, a set of tables with the positions of stars and planets in heaven as observed in Toledo in the year 1252, accompanied with the instructions (canons) to use them.[75] Only the Castilian canons are now extant. The authors of these tables were two Jews: Judah ben Moses and Isaac ibn Said.

In the prologue, the authors stressed the importance of observation and of the collaboration of several scientists for long periods of time in order to establish the positions of stars with accuracy:

> The science of astrology[76] is a subject that cannot be investigated without observations. Yet, the observations made by experts in this discipline cannot be completed by a single man; indeed, they cannot be completed in the lifetime of one man. On the contrary, when a result is attained, it is attained through the work of many men, laboring one after another for a long time. The reason for this is that among the celestial motions are some that are so slow that they only complete a circuit after thousands of years. It is therefore necessary to continue making observations because, by proceeding in this way, phenomena will become apparent at one time that were not apparent at another time.[77]

In spite of this remark, no specific dated observations are mentioned in the fifty-four chapters that follow this prologue.[78] In fact, what the king ordered his astronomers was to correct previous

[74] Goldstein, "Neutral Zone," 165.

[75] José Chabás and Bernard R. Goldstein, *The Alfonsine Tables of Toledo* (Dordrecht: Kluwer Academic Publisher, 2003), and Goldstein, "Neutral Zone," 165-167.

[76] The term "astrology" in the Middle Ages frequently refers to both astronomy and astrology.

[77] Chabas and Goldstein, *Alfonsine Tables*, 136-37, and B. R. Goldstein, "Neutral Zone," 166.

[78] Goldstein, "Neutral Zone," 167.

astronomical tables, although according to Bernard Goldstein, it is not entirely clear which set of tables he had in mind:

> [Don Alfonso] ordered us to rectify and correct the divergences and disagreements that had appeared in some positions of some of the planets and in other motions. We obeyed his order as he demanded of us, reconstructing the instruments as best we could.[79] We worked at making observations for a certain length of time and proceeded to observe the Sun throughout a complete year. [...] We made some observations in which we had doubts but repeated them many times to resolve the doubt; we did not abandon searching and investigating anything until the way to correct that which was in need of correction became evident to us.[80]

The *Alfonsine Tables* served as the standard guide to the practice of mathematical astronomy until the sixteenth century in Christian countries north of the Pyrenees; however, there is no evidence that these tables were used by anyone in Spain until 1460, when Nicholas Polonius arrived in Salamanca to hold the chair of astronomy at the University of Salamanca. Polonius, who came from Poland, made use of the *Alfonsine Tables* to write a text for his students on astronomical matters.[81]

Judah ben Moses and Isaac ibn Said also participated in the preparation of the *Libro del saber de astronomía* (The Book of Astronomical Knowledge), a compilation of treatises on the construction of astronomical instruments, clocks and astrolabes.

Abraham Zacut and the Last Chapter of Jewish Science in Medieval Iberia

Abraham Zacut marked the end of Jewish science in medieval Iberia. Born in Salamanca in 1452, he was active as an astronomer and astrologer in Salamanca and other places in Castile before the expulsion of the Jews in 1492. Afterwards he spent some time in

---

[79] This refers to the instruments used for astronomical reckoning, such as the armillary sphere and the astrolabe.

[80] Chabas and Goldstein, *Alfonsine Tables*, 136-37, and B. R. Goldstein, "Neutral Zone," 166.

[81] José Chabás, "Astronomy in Salamanca in the Mid-fifteenth Century: The *Tabulae resolutae*," *Journal for the History of Astronomy* 29 (1998): 167-175.

Portugal, North Africa and then in Jerusalem.[82] In 1478 he finished his masterpiece on astronomy and astrology in Hebrew, *Ha-hibbur ha-gadol* (The Great Composition), consisting of astronomical tables and canons in which the author explained how to use the tables. In the introduction to the canons, Zacut expressed his main goal in writing this work:

> With the elaboration of these Tables we have achieved the most important object of astronomy for our Law, which is to fix the new moons and the feasts, and to teach how to calculate the day of the new moon, according to what R. Moses ben Maimon wrote in the ordinances for the *Sanctification of the New Moon*.[83]

Therefore, this treatise will help to fix the Jewish calendar by providing the scientific basis for implementing such a task. Even though this work was directed to a Jewish audience, it contains relevant data for the Christian and the Muslim calendars, which proves that the *Hibbur* could be useful for people of all three monotheistic religions. In fact, in 1481 this work was translated into Castilian by Juan de Salaya, who held the chair of astronomy at the University of Salamanca, with the assistance of Zacut himself. This translation was probably intended for Christian intellectuals at the university, in particular those professors and students interested in astronomy.[84]

Zacut also composed the *Tratado en las ynfluencias del cielo* (Treatise on the Influences of Heaven) in Castilian, with the purpose

---

[82] The best analysis of astronomy in the Iberian Peninsula at the end of the Middle Ages and specifically that of Abraham Zacut is José Chabás and Bernard R. Goldstein, *Astronomy in the Iberian Peninsula: Abraham Zacut and the Transition from Manuscript to Print* (Philadelphia: American Philosophical Society, 2000).

[83] Francisco Cantera, *El judío salmantino Abraham Zacut* (Madrid: Academia de Ciencias, 1931), 186.

[84] Abraham Zacut is best known for the *Almanach perpetuum*, published in Leiria, Portugal, in 1496. Although it has been demonstrated that the author is not Zacut but Joseph Vizinus, this work is very similar in content to the *Hibbur*. (Chabás and Goldstein, *Astronomy in the Iberian Peninsula*, 90-160.) The *Almanach* had also a significant impact in the Muslim world. There are at least two versions of this work in Arabic, one made in Istanbul and the other in the Maghrib. On the changing identity of the works written by or attributed to Zacut, see Mariano Gómez-Aranda, "Science and Jewish Identity in the Works of Abraham Zacut (1452-1515)," in *Medieval Jewish Identities: Al-Andalus and Beyond*, ed. C. Caballero-Navas and E. Alfonso (New York: Palgrave Macmillan, forthcoming).

of providing the astrological information necessary to be used in medicine. He affirmed:

> The perfection of the astrologer lies in knowing all natural things and mastering the art of medicine. He will help with the effects of the stars by preparing the passive ones to receive the good influences of the agents and by deviating the bad ones from them.[85]

In the Middle Ages, it was believed that the stars could exert an influence on the treatment of patients. Some physicians used to consult the positions of stars and planets before performing medical operations or making a diagnosis.

After the expulsion of the Jews from Portugal in 1496, Zacut settled in Tunis, where in 1504 he wrote (or completed) his *Sefer Yuḥasin* (Book of Genealogies), a work completely different from anything he had previously written. Zacut decided to change his scientific interests and focus on Jewish history and tradition for the remainder of his life. The very beginnings of the introduction to the book, in which he compared Israel and the Jewish Sages with the stars in heaven, expressed how Zacut felt about the evolution of his own intellectual interests post-expulsion:

> The people of Israel are compared to the stars by name and number, akin to gold implements and the most precious stones. Even more so are the Sages and pious men, for it is said "those who are wise shall shine like the brightness of the sky, and those who lead many to righteousness, like the stars forever and ever" (Dan. 12:3). [...] The star that shines light in the celestial sphere is like the soul in the body. The Sages of the Mishnah and the Talmud and all those who came after them enlighten our souls with the books they wrote to benefit us.[86]

If, until that moment, Zacut had dedicated himself to the transmission of scientific knowledge to both Jews and Christians, after the expulsion he changed his focus of interest to concentrate on "The Jewish Tradition." In those moments of misery, the Jewish tradition

---

[85] Joaquim de Carvalho, "Dois inéditos de Abraham Zacuto," in *Estudos sobre a Cultura Portuguesa do século XVI* (Coimbra: Atlanida, 1947), vol. I, 95-183: 109.

[86] Abraham Zacut, *Sefer Yuḥasin ha-shalem*, ed. H. Filipowski (London: The Society of Hebrew Antiquities, 1857), 1. For an English translation, see Abraham Zacuto, *The Book of Lineage or Sefer Yohassin*. Translated and edited by Israel Shamir (Tel Aviv: Zacuto Foundation, 2005).

provided consolation, hope, and, most importantly, roots to a people who felt displaced. However, Zacut did not abandon science completely after the expulsion. He continued elaborating on astronomical tables, probably for his livelihood, and wrote a short astrological work entitled *Judgments of the Astrologer*. In this work, he made the following prediction:

> In the year 1524 there will be a conjunction of the planets unlike any that came before it. It indicates that there will be great woes in Christian countries to the West, and that the sea will rise and some of their lands will be flooded. Happy is he who waits and reaches that year in repentance, upright in heart, and in good deeds. And in that year will be redemption and salvation for Israel [...] and the coming of the Messiah, son of David, may God be blessed for the sake of His name, may He help us and support us and maintain us with His righteous right hand, and may He inscribe us for a good life with all that is written for life, to look upon the goodness of God in the land of life. Amen, may it be His will.[87]

Zacut's aim was to use all his astrological knowledge—and by extension, all his scientific knowledge—to compute the date of the advent of the Messiah. Astronomy, astrology, and mathematics, then, proved their utility for the expelled Jews as a way to provide the necessary knowledge for the calculation of the date of the coming of the Messiah. They were also useful in bringing consolation, comfort, and hope to all the Jews who felt desperate and disillusioned by the terrible experience of the expulsion. If the history of the Jewish people concludes with the coming of the Messiah from a theological point of view, the final chapter of the history of the Jewish science in medieval Iberia also concludes with the astrological calculations to predict scientifically the coming of the Messiah and the final triumph of the people of Israel.

---

[87] Chabás and Goldstein, *Astronomy in the Iberian Peninsula*, 173-174.

Works Cited

Abraham bar Hiyya. *Sefer ha-Ibbur*. Edited by H. Philipowski. London: Longman, Brown, Green and Longmans, 1851.

------. *Chibur ha-Meschichta weha-Tischboret*. Herausgegeben und mit Ammerkungen versehen von Dr. M. Guttmann. Berlin: Mekitse Nirdamim, 1913.

------. *Sefer Megillat ha-Megalleh*. Zum ersten Male herausgegeben von Dr. A. Poznanski. Revidiert und mit Einleitung versehen von Prof. Dr. J. Guttmann. Berlin: Mekize Nirdamim, 1924.

------. *La obra enciclopédica Yěsodé ha-Těbuná u-Migdal ha-Ěmuná*. Edición crítica con traducción, prólogo y notas por J. M. Millás Vallicrosa, Madrid-Barcelona: CSIC, 1952.

------. *La obra Forma de la Tierra*. Traducción del hebreo con prólogo y notas por J. M. Millás Vallicrosa. Madrid-Barcelona: CSIC, 1956.

------. *La obra Séfer Ḥešbón mahlekot ha-kokabim*. Edición crítica, con traducción, introducción y notas por J. M. Millás Vallicrosa. Barcelona: CSIC, 1959.

Abraham ibn Ezra, *Sefer ha-Ibbur*. Edited by L. Silbermann. Lyck: Mekitse Nirdamim, 1874.

------. *Sefer Ha-Mispar. Das Buch der Zahl*. Ein hebräisch-arithmetisches Werk des R. Abraham ibn Esra. Zum ersten Male herausgegeben, ins Deutsche übersetzt und erläutert von Dr. M. Silberberg. Frankfurt am Main: J. Kauffmann, 1895.

------. *The Beginning of Wisdom*. Edited by R. Levy and F. Cantera. Baltimore: The Johns Hopkins Press, 1939.

------. *El comentario de Abraham ibn Ezra al libro del Eclesiastés*. Introducción, traducción y edición crítica de M. Gómez Aranda. Madrid: CSIC, 1994.

------. *The Secret of the Torah*. Translated and Annotated by H. Norman Strickman. Northvale, New Jersey: Jason Aronson Inc. 1995.

------.*Commentary on the Pentateuch: Exodus (Shemot)*. Translated and Annotated by H. N. Strickman and A. M. Silver. New York: Menorah Publishing Company, 1996.

------. *El Comentario de Abraham Ibn Ezra al Libro de Job.* Edición crítica, traducción y estudio introductorio de M. Gómez Aranda. Madrid: CSIC, 2004.

------. *The Book of Reasons*: A Parallel Hebrew-English Critical Edition of the Two Versions of the Text by S. Sela. Leiden: Brill, 2007.

------. *Yesod Mora ve-Sod Torah: The Foundation of Reverence and the Secret of the Torah.* An Annotated Critical Edition. Second revised and enlarged edition by J. Cohen and U. Simon. Ramat Gan: Bar-Ilan University Press, 2007.

------. *The Book of the World.* A Parallel Hebrew-English Critical Edition of the Two Versions of the Text Edited, Translated and Annotated by S. Sela. Leiden: Brill, 2010.

Abraham Zacut. *Sefer Yuhasin ha-shalem.* Edited by H. Filipowski. London: The Society of Hebrew Antiquities, 1857.

------. *The Book of Lineage or Sefer Yohassin.* Translated and Edited by Israel Shamir. Tel Aviv: Zacuto Foundation, 2005.

Allard, A. "The Arabic Origins and Development of Latin Algorisms in the Twelfth Century," *Arabic Sciences and Philosophy* 1 (1991): 233-283.

Cantera, Francisco. *El judío salmantino Abraham Zacut.* Madrid: Academia de Ciencias, 1931.

Chabás, José and Bernard. R. Goldstein. *Astronomy in the Iberian Peninsula: Abraham Zacut and the Transition from Manuscript to Print.* Philadelphia: American Philosophical Society, 2000.

------. *The Alfonsine Tables of Toledo.* Dordrecht: Kluwer Academic Publisher, 2003.

Chabás, José. "Astronomy in Salamanca in the Mid-fifteenth Century: The *Tabulae resolutae*," *Journal for the History of Astronomy* 29 (1998): 167-175.

Frank, Daniel H., and Oliver O. Leaman, eds. *The Cambridge Companion to Medieval Jewish Philosophy.* Cambridge: Cambridge University Press, 2003.

Frank, Daniel H. "Maimonides and Medieval Jewish Aristotelianism." In *The Cambridge Companion to Medieval Jewish Philosophy*, edited by D. H. Frank and O. Leaman, 136-156. Cambridge: Cambridge University Press, 2003.

Fontaine, Resianne. "Judah ben Solomon ha-Cohen's *Midrash ha-Hokhmah*: Its Sources and Use of Sources." In *The Medieval Hebrew Encyclopedias of Science and Philosophy*, edited by S. Harvey, 191-210. Dordrecht-Boston-London: Kluwer Academic Publishers, 2000.

Freudenthal, Gad. "Providence, Astrology, and Celestial Influences on the Sublunar World in Shem-Tov Ibn Falaquera's *De'ot ha-Filosofim*." In *The Medieval Hebrew Encyclopedias of Science and Philosophy*, edited by S. Harvey, 335-370. Dordrecht: Kluwer Academic Publishers, 2000.

Gil, José S. *La escuela de traductores de Toledo y sus colaboradores judíos*. Toledo: Instituto Provincial de Investigaciones y Estudios Toledanos, 1985.

Goldstein, Bernard R. "Star Lists in Hebrew," *Centaurus* 28 (1985): 185-208.

------. "Astronomy as a 'Neutral Zone': Interreligious Cooperation in Medieval Spain," *Medieval Encounters* 15 (2009): 159-174.

Gomez-Aranda, "Aspectos científicos en el Comentario de Abraham ibn Ezra al libro de Job," *Henoch* 23 (2001): 81-96.

------. "The Meaning of Qohelet According to Ibn Ezra's Scientific Explanations," *Aleph* 6 (2006): 339-370.

------. "The Contribution of the Jews of Spain to the Transmission of Science in the Middle Ages," *European Review* 16 (2008): 169-181.

------. "Enciclopedias hebreas en la época medieval," in *Las Enciclopedias en España antes de l'Encyclopédie*, edited by A. Alvar Ezquerra, 105-124. Madrid: CSIC, 2009.

------. Mariano. "Science and Jewish Identity in the Works of Abraham Zacut (1452-1515)." In *Medieval Jewish Identities: Al-Andalus and Beyond*, edited by C. Caballero-Navas and E. Alfonso, 266-290. New York: Palgrave Macmillan, 2010.

Goodman, Lenn E., ed. *Neoplatonism and Jewish Thought*, New York: SUNY Press, 1992.

Harvey, Steven, "Science in the Jewish Communities of the Iberian Peninsula: An Interim Report." In *The Jews and the Sciences in the Middle Ages*, 1-54. Aldershot: Ashgate Variorum, 1999.

------, ed. *The Medieval Hebrew Encyclopedias of Science and Philosophy*, Dordrecht: Kluwer Academic Publishers, 2000.

------. "Shem-Tov Ibn Falaquera's *De'ot ha-Filosofim*: Its Sources and Use of Sources." In *The Medieval Hebrew Encyclopedias of Science and Philosophy*, edited by S. Harvey, 211-237. Dordrecht: Kluwer Academic Publishers, 2000.

------. "Maimonides' Repudiation of Astrology." In *Maimonides and the Sciences*, edited by R. S. Cohen and H. Levine, 131-157. Dordrecht: Kluwer Academic Publishers, 2000.

Levinger, Jacob. "Maimonides' *Guide of the Perplexed* on Forbidden Food in the Light of His Own Medical Opinion." In *Perspectives on Maimonides: Philosophical and Historical Studies*, edited by J. L. Kraemer, 195-208. Oxford: Oxford University Press, 1991.

Levy, Raphael. *The Astrological Works of Abraham ibn Ezra*. Baltimore: Johns Hopkins Press, 1927.

------. Lévy, Tony. "Abraham ibn Ezra et les mathematiques: remarques bibliographiques et historiques." In *Abraham ibn Ezra, savant universel*, edited by P. J. Tomson, 60-75. Brussels: Institutum Iudaicum, 2000.

------. "Les débuts de la litterature mathématique hébraïque: La géométrie d'Abraham bar Hiyya (XIe-XIIe siècle)," *Micrologus* 9 (2001): 35-64.

Lindberg, David C. *The Beginnings of Western Science*. Chicago: The University of Chicago Press, 1992.

Maimonides. *The Guide of the Perplexed*. Translated and with an Introduction and Notes by S. Pines. Chicago: The University of Chicago Press, 1963.

McGinn, Bernard. "Ibn Gabirol: The Sage among the Schoolmen." In *Neoplatonism and Jewish Thought*, edited by L. E. Goodman, 77-109. New York: SUNY Press, 1992.

Pessin, Sarah. "Jewish Neoplatonism: Being Above Being and Divine Emanation in Solomon ibn Gabirol and Isaac Israeli." In *The Cambridge Companion to Medieval Jewish Philosophy*, edited by D. H. Frank and O. Leaman, 91-110. Cambridge: Cambridge University Press, 2003.

Romano, David. "The Jews' Contribution to Medicine, Science and General Learning." In *Moreshet Sepharad: The Sephardi Legacy*, edited by H. Beinart, vol. 1, 240-260. Jerusalem: The Magnes Press, The Hebrew University, 1992.

Rosner, Fred. *Medicine in the* Mishneh Torah *of Maimonides*. New York: Ktav Publishing House, 1984.

Roth, Norman. "The 'Theft of Philosophy' by the Greeks from the Jews," *Classical Folia* 32 (1978): 53-67.

Rubio, Mercedes, "The First Hebrew Encyclopedia of Science: Abraham bar Hiyya's *Yesodei ha-Tevunah u-Migdal ha-Emunah*." In *The Medieval Hebrew Encyclopedias of Science and Philosophy*, edited by S. Harvey, 140-153. Dordrecht: Kluwer Academic Publishers, 2000.

Sánchez Faba, Francisco. "Abraham bar Hiyya (1070-1136) y su *Libro de Geometría*," *Gaceta matemática* 32 (1982): 101-115.

Sela, Shlomo, and Gad Freudenthal. "Abraham ibn Ezra's Scholarly Writings: A Chronological Listing," *Aleph* 6 (2006): 13-55.

Sela, Shlomo. "Abraham ibn Ezra's Scientific Corpus: Basic Constituents and General Characterization," *Arabic Sciences and Philosophy* 11 (2001): 91-149.

------. "The Fuzzy Borders between Astronomy and Astrology in the Thought and Work of Three Twelfth-Century Jewish Intellectuals," *Aleph* 1 (2001): 59-100.

------. *Abraham ibn Ezra and the Rise of Medieval Hebrew Science*. Leiden: Brill, 2003.

------. "Abraham ibn Ezra's Appropriation of Saturn," *Kabbalah: Journal for the Study of Jewish Mystical Texts* 10 (2004): 21-53.

------. "Abraham Bar Hiyya's Astrological Work and Thought," *Jewish Studies Quarterly* 13 (2006): 128-158.

Simon, Uriel. "Abraham ibn Ezra." In *Hebrew Bible/Old Testament: The History of Its Interpretation*. Volume I: *From the Beginnings to the Middle Ages (Until 1300)*. Part 2: *The Middle Ages*, edited by M. Sæbø, 377-387. Göttingen: Vandenhoeck and Ruprecht, 2000.

Sirat, Collete. *A History of Jewish Philosophy in the Middle Ages*. Paris: Editions de la Maison des Sciences de l'Homme-Cambridge University Press, 1985.

Tomson, Peter J., ed. *Abraham ibn Ezra, savant universel*. Brussels: Institutum Iudaicum, 2000.

Vegas González, Serafín. "Significado histórico y significación filosófica en la revisión de los planteamientos concernientes a la Escuela de Traductores de Toledo," *Revista Española de Filosofía Medieval* 12 (2005): 109-134.

Vignau, Vicente, "Carta dirigida á D. Juan II de Aragón, por su médico, fijándole día para operarle los ojos," *Revista de Archivos, Bibliotecas y Museos* 4 (1874): 135-137, 230-231.

Zonta, Mauro, "The Place of Aristotelian Metaphysics in the Thirteenth-Century Enciclopedias." In *The Medieval Hebrew Encyclopedias of Science and Philosophy*, edited by S. Harvey, 414-426. Dordrecht: Kluwer Academic Publishers, 2000

The Jewish Physician in Medieval Iberia (1100-1500)

····································· Maud Kozodoy

Any comprehensive view of Jewish society in medieval Iberia must take into account the figure of the physician. In late medieval Christian Spain and Provence, the number of Jews working as doctors was far out of proportion to their percentage of the general population. Next to money-lending, medicine was the most common form of employment for Jews.[1] Those who chose it as a profession comprised a discernible group, united by professional loyalties, distinct social privileges, and a shared corpus of knowledge and practice.

The significance of this group for our understanding of the period has rarely been acknowledged but deserves closer scrutiny. Since Jewish healers served Jewish and Christian patients of all social ranks, from kings and popes to the poorest members of society, they were involved in many of the most intimate social interactions between the Jewish and Christian communities. At the highest levels of the profession stood the court physician, an authoritative figure with personal access to the royal family, com manding a status comparable to that of the financially powerful

I am deeply grateful to Gad Freudenthal and Gerrit Bos for reading and commenting on an earlier version of this article.

[1] Joseph Shatzmiller, *Jews, Medicine and Medieval Society* (Berkeley, CA: University of California Press, 1994), 1.

Jewish courtier. Sometimes the two roles were combined in one person. And this exalted figure was only one element in a broader societal phenomenon that affected the self-image of Iberian Jews in general. In examining here both the intellectual heritage of medieval Jewish medicine and the social typology of Jewish physicians, we may hope to cast fresh light on the nature of Jewish society in medieval Spain and on the self-understanding of Iberian Jews.

During the four centuries between 1100 and 1500, hundreds of Jewish physicians and surgeons attended patients throughout Christian Iberia and Provence. Particularly in the latter two centuries, for which we have the most data, the numbers of Jewish doctors are strikingly disproportionate, even "astonishing."[2] But the phenomenon has its roots in the earlier era, including the period up to the end of the eleventh century, when most Jewish physicians in the Iberian Peninsula lived not in Christian but in Muslim Spain, or al-Andalus. During this time, about which we have much less concrete information, Jewish courtiers served in cultural and political centers such as Córdoba and later Seville, Granada, and Saragossa. Some were expert enough to have earned reputations as skilled physicians, and their roles may have included providing treatment to the ruler and his family—or, like Yusuf ben Ishaq ibn Baklarish at the end of the eleventh century, writing a medical text in his honor.[3]

From Cairo Geniza material, we know something about the commerce in pharmaceutical ingredients and have evidence of common medical practices throughout the Islamic Mediterranean. From Geniza letters and other documents, for example, we know that Jewish physicians also practiced in the marketplace and in local shops where they would have examined patients complaining of minor ailments, sold syrups and medicinal pastes, and perhaps let blood and performed minor surgeries.[4]

---

[2] Michael McVaugh, *Medicine before the Plague: Doctors and Patients in the Crown of Aragon, 1285-1335* (Cambridge, UK: Cambridge University Press, 1993), 55.

[3] Charles Burnett, ed. *Ibn Baklarish's Book of Simples: Medical Remedies between Three Faiths in Twelfth-Century Spain* (Oxford: Oxford University Press, 2008).

[4] See S. D. Goitein, "The Medical Profession in the Light of the Cairo Geniza Documents," *HUCA* 34 (1963): 177-194, and his *A Mediterranean Society, Volume II: The Community* (Berkeley, CA: University of California Press, 1971), 240-261.

Muslim writers occasionally mention the presence of Jewish physicians in Iberian lands. The scholar Sa'id al-Andalusi, who was born in Almeria in 1029 and settled in Toledo as a young man, described the scientific activities of the eight nations of the earth, including that of the Jews, or "Banu Israel." In particular, al-Andalusi cites four Jewish physicians from al-Andalus, with one of whom (Ishaq ibn Qistar) he had been personally friendly in Toledo. A second was Hasday ibn Ishaq, known to Jewish history as Hasdai ben Isaac ibn Shaprut, the famous tenth-century patron of the poets Dunash ibn Labrat and Menahem ibn Saruq and courtier to 'Abd al-Rahman III. The other two—Manahym ibn al-Fawwal and Marwan ibn Jinah—lived in Saragossa, and the latter, al-Andalusi notes, wrote a work on simples (single-ingredient drugs) and their doses.

Accounts of Jewish physicians in al-Andalus also offer a window onto their daily lives. In his book on love, the Muslim theologian Ibn Hazm (994-1069), who was born in Córdoba and spent years traveling around al-Andalus, includes a brief glimpse of a Jewish doctor with his own shop. In Ibn Hazm's rendering, the Muslim clientele are bent on testing the doctor's skill:

> I was seated one day at Almería, with a knot of other people, in the shop of Isma'il b. Yunus, the Hebrew physician, who was also a very shrewd and clever physiognomist. Mujahid ibn al Hasin al-Qaisi said to him, pointing to a certain man named Hatim [...] who was withdrawn apart from the rest of us, "What do you say about this man?" He looked at him for a brief moment, and then said: "He is passionately in love." Mujahid exclaimed: "You are right; what made you say this?" Isma'il answered, "Because of an extreme confusion apparent in his face. Simply that; otherwise all the rest of his movements are unremarkable. I knew from that he is in love, and not suffering from any mental disorder.[5]

Ibn Hazm's story is intended to show the skill of an expert in the science of physiognomy, the art of determining temperament from outward appearances, such as facial indications—a regular part of medieval medical diagnosis. One might, for example, diagnose a liver complaint from a man's yellowed eyes, or from other signs

---

[5] Ali Ibn Ahmad Ibn Hazm, *The Ring of the Dove*, trans. Anthony Arberry (London: Luzac, 1994), 45.

detect a general tendency toward one humor or another, or, in this case, whether a patient is sick only with love. But the story also tells us a little about the social acculturation of medical professionals in the Arabic world of the Middle Ages. From all indications, a doctor's religious status was less important to his patients than his reputation, his skills, and his learning.

Similarly, there is ample evidence that Jewish medical students schooled with Muslim masters, and vice-versa.[6] Educated Jews were well-versed in Arabic, and thus benefited from the accessibility of medical writings in Arabic, the language of scientific literature in al-Andalus and the East. And the benefits flowed in more than one direction: one Arab chronicler reports that Hasdai ibn Shaprut collaborated with a Christian monk and Muslim experts on an Arabic translation of Dioscorides' *Materia medica* for 'Abd al-Rahman III, one indication of the level to which Jews were integrated into the wider Muslim world, especially in the area of the sciences.

Many of the same factors operating in Muslim Iberia prior to 1100 would be no less present in Christian Iberia during the centuries covered in this volume—when, as noted above, medicine became so significant in the social and economic landscape. In the early fourteenth century, Jews made up a third of the doctors listed in the archives of Barcelona, a city whose Jewish population stood at approximately 5% of the total. In the city of Valencia around the same time, the proportions were more or less the same. In the much smaller city of Huesca, where Jews comprised 10-15% of the population, more than half of physicians and surgeons were Jews, and in 1310-11, all four doctors in the city were Jewish. The fifteenth century was no different.[7] It has been estimated that even after the Black Death in the mid-fourteenth century, 20-30% of the medical professionals serving the Christian community in Catalonia, Aragon, Valencia, and Mallorca were Jews.[8]

---

[6] Peter E. Pormann and Emilie Savage-Smith, *Medieval Islamic Medicine* (Washington, DC: Georgetown University Press, 2007), 101

[7] For these numbers, see Shatzmiller, *Jews, Medicine and Medieval Society*, 1; McVaugh, *Medicine before the Plague*, 55-56; Eugenio Benedicto Gracia, "Los médicos judíos de Huesca, según los protocolos notariales del siglo XV," *Sefarad* 68 (2008): 55-87.

[8] Luis García Ballester, "Ethical Problems in the Relationship between Doctors and Patients in Fourteenth-Century Spain: On Christian and Jewish Practitioners," in *Medicine*

As in al-Andalus, but on a greater and more complex scale, Jewish doctors in Christian Iberia occupied a variety of positions and functioned in a variety of social roles. The range of skill, learning, and financial success was striking. Some doctors served kings and royal families; others were hired by monasteries and municipalities; still others catered to private patients. Some did a little of each. And while some were leaders of the Jewish community, many others were not. Not only did Jews treat both Jewish and Christian patients of all stations, they also engaged in the study and transmission of medical traditions and medical knowledge, a crucial role to which we now turn.

Medical Traditions and Their Transmission

In general, scientific medicine in medieval Iberia—both the Muslim- and Christian-ruled parts—developed and was transmitted on a theoretical foundation inherited from the Greeks. This tradition is called Galenic, after the second-century Greek physician on whose writings it is based. Galen himself built on an older medical and philosophical tradition, writing lengthy commentaries on a group of medical works mostly composed between 420 and 350 BCE and attributed to Hippocrates. Galen harmonized the medical principles of these texts with Aristotle's theories of matter, and the resulting system—rationalist and highly philosophical—became the conceptual framework for scientific medicine in both the Muslim Mediterranean and the Latin West throughout the medieval period.

Very briefly, the main principles of that system are as follows. The body is composed of a mixture (called a temperament or complexion) of four humors: blood, red (or yellow) bile, black bile, and phlegm. Each humor, like everything else in the sub-lunar world, is made up of some combination of the four elements—earth, air, fire, and water—and each humor thus tends toward two of the four primary qualities: heat, cold, dryness, and moisture. For example, blood, produced by the liver, has the qualities of heat and moisture (like the

and Medical Ethics in Medieval and Early Modern Spain: An Intercultural Approach, ed. Samuel S. Kottek and Luis García Ballester (Jerusalem: Magnes Press, 1996), 11-32, 31.

element air). Black bile, a residue left over from the production of blood, and located in the spleen, is cold and dry (like earth).

Each person, it was believed, had a natural tendency toward a particular temperament, based on his parents' "genetic" contributions and the astral configuration at the moments when he was conceived and born. In addition, six external (called non-natural) factors were thought to affect the humoral balance in a person: air (generally speaking, climate and physical surroundings), food and drink, movement and rest, emotions, sleeping and wakefulness, excretion and retention. Sexual activity was often taken into account as well.

Illness was caused by an imbalance in the humors, usually an excess of a particular humor in one part of the body or in the body as a whole. A correct diagnosis of the imbalance and the illness could be determined by—among other things—an examination of the patient's urine, namely, its color, sediment, thickness, foam, odor, etc. This then led to the proposed treatment: regulating and controlling the imbalance, by means of diet, drugs, purges, and surgical techniques, so as to maintain or restore health. Injuries and wounds could be treated by similar means as well.

Al-Andalus played a special role in the transmission of this medical tradition from antiquity to the medieval world. From the middle of the ninth century to the fall of the Córdoban caliphate in 1031, Andalusian medicine was strongly influenced by the traditions of the Muslim East, especially as conveyed by Al-Razi (864-930, Bukhara), known in the Latin West as Rhazes, and Ibn Sina (980-1037, Persia), the famous philosopher and physician known as Avicenna. Ibn Sina's systematic and lengthy discussion of theoretical and practical medicine, called the *Qanun fi-l-tibb* ("Canon of Medicine"), in particular came to represent the zenith of Arabic medical theory.

After the eleventh century, scientific development in Muslim Spain gained greater independence from the East. Indeed, three of the most important Muslim physicians of the eleventh and twelfth centuries were from al-Andalus: Al-Zahrawi (936–1013, b. near Córdoba), known as Abulcasis, Ibn Zuhr (b. Seville, 1092-1161[9]),

---

[9] See Rosa Kuhne, "Hacia una revisión de la bibliografia de los Banu Zuhr," *Al-Qantara* 13.2 (1992) 581-585.

known as Avenzoar, and the philosopher Ibn Rushd (b. Córdoba, 1126-1198), known as Averroes. These three figures consolidated the Arabic medical tradition. In Latin translation, the texts of this tradition entered the European universities in the thirteenth century, transforming Latin scholastic medicine and remaining influential until the sixteenth century.

The same tradition helped shape the work of the great Jewish scholar Moses ben Maimon, or Maimonides (1138-1204), who occupies a place of his own in the chain of medical transmission. Though he lived in Córdoba only until the age of ten or so, his medical writings, completed in Egypt, were, in the end, highly influential in Christian Iberia and Provence. Maimonides considered Galen the greatest physician of all, but in addition showed a marked preference for medical writings from al-Andalus, whether out of personal loyalty to his own teachers or, as has been suggested, because of something distinctive about the Andalusian medical tradition.[10] His works, written in Arabic and often intended as instructions for individual Muslim patients, also offer general medical advice. For example, the treatise called *On Asthma*, in addition to discussing the causes of the particular patient's condition and prescribing a series of measures for his diet and bathing, includes some general suggestions for healthy living and a lengthy lecture concerning the dangers presented by incompetent physicians. Thus, despite the fact that these works by Maimonides were tailored to individual patients, they would be studied and mined for their general information not only by Iberian Jewish doctors (in both the original Arabic and in mostly thirteenth-century Hebrew translations) but also by Christian physicians in late-thirteenth- and early-fourteenth-century Latin translations.

As for the influx of Greco-Arabic medicine into Christian Iberia, this was a highly complex process in which Jews played a major part. For Christian physicians interested in reading Arabic medical texts in either Latin or one of the newly developing vernaculars, Jewish physicians might either translate from Arabic into the vernacular, which might then be turned into Latin, or, occasionally, help a Christian otherwise familiar with Arabic to decipher an Arabic text

---

[10] Y. Tzvi Langermann, "Science in the Jewish Communities of the Iberian Peninsula: An Interim Report," in his *The Jews and the Sciences in the Middle Ages* (Aldershot: Ashgate, 1999), 1-54, 26.

written in Hebrew characters.[11] The first medical translation into the Catalan vernacular (1296-1297) was done by two Jewish physicians from Saragossa by order of King Jaume II. In 1313, another medical text was translated from Arabic into Catalan by a Jewish doctor, Jafuda Bonsenyor, who was paid from the royal treasury. In 1302, at Jaume's instruction, a professor of medicine at the University of Lerida borrowed Arabic medical works from Jews to correct texts rented by medical students for copying.[12]

Latin medicine itself, though based, like Arabic medicine, on Greek theory, would take on a somewhat different complexion from the Arabic tradition. A set of core texts—Hippocrates' *Aphorisms* and *Prognostics*, two Byzantine diagnostic works on urine and the pulse, Galen's summary of medicine, and Hunayn ibn Ishaq's introduction to Galen—composed the nucleus of the curriculum of the medical school at Salerno, the most important center of scientific medicine in twelfth-century Western Europe. This core, called the Articella, supplemented by writings of the Salernitan masters, was then brought to the developing medical schools in Montpellier and Paris. The thirteenth-century addition of Latin versions of works of Galen and Ibn Sina's *Qanūn fi-l-tibb* encouraged a far more systematically philosophical approach to medicine as a science. With these and other expansions—notably including Latin translations of four works by the tenth-century Jewish physician Isaac Israeli—the group of texts became known as the *Ars medicina* ("The Art of Medicine"), providing a curriculum for medical teaching in the universities for the next centuries.

One of the most famous centers of medical learning in all medieval Europe was in the city of Montpellier, which now lies within the borders of France but, from 1066 to 1081 and again from 1213 to 1349, was a possession of the Crown of Aragon. Elsewhere in the Crown of Aragon, medical faculties were founded at Lerida in 1300, Perpignan in 1350, and Barcelona in 1450. In Castile, on the other hand, the universities were both weaker and later to develop, as were the schools of medicine. The university at Salamanca does

---

[11] Michael McVaugh and Lola Ferre, *The "Tabula Antidotarii" of Armengaud Blaise and Its Hebrew Translation*, (Philadelphia: American Philosophical Society, 2000), 3.

[12] See Lluís Cifuentes i Comamala, *La ciència en català a l'Edat Mitjana i el Renaixement* (Barcelona: Universitat de Barcelona, 2002), 62-3.

not seem to have had a functioning medical school until the fifteenth century. The curriculum there was equally slow to take advantage of the new trends. In thirteenth-century Castile, the monasteries and nascent universities were still offering pre-Salernitan and Salernitan medicine. The Greco-Arabic material was circulating, but only in the original Arabic, not in the Latin translations then beginning to dominate medicine in northern Spain and southern France.[13]

Through the twelfth and most of the thirteenth century, it was Toledo, capital city of Castile, that saw the steadiest and most intense copying of Arabic medicine in Christian Iberia. Of the 43 extant Arabic medical manuscripts copied there, all were produced for Jewish physicians.[14] In the first third of the thirteenth century, Ishaq ben Shushan al-Israili bought an Arabic manuscript of Dioscorides that had been copied in Almería and made its way to the library of a Rabbi Fanhash in Toledo.

Castilian Jewish doctors also composed original medical works in Arabic. Solomon ben Abraham ibn Ya'ish (d. 1345) wrote a lengthy and highly scholastic Arabic commentary to Ibn Sina's "Canon,"[15] and an anonymous Jew, physician to Ferdinand IV (1295-1312), composed the important *Kitab al-tibb al-qastali al-maluki* ("Book of Royal Castilian Medicine").[16] From references in the book, the author seems to have lived and worked in numerous towns and cities throughout León and Castile. He refers to other physicians and assumes the existence of a community of Jewish physicians interested in medical-philosophical controversies.[17]

As we have seen, Jews were active participants—as translators—in the transmission of Greco-Arabic medicine to the Latin West. Still, the fact that they lacked access to the university world placed

---

[13] Luis García Ballester, "Medical Science in Castile: Problems and Prospects," *Bulletin of the History of Medicine* 61 (1987): 183-202, 189, 197.

[14] Ballester, "A Marginal Learned Medical World," 373.

[15] See Y. Tzvi Langermann, "Solomon Ibn Yaish's Commentary on the Qanun of Ibn Sina" (Heb.), *Kiryat Sefer* 63 (1990-1991): 1331-1333.

[16] See Luis García Ballester, *La búsqeda de la salud: Sanadores y enfermos en al España medieval* (Barcelona: Ediciones Península, 2001), 455-472.

[17] Natan ben Yoel Falaquera, though he wrote in Hebrew in the previous century, also includes a number of such controversies in his medical compendium. Gerrit Bos and Resianne Fontaine, "Medico-philosophical controversies in Nathan b. Jo'el Falaquera Sefer Zori ha-Guf," *Jewish Quarterly Review* 90 (1999): 27-60.

them at a distance from new academic developments. As for Latin, it was in general even less readily accessible than Arabic to the majority of Jewish physicians. Hebrew was their learned language, and throughout the thirteenth, fourteenth, and fifteenth centuries, Arabic and later Latin and vernacular medical works were translated into Hebrew by Jewish doctors for their own use, and for that of their colleagues. As a result of this mixed heritage, the medical literature used by Jewish physicians was not precisely identical with that used by their Christian colleagues.

This proved an advantage in the first half of our period, the twelfth and thirteenth centuries, when Latin medicine was only just beginning to absorb Greco-Arabic medical texts, and Jewish physicians might be using Arabic texts either in the original or in their Hebrew translations. Ibn Sina's *Qanun* is a case in point. To judge by its influence, it was the most important medical compendium for Jewish physicians. Sometimes studied and consulted in Arabic, it was ultimately translated into Hebrew more frequently and appears in more extant manuscripts than any other medical work.[18] In the thirteenth century, the *Qanun* might have been considered cutting-edge medicine. By the fifteenth, however, while the Hebrew translation was still being copied by Jewish physicians and indeed was the first Hebrew medical work to be printed (1491, Naples), knowledge of the *Qanun* no longer represented an advance over Latin medicine, as it had now been long included in the Christian scholastic medical curriculum.

The Jews of Castile continued to retain Arabic for medical literature until the sixteenth century, yet among the Jews of the Crown of Aragon it fell more quickly out of favor. In the fourteenth century, as Latin scholastic medicine began to develop independently, Arabic medical texts were relied on with decreasing frequency. By then, the writings of the Montpellier medical scholars were exerting a strong influence on both Christian and Jewish physicians in Iberian lands.

While we find translations of the core Latin medical texts into Hebrew being prepared as early as the late twelfth century by a Provençal Jew writing under the pseudonym Do'eg ha-Edomi,

---

[18] Benjamin Richler, "Manuscripts of Avicenna's Canon in Hebrew Translation: A Revised and Up-to-date List," *Korot* 8 (1982): 145-168. See also Lola Ferre, "Avicena Hebraico: La traducción del *Canon de Medicina*," *MEAH* 52 (2003): 163-182.

Hebrew versions of medical works from Latin increased in the fourteenth century, including those by the three great physicians associated with the medical school in Montpellier: Arnald of Villanova, Bernard of Gordon, and Gérard de Solo. In 1383, Jacob ben Judah Cabret of Barcelona made an abridgement in Hebrew from Arnald's book on astrological medicine.[19] Bernard's *Lilium medicinae*, written between 1303-1305, was translated twice into Hebrew, once in Seville in 1362 by a converted Jew, Juan de Aviñon, and again in 1387 by another Jewish physician, Yekutiel ben Shlomo. The works of Gérard were translated into Hebrew in the second half of the fourteenth century by Abraham Avigdor (1351-1402), who reports that he studied medicine in Montpellier and learned Latin there,[20] by Leon Joseph of Carcassonne (1365-c. 1418), who lived in Perpignan, and by Tobiel ben Samuel of Leiria (fl. c. 1388), who worked in the Portuguese city of Coïmbra.[21]

Not only were these works translated into Hebrew and widely circulated, but Jewish physicians had direct contact with Christian scholars associated with the school. For example, around the turn of the century, Jacob ben Machir ibn Tibbon (1236-1307), nephew of the translator Moses ibn Tibbon, collaborated with Montpellier scholars—including Armengaud Blaise, nephew of the famous Catalan physician Arnald of Villanova (1235-c.1313)—in the translation of medical works from Latin to Hebrew and, perhaps no less significantly, from Hebrew to Latin. In addition, for a very brief period in the mid-fourteenth century, some Jews even studied at Montpellier, though whether they were officially enrolled is not clear.[22]

Starting in the fourteenth century, too, we find Latin prescriptions added as notes to Hebrew-language manuscripts, as well as Hebrew

---

[19] David ben Yom Tov, *Kelal Qaṭan: Hebrew Medical Astrology*, ed. Gerrit Bos, Charles Burnett, and Y. Tzvi Langermann (Philadelphia: American Philosophical Society, 2005), 21.

[20] Anne-Sylvie Guénon, "Les traductions en Hébreu de l'oeuvre du médecin Gérard de Solo (XIVe siècle)," *Revue des études juives* 164 (2005): 463-488.

[21] Guénon, "Les traductions en Hébreu," 466.

[22] Joseph Shatzmiller, "In Search of the 'Book of Figures': Medicine and Astrology in Montpellier at the Turn of the Fourteenth Century," *AJS Review* 7 (1982): 383-407, at 28-31. Armengaud himself translated six works from Hebrew into Latin between 1284 and 1305, and at least five works from Arabic, including Maimonides' *On Asthma* (1294) and his *On Poisons* (1305).

annotations on Latin medical works: testimony to the fact that Jewish physicians were becoming increasingly familiar with the language.

The vernacular, too, appears in glosses in Hebrew transliteration and Jewish physicians were likely accustomed to writing prescriptions in the vernacular. According to regulations instituted in Valencia in 1329, all physicians were henceforth required to write their prescriptions "in the vulgar tongue, naming herbs and other medicinal things by their common or popular names."[23] Jews as well as Christians would have been expected to conform with this regulation. For this purpose, it was necessary to know the local, vernacular names of those "herbs and medicinal things" that featured in medical texts. Indeed, numerous lists of herbs and medicaments written in the Hebrew alphabet are extant in manuscript, giving synonyms in various languages, commonly the vernacular, but also including Arabic, Latin, and sometimes Hebrew. Such lists were often included in collections of medical works or appended to a text requiring a glossary. Castilian does appear among the vernaculars, but the one most often in evidence appears to be a mix of Old Catalan and Old Occitan, indicating not only the close relationship of the two dialects but also the ties between Catalonia and Languedoc—and signaling, in addition, the presence of Jewish physicians and medical translators in the region near the medical school of Montpellier.[24]

In 1348, the Iberian Peninsula was hit by the Black Death. Lasting until the spring of 1350, and returning sporadically thereafter, it cut down somewhere between a quarter and a third of the total Iberian population, including, for obvious reasons, many physicians. Not only were numerous plague treatises translated into Hebrew from Latin and the vernaculars in this period, but several original works in Hebrew and Arabic were dedicated to the medical causes of the Black Death.[25] Abraham ben David Caslari in Besalú wrote *Ma'amar*

---

[23] "En romanç, declaren los noms de les erbes e de les altres coses medicinal en lur nom comú e vulgar." Luis García Ballester, Michael R. McVaugh, Agustín Rubio, *Medical Licensing and Learning in Fourteenth-Century Valencia* (Philadelphia: American Philosophical Society, 1989), 60-61.

[24] Gerrit Bos and Guido Mensching, "The Literature of Hebrew Medical Synonyms: Romance and Latin Terms and their Identification," *Aleph* 5 (2005): 169-211.

[25] See Ron Barkai, "Jewish Treatises on the Black Death (1350-1500): A Preliminary Study," in *Medicine from the Black Death to the French Disease*, ed. Roger French, Jon Arrizabalaga, Andrew Cunningham and Luis García Ballester (Aldershot: Ashgate, 1998), 6-25.

be-qadahot divriyyot u-minei qadahot ("A Treatise on Pestilential Fevers and Other Kinds of Fevers") soon after the plague broke out:

> My heart awakened me to write this treatise because of what happened in the summer and the late spring. Fevers overcame the entire province and all of Catalonia and Aragon, and there was no city which was safe from the fevers.[26]

Caslari's student, Moses Narboni (1300-1362), a renowned philosopher, after a youth spent in Perpignan, led a peripatetic life practicing medicine throughout northern Iberia.[27] His Hebrew medical treatise, *Orah Hayim* ("The Way of Life"), was completed at some point between 1350 and 1362. The work belongs to a common genre in medical writing: a book of diseases. Unusually for this type of work, it includes sections on the care and education of children, as well as the particular treatment of the elderly. It also incorporates a report of the author's experience during the Black Death: "I witnessed last year, namely 1349, a great plague throughout this whole region which had a lethal effect because of the pestilential fevers, with terrible toxic abscesses. . . . Not one in a thousand was saved."[28] The long-term effects of the plague on the development of medieval medicine are still not fully understood.

Practicing Medicine

A learned Jewish physician not only could speak knowledgeably about theory but also had specific methods for diagnosing disease, foretelling the course of an illness, and—if lucky—effecting cures. How did the physician master his craft? In the Muslim world, a would-be doctor would have studied with an established physician, often receiving a certificate or letter attesting to the particular areas and techniques covered. Often, fathers taught their sons, in a system that, among Jews and Muslims, appears to have continued

---

[26] Barkai, "Jewish Treatises on the Black Death," 10.

[27] Narboni says that he studied with Caslari as a young man and that he based his discussion of fevers on Caslari's treatise. Gerrit Bos, "R. Moshe Narboni: Philosopher and Physician, A Critical Analysis of Sefer Orah Hayyim," *Medieval Encounters* 1.2 (1995): 219-251, 226.

[28] Bos, "R. Moshe Narboni: Philosopher and Physician," 219.

to function during the Christian period as well. From the numerous instances in Christian Iberia of Jewish medical dynasties within a single family, including occasional evidence of contracts between fathers and sons-in-law, such direct, inter-generational teaching appears to have remained a primary channel for the transmission of medical knowledge.[29]

Of course, such personal teaching would rely on books as well as practical, hands-on advice and apprenticeship. Some medical texts were primarily oriented toward theory, discoursing on anatomy, physiology, and etiology: i.e., the structure and workings of the body and the causes of illness. Others, aimed at working physicians and meant to be used in practice, typically offered only a very brief description of a disease and its causes, concentrating most strongly on therapy.

Technical medical writing, in fact, came in numerous different forms: glossaries of foreign terminology, tables of drug or plant effects, treatises on pharmaceutical theory, didactic question-and-answer handbooks, collections of prescriptions or case studies, specialized works on surgery, the plague, or other particular conditions or diseases, texts versified for memorization, and more. In the introduction to his medical compendium, Natan ben Yoel Falaquera, a thirteenth-century Iberian physician, asserts that he learned his craft by studying Arabic medical texts with his father. In the Crown of Aragon and in Castile, as we have just seen, Jews without access to universities or medical schools read and studied Arabic and Hebrew texts independently.[30]

Maimonides studied at some point with senior physicians,[31] and even while practicing medicine continued to question other doctors

---

[29] Shatzmiller, *Jews, Medicine, and Medieval Society*, 22-27. Note that when Leon Joseph of Carcassonne praises the teaching of the Christian physician Jean de Tournemire, he says that Jean teaches "like a father to a son." Luis García Ballester, Lola Ferre, and Eduard Feliu, "Jewish Appreciation of Fourteenth-Century Scholastic Medicine," *Osiris* 6 (1990): 85-117, 112.

[30] Luis García Ballester, "A Marginal Learned Medical World: Jewish, Muslim and Christian Medical Practitioners, and the Use of Arabic Medical Sources in Late Medieval Spain," in *Practical Medicine from Salerno to the Black Death*, ed. Luis García Ballester, Roger French, Jon Arrizabalaga, and Andrew Cunningham (Cambridge: Cambridge University Press, 1994), 353-394.

[31] Gerrit Bos, "Maimonides' Medical Works and their Contribution to his Medical Biography," *Maimonidean Studies* 5 (2008): 243-266, esp. 244-246.

about their cases in hopes of profiting from their experience.[32] At the same time, he both returned to the classical texts and endeavored to keep up with the current literature. Here is Maimonides writing in 1187 or 1190 to his student Joseph ben Judah ibn Shim'on:

> When I come home to Fustat [after attending the Sultan], the most that I can do during what is left of the day and the night is to study that which I may need to know from the medical books. For you know how long and difficult this art is for someone who is conscientious and fastidious, and who does not wish to say anything without first knowing its proof, its sources, and the type of reasoning involved.[33]

And here he is later, in *On Asthma*, still remarking upon the difficulty of mastering the field:

> In our generations . . . physicians have but little experience, while much memorizing is needed, since the different parts of medicine have become so lengthy! Consequently, a lifetime is too short to attain perfection in even one part of it.[34]

Shem Tov ibn Falaquera (ca. 1225–1295), a philosopher, translator, and poet as well as a physician, composed a charming work, *Sefer ha-Mevaqqesh* ("Book of the Seeker"), whose hero progressively interviews a series of human types in search of ultimate truth. In his interview, the doctor describes his profession as necessarily imperfect, one in which sometimes the physician makes mistakes and sometimes the illness is simply too catastrophic to be treated. Using a common simile, he likens the physician to "a captain who prepares all the implements and makes the calculations necessary for navigating his ship. What can he do, however, if a great storm breaks out and destroys the craft?" What the physician *can* do is to serve nature, which normally acts to preserve the health of man. He can also provide "the materials that [the body] requires *in the proper amounts*: air, movement, reclining, bathing, food, sleep, intercourse,

---

[32] Bos, "Maimonides' Medical Works," 246-247.

[33] Y. Tzvi Langermann, "Maimonides on the Synochous Fever," *Israel Oriental Studies* 13 (1994): 175-198, 176.

[34] Maimonides, *On Asthma* 13.20, in *On Asthma: A Parallel Arabic-English Text*, ed. and trans. Gerrit Bos (Provo, UT: Brigham Young University Press, 2002), 91.

and activity. When a man falls ill, the physician's task is to apportion to him the remedies and curatives which will restore him to health."[35]

To illustrate medical theories at work, Ibn Falaquera has the physician answer a series of challenges posed by the Seeker. For diagnosis by urine (which as we have seen was a physician's main diagnostic tool), the Seeker asks: what if the color is ambiguous? Dark urine may indicate fever or it may indicate a bad chill. How can the same symptom reflect two utterly opposite conditions, and how do you tell them apart? The doctor responds: "Both warmth and cold create darkly colored urine. Products of heat are, of necessity, accompanied by colors that reveal its presence, as in the case of burned matter. Coldness too is accompanied by a dark green . . . color. But urine resulting from the prevalence of heat has a bad odor, whereas this is not the case with dark urine produced by cold."[36]

This type of diagnosis was taken seriously not only by physicians and their patients but by courts of law. In a malpractice case from 1318 in a small town in Valencia, a Jewish physician named Abrahim Abengalell administered a fatal purgative to a woman who turned out to have been pregnant with a boy. Abrahim, accused of negligence in his treatment, was exonerated when a Christian physician testified that he himself had analyzed the woman's urine only days earlier, and she had not been pregnant at the time.[37]

Diagnosing a condition from urine alone was a tricky matter, and sometimes patients (like the hangers-on at the shop described by Ibn Hazm) would test a doctor's skill at it. Numerous texts suggest ways of detecting whether a patient has brought an adulterated or false sample to make a fool of the physician. In the later medieval period, analysis from urine alone came to be associated with a lower class of doctors, while university-educated physicians also included careful analysis of the pulse and blood.[38] The more factors taken into

---

[35] Shem Tov Ibn Falaquera, *Book of the Seeker*, trans. M. Herschel Levine (New York: Yeshiva University Press, 1976), 44-45.

[36] Ibn Falaquera, *Book of the Seeker*, 51.

[37] Carmel Ferragud Domingo, "Organització social i atenció mèdica a la Cocentaina Baixmedieval: El process a Abrahim Abengalell (1318)," *Asclepio* 57 (2005): 3-24.

[38] Michael R. McVaugh, "Beside Manners in the Middle Ages," *Bulletin of the History of Medicine* 71 (1997): 201-223.

consideration, the better were the doctor's chances of making an accurate diagnosis and avoiding blunders.

The physician's task was to prevent sickness, but if necessary to cure it as well. For both prevention and treatment, a doctor started with diet. Like humors, foods had their own mixture of qualities, and these could be exploited to effect changes in the patient's system. For example, by consuming hot, moist foods, one could increase and improve the amount of blood in the body. If one's blood were overabundant, one might consume mainly cold and dry foods. For particularly important clients, a physician would draw up a custom "regimen" detailing which foods to consume and which to avoid. Over the course of the thirteenth and fourteenth centuries, with interest in medical advice intensifying at every level of society, such "regimens of health" circulated more and more widely.

Ibn Falaquera's Seeker ends up spending some time studying medicine with the fictional physician. As the Seeker takes his leave, he requests some final advice in the form of a condensed "regimen." The doctor offers two Hippocratic injunctions favored by Maimonides, and they still ring true: "Guard your health by eating only to the point of satiety, and not to excess. Refrain from sloth by sufficient exercise."[39]

Maimonides himself included a chapter in his code of Jewish law, *Mishneh Torah*, that functions as a rough set of medical guidelines: a regimen of health for every Jew. Here is an excerpt:

> A man should never eat unless he is hungry; nor should he drink unless he is thirsty. . . . A man should not eat to the point that he has filled his belly, but should leave off at about a quarter short of satiety. Nor should he drink water during a meal, except just a little and mixed with wine. And when the food begins to digest in his entrails, he should drink what he needs to drink, but not too much water, even once the food is digested. He should not eat unless he has attended very well to his functions of excretion. A man should not eat unless he has walked before eating, so that his body has begun to warm up, or done some work or tired himself with some labor. The rule of the matter: he should exercise his body and tire it every day in

---

[39] Ibn Falaquera, *Book of the Seeker*, 54.

the morning until his body begins to warm up, and he should rest a little until his spirit is composed—and [then] he should eat.[40]

The chapter continues with recommendations as to which foods to avoid, how much to sleep, and so on.

This genre of writing came to be extremely popular. Later in the thirteenth century, Arnald of Villanova composed a regimen of health for the king of Aragon (in Latin, though a Catalan version was soon provided as well). The work was rapidly translated from the Catalan into Hebrew. Over the fourteenth century, the growing audience for this type of advice spurred an entire literature in which foods were categorized according to their medical qualities.[41]

Aside from long-term dietary regimen, there were other expedients available to a doctor. Drugs were an important part of therapy, for their effects were often powerful and immediately obvious. Excess humors could also be physically removed from the body. Too much blood was a problem easily solved; choosing the right time and the right part of the body, a physician would make an incision to draw off the excess. Bloodletting, indeed, was one of the most common medical procedures, performed by doctors at all levels of rank and experience. Blood might be let not only to cure illness, but to keep one healthy. Still another method was purging—that is, inducing either vomiting or diarrhea.

Not all practice was based on theoretical principles. Supplementing these were traditions of recipes and procedures that had accumulated over centuries. Geniza fragments testify to the widespread use of methods that would now be regarded as more magical than medical, such as those in the *Sefer ha-Nisyonot* ("The Book of Experiences"), a work long attributed to the twelfth-century Andalusian poet, grammarian, astronomer, and astrologer Abraham ibn Ezra. Prescriptions taken from it appear in numerous later Hebrew works. Among the cures listed, some properly fall into a medical category, such as this prescription for stomachache: "If you anoint the chest with sweet almond oil mixed with butter from

---

[40] *Hilkhot deʿot* 4: 1-2, Maimonides, *Mishneh Torah, Sefer ha-maddaʿ*, ed. Moses Hyamson (Jerusalem and New York: Feldheim, 1981), 50a-b.

[41] See Marilyn Nicoud, *Les régimes de santé au Moyen Âge: naissance et diffusion d'une écriture médicale, XIIIe-XVe siècle* (Rome: École française de Rome, 2007).

cattle, it will greatly relieve pain in the stomach and is also good for oppression in the chest."[42] Others are plainly magical, like this one for nosebleed: "If you write on the patient's forehead the following three names with the blood issuing from his nostrils, it will stop immediately. And these are the three names: 'Kita', 'Zvi', and 'Lekh.'"[43]

Jewish medical writing also included works devoted to women's issues, with advice about cosmetics, gynecology, and obstetrics. Some tended to include a similar mix of medical and magical advice. A recently published example, surviving in a single late-fifteenth-century copy, is the anonymous Hebrew *Sefer Ahavat Nashim* ("Book of Women's Love"). It consists for the most part of recipes and prescriptions said to derive from Muslim or Christian practices or copied from other medical works. Several are also featured in *Sefer ha-Nisyonot*.

The first of the book's three sections is largely devoted to making people fall in or out of love: love potions and spells. One typical love spell, attributed to the biblical Rachel, suggests writing mystical names on a parchment with pigeon's blood, rinsing them off with water, and, on the third day of the month, making the man drink the rinse water.[44] The second section deals with sexual matters, including impotence and infertility, abortion and miscarriage. The third focuses on cosmetics. An example of the more medically-oriented instructions: "To increase a woman's milk, take rue leaves and clean branches of vine shoots and boil them in goat's milk; she must drink it regularly, it will be helpful."[45] Though there is ample evidence in the archives that medieval Jewish women served as healers and even taught medicine, most texts dealing with women's medicine, including this particular work, are written in the form of instructions for a male physician treating female patients.

Some seemingly odd cures could be found in the Talmud and were in general avoided by medieval Jewish physicians, but others, equally difficult to rationalize, originated in the authoritative

---

[42] Ps. Abraham Ibn Ezra, *Sefer haNisyonot: The Book of Medical Experiences*, ed. Joshua Otto Leibowitz, Shlomo Marcus (Magnes Press, Hebrew University, 1984), 201.

[43] Ibn Ezra, *Sefer haNisyonot*, 183.

[44] Carmen Caballero Navas, ed. *The Book of Women's Love and Jewish Medical Literature on Women: Sefer Ahavat Nashim* (London: Kegan Paul, 2004), 112.

[45] Navas, ed. *The Book of Women's Love*, 140

Greek and Arabic (and Latin) texts.[46] And yet, even if they could not be derived from theoretical principles, they were not for that reason rejected as ineffective or imaginary. "Experience" had demonstrated their efficacy—and not just the personal experience of the individual doctor but, as Maimonides writes, "the sum of the experience acquired over the course of past generations, [even] before the time of Galen."[47] Despite being at odds with the physical and philosophical principles underlying the theory of medicine, such cures were sometimes offered by even the most rationalist physicians throughout the medieval period, including Maimonides.

Astrology too was sometimes a part of medicine, eventually being included in official examinations for medical licenses. In Aragon, 1382, one Benedit Caravida was tested not only "in the art of medicine and physics, but also in metaphysics, in natural sciences, and in some part of astrology."[48] To at least a limited extent, Jewish physicians engaged in astrological calculations, but it appears that few went so far as to cast the horoscopes that were the specialty of professional astrologers. Rather, they ranged from choosing or avoiding a particular hour of the day or day of the week (or month) for delicate procedures like bloodletting or surgery, to assessing the course of an illness or the outcome of a wound according to the position of the moon in its path through the heavens.

The only significant extant Hebrew text on astrological medicine was written by David ben Yom Tov in Perpignan during the first half of the fourteenth century, a period that saw a surge of interest in medical astrology in southern France and Catalonia.[49] This work, strongly influenced by Abraham ibn Ezra's astrological work *Sefer ha-Me'orot*, asserts that "knowledge of the forces of the spheres and their application to individuals is part of the perfection of the physician." For example: "If you want to administer a foodstuff or potion in order to purge [the body of a patient], do so when the

---

[46] For the Talmud, for example, b. Gittin 68b-70a; M. J. Geller, "Akkadian Healing Therapies in the Babylonian Talmud," *Max-Planck-Institut für Wissenschaftsgeschichte Preprint* 259 (2004): 1-60. For magical folk remedies see Richard Kieckhefer, *Magic in the Middle Ages* (Cambridge, UK: Cambridge University Press, 1989), 56-79.

[47] Maimonides, *On Asthma*, 13.29, (ed. and trans. Bos, 96).

[48] Shatzmiller, *Jews, Medicine, and Medieval Society*, 39-40.

[49] Ben Yom Tov, *Kelal Qaṭan*, 26.

moon is in the sign similar to the humor you want to expel. Thus, if you want to expel yellow bile, do so when the moon is in one of the fiery signs, namely, Aries, Leo, or Sagittarius."[50]

But astrology had been known to fail. A physician might cast a horoscope prognosticating the imminent death of his patient and yet the patient might live. At the end of his treatise, David ben Yom Tov attributes such failures not to a flaw in the system per se but, primarily, to contradictions between the birth horoscope and the disease horoscope—that is, the patient might instead be fated to die ten years hence. Other possible explanations: the patient has engaged in "repentance and good deeds, which annul a [divine] decree, or the physician does not know all the principles of this science."[51] The religious note ("repentance and good deeds..."), invoking the liturgy of Yom Kippur, is sounded here only in passing, but it suggests how an astrological system can also allow for free will.

Indeed, pious expressions of trust in God were often and easily combined with rationalist medicine performed by skilled physicians. Prescriptions uncovered in the Geniza, mostly written by pharmacists and validated by the physician, nearly universally invoke divine help in healing, often ending in a phrase like "It [the prescription] will help, if God will."[52] The great poet Judah Halevi (c.1075–1141), who made his living from medicine, composed a prayer for healing that expresses not only just such trust in God but radical modesty on the part of the Jewish physician.[53]

> Heal me, Lord, and I will be healed.
>   Let me not perish in your anger.
> All my balms and potions are Yours,
>   leading to weakness or to vigor.
>
> It is You alone, not I, who choose;
>   You who know best what is flawed and what pure.
> It is not my medicine on which I rely—
>   I look instead toward Your cure.[54]

---

[50] Ben Yom Tov, *Kelal Qaṭan*, 83, 87.

[51] Ben Yom Tov, *Kelal Qaṭan*, 92-93

[52] Goitein, *A Mediterranean Society II*, 254.

[53] See S. D. Goitein, "The Biography of Rabbi Judah Ha-Levi in the Light of Cairo Geniza Documents," *PAAJR* 28 (1959): 41-56.

[54] Judah Halevi in *The Dream of the Poem: Hebrew Poetry from Muslim and Christian Spain 950-1492*, ed. and trans. Peter Cole (Princeton: Princeton University Press, 2007), 154. See

Jewish Physicians as Professionals

With the Almohad invasion of the Iberian Peninsula in 1148, many Jewish physicians left Muslim al-Andalus and moved north—where, over the course of the twelfth and thirteenth centuries, city after city that had been under Muslim rule was falling to the Christian *Reconquista*. In al-Andalus, as we saw early on, some Jews served Muslim rulers as court physicians, while others served as secretaries or even viziers and some, like Hasdai ibn Shaprut, combined the two roles. Here too, in Aragon and Castile, the skills of some educated Jews in medicine and in Arabic (recently valuable for diplomatic service) led to positions of power in the new Christian governments. That is, the rulers of Christian Iberia during the High Middle Ages came to employ individual Jews in a position known as the *alfaquim* that could combine functions ranging from expert in Arabic (linguist or translator[55]) to bailiff to physician. Depending on skills and knowledge, then, the medical role might be primary or secondary.

Aside from elite physicians who might be hired by the king, hundreds of less exalted Jewish doctors were able to earn a living from their profession. Some might be hired by the municipal council of a town or by a monastery or convent to be doctors "on call." They were often given a contract to provide medical services for a given period of time, usually not more than five years. At a minimum, the contract would cover treating any diseases or problems that might occur; it might also involve setting a regimen—diet, bathing, purging, and so forth—in order to maintain patients in health. One such contractual physician was Abraham ben David Caslari, who together with his physician father David (d. 1315/6) had joined the great exodus of Jews from France after the expulsion edict of 1306. In his 1316 contract with the town of Besalú, where he had settled,

---

also the poem by the physician Ibn al 'Ammani of Alexandria, cited by Goitein in his *A Mediterranean Society II*, 259-260.

[55] See the description of Astruc Bonsenyor and his duties in the *Book of Deeds* by James I of Aragon, where Astruc is called "our scribe for Arabic" and "our interpreter" (315), but also appears involved in transporting charters (308) between the Muslims and the king. One Bahiel, who is called *alfaquim*, also interprets (98) and his brother Salomó is *alfaquim* of Saragossa and involved with writing letters in Arabic. *The Book of Deeds of James I of Aragon*, trans. Damien J. Smith and Helena Buffery (Farnham, UK: Ashgate, 2003).

Abraham agreed to "look at and assess all the urines brought to me by the citizens, whom I will advise as to bloodletting and diet, and generally as to their manner of life, and I will visit two or three times all the sick of the town who ask me to attend them."[56] He was particularly successful, and somewhat later was employed by the royal family and eventually treated the three children of Jaume III.[57] As time went on, Jewish physicians serving the crown might receive royal privileges of various sorts, such as freedom of movement (for themselves and their patients) and exemption from taxation or from wearing identifying clothing.[58]

As this suggests, Jewish physicians did not practice solely in their own quarter. Nor were they restricted to the cities. Like Muslim and Christian doctors, many were itinerant—in part because of the time-limited nature of their contracts and in part because of changing markets. The confraternities that developed at the beginning of the fourteenth century included *biqqur holim* ("visiting the sick") societies, in some cases helping to pay for healthful food and medicines for the ailing poor.[59] But individuals, too, had the option of securing the services of a physician, either in advance or at a fee for a particular service.

Over the course of the thirteenth and fourteenth centuries, as medical advice came to be increasingly sought out and indeed to be considered a public good, and as physicians were accorded greater social honor, royal and municipal governments established licensing procedures for medical practitioners. These regulations were first applied to physicians and surgeons and later extended to barbers and apothecaries. In Monzón, a small city in the Crown of Aragon, physicians and surgeons were subjected in 1289 to the same requirement as that imposed on lawyers, being allowed to practice only if previously examined by the municipal councilors and other physicians. This procedure appears to have governed medical practice in Catalonia and Aragon through the first third of the fourteenth

---

[56] McVaugh, *Medicine Before the Plague*, 192.

[57] McVaugh, *Medicine Before the Plague*, 59.

[58] Yom Tov Assis, "Jewish Physicians and Medicine in Medieval Spain," in *Medicine and Medical Ethics in Medieval and Early Modern Spain*, 33-49, at 38-40. See Joseph Shatzmiller, *Jews, Medicine, and Medieval Society*, 58-60.

[59] Assis, "Jewish Physicians and Medicine in Medieval Spain," 41.

century.[60] In 1329, as mentioned earlier, the kingdom of Valencia enacted even more detailed rules, including the requirement of a university education; similar rules were promulgated in Catalonia in the 1330s, and in 1359 the Valencia rules were officially extended to the rest of the Crown of Aragon.

Jewish physicians throughout the Crown of Aragon had to be licensed if they wished to treat Christian patients. Special provisions were made for the legal issues thereby entailed, including the need to circumvent the requirement of a university degree. Those already practicing in 1329, when the requirement was established, were allowed to procure a license on the basis of an examination alone, and the same exception came to apply customarily in the case of all Jewish medical professionals seeking to be licensed.[61] Other accommodations were made as well: Jews (and Muslims) were permitted to take the licensing oath on their own scriptures (with Jews swearing on the "ten commandments"). In 1363, it was stated explicitly by the *cortes* of Monzón that Jews were to be examined by a physician of their own religion, assisted by a Christian physician. If no Jewish physicians were to be found, two Christians would conduct the examination.[62]

Despite the growing professionalization of medicine at the higher levels, practitioners continued to come in a wide range, from the licensed physician, surgeon, barber, or apothecary to the unlicensed midwife, and everything in between. Many practicing doctors were women, appearing in archival documents under the feminine form of the official titles given to men: from *physica* to *chirugica*. Women could be formally licensed, such as two from Lerida who won their certifications in 1387.[63]

Jewish healing skills may have been esteemed by both kings and municipalities, but it appears that the fees for medical care by Jewish physicians were significantly lower than those commanded by university-trained Christians. A disadvantage to the individual

---

[60] Ballester, McVaugh, Rubio, *Medical Licensing and Learning*, 2.

[61] Ballester, McVaugh, Rubio, *Medical Licensing and Learning*, 27. Eventually, the requirement was dropped even for Christians. (Ballester, McVaugh, Rubio, *Medical Licensing and Learning*, 54.)

[62] Ballester, McVaugh, Rubio, *Medical Licensing and Learning*, 28.

[63] Shatzmiller, *Jews, Medicine, and Medieval Society*, 109.

physician, this was a benefit of some importance not only to merchants and municipalities but also to chronically cash-strapped monarchies. Jews suffered from another liability as well: they found it more difficult to collect payment from non-Jewish patients.[64]

In an age of increasing professionalism and regulation, Jewish physicians could only have chafed at the restrictions that barred them from universities and precluded their winning the title of "*magister in medicina*," granted only to Christians. This may help account for the rapidity with which Jewish physicians emerged with that title after having been forcibly converted to Christianity in 1391 or later. Whatever their other burdens during the radical social upheavals of the 1391 riots and their aftermath, many clearly took advantage of their new religious status to improve their professional status.[65]

Image and Self-image

Medical knowledge, medical ideas, and medical terminology permeated the intellectual discourse of Jews in medieval Iberia to a surprising extent, constituting an essential element of cultural literacy and serving to cement the self-image of the Jewish elite. Medical themes, anatomical descriptions, and technical allusions taken from medicine appear in poetry, belles-lettres, ethical writings, biblical commentary, legal treatises, and works of philosophy. As early as the twelfth-century, the Barcelona physician Joseph ibn Zabara wrote a Hebrew proto-novel featuring a physician, also named Joseph ibn Zabara, as his protagonist. He dedicated the book to Sheshet Benveniste, courtier-*nasi* in the court of the kings of Aragon in Barcelona, a scion of one of the four dominant families in the Jewish community and a man reputed to be highly learned in medicine.

As *Sefer Sha'ashuim* ("The Book of Delight") opens, the protagonist introduces himself as a person who to his friends is both "servant and healer," who "with the help of his Creator, and according to his craft and knowledge . . . is busy with their illness, works for them, and serves them with love and compassion, [treating]

---

[64] McVaugh, *Medicine before the Plague*, 177, 181.
[65] Richard Emery, "Jewish Physicians in Medieval Perpignan," *Michael* 12 (1991): 113-134.

the young man in accordance with his youth and the old man in accordance with his age."[66] Joseph is resting from what he describes as exhausting labor. Even in sweet sleep, however, he cannot resist musing on medical topics, conjuring up maxims from Hippocrates, Aristotle, Galen, and Johannitius on the medical benefits of slumber. Soon his peace is broken by the vision of a man, also claiming medical expertise, who by the end of the novel will turn out to be a demonic personification of, seemingly, Joseph's own evil impulse.[67] Throughout the book, medicine is a recurrent theme, incidentally providing some of its most entertaining and humorous moments.

Joseph ibn Zabara was completely at ease writing for an audience familiar with medical theory and sympathetic with professional medical concerns, an audience that could be counted upon to be amused by jokes about incompetent doctors, and that could identify with a physician-protagonist. Many in this audience would not have been practicing doctors themselves, or, if trained in medicine, might have been mainly engaged in other activities. One may point to the later figure of Nahmanides (1194-1270), the rabbi, communal leader, and kabbalist who also wrote a monograph, *Torat ha-Adam*, that includes a discussion of the practice of medicine,[68] and who was reported to have accepted money for treating a female Christian patient and to have used lion-shaped amulets to heal kidney ailments.[69]

In short, Ibn Zabara was writing not just for Sheshet Benveniste but for a larger Jewish elite, some of whom are well known to history and all of whom shared his and Benveniste's education, tastes, and cultural values. In late thirteenth-century Castile, Isaac ibn Sahula had a similar audience in mind when he incorporated medical and

---

[66] Joseph ben Meir Ibn Zabara, *Sefer Sha'ashuim: A Book of Mediaeval Lore*, ed. Israel Davidson (New York: Jewish Theological Seminary of America, 1914); in English translation as *The Book of Delight*, trans. Moses Hadas (New York: Columbia University Press, 1932).

[67] Raymond P. Scheindlin, "*Sefer Sha'ashu'im*: Maqama or Medieval Bildungsroman?" (Heb.) *HaDoar* (1986): 26-29.

[68] Samuel S. Kottek, "Medical Practice and Jewish Law: Nahmanides' Sefer Torat haAdam," in *Medicine and Medical Ethics in Medieval and Early Modern Spain*, 163-172.

[69] For the first, see Y. Tzvi Langermann, "Fixing a Cost for Medical Care: Medical Ethics and Socio-Economic Reality in Christian Spain as Reflected in Jewish Sources," in *Medicine and Medical Ethics in Medieval and Early Modern Spain*, 154-162; for the second, Joseph Shatzmiller, "In Search of the 'Book of Figures': Medicine and Astrology in Montpellier at the Turn of the Fourteenth Century": 383-407, 400.

astrological material into his story collection, *Meshal ha-Qadmoni,* certain that his readers would relish explanations of Galen's humoral pathology in biblically-inflected rhymed prose.[70]

Out of the relatively broad knowledge of medicine among educated Andalusian Jews emerges the image of the professional Jewish physician: a type that later, in Christian Iberia, appears in one or another incarnation and at one or another level of social status. Let us briefly tease out a few of his cultural manifestations.

At the uppermost stratum, with some chronological overlap, there appear two related but distinct prototypes. One is the *alfaquim* of the High Middle Ages, a figure like Sheshet Benveniste, in whom medical knowledge vies with linguistic, diplomatic, and administrative skill.[71] The other, later, figure is the royal physician, in whom medical expertise is the primary and defining feature. Prominent examples include Abraham ben David Caslari and Moses Zarzal.[72] Jewish physicians who served the kings had an especially privileged position. Even after Jews were ordered out of the Aragonese royal administration near the end of the thirteenth century, Jewish doctors continued in royal service.[73]

But *alfaquims* and royal physicians were not the only privileged Jewish members of the medical profession. Throughout Christian Iberia and Provence, they and the successful physicians slightly below them made up a kind of miniature caste or guild, practicing their medical skills and deploying their resulting revenues in various fields including commerce and money-lending. The status enjoyed by such men offered both financial and social rewards, advantages like tax exemptions and the freedom to travel, even a measure of respect from Christian society at large. Although they might still have to accept lower salaries than Christian doctors, or experience an extra vulnerability to lawsuits from patients,[74] appreciation of their medical expertise elevated them above the common run of

---

[70] Isaac Ibn Sahula, *Meshal Haqadmoni: Fables from the Distant Past,* ed. and trans. Raphael Loewe (London: Litmann Library, 2004).

[71] Elka Klein, *Jews, Christian Society, and Royal Power in Medieval Barcelona* (Ann Arbor, MI: University of Michigan Press, 2006), 83.

[72] See Assis, "Jewish Physicians and Medicine in Medieval Spain," 46-48.

[73] Assis, "Jewish Physicians and Medicine in Medieval Spain," 47.

[74] Shatzmiller, *Jews, Medicine, and Medieval Society,* 116-118.

their co-religionists. As Leon Joseph of Carcassonne, a fourteenth-century Jewish physician working in Perpignan, reports: "When I lived among the Christians, I was of an inferior condition in their eyes, for there is none of our nation who is honored in their eyes except him who is a physician and who cures of them of their ills; in such a case, he sits at the table of kings and remains standing before them, whether he be of humble birth or of high rank, owing to his knowledge of medical science."[75]

Whether a person was an *alfaquim*, royal physician, or successful doctor, medical knowledge functioned as a key to privilege, access, and trust. Moreover, the prominence of such men, and the honor accorded them, had a ripple effect on their fellow Jews. From the numerous dedications of Jewish books to such figures and the hint of vicarious pride in testimonials like Leon Joseph's, and from the virtual absence of any criticism directed at them from within the Jewish community,[76] it is plain that the Andalusian ideal continued not only to animate the pride of these privileged figures themselves but to stir widely shared feelings of Jewish religious and national honor.

Among non-Jews, a different dynamic should be noted. The image of the Jewish physician as reliable confidant to kings and as expert healer and possessor of medical wisdom conflicted with the principle that the Jews were an inferior people whose repression was the fitting token of Christian triumph. It has been suggested that the image of the Jew as poisoner, which likely spurred the accusations of well-poisoning by Jews during the time of the Black Death, owed some of its power to Christian discomfort with the visible success of some very visible Jewish physicians; similar motifs appear in Islamic literature as well.[77]

In the thirteenth century, anti-Jewish legislation entered the medical realm, increasingly restricting Jewish access to

---

[75] Ballester, Ferre, Feliu, "Jewish Appreciation of Fourteenth-Century Scholastic Medicine," 110.

[76] Despite some indications of tension over the privileges accorded to doctors, the archives are said to contain "few records indicating a widespread feeling of resentment within the Jewish community against physicians." Assis, "The Jewish Physician in Medieval Spain," 48.

[77] Shatzmiller, *Jews, Medicine, and Medieval Society*, 85-90. Moshe Perlmann, "Notes on the Position of Jewish Physicians in Medieval Muslim Countries," *Israel Oriental Studies* 2 (1972): 315-319.

pharmaceuticals. The thirteenth-century law code the *Siete Partidas* ruled that Christians were not allowed to take medicines compounded by Jews; in 1227 in Trier, no drink or medicine was to be accepted from a Jew, nor could one seek medical help from Jews. Similar rules were enacted throughout the thirteenth century in the Crown of Aragon. If they had little effect on actual behavior, the Jew as potential poisoner continued to be a salient theme in anti-Jewish polemics. The fifteenth-century Alfonso de Espina accused Jews of perpetrating cruel deeds on Christians, "commonly . . . in the administration of medicines."[78]

Objections to Jewish physicians were also voiced by Christian physicians, including Arnald of Villanova, and sometimes even more virulently by Jewish converts to Christianity. The *converso* physician Alfonso Chirino (c. 1365-1429), in his *Espejo de medicina* (1414-1418), attacked by implication the two personal physicians of Enrique III, Moses ibn Zarzal and Meir Alguades. More generally, he objected to the fact that Jewish physicians could attain a certain level of power: "By means of their malevolent tricks they build their reputation among the ignorant. They sow the seeds of lies and harvest vanity, thus becoming the physicians of powerful noblemen and -women. Through these notables, some of these physicians are introduced to the kings and queens and the grandees; and once they have their favor, they exert their power to do whatever harm they wish."[79]

Whether independently of Christian animosity, or in reaction to it, or both, Jewish physicians in the later medieval period exhibited a marked sense of professional solidarity. This feeling may well have been enhanced by the development of guilds in general. But the separate tradition of Hebrew (and Arabic) medical texts, inaccessible to Christian physicians and—formerly—sought after by kings, would only have strengthened the mutual ties among Jewish doctors, whom Leon Joseph of Carcassonne does not hesitate to term a community

---

[78] Marcelino V. Amasuno, "The Converso Physician in the Anti-Jewish Controversy in Fourteenth-Fifteenth Century Castile," in *Medicine and Medical Ethics in Medieval and Early Modern Spain*, 92-118, 103, 106.

[79] Amasuno, "The Converso Physician," 115.

(*'adat ha-rof'im*).[80] In a striking illustration of this strong sense of solidarity, Jewish physicians regularly sought out, copied, or translated the most valuable medical texts to be distributed for use by their fellow physicians.

Sometimes the sense of professional solidarity even crossed religious boundaries. Moses ben Samuel of Roquemaure (a.k.a. Juan of Aviñon), who converted to Christianity in 1353 and whose later work displays a certain anti-Jewish bias, completed his Hebrew translation of Bernard of Gordon's *Lilium medicine* apparently for the use of Jewish physicians, a gesture that points to relatively permeable relations between Jews and *conversos* during this period.[81] At the same time, it is fascinating to note that professional loyalties also linked Jewish and Christian doctors together when, for example, faced with patient mistrust (as in a malpractice suit) or competition from unlicensed and non-learned healers.[82] And in Valencia, Jewish and Muslim medical practitioners worked and consulted together into the middle of the fifteenth century.[83]

Medieval Iberian Jewish physicians were so various and so ubiquitous as to resist being reduced to a single social type. Nevertheless, three common features may be identified: the association of medical knowledge with the Andalusian Jewish cultural ideal; the identification of medical skill with Jewish access to social advancement and possible real power, with consequences for good or for ill; and a loyalty and solidarity among Jewish doctors that could cross socioeconomic lines, as well as a professional loyalty that would sometimes even cross religious lines.

---

[80] Ballester, Ferre, Feliu, "Jewish Appreciation of Fourteenth-Century Scholastic Medicine," 110.

[81] On Juan of Aviñon, see Ballester, *La búsqeda de la salud*, 435-438.

[82] Domingo, "Organització social i atenció mèdica," 16-18.

[83] Mark D. Meyerson, *A Jewish Renaissance in Fifteenth-Century Spain* (Princeton: Princeton University Press, 2004), 154-155.

Works Cited:

Ali ibn Ahmad ibn Hazm. *The Ring of the Dove.* Translated by Anthony Arberry. London: Luzac, 1994.

Amar, Zohar, and Yiron Sari. "Remnants of the Dictionary of Medical Terms of R. Yonah Ibn Janah." (Heb.) *Leshonenu* 63 (2000-2001): 279-291.

Benedicto Gracia, Eugenio. "Los médicos judíos de Huesca, según los protocolos notariales del siglo XV." *Sefarad* 68 (2008): 55-87.

Bos, Gerrit. "R. Moshe Narboni: Philosopher and Physician, A Critical Analysis of *Sefer Orah Hayyim.*" *Medieval Encounters* 1 (1995): 219-251.

------. "Editing medieval Hebrew medical manuscripts: R. Barkai, *A history of Jewish gynaecological texts in the Middle Ages,*" *Jewish Quarterly Review* 89 (1998): 101-21.

------. "Maimonides' Medical Works and their Contribution to his Medical Biography." *Maimonidean Studies* 5 (2008): 243-266.

Bos, Gerrit, and Resianne Fontaine. "Medico-philosophical controversies in Nathan b. Jo'el Falaquera Sefer Zori ha-Guf." *Jewish Quarterly Review* 90 (1999): 27-60.

Bos, Gerrit, and Guido Mensching. "*Macer Floridus*, 'A Middle Hebrew Fragment with Romance Elements.'" *Jewish Quarterly Review* 91 (2000): 17-51.

------. "The Literature of Hebrew Medical Synonyms: Romance and Latin Terms and their Identification." *Aleph* 5 (2005): 169-211.

Burnett, Charles, ed. *Ibn Baklarish's Book of Simples: Medical Remedies between Three Faiths in Twelfth-Century Spain.* Oxford: Oxford University Press, 2008.

Caballero Navas, Carmen, ed. *The Book of Women's Love and Jewish Medical Literature on Women: Sefer Ahavat Nashim.* London: Kegan Paul, 2004.

Cabré, Monserrat. "Women or Healers?: Household Practices and the Categories of Health Care in Late Medieval Iberia." *Bulletin of the History of Medicine* 82 (2008): 18-51.

Cardoner i Planas, Antoni. *Història de la medicina a la Corona d'Aragó (1162-1479)*. Barcelona, 1973.

Cifuentes i Comamala, Lluís. *La ciència en català a l'Edat Mitjana i el Renaixement*. Barcelona: Universitat de Barcelona, 2002.

Cole, Peter, ed. and trans. *The Dream of the Poem: Hebrew Poetry from Muslim and Christian Spain 950-1492*. Princeton: Princeton University Press, 2007.

David ben Yom Tov. Kelal Qatan: *Hebrew Medical Astrology*. Edited by Gerrit Bos, Charles Burnett, and Y. Tzvi Langermann. Philadelphia: American Philosophical Society, 2005.

Emery, Richard. "Jewish Physicians in Medieval Perpignan." *Michael* 12 (1991): 113-134.

Ferragud Domingo, Carmel. "Organització social i atenció mèdica a la Cocentaina Baixmedieval: El process a Abrahim Abengalell (1318)." *Asclepio* 57 (2005): 3-24.

Ferre, Lola. "Hebrew Translations from Medical Treatises of Montpellier." *Korot* 13 (1998-99): 21-36.

------. "Avicena Hebraico: La traducción del *Canon de Medicina*." *MEAH* 52 (2003): 163-182.

------. "Dissemination of Maimonides' Medical Writings in the Middle Ages." In *Traditions of Maimonideanism*. Edited by Carlos Fraenkel, 17-31. Leiden: Brill, 2009.

French, Roger, Jon Arrizabalaga, Andrew Cunningham and Luis García Ballester, eds. *Medicine from the Black Death to the French Disease*. Aldershot: Ashgate, 1998.

Freudenthal, Gad. "Les Sciences dans les communautés juives médièvales de Provence: Leur appropriation, leur role." *Revue des études juives* 152 (1993): 29-136.

------. "Science in Medieval Jewish Culture." *History of Science* 33 (1995): 23-58

García Ballester, Luis. "El papel de las instituciones de consume y diffusion de ciencia médica en la Castilla del siglo III: El Monasterio, la cathedral y la Universidad." *Dynamis* 4 (1984): 33-63.

------. "La circulación de las ideas médicas en la Castilla de Alfonso X el Sabio." *Revista de Occidente* 43 (1984): 85-107.

------. "Medical Science in Castile: Problems and Prospects." *Bulletin of the History of Medicine* 61 (1987): 183-202.

------. *La búsqeda de la salud: Sanadores y enfermos en al España medieval.* Barcelona: Ediciones Península, 2001.

García Ballester, Luis, Lola Ferre, and Eduard Feliu. "Jewish Appreciation of Fourteenth-Century Scholastic Medicine." *Osiris* 6 (1990): 85-117.

García Ballester, Luis, Roger French, Jon Arrizabalaga, and Andrew Cunningham, eds. *Practical Medicine from Salerno to the Black Death.* Cambridge, UK: Cambridge University Press, 1994.

García Ballester, Luis, Michael R. McVaugh, Agustín Rubio, *Medical Licensing and Learning in Fourteenth-Century Valencia* (Philadelphia: American Philosophical Society, 1989).

Geller, M. J. "Akkadian Healing Therapies in the Babylonian Talmud." *Max-Planck-Institut für Wissenschaftsgeschichte Preprint* 259 (2004): 1-60.

Goitein, S. D. "The Biography of Rabbi Judah Ha-Levi in the Light of Cairo Geniza Documents." *PAAJR* 28 (1959): 41-56.

------. "The Medical Profession in the Light of the Cairo Geniza Documents." *Hebrew Union College Annual* 34 (1963): 177-194.

------. *A Mediterranean Society, Volume II: The Community.* Berkeley, Los Angeles, London: University of California Press, 1971.

Guénon, Anne-Sylvie. "Les traductions en Hébreu de l'oeuvre du médecin Gérard de Solo (XIVe siècle)." *Revue des études juives* 164 (2005): 463-488.

Hasani, M. "A Unique Manuscript of the Medieval Medical Treatise al-Iktifa' by Abu-l-Mutrib 'Abd al-Rahman." *Manuscripta Orientalia* 5 (1999): 20-24.

Hasselhoff, Görge K. "The Reception of Maimonides in the Latin World: The Evidence of the Latin Translations in the 13th-15th Century." *Materia guidaica* 6 (2001): 258-280.

Hourani, George F. "The Early Growth of the Secular Sciences in Andalusia." *Studia Islamica* 32 (1970): 143-156.

Isaac ibn Sahula. *Meshal Haqadmoni: Fables from the Distant Past.* Edited and translated by Raphael Loewe. London: Litmann Library, 2004.

Joseph ben Meir ibn Zabara. *Sefer Sha'ashuim: A Book of Mediaeval Lore.* Edited by Israel Davidson. New York: Jewish Theological Seminary of America, 1914.

------. *The Book of Delight.* Translated by Moses Hadas. New York: Columbia University Press, 1932.

Juan de Aviñon. *Sevillana medicina.* Sevilla, 1885.

Kieckhefer, Richard. *Magic in the Middle Ages.* Cambridge, UK: Cambridge University Press, 1989.

Klein, Elka. *Jews, Christian Society, and Royal Power in Medieval Barcelona.* Ann Arbor, MI: University of Michigan Press, 2006.

Kottek, Samuel S., and Luis García Ballester, eds. *Medicine and Medical Ethics in Medieval and Early Modern Spain: An Intercultural Approach.* Jerusalem: Magnes Press, 1996.

Kuhne, Rosa. "Hacia una revisión de la bibliografia de los Banu Zuhr." *Al-Qantara* 13 (1992): 581-585.

Langermann, Y. Tzvi. "Solomon Ibn Yaish's Commentary on the Qanun of Ibn Sina." [In Hebrew] *Kiryat Sefer* 63 (1990-1991): 1331-1333.

------."Maimonides on the Synochous Fever." *Israel Oriental Studies* 13 (1994): 175-198.

------. "Science in the Jewish Communities of the Iberian Peninsula: An Interim Report." In his *The Jews and the Sciences in the Middle Ages*, 1-54. Aldershot: Ashgate, 1999.

Lewis, Bernard. *Islam: From the Prophet Muhammad to the Capture of Constantinople*, Vol. II. New York: Harper and Row, 1974.

Maimonides. *Mishneh Torah, Sefer ha-madda'.* Edited and translated by Moses Hyamson. Jerusalem and New York: Feldheim, 1981.

------. *On Asthma: A Parallel Arabic-English Text.* Edited and translated by Gerrit Bos. Provo, UT: Brigham Young University Press, 2002.

------. *Medical Aphorisms, 1-5: A Parallel Arabic-English Edition.* Edited and translated by Gerrit Bos. Provo, UT: Brigham Young University Press, 2004.

------. *Medical Aphorisms, 6-9: A Parallel Arabic-English Edition.* Edited and translated by Gerrit Bos. Provo, UT: Brigham Young University Press, 2007.

------. *On Asthma, vol. 2: Critical Editions of Medieval Hebrew and Latin Translations.* Edited and translated by Gerrit Bos and Michael R. Mc Vaugh. Provo, UT: Brigham Young University Press, 2008.

------. *On Poisons: Critical Edition of the Arabic Text, Medieval Hebrew and Latin Translations, with English Translation.* Edited and translated by Gerrit Bos and Michael R. McVaugh. Provo, UT: Brigham Young University Press, 2008.

McVaugh, Michael R. *Medicine before the Plague: Doctors and Patients in the Crown of Aragon, 1285-1335.* Cambridge, UK: Cambridge University Press, 1993.

------. "Bedside Manners in the Middle Ages." *Bulletin of the History of Medicine* 71 (1997): 201-223.

McVaugh, Michael R. and Lola Ferre, eds. *The "Tabula Antidotarii" of Armengaud Blaise and Its Hebrew Translation.* Philadelphia: American Philosophical Society, 2000.

Meyerson, Mark D. *A Jewish Renaissance in Fifteenth-Century Spain.* Princeton: Princeton University Press, 2004.

Nicoud, Marilyn. *Les régimes de santé au Moyen Âge: naissance et diffusion d'une écriture médicale, XIIIe-XVe siècle.* Rome: École française de Rome, 2007.

O'Boyle, Cornelius. *The Art of Medicine: Medical Teaching at the University of Paris, 1250-1400.* Leiden: Brill, 1998.

Perlmann, Moshe. "Notes on the Position of Jewish Physicians in Medieval Muslim Countries." *Israel Oriental Studies* 2 (1972): 315-319.

Pormann, Peter E. and Emilie Savage-Smith. *Medieval Islamic Medicine.* Washington, DC: Georgetown University Press, 2007.

Ps. Abraham ibn Ezra. *Sefer haNisyonot: The Book of Medical Experiences.* Edited and translated by Joshua O. Leibowitz and Shlomo Marcus. Jerusalem: Magnes Press, 1984.

Richler, Benjamin. "Manuscripts of Avicenna's Canon in Hebrew Translation: A Revised and Up-to-date List." *Korot* 8 (1982): 145-168.

Sa'id al-Andalusi. *Science in the Medieval World*, "Book of the Categories of the Nations." Edited and translated by Sema'an I. Salem and Alok Kumar. Austin, TX: Texas University Press, 1991.

Scheindlin, Raymond P. "*Sefer Sha'ashu'im*: Maqama or Medieval Bildungsroman?" [In Hebrew] *HaDoar* (1986): 26-29.

Shatzmiller, Joseph. "In Search of the 'Book of Figures': Medicine and Astrology in Montpellier at the Turn of the Fourteenth Century." *AJS Review* 7 (1982): 383-407.

------. *Jews, Medicine and Medieval Society*. Berkeley and Los Angeles: University of California Press, 1994.

Shem Tov ibn Falaquera. *Book of the Seeker*. Translated by M. Herschel Levine. New York: Yeshiva University Press, 1976.

Smith, Damien J. and Helena Buffery, trans. *The Book of Deeds of James I of Aragon*. Farnham, UK: Ashgate, 2003.

van Koningsveld, P. Sj. "Andalusian-Arabic Manuscripts from Christian Spain: A comparative Intercultural Approach." *Israel Oriental Studies* 12 (1992): 75-110.

The Unknown Jewish Artists of Medieval Iberia

.... Vivian B. Mann

It is often said that only with the Emancipation in the nineteenth century did Jews become artists. A related assumption is that most medieval Jews earned their living by lending money or by pawnbroking. Many of those who admit Jews functioned as artists in the medieval period assume that the writing and decorating of Hebrew manuscripts was the only artistic genre they practiced; very few have had a broader view.[1] History books devoted to the Jewish experience have long contributed to misconceptions about the existence of medieval Jewish art since they often group artists who produced significant medieval genres—silversmiths, weavers, or painters of manuscripts and altarpieces—with craftsmen like shoemakers and tailors.[2] None of these statements is accurate for the kingdoms of medieval Spain, since they are based on a narrow view of the Jewish community, and on a similarly narrow definition of medieval art.

During the medieval period, most of the Jewish population lived in Muslim lands, rather than in countries ruled by Christians. Mark

---

[1] The subject of this essay was first discussed by Franz Landsberger almost seventy years ago: "Jewish Artists before the Period of Emancipation," *Hebrew Union College Annual*, 16 (1941): 358-59.

[2] Mark Wischnitzer, *Jewish Crafts and Guilds* (New York: Jonathan David, 1965).

Cohen has compared the legal and economic status of medieval Jews who lived as *dhimmis* under Muslim rulers, that is people of the Book who were considered to have a revealed Scripture, with those living under Christian rule in Europe – who were viewed as rejecting the truth of Christianity.[3] The greater consistency by which Islamic law treated the *dhimmis* contributed to the continuity of Jewish life in Muslim lands; in many countries their history stretches from antiquity to the mid-twentieth century. In contrast, the frequent changes in the law and status of Jews in Christendom yielded greater uncertainty and more frequent persecutions. As a result the range of Jewish artistic activity in the medieval world varied from country to country and was determined by the laws of the predominant religion and the rulers who governed in its name. As William Brinner has written about Islamic countries, "In the absence of European-type guilds… there was a great deal of cohesion and cooperation within trades and professions; thus at all levels Jews interacted with their Muslim… counterparts."[4] The same was true in medieval Spain, whose art created under Christian rule was, to a great extent, based on the arts practiced under Muslim rulers—the weaving of textiles, woodworking, calligraphy, silversmithing, and jewelry making— with the addition of art required by the Church.

In considering the historical question of whether Jews were artists in late medieval Spain, one must first consider the genres of art that were important at that time. In most Christian lands, in addition to painting and sculpture, the so-called "decorative" or "treasury arts" were prominent. The distinction between the so-called "fine arts" and the "decorative arts" was a product of the later European Renaissance, and related to a shift in emphasis on the artist's skill and away from the contractual definition of his work—of its subject, media, and composition.[5] In the Middle Ages, the designers and weavers of textiles, jewelers, and silversmiths were praised for their

---

[3] Mark R. Cohen, *Under Crescent & Cross: The Jews in the Middle Ages* (Princeton: Princeton University Press, 1994), chs. 3 and 4.

[4] William Brinner, "The Jewish, Christian, and Muslim Communities in Egypt," in *Fortifications and the Synagogue: The Fortress of Babylonia and the Ben Ezra Synagogue, Cairo*, ed. Phyllis Lambert (London: Weidenfeld & Nicolson, 1995), 14-15.

[5] Michael Baxandall, *Painting and Experience in Fifteenth-Century Italy* (Oxford: Oxford University Press, 1986), 23.

skill, the beauty of their compositions, and the colors they used; they were artists on a par with painters and sculptors. The medieval illuminator who decorated manuscripts with elaborate miniatures was equal to the artist of panel paintings or frescoes. Archival records mention Jews as practitioners of these arts and also as painters.[6]

Occasionally the same artist worked in more than one genre. For example, an atelier active in fourteenth-century Barcelona under the leadership of the artist Ferrer Bassa (d. ca. 1348), known for a long time as the Workshop of San Marco, produced manuscripts in both Hebrew and Latin as well as *retablos* or altarpieces.[7] In a 1348 edition of Maimonides' great philosophical treatise *The Guide of the Perplexed* from Bassa's workshop (Copenhagen, Royal Library, Cod. Heb. xxxvii), Christian illuminators worked together with a Hebrew scribe responsible for the text. One miniature of the Maimonides manuscript featuring the Four Beasts of Ezekiel's vision (fol. 202r) demonstrates the passage of Christian iconography to a Jewish work.[8] The composition, developed initially in Byzantium to encompass the symbols of the Four Evangelists, migrated to the West and appears in works like the English *Bury Bible* of the twelfth century. In the Hebrew text from Barcelona, they represent their original literary source, the Four Beasts of the heavenly chariot.

The existence of the San Marco atelier is of great significance when considering the genesis of the illuminated haggadot produced in Barcelona and its environs during the second and third quarters of the fourteenth century. These haggadot have always been viewed as a unique phenomenon within Spanish Jewish art, whose origins ca. 1300 have never been satisfactorily explained.[9] When their biblical

---

[6] Asunció Blasco Martínez, "Pintores y Orfebres Judíos en Zaragoza (Siglo XIV)," *Aragon en la Edad Media* VII (1989): 113-31; Encarnación Marín Padilla, presents the case of two Jewish painters, Isaac Avençur and Moses Beçudo, who apprenticed to a Christian painter in 1470 in order to learn the art of applying gold leaf. ("Varia," *Sefarad* XLVII, 1(1987): 183)

[7] Pioneering work on the San Marco workshop was done by Millard Meiss: "Italian Style in Catalonia and a Fourteenth-Century Catalan Workshop," *Journal of the Walters Art Gallery*, 4 (1941): 45-87.

[8] For the miniature in the *Guide of the Perplexed,* see Vivian B. Mann, Thomas Glick and Jerilynn Dodds, *Convivencia: Jews, Muslims and Christians in Medieval Spain* (New York: George Braziller, 1992), fig. 51.

[9] For a recent iconographic study of six of the manuscripts, see Katrin Kogman-Appel, *Illuminated Haggadot from Medieval Spain: Biblical Imagery and the Passover Holiday* (University Park: University of Pennsylvania Press, 2006).

and genre scenes are viewed in the context of altarpieces, and their
style is considered, the place of the haggadot within Spanish art
becomes more apparent.

Fig. 1. Hispano-Mauresque Haggadah, Castile, ca. 1300.

An early Spanish haggadah, a late thirteenth-century "Hispano-
Moresque" manuscript in the British Library (Or. 2737, fig. 1)
is related stylistically to scenes from the Life of Christ on a
fragmentary late thirteenth-century Iberian altarpiece now in The
Cloisters (New York, Metropolitan Museum of Art, 55.62 a, b and
1977.94, fig. 2) and to similar *retablos*. In these works, the scenes
are set in architectural frames, often of deep red, above which are
rubrics indicating the content of the scene (Latin on the altarpiece;
Hebrew in the haggadah). The languages of these rubrics, assuming
they served as instructions to the artists, symbolize that both Jewish

and Christian artists were active in producing Hispano-Moresque works.[10]

Fig. 2. Anonymous, Panels with scenes from the Life of Christ, Spanish, thirteenth century.

---

[10] That they were not titles for the finished miniatures is indicated by the discrepancies between the texts and the subjects depicted.

The action takes place against blank backgrounds, with only the minimal props required by the narrative. Terracotta red, green, and ochre are the dominant colors on both works, and they appear saturated rather than shaded. Often, the size of key figures, like Jesus in the altarpiece, is enlarged to indicate a subject's importance. Still, stylistic differences between the two works indicate that more than one artist was responsible for the haggadah and the *retablo*.

Fig. 3. Anonymous, "Scenes of Creation," The Golden Haggadah, Barcelona or Lleida, ca. 1320.

Fig. 4. Master of Roussillon (?), "Creation Scenes," Retable with Scenes from the Life of
St. Andrew, Perpignan (?), ca. 1420-30.

Another comparison between a Christian and Jewish work of
the same date could be made between the most lavish Passover
manuscript of the period, the Golden Haggadah in the British
Library of around 1320 (Add. 27210, fig. 3), and a second *retablo*
in the Cloisters, one dedicated to Saint Andrew (Metropolitan
Museum, 25.120.257; fig. 4). Five scenes of the Creation story appear
in the Golden Haggadah: Adam Naming the Animals occupies one
frame and the remaining four are combined in a single frame. The
sequence reads chronologically from right to left, the direction in
which Hebrew is read: Adam Naming the Animals (Gen. 2: 20), the
Creation of Eve (Gen. 2:21–22), the Temptation of Eve (Gen. 3:1–5),
the Man and his Wife with Loincloths (Gen. 3:7) and God (in the
guise of an Angel) Reproaching Adam and Eve (Gen. 3:16–18). In
the second, composite frame, the figure of Eve is shown tempted
by the Serpent and simultaneously covering herself with a loincloth,

while Adam both covers himself and raises his head as the angel reproaches him.[11] The rubric for the second frame, "Adam and his Wife were Naked," refers to the episode of the Man and his Wife with Loincloths. The *retablo* originally included seven Creation scenes, but the location of the three is unknown. With one exception, each of the altarpiece scenes is given its own pictorial space: God Creates the Creatures of the Waters and the Birds (Day 5; Gen. 1:20–23), the Creation of Man (Day 6; Gen. 1:26–27), God Casts a Deep Sleep on Adam (Gen. 2:21), God Presents Eve to Adam (Gen. 2:22, God Commands Adam and Eve Not to Eat from the Tree of Knowledge (Gen. 2:16–17), the Temptation and Reproach (Gen. 3:1–6; 11), and the Expulsion (Gen. 3:24). All of the *retablo* and haggadah scenes are set against diapered backgrounds with the foregrounds made up of landscape elements: earth and stylized trees. The patches of earth on the *retablo* are composed of stylized forms stacked up against one another, while in the haggadah the landscape is a continuous, shaded mass. On the altarpiece, God dominates through his size or his appearance in a mandorla; in the haggadah scenes he is absent. Despite differences in iconography and figure style between the haggadah and the altarpiece—the *retablo* figures are more linear— there are striking similarities between the two works, in particular their devotion of considerable space to the story of Creation and their emphasis on a few important figures in scenes that are set against a diapered background and anchored to a foreground of earth and stylized trees.

One image on the Saint Andrew altarpiece, a combination of the Creation of the Creatures of the Waters and the Birds on Day 5 with the Creation of the Beasts and Cattle on Day 6, may be related to the same scene in another haggadah manuscript from fourteenth-century Iberia found in Sarajevo.[12] In both images, the creatures of the water are seen swimming, while above them are birds, cattle, and wild animals. The role of God in the haggadah Creation scene

---

[11] This composition, showing Adam and Eve hiding their genitals with large leaves and standing on either side of the Tree of Knowledge around which the serpent coils, is known as early as the fourth century and ca. 1000 in Spanish art. (See an engraved bowl in Jeffrey Spier et al., *Picturing the Bible: The Earliest Christian Art* [New Haven: Yale University Press, 2007], fig. 4).

[12] Cecil Roth, *Sarajevo Haggada* (Belgrade: Beogradski Izdavačko-Grafički Zavod, 1975), 2.

is symbolized by a cone of gold rays emanating from the heavens. On the *retablo*, God is anthropomorphic and ensconced in heavenly clouds.[13] The image of the second day when the earth was separated from the firmament is shown in a similar way in the Sarajevo Haggadah and in the Harburg Pamplona Bible, a manuscript commissioned by King Sancho the Strong of Navarre (1194–1234).[14] The representation of the earth as a sphere in these miniatures also appears on two capitals of the twelfth-century Puerta del Palau of Valencia's Cathedral.[15] Another parallel between the Pamplona Bibles and the haggadot occurs in the scene of the Crossing of the Red Sea, in which the water is depicted as a series of bands.[16] These interlocking relationships between art created under Christian auspices and the haggadot represent artistic interchange between Jews and Christians. Two other types of cross-cultural relationships remain to be discussed: the work of Jewish artists for the Church and the depiction of Jews by Christian artists.

Our knowledge of the role of Jewish artists in medieval Spanish art is based on three types of evidence: works signed by Jewish artists; works whose nature presumes Jewish authorship; and texts mentioning or describing works made by Jews. An example of the first type is the illuminated Hebrew manuscript. The decorative scheme of biblical manuscripts produced in Spain can be traced back to those produced in the Land of Israel and Egypt during the tenth and eleventh centuries. One form of manuscript decoration is micrography, the use of the written word to create designs, a technique that can also be seen in later Qur'ans. Another type of decoration is the carpet page, miniatures whose composition imitates those

---

[13] In the early twelfth-century Creation Tapestry in Girona cathedral, the fifth day is similarly depicted: at bottom are the creatures of the water, above are the birds craning their heads toward Jesus enthroned at center. Missing are the wild animals in the zone of the birds that appear in both the haggadah and the *retablo* scene. See Joseph Calzada i Oliveras, *Die Kathedrale von Girona* (Barcelona, Escudo de Oro, S.A., 1988), 78-81.)

[14] François Boucher, *The Pamplona Bibles* (New Haven: Yale University Press, 1970), pl. 3. The two scenes of Adam and Eve in the manuscript are not comparable to those under discussion here.

[15] For a discussion of the creation cycle in the Sarajevo Haggadah and its iconographic relationship to both earlier and later manuscripts, see Herbert R. Broderick, "Observations on the Creation Cycle of the Sarajevo Haggadah," *Zeitschrift für Kunstgeschichte*, 3(1984): 320-32.

[16] Boucher, *Pamplona Bibles*, pl. 118; Bezalel Narkiss et al., *Hebrew Illuminated Manuscripts in the British Isles* (Oxford: Oxford University Press, 1982), Vol. 1, Pt. 2, fig. 294.

of textiles and was probably intended as a replacement for cloths placed between miniatures to preserve them, which appears in both Hebrew and Islamic manuscripts. The usual motifs of these carpet pages are geometric or floral, but the manuscript known as the First Leningrad Bible, created in 929 by Solomon ben Levi ha-Bouya'a in Egypt, introduces a new composition which was repeated in Spain until the Expulsion. It is a page of the Temple Implements, which became a sign for Spanish Jewry of the hope and belief in the rebuilding of the ancient center of Jewish worship.[17] That similar decoration exists in the Hebrew Bibles and Qur'ans of Spain, as it had in the Maghrib, must have been due to cooperative relationships between Jewish and Muslim artists and the result of interreligious partnerships. Maimonides (1135-1204) discussed one such example in a responsum:

> What does our Master say with regard to partners in a workshop, some being Jews and some Muslims, exercising the same craft. The partners have agreed between themselves that the [gains made on] Friday should go the Jews and those made on Saturday to the Muslims. The implements of the workshop are held in partnership; the crafts exercised are in one case goldsmithing, in another the making of glass.[18]

Maimonides allowed the arrangement as long as the Jewish craftsman did not benefit from revenues earned on Saturday. That inter-religious ateliers existed in Christian Iberia as well is proved by the San Marco workshop whose creations included both Latin and Hebrew manuscripts and altarpieces.

Some of the works produced in the 200 years before the Expulsion of 1492 are known only from documents. A unique, surviving contract written in Mallorca in 1335 between the patron, David Isaac Cohen, and two fellow Jews, Abraham Tati and Bonnim Maymo, stipulates that Maymo will provide three books with illuminated letters: a Bible with gold letters, Maimonides' *Guide of the Perplexed*,

---

[17] Narkiss, *Hebrew Illuminated Manuscripts* (Jerusalem: Keter Publishing House, Ltd., 1969), 42.

[18] S. D. Goitein, *A Mediterranean Society. The Jewish Comunities of the World as Portrayed in the Documents of the Cairo Geniza. Vol 2: The Community* (Berkeley: University of California Press, 1999), 296; see also Cohen, *Under Crescent & Cross*, 95-96.

and a second Maimonidean treatise.[19] Maymo was a minor at the time that the contract was written, which explains the involvement of Tati who was a silk maker. Other Spanish Hebrew manuscripts have colophons naming their creators. In 1260, Menahem ben Abraham ibn Malik recorded in the colophon of his manuscript that it was finished in Burgos in 1260 (Jerusalem, National Library, Ms. Heb. 4°790).[20] It is the first Spanish Hebrew Bible whose decorative scheme of carpet pages both reflects the earlier manuscripts from the Land of Israel and North Africa and presents a model for those produced until the Expulsion. The floral motifs of the carpet pages are drawn from Islamic art like stucco work; they are surrounded by large and small framing inscriptions. In 1299, Joseph the Frenchman worked as an illuminator for the scribe of the Cervera Bible, leaving a colophon in zoomorphic letters, a feature derived from Latin manuscripts (Lisbon, Biblioteca Nacional de Lisboa, Ms. Hebr. 72, fol. 449).[21] This text served as a model for the colophon of the Kennicott Bible illustrated by Joseph Ibn Hayyim in 1476.[22] Another signed manuscript is the Farhi Bible written between 1366 and 1382 by Elisha ben Abraham ben Benveniste ben Elisha, called Crescas (Jerusalem: Sassoon Collection, Ms. 368).[23] It includes the double page of Temple Implements seen in the First Leningrad Bible, and in later Hebrew Bibles from Spain.

Some Jewish artists undertook to work on manuscripts for Christian patrons. Vidal Abraham illuminated a Book of Privileges for the government of Mallorca in 1341. Fragments of it still exist, showing that the artist created large initials (some with gold), smaller ones of red and blue ink, plus chapter markings,[24] a decorative scheme common to both Hebrew and Christian Bibles.[25] Another,

---

[19] J. N. Hillgarth and Bezalel Narkiss, "A List of Hebrew Books (1330) and a Contract to Illuminate Manuscripts (1335) from Mallorca," *Revue des Études Juives* 3 (1961): 304-08, 316-320.

[20] Narkiss, *Hebrew Illuminated Manuscripts*, 50-51.

[21] Joseph Gutmann, *Hebrew Manuscript Painting* (New York: George Braziller, 1978), pl. 8.

[22] Gutmann, *Hebrew Manuscript Painting*, fig. 9.

[23] Bezalel Narkiss, *Decorated Hebrew Manuscripts* (Jerusalem: Keter Publishing, 1984), 98-99 (Hebrew).

[24] Hillgarth and Narkiss, "A List of Hebrew Books (1330) and a Contract to Illuminate Manuscripts (1335) from Mallorca," 305.

[25] See for example, Sonsoles Herrero Gonzáles, *Codices Miniados en el Real Monasterio de Las Huelgas* (Barcelona: Editores Lunwerg, 1988), fig. 71, for a Christian Bible from Burgos

more specialized, work by a Mallorcan Jewish scribe and artist was the Catalan Atlas drawn and illustrated by Abraham Cresques (1325-1387) in 1375; it was recorded as having been in the library of Charles V of France five years later.[26] The numerous illustrations of human figures, animals, flora and cities appearing throughout the map are akin to manuscript decoration. Two letters of 1381 written by Juan, the Infante of Aragon, mention "Cresques the Jew, a leading master of maps of the world and of compasses." In 1422, Rabbi Moses of Arragel was asked by Don Guzman, Master of the Order of Calatrava, to translate the Hebrew Bible into Castilian, and to produce commentaries and illustrations for the text.[27] The history of the commission is related in a lengthy preface to the text of the Bible. Rabbi Moses demurred, citing the biblical prohibition against images. To accommodate the rabbi, Don Guzman hired Christian artists from Toledo to produce the miniatures. When finished, the manuscript included 334 miniatures that were modeled on a manuscript from the Cathedral in Toledo, which is astonishing testimony to the Christian preservation of a large body of scenes from the Hebrew Bible.[28] In effect, Rabbi Moses and the Christian illuminators with whom he worked formed a mixed shop, such as Fernand Bassa's atelier.

In the second quarter of the fourteenth century, acting to implement the ruling of the Fourth Lateran Council of 1215 requiring congregants to see the moment of Transubstantiation during mass, Spanish churches moved their paintings off the altar to a position behind it. The *retablos*, as they came to be called, were thereby freed from the spatial constraints of ordinary altarpieces,

---

of the twelfth century, and New York Public Library, *Tesoros de España. Ten Centuries of Spanish Books*, exhibition catalogue, 1985, 48.

[26] Jean Michel Massing, "Abraham Cresques : Catalan Atlas," in *Ca. 1492. Art in the Age of Exploration*, ed. Jay A. Levenson (Washington: National Gallery of Art and Yale University Press, 1991), no. 1 (there the older literature).

[27] Moses of Arragel, trans., *La Biblia de Alba*, ed. Jeremy Schonfeld (Madrid, 1992), there the older bibliography. The iconography of the scenes was discussed by Carl-Otto Nordström (*The Duke of Alba's Castilian Bible: A Study of the Rabbinical Features of the Miniatures* (Uppsala: Almquist and Wiksells, 1967)).

[28] An earlier example of the Christian transmission of biblical iconography are the hundreds of scenes in the eleventh-century Pamplona Bibles, some of which preserve the compositions of wall paintings in the Dura Europos Synagogue, dated ca. 244 CE. (Boucher, *The Pamplona Bibles*).

and grew in size, often reaching the height of the church vaults, as at Teruel and Ejea de los Cabelleros. This new art form allowed for many more panels and subjects surrounding the central depictions of saints or holy figures. The artists responsible for creating *retablos* were challenged to provide more complex iconographic programs than before, and the manner in which they met this challenge forms part of the present discussion.

Notarial documents dating from the fourteenth century reveal the existence of several Jewish painters who worked on large-scale projects for Christian patrons, often involving Christian religious themes. One such artist was Abraham de Salinas who signed a contract with the See of Saragossa in 1393 to produce a *retablo* on the theme of the Life of the Virgin.[29] Another contract records the employment of Bonafós Abenxueu, a Jewish silversmith, to create a frame for Abraham's retable that was to include six cartouches with scenes of the Annunciaton to Mary. From the notarial texts, we know that Abraham de Salinas painted at least four *retablos* for the churches of San Felipe and La Puebla de Alborton in the See of Saragossa, but he may also have produced others whose records are lost. That Abraham de Salinas was given the commissions just mentioned, including repeat commissions from the same churches, testifies both to the fact that he was esteemed as a painter, and that he was able to produce various Christological themes that satisfied his patrons. Abraham's commissions also suggest that Jewish artists knew visual models of Christian iconography.

Other painters of altarpieces were conversos. Born and educated in the Jewish community, they later converted to Christianity, taking their Jewish educations with them. Among them were two brothers, Juan and Guillén de Leví, whose family name indicates a Jewish origin. Nothing is known of Guillén until the 1380's, when he is listed as a painter. Juan is undocumented until 1402 when he is similarly listed. The lack of early records is an indication of Jewish origins.[30] Juan de

---

29 Martínez, "Pintores y Orfebres Judíos en Zaragoza (Siglo XIV)," 115-18.

30 María Teresa Ainaga Andrés et al., *Retablo de Juan de Leví y su restauración: Capilla de los Pérez Calvillo. Catedral de Tarazona* (Saragossa: Felix Arilla, 1984), 11 and 30, n. 10; Judith Berg Sobré, *Behind the Altar Table: The Development of the Painted Retable in Spain, 1350-1500* (Columbia, MO: University of Missouri Press, 1989), 93. n. 31. The existing biographical information on the Pérez Calvillo brothers begins only at the point of their service to the church, which raises the possibility that they, too, were converts. It is well-

Leví created a *retablo* for the tomb of the bishops of Tarazona, Pedro and Fernando Pérez Calvillo, brothers who succeeded one another in office.[31]

In the church of Rubielos de Mora is a *retablo* dated ca. 1420 that may be a work by a member of the de Levís atelier. The proportions of the panels and the Gothic framing devices are similar to those of the Tarazona altarpiece, and the palette appears similar: for example, red clay earth is used in outdoor scenes.[32] The facial type of Jesus in the scene among the doctors at Rubielos is similar to that of St. Prudencio in the scene of his consecration in Tarazona. Both have pudgy faces, arched eyebrows, small eyes and mouths, features that appear to sit on the surface rather emerging from the planes of the face. Their idealization contrasts with the Jewish figures in the scene of Jesus among the doctors, whose faces are individualized by features such as large noses. The Jews hold books with accurately formed Hebrew letters that suggest the texts were written by someone who had studied the Hebrew language, not surprising if the painter came from the de Leví's atelier. The *sottobanco*, the lowest register of the altarpiece, at the eye level of the viewers, is devoted to the depiction of twelve Hebrew prophets, an unusually large number on one *retablo* and a reflection of the significance of prophetic writings in Christian attempts to convince Jews to convert. Other converso artists who painted altarpieces were Nicolás and Bonanat Zahortiga, who were active in the first quarter of the fifteenth century.[33] Among their works is a large *retablo* for the collegiate church of Santa María de Borja.

Jews were also subjects on Spanish *retablos* in scenes that were sometimes laudatory and in others depicted persecution: representation of biblical worthies like King David or the Prophets; portrayals of libels like the desecration of the host; forced baptism;

---

known that conversos often had dealings with one another, and a similar sense of fraternity may have led Bishop Fernando to commission the altarpiece for his brother's tomb from Juan de Leví in 1408.

[31] Ainaga Andrés, et al., *Retablo de Juan de Leví y su restauración*, 11.

[32] Ainaga Andrés, et al., *Retablo de Juan de Leví y su restauración*, 37.

[33] On the Zahortigas, see José María Azcárte, *Arte gotica en* España *(Madrid: Ediciones Cátedra, 2007, 343; Berg Sobré, *Behind the Altar Table*, 18 passim; F. Olivan Bayle, *Bonanat y Nicolás Zahortiga y la pitura del siglo XV* (Saragossa: Ayuntimento de Zaragoza, Comisión de la Cultura, 1978).

and scenes from early and contemporary church history. A scene expressing the uneasy relationship between Jews and Christians in the late Middle Ages is the Disputation between Moses and St. Peter, a predella panel of an altarpiece dedicated to the Mother of God painted for the Monastery of Santes Creus by Pere Serra, Guerau Gener, and Lluís Borassa in the early fifteenth century.[34] The subject is based on actual debates between Church prelates and rabbis, in which Jews were forced to participate. An unusual feature of the painting is that Moses holds a decalogue with accurately written Hebrew inscriptions, while Peter's scroll is blank, an indication that the artist did not know Latin, but did know Hebrew and was a Jew or a Converso.

Representations of contemporary reality infiltrated historical scenes like the episodes from the lives of Jesus and early saints that surrounded the central image of the holy figure who was the focus of the altarpiece. For example, late medieval Jews appear in a presentation of Jesus in the Temple, part of the *retablo* in the Church of San Salvador in Ejea de los Caballeros painted by Blasco de Grañén and Martín de Soria beginning ca. 1440 (fig. 5).[35] In this painting, the primary Christian figures of Jesus and Mary are idealized in their form and dress and crowned by circular haloes whose shape symbolizes perfection. The Jewish figures of the narrative, Joseph and the High Priest, possessed of a lesser degree of holiness, wear cusped haloes above faces that are individualized and portrait-like in contrast to the ethereal, blemish-free figures of Jesus and Mary. The Jews' appearance also reflects discriminatory regulations enacted by the kings of Spain after the Lateran Council. The influential law code of Alfonso X of Castile (1252-84) elaborates on this point:[36]

---

[34] Francesc Ruiz y Queseda, ed., *L'Art Gòtic a Catalunya. Pintura II: El corrent internacional* (Barcelona: Enciclopèdia Catalana, 2005), 44-45. The disputation scene is incorrectly labeled as a depiction of "Prophets."

[35] On the Ejea *retablo*, see María del Carmen Lacarra Ducay, *Blasco de Grañén, pintor de retablos (1422-1459)* (Saragossa: Institución "Fernando el Católico," 2004), 44-90; María del Carmen Lacarra Ducay, "Retablo de San Salvador: Ejea de los Caballeros," in *Joyas de un Patrimonio* (Saragossa: Diputación de Zaragoza, 1990), 12-79. Some of the costs of the Ejea altarpiece was financed by a loan from Faym Baco, a Jew of Albalate de Cinca. (Achivio Parroquial de Ejea, *Sección Pergaminos*, s/n. Ejea, 19 de febrero de 1472).

[36] Jacob Rader Marcus, *The Jew in the Medieval World: A Source Book: 315-1791.* 2nd ed. (Cincinnati: Hebrew Union College Press, 1990), 39-40.

Many crimes and outrageous things occur between Christians and Jews because they live together in cities, and dress alike; and in order to avoid the offenses and evils which take place for this reason, we deem it proper and we order that all Jews, male and female, living in our dominions shall bear some distinguishing mark upon their heads so that people may plainly recognize a Jew, or a Jewess.

Fig. 5. Blasco de Grañén (a. 1438-54), "Presentation of Jesus in the Temple," Altarpiece of San Salvador, Ejea de los Caballeros, ca. 1441-1459.

Alfonso's father-in-law, James I of Aragon, decreed in 1263 that his Jewish subjects wear a dark cloak out-of-doors emblazoned with a rotulus[37] and, in 1412, Jews and Muslims were prohibited from trimming their hair and beards so that unkempt hair became a compulsory sign of alterity.[38] The imposition of these restrictions

---

[37] For a discussion of clothing restrictions, see Jonathan Ray, *The Sephardic Frontier: The Reconquista and the Jewish Community in Medieval Iberia* (Ithaca: Cornell University Press, 2006), 156-64.

[38] Wild hair was a sign that also marked heretics in the *Bible Moralisée*, the large picture Bibles written and illuminated in the first half of the thirteenth century for the kings of France. Jews were often conflated with heretics. (Sara Lipton, *Images of Intolerance: The Representation of Jews and Judaism in the* Bible Moralisée, [Berkeley: University of California Press, 1999] 86-87.)

provoked the following response from the Spanish Jew Solomon Alami (1370-1420):

> We have suffered measure for measure. Because we adopted their dress, they required different vestments so that we would seem to be strangers among them, and because we shortened the corners of our hair and beards, they forced us to let our hair grow as if we were plunged into deep mourning.[39]

The presence of recognizable Jews in Christological scenes served to underscore the Christianity of holy figures, much as black figures in exotic clothes emphasized the European character of those who sat for portraits during the Renaissance. Differences in the clothing or appearance of the Jews reinforced their Otherness. That these regulations were necessary suggests the visual homogeneity of the Spanish population, a homogeneity that required artificial means of differentiation.[40] In other words, Jews and Christians looked very much alike. On the Iberian Peninsula, sartorial differentiation had first been instituted by the Muslim rulers of Al-Andalus, to signify the subordinate status of *dhimmi* or protected minorities.[41] Some articles of dress required by the Muslims, such as the *zunnar*, a rope belt, appear in the later Christian art of Aragon, for example, in a scene of the Expulsion of Joachim and Anna from the Temple. The designation of clothing as a symbol of minority status was part of a general medieval view of dress as denoting class or occupation and an individual's place in society.[42] They were not "fashion" in the contemporary use of the term. The dingy clothing and wild hair of

---

[39] Solomon Alami, *Iggeret haMusar [Treatise on Moral Behavior]*. The mention of deep mourning refers to the Jewish prohibition against shaving and haircutting while in mourning for a close relative.

[40] Janina M. Safran, "Identity and Differentiation in Ninth-Century Al-Andalus," *Speculum* 76 (2001), 582.

[41] Cohen, *Under Crescent & Cross*, 62-64; Safran, "Identity and Differentiation in Ninth-Century al-Andalus," 582-83. The *zunnar* or rope belt worn by Joachim was required of dhimmi or minority populations in Muslim lands as early as the reign of the Abassid caliph al-Mutawakkil in the mid-ninth century; he also required a hood *(taylasan)* and a conical cap (qalansuwa). The caliph's specification that the *zunnar* be made of rope or cord marked a turning point in the meaning of the belt. Once a sign of honor, its material requirements transformed the *zunnar* into a sign of degradation, of second-class status.

[42] Ann Rosalind and Jones & Peter Stallybrass, *Renaissance Clothing and the Materials of Memory* (Cambridge: Cambridge University Press, 2002), 54-55.

Jews were signs of their exclusion from Christian society and of their defeat by a victorious Christianity.

The presence of discriminatory markers on Jews in the Ejea Presentation of Jesus in the Temple are a contemporary intrusion into the subject, as is the setting of the scene in a Gothic building with detailed pier capitals. That the building is not a church but a synagogue is indicated by the Torah Case or *tik* that is on the altar. A cylindrical case of wood or silver to hold a Torah scroll upright in the synagogue first came into use during the eleventh century in the Maghrib in the same period that the Qur'an box became a feature of mosques.[43] It was used in Spain until the Expulsion, as an alternative to textile coverings (mantles) for the Torah scroll. That the cylindrical case was understood as a Jewish appurtenance is explicit in a version of the "Presentation in the Temple" on the Retablo de la Gozos de la Virgin, dated ca. 1449/50 (Valencia: Museo de Bella Artes, n° Inv. 278) where the *tik* on the altar bears a band of Pseudo-Kufic Arabic script around its middle; the Kufic writing substitutes for Hebrew. A 1515 scene of Jesus among the doctors on the main altarpiece in the Real Monasterio de Santa María de Sijena in Aragon includes a partially open *tik* revealing two round-topped Tablets of the Law with five lines of "writing" on each, corresponding to the Ten Commandments. Another detail of the Ejea panel, Joseph's basket with two doves, the post-partum Temple offering of a woman of modest means, indicates that the architecture is meant to be understood as the Temple, although its form reflects contemporary synagogues. In other words, if the Jews of the late Middle Ages could be construed as representatives of Jews alive during the early history of the Church, by the same reasoning the contemporary Jewish house of worship could serve as a stand-in for the Temple of antiquity.[44] Another "Presentation of Jesus" in the Hispanic Society of New York

---

[43] Vivian B. Mann, "The Covered Gospels, the Torah Case and the Qur'an Box," *Art & Ceremony in Jewish Life: Essays in the History of Jewish Art* (London: Pindar Press, 2005), 177-94.

[44] The one exception to the modeling of the Temple on local synagogues is a scene of the Presentation of Jesus on an altarpiece in Palencia, in which all the figures stand in a hexagonal structure with a domed roof. Medieval circular or polygonal structures were thought to imitate the Church of the Holy Sepulchre, the most important Christian building in Jerusalem. (Richard Krautheimer, "Introduction to an Iconography of Medieval Architecture," *Studies in Early Christian, Medieval and Renaissance Art* [New York: New York University Press and London University Press Limited, 1969], 115-50.)

includes further contemporary details: a curved circumcision knife and a beaker to hold wine blessed after the circumcision.

In fact, all scenes on the *retablos* that were supposed to have taken place in the Temple are shown in synagogue spaces: The Presentation of Jesus in the Temple (sometimes represented as his Circumcision), the most commonly depicted Temple narrative; Jesus Speaking to the Doctors; The Annunciation to Zacharias, the father of John the Baptist; and The High Priest Expelling Joachim and Anna from the Temple. All of these scenes are staged in Gothic buildings that are sometimes a combination of nave-like spaces and apses or are simply rectangular halls. One *retablo* includes another detail, an outside staircase leading to a second storey,[45] presumably providing access to the women's balcony found in several synagogues, for example in Córdoba, and Toledo (El Transito). The identification of these painted buildings as synagogue spaces depends on the placement of a *tik* or cylindrical case for the Torah on the altar and the absence of any Christian accoutrements such as a cross. In the "Expulsion of Joachim and Anna," a noteworthy detail is the decoration of the *tik* with a scarf or cloth, a custom still practiced in the Sephardi diaspora and in eastern Jewish communities today.

A scene of the Annunciation to Zacharias, the saint's father, of the impending birth of his son is at the top left on a *retablo* dedicated to St. John the Baptist now in The Cloisters in New York (No. 25.120.929; fig. 6). According to Christian lore, Zacharias was an ordinary priest in the Temple, but in an extraordinary scene on the New York altarpiece, Zacharias perform the duties of the High Priest on Yom Kippur, the Day of Atonement, the holiest day of the Jewish year. A priest holds a chain attached to the leg of Zacharias who entered the Holy of Holies alone, so that should he die or faint in the divine presence, his body could be retrieved. Small bells were sewn to the hem of the High Priest's skirt so that those outside would know that he was performing his duties and was not in distress. Yet, as in other *retablo* depictions of the Temple, there is a Torah case on the altar, which is a synagogue appurtenance. The service depicted in this extremely detailed and particularized scene is based on the Jewish mystical text the *Zohar*, which first appeared in Castile in

---

[45] Rosa Alcoy i Pedrós, *L'Art gòtic a Catalunya: I. De l'inicio a l'italianisme* (Barcelona: Enciclopèdia Catalana, 2005), 189.

the late thirteenth century. The wealth of detail suggests that the Christian artist Domingo Ram (a. 1464-1507) either consulted with a rabbi or had a Jewish assistant.

Recent excavations in the Murcian town of Lorca prove the accuracy of the synagogue architecture painted on *retablos*. In 2003, the remains of a synagogue were found near the local fortress, consisting of a vestibule leading to a rectangular hall whose perimeter is surrounded by stone benches. The ruins of the Torah ark are on one of the short ends and the center of the hall is filled with the remains of a reader's desk that was reached by a flight of steps. A painted version of this synagogue type appears in a *retablo* panel now in the Metropolitan Museum in New York (No. 32.100.423; fig. 7), where the scene is enlivened by Jewish worshippers seated along the walls and by Mary and Joseph watching Jesus ascend the steps of the *teivah* or reader's desk. The space is illuminated by glass "mosque" lamps and, in a case of life imitating art, a large cache of glass shards was found beneath the *teivah* at Lorca and the lamps were reconstructed.[46]

Fig. 6. Domingo Ram (a. 1464-1507), "Annunciation to Zacharias," Altarpiece of Saint John the Baptist, 1480.

---

[46] Juan García Sandoval, "El Resplandor de las Lámparas de Vidrio de la Sinagoga de Lorca. Estudio Tipológico," *Lorca. Luces de Sefarad*: 259-304.

The substitution of contemporary synagogue buildings for the ancient Temple in these works may have been due to the fact that the actual appearance of the Temple was unknowable to medieval men and woman.[47] Or the substitution may have been encouraged by a common Jewish usage that terms the synagogue a "small sanctuary" (*mikdash me'at*), a play on the name of the Temple in Jerusalem, the *beit ha-mikdash*, the House of Sanctuary. In medieval Spain, the phrase was used in the Hebrew dedicatory inscription of the Córdoba synagogue:

> Isaac Mehab, son of the honorable Ephraim, has completed this lesser sanctuary (*mikdash me'at*) and he built it in the year 75 [1314-1315] as a temporary abode. Hasten, O God, to rebuild Jerusalem.[48]

Fig. 7. Anonymous, "Jesus among the Doctors," Catalonia, early fifteenth century.

Of the architecture associated with Jewish life in the Crown of Aragon, the most common form still standing is the arcuated gate to the *judería*, the Jewish quarter. The use of this defining structure

---

[47] Walter Cahn, "Solomonic Elements in Romanesque Art," in *The Temple of Solomon: Archaeological Fact and Medieval Tradition in Christian, Islamic and Jewish Art*, ed. Joseph Gutmann (Missoula: Scholar's Press, 1976), 58.

[48] For the Hebrew original, see Mann, et al., *Convivencia: Jews, Muslims and Christians in Medieval Spain*, 216.

to situate an episode from fourth-century Christian history within the ambience of late-fifteenth-century Jewish life is evident in a portrayal of Saint Helena in the Holy Land questioning Judas, a Jew who claimed to have knowledge of the burial spot of the True Cross (fig. 8). The scene is part of an altarpiece devoted to the True Cross by Miguel Jiménez and Martín Bernat painted in 1485-1487 for the Parish Church of Santa Cruz de Blesa in Teruel. It is staged on local Jewish turf, just inside the arcuated gate to an Aragonese *judería*, while the house behind is based on the architecture of Jewish houses still existing in former Jewish quarters. In this painting, the *judería* symbolizes the land of the Jews, the Holy Land.

Fig. 8. Martín Bernat (1469-1497) and Miguel Jiménez (ca. 1466-1505), "Saint Helena Questioning Judas," Altarpiece of the True Cross from the Parochial Church of Santa Cruz de Blesa (Teruel), 1481-1487.

The scene of St. Helena is also remarkable for its representation of fifteenth-century dress. The Jew Judas is dressed in the dark cloak mandated by decree of Pedro III of Aragon in 1263; his hair and beard grow wild because of the decree of 1412. But Helena and her ladies are dressed in rich silks and jewels. She wears a red gown with ermine cuffs and hem, a silk brocade cloak with gold threads and an elaborate crown. The lady directly behind her wears a diadem with bosses that imitate pearls. In the High Middle Ages, scarlet cloth gave status to the wearer and was reserved for the elite, and silk brocade was a mark of royalty.[49] Various sources indicate that wealthy Jews were capable of wearing clothing similar to the robes of royalty depicted on the altarpieces. According to the sumptuary laws passed at a meeting of Castilian Jews convened at Valladolid in 1432:[50]

> No woman unless unmarried or a bride in the first year of her marriage, shall wear costly dresses of gold-cloth, or olive colored material [a Chinese silk] or fine linen or silk, or of fine wool. Neither shall they wear on their dresses trimming of velvet or brocade or olive-colored cloth. Nor shall they wear a golden brooch nor one of pearls, nor a string of pearls on the forehead, nor dresses with trains on the ground more than one third of a *vara* in measure, nor fringed Moorish garments, nor coats with high collars, nor cloth of high reddish color, nor a skirt of *hermeia* thread...nor shall they make wide sleeves on Moorish garments of more than two palms in width, but they may wear jewelry like silver broaches and silver belts provided that there is not more than four ounces of silver on any of them.

Although not identified as such in the sumptuary laws, the bridal costumes described are similar to the royal dress of Helena and her courtiers. Nevertheless, the Jewish women in the open windows of the house in the background of the scene wear subdued dresses and headgear. The artist created a single, nuanced facial type and

---

[49] Françoise Piponnier & Perrine Mane, *Dress in the Middle Ages*, trans. Caroline Beamish (New Haven: Yale University Press, 2007), 16, 20.

[50] Yolanda Moreno Koch, "De iure hispano-hebraico: Las Taqqanot de Valladolid de 1432. Un estato comunal renovador," *Fontes Iudaeorum Regni Castellae*, V (1987): 9-105. In 1456, the Jewish community of Morvedre passed sumptuary laws regulating Jewish women's dress and the amount of jewelry that could be worn in order to prevent ostentatious display that might lead to an increase in taxes. (Meyerson, *A Jewish Renaissance in Fifteenth-Century Spain*, 89.)

then used it for all four women, but varied their dresses, which have different necklines and trim and are of differently colored textiles. Emphasis is given to the rendering of the white silk sleeves that appear to be a separate garment worn together with the gowns, like those described in the sumptuary laws. Despite the rich details on these panels, there is an air of tension to the confrontation between Helena and Judas that is generated by the sober expressions of the figures. The depiction of the Christian Queen Helena interrogating the Jew, Judas, may have been intended to reflect the activities of the Inquisition, established in Aragon in the second half of the thirteenth century.

Fig. 9. Workshop of Jaime Huguet, Exodus from Egypt, Altarpiece of Saint Bernardi and the Guardian Angel, 1462-82.

The identification of Jewish women in Christian art of the fourteenth and fifteenth centuries depends on their clothing and the narrative context in which they are seen, since they lacked the identifying beards of Jewish men and their hair was generally covered. One of the scenes from the Hebrew Bible, an Exodus from Egypt included in the *Retablo de San Bernardi i l'Angel Custodi* of 1462-82 (Barcelona: Diocesan Museum), is the work of a painter from the atelier of the Christian artist Jaime Huguet (fig. 9).[51] The

---

[51] Joan Molina i Figueras, "Al Voltant de Jaume Huguet," *L'Art Gòtic a Catalunya: Pintura III. Darreres manifestacions* (Barcelona: Enciclopèdia Catalana, 2006, 142-43).

panel preserves the traditional v-shaped composition in which the drowning Egyptians appear in a lower corner, while the Israelites stride along the Red Sea, a composition that appeared in early Christian and Jewish art.[52] A manuscript or copy book may have been the means by which this iconography was transmitted from the east to medieval Spain. Although the scene is composed traditionally, the Israelites are represented as contemporary Jews. The painter took great care to individualize their faces and to vary their dress. The foremost Jewish figures, representing Moses and Aaron, are thought to be portraits of the leading Jewish residents of the Catalan town of Banyoles where the *retablo* first hung. The figure guided by the Guardian Angel is tentatively identified as Bonjuà Cabrit, who was doctor-surgeon to the Royal House of Barcelona.[53] He wears a striped garment over his head, probably a *tallit*, or prayer shawl, and a gold-bordered cloak, and carries a codex with gilt edges. Although most of the women leaving Egypt wear simple scarves over their heads, one near the end of the procession wears an elaborate headdress with chin strap that forms a roll around her head and has a protruding element at top dotted with pearls. Attention is drawn to this elaborately dressed woman by her bright red cloak, which visually links her to Bonjuà Cabrit, the man at the head of the procession who may have been her husband.[54] The same headdress worn in the Exodus is used on Christian sculptures and altarpieces to identify Jewish women, which indicates that this headgear was considered distinctive. It appears, for example, on a *retablo* panel of the Massacre

---

[52] For the composition on the Via Latina fresco, see Kurt Weitzmann, *The Age of Spirituality: Late Antique and Early Christian Art, Third to the Seventh Century* (New York: Metropolitan Museum of Art, 1979), fig. 43; on the mosaic in Sta. Maria Maggiore, see Wolfgang Fritz Volbach, *Early Christian Art* (New York: Harry N. Abrams, 1962), fig. 129.

[53] Bonjuà Cabrit is cited in legal records as possessing a copy of *Avicenna* that was stolen from Meir of Figueras, the son of a deceased physician. (Robert I. Burns, *Jews in the Notarial Culture: Latinate Wills in Mediterranean Spain 1250-1350* [Berkeley: University of California Press, 1996], 64).

[54] See Roth, *The Sarajevo Haggada*, no pagination; and Narkiss, *Hebrew Illuminated Manuscripts in the British Isles*, fig. 209. Knowledge of this headdress spread to Germany by the beginning of the fifteenth century. In a scene of the birth of Mary on the Buxtehuder Altar, Meister Bertram painted the woman serving Elizabeth wearing a headdress with chin strap and circular element atop her head. (Jürgen Wittstock,ed., *Aus dem Alltag der mittelalterlichen Stadt: Hefte des Focke Museums, no. 62* [1982]: 165, fig. 7.)

of the Innocents dated 1390-1400, now in the Saragossa Museum,[55] and worn by a group of women on a fourteenth-century capital in the cloister of Barcelona Cathedral.[56] In Jewish art, such as the seder scenes in the Sarajevo Haggadah (Sarajevo, National Museum) and in the Sister of the Golden Haggadah (London, British Library, Or, 2884; fig. 13), the women wear elaborate pleated headcoverings with a raised flower-like element in the center of the forehead.

The profound knowledge of Jewish beliefs and customs evident on the altarpieces could have been the result of the employment of Jewish artists or conversos on a project, but it also could have been due to the small size of villages like Ejea, whose parish churches commissioned *retablos* from major artists. In small towns and cities, the mingling of Jewish, Christian, and even Muslim residents was inevitable. At the time Blasco de Grañen and Martín de Soria painted its altarpiece, Ejea was home to some 250 Jews out of a total population of a thousand.[57] In addition, Jewish scholars became knowledgeable about Christian lore as the result of their own interest or out of the need to counter the claims made by Church spokesmen, often conversos, in disputations and conversionist sermons. They voluntarily attended sermons in churches and cathedrals,[58] where they could have been exposed to scenes from the Hebrew Bible on altarpieces and on sculpture. Christians attended sermons in synagogues out of curiosity, and their firsthand experience of Jewish houses of worship could have served as the inspiration for scenes on *retablos*. All the ways that Christians and Jews mixed in the fourteenth and fifteenth century, for business, as doctors attending patients, as workers and servants in each other's home, as artists

[55] Alfredo Romero Santamaría, ed., *Hebraica aragonalia: El legado judío en Aragón*, vol. 1 (Saragossa: Palacio de Sastago - Diputación de Zaragoza, 2002), 155.

[56] For the capital, see Elena Romero, ed., *La Vida Judía en Sefarad* (Toledo: Ministerio de Educacion y Cultura, 1991), 60.
Until early in the twentieth century, the Jewish women of Salonica wore headdresses whose constituent elements were similar to those depicted in Spanish art, but whose proportions were somewhat different. (Batsheva Goldman-Ida, "The Sephardic Woman's Head-Dress," in *From Iberia to Diaspora: Studies in Sephardic History and Culture*, ed. Yedida K. Stillman and Norman A. Stillman (Leiden: Brill, 1999), 525-30.

[57] Miguel Angel Motis Dolader, *Los Judíos en Aragon en la Edad Media (Siglos XIII-XV)* (Aragon: Caja de Ahorros de la Inmaculada, 1990), 52.

[58] Ram Ben-Shalom, "Between Official and Private Dispute: The Case of Christian Spain and Provence in the Late Middle Ages," *AJS Review* 27 (2003): 30, 35.

and artisans, and as colleagues exploring intellectual issues, allowed exposure to each other's way of life and art.

But, we must ask: what was the effect of the art created during the fourteenth and fifteenth centuries on its viewers? The Jewish art remaining from Spain largely consists of manuscripts, although recent excavations have brought to light more ceremonial objects and visual culture.[59] Most of the illuminated manuscripts are Bibles and haggadot, although other genres like philosophical and scientific treatises exist. Manuscripts were an art form that was enjoyed privately in the Middle Ages. The opposite is true of the Christian *retablos*. Altarpieces are definitely public art meant to teach, to inspire, and to invest the church with grandeur.[60] The artists' practice of populating scenes from the Gospels and the lives of saints with figures modeled on local Jews, who were dressed in costumes visible in the course of daily life, whose unkempt hair and beards were the result of royal edicts, must have had an effect on the worshippers standing before large and impressive altarpieces. These depictions attempted to brand contemporary Jewry with the guilt of their ancestors, who tormented Christ and the martyrs of the church.[61] The portrayals were reminders of the Christian doctrine that the Jews of any era were equivalent to those alive during the early centuries of the Church. Jews were witnesses to the truth of Christianity and were, therefore, allowed to survive; still they embodied the guilt of their ancestors. The negative message of historical scenes was compounded by representations of contemporary arenas of conflict between Jews and Christians. Two altarpieces from the Cistercian monastery of Vallbona de los Monges painted in 1349-50 with their scenes of the Desecration of the Host were expressions of anti-Judaism linking the Black Plague to Jewish transgressions.[62]

[59] Angel Iniesta Sanmartin, et al., *Lorca. Luces de Sefarad* (Murcia: Industrias Gráficos Libecom, 2009); Isidro Bango Treviso, *Memoria de la Sefarad* (Madrid: Sociedad Estatal para la Acción Cultural Exterior, 2002), 111-29, 142-57.

[60] Michael Baxandall, *Patterns of Intention. On the Historical Explanation of Pictures* (New Haven: Yale University Press, 1985), 106.

[61] Jonathan Elukin, *Living Together, Living Apart: Rethinking Jewish-Christian Relations in the Middle Ages* (Princeton: Princeton University Press, 2007), 4.

[62] Carmen Muñoz Párraga, "Los Judíos en Aragón: Del Mundo del Medievo al del Renacimento," in *Encrucijada de Culturas* (Saragossa: Típolinea, 2008), 104. For the altarpieces, see Alcoy i Pedrós, *L'Art gòtic a Catalunya: I. De l'inicio a l'italianisme*, 127-29.

Another arena of conflict was the conversionist sermon that became a popular tactic of Christians seeking to convert Jews after 1242, when James I of Aragon and other secular rulers permitted Christian missionaries to preach in synagogues.[63] Scenes of conversionist sermons appear on altarpieces dedicated to St. Stephen, who was known as a zealous preacher and died in Jerusalem ca. 35 CE. A *retablo* by Jaime Serra ca. 1385 shows St. Stephen in a Gothic building that might be a church or a synagogue, flanked by Jewish men who are reacting to his sermon (fig. 10). Interestingly, given the placement of the representation on an altarpiece, the Jews are shown responding in diverse ways to what they have heard. An elderly man in the right foreground holds his Bible or prayer book up to the saint and appears to argue with Stephen. Behind him is a man who covers his ears in order not to hear blasphemy, and between the two is a man tearing up his Hebrew book having been convinced by the saint to abandon Judaism. The same actions are repeated by the Jews standing at left. Similar responses are depicted in a scene of Jesus before the Doctors on a contemporaneous *retablo* by Lluís Borrassà.[64] Unlike Jews' attendance at Christian sermons out of intellectual curiosity, these scenes record a different, malevolent purpose.

Fig. 10. Jaime Serra (a. 1358-89), "St. Stephen Preaching to Jews," Altarpiece of St. Stephen from the Church of Santa Maria de Gualter, La Noguera, ca. 1385.

---

[63] See, for example, a discussion of medieval Jews' knowledge of Christianity in Robert Chazan, *Fashioning Jewish Identity in Medieval Western Christendom*, (Cambridge: Cambridge University Press, 2005), 324-329.

[64] Elena Romero, *La Vida Judía en Sefarad*, 72.

There are two unusual renderings of the Miracle of the Loaves and the Fishes that express a reconciliation of Jews and Christians, albeit in a Christian context. On the altarpiece of San Salvador in Ejea de los Caballeros (fig. 11) and on the Altarpiece of the Transfiguration painted by Bernat Martorell between 1445 and 1452, the stream of people approaching Jesus is made up of both Christians and Jews, the Jewish men identifiable by their dark cloaks and untrimmed hair and beards. This treatment of the subject reflects the teachings of ecclesiastics such as Abbot Joachim of Fiore (ca. 1135-1202), who saw a future in which Jews and Christians would join as one flock.[65] On another *retablo* painted by Martorell ca. 1435-45 on the theme of St. John the Baptist, two scenes on the right present Christians and Jews acting together.[66] Both Christian and Jewish women attend Anna in a scene of the birth of the saint, and St. John preaches to a mixed group of Jews and Christians.

Fig. 11. Blasco de Grañén (a. 1438-54) and Martín de Soria (a. 1454-76), "Miracle of the Loaves and the Fishes," Altarpiece of San Savador, Parish Church of Ejea de los Caballeros, 1454

[65] Robert E. Lerner, *The Feast of Saint Abraham: Medieval Millenarians and the Jews* (Philadelphia: University of Pennsylvania Press, 2001), 1.

[66] For an illustration see Francesc Ruiz i Quesada, ed., *L'Art Gòtic a Catalunya. Pintura II: El corrent internacional,* 239.

Joachim of Fiore was perhaps the first theorist of incremental progress ending in a "mutually beneficial union of Christians and Jews."[67] His ideas spread throughout western Europe in the books of his followers, among them Arnold of Villanova, influential in Spain in the early years of the fourteenth century, and in writings of the Franciscan monk Francesc Eiximenis, born in Girona in 1327, who served Peter the Ceremonious of Aragon (1336-87) and other members of the royal family.[68] Eiximenis' writings, which spread Joachite ideology throughout Spain, were written in the last quarter of the fourteenth century. The Franciscan expanded Joachim's philosophy to include the concept that the "saints" of the Old Testament would be venerated along with those of the New: that is Saint Abraham, Saint David, Saint Isaiah and others.[69] A reflection of this syncretist vision may be the altarpiece scenes discussed above and the many portraits of Israelite kings and prophets on the *retablos*, although the prophets served a dual role as predictors of the coming of Jesus as the Messiah.

The record of Jewish life on the altarpieces of Aragon is a precious one. Manuscripts were the only art form Jews were allowed to take with them into exile in 1492, and the few genre scenes they contain yield only a partial glimpse of Jewish life. The figures that inhabit the miniatures of the preparations for and celebration of Passover in the haggadot are mostly stereotypical. But the larger scale of the altarpieces and the superior skill of their artists afford us actual, particularized portraits of Jews who lived in the fourteenth and fifteenth centuries and details of their dress and their surroundings. Some of the paintings include Jewish figures as part of the daily life of medieval Aragon, like the shoemakers of a *retablo* now in Manresa, or the Jew on horseback depicted behind the Virgin Mary in a Pietà by Barolomé Cárdenas of 1490.[70] A similar rider is shown leaving a

[67] Lerner, *The Feast of Saint Abraham: Medieval Millenarians and the Jews*, 19 and 24.

[68] Marjorie Reeves, *The Influence of Prophecy in the Later Middle Ages: A Study in Joachimism* (Notre Dame: University of Notre Dame Press, 1993), 221.

[69] Lerner, *The Feast of Saint Abraham: Medieval Millenarians and the Jews*, 110.

[70] For the shoemakers, see Vivian B. Mann, *Uneasy Communion: Jews, Christians and the Altarpieces of Medieval Spain* (New York: Museum of Biblical Art and D. Giles Limited, 2010), 81-85; for the horseman, see J. M. Martí Bonet, *La Cathedral de Barcelona* (Barcelona: Editorial Escudo de Oro and Arxiu Diocesà de Barcelona, n.d.), 111.

city on an altarpiece in Palma de Mallorca.[71] Their inclusion on the *retablos* exemplifies the social interaction that characterized Iberian society, and which has been termed *convivencia*.[72]

The broad nature of Jewish participation in the art of painting on the Iberian Peninsula is indicated by a treatise on colors, the *Libro de Como se Fazen as Cores*, written by Abraham Ibn Hayyim during the late thirteenth century.[73] Abraham wrote his manuscript in 1262 in Judeo-Portuguese, which presumes that there was an audience of other Jewish artists who could understand the text. At the time Abraham composed the twenty-eight chapters of his *Libro*, the first translations of early treatises describing techniques of painting, glassmaking and metalworking appeared. The number of color recipes in Abraham's book, which is greater than those found in the popular *Various or Divers Arts* by Theophilus, indicates that the author used an additional source for his own work.

Only one work of art produced by a Jew survives from the period of Islamic rule. It is an extraordinary work in silver with a Kufic inscription noting it was made for the caliph Alhakem, by the Jew Juden ben Bazla.[74] It is now in the museum of the Girona Cathedral. The prominence of Jews in silversmithing even after the *Reconquista* may be a heritage from their roles in areas previously under Muslim rule, since the *hadith*, the religious traditions of Islam, viewed metalworking as degrading and left it to Jews. Bonafós Abenxueu, who made the frame for the La Seo altarpiece by Abraham de Salinas, was a silversmith, one of the many Jewish silversmiths of Saragossa, who were numerous enough to support their own synagogue.[75] Confraternities of artists and craftsmen, both Jewish and Christian, organized to protect their religious concerns and for mutual support in areas of social welfare, were more numerous in Aragon than

---

[71] Montserrat Blanch, *El Arte Gotico en España* (Barcelona: Ediciones Poligrafa, 1972), 316.

[72] Ray, *The Sephardic Frontier*, 174.

[73] S. Blondheim, trans., "An Old Portuguese Work on Manuscript Illumination," *Jewish Quarterly Review*, 19 N. S. (1928-29): 97-135.

[74] For a photograph, see Jerrilynn Dodds, *El Andalus* (New York: Metropolitan Museum of Art, 1992), 64-65; for the inscription see Gabriel Roura, *L'arquet aràbiga d'Al-Hakam, Girona Carolíngia* (Girona: Diputació de Girona y Ajuntament de Girona, 1980).

[75] Blasco Martínez, "Pintores y Orfebres Judíos en Zaragoza (Siglo XIV)," 120. The Jewish weavers' guild of Catalyud also had their own synagogue. (Wischnitzer, *A History of Jewish Crafts & Guilds*, 109.)

elsewhere in Christian Spain, and most Jewish confraternities were in Aragon, particularly in Saragossa.[76] The earliest recorded silversmith in Morella, Aragon, was the Jew Mose Alafoydar, nicknamed "the Jewish silversmith" in documents of 1334–35.[77] Mose had two brothers, Salomon and Caquo, who were also silversmiths. The Santalinea family of silversmiths who flourished in Morella during the second half of the century were conversos. In the Valencian town of Morvedre, silversmiths were the foremost artists in the Jewish community. Their work was so highly esteemed that they established branch workshops in other locales to which they regularly traveled, and apprentices from other cities came to study with them.[78] Their knowledge of the forms of church vessels could have been acquired during the times that church silver was pawned with Jews or from works given to them as models for new commissions. In 1380, the sister of the Bishop of Tarazona and the sacristan of the church in Borja pawned a silver cross, a reliquary, a censer, and an incense vessel with its ladle of silver with the Jew, Yuçe Francés.[79]

Visual representations of Jews as silversmiths under Christian rule appear in the *Vidal Mayor*, the law code of James I of Aragon dated to the second half of the thirteenth century.[80] Among the recorded cases are four involving Jews, each text accompanied by an illuminated initial. Jews are shown as silversmiths, as merchants of metalwork, as pawnbrokers (accepting metalwork as surety for a loan), and as litigants before the king in a case involving metalwork.

---

[76] Yom Tov Assis, ed., *The Jews in the Crown of Aragon: Regesta of the Cartas Reales in the Archivo de la Corona de Aragón. Part II: 1328-1493* (Jerusalem: Akademon, 1995), vii. See Miguel Angel Motis Dolader, *Los Judíos en Aragon en la Edad Media (Siglos XIII-XV)* (Aragon: Caja de Ahorros de la Inmaculada, 1990), 152-60, for an analysis of Jewish artisanal trades and their integration into the Aragonese economy.

[77] Núria de Dalmases i Balañà, "Approximción a la orfebrería morellana," *La memòria daurada: Obradors de Morellas. XIII-XVI* (n.p.: Pliego Digital, 2000), 120.

[78] Meyerson, *A Jewish Renaissance in Fifteenth-Century Spain*, 110, 129-31.

[79] Archivo Capitular de Tarazona, Protocolo de Làzaro de Larraz, 1380, fols. 22v.-23. For papal denunciations of pawning church vessels to Jews, see Solomon Grayzel, *The Church and the Jews in the XIIIth Century*, Vol. II: 1254-1314, ed. Kenneth R. Stow (New York: Jewish Theological Seminary of America and Wayne State University Press, 1989), 62-64.

[80] A. Ubierto Arteta, J. Delgado Echeverría, J. A. Frago Gracía and M. del C. Lacarra Ducay, *Vidal Mayor: Estudios* (Hesca: n. p., 1984), there the older literature; Mann, Glick and Dodds, *Convivencia*, fig. 1 and 24.

With the Expulsion of 1492, silversmiths were among those who sought refuge in North Africa, to the extent that Leo Africanus, in his description of Morocco published in 1556, wrote that the majority of the goldsmiths in Fez were Jewish. They also settled in Jerusalem, where they belonged to the same guild as Muslims.

The responsa of Rabbi Solomon ben Abraham Ibn Adret (1235–1310) reveals another métier of Jewish artists in medieval Spain. He wrote:

> Those images of crosses that women weave in their silks [made] for non-Jews should be forbidden. Nevertheless, they can be deemed permissible because non-Jews do not worship their deity in this way. The [women] make nothing with their looms but [designs] for beauty in the manner of drawings. Even though the same images are worshipped on other articles, since it is not customary to worship them in this manner, [the images are] permissible.[81]

Ibn Adret's responsum is noteworthy for the information that the Jewish women of Toledo were weavers of deluxe silk textiles in the thirteenth century. Muslims had introduced the production of silk cloth to Spain in the early tenth century, three centuries prior to its manufacture in the rest of Europe.[82] The silks produced by Muslims and Jews during the *Reconquista* were thought to be the finest in Spain, and were purchased and used by the Catholic kings and queens.[83] Jews also predominated in the production of silk in Sicily, which in 1282 became part of the Crown of Aragon. Jewish travelers, like Benjamin of Tudela in the twelfth century and Elijah of Ferrara in the fifteenth century, recorded the activity of Jewish silk weavers in many countries under both Christian and Islamic rule. The sum of all these accounts is that Jewish involvement in the weaving and trade of silk textiles was widespread in Muslim countries and in Christian Iberia.

---

[81] Isidore Epstein, *The "Responsa" of Rabbi Solomon ben Adreth of Barcelona (1235-1310) as a Source for the History of the Jews of Spain and The Responsa of Rabbi Simon b. Zemah Duran as a Source of the History of the Jews in North Africa*, 2nd ed. (New York: Ktav Publishing House, 1968), 14 and fn. 20.

[82] Juan Zozaya, "Material Culture in Medieval Spain," in Mann, Glick and Dodds, eds., *Convivencia*, 159.

[83] Concha Herrero Carretero. *Museo de Telas Medievales : Monasterio de Santa María la Real de Huelgas* (Madrid: Patrimonio Nacional, 1984), for example, 54-55, 61, 83.

Jewish artists and traders participated in transmitting artistic models and techniques from one land to another. In peaceful times, this cultural interchange took place as the result of trade. In the eleventh century, for example, a Jewish trader shipped Muslim prayer rugs from Kairouan to Iberia, according to a record found in the Cairo Geniza that is the earliest written documentation of prayer rugs.[84] Times of persecution, like the pogroms of 1391 and the Expulsions from Spain in 1492 and from Portugal in 1497, resulted in the migration of artists and the diffusion of artistic genres. For example, one third of the Jewish refugees from Spain who settled in Safed at the end of the fifteenth century engaged in the manufacture of wool and its weaving. They were familiar with textile manufacturing processes on the Iberian Peninsula, and encountered an established wool and silk industry in Safed on which they could build.

Other examples of cultural transmission by medieval Jewish artists are the introduction of Spanish weaves to Morocco, which were recreated on "Fez belts" well into the twentieth century, and the establishment of manufactories of majolica and *corami* (decorated leather wall hangings) in Italy, which bears a discussion of its own.

The production of beautiful lusterware was an art form introduced by the Arabs to Spain. The wares excavated in *juderías* such as that of Teruel can be presumed to have been used by Jews, but these works cannot be differentiated from the pottery of other population groups, unless they are painted with Jewish symbols such as the Star of David and the *hamsa*.[85] Some medieval forms appear to have been made exclusively for Jews, like a dish from Teruel with five affixed containers that appears to have been a Seder plate.[86] Fragments of ceramic Hanukkah lamps found in the Jewish quarters of Teruel, Burgos, Saragossa and Lorca are the most commonly excavated Jewish type.[87] Another ceramic, a large platter with a prominent cavetto and deep center, bears a Hebrew inscription naming the three

---

[84] Richard Ettinghausen, "Introduction," *Prayer Rugs* (Washington, DC: Textile Museum, 1974/5), 15.

[85] Isidro G. Bango Torviso, "El Menaje del hogar," *Memoria de Sefarad*, 132.

[86] Mann, Glick and Dodds, *Convivencia*, cat. no. 85.

[87] Bango Torviso, *Memoria de Sefarad*, cat. nos. 139-142; Iniesta Sanmartin, et al., *Lorca: Luces de Sefarad*, 372-85. The Saragossa example is unpublished.

most important symbols of the ritual Passover meal, the Seder.[88] A similar plate appears in the Sister of the Golden Haggadah to hold *matzot* that a householder distributes.[89]

By the mid-fifteenth century, these ceramics were imported into Italy from Mallorca, which led to their being called majolica.[90] Some of the earliest workshops were established by Jews. In the ceramics centers of Savona and Albisole near Genoa, one of the first majolica factories was established by the Salomone family, who used the hexagram as their symbol from the late fifteenth century until the twentieth, long after the family had converted to Christianity.

Another art form that arrived in Italy with the expelled Sephardim was *corami*, or painted leather hangings that functioned much as did medieval tapestries. Hung on the walls, they protected inhabitants from cold and damp and provided a luxurious shimmering surface. The center of Renaissance *corame* production was Venice, and portions of two sets of these leather hangings made for the Scuola Spagnola in that city are still extant, one from the sixteenth century,[91] in addition to others made for various patrons. The tradition of hanging *corami* in Sephardi synagogues can be seen in the decorated leather lining of the Torah ark in the Bevis Marks Synagogue of London, which was established by Sephardi immigrants. Jews in Rome both sold *corami* and rented them for special occasions.

In sum, Jewish participation in the artistic life of the Iberian Peninsula was significant and varied. Yet none of the historians concerned with the nature of Jewish–Christian coexistence in the fourteenth and fifteenth centuries has analyzed the art of the period and the history of its production as a source for understanding relationships between Christians and Jews, or as evidence for knowledge of each other's religious praxis. The fact that Jews worked as artists for Christians suggests they were knowledgeable about Christian history and beliefs, and that Christian artists demonstrated an intimate knowledge of Jewish life by setting scenes from the

---

[88] Bango Torviso, *Memoria de Sefarad*, 171.

[89] Narkiss, et al., *Hebrew Illuminated Manuscripts in the British Isles*, fig. 186.

[90] Harold Osborne, ed., *The Oxford Companion to the Decorative Arts* (Oxford and New York, 1985), 132-33.

[91] Vivian B. Mann, *Gardens and Ghettos: The Art of Jewish Life in Italy* (Berkeley: University of California Press, 1989), cat. no. 102.

Gospels and Christian lore within Jewish architectural and ceremonial contexts. Sadly, the implications of these artistic themes have thus far been ignored.[92] The failure to exploit this historical source may be due to a lack of knowledge of the art-historical methodologies necessary to an understanding of medieval works of art. With easier access to original sources made available by the computer and the internet, together with the traditional forms of scholarly exchange, we can examine the evidence anew and reexamine our assumptions regarding Jews and art in the Middle Ages.

---

[92] See, for example, a discussion of medieval Jews' knowledge of Christianity in Robert Chazan, *Fashioning Jewish Identity in Medieval Western Christendom*, 324–29. Chazan confines his discussion to the evidence of polemical literature. See also Ram Ben-Shalom, "Between Official and Private Dispute: The Case of Christian Spain and Provence in the Late Middle Ages," *AJS Review* 27:1 (2003): 23–72. Ben-Shalom discusses not only conversionist sermons and the well-known disputations at Barcelona and Tortosa, but also the various types of disputes which took place between Jews and Christians, some of them on a friendly plane.

Works Cited:

Abrahams, Israel. *Jewish Life in the Middle Ages*. Philadelphia: Jewish Publication Society, 1896.

Alami, Salomon. *Iggeret haMusar [Treatise on Moral Behavior]*. Jerusalem: Mosad ha-Rav Kook, 1946.

Alcoy i Pedrós, Rosa. *L'Art gòtic a Catalunya. I. De l'inicio a l'italianisme*. Barcelona: Enciclopèdia Catalana, 2005.

Anaga Andrés, María Teresa, et al. *Retablo de Juan de Leví y su restauración. Capilla de los Pérez Calvillo. Catedral de Tarazona*. Saragossa: Felix Arilla, 1984.

Assis, Yom Tov, ed. *The Jews in the Crown of Aragon. Regesta of the Cartas Reales in the Archivo de la Corona de Aragón. Part II: 1328-1493*. Jerusalem: Akademon, 1995.

Azcárate, José María de. *Arte gótico en España*. Madrid: Ediciones Cátedra, 2007.

Bango Torviso, Isidro. *Memoria de la Sefarad*. Madrid: Sociedad Estatal para la Acción Cultural Exterior, 2002.

Baxandall, Michael. *Patterns of Intention. On the Historical Explanation of Pictures*. New Haven and London: Yale University Press, 1985.

Bayle, F. Olivan. *Bonanat y Nicolás Zahortiga y la pitura del siglo XV*. Zaragoza: Ayuntimento de Zaragoza, Comisión de la Cultura, 1978.

Baxandall, Michael. *Painting and Experience in Fifteenth-Century Italy*. Oxford and New York: Oxford University Press, 1986.

Ben-Shalom, Ram. "Between Official and Private Dispute: The Case of Christian Spain and Provence in the Late Middle Ages." *AJS Review*, 27 (2003): 23-72.

Berg Sobré, Judith. *Behind the Altar Table. The Development of the Painted Retable in Spain, 1350-1500*. Columbia, MO: University of Missouri Press, 1989.

Blanch, Montserrat. *El Arte Gotico en España*. Barcelona: Ediciones Poligrafa, 1972.

Blasco Martínez, Asunció. "Pintores y Orfebres Judíos en Zaragoza (Siglo XIV), *Aragon en la Edad Media* 7 (1989): 113-31.

Boucher, François. *The Pamplona Bibles.* New Haven and London: Yale University Press, 1970.

Broderick, Herbert R. "Observations on the Creation Cycle of the Sarajevo Haggadah." *Zeitschrift für Kunstgeschichte* 3 (1984): 320-32.

Burns, Robert I. *Jews in the Notarial Culture. Latinate Wills in Mediterranean Spain 1250-1350.* Berkeley: University of California Press, 1996.

Cahn, Walter. "Solomonic Elements in Romanesque Art." In *The Temple of Solomon. Archaeological Fact and Medieval Tradition in Christian, Islamic and Jewish Art,* edited by Joseph Gutmann, 45-72. Missoula: Scholar's Press, 1976.

Chazan, Robert. *Fashioning Jewish Identity in Medieval Western Christendom.* Cambridge: Cambridge University Press, 2005.

Mark R. Cohen, *Under Crescent & Cross. The Jews in the Middle Ages.* Princeton: Princeton University Press, 1994.

De Dalmases i Balañà, Núria. "Approximación a la orfebrería morellana." In *La memòria daurada. Obradors de Morella s. XIII-XVI,* edited by Josep Alanyà i Roig. [Morella]: Pliego Digital, 2003.

Dodds, Jerrilynn. *El Andalus.* New York: Metropolitan Museum of Art, 1992.

Elukin, Jonathan. *Living Together. Living Apart. Rethinking Jewish-Christian Relations in the Middle Ages.* Princeton: Princeton University Press, 2007.

Epstein, Isidore. *The "Responsa" of Rabbi Solomon ben Adreth of Barcelona (1235-1310) as a Source for the History of the Jews of Spain and The Responsa of Rabbi Simon b. Zemah Duran as a Source of the History of the Jews in North Africa,* 2nd. ed. New York: Ktav Publishing House, 1968.

Ettinghausen, Richard. "Introduction," *Prayer Rugs.* Washington, DC: Textile Museum 1974/5.

Grayzel, Solomon. *The Church and the Jews in the XIIIth Century. Vol. II. 1254-1314.* Edited by Kenneth R. Stow. New York: Jewish

Theological Seminary of America and Wayne State University Press, 1989.

Goitein, S. D. *A Mediterranean Society. The Jewish Communities of the World as Portrayed in the Documents of the Cairo Geniza.* Berkeley: University of California Press, 1999.

Gutmann, Joseph. *Hebrew Manuscript Painting.* New York: George Braziller, 1978.

Herrero Carretero, Concha. *Museo de Telas Medievales. Monasterio de Santa María la Real de Huelgas.* Madrid: Patrimonio Nacional, 1984.

Herrero Gonzáles, Sonsoles. *Codices Miniados en el Real Monasterio de Las Huelgas.* Barcelona: Lunweg Editores, 1984.

Hillgarth, J. N. and Bezalel Narkiss. "A List of Hebrew Books (1330) and a Contract to Illuminate Manuscripts (1335) from Mallorca." *Revue des Études Juives*, 3rd Series, 3 (1961): 304-320.

Jones, Ann Rosalind and Peter Stallybrass. *Renaissance Clothing and the Materials of Memory.* Cambridge: Cambridge University Press, 2002.

Krautheimer, Richard. "Introduction to an Iconography of Medieval Architecture," In *Studies in Early Christian, Medieval and Renaissance Art*, edited by R. Krautheimer, 115-150. New York and London: New York University Press and London University Press Limited, 1969.

Kogman-Appel, Katrin. *Illuminated Haggadot from Medieval Spain. Biblical Imagery and the Passover Holiday.* University Park: Pennsylvania State University Press, 2006.

Lambert, Phyllis, ed. *Fortifications and the Synagogue, The Fortress of Babylonia and the Ben Ezra Synagogue, Cairo.* London: Weidenfeld & Nicolson, 1994.

Lacarra Ducay, María del Carmen. "Retablo de San Salvador. Ejea de los Caballeros." In *Joyas de un Patrimonio*, 12-79. Saragossa: Diputación de Zaragoza, et al., 1990.

------. *Blasco de Grañén, pintor de retablos (1422-1459).* Saragossa: Institución "Fernando el Católico," 2004.

Landsberger, Franz, "Jewish Artists before the Period of Emancipation," *Hebrew Union College Annual* 16 (1941): 321-414.

Lerner, Robert E. *The Feast of Saint Abraham. Medieval Millenarians and the Jews.* Philadelphia: University of Pennsylvania Press, 2001.

Lipton, Sara. *Images of Intolerance. The Representation of Jews and Judaism in the* Bible *Moralisée.* Berkeley, Los Angeles and London: University of California Press, 1999.

Mann, Vivian B. *Gardens and Ghettos. The Art of Jewish Life in Italy.* Berkeley: University of California Press, 1989.

------. *Art & Ceremony in Jewish Life. Essays in the History of Jewish Art.* London: Pindar Press, 2005.

------. *Uneasy Communion. Jews, Christians and the Altarpieces of Medieval Spain.* New York and London: Museum of Biblical Art and D. Giles Limited, 2010.

Mann, Vivian B., et al., eds. *Convivencia: Jews, Muslims and Christians in Medieval Spain.* New York: George Braziller, 1992.

Marcus, Jacob Rader, ed. *The Jew in the Medieval World. A Source Book: 315-1791.* 2nd ed. Cincinnati: Hebrew Union College Press, 1990.

Marín Padilla, Encarnación. "Un pintor Aragonés enseña a dos judíos castellanos." *Sefarad,* 47 (1987): 182-84.

Martí Bonet, J. M. *La Cathedral de Barcelone.* Barcelona: Editorial Escudo de Oro and Arxiu Diocesà de Barcelona, n.d.

Meiss, Millard. "Italian Style in Catalonia and a Fourteenth-Century Catalan Workshop." *Journal of the Walters Art Gallery* 4 (1941): 45-87.

Molina i Figueras, Joan. "Al Voltant de Jaume Huguet." In *L'Art Gòtic a Catalunya. Pintura III. Darreres manifestacions,* edited by Joan Sureda i Pons. Barcelona: Enciclopèdia Catalana, 2006.

Moreno Koch, Yolanda. *De iure hispano-hebraico. Las Taqqanot de Valladolid de 1432. Un estato comunal renovador, Fontes Iudaeorum Regni Castellae* 5. Salamanca: Universidad Pontificia de Salamanca, 1987.

Moses of Arragel, trans., *La Biblia de Alba.* Edited by Jeremy Schonfeld. Madrid: Fundación Amigos de Sefarad, 1992.

Motis Dolader, Miguel Angel. *Los Judíos en Aragon en la Edad Media (Siglos XIII-XV)*. Zaragoza: Caja de Ahorros de la Inmaculada, 1990.

Muñoz Párraga, Carmen. "Los Judíos en Aragón. Del Mundo del Medievo al del Renacimento." In *Encrucijada de Culturas*. Saragossa: Típolinea, 2008.

Narkiss, Bezalel. *Hebrew Illuminated Manuscripts*. Jerusalem: Keter Publishing, 1969.

------. *Decorated Hebrew Manuscripts*. Jerusalem: Keter Publishing, 1984. (Hebrew)

Narkiss, Bezalel et al. *Hebrew Illuminated Manuscripts in the British Isles*. Oxford: Oxford University Press, 1982.

New York Public Library. *Tesoros de España. Ten Centuries of Spanish Books*, exhibition catalogue, 1985.

Nordström, Carl-Otto. *The Duke of Alba's Castilian Bible: A Study of the Rabbinical Features of the Miniatures*. Uppsala: Almquist and Wiksells, 1967.

Piponnier, Françoise and Perrine Mane. *Dress in the Middle Ages*. Translated by Caroline Beamish. New Haven and London: Yale University Press, 2007.

Ray, Jonathan. *The Sephardic Frontier. The* Reconquista *and the Jewish Community in Medieval Iberia*. Ithaca, NY: Cornell University Press, 2006.

Reeves, Marjorie. *The Influence of Prophecy in the Later Middle Ages. A Study in Joachimism*. Notre Dame and London: University of Notre Dame Press, 1993.

Romero Santamaría, Alfredo, ed. *Hebraica aragonalia. El legado judío en Aragón*. Zaragoza: Palacio de Sastago - Diputación de Zaragoza, 2002.

Romero, Elena, ed. *La Vida Judía en Sefarad*. Toledo, 1991.

Roth, Cecil. *Sarajevo Haggadah*. Belgrade: Beogradski Izdavač-Grafički Zavod, 1975.

Roura, Gabriel. *L'arquet aràbiga d'Al-Hakam, Girona Carolíngia*. Girona: Diputació de Girona y Ajuntament de Girona, 1980.

Ruiz y Queseda, Francesc, ed. *L'Art Gòtic a Catalunya. Pintura II. El corrent internacional.* Barcelona: Enciclopèdia Catalana, 2005.

Safran, Janina M. "Identity and Differentiation in Ninth-Century Al-Andalus." *Speculum,* 76 (2001): 573-598.

Spier, Jeffrey et al. *Picturing the Bible. The Earliest Christian Art.* New Haven: Yale University Press, 2007.

Ubierto Arteta, A., J. Delgado Echeverría, J. A. Frago Gracía and M. del C. Lacarra Ducay, *Vidal Mayor: Estudios* Huesca, [n. p.], 1984.

Volbach, Wolfgang Fritz. *Early Christian Art.* New York: Harry N. Abrams, 1962.

Weitzmann, Kurt. *The Age of Spirituality. Late Antique and Early Christian Art, Third to the Seventh Century.* New York: Metropolitan Museum of Art, 1979.

Wischnitzer, Mark. *Jewish Crafts and Guilds.* New York: Jonathan David, 1965.

The Jews of Barcelona in Maritime Trade with the East

....   Yom Tov Assis

In many respects, the thirteenth century is regarded as the golden age of the Jews of Christian Spain.[1] Their involvement in economic life was very extensive. In lending money, tax farming, and domestic commerce, the Jews showed ability that aroused admiration and envy. Jews continued their vigorous economic activity long after the thirteenth century in places and fields where none could replace them.[2]

---

*This chapter is based on an article which appeared in Hebrew in *Exile and Diaspora: Studies in the History of the Jewish People Presented to Professor Haim Beinart on the Occasion of His Seventieth Birthday* (Jerusalem: Ben-Zvi Institute, 1988), 257-283.

[1] On the Jews of Christian Spain in the thirteenth and fourteenth centuries, see Yitzhak Baer, *A History of the Jews in Christian Spain* (Philadelphia: Jewish Publication Society, 1966), vol. 1, 111-378; vol. 2, 1-94. On the Jews of the Crown of Aragon, see Yom Tov Assis, *The Golden Age of Aragonese Jewry: Community and Society in the Crown of Aragon, 1213-1327* (London: Littman Library, 1997).

[2] The place of the Jews of Spain in the economic life of the country requires extensive research. For an estimate of the part of the Jews of Aragon in the kingdom's economy see: J. N. Hillgarth, *The Spanish Kingdoms 1250-1516* (Oxford: Clarendon, 1976) vol. 240; Baer, *History,* 1, 197- 212. On the Jews in the economic life of the Crown of Aragon, see Yom Tov Assis, *Jewish Economy in the Medieval Crown of Aragon, 1213-1327; Money and Power* (Leiden: Brill, 1997).

Envy and anger at their economic activity distressed the Jewish businessmen, of course, but so long as no serious competitors arose who were ready and able to replace them, their activity was not fundamentally harmed. According to all the evidence, the extent of loans made by Jews to every stratum of society steadily grew in many areas of Spain. Toward the end of the thirteenth century, there was a considerable rise in this area, which provoked opposition and criticism among various circles.[3] The decisions of the Cortes in Catalonia during the thirteenth century express the resentment of these circles, chiefly the Church and the bourgeoisie.[4]

At that time, an urban class began to flourish in northeastern Spain that regarded the Jews as extremely serious competitors. In the mid-thirteenth century this class controlled the *Consell de Cent*

---

[3] On Jewish moneylenders in Spain in the thirteenth and fourteenth centuries, see: F. Cantera Burgos, *La usura judía en Castilla*, Salamanca 1932; C. Sánchez Albornoz, *España, un enigma histórico* (Barcelona: Edhasa, 1973), vol. 2, 190-206; R. Emery, *The Jews of Perpignan in the Thirteenth Century* (New York: Columbia University Press, 1959); M. Delcor, "Les Juifs de Puigcerdà au XIIIᵉ siècle," *Sefarad*, 26 (1966): 17-45; Yom Tov Assis, *The Jews of Santa Coloma de Queralt in the Thirteenth Century* (Jerusalem: Magnes Press, 1988); A. Altisent, "El monasterio de Poblet y unos judíos prestamistas de la Segarra (S. XIV-XV)," *Sefarad* 27 (1967): 282-289; A García Sanz, "Los intereses de los préstamos de los judíos de Vich durante la primera mitad del siglo XIV," AUSA, 4 (1962): 247-255; L. Piles Ros, "Situación económica de Valencia a comienzos del Siglo XIV, a través de los préstamos judaicos," in *XI Congresso di Storia della Corona d'arragona* (Palermo: Società Siciliana per la historia patria, 1984), 63-88; I. Ollichi Castanyer, "Aspectes económics de l'activatat dels jueus de Vic, segons els 'Libri Iudeorum' (1266-1278)," in Els 'Libri Iuderoum' de Vic de Cardona, *Miscellània de Textos Medievals*, 3 (Barcelona: CSIC, 1985), 3-118; M. Casas i Nadal, "El 'Liber Iudeorum' de Cardona (1330-1334), edició i estudi," 121-314; Assis, *Jewish Economy*, 118-131; J. Carrasco Pérez, "Acerca del préstamo judío en Tudela a fines del siglo XIV," *Príncipe de Viana*, 166-167 (1982): 909-948; J. Carrasco Pérez, "Los judíos de Viana y Laguardia (1350-1408): aspectos sociales y económicos," in *Vitoria en la Eda Media*, ed. Victoria-Gasteiz 1982, 419-447; J. Carrasco Pérez, "La actividad crediticia de los judíos en Pamplona (1349-1387)," in *Minorités et Marginaux en France méridionale et dans la Peninsule ibérique (VIIᵉ-XVIIIᵉ siècles)* (Actes du Colloque de Pau, 27-29 mai 1984), (Paris: Presses du CNRS, 1986), 221-263; J. Carrasco Pérez, "El crédito judío en la villas navaras del camino de Santiago (1339-1408)," in *Local and International Credit in the Middle Ages and the 16ᵗʰ Century,* Ninth International Economic History Congress (Bern: International Economic History Association, 1986), 8-14; B. Leroy, *The Jews of Navarre in the Late Middle Ages* (Jerusalem: Magnes Press, 1985), chapter 3; J. Hinojosa Montalvo, "El préstamo judío en la ciudad de Valencia en la segunda mitad del siglo XIV," *Sefarad* 45 (1985): 315-339; Y. Assis and R. Magdalena, *The Jews of Navarre in the Late Middle Ages*, Jerusalem: Zalman Shazar Center, 1990 (Hebrew).

[4] On the decisions of the Cortes in Catalonia, see *Cortes de los antiguos reinos de Aragón y de Valencia y principado de Cataluña* I (Madrid, 1896).

(the Council of the Hundred) of the city of Barcelona, which was the most important commercial and economic center in the region. Under the inspiration of the *Consell de Cent*, several municipal ordinances against the Jews were passed.[5] Despite all the measures taken to hinder Jewish money lenders, their activity continued for a long time and even grew in strength. This continued activity was made possible mainly because of the benefit it brought to the entire society, which needed cash, and because of the considerable profits that it passed on to the royal treasury. The practical dependence of the nobility and clergy on Jewish money helped to frustrate every effort aimed at preventing the Jews from lending money at interest. The gap between law and practice, between what was desired and what actually took place, stands out in this matter and demonstrates one of the foundations of Jewish life in the Middle Ages, a foundation valid in Spain as well.

No one can deny that the main success of the Jews was in fields that were favored by the authorities and the general society. This success depended to no small degree on the explicit or implicit agreement of the authorities and other influential factors. That is to say, the Jews' lending of money at interest continued throughout the thirteenth and fourteenth centuries with full impetus because it was needed by Christian society, especially by those with the power to halt it. Additional proof that Jewish financial activity was only possible to the degree that these elements permitted it can also be found in the maritime trade of Iberian Jews with the East.

The Catalans in Maritime Commerce

In the mid-thirteenth century, with the end of the second stage of the *Reconquista*, the Crown of Aragon controlled the Mediterranean coast of the Iberian Peninsula and the Balearic Islands.[6] This control opened the path for eastward overseas expansion for the Crown of

---

[5] On the development of the urban population in Spain, see L. García de Valdeavellano, *Sobre los burgos y los burgueses de la España medieval* (Madrid: Real Academia, 1969).

[6] On the part played by the Crown of Aragon and its achievements in the *Reconquista* of the thirteenth century, see J. N. Hillgarth, "The Problem of a Catalan Mediterranean Empire 1229-1327," *The English Historical Review*, Supplement 8 (1975).

Aragon, and particularly for Catalonia. This expansion was doubly important since, due to the Castilian control of Murcia, the Catalans could not continue the *Reconquista* in the south. The turn eastward eventually led to the rule of the Crown of Aragon-Catalonia over Sicily, Sardinia, and other islands in the Mediterranean. It is difficult to determine with certainty the relationship between conquest and trade: did the conquest bring in its wake the expansion of trade, or did the desire to expand Catalan trade lead the Crown of Aragon to make overseas conquests? Nevertheless, the connection between political and commercial expansion is self-evident.[7] In the thirteenth century, which was a time of prosperity throughout Europe, the two main Christian monarchies on the Iberian Peninsula flourished as well. Castile produced and exported wool, and Catalonia engaged in Mediterranean trade.

In Catalonia, maritime trade in the Mediterranean basin opened markets and possibilities for enormous economic expansion. In certain respects sea routes were easier than land routes, and merchandise sent down the Ebro from Aragon was now exported from Catalonia to various Mediterranean ports, mainly those in Sicily, Italy, Provence-Languedoc, Sardinia, Granada, and North Africa. Ships from Catalonia reached the East as well: Greece, Constantinople, Crete, Cyprus, and Alexandria, Egypt. They were laden with cloth, olive oil, and oranges, and they returned with spices like pepper and ginger, indigo, frankincense, wax, and ivory. The Catalans showed great expertise in maritime transportation and ship-building, and in fact during the fourteenth century the Crown of Aragon was the only Christian kingdom with its own merchant navy. In 1227 Jaume I forbade the shipping of merchandise from Barcelona in foreign ships if a Catalan ship was anchored in the port.[8]

---

[7] This subject is discussed by a number of scholars. See especially M. del Treppo, *Els mercaders catalans: l'espansió de la Corona Catalono-Aragonesa al segle XV*, Trans. J. Riera i Sans, (Barcelona: Curial, 1976), 15-25; J. Vicens i Vives, *España: Geo-polític del estado y del imperio* (Barcelona: Yunque, 1940), 111; J. Lalinde Abadia, *La Corona de Aragón en el mediterráneo medieval (1229-1479)* (Zaragoza: Institución Fernando el Católico, 1979), 87.

[8] A. de Capmany Surís y de Montpalau, *Memorias históricas sobre la marina, comercio y artes de la antigua ciudad de Barcelona* (Barcelona: A. de Sancha, 1779-1792), vol. 2, 11. For technical reasons I was forced to use two different editions of this book, and in every instance I have indicated the first edition with a superscript '1' and the second edition, Barcelona 1962, with a superscript '2.'; Hillgarth, *Kingdoms*, vol. 1, 40-42.

Although the Church had forbidden trade with Muslim countries,[9] Catalonia maintained and developed its commercial ties with them. Nor was the prohibition against the sale of iron, weapons, wood, and food strictly observed.[10] Control over Mallorca and Sicily enabled the Crown of Aragon to take a highly significant part in trade with Tunisia, Bugia, and Tlemcen,[11] and the colony in Alexandria of Catalan merchants from the Crown of Aragon, which already existed at the time of Benjamin of Tudela's visit there, was strengthened and institutionalized with the founding of the consulate in 1264. During the fourteenth century it enjoyed clear commercial hegemony. In several important cities of the East, such as Alexandria and Beirut, the Catalan merchants had their own neighborhoods, with self-rule headed by the consuls, who were appointed by the king of Aragon-Catalonia, and, after 1266, by the city of Barcelona.[12] The importance of maritime trade is reflected in the establishment of guilds of merchants and seamen—the *Consulat del Mar* [Consulate of the Sea] in Barcelona, Valencia, and Mallorca—which laid the foundations for an extensive system of laws of maritime trade.[13]

[9] The prohibition against trade with Muslims was declared at the General Councils of 1179, 1215, and 1245, and Popes Innocent III in 1198 and Gregory X in 1272 demanded its imposition; W. von Heyd, *Histoire du commerce du Levant au Moyen Age* (Leipzig: Harrassowitz, 1885), vol. 1, 386 (for reasons of convenience I used the French translation); Nicolao Doliver, *Catalonia*, 34-29; on the decisions of the Councils see C. J. Hefele, *Histoire des Conciles* (Paris: Letouzey et Ané, 1913), Vol. 2, 1104, can. 24 (1179), 1394 (1215), and 1660 (1245) [translated from German; there is an English translation *History of the Church Councils*, (New York, 1972) (reprint of Edinburgh ed. 1883-1896)]; on the prohibition by the Church and the reactions it provoked see: Capmany[2], vol. 2, 241 ff.

[10] After 1274 Jaume I reduced the prohibition against vital merchandise. See Capmany[1], vol. 2, 36.

[11] On the Crown of Aragon and the states of North Africa see: A. Masía de Ros, *La Corona de Aragón y los estados del Norte de Africa* (Barcelona: Instituto de estudios mediterráneos, 1951); Ch. E. Dufourcq, *L'Espagne catalane et le Maghrib*, Paris 1966; and Yom Tov Assis, "Jewish Diplomats from Aragon in Muslim Lands (1213-1327)," *Sefunot* 18 (1985): 11-34 (Hebrew).

[12] On the Catalan consulates see: A. B. Hibbert, "Catalan Consulates in the Thirteenth Century," *Cambridge Historical Journal* 9 (1949): 352-358. On the initiative to establish the consulate and hostel in Alexandria see: J. Miret y Sans, *Itinerari de Jaume I "el Conqueridor,"* (Barcelona: Institut d'Estudis Catalans, 1918), 325; on the appointment of the first consul in 1264 see 349. On the testimony of Benjamin of Tudela, see M. N. Adler, *The Itinerary of Benjamin of Tudela* (London: H. Frowde, 1907), 76, and for the Hebrew part, 68.

[13] J. F. O'Callaghan, *A History of Medieval* Spain (Ithaca, NY: Cornell University Press, 1975), 483-485; in 1283 a maritime consulate was established in Valencia, and shortly afterward in Barcelona and Mallorca. See: A.de Capmany, *Libro del Consulado del*

As noted, the prohibition against trade with Muslim countries was not in fact observed, and after Jaume I was excommunicated, he resumed almost entirely free trade with them. This policy was continued by Pere III, and in the reigns of Alfonso III and his brother Jaume, who was the King of Sicily, a trade agreement was signed with the Sultan of Egypt. All the prohibitions and restrictions from the time of Jaume I were rescinded, and a political treaty was reached with Egypt, while France and the Papacy became the enemies of the Crown of Aragon.[14] The treaty was ratified in 1293 by Jaume II. Although a large part of the Crown of Aragon's trade was diverted to North Africa after the fall of Acre, Catalonia-Aragon did continue to trade with Muslim countries in general and with Egypt in particular, despite the increased severity of the prohibition and admonitions in the final decade of the thirteenth century. The treaty of Anagni, which was signed with the Pope, and the reconciliation between the King of Aragon and the Church, which was achieved, at least in appearance, in 1302, were insufficient to put an end to the commercial ties that had developed.[15] Jaume II was forced to prohibit the trade; however, at the same time he issued many special permits to merchants, and the Council of the Hundred was even more flexible. The Catalans were unwilling to forgo their special status and their commercial achievements in Egypt.

Most of the ships that departed from Barcelona to the East passed through Cyprus and Crete. In fact, the sources indicate that every ship that anchored in Cyprus had also passed through Crete.[16] Cyprus, from which two major international sea routes departed,

Mar, reedición Barcelona, 1965. On the activities of Catalan merchants in the western Mediterranean during the thirteenth century, see: D. Abulafia, "Catalan Merchants and the Western Mediterranean, 1236-1300: Studies in the Notarial Acts of Barcelona and Sicily," *Viator* 16 (1985): 209-242. This article contains interesting material about Jewish merchants and about the subject of our research.

[14] Heyd, vol. 1, 422-439; on the relations of the Crown of Aragon and Egypt in general, see A. S. Atiya, *Egypt and Aragon* (Leipzig, 1938; republished Nendeln, 1966).

[15] On ratification of the treaty with Egypt see: V. Salvert Roca, "El tratado de Anagni y la expansión mediterránea de la Corona de Aragón," *Estudios de Eda Media de la Corona de Aragón*, 5 (1952): 209-360.

[16] Crete was under Venetian control since 1204, and its location made it a necessary way station between the two ends of the Mediterranean Basin. As noted, almost all the sources of the Archivo Municipal de Barcelona and those of other archives that served as a basis for the present study show that the port of Candia was included in almost every voyage to Cyprus. See also Nicolao Doliver, *Catalonia*, 209.

became an important commercial destination. One route passed through Damascus and the Persian Gulf, and on to India. The other passed through Lesser Armenia before reaching the Persian Gulf and then India. Both of these routes departed from the island of Cyprus, where the remains of a Crusader kingdom were present. The island, especially the port of Famagusta, became a meeting point of traders from the West. At the end of the thirteenth century the Catalans retained a foothold on Cyprus after the fall of Acre. They strove to strengthen political and economic relations with the island, whose strategic and commercial importance for the Catalans increased after the expansion of the Crown of Aragon into Sicily, Athens, and the Morea peninsula. Two branches of the royal family of Aragon, the Catalan and the Sicilian, made a marital alliance with the Cypriot royal family in the second decade of the fourteenth century. The ports of Cyprus helped the Catalans to circumvent the prohibition against trade with Muslims, and this function continued to increase the importance of Cyprus as a link between Barcelona and Alexandria.[17]

The Jews of Catalonia in Maritime Trade

The development of sea trade entailed the rise of the bourgeoisie, the class of merchants and seamen. The flourishing of the new urban class led to social instability and a gap between the rich and the poor.[18] The rise of the urban class, which began in Catalonia and later spread to Valencia and Mallorca, had many consequences for the status of the Jews, who mainly lived in cities. The Catalan urban populace regarded the Jews as competitors and obstacles in economic life, and neutralizing them became, in their view, a vital goal in the desire to increase their profits. In two main areas the Jews enjoyed a prominent place in economic life and a huge slice of the national wealth: money lending and commerce. As noted, the Jews played a major role in lending money at interest, and this led to enmity between them and

---

[17] Capmany¹, II, 81; Heyd, vol .2, 4, 15, and esp. n. 15; Nicolao Doliber, *Catalonia*, 164-166; See E. González Hurtebise, *Libros de Tesorería de la Casa Real de Aragón*, I (Barcelona: Luis Benaiges, 1911), par. 411, regarding the Catalan merchants who sailed from Candia, Crete, to Alexandria.

[18] Hillgarth, *Kingdoms*, vol. 1, 42, 72-74; Lalinde, 86-88.

the Christian bourgeois class that had accumulated capital. In time that class was to inherit the place of the Jews, after major Christian banking families arose in Catalonia. In Castile and Portugal, where there was as yet no urban class worthy of the name, the Jewish money lenders continued their activities and retained their control over commerce in the thirteenth and fourteenth centuries and beyond. In Catalonia, the Jewish money lenders were ultimately shunted aside after a prolonged period of struggle; the outcome was delayed because of the deep and longstanding establishment of the activity of the Jewish money lenders there.[19]

The Jews were appropriate candidates with respect to their capital, their connections, and their talents to take part in the maritime trade whose enormous development during the thirteenth century opened the door to new sources of livelihood and profit for the Catalan merchants. What part did the Jews play in the maritime trade with the East, and to what degree did they succeed in sharing the prosperity that this trade brought with it? What was the response of the Catalan merchants to the efforts of the Jews to gain a share of their profits, and what was the status of the Jewish merchants in the system of consulates which had become institutionalized, and whose purpose was to protect the rights of Catalan merchants and seamen in the cities of the East? What were the consequences of the organization of guilds of merchants and seamen, the *Consulat del Mar*, for the Jewish merchant? Were there any factors that were interested in Jewish participation in maritime trade with the East? Were the Jews able to exploit their wealth and talents in this branch as they had in money lending? I set about answering these questions and others of similar scope, and what follows is the result of my examination of dozens of new sources found in three archives in Barcelona: the Archivo de la Corono de Aragón (ACA), the Archivo de la Catedral (Capitular) de Barcelona (ACB), and the Archivo Histórico de Protocolos de Barcelona (AHPB).

In many respects it was appropriate for the Jews to play an important role in maritime trade with the East. Some of them had liquid assets they could devote to this economic outlet. Moreover, Jews in the port cities of the East served as intermediaries and agents,

---

[19] O'Callaghan, 486.

and they could find assistance among Jews in various areas. The local Jewish community served them in certain respects as a base parallel to the Catalan *rua,* or colony. Moreover, quite a few Jews knew Arabic and were familiar with Muslim society and the customs of trade in the East. In these areas they enjoyed a clear advantage over Christian merchants. Thus, for example, in 1294, in Barcelona itself, two local Jews served as translators for Muslim merchants from Tunis who did not know Catalan and needed the services of a notary.[20] Indeed, sources from earlier than the thirteenth century refer to the entry of Iberian Jews in maritime trade with the East. Jews from Mallorca, Valencia, Aragon, and Catalonia maintained close commercial ties with Jews of North Africa and, through them, sold merchandise to Muslims in distant and remote regions.[21] The Jewish intermediary in Muslim lands paid the Jewish merchant from the Crown of Aragon in money or in kind[22] only after the sale of the merchandise in the interior. It seems that in the first stages of commercial activity in new markets there was an identity of interest between the Jews, the Crown, and Christian merchants. The Jews were usually pioneers and a key link in sea trade between the Iberian Peninsula and Muslim lands.[23] As late as the last decade of the thirteenth century there were still partnerships between Jewish and Christian merchants as an expression of this common interest, which was then in its final stages.[24]

Methods of Commerce in the Thirteenth Century

The Jewish merchants used the methods of sea trade and the means of financing it that had been practiced by Catalan merchants, so it is appropriate to present a short description of these methods before discussing the activity of the Jews in this area at the end of the thirteenth and the beginning of the fourteenth centuries. As a

---

[20] ACB, Notaria Capitular, Bernat de Vilarrubia 1292-1297, f. 65v-66.

[21] "In partibus distantibus et remotis." See above, note 20.

[22] "in rebus" or "in pecunia."

[23] See Dufourcq, 143.

[24] See, for example, ACB, Notoria Capitular, Bernat de Vilarrubia 1295, f. 3r. & v. regarding the partnership between Bonjua Bolax de Fez and Jacob David, Jews from Barcelona, on the one hand, and two Christians, Joan Cap and Perez Ris, also from Barcelona, on the other.

consequence of their connections with Italy, the Catalan merchants adopted commercial patterns similar to those that were common there.

Usually the investor did not run a personal, physical risk by taking part in the voyage, for the active partner was responsible for selling the merchandise overseas. The active partner was often the owner of a ship. Every transaction was made separately, and the partnership would end when it was completed. Even the maritime companies (*societas maris*) that were common in the fourteenth century would be dissolved at the end of the voyage.[25] When the investment took the form of a loan, its payment was without conditions, but the payment of a maritime loan, *nauticum foenus*, was obligatory only if the ship reached port. Mainly the *commendatio* or *comanda*[26] system was prevalent, according to which the investor gave money or merchandise to the merchant who was setting forth. At the end of the voyage, the investment was returned, and the profits were shared between the investor, who received three-quarters, and the merchant, who received one quarter. In the *collegantia* system, used by companies, the merchant also invested something. However, because of the dangers, the merchant usually preferred the *comanda* system of commercial deposit. This is the only system mentioned in the regulations of the maritime consulate.[27]

When the financing of a transaction entailed contracting loans with neither the deposit nor the *comanda* system, the loan was straightforward and included interest. Usually the deposit or loan was repaid according to the request of the investor. The commercial deposit was usually money, but occasionally merchandise, whose monetary value was stipulated in the contract. Of course, the merchant, the active partner, did not set out with only a single order—

---

[25] O'Callaghan, 485.

[26] Comanda – cum mandare (manui dare) – to make a deposit. See Du Cange, *Glossarum Mediae et Infinae Latinitatis*, editio nova, L. Favre, Niort, 1883; J. F. Niermeyer, *Mediae Latinatis Lexicon Minus*, (Leiden: Brill, 1976; B. Oliver, *Historia del derecho en Cataluña* (Madrid, 1881), vol. 4, 190; A. E. Sayous, "Let méthodes commerciales de Barcelone au XIIe siècle, d'après les documents inédits des Archives de sa Cathédrale," *Estudis Universitaris Catalans* 16 (1931): 165 and docs. A, B; on *Comandas* in Barcelona during the thirteenth and fourteenth centuries, Marimón and Sanz, vol. 2, 62 ff.

[27] Sayous, 157, 160, 163; on the division of the investment and the profits, see Sayous, 178.

unless the investment or the merchandise was very valuable—and therefore he would receive many deposit orders.

The funds or merchandise of the investor were transferred in three ways: via the owner of the ship, via a third party, or via a merchant who was traveling to the East.[28] It could be that the Jews were the main reason why the maritime loan [*nauticum foenus*] did not fully develop.[29] In this form of investment, repayment was conditional upon the ship's arrival in port, whereas simple loans, which were more common, were repaid under any conditions. Even after the Catalan merchants managed to drive the Jews out of maritime trade with the East, Jews remained passive investors or partners in many transactions, and thus they continued to take part in this trade. Their active partnership encountered obstacles, as we shall see below, but their financing of trade did not cease. The Jews' deposits were vital, and it was almost impossible to prevent them, because they could be transacted as entirely ordinary loans. When the Jews finally withdrew from active partnership in maritime trade, as a result of the obstacles to be described below, they agreed to deposit money in the form of loans, but they refused to accept any risk and demanded repayment as of an ordinary loan.

The Jews between Barcelona and Alexandria

The thirteenth century, when the markets of the East were opened to the merchants of the Crown of Aragon, was the best time of all for the Jews of that country. However, there are no indications that the role of the Jews in trade with the East was as great as in other economic fields. Nevertheless, from the Jews' point of view, nothing prevented them from gradually integrating in that trade. At that time, connections were made between the Jews of Barcelona and those of Alexandria, the two main port cities in their respective countries. Jews from both cities made reciprocal visits for business purposes

---

[28] Sayous, 176-177. He claims that in the sources from the ACB none indicates a multiplicity of *Comandas*, and that is not true. His claim that all the *Comandas* in the sources are in merchandise or a mixed transaction in merchandise and money is not exact, as we shall see below. On the manners of payment, see Sayous, 180.

[29] This is Sayous' opinion, 184, though he did not explain or justify it.

and found valuable support in the host community, providing many services and advantages greater than those provided by the *fondaco* that the Catalan merchants established in Alexandria. In addition to the preferential treatment that the Jewish merchants found in the host Jewish community, they also received protection from the king-count of Aragon-Catalonia. Jews from Alexandria who sojourned in Barcelona enjoyed royal protection, and some of them settled permanently there. In 1270 Jaume I extended protection to two Jewish brothers and their families, who had arrived in the Crown of Aragon from Alexandria. Perhaps the presence of the two brothers' families indicates their intention to settle, and such an intention indicates the existence of close ties between the two Jewish communities and commercial activity in both directions.[30]

Naturally, business trips and commercial ties did not always go smoothly, and occasionally controversies arose between the parties. The Jewish party, especially, required the support of the authorities to settle matters. Although according to the practice in Barcelona, a merchant could not be sued while in the midst of a commercial voyage, in 1289 Alfonso III responded to a request from the Egyptian sultan and held a judicial inquiry into a dispute between a Jew from Alexandria and a Catalan merchant who was in his debt.[31]

Among the Jews from Alexandria who came to dwell in Catalonia was the Ascandrani family, which was quickly absorbed by the Barcelona community. One of its daughters was married to Isaac Cap, whose commercial activities in the Mediterranean Basin undoubtedly took off and received a new dimension after his marriage. The Ascandrani family did not cut its overseas ties, nor did it give up its assets abroad, and thus it was one of those that contributed to the increase of the share of the Jews in maritime trade. Their activity in international trade made life rather complicated for members of the family.[32] Isaac ben Samuel Cap also encountered

---

[30] ACA, R 16, f. 199 (J. Régné, *A History of the Jews in Aragon*, ed. Yom Tov Assis [Jerusalem: Magnes, 1978], no. 443). These sources were originally published in *REJ* in 1910-1925, under the title: "Catalogue des actes de Jaime Ier, Pedro III et Alfonso III d'Aragon, concernant les Juifs; Catalogue d'Actes pour servir à l'Histoire des Juifs de la Couronne d'Aragon sous le règne de Jaime II (1291-1327)."

[31] ACA, R 80, f. 52 (Régné, no. 2003).

[32] On the Askandrani family in Catalonia, see Baer, *A History*, I, 209-210; also Régné, nos. 72, 679, 705, 739, 785, 88; these sources describe the dangers of maritime trade very

difficulties and went bankrupt. In 1280 he disappeared while in possession of the deposits of Catalan merchants and others. Among those who suffered damage were the consuls of Pisa and Venice and representatives of the king of Cyprus and the Templars. They confiscated merchandise belonging to Jews in response to the losses that Isaac Cap caused them, and the king of Aragon had to intervene on behalf of the Jews who suffered damage though they were not at fault.[33]

The Jews in Trade with Alexandria

In the last decade of the thirteenth century, when the king of Aragon continued to trade with Muslim lands in general and with Egypt in particular, the sources testify to the vigorous participation of Jews in this commerce. There are signs that after the ratification of the treaty with Egypt in 1293, the volume of trade between the two countries increased.

Jews from Barcelona also participated in trade with Muslims in the eastern Mediterranean Basin. Evidence of this can be found in the notarial register of Bernat de Vilarrubia of 1295, in ACB. From the end of March until almost the end of August, 1295, thirteen Jews are listed as planning voyages to Alexandria. There is no indication that these merchants encountered any special difficulty because they were Jewish. Like the Catalan merchants, they listed their transactions openly and legally with the notary. Without doubt this notarial register was not the only one, and the presence of eighteen notarial records connected with Jews who were engaged in trade with

---

well. On the family, see also in J. Miret y Sans and M. Schwab, "Documents sur les Juifs catalans aux XIe, XIIe et XIIIe siècles," *REJ* 68 (1914): 182-183; on 184-185 is the will of Astrug Scandarani filius Abrahim de Alexandria. On his daughter Bona Dona, who was the wife of Rabbi Juda de Porta, see 188-189. On Astrug Scandarani, Abrahim de Alexandria, Bonadonina the daughter of Astrug and his wife Boniuda de Porta, see: Archivo Diocesano de Barcelona, Pergaminos de Santa Anna, Carpeta 1, Bolsa 4, No. 19; Carpeta 2-A, No. 299; ACT, 1-6, doc. 2802. See also Miret y Sans and Schwab, "Documents sur les Juifs catalans," 49-50, no. 32; 53, no. 36.

[33] Baer, *A History*, vol. 1, 209-210; ACA R 48, f. 67v., and see B. Z. Dinur, *Israel in the Diaspora*, volume 2, book 1, 528, no. 2 (Hebrew); ACA, R 49 f. 5v (Régné, no. 857), and see Régné, no. 1534; J. Miret y Sans and M. Schwab, "Documents sur les Juifs catalans aux XIe, XIIe et XIIIe siècles," *REJ*, 68 (1914): 184 ff.; and on him, see below.

Alexandria in a register consisting of 132 pages is not coincidental. The proportion of Jewish merchants among Catalan merchants involved in trade with Alexandria was evidently greater than the proportion of Jewish merchants among the total population of merchants in the Mediterranean coastal region of Spain. Moreover, it is unlikely that Jewish merchants would be satisfied with fewer than a reasonable number of *comandae* or commercial deposits when they set out on the long, difficult, and expensive journey to Alexandria. Thus, we must assume that the single *comanda* listed in the aforementioned register was representative of other transactions whose records are not in our possession.

On March 28, 1295, Bonjua Bolax (or Belaish) de Fez and Jacob David of Barcelona signed an agreement with Perez Ris and Joan Cap, residents of the city, promising to transfer the merchandise of these Jews to Alexandria.[34] From other sources it is clear that these two Jewish merchants intended to sail to Alexandria, and the contract they signed with the two Catalan merchants was meant to assure the success of the voyage. Two weeks later the two Jews received merchandise from Momet Bonafeu to be sold in Alexandria.[35] At the end of May, the two Catalan merchants confirmed that they had received additional merchandise from the two, which was also destined for Alexandria.[36] On August 5, Bunjua and Jacob admitted that they had received the sum of £24 4s 1d from Vidal Crespi of Tarragona and Isaac David of Barcelona as a commercial deposit for the voyage they were about to undertake to Alexandria.[37] Most likely these transactions were a small fraction of their shared activities in Alexandria, and Bunjua Bolax will appear later in commerce with the East. His partner Jacob David was certainly suited for trade with Muslim countries, for he knew the Arabic language well and in 1294 he and Salamo Corareif were active as interpreters when Muslims

---

[34] See n. 24 above.

[35] ACB Notaria Capitular, Bernat de Vilarrubia, 1295, f. 13v. The owner of the merchandise was Momet Bonafeu.

[36] ACB, Notaria Capitular, Bernat de Vilarrubia, f. 61v.

[37] ACB, Notaria Capitular, Bernat de Vilarrubia, f. 119v. The currencies of the four components of the Crown of Aragon (Catalonia, Aragon, Valencia and Mallorca) were composed of three denominations of the £, which consisted of 20 solidi (s) and each solidus or sous of 12 denarii (d).

from Tunisia who did not know Catalan appeared before the notary.[38] Bunjua himself was apparently of North African origin, born to a family that had settled in Barcelona, as his name indicates: a Catalan first name and a family name that derived from North Africa.

Another group of Jewish partners who sailed from Barcelona to Alexandria included Samuel Salvat, David Astruc, and at a certain stage Juce Sullam. They received three *comandae* from three Jews of Barcelona in May and June 1295. The sum of the *comandae*, 136 s and £16, was converted into Alexandrian coin, as was usually the practice, while the sum of a third transaction, £9 18s was used to buy merchandise for export.[39] Before the voyage David Astruc saw fit to give his wife and his brother power of attorney to collect the deposit from Salamo de Porta, in the amount of 20.5 Old Byzants of Alexandria.[40]

In the summer of 1295 Rovem (Reuven) Astruc de (Sa) Real, along with two partners, Bonet Aninay and Jacob Guago (or Gangio) began preparations for a voyage to Alexandria. Momet Bonafeu, whose other investments were mentioned above, deposited *comandae* in various sums in June and July of that year. In three notarial records the merchants attest to receiving various sums, in return for which they obligated themselves to take merchandise for sale in Egypt.[41]

Three other Jewish merchants are known to us who planned to sail to Alexandria in July and August of 1295: Bonjuda son of Astruc Cap,[42] Jucef Abraham Tavell,[43] and Salomo Llop.[44] Bunjuda Cap received a deposit from a Christian, whereas the other two received them from Jews of Barcelona: the wife of Joce Habib, and

---

[38] See n. 20 above.

[39] ACB, Notaria Capitular, Bernat de Vilarrubia, f. 41v, 71, 82v.

[40] ACB, Notaria Capitular, Bernat de Vilarrubia, f. 67v-68.

[41] ACB, Notaria Capitular, Bernat de Vilarrubia, f. 78v, 84v, 96; the senior partner, Rovem Astruc de (Sa) Real, appears later under his Hebrew name Reuven in connection to another voyage to Alexandria in 1299, AHPB, Pere Portell, 1299, Lligall 1, f. 8, 9v; the two other partners were also from Barcelona: Jacob Guago (or Gangia) and Bonet Aninay. The former (Gangio) appears in September 1299 in a voyage to Crete and Cyprus (AHPB, f. 54 & v). A Jew whose name was the same as the latter partner was one of the leaders of a group of the communities (*colecta*) of Gerona-Besalú in 1274-1281; ACA, R 37, f. 61v (=Régné, no. 599); ACA, R 50, f. 184 v. (Régné, no. 882).

[42] ACB, Notaria Capitular, Bernat de Vilarrubia, f. 116r (Bonjuda Cap).

[43] ACB, Notaria Capitular, Bernat de Vilarrubia, f. 188r & v (Jucef Abraham Tavell).

[44] ACB, Notaria Capitular, Bernat de Vilarrubia, f. 132r & v (Salomo Llop).

David Abraham. The deposits were converted to the currency of Alexandria, or merchandise. It should be pointed out that not all those who made deposits invested only money, as is indicated by the deposit of David Abraham. It appears that of the £16 that he deposited with Salamo Llop, only £3 was his money, whereas £13 was the investment of Samuel de Marsilia, a Jew from Narbonne.[45] From a source dated August 1295 we know of the voyage to Alexandria made by Isaac de Castello, upon which he had received a *comanda* of £42 7s 4d from Josef Benvenist, a Jew from Barcelona, and in return for which he brought merchandise to the depositor.[46]

Jews in Trade with Crete and Cyprus

For the period from the end of August 1295 to September 1299, we possess no sources regarding the participation of Jews in maritime trade with the East. When the information is renewed, in September 1299, it contains a surprise: Alexandria appears explicitly as the destination of only four Jewish merchants who departed from Barcelona. In contrast, Crete and Cyprus emerge as destinations for many voyages with the participation of Jews from Barcelona. Three Jews who reached Alexandria at that time were Maimon ben Isaac Tavell, Salamo Bonsenior, and Rovem Astruc, who is known to us from his earlier voyage in 1295. Another Jew, Ahomar de Mallorca, gave power of attorney to Vides Juce, also known as Vides Malakhi, to collect six old Byzants of Alexandria from Maimon Tavell, who was in Alexandria. The sum had been deposited with him as a *comanda*.[47] After a few days, Salamo Bonsenior of Barcelona acknowledged that he owed five Byzants and sixteen gold corats of Alexandrian currency to Rovem Astruc, and he promised to pay the sum within fifteen days of arriving in Alexandria.[48] Rovem Astruc sold merchandise valued at 100s to Maimon Tavell, who promised to

---

[45] ACB, Notaria Capitular, Bernat de Vilarrubia, f. 132v (notarial record of August 23, 1295, the same date as the registry of the *comanda*).

[46] ACB, Notaria Capitular, Bernat de Vilarrubia, f. 123.

[47] AHPB, Pere Portell, 1299, Lligall 1, f. 1v & av-2. Both of these sources are damaged, but they complement one another.

[48] AHPB, Pere Portell, 1299, Lligall, f. 8.

pay eight old Byzants one month after arriving in Alexandria.[49] These notes, which were written and signed before the notary in Barcelona over the course of only seven days, indicate extensive and complex activity beyond these documents; they show that many contracts and agreements were made during preparations for a voyage, and that Jews and Catalan Christians continued to do business while in Alexandria.

Though it is clear that these sources about the trade of Jews from Barcelona in Egypt represent only part of this activity in 1299, to the same extent we must regard the sources about the trade of Jews in Crete and Cyprus as partial. This is the first evidence we have of voyages by Jewish merchants to these destinations, and it shows that they sailed there five times more frequently than to Alexandria in that period. From September 18 to October 2, 1299, just fifteen days, fourteen voyages by Jews to Crete and Cyprus are listed, in which nineteen Jews participated. Maimon ben Isaac Tavell received *comanda* contracts from Christians, which were converted into merchandise, which he brought to Crete and Cyprus;[50] Abraham de Tolosa from Tarragona and his partner received a *comanda* valued at £18 5s 8d on a similar voyage from a Jew from the Cap family, apparently Abraham son of Samuel Cap.[51] Solam Ruben Jafia, a Jewish merchant from Barcelona, received deposits from Jews and Christians to export merchandise to Crete and Cyprus.[52]

Four pairs of Jewish partners made journeys to these two places, and various deposits that they had received were listed with the notary Pere Portell in September. The partners from Barcelona were Jose Zerah and Jacob Gangin,[53] Bolax Jassua and Mosse Isaac,[54]

---

[49] AHPB, Pere Portell, 1299, Lligall, f. 9v.

[50] AHPB, Pere Portell, 1299, Lligall, 1 & 1v.

[51] AHPB, Pere Portell, 1299, Lligall, 1v.

[52] Between September 18 and September 24, Solam Ruben Jafia received deposits from the Jew Vidal Reuven (f. 2) and received two from Bartomeu de Besalú, a cobbler from Barcelona (f. 5v, 10).

[53] On September 22, they received a *comanda* for the sum of £25 from Vidal Hakham (AHPB, Pere Portell, 1299, Lligall, f. 5r & v).

[54] Bolax Jassua and Mosse Isaac received the sum of £25 14s 3d from Ramon Dilmer, a resident of Barcelona (f. 11v).

Salamo Jacob and Vidal Moacel.[55] The fourth pair of partners who made a business voyage to Crete and Cyprus were Abraham de Torre Moales and Isaac de Torre Malforgia, from two towns in the Tarragona region.[56]

In that month, Jewish merchants from Barcelona received deposits of various sums from Jewish and Christian investors before their departure for Crete and Cyprus. These merchants were Samuel Jucef, Isaac Adret, Vides Jucef, Meir Samuel, Reuben Astruc, Santo Bonjuda, and Maimon Danan.[57] Some of them were very active. In addition to his voyage in 1299, Meir Samuel and his partner Astruc Abraham made another voyage in the summer of 1301.[58] Maimon Danan was one of the most active merchants. On October 30th, he signed a receipt for a *comanda* in money or merchandise from Vidal Hakham, Salamo Astruc, and Juda Bolax.[59]

As noted, the main destination was Cyprus, but every ship on its way there also passed through Crete and made a stop at Candia. What caused this clear change in destination among the Jewish merchants of Barcelona? Why did Cyprus and Crete largely replace Egypt? When Acre fell, and the court of the kingdom of Jerusalem retreated from the Land of Israel to Cyprus, the importance of the island rose in the estimation of European Christian merchants, given its strategic location on the international trade route. The island became a large and important center; many merchants from Christian countries were concentrated there, and from there they set out for the various markets of the Muslim East and for those of Byzantium. As noted, Cyprus became a focus of political and commercial interest for Aragon. Moreover, the location of the island made it possible for many Catalans to circumvent the prohibition imposed by the Church on trade with Muslims. This was particularly

---

[55] Salamo Jacob and Vidal Moacel (f. 13r & v). See J. Mª Madorell Merimón and A. García Sanz, *Comandas comerciales barcelonesas de la baja edad media*, (Barcelona: Colegio Notarial de Barcelona, 1973) doc. 70; Abulafia, "Catalan Merchants," 224.

[56] These two men received deposits from Abraham son of Samuel Cap of Barcelona totalling £30 35s, and in the name of Astruga, the wife of Isaac Llop from Tarragona from Abraham Joseph of Mallorca, 74s.

[57] AHPB, Pere Portell, 1299, Lligall, f. 14v; ff. 2v, 7, 9v, 10v, 11, 15, 15v-16, 19. See also the single page torn from the register of Pere Portell, 1299, Lligall 1.

[58] ACB, Notaria Capitular, Bernat de Vilarrubia 1301, f. 58r & v.

[59] AHPB, Pere Portell, 1299, Lligall 1, f. 15v.

important after relations between the Crown of Aragon and the papacy improved, at least formally, and the Crown of Aragon was forced to pay lip service to the prohibition. The Treaty of Anagni, signed in 1295, created such an opportunity, and consequently it became possible for Aragon to increase its activity and expansion in the Mediterranean. The commercial and strategic importance of Crete, which had been under Venetian rule since 1204, also attracted many Catalan merchants, including Jews. The latter doubtless were assisted by their brethren who lived on the island in creating commercial ties. Perhaps after 1295, when the activity of Jewish merchants from Barcelona in Alexandria achieved impressive results, the king sought to impose the prohibition against trade with Muslims on them. The Jews therefore found in Cyprus a way to circumvent that obstacle. Nor is it impossible that this prohibition was exploited by Catalan Christians who regarded the activity of the Jewish merchants as insupportable competition. One way or another, the result was the sudden rise of the proportion of Jews involved in Mediterranean trade in the direction of Crete and Cyprus. However, the true destination remained Alexandria.[60]

We possess clear proof that most of the merchants whose destinations were listed in the notarial registers as Crete and Cyprus intended to continue on to Alexandria. On September 18, 1299, various *comandas* were recorded by the notary in Barcelona, which had been deposited with Maimon son of Isaac Tavell of Barcelona, who intended to bring them with him on the voyage to Candia and Cyprus that he was planning.[61] On the same day, Vides Jucef signed a note before the same notary in which he stated that Ahomar de Mallorca had given him power of attorney to collect six old Byzants of Alexandrian coin from Maimon Tavell when he was in Alexandria. Vides Jucef promised to retain this sum as a *comanda* to trade with it.[62] In a notarial record of September 23, 1299, it is stated that Vides

---

[60] On the Treaty of Anagni see Salvert Roca; see H. Finke, *Acta Aragonensia*, Berlin and Leipzig, 1908-22, I, doc. 30; on Cyprus, see D. Alastos, *Cyprus in History* (London: Zeno Publishers,1976), 185 ff. On the Jews of Crete, see Sh. Marcus, "History of the Jews in the Island of Crete," *Otsar Yehudei Sefarad* 3 (1963): 135-139 (Hebrew). J. Starr, "Jewish Life in Crete under the Rule of Venice," *PAAJR* 12 (1942): 59-114, repub. in *Medieval Jewish Life*, ed. R. Chazan (New York: Ktav, 1976), 233-288.

[61] AHPB, Pere Portell, 1299, Lligall, f. 1, 1v.

[62] AHPB, Pere Portell, 1299, Lligall, f. 1v, 1v-2.

received a *comanda* in an equal sum from Ahomar de Mallorca in order to trade on his voyage to Crete and Cyprus.[63] We do not know whether these two Jewish merchants met in Cyprus or in Alexandria, but it is clear that Maimon Tavell, who had departed for Crete and Cyprus, arrived in Alexandria. Additional proof that he stopped in Alexandria is found in a notarial record dated September 24, 1299, in which he acknowledged a debt in Alexandrian coin to Reuben Astruc, who had sold merchandise to him. Maimon obligated himself to pay the sum within a month of his arrival in Alexandria.[64] Thus it is clear that Reuben Astruc intended to stay in Alexandria. However, on September 30, Reuben Astruc received a *comanda* from Ramon de Castelet, which was converted into merchandise, and which he was supposed to take on his voyage to Crete and Cyprus.[65] For the reasons mentioned above, the final destination was concealed, and the voyage was therefore registered as headed for Crete and Cyprus, although Alexandria was included in the itinerary and might also have been the main destination.

Further evidence that many if not all of the Jewish merchants included Alexandria in their voyages is found in the currency mentioned occasionally in the notarial registers. In some of the sources where the destinations of Candia and Cyprus are mentioned, the value of the deposit is given in the coin of Barcelona along with its value in the old Byzants of Alexandria.[66] The use of the specific currencies is indicative of the real destination of the Catalan Jewish merchants.[67]

---

[63] AHPB, Pere Portell, 1299, Lligall, f. 7.

[64] AHPB, Pere Portell, 1299, Lligall, f. 9v.

[65] AHPB, Pere Portell, 1299, Lligall, f. 15v-16.

[66] AHPB, Pere Portell, 1299, Lligall, f. 5r & v, 7; see also the sources from 1301: ACB, Notaria Capitular, Bernat de Vilarrubia 1301, f. 24, 78 r-v, 87.

[67] Until 1285, the coin of the kingdom of Cyprus was the gold "white Byzant," which was an imitation of a Byzantine coin. During the reign of Henry II (1285-1324) the coin was changed to the silver gross and the half-gross, without halting use or minting of the Byzant. It is difficult to explain the mention of the old Byzants of Alexandria, unless Egypt remained the destination of the Jewish merchants who listed their ports of destination as Crete and Cyprus, just as it remained the destination of the Christian Catalan merchants. A. Engel & R. Serrure, *Traité de Numismatique du Moyen-Age* (Paris, 1894), vol. 2, 915-916; (Paris: Leroux, 1905), vol. 2, 1410-1411; until the thirteenth century various coins in Europe and the Middle East were called "Byzants," like the original coins of Byzantium. See R. A. G. Carson, *Coins, Ancient, Mediaeval and Modern, II: Coins of Europe* (London: Hutchinson,

Sources from the archive of the cathedral of Barcelona from the summer of 1301 indicate the continuation of voyages by Jewish merchants from Barcelona in the direction of Candia and Cyprus. From June 16 to August 8, 1301, the notarial register of Bernat de Vilarrubia contains records of ten voyages by sixteen Jews to those destinations. In five cases the records refer to partnerships between two Jews. In two cases we possess copies of the contracts between the partners.[68] Usually the merchants received deposits of money, which were invested in merchandise for export. It should be mentioned that half of the deposits were from Christians, and half were from Jews.[69]

The question that interests us here is whether at the beginning of the fourteenth century Alexandria continued to be a principal or additional destination for the Jewish merchants who declared their intention of sailing to Crete or Cyprus. According to some of the sources, sums that Jewish and Christian residents of Barcelona invested in the local currency were converted to old Byzants of Alexandria, leading us to conclude that these merchants continued to visit the port of Alexandria, despite the prohibitions, which were constantly renewed.[70] Notarial sources from Candia dated 1300 confirm our conclusion. They reveal that Jewish merchants from Barcelona who reached Candia signed on transactions there before sailing to Alexandria. Salamo Sirot of Barcelona received a certain quantity in Candia, which he obligated himself to transfer to Alexandria. Another Jew from Barcelona, Isaac Gracian, who needed money while he was in Candia, received a loan and obligated himself to repay it within four months; or, if the ship were to reach

---

1971), 195, and see González Hurtebise, par. 411, regarding Catalan merchants who went from Candia in Crete to Alexandria in Egypt.

[68] ACB, Notaria Capitular, Bernat de Vilarrubia, 1301, f. 5r & v, 24r & v. The first partners were Habib Vidal and Mosse de Tolosa from Barcelona; their contract states that their destination was "Candia and other places." The other partnership was between two Jews from Gerona, Reuben Curtavini and Isaac Gabinti, who established a commercial company that planned a voyage to Candia and Cyprus in the ship belonging to Bernat Marquet.

[69] On the investment of deposits, see ACB, Notaria Capitular, Bernat de Vilarrubia, f. 58r & v, 68v-69, 95, 112. On deposits from Christians, see: ACB, Notaria Capitular, Bernat de Vilarrubia, f. 24, 58r & v, 68v-69, 78r-v. On the deposits from Jews, see: f. 86v, 87, 95, 112.

[70] ACB, Notaria Capitular, Bernat de Vilarrubia, f. 24, 78r &v, 87.

Alexandria before that time, to pay his debt within fifteen days.[71] Without doubt, then, close to the time of the renewal of the prohibition against trade with Muslims, following the agreement with the Pope, Jewish merchants from Barcelona continued to reach the port of Alexandria.

Trials and Persecution

On June 17, 1302, Jaume II proclaimed the prohibition against trade with Alexandria in particular and with Muslim lands in general, in accordance with the demands of the Pope. The prohibition was renewed in 1305, and then emphasis was placed on merchandise that could be used for military purposes and thus was forbidden to be exported.[72] Christian merchants who violated the decisions of Pope Clement V were excommunicated; however, in 1309 it was proposed to rescind these excommunications for any resident of the Crown of Aragon who joined in the Crusade against Granada.[73] Without doubt, the prohibition that was proclaimed by Jaume II was motivated by political expediency. When it was convenient for him, he ignored the prohibition and followed the traditional policy of the kings of Aragon. On the one hand, he collected fines that were imposed on delinquent merchants, and these became an important source of revenue for his treasury; on the other hand, he issued licenses to merchants to trade with Muslims. In 1305 he allowed his ambassador to Egypt to export merchandise to that country, and he issued licenses to trade with Muslims to many merchants, including Jews. In 1318, Pope John XXIII offered to pardon the king's transgression against the decree of Clement V, when he permitted trade with Muslims in Alexandria and Egypt.[74] Even after the prohibition was proclaimed, it is doubtful

---

[71] *Pietro Pizolo, notaria in Candia*, I, ed. S. Carbone (Venice, 1978), no. 101; E. Ashtor, "The Jews in the Mediterranean Trade in the Late Middle Ages," *HUCA* 55 (1984): 162.

[72] On the prohibition of 1302, see Ashtor, 163, and n. 16 there; on renewal of the prohibition in 1305, see ACA, R236, f. 71v (Masía di Ros, doc. 4), and cf. docs. 5-20; see also Finke vol. 2, doc. 461.

[73] F. J. Miquel Rosell, *Regesta de letras pontíficas del Archivo de la Corona de Aragón, sección Cancillería Real (pergaminos)* (Madrid: Góngora, 1948), Nos. 325 (1306); 355 (1309).

[74] On the Pope's offer in 1318 to pardon the king, see Rosell, *Regesta de letras pontíficas*, no. 44; on the king's permission to his ambassador to trade in Egypt and on the licenses that he distributed to merchants, including Jews, see Ashtor, 163, n. 17.

whether there was any true intention to put an end to the profitable commercial ties between Barcelona and Alexandria. However, with respect to the Jews, the king's official adoption of the prohibition was a sign of a turn for the worse, and it was used by various agents to displace them from commerce between the two cities. After 1302, the year the prohibition was imposed, reports of the arrest of Jewish merchants who had traveled to Alexandria became more common.

Upon their return to Barcelona, many Jewish merchants were placed under arrest for participation in forbidden trade with Muslims and dealing in items that it was forbidden, with increased severity, to sell to "infidels." There is reason to doubt the veracity of the charges, which went beyond economic crimes, and the sincerity of the intentions that officially lay behind the prosecution of Jewish merchants who had been to Alexandria.

The most interesting trial was that of three Jews: Bonsenyor Astrug, Sento de Forn, and Mosse Toros. On June 11, 1302, the Dominican Joan de Lotger, who headed the Inquisitional tribunal, announced the investigation that he was conducting, along with the bishop elect of Barcelona, against the three, who were under arrest. They were accused of having reviled the Virgin Mary during their stay in Alexandria and acting contemptuously toward her while in the courtyard of the Greek church of the city. According to the testimony of one of the priests of the church—testimony that was given to Christians, who passed it on to the investigators in Barcelona—the accused had desecrated the church, thrown stones at a statue of the Virgin, and spat on the floor in contempt. In a letter to the king it was related that the three appeared before the consul of the Catalans, P. Ruuira, and many Catalan merchants, to examine the deed, and the investigators asked the king's permission to inquire into the matter.[75] It would be surprising that a group of Jewish merchants from Barcelona felt such a great urge to express feelings of contempt in deed and word, in public, before witnesses, in front of the great church of Alexandria. They could just as easily voice pejorative

---

[75] ACA, Cartas Reales (CR), Jaime II, Caja 135, No. 397. The letter was published by Finke, vol. 3, doc. 49. The system used by Finke for numbering the documents is no longer valid. See *The Jews in the Crown of Aragon; Regesta of the Cartas Reales in the Archivo de la Corona de Aragón*, Part I: 1066-1327, ed. Yom Tov Assis; compiled by Mª. Cinta Mañe & G. Escribà (Jerusalem: Hispania Judaica, 1993), doc. 540, 218.

expressions and perform acts of contempt in Barcelona itself, at the cathedral, which was near the Jewish quarter, in secret, in the dark, alone. Such insults against the Church and its saints would certainly not have been unheard of among the Jews. However, their purported appearance before the consul of the Catalan settlement and before many Catalan merchants strengthens our suspicion that the entire affair was a conspiracy. The odor of commercial competition arises from it. There are grounds to assume that the Catalan community in Alexandria was not at all pleased by the presence of Jewish merchants from their homeland. While they could do very little against other merchants, they had many possibilities of taking action against Jews from Barcelona, if not in Alexandria, then back at home. Thus the defense of the honor of the Church was merely an excuse and a tool in the hands of those who were interested in deterring the Jews from trading in the East, intimidating them, and impoverishing them until they were finally driven out of maritime commerce. The fate of the three accused was meant to show very clearly that it did not pay to persist in trading with Muslims. Even after the king came to their assistance and pardoned them, they were required to pay the sum of 6,000 sous of Barcelona (sb), as can be seen from the record in the register of the royal treasurer from June 22, 1302.[76]

The fines that the Jews were forced to pay for insulting Christianity or for trading with Muslims destroyed the profit for which they had taken so many chances. These risks were increased with the passage of time and made trade with Alexandria a dangerous enterprise. One episode worthy of our attention concerns Isaac Vives, a leader of the Barcelona Jewish community during the reign of Pedro III and Alfonso III, who developed important commercial ties with Alexandria.[77] Thanks to well-planned commercial activity, he amassed a huge fortune. Many commercial deposits were made with him by many Jews. After his death, his wealth and property attracted the attention of the authorities. The owners of *comandas*

---

[76] González Hurtebise, pars. 25, 209 and see also Finke, vol. 3, 112, who cites a letter from the king to his treasurer Pedro Boyl in which he mentions the sum paid by the three (ACA, R294, f. 251); regarding the pardon granted by the king to the three Jewish merchants on June 24, 1302, see ACA, R 199, f. 95r & v, 96 (Régné, no. 2781, 2782).

[77] ACA, R 57, f. 129 (Régné, no. 1391); and see: Dinur, *Israel in the Diaspora*, Book 2, Vol. 3, 272-273; ACA, R 66, f. 162v (Régné, no. 1615).

also encountered difficulties because of trade with Alexandria.[78] Putting him on trial posthumously provides incontrovertible proof of the disingenuous nature of the judicial system, which prosecuted the Jews who traded with the Muslim East in contravention of the directives of the Church. On August 21, 1307, a letter was sent from a royal judge and his scribe regarding the trial against the late (!) Isaac Vives, who, according to the prosecution, had traveled frequently to Alexandria. The appellants asked the king not to include Isaac Vives with many other Jews who were about to sign a payment agreement with the king, which would absolve the Jews from legal prosecution because of their voyages to Alexandria, until the king received a full report about him.[79] Two days later the king granted a pardon to the heirs of Isaac Vives and the executors of his estate, in return for the enormous sum of 40,000 sb, which was meant to cancel the forfeits for which he was liable because of his voyages to Alexandria.[80] This huge fine did not resolve everything. On August 30 the king's adviser, Bernat de Sarria, sent a letter to Jaume II about the investigation of the case of Isaac Vives and the commercial deposits he had taken on his voyages to Alexandria. In his letter the adviser claimed that the deceased was guilty and that two Jews would testify to that. He also informed the king about the size of Isaac Vives' fortune, which came to 160,000 sb, which would fall into the king's hands if he were found guilty.[81] Perhaps this incident can explain the multitude of trials and the crown's willingness to remove the Jews from commercial activity in the East. However, we must emphasize that one cannot draw general conclusions from this episode.

In December 1302, the royal treasurer issued a receipt for 173 sb as a fine paid by Samuel Salvat and Yucef Sullam from Barcelona for traveling to Alexandria. The amount of the fine was at the rate of 2s

---

[78] ACA, CR, Jaime II, Caja 149, No. 519.

[79] ACA, CR, Jaime II, Caja 23, no. 2972 (Masía de Ros, doc. 22). In Masía de Ros the documents are numbered according to the old system. See Finke, vol. 2, doc. 587.

[80] ACA, R. 204, f. 88 (Régné, no. 2878); the document was published in Masía de Ros, doc. 91. See also docs. 18, 82. On the receipt of the royal treasurer see ACA, Archivo del Real Patrimonio (ARP), Maestre Racional (MR), Tesoría Real de Aragón, Tesorería del Rey (Libros Ordinarios), No. 270, Tesorero Pere March, f. 17 (IX-1307).

[81] ACA, CR, Jaime II, Caja 135, No. 398 (*The Jews in the Crown of Aragon*, 1, doc. 541, p. 219).

per libra, that is, 10%.[82] From a payment made to the royal treasury in July 1302 we know of *comandas* deposited with another Jew from Barcelona, Gangya (or Guago), whose commercial activity a few years earlier has been discussed above.[83] Payment at the rate of 2s for merchandise valued at a libra was collected from all the merchants, both Christians and Jews, who traded with Muslim countries. From 1302 on fines were levied against many Christians for their voyages to Alexandria in violation of the ban, as recorded by the royal treasurer, Pedro Boyl.[84] Most likely there were Jews among the many merchants whose names were not recorded in the treasurer's account book.

The collection of fines from those who had traveled to Alexandria against the ban became an important source of current revenue—so much so that the king even promised payment from future income from fines.[85] In fact, special officials were appointed at a set salary and stationed in the port of Barcelona for the purpose of announcing the arrival of ships in the harbor whose itinerary included Alexandria.[86] Indeed, the list of merchants and ships that were fined for this reason continued to swell. The names of many Jews figure on the list of exporters who were required to pay a total of 16,000s in March 1305 for merchandise that was sent on one ship. Thus we have evidence of continued Jewish participation in this trade, despite the restrictions and prohibitions.[87] In early June, 1305, many merchants who had sailed to Alexandria in 1304 were required to pay the fine, which, at the rate mentioned above, came to 18,000 sb, showing, like the previous sum, both the volume of trade and the large number of Jewish merchants. This sum did not include the fine for the export of forbidden merchandise, which was paid separately.

---

[82] González Hurtebise, par. 386.

[83] González Hurtebise, par. 37; on the earlier activity of Ganyo see above, n. 41. He belonged to a group of Jews who received licenses to trade in Alexandria in 1305. See Ashtor, 163.

[84] González Hurtebise, pars. 14, 15, 33, 34, 46, 353, 373-375, 409, 411-413, 807, 925-923, 927-928, 931, 1360, 1371.

[85] González Hurtebise, par. 116.

[86] González Hurtebise, par. 1305, and see Finke, vol. 1, doc. 65.

[87] ACA, R 203, f. 131 (Masía de Ros, doc. 75). Among the merchants, the following Jews are listed: Salamon Jaffie, Aaron Jaffie, Issach David, Isaach Mapaluff, Triuhell, Bonjua Iuceff (Masía de Ros, doc. 109).

The appearance of Senton de Forn among the Jewish merchants who sailed to Alexandria in 1304, two years after the Inquisition trial in which he was involved, shows the stubborn perseverance of the Jewish merchants, who did not easily give up the profit they could expect from their mercantile ties with Egypt.[88] His partner in that voyage was Mosse Toros, who had been tried with him by the Inquisition and who had paid a fine of 300 sb in August 1303 for sailing to Alexandria.[89] In May 1305 the king granted a pardon to Juceff Besers of Villafranca and to Astrug Biona from Barcelona, in return for payment of 800 sb at the rate of 2s for every libra of forbidden merchandise that had been exported to Muslim countries. The former was prosecuted for two voyages, the second, for a single voyage, and both of them together for a joint voyage that they made to Alexandria via Cagliari.[90]

These measures do not appear to have deterred many Jews, who continued to trade with Egypt. From a letter of Jaume II to the bailiff of Barcelona in September 1305, we learn of a company that had been established shortly beforehand by Maimo Avinyena (ibn Yona) and Rossel Acerii to export and import merchandise between Barcelona and Alexandria. At about the same time, Vitalis Bonsenyor of Tortosa organized a similar voyage to Alexandria, having received *comandas* from merchants in Catalonia.[91] Some of the Jews who were arrested for the crime of trade with Alexandria were subjects of foreign countries. Two Jews from Morocco, who were arrested in Barcelona in 1311 after arriving from Alexandria, were not deterred

---

[88] ACA, R 203, f. 36v (Masía de Ros, doc. 79). Aside from Senton de Forn, the following Jews appear: Vital Bonsenyor from Tortosa, Salamon Adret, who was perhaps a relative, even a grandson of the RASHBA (Rabbi Salomon ben Adret [1235–1310], who was still alive), Jaco Dalell, Samuel Alfaquin, Samuel Xarquia, Jaffuda Samuel, and Vital Annen.

[89] González Hurtebise, par. 926.

[90] ACA, R 203, f. 17v-18 (Régné, no. 2840).

[91] On these two partners, Maimon and Rosil, see: ACA, R 136, f. 249 (F. Baer, *Die Juden im christlichen Spanien, I: Aragonia und Navarra* [Berlin, Akademie, Verlag 1929], doc. 158); cf. Baer, *Juden*, doc. 152. On Vitalis Bonsenyor, see Baer, *Juden*, 189; the source dates from 1307. On those who were fined in 1308, including Jews from Gerona and Tortosa, see in the latter source, at n. 80, ACA, ARP, MR, Tesorería, 80 Real, no. 271, fol. 8v, 12, 13. The Jews from Tortosa were Vidal Bonsenyor, Jucef Avinatara, David Ximblell, Jucef Quiva, Jamila viuda de Abincema, Issach Avinatara, and Juceff Abinaig (f. 13); they paid 3,000 sb; Juceff Bados of Gerona and Crescas Catora paid 10,000 sb (f. 8v); Samuel de Piera paid 2,000 sb. by means of Bonjua de Piera (f. 12).

from threatening that their continued detention would arouse retaliation, in the wake of which merchants from Barcelona who were sojourning or dwelling in Morocco would suffer.[92] Two years later the king granted a pardon to the Jews Abraham Bisba, Salamo Hakim, Maimon Abraham, and Benvenishti Salamo of Barcelona, who had violated the decree and exported merchandise to Egypt. The total fine on the crew of the ship and the merchants came to 18,500 sb. Hence, according to the customary rate, the value of the merchandise came to the huge sum of over £9,000. Two Jews, Salamon Bisbe and Salamon Jaffia, were fined 682s 3d for a similar voyage, which they made in 1312. After selling their merchandise to Muslims in Alexandria, they imported merchandise from there that was valued at £327 10sb, and they paid the aforementioned fine for it, at the rate of 2s 1d for every libra of merchandise.[93]

The extent of trade with Alexandria by Jewish merchants, despite everything, and the continued, routine collection of fines, can be inferred from a decision made by the king in 1319 regarding the estate of Juceff Ferrer of Bisalú. The king, in return for 2,000 sb, granted a pardon to Juceff's heirs—he had died without legitimate descendants and was accused of various infractions. The king emphasized that the pardon would not be valid if it turned out that the deceased had violated the prohibition against trading with Muslims in Alexandria. The need for this condition shows the frequency of this sort of thing at the end of the first decade of the fourteenth century.[94]

Although Jewish and Christian merchants ostensibly suffered equally from the imposition of the prohibition against trading with Muslims, the damage to the Jewish mercantile activity was much greater. The Catalan merchants and churchmen exploited the opportunity to weaken and even to halt completely the participation of Jews in maritime trade. The Jews did not own ships, and this

---

[92] Archivo Municipal de Barcelona, Llibre del Consell, serie 1, núm. 2 f. 14. The source was published in Masía de Ros, doc. 95.

[93] ACA, R 210, f. 96v-97, 112v-113 (Régné, no. 2975, 2983).

[94] ACA, R 216, f. 119v (Régné, no. 3104); on the validity of the prohibition in 1313 see J. Vincke, *Selecta mutuas civitatis Arago-Cathalaunicae et ecclesia relationes illustrantia*, Barcinone, MCMXXXVI, No. 335; and see the letters of Pope John XXII and Gregory XI, Régné, no. 476, 643; and on trade by Jews at that time, see also F. Giunta, *Aragonesi e Catalani del Mediterraneo*, (Palermo: Società Siciliana per la historia patria, 1972-1973), vol, 2, 126.

made it difficult for them to recover, even when the prohibition was temporarily lifted. Their rivals made certain they did not succeed in rehabilitating their activity, and despite evidence of Jewish participation in trade with Alexandria during the 1340s and 1360s, conditions became more difficult from day to day, and the Jews were restricted to commercial deposits. In 1381 the municipal council of Barcelona forbade the consul of the Catalans in Alexandria from renting out rooms and shops in the Catalan inn to Jews. Even if the Jews had been able to overcome this obstacle, this prohibition reflects the hostility of the Christian merchants and their representatives in Barcelona about ten years before the end of the community in 1391.[95]

Systems of Finance and Raising Capital

As noted, the part played by the Jews in the consolidation and adoption of the *comanda* system (or commercial deposit) was apparently decisive, and like the Catalan merchants, they used it almost exclusively. We have already described the system above and the reasons for preferring it and especially its appropriateness for the Jews. By means of the *comanda* it was possible in fact to get around any prohibition and obstacle placed before Jewish merchants: the *comanda* was executed like a loan in every respect, and the Jew acted as a lender.[96] Naturally we cannot trace all of the many *comandas* deposited by Jews with Christian merchants: many of them appear as simple loans, and only in cases when the merchant fell into difficulties did the names of Jews come to light as having made deposits and taken part in financing the voyage. Nevertheless,

---

[95] On commerce with Muslim lands, Syria, and Egypt, in the 1340s, despite the prohibition, see: Baer, *Juden*, doc. 212; many Jews from Catalonia were involved in that trade. Sometimes they used Cyprus to disguise their true destination. See *Sheelot uTeshuvot haRaN (R. Nisim Gerondi)*, ed. A. Feldman (Jerusalem: Moznaim, 1984), nos. 38, 43. On trade during the 1360s see: Ashtor, 169, no. 26; on the attitude of the municipal council and its decisions see F. de Bofarull y Sans, "Ordinaciones de los concelleres de Barcelona sobre los judíos en el siglo XIV," *Boletín de la Real Academa de Buenas Letras de Barcelona* 6 (1911): 97-102. Capmany[1], vol. 2, 156 ff.; 429; on the prohibition against renting out rooms and shops in the Catalan inn in Alexandria see Capmany[2], vol. 2, part 1, doc. 214, 321: "Item, que'l dit consol, ne hom per ell, ne gos logar ne prestar alcuna cambre ne casa o botiga del afondech a alcum moro ne juheu en negun cas; ans aço deje esquivar sobre totes coses."
[96] See above, notes 26-29.

the sources in our possession show that the phenomenon was quite common.[97]

Regarding the Jewish merchants who were active partners and sailed to the East, we have precise and detailed information. About two thirds of the investors who deposited *comandas* with them were Jews.[98] Despite their small number with relation to Jewish investors, it appears that Christian investors did not refrain from depositing *comandas* with Jewish merchants, thus becoming silent partners. The Christian investors, who were all residents of Barcelona, practiced various professions—merchants, artisans, pharmacists—and they belonged to various classes.[99] There is evidence that some of the depositors of *comandas* were themselves agents, and their investment included other people's money. In most cases we cannot discover who the investors were, and it is quite probable that if sources are extant about complex *comandas* of this kind, they are in other archives and sections. However, the sparse evidence in our possession is certainly indicative of the general situation.[100]

Some trade with the East was financed by simple loans recorded with the notary and not as a commercial deposit, though there was a real difference between the two methods. Jews lent money to Catalan merchants who traded with Muslims. These loans were sometimes recorded in Alexandrian currency, and in that manner we may infer their nature. Joan Cap and Perez Ris, who were mentioned above, managed to raise considerable sums from Jewish lenders. Naturally these merchants often needed financing in order to import

---

[97] ACB, 1-6, doc. 1900; Notaria Capitular, Bernat de Vilarrubia 1295, f. 3r & v, 61v, 101-102, 104v-105.

[98] ACB, Notaria Capitular, Bernat de Vilarrubia, 1295, f. 13, 41v, 67v-68, 71, 78v, 82v, 84v, 96, 118r & v, 119v, 123, 132r & v; ACB, Notaria Capitular, Bernat de Vilarrubia 1301, f. 86v, 87, 95, 112; AHPB, Pere Portell, 1299, Lligall 1, f. 1v-2v, 5r & v, 7, 9v, 10v-11, 12v, 14v, 15r & v, 19; ACA, CR, Jaime II, Caja 135, No. 398 (*The Jews in the Crown of Aragon*, I, doc. 541, 219).

[99] ACB, Notaria Capitular, Bernat de Vilarrubia 1295, f. 116; AHPB, Pere Portell, 1299, Lligall 1, f. 1r & v, 5v, 10, 11v, 15v-16; ACB, Notaria Capitular, Bernat de Vilarrubia 1301, f. 24, 58r-v, 68v-69, 78r-v, 111; ACB, Notaria Capitular, Bernat de Vilarrubia 1308, f. 172v-173.

[100] On an especially interesting case, in which David Abraham, a Jewish merchant from Barcelona, admits that of £16 that were deposited with him by Salamo Llop, £13 belong to Samuel of Marsilia, a Jew from Narbonne, see: ACB, Notaria Capitular, 1295, f. 132r & v, 132v.

merchandise from Alexandria to Barcelona, and, interestingly, they occasionally found Jews from Barcelona who were staying in Alexandria for business purposes and borrowed money or received *comandas* from them.[101] The shipowners usually engaged in maritime trade themselves and were not content with merely transporting goods. Thus, for example, one of them, Arnau de Cornela, borrowed money from a Jew, Aaron Israel, in 1314 and promised to pay his debt in any port where his ship might anchor. Jewish merchants, too, made use of their brethren's capital and borrowed money to finance their business, both import and export, between the two coasts of the Mediterranean. Here, too, some of the lenders themselves took part in sea trade with Alexandria, and it could be that these loans were part of commercial transactions that were more complex than meets the eye from initial perusal of the source.[102]

The Value of Trade between Barcelona and the East

The merchant who received deposits in effect became the investors' active partner, and he used their money to buy merchandise for export. The amounts of the deposits varied, of course, ranging between the small sum of 5s 3d and the considerable sum of £100. Of forty-eight transactions about which we possess information, the sums of the *comandas* are recorded. These sums are denominated in one of two currencies or in both: Barcelona coin (*sous* or *solidi* [s] of Barcelona) in units of the libra (£) and denarius (d), and the currency of Egypt, old Byzants of Alexandria. In the thirteenth century the Crown of Aragon adopted the Anglo-French system, and the silver *gros* or the *croat* was minted, the value of which was one *sou* or one *sueldo*. This system supplanted the earlier currency

---

[101] ACB, Notaria Capitular, f. 101-102, 104v, 104v-105. These are the names of the Jewish lenders and the amounts of their loans: Llobell Issac: 54 old Byzants of Alexandria; Llobell Issac: 134 Byzants; Bonjuha Bellcaire: 80 Byzants. On a *comanda* from a Barcelonian Jew who was staying in Alexandria, see González Hurtebise, par. 61.

[102] Here, too, some of the lenders themselves took part in sea trade with Alexandria, and it could be that these loans were part of commercial transactions that were more complex than meets the eye from initial perusal of the source. On ship owners who borrowed money from Jews, see: AHPB, Pere de Torre, 1314, Lligall 1, f. 12. In this case it is clear that the Jew sailed on the same ship. On the participation of moneylenders in maritime trade, see, for example, AHPB, Pere Portell, 1299, Lligall 1, f. 8, 9v.

of the *denarius* or *dinero*. In both systems, the other units were used solely for calculation and did not exist in reality.[103] In Alexandria during the thirteenth century the coin mainly in use was the gold Byzant, *bisancio*, or *besante*, or, as it is known in the sources, *bisancii veteri de Alexandria aura fini*. It was worth one Florentine *ducado*, and one Byzant was worth 16s of Barcelona; a Byzant was also worth twenty-four *kirato*, so that two *solidi* were worth three *kiratos*.[104] The exchange rates between currencies were well known, for they are recorded in the sources upon which this study is based.[105]

Calculating the value of the *comandas* is a very complex matter, and among other things one must determine the purchasing power of each of the coins, prices, and the wages that were customary at that time, and this is not the place to deal with that topic.[106] Making an arbitrary division of libras into deciles produces the following table, in which the *comandas* are divided in a way that can offer a general impression.

The Amounts of the Comandas (according to the number of smallest and largest sums in each decile).

		£10	–		3d	5s		28
8d	5s	£18	–			11s	£11	5
3d	14s	£25	–			4s	£24	5
4d	15s	£33	–			3s	£30	2
	4s	£46	–	4s		7s	£42	2
	4s	£58	–				£50	3
							£64	1
							£100	1

---

[103] On the coins used in the Crown of Aragon, particularly in Catalonia, during the thirteenth and fourteenth centuries, see J. Botet i Sisó, *Les monedes catalanes* (Barcelona 1908-1911); F. Mateu i Llopis, *Glosario hispánico de numismática* (Barcelona, 1946); O. Gil Farrés, *Historia de la moneda española* (Madrid: Diana, 1949); Dufourcq, 525-531; Hillgarth, *Kingdoms*, vol. 2, 629-633.

[104] Capmany², vol. 2, Part 2, 1056-1057; but see Mateu i Llopis, s.v. Besante de Alejandría.

[105] ACB, Notaria Capitular, Bernat de Vilarrubia 1295, f. 71v (£16=20 besant); f116 (80 sb=5 besant); AHPB, Pere Portell, 1299, Lligall 1, f. 7 (80s=6 besant); f. 9v (100s=8 besant); ACB, Notaria Capitular, Bernat de Vilarrubia, 1301, f. 24 (£51=70 besant).

[106] Emery, *The Jews of Perpignan in the Thirteenth Century*, 128-130; Dufourcq, 540-556; 566-469.

The table clearly shows that more than seventy percent of the deposits were less than £20 or 27 old Byzants of Alexandria. Since the information in our possession is partial, the important question—what was the average general sum that a merchant would bring in both directions from Barcelona and Alexandria or Cyprus, which was regarded by him as being worthwhile from a commercial point of view—regrettably remains unanswerable. However, in some instances we know the total value of the merchandise shipped on a single voyage from Barcelona to Alexandria. In March 1305 the sum of 16,000 s was paid in customs at a rate of 2s for every libra of merchandise that was on board the San Joan. Accordingly, the value of the merchandise was £8,000. The merchandise belonged to eighteen merchants, including six Jews. In June 1305 a customs duty of 18,000 s was paid for the merchandise on board the San Francisco, so that the value of the merchandise was £9,000, and once again among the owners of the cargo were eight Jews.[107]

In two other cases we have information about the value of the merchandise brought by Jews to Alexandria or from there to the Iberian Peninsula. In 1312 two Jews from Barcelona, Salamo Bisba and Salamo Afia, shipped various merchandise that they sold in Egypt. They returned to Barcelona with goods valued at £327 10s. As noted, they were fined for trading with Egypt when they returned to Catalonia. A year later, four Jews resident in Barcelona exported merchandise to Alexandria on the Santa Eulalia, and they sold it in that region. We saw above that after their return to Barcelona they were put on trial, and the king granted them a pardon in return for 18,500 s. According to the customary rate, their merchandise was valued at £9,250, quite a considerable sum.[108] We cannot propose an average amount on the basis of only four shipments, but we would maintain that these instances do permit us to make a rather well founded estimate.

---

[107] About the San Joan, see above, n. 87; on the San Francisco, see above, n. 88.
[108] See above, n. 93.

The Merchandise

In the notarial sources in our possession, along with the sums of the *comandas*, the merchandise that the Catalan merchants exported to the East is often mentioned along with the goods they imported on their way back. However, because the main purpose of these sources was to list the amounts of money deposited with the merchants, who converted it into merchandise, occasionally there is no mention of the items exported. European merchants, including Catalans, exported gold, silver, tin, lead, copper, mercury, amber, and coral to Egypt and thence to the countries of the East. Egypt also needed material for shipbuilding—lumber, tar, resin, and iron. The Egyptians mainly imported textiles from Spain: wool and silk cloth, olive oil, honey, walnuts, almonds, and saffron. From Eygpt, the Spanish merchants imported many spices, sugar, silk, indigo, ivory, gold, and slaves.[109]

According to a document dated September 1299, Maimon Denan exported four jugs of oil for 108 s, which Salamo Astruc deposited with him. The merchandise was on board a ship that sailed to Cyprus but, as noted, the merchandise apparently reached a Muslim market. In that year Sullam Ruben Jahia received a *comanda* from Vidal Roven consisting of various textiles, clothing, candle wicks, and from a Christian, saffron and a woolen blanket. All this merchandise was to be shipped to Candia and Cyprus.[110] In 1301 Salamo Sullam of Barcelona and Samuel Asday of Villafranca received a *comanda* from Ramon de Tolosa for the sum of £24 4s. They converted the money into 22 libras worth of saffron, which they shipped to the same destination.[111] In a *comanda* for the sum of 39s, which Jusef

---

[109] See Capmany[2], 237 ff.; Masía de Ros, 242-260, where all the commodities are listed. Also see Marimón and Sanz, 41-44 and doc. 14 (export of textiles), 41 (import of lacquer), 57 (import of aloe and pepper); and regarding the fourteenth century, docs. 114, 116, 136, 138, 140, 151. On the Egyptians' need to import building materials, see M. Lombard, "Arsenaux et bois de marine dans la Mediterranée musulmane (VIIe-XIe siècles)," *Le Navire et l'économie maritime du Moyen-Age au XVIIIe siècle* (Paris: S.E.V.P.E.N, 1958), 86-87. This is the cause of the extremely severe prohibition by the church against the export of these materials to Islamic countries, to prevent them from building warships. See, for example, ACA R 210, f. 96v-97 (Régné no. 2975).

[110] AHPB, Pere Portell 1299, Lligall 1, f. 2, 5v, 15v, and see Marimón and Sanz, docs. 62, 64.

[111] ACB, Notaria Capitular, Bernat de Vilarubia 1301, f. 68v-69. In southern Catalonia saffron was an important item on the local market and for export purposes.

Abraham Tavell received from Jusef Habib's wife, three dozen genuine diamonds were purchased, which were intended for sale in Alexandria.[112] Finally, there was an interesting transaction in which Roven Astruc de Real received a deposit of £6 from Momet Bonafeu, a Jew from Barcelona, in return for which he exported to Alexandria in that year golden thread from Montpellier.[113]

Among the goods imported from Alexandria or via that city our sources mention a number of items. In 1295 Jusef Benvenist imported pepper that Isaac de Castello had ordered according to a *comanda* valued at £42 7s 4d. In September 1299 Sullam Roven imported ginger from Cyprus, which doubtless originated in Alexandria, according to an order from a Christian cobbler from Barcelona who had made a deposit with him. Vides Jucef bought sugar in Alexandria according to the request of a Jew from Mallorca.[114]

Companies and Partnerships

Almost half of the voyages of Jewish merchants to the East were undertaken by partners. In most cases the partnership remained in force only until the end of the voyage and the completion of the transaction that was connected with it. By entering into such partnerships, the Jews sought to increase the chances of success by increasing the capital available to them, to diminish the dangers of a voyage to distant ports, and to share the losses that might be incurred. In a small number of voyages there were three partners,[115] but in most there were two.[116]

---

[112] ACB, Notaria Capitular, Bernat de Vilarrubia, 1295, f. 118r & v.

[113] ACB, Notaria Capitular, Bernat de Vilarrubia, fol. 78v.

[114] ACB, Notaria Capitular, Bernat de Vilarrubia, fol 123; AHPB, Pere Portell 1299, Lligall, f. 5v, 7 (pepper); Marimón and Sanz, docs. 64, 67 (ginger and sugar).

[115] ACB, Notaria Capitular, Bernat de Vilarrubia, f. 71 (Samuel Salvat, David Astruc, Jucef Sullam); f. 84v (Roven Astruc de SaReal, Bonet Aninay, Jacob Guago); González Hurtebise, par. 25, Sento de Forn, Salomo Bonsenyor, Mosse Toros Gracia.

[116] ACB, Notaria Capitular, Bernat de Vilarrubia, f. 3r &v, 13, 61v, 119v (Bonjuda Bolax, Jacob David); AHPB, f. 1v (...[?], Isaac); f. 12v, 13r & v (Isaac Abraham de Torre, Isaac Salamo de Torre); f. 134 & v (Salamo Jacob, Vidal Moacel); ACB, Notoria Capitular, Bernat de Vilarrubia 1301, f. 5r & v (Salamo Tholosa, Fabib Vidal); f. 24 (Jucef Corayef, Abraham Tavell); f. 24r & v (Roven Curtavini, Isaac Gabinti); f. 58r & v (Mayr Samuel, Astruc Abrafim); f 68v-69 (Salamo Soylam, Samuel Açday); ACB, Notaria Capitular, Bernat

The agreement between the partners and of course the establishment of a company was transacted according to rules, and the contract between the partners was signed according to law before a notary. At the end of September 1299, Salamo Jacob and Vidal Moacel, Jews from Barcelona, established a commercial company and signed an agreement for dividing the profits at the end of a voyage to Crete and Cyprus.[117] In mid-June 1301 a company was established by two Jews from Barcelona, Fabib Vidal and Mosse de Tholosa, to make a voyage to Candia and other places.[118] On June 23, 1301, Roven Curtavini (or Cortobi) and Isaac Gabinti of Gerona signed a contract in Barcelona to establish a commercial company for the purpose of a voyage they planned to make on a ship belonging to Bernat Marquet to Crete and Cyprus. According to the contract, they were to divide the profits equally.[119] The importance of the official founding of a company is quite clear. A controversy between partners, deviation from the plan, breakdowns along the way, the death or absence of one of the partners—all of these contingencies required the writing of a contract.

A company established by two Jews from Barcelona in the early fourteenth century is worthy of our attention. Maymo Avinyena and Rossel Acerii planned a voyage to Alexandria. On their way back they were delayed in Cagliari, where Rossel remained with the merchandise of the company, and Maymo continued on his way. After some time Rossel died, and his partner did not receive his share, although he had a document that confirmed the partnership. Rossel's widow refused to give her husband's partner his share, and Maymo addressed the king to ask his assistance.[120] Two years earlier two brothers, Perfet and Bonafos Saltell, had lodged a complaint

---

de Vilarrubia 1308, f. 172v-173 (Isaac Salamo, Mosse Teros); González Hurtebise, par. 386 (Samuel Salvat, Juceff Sullam); Baer, *Juden*, doc. 158 (Maymo Avinyena, Rossell Acerii).

[117] AHPB, f. 13r & v. The contract was published in Marimón and Sanz, doc. 70; details of this contract and its conditions and the contracts mentioned below will be published and discussed in a study presently being prepared.

[118] ACB, Notaria Capitular, Bernat de Vilarrubia, f. 5r & v; among the witnesses figures Astruc Saltell.

[119] ACB, Notaria Capitular, Bernat de Vilarrubia, f. 24r & v. Among the signatures of the witnesses appears that of Bonjuda Aninay. In the three contracts mentioned above, a mark of ratification is found, and in the latter two the word "iuravit" (he swore).

[120] ACA, R 136, f. 249 (Baer, *Juden*, doc. 158).

against Maymo and Rossel, who had agreed to return the deposit placed with them upon their return to Barcelona. Instead, the partners remained in Cagliari and did not return the deposit, and the two brothers addressed the authorities.[121] The company of Isaac Salamo of Villafranca and Mosse Toros, who is well known to us, encountered difficulties after the former died. The two partners, who had traveled to Crete and Cyprus, had received a *comanda* of 1,000 sb from Bernat de Moguera. In January 1309 Saltell Gracia of Barcelona admitted that he owed 800 sb out of a total of 1,000 sb that his late son Salamo Isaac was supposed to have paid in his father's name. Saltell was apparently the guarantor. His wife Druda confirmed the obligation of her husband and thereby certainly forfeited the priority of her marriage contract, and the couple also produced their sons Astruc and Bonjuda Saltell as guarantors.[122]

Usually partnerships were short term, for the duration of only a single voyage, and when that voyage ended, the partnership was dissolved. Nevertheless, some companies were of long duration, and some partnerships were reconstituted with new contracts with an eye to another voyage to the East. Samuel Salvat and Jusef Sullam may serve as an example of a longstanding partnership. The two were the partners of David Astruc in 1295 on a business voyage to Alexandria,[123] and in December they appear again as partners who were fined 173 sb for a voyage to Alexandria in contravention of the king's orders.[124] However, these exceptions do not disprove the rule: most of the companies and partnerships were created for a single voyage.

Risks and Dangers

The dangers that lurked on the path of a merchant on his voyage and those he could expect at his destination also contributed to the short duration of companies and partnerships. Pirates who

---

[121] ACA, R 130, f. 208 (Baer, *Juden*, doc. 152).

[122] ACB, Notaria Capitular, Bernat de Vilarrubia, 1308, f. 172v-173. Among the witnesses appears Bonjuda Cortobi.

[123] ACB, Notaria Capitular, Bernat de Vilarrubia, 1295, f. 71.

[124] González Hurtebise, par. 386.

threatened trading ships were not criminals marginal to society. They came from every country and acted against anyone whose path they crossed. All the agreements among states to eliminate the phenomenon were fruitless, and every party was liable to violate such an agreement when it seemed opportune to do so. The merchants, too, and especially the shipowners themselves, indulged in piracy when they had an opportunity: Catalans against Mallorcans, Sicilians against Sardinians, Muslims from Granada and North Africa against Christians, and everyone against everyone else. Christian prisoners were redeemed in Mallorca, Muslim prisoners were redeemed in Granada, and in this volatile world the Jews were more vulnerable than anyone.[125]

The Jewish merchant who was robbed not only lost his money and his wares, but he also lost the deposits that many Christians and Jews had placed with him, because there was not a single merchant who did not receive *comandas*. If he suffered no physical injury and was not captured, upon reaching Barcelona, before he managed to recite the blessing for being saved from disaster, he was greeted by many of those who had invested their money with him on the voyage, expecting profits. Not only did he have to compensate them, especially if he intended to continue overseas commercial activity, but he also had to make certain that he was not sued by the many people who had invested their money with him. As noted, some of the owners of *comandas* had deposited money with the merchant that they had received from others. The Jewish merchant was therefore required to obligate himself to pay back the deposits and to take the responsibility upon himself.

At the end of December, 1303, Isaac Llobell declared that two Christian merchants from Barcelona, whose merchandise he had received as a *comanda*, had disappeared when their ship was lost, and therefore they would not be responsible to any person.[126] In July 1289 many Jews from Mallorca, headed by Saadon Benaade, lodged a complaint with the *baile* of Mallorca against Pere Rubio of Valencia, who had captured the ship of Ramon de Rose of Mallorca on June 25th at Athens and plundered nine bundles of merchandise. He also

---

[125] Dufourcq, 574-576; Hillgarth, *Kingdoms*, vol. 1, 42-44.
[126] ACB, Notaria Capitular, Bernat de Vilarrubia, 1301-1307, f. 111.

captured a Jew named Jacob Bendellell, a resident of Mallorca, who was carrying cash. Following that complaint, judicial proceedings were opened.[127]

The risks and dangers of sea travel were many and multifarious. In February 1277 Pedro III ordered all of his officials in Tortosa to force two residents of the city and their partners in crime to return to Mosse Ascandran, who represented a Jew named Abraham, everything they, together with the robbers, had stolen from Bondia, who was working for the aforementioned Abraham. A year and a half later, we find a Mosse Ascandaran involved in a suit against the king's physician. The physician, who was on a voyage overseas, was found guilty by the judge. That physician, along with Domiro de Castilit, one of two Christians from Tortosa who were found guilty of piracy, was condemned by the same judge for the crime of theft from a Mosse Ascandran in July 1279. This same Mosse was interested in collecting money due to him from residents of Tortosa, who owed money to Romero. The king was hesitant and changed his instructions several times. He ordered the Tortosa authorities to allow Romero to enter the city so the trial could be held properly. From a source dated October 1281, we learn that the problem had not yet been resolved, and it appears that the main claim of Mosse against the knight of Tortosa was a theft he had committed against Mosse's father, apparently at high sea. This episode shows us some of the problems, complications and delays in lodging a lawsuit that Jews encountered when they wished to make money from maritime trade.[128]

Taxes and Customs Duties

The rulers of Egypt, who encouraged trade between Christian countries and their own, derived great benefit from this activity. They made their country into a link between Christian Europe and the Far East by preventing European merchants from continuing on to the Orient. The benefit they derived came first of all from the imposts that the sultan placed upon various items that passed

[127] ACA, CR, Jaime II, Caja 135, No. 405 (*The Jews in the Crown of Aragon*, I, 221, no. 546.)
[128] On that incident, see Régné, nos. 679, 705, 739, 785, 883.

through Egypt.[129] In parallel, the kings of Aragon collected customs duties from goods imported into their country and on merchandise exported from its ports.[130] The king of Aragon imposed a duty of 2s per libra, that is, ten percent. This would appear to be a fine which, as noted, was imposed for trading with a Muslim country against the king's directives, and one might be tempted to conclude that there was no essential difference between the king's position in fact and his declared position in principle, which was proclaimed whenever good relations prevailed between him and the Pope. However, when speaking of a fine, the violation of the king's order is mentioned explicitly.[131] One might argue that this wording was used in accordance with circumstances, whereas the levy itself was constant and stable. However, a source from 1305 refutes that argument. In this source two payments are mentioned, the payment of customs duties for exported merchandise and payment at the same rate for goods which were not allowed to be exported to Muslim countries (as noted, special officials were appointed to collect that fine).[132] Thus, the rate of customs on the import of goods and the rate imposed for export, including forbidden goods, were identical. Let us note that according to a source dated September 1299, every merchant who sailed to Crete and Cyprus had to pay a license fee of 80s.[133]

Conclusion

At the end of the thirteenth and the beginning of the fourteenth centuries, Jews of Catalonia sought to take part in trade between Barcelona and Alexandria, which began to develop in parallel to the political and commercial expansion of the Crown of Aragon in the Mediteranean basin.[134] The Jews' efforts had good chances to

---

[129] See for example: Capmany2, 235 ff.

[130] Thus, for example, on pepper that was imported in February 1302, González and Hurtebise, par. 410.

[131] "La pena posada a aquells qui contra vet del SR navegaren a Alexandria," see above, n. 124, and the many sources mentioned there.

[132] See above, n. 88. On the special official, see above n. 86.

[133] AHPB, Pere Portell, 1299, Lligall 1. The source is found on a single sheet in the aforementioned register.

[134] See the comprehensive discussion on this subject in the article by Hillgarth (above n. 6); and see the article by Abulafia, "Catalan Merchants" (above, n. 13).

succeed. They possessed the capital, connections, talents, and will that were necessary for such success. However, the effort did not go well. Catalan expansion came at the end of the main period of the Catalano-Aragonese *Reconquista*, when there was a significant decline in the political status of the Jews. Their importance to the king diminished to a degree that made it difficult for them to assume a primary place or to take a true part in the development that emerged under the new conditions of the end of the thirteenth century.

A major obstacle to the interesting initiative of Jewish merchants was the growth of a new middle class in Catalonia, for whom maritime commerce was one of the most important channels of development and consolidation. This pioneering group of merchants was, in many cases, the main factor in the creation of the infrastructure for the commercial activity that spread throughout the entire Mediterranean, and which was parallel to the Crown's political expansion. In fact, it is difficult to distinguish between the two trends, the commercial and the political. Catalan merchants established colonies in the important cities of the East, both in Muslim lands and on the important islands of the Mediterranean, in Athens, in Constantinople, and even on the Crimean peninsula. They had no reason to share the profits that they hoped to gain from this widespread activity with the Jews. They viewed the Jews as competitors, and in the resolutions of the councils of the cities of Catalonia they expressed hostility toward them.

In the efforts of the new bourgeois to displace the Jews in maritime commerce, they were assisted by a number of factors and phenomena. The political decline of the Jews from the 1280s on was timely for them. Pressure from the Church, mainly in the initiative of the Dominicans, with the help of the Papal Inquisition, also contributed quite a bit.[135] The prohibition imposed by the church on trade with Muslim countries was apparently supposed to damage the Catalan merchants, but all the evidence shows that they continued to pursue that trade and ultimately overcame the artificial obstacle, about which no Count-King of Aragon-Catalonia, although officially supposed to enforce it, was enthusiastic. The prohibition

---

[135] Yom Tov Assis, "The Papal Inquisition and Aragonese Jewry in the Early Thirteenth Century," *Mediaeval Studies* 49 (1987): 391-410.

acted mainly against the Jews, and its consequences for them were long term.

From this chapter in the history of the Jews of the Iberian Peninsula a historical conclusion of the highest significance emerges, one that is incontrovertible. Although lending money at interest was sharply criticized and restricted, that activity was never halted, and Christian society did not produce a substitute for the Jewish money lender. In contrast, the participation of Jews in maritime trade in the first stages of this commerce with Islamic lands was eventually brought to an end when Catalan merchants understood that they could take it over without sharing profits with the Jews. In maritime trade the Jews were dangerous rivals, and for that reason they were removed from the field by various stratagems, whereas in lending money at interest, they remained useful to society. Lacking institutions that could provide cash and credit, because of the Christian religious prohibition against taking interest, the Jews were permitted to continue working in this field. The legislation and the complaints, the opposition and the criticism to Jewish participation in money lending, cannot disguise the benefit that Christian society derived from Jewish loans.[136] In contrast, Jewish merchants trading between Barcelona and Alexandria were a hindrance to Christian merchants. Hence, they were eventually prohibited from participating in this activity.

---

[136] See Assis, *Jewish Economy*, passim.

Works Cited:

Abulafia, David. "Catalan Merchants and the Western Mediterranean, 1236-1300: Studies in the Notarial Acts of Barcelona and Sicily." *Viator, Medieval and Renaissance Studies* 16 (1985): 209-242.

Adler, M. N. *The Itinerary of Benjamin of Tudela.* London: H. Frowde, 1907.

Alastos, Doros. *Cyprus in History.* London: Zeno, 1976.

Altisent, Agustín. "El monasterio de Poblet y unos judíos prestamistas de la Segarra (S. XIV-XV)." *Sefarad* 27 (1967): 282-289.

Ashtor, Eliyahu. "The Jews in the Mediterranean Trade in the Late Middle Ages." *Hebrew Union College Annual.* 55 (1984): 159-178.

Assis, Yom Tov. "Jewish Diplomats from Aragon in Muslim Lands (1213-1327)." *Sefunot* 18 (1985): 11-34. (Hebrew)

------. "The Papal Inquisition and Aragonese Jewry in the Early Thirteenth Century." *Mediaeval Studies* 49 (1987): 391-410.

------. *The Jews of Santa Coloma de Queralt in the Thirteenth Century.* Jerusalem: Magnes Press, 1988.

------. *The Golden Age of Aragonese Jewry, Community and Society in the Crown of Aragon, 1213-1327.* London and Portland, OR: The Littman Library, 1997.

------. *Jewish Economy in the Medieval Crown of Aragon, 1213-1327; Money and Power.* Leiden: Brill, 1997.

Assis, Yom Tov and José Ramón Magdalena Nom de Deu. *The Jews of Navarre in the Late Middle Ages.* Jerusalem: Zalman Shazar Center, 1990 (Hebrew).

Assis, Yom Tov, ed., and María Cinta Mañe and Gemma Escribà, compilers. *The Jews in the Crown of Aragon; Regesta of the Cartas Reales in the Archivo de la Corona de Aragón,* Part I, 1066-1327. Jerusalem: Hispania Judaica & The Central Archives, 1993.

Atiya, A. S. *Egypt and Aragon.* Nendeln, Liechenstein: Kraus, 1966.

Baer, Fritz. *Die Juden im christlichen Spanien, I: Aragonia und Navarra.* Berlin: Akademie, Verlag, 1929.

Baer, Yitzhak. *A History of the Jews in Christian Spain.* Philadelphia: Jewish Publication Society, 1966.

Bofarull y Sans, Francisco de. "Ordinaciones de los concelleres de Barcelona sobre los judíos en el siglo XIV." *Boletín de la Real Academa de Buenas Letras de Barcelona* 6 (1911): 97-102.

Botet i Sisó, Joaquim. *Les monedes catalanes.* Barcelona: Institut d'Estudis Catalans, 1908-1911.

Cantera Burgos, Francisco. *La usura judía en Castilla.* Salamanca: Calatrava, 1932.

Capmany Surís y de Montpalau, Antonio de. *Memorias históricas sobre la marina, comercio y artes de la antigua ciudad de Barcelona, Vol II.* Barcelona: A. de Sancha, 1779-1792.

Carrasco Pérez, Juan. "Acerca del préstamo judío en Tudela a fines del siglo XIV." *Príncipe de Viana,* 166-167 (1982): 909-948.

------. "Los judíos de Viana y Laguardia (1350-1408): aspectos sociales y económicos." In *Vitoria en la Eda Media,* 419-447. Victoria-Gasteiz: [n. p.], 1982.

------. "La actividad crediticia de los judíos en Pamplona (1349-1387)." In *Minorités et Marginaux en France méridionale et dans la Péninsule ibérique (VIIe-XVIIIe siècles)* (Actes du Colloque de Pau, 27-29 mai 1984), 221-263. Paris: Presses du CNRS, 1986.

------. "El crédito judío en la villas navaras del camino de Santiago (1339-1408)." In *Local and International Credit in the Middle Ages and the 16th Century,* Ninth International Economic History Congress, 8-14. Bern: International Economic History Association, 1986.

Carson, R. A. G. *Coins, Ancient, Mediaeval and Modern, II: Coins of Europe.* London: Hutchinson, 1971.

Cortes de los antiguos reinos de Aragón y de Valencia y principado de Cataluña I. Madrid: [n. p.], 1896.

Delcor, Maties. "Les Juifs de Puigcerdà au XIIIe siècle." *Sefarad* 26 (1966): 17-45.

Dinur, Ben Zion. *Israel in the Diaspora,* book II, vol. III. Tel Aviv: Dvir & Bialik, 1968. (Hebrew)

Du Cange, Charles du Fresne. *Glossarum Mediae et Infimae Latinitatis,* editio nova. London, L. Favre, Niort, 1883.

Dufourcq, Charles E. *L'Espagne catalane et le Maghrib.* Paris, Presses universitaires France, 1966.

Emery, Richard. *The Jews of Perpignan in the Thirteenth Century.* New York, Columbia University Press, 1959.

Engel, Arthur, and Raymond C. Serrure, R., *Traité de Numismatique du Moyen-Age,* vol. II, Paris: Leroux, 1894; and vol. III, Paris: Leroux, 1905.

Finke, Heinrich. *Acta Aragonensia.* Berlin and Leipzig: Rothschild, 1908-22.

García Sanz, Arcadio. "Los intereses de los préstamos de los judíos de Vich durante la primera mitad del siglo XIV," AUSA 4 (1962): 247-255.

García de Valdeavellano, Luis. *Sobre los burgos y los burgueses de la España medieval.* Madrid: Real Academia, 1969.

Gerondi, Nissim ben Rueben. *Sheelot uTeshuvot haRaN (R. Nisim Gerondi).* Edited by A. Feldman. Jerusalem: Moznaim, 1984.

Gil Farrés, Octavio. *Historia de la moneda española.* Madrid: Diana, 1949.

Giunta, Francesco. *Aragonesi e Catalani del Mediterraneo, vol. II.* Palermo: Società Siciliana per la historia patria, 1973.

González Hurtebise, Eduardo. *Libros de Tesorería de la Casa Real de Aragón,* I. Barcelona: Luis Benaiges, 1911.

Hefele, C. J., *Histoire des Conciles,* Paris: Letouzey et Ané, 1913.

Heyd, Wilhem von, *Histoire du commerce du Levant au Moyen Age.* Leipzig: Harrassowitz, 1885.

Hibbert, A. B. "Catalan Consulates in the Thirteenth Century." *Cambridge Historical Journal* 9 (1949): 352-358.

Hillgarth, Jocelyn N. "The Problem of a Catalan Mediterranean Empire 1229-1327," *The English Historical Review,* Supplement 8 (1975).

------. *The Spanish Kingdoms, 1250-1516.* Oxford: Clarendon, 1976.

Hinojosa Montalvo, José. "El préstamo judío en la ciudad de Valencia en la segunda mitad del siglo XIV." *Sefarad* 45 (1985): 315-339.

Lalinde Abadia, Jesús. *La Corona de Aragón en el mediterráneo medieval (1229-1479).* Zaragoza: Institución Fernando el Católico, 1979.

Leroy, Béatrice. *The Jews of Navarre in the Late Middle Ages.* Jerusalem: Magnes, 1985.

Lombard, M. "Arsenaux et bois de marine dans la Mediterranée musulmane (VIIe-XIe siècles)." In *Le Navire et l'économie maritime du Moyen-Age au XVIIIe siècle.* Edited by M. Mollat, 53-106. Paris: S.E.V.P.E.N, 1958.

Madorell Merimón, José Mª, and Arcadio García Sanz. *Comandas comerciales barcelonesas de la baja edad media.* Barcelona:Colegio Notarial de Barcelona, 1973.

Marcus, Shimon. "History of the Jews in the Island of Crete." *Otsar Yehudei Sefarad* 3 (1963): 135-139. (Hebrew)

Masià de Ros, Àngels. *La Corona de Aragón y los estados del Norte de Africa.* Barcelona: Instituto de estudios mediterráneos, 1951.

Mateu i Llopis, Felipe. *Glosario hispánico de numismática.* Barcelona: CSIC, 1946.

Miquel Rosell, F. J. *Regesta de letras pontificias del Archivo de la Corona de Aragón, sección Cancillería Real (pergaminos).* Madrid: Góngora, 1948.

Miret y Sans, Joaquim. *Itinerari de Jaume I "el Conqueridor."* Barcelona: Institut d'Estudis Catalans, 1918.

Miret y Sans Joaquim and Moise Schwab. "Documents sur les Juifs catalans aux Xie, XIIe et XIIIe siècles." *Revue des Études Juives* 68 (1914): 49-83, 174-197.

Niermeyer, J. F. *Mediae Latinatis Lexicon Minus,* Leiden: Brill, 1976.

O'Callaghan, Joseph F. *A History of Medieval Spain.* Ithaca: Cornell University Press, 1975.

Oliver, B. *Historia del derecho en Cataluña.* Madrid: Ginesta, 1881.

Ollich i Castanyer, Immaculada. *Aspectes económics de l'activitat dels jueus de Vic, segons els 'Libri Iudeorum' (1266-1278), Els 'Libri Iuderoum' de Vic de Cardona.* Barcelona: CSIC, 1985.

Pietro Pizolo. *Pietro Pizolo, notaio in Candia*. Edited by Salvatore Carbone. Venice: Comitato per la pubblicazione delle fonti relative alla storia di Venezia, 1978.

Piles Ros, Leopoldo. "Situación económica de Valencia a comienzos del Siglo XIV, a través de los préstamos judaicos." In *XI Congresso di Storia della Corona d'aragona*, 63-88. Palermo: Academia de Scienze Letter e Arti, 1984.

Régné, Jean. *A History of the Jews in Aragon*. Edited by Yom Tov Assis. Jerusalem: Magnes Press, 1978.

Salavert y Roca, Vicente. "El tratado de Anagni y la expansión mediterránea de la Corona de Aragón." *Estudios de Eda Media de la Corona de Aragón* 5 (1952): 209-360.

Sánchez Albornoz, Claudio. *España, un enigma histórico*. Barcelona: Edhasa, 1973.

Sayous, A. E. "Let méthodes commerciales de Barcelone au XIIe siècle, d'après les documents inédits des Archives de sa Cathédrale." *Estudis Universitaris Catalans* 16 (1931): 155-198.

Starr, Joshua. "Jewish Life in Crete under the Rule of Venice," *PAAJR* 12 (1942): 59-114 (repub. in *Medieval Jewish Life*. Edited by R. Chazan, New York: Ktav, 1976, 233-288).

Treppo, Mario del. *Els mercaders Catalans i l'expansió de la Corona Catalano-Aragonesa al segle XV*. Translated by J. Riera i Sans. Barcelona: Curial, 1976.

Vicens Vives, Jaime. *España: Geopolítica del estado y del imperio*. Barcelona: Yunque, 1940.

Vincke, Johannes. *Selecta mutuas civitatis Arago-Cathalaunicae et ecclesia relationes illustrantia*. Barcelona: Editorial Balmes, 1936.

Jews and Finance in Medieval Iberia

Gregory B. Milton

The Jewish lender has long been an archetype of medieval history, whether considered within the political and religious polemic of contemporary medieval culture, or as a category of activity by modern historians. The significance of the image and of the actual role of Jews as lenders has long been accepted as part of the history of Iberian society during the Middle Ages, although historians have not yet sufficiently melded two threads of activity for medieval society on and off the Iberian Peninsula: the development and expansion of commercial finance on one side and the full economic activity of Jews on the other. Recent scholarship has begun to address both aspects of the relationship between Jews and finance, at least as it was experienced in Iberia from the twelfth to the fourteenth centuries. Jews were important economic actors within Iberian society, and their activity included extending credit as part of the developing commerce of Iberia from at least the twelfth century. Yet, credit did not encapsulate all Jewish economy by any means, nor were all credit and financial activities conducted by Jews. An extensive credit economy existed by the thirteenth century in all areas of Christian-controlled Iberia, and the majority of creditors were Christian. Christians and Jews worked together to utilize credit, and at times Christians acted as hidden partners investing in the activity of Jewish lenders. The relationship between Jews and finance, then, must be considered within the full context of the wider credit economy.

Economic studies have too often assumed that lending, usury, and Jews were interconnected elements of Iberian society,[1] even as the negative stereotypes of the Jewish lender have been properly rejected. In his study of medieval Provence, Joseph Shatzmiller proposed that two cultural concepts of the Jewish moneylender in the early fourteenth century existed in the minds of medieval Christians: the well-known "Shylock" stereotype of the oppressive and exploitive lender on one hand, and the good neighbor/charitable lender on the other. Shatzmiller's work describes an economic society in which lending and interest by Jews occurred regularly. Some Christians spoke up for Jewish lenders as good neighbors whose credit activity served useful, friendly purposes. Others at times complained about oppressive Jewish creditors illegally extracting interest for outstanding debts. Shatzmiller's investigation focused on Jewish lending exclusively however, where interest rates of 33-50% were the norm and total repayment figures often reached four or five times the original amounts of the debts.[2] As we shall see, Jewish lending was much more varied and part of a wider world of commercial credit in Christian Iberia.

Examination of the complex roles of Jews within the financial and commercial exchanges of Iberia has only begun recently. For much of the twentieth century, proponents of commercial development originating in eleventh- and twelfth-century European cities often assumed a Jewish monopoly of financing in Iberia. These historians dismissed its "positive" effects when compared to the Italian and Flemish Christian activity that they studied and which allowed for the expansion of long-distance trade and the development of a vibrant commerce across Europe. Within this interpretation, Jewish lenders provided consumptive loans, usually considered unproductive in light of the more acceptable accounting, investing,

---

[1] Yitzhak Baer, *A History of the Jews in Christian Spain*. 2 vols. (Philadelphia: Jewish Publication Society, 1961), especially vol. 1, 116-118, 201-208; Yom Tov Assis, *Jewish Economy in the Medieval Crown of Aragon, 1213-1327: Money and Power* (Leiden: Brill, 1997).

[2] Joseph Shatzmiller, *Shylock Reconsidered: Jews, Moneylending and Medieval Society* (Berkeley: University of California Press, 1990), 72-79.

and banking activity of non-Iberian Christians.[3] However, these older interpretations do not best reflect the commercial activity of Iberia, in which Jews and Christians participated in financing long-distance as well as local trade through a variety of productive and effective financial mechanisms. Iberia from the twelfth to the fourteenth centuries, with its mix of Muslim, Christian, and Jewish populations, created a vibrant economic society. Not only must our understanding of the Jewish credit economy be expanded to acknowledge Christian activity within the financial field, but our understanding of medieval commercial credit must recognize the role and significance of Jewish creditors within their proper context.

Interpreting Cultural Representations

Cultural representations of Jews and lending, many created in the thirteenth century, are often deployed to demonstrate the dominant real-economy role of Jews as creditors in Iberia. The most common references are to *The Song of The Cid*, written in the early thirteenth century, and to the *Cantigas de Santa Maria (Songs of Saint Mary)*, originating in the later thirteenth century. *The Song of The Cid* presents a well-known scene involving Jewish lenders. At the beginning of the first canto, the Cid, sentenced to exile, conspires with his man, Martín Antolínez, to raise 600 marks from two Jews of Burgos, Raquel and Vidas, by providing two coffers of "treasure" as security for a loan. The coffers, of course, are filled with sand and the Cid has no intention of paying back the loan. As the negotiations progress, Martín Antolínez even manages to gain a piece of fine

---

[3] Henri Pirenne, *Economic and Social History of Medieval Europe*. Trans. I. E. Clegg. (London: Kegan Paul and Co., 1936), 131-133 and 156-157, considers Jewish money lending a "small affair" and "much exaggerated" except for in Spain, where Jews "possessed sufficient capital" to support expanding trade. Nevertheless, Catalonia was not a center of commercial capitalism according to Pirenne. Robert S. Lopez, *The Commercial Revolution of the Middle Ages, 950-1350* (Englewood Cliffs, NJ: Prentice Hall, 1971), 60-62, recognizes the role of Jews as intermediaries in long-distance trade in the tenth and eleventh centuries, but the primary agency of his commercial revolution remains Christian merchants and bankers. Edwin S. Hunt and James M. Murray, *A History of Business in Medieval Europe, 1200-1550* (Cambridge: Cambridge University Press, 1999), 70-71, 215-216, claims that small, consumptive loans, typically provided by Jewish lenders or pawnbrokers, did little to develop the medieval economy.

leather, some good cloth, and 30 marks from Raquel and Vidas for his efforts mediating the transaction.[4] Most scholars refer to this scene to demonstrate the common identification of Jews as lenders in twelfth- and thirteenth-century Castile, and perhaps to represent the cultural distrust of lenders that existed within the feudal society of the period.[5]

A fuller consideration of the scene, however, illustrates something else. The interaction of the Cid and Martín Antolínez with Raquel and Vidas does not focus on the two Jews as economic actors, but instead demonstrates the legitimacy—within the perspective of the medieval author and his audience—of fraud by Christian debtors towards Jews. The Cid, having "used up all [his] gold, and [his] silver," intentionally provides two locked coffers of sand, swearing that they were filled with golden treasure, in order "to pawn it at some fair price"; meaning whatever he could get by false promises.[6] Once the exchange is complete, the Christian nobles prepare to hurry away: as Martín Antolínez says, "there's six hundred marks for you, and thirty for me. Let's pack up the tents and leave in a hurry...."[7] Most significantly, the issue of the Jewish loan does not end there. The author of *The Song of The Cid* deliberately reminds the audience of the loan and its non-repayment—seemingly unnecessarily in relation to the plot—in the middle of the second canto, when Raquel and Vidas approach the Cid's representative to Alfonso VI, Minaya Alvar Fâñez, as he rides through Burgos. There they beg Minaya to intercede for them so that the Cid would pay back the amount lent.

While no further action concerning this loan is mentioned in the rest of the epic, it is clear that these scenes do not represent an anti-Jewish polemic concerning lending. On the contrary, the two Jewish

---

[4] *The Song of the Cid: A Dual-Language Edition With Parallel Text.* Trans. Burton Raffel (New York: Penguin, 2009), 9-17, Canto One, Verses 6-11.

[5] See, for example, Baer, *A History of the Jews in Christian Spain.* vol. 1, 58; Enrique Cantera Montenegro," Cristianos y judíos en la Meseta Norte castellana: la fractura del siglo XIII," in *Del pasado judío en los reinos medievales hispánicos: Afinidad y distanciamient. XIII. Curso de Cultura Hispanojudía y Sefardí de la Universidad de Castilla-La Mancha,* ed. Yolanda Moreno Koch and Ricardo Izquierdo Benito (Cuenca: Universidad de Castilla La Mancha, 2005), 61; Jonathan Ray, *The Sephardic Frontier: The Reconquista and the Jewish Community in Medieval Iberia* (Ithaca: Cornell University Press, 2006), 55.

[6] *The Song of the Cid,* 9, Canto One, Verses 6-7.

[7] *The Song of the Cid,* 17, Canto One, Verse 11.

lenders are portrayed rather moderately. In the second scene, Raquel and Vidas only ask for the return of their money: "We forgive him the interest, if he'll pay back the loan."[8] The author, moreover, does not attempt to justify the Cid's non-repayment on any anti-Jewish grounds. We must recognize that the portrayal of these scenes regarding Raquel and Vidas is deliberate. The deception and fraud, in an economic sense, remain fully reflective of the Christian debtor's actions, not the Jewish lenders'. However, Raquel and Vidas may be interpreted as at fault in one way: they lent with an eye towards future profit, rather than giving freely in friendship. The giving of elaborate gifts without expectation of return, especially exemplified by the Cid's continuous generosity throughout the poem, is a heavily-stressed, highly-valued activity of heroic quality. As we shall see, these scenes reflect the divide between cultural beliefs about commercial finance—specifically the opportunity that Christians had to accuse Jewish creditors of illegality—rather than the actuality of Jewish and Christian participation in credit transactions.

The other often-referenced source of anti-Jewish literary representation in Iberia is the monumental *Cantigas de Santa Maria*, produced in the second half of the thirteenth century under the patronage of Alfonso X of Castile.[9] These poem-songs provide miracle stories of the Virgin Mary and reflect a variety of perspectives of popular religion, including, but not limited to, attitudes towards Jews. Out of the four hundred and twenty-seven stories, twenty-three involve Jews as agents of anti-Christian activity, as targets of conversion, and as symbols of religious ambiguity. Only Cantiga 25, however, focuses specifically on Jewish lending. Nonetheless, scholars place significant importance on this one text as representative of Jewish economic activity in thirteenth-century Iberia.[10] In Cantiga 25, a Christian man contracts a loan from a

---

[8] *The Song of the Cid*, 103, Canto Two, Verse 83.

[9] All citations and translations of the *Cantigas de Santa Maria* text are derived from The Centre for the Study of the 'Cantigas de Santa Maria' of Oxford University, *The Oxford 'Cantigas de Santa Maria' Database*. http://csm.mml.ox.ac.uk/

[10] Albert I. Bagby, "The Jews in the Cántigas of Alfonso X, El Sabio," *Speculum* 46 (1971): 680-83, examines Cantiga 25 in detail as one highly important poem, due to its many associated illuminated miniatures. Bagby classifies this as one of five cantigas demonstrating Jewish avarice, although Cantiga 25 is really the fullest example of this potential. As with many scholars studying Jews in Iberia, little attention is paid to the 404 other cantigas that do not depict Jews.

Jewish lender, after exhausting his money giving charity. The man offers his creditor "Mary and Christ as his warrantors." When the loan is due, the Christian man is overseas, so he has a chest with his payment thrown into the sea, praying for it to be guided to his creditor, which occurs. However, the Jewish lender, having retrieved the chest, pretends that he did not recover the money, instead demanding repayment from the debtor upon his return to the city. The Christian merchant claims that the Virgin Mary would provide proof of the repayment, which is done in the church when a statue of the Virgin Mary miraculously speaks, stating that "the Jew had indeed received the money. When the Jew heard this, he converted to Christianity."[11]

The story of Cantiga 25 is clearly anti-Jewish. The Jewish lender exhibits greed and duplicity, and the series of miracles described lead to the fundamental, desired conclusion: conversion of the Jewish man to Christianity. However, this story is only one representation of a Jewish creditor among twenty-three cantigas concerning Jews. Significantly, it is also the only one of the three cantigas concerned with lending and usury generally which addresses lending by Jews. Both Cantiga 62 and Cantiga 75 provide miracles stories related to lending at interest, but address only Christian characters. The miracle story in Cantiga 62 depicts a release from debt for a Christian widow and her son, the latter having been held hostage by the Christian creditor to gain repayment of the debt, after the widow prays for protection from the Virgin Mary.[12] Cantiga 75 presents a warning to the "corrupt, vain and arrogant" who enriched themselves through avarice, and those around them who hoped to benefit from those riches. The story balances the deathbed action of a Christian usurer and a poor Christian widow. The latter prays to the Virgin Mary, and even though the local chaplain refuses to attend the widow in order to focus his efforts on gaining a bequest from the rich man, it is the widow's soul that goes to heaven. The usurer's home is surrounded

---

[11] *The Oxford 'Cantigas de Santa Maria' Database*, Cantiga 25 "Pagar ben pod' o que dever." http://csm.mml.ox.ac.uk/

[12] *The Oxford 'Cantigas de Santa Maria' Database*, Cantiga 62 "Santa Maria sempr' os seus ajuda." http://csm.mml.ox.ac.uk/

and filled by devils who end up "taking the soul from the rich man's body to a place of perpetual punishment."[13]

Concerning lending and usury, then, the lessons of the *Cantigas de Santa Maria* are not simply about Jews. In fact these miracle stories fit very well into the larger theological concerns of Christian society. Jacques Le Goff demonstrates that the vast majority of European anti-usury sermons and penitential *exempla* focused on Christian behavior, inner intent and the true repentance of individual members of the faith.[14] As Jeremy Cohen has demonstrated for anti-Jewish theological polemic, thirteenth- and fourteenth-century mendicant preachers were rarely concerned with Jewish lending systematically. Instead, the development of anti-Jewish polemic reflected concerns with the impropriety of a living religion for medieval Jews, in which Jews were equated with heretics for not fulfilling the Christian concept of "proper" Judaism.[15]

Usury, Church and State

Charging interest and gaining profit, the economic goal of medieval merchants, craftsmen, and financiers, created cultural discomfort for some elements of medieval society. The medieval church particularly attempted to control the commercial activities beginning to develop in the eleventh century, yet rarely to the point of outright prohibitions against them. Charging interest itself was classified as the sin of usury, yet this was a slippery term that changed definition over time and place.[16] In the modern sense, usury is the charging of excessive interest, with a standard defined legally. In the most absolute sense, usury could be defined as the charging of any interest at all. Generally, non-specialists confuse medieval

---

[13] *The Oxford 'Cantigas de Santa Maria' Database*, Cantiga 75, "Omildade con pobreza." http://csm.mml.ox.ac.uk/

[14] Jacques Le Goff, *Your Money or Your Life*. Trans. Patricia Ranum (New York: Zone, 1998).

[15] Jeremy Cohen, *The Friars and The Jews: The Evolution of Medieval Anti-Judaism* (Ithaca: Cornell University Press, 1982), 77-99. In Cohen's argument, polemics against Jewish lending were not significant and fairly limited, see 82-84.

[16] Bernard J. Meislin and Morris L. Cohen, "Backgrounds of the Biblical Law Against Usury." *Comparative Studies in Society and History* 6 (1964): 250-267.

concern about usury with the belief that usury was consistently prohibited following the absolute definition. In contradiction to this misunderstanding about medieval attitudes, however, definitions of usury deployed by medieval people adapted to the reality of regular credit as part of medieval financial commerce. The institutional Church argued that usury, defined in multiple ways, was a sin, while secular states often created legal standards and definitions that regulated—and profited from—forms of credit finance.[17]

Medieval discourse about usury had biblical foundations, and both medieval Jews and Christians struggled with the propriety of extending credit and charging interest within and between religious communities. As Christians were the majority of the population in high and late medieval Iberia, as well as in Europe more widely, their perspective had the greatest effect on credit activity, yet Jews also had ambivalent attitudes about usury, both for its use within the Jewish community and outward to the majority Christian society. Four scriptural citations informed the medieval debate on justifying the continuation or prohibition of usury, three from the Hebrew Bible—Exodus 22:25-27, Leviticus 25:35-37, and Deuteronomy 23:19-20—and one from the New Testament—Luke 6:34-35.[18] As with most biblical exegesis, all four references allowed for varying

---

[17] John T. Gilchrist, *The Church and Economic Activity in the Middle Ages* (New York: Macmillan, 1969); Lester Little, *Religious Poverty and the Profit Economy in Medieval Europe* (Ithaca, NY: Cornell University Press, 1978); William C. Jordan, *The French Monarchy and the Jews: From Philip Augustus to the Last Capetians* (Philadelphia: University of Pennsylvania Press, 1989); Shatzmiller, *Shylock Reconsidered*, 43-70; Mark D. Meyerson, *Jews in an Iberian Frontier Kingdom: Society, Economy and Politics in Morvedre (1248-1391)* (Leiden: Brill, 2004), 189-190.

[18] Exodus 22:25 suggests that profiting from lending to those in need should be avoided: "If you lend money to one of my people among you who is needy, do not be like a moneylender; charge him no interest." The sentiment is mirrored in Leviticus 25:35-37. However, Deuteronomy 23:19-20 creates more specific categories, "do not charge your brother interest, whether on money or food or anything else that may earn interest. You may charge a foreigner interest but not a brother Israelite." Luke 6:34-35 states that, "If you lend to those from whom you expect repayment, what credit is that to you? Even 'sinners' lend to 'sinners' expecting to be repaid in full. But love your enemies, do good to them, and lend to them without expecting to get anything back. Then your reward will be great, and you will be sons of the Most High..." The passage from Luke seems to direct believers to provide charity rather than loans. Carl F. Taeusch examines the development of usury as a concept, considering the three Hebraic Biblical passages along with a definition of Aristotle's, but not the New Testament passage, in "The Concept of 'Usury': the History of an Idea," *Journal of the History of Ideas* 3 (1942): 291-318.

interpretations. The three biblical passages shared by both Jews and Christians indicated that charging interest could be acceptable under certain circumstances, although some theologians could argue that a debtor was 'needy' simply by the nature of requiring a loan, meaning these passages precluded any legitimate charged-interest. The one Christian scripture on the topic, Luke 6:34-35, exhorted the faithful to charity rather than lending.

The effectiveness of religious regulation of usury cannot be assumed. Among Jews in the Middle Ages, rabbinical guidance allowed Jews to lend to non-Jews but not to their fellow believers, without attempting to address Christian activity in terms of credit and interest at all. Considering economic need, Jewish religious authority defined Christians as "foreigners" to whom Jews could lend money, rather than "brothers" to whom they could not. Thus, Jews could lend to Christians. "The economic necessity of earning their livelihood through money lending, however, scarcely allowed them any other interpretation."[19] Christian attempts at regulation were more complex, less clearly understood by the wider society, and aimed at the control of non-Christian activity as well as that of Christians. The emphasis of ecclesiastical discourse on usury as a significant, spiritual problem in the commercial revolution after the eleventh century obscured the fact that lending was a regular and necessary part of economic life, which helped make Jews viable and important members of medieval society, especially in Iberia.

These religious concerns about charging interest operated within an economic reality in which many people utilized credit on a daily basis, a fact which must be taken into account when deconstructing the prevailing counter-usury attitudes. The medieval church's concern with the issue of usury corresponds for the most part to the commercial expansion of the eleventh, twelfth and thirteenth centuries. Although a prohibition against usury was included among the canons of the Council of Nicea as far back as 325, stating that any cleric "taking interest" or "dealing in usury" should "be deposed and

---

[19] David B. Ruderman, "Champion of Jewish Economic Interest" in *Essential Papers on Judaism and Christianity in Conflict*, 516. Originally published in *The World of a Renaissance Jew: The Life and Thought of Abraham ben Mordecai Farissol* (Cincinnati: Hebrew Union College Press, 1981), 85-97.

removed from his order,"[20] the ecumenical councils of late Antiquity and the Early Middle Ages attempted no further restriction of usury. Commercial expansion inspired church concern with the charging of interest, generating six statutes concerning usury which were promulgated in ecumenical councils from the twelfth to fourteenth centuries. Beginning with the Second Lateran Council of 1139, usury merited attention, this time with a general and full condemnation of "that detestable, shameful and insatiable rapacity of moneylenders."[21] This council's decree prohibited lending, without specificity and without much apparent effect. Forty years later, the Third Lateran Council of 1179 changed focus, condemning "notorious usury," and demonstrating an acceptance of commercial lending to some extent.[22] By creating this 'unacceptable' category of charging interest, the decree implied a category of 'acceptable,' or at least ignored, interest. In 1215, the Fourth Lateran Council switched focus once more, acting "to protect the Christians against cruel oppression by the Jews" in an attempt to end excessive usury between Jews and Christians.[23] Church councils returned to the issue of Christian usury in 1245 and again in 1274 at successive meetings held in Lyons.[24] Finally, the Council of Vienne of 1311-1312 attempted to refute the actions of secular authorities who provided protection to lenders by extending exemptions from prosecution for excessive usury to local communities.[25] The acts of this council indicate a potential struggle—perhaps desired on the part of the higher clergy—between ecclesiastical and secular authority for jurisdiction over complaints

[20] Nicea I (325), Canon 17. *Conciliorum Oecumenicorum Decreta*, 3rd Ed., ed. Huberto Jedin (Bologna: Instituto per le Scienze Religiose, 1973), with English translations from *Decrees of the Ecumenical Councils*, vol. 1, ed. Norman P. Tanner S.J., (Washington, D.C.: Georgetown University Press, 1990), 14. While occasional secular and/or local prohibitions during the period between 325 and 1139 did repeat the earliest prohibition, usury was not an economic phenomenon of great concern until commercial expansion began in the eleventh century.

[21] Lateran II (1139), Canon 13, *Decrees*, vol. 1, 200.

[22] Lateran III (1179), Canon 25, *Decrees*, vol. 1, 223.

[23] Lateran IV (1215), Constitution 67, *Decrees*, vol. 1, 265-266.

[24] Lyons I (1245), Constitution 1 of the second collection of decrees produced by the council, *Decrees*, vol. 1, 293-295, see the discussion of the decrees in the introduction to this council, 273-277; also Lyons II (1274), Constitutions 26 and 27, 328-330.

[25] *Decrees*, vol. 1, Vienne (1311-1312), Decree 29, 384-385. These decrees addressing secular exemptions of usury accusations related directly to royal policies in Iberia. See below.

of excessive interest. As with earlier decrees, the concept of usury as excessive interest implicitly created a category of acceptable interest rates.

Aside from the Fourth Lateran Council, which marked an exceptional anti-Jewish moment in medieval ecclesiastical legislation of finance, all of the decrees deriving from the ecumenical councils of the High Middle Ages focused on Christians lending and taking interest. The decree of 1139, in fact, was the only one to forbid the practice of charging interest completely. All the others instead concerned themselves with excessive usury, in which the interest charged became oppressive. This shift represents the gradual, if grudging, acceptance by Church authorities of a commercial money economy. Posing a distinct conflict between spirituality and economy, John T. Gilchrist argues that this change was linear and reciprocal: the movement from an absolute moral proscription of usury to an acceptance of charging interest, within determined limits, was balanced by a "gradual decline in the spiritual life of the Church."[26]

Canonical attention to, and definition of, the problem of usury came to be reflected in approaches to popular religion through sermon *exempla* and confessionals, which focused on Christian lending rather than on Jewish credit activity. Jacques Le Goff argues that church authority in the thirteenth and fourteenth centuries considered usury a corruptive threat to the spiritual well-being of Christians.[27] Implicit in this consideration was the actuality that interest was a permanent part of economic life. Jeremy Cohen demonstrates that the anti-Jewish polemic created by mendicant preachers in this same period had limited concern with usury as a particular issue. Public accusation and preaching against Jews because of usurious activities seem to have been symbolic motivators—and yet quite powerful ones—as a means to focus the attention of Christians on their own spiritual status, rather than as reflections of concrete concerns generated by economic reality. Medieval morality might have shaped concern over economic life,

[26] Gilchrist, *The Church and Economic Activity*, 4-10, and 138-139.
[27] Le Goff, *Your Money or Your Life*, 17-32; see also Little, *Religious Poverty*, 34-41.

especially usurious transactions, but did not necessarily originate in the real experience of the people involved in economic activity.[28]

The effectiveness of attempted religious proscriptions against charging interest is questionable, as continued economic development included the increased use of financial credit mechanisms of many types throughout the twelfth, thirteenth and fourteenth centuries. Secular authority had a more direct impact on shaping both attitudes and real actions of medieval people than did religious beliefs, although one could argue that secular rulers simply adapted more quickly to reality than the religious hierarchy. In Iberia, the thirteenth and fourteenth centuries saw a growth in state regulation of economic activity, especially relating to lending and Jews, but rarely did this regulation attempt to prohibit the charging of interest. Instead, Iberian governments acted to control excesses in credit transactions as they defined them, to establish procedures for recording debt and judicial complaints, to set limits on interest rates and periods of repayment, and then to collect fees, payments, and fines for their regulation.

In Castile-Léon complaints and legislation recorded in meetings of the representative body known as the Cortes (Catalan: Corts) present a picture of interest charged on Jewish loans as following patterns similar to those offered by historians of areas outside Iberia: rates of 33% to 50%, and total payments far exceeding the principal owed. Legislation at successive meetings of the Cortes at Valladolid (1258), Jerez (1268), Valladolid (1293), and Carrión (1317), addressed complaints made against Castilian Jews by regulating their debt contracts, such as in 1293, when the Cortes set a limit on interest at "tres por cuatro al año" or 33% annually.[29] As in France and England, this legislation often reflected internal political tensions and was not limited to, nor perhaps even focused upon, the actuality of lending in Castile-Léon. Noble and urban resistance to the strong

---

[28] Le Goff, *Your Money or Your Life*, 65-84; Little, *Religious Poverty*, 146-169 and 197-217; Cohen, *The Friars and The Jews*, 82-84; and Meyerson, *Jews in an Iberian Frontier Kingdom*, 189-194 and 203-205.

[29] *Cortes de los antiguos reinos de Léon y Castilla*, 2 vols., ed. Don Manuel Colmeiro, (Madrid, 1883-4). For Valladolid (1258), 156; Jerez (1268), 158-160; Valladolid (1293), 180-181; and Carrión (1317), 235 and 241.

royal authority of Castile, based on the military successes of the re-conquest, found expression in complaints against Muslims and Jews.

Within the Crown of Aragon, Catalan legislation and royal charters reflect a greater acceptance of credit exchange than exists in documentation from Castile, providing regulation of lending activity with more measured prescriptions. Jaume I (r. 1213-1276) promulgated the earliest regulations concerning interest within the Crown of Aragon. At the Corts of Villafranca in 1228, the interest charged by Jewish lenders was limited to 20%, to accrue for no more than two years, and not to exceed the capital of the loan.[30] Jaume I renewed the limit of 20% at the ecclesiastical council and Corts of Tarragona in 1235.[31] In 1241, the king and the Corts of Girona added a limit of 12% for Christian lending along with a confirmation of the previous limit on Jewish lending.[32] These early statutes, coincident in time with the much more prohibitive legislation and inquests occurring in territories north of the Pyrenees, not only indicate an acceptance of credit transactions by Jews and Christians but also set the standard for lending at interest in the Crown of Aragon over the next century. In June of 1301, the Jews of the Crown of Aragon received a license to lend at interest to Muslims within the limits established by Jaume I over seventy years before.[33] Jaume II (r. 1291-1327) extended the same regulations for charging interest to the Muslims of Tortosa, ordering that they respect the level of 4 *denarii* per *libra* per month (20%) set by Jaume I.[34]

By the last decades of the thirteenth century, however, complaints about Jewish lending in particular started to shape the relationship between royal authority and the Jews of the Crown of Aragon, as Jewish communities began to provide subsidies to the crown to gain exemptions from potential prosecutions of complaints. Accusations and the exemptions usually made reference to Jaume I's original

[30] Jean Régné, *History of the Jews in Aragon: Regesta and Documents 1213-1327*, ed. Yom Tov Assis (Jerusalem: Magnes Press, 1978), no. 4. Hereafter cited as Régné.

[31] Régné nos. 9 and 10.

[32] Régné no. 28; also M. Cinta Mañé and Gemma Escribà in *The Jews in the Crown of Aragon Regesta of the Cartas Reales in the Archivo de la Corona de Aragón*, vol. 1, *Sources for the History of the Jews in Spain* 4 (Jerusalem: Hispania Judaica, 1993), no. 5. Hereafter cited as Mañé.

[33] Mañé no. 81.

[34] Mañé no. 230.

statutes. Alfons II (r. 1285-1291) granted the Jews of Calatayud in November of 1287 an exemption from prosecution for violating the maximum interest established at the Girona Corts.[35] In June 1290, F. Lull accused two Jews of Mallorca, Maymo Benenono and Jucef Abenahar, of charging interest in excess of the limit fixed by Jaume I. The king ordered that an inquest be conducted to investigate the charge.[36] Perhaps in response to a similar inquest, Vidal Baron, a Jew of Cardona, swore before two magistrates (*veguers*) of the king in February of 1299 that he observed the statutes of Jaume I concerning the legal amount of interest charged.[37] While many similar cases can be found in the royal registers, the permanence of Jaume I's legislation demonstrates an element unique to Catalonia's economic development. Unlike many other rulers in Western Europe, the count-kings allowed and regulated lending and interest, while providing a stable environment for economic exchange involving credit by both Jews and Christians.

While their policies remained consistent and supportive of credit activity, by the late thirteenth century Catalan rulers were finding methods to use this longstanding regulation to their financial advantage. Rather than prohibiting and confiscating loans, as the French monarchs did, the count-kings benefitted from regulating them. Providing justice regarding accusations against violators of the statutes resulted in judicial fines for the royal fisc. For example, in August of 1321, Thomas Perez of Fochs, with proof provided to the royal court of Jaume II, accused Muça Abnalcavit, Vidal Abulbaca and Abrahim Arapinaz, Jews of Huesca, of extorting interest from him. The court confiscated the amount of the debt and interest, 5,000 *solidi* of Jaca, half profiting the king and half to Thomas Perez. In addition, the accused usurers had to pay another 5,000 *solidi* to the royal fisc in amends.[38]

---

[35] Régné no. 1810.

[36] Régné no. 2155.

[37] Régné no. 2717.

[38] Régné no. 3195 and no. 3213. Thomas Perez was involved in another case the day previously, Régné no. 3193, in which the accused, Bonafos Jucef and Vidal Gallipapa, Jews of Montclus, bought a royal remission for 3,300 *solidi* of Jaca. The amount equaled double the capital and interest charged, of which 2,000 *solidi* went to the royal treasury and 1,300 *solidi* to the debtor.

The count-kings found even greater profit by selling exemptions from prosecution to entire Jewish communities. Jaume I provided exemptions, without noting the price paid for the service, to the Jews of Mallorca in 1254 and to the Jews of Lleída in 1262.[39] Alfons II received 95,000 *solidi* from the Jewish *aljama* of Barcelona for an exemption in 1290.[40] At the same time the Jews of the city and kingdom of Mallorca paid the king 37,000 *solidi* for their own exemption.[41] In 1298, the Jews of the Catalan town of Santa Coloma, as one of the communities subordinate to the *aljama* of Barcelona, helped pay 100,000 *solidi* for general letters of remission to absolve them from fault for charging interest in excess of 4 *denarii* per *libra* per month.[42] These exemptions covered any and all violations of the law—presumed or real—which had already occurred. Exemptions for future behavior also were granted, such as the five-year exemptions which Jaume II gave to the Jews of Lleída and to the Jews of Huesca in 1298.[43] It was most likely this latter type of exemption that Decree 29 of the Council of Vienne addressed when it condemned the protection provided by secular rulers to those accused of excessive, usurious interest. Through judicial fines engendered by complaints of usury and payments for exemptions from such accusations, the count-kings found a useful and profitable stream of revenue by extorting taxes and special payments from Jews under their authority. These exemption payments should not be seen as proof that Jewish lenders charged excessive interest. Buying exemptions from the crown simply precluded the severe risk that prosecution of complaints posed for any Jewish creditor. Of course, the continued negotiation of exemptions with the crown could lead some creditors from Jewish communities to increase charged interest and press harder to collect debts, either as opportunity for personal profit or as necessity to raise sufficient money to pay for the subsidies. Perhaps more significantly, the exemptions could provide the perception

---

[39] Régné no. 51 and no. 152.

[40] Régné no. 2130 and no. 2139.

[41] Régné no. 2163.

[42] Régné no. 2683. The 100,000 *solidi* bought letters of remission for the aljama of Barcelona and for the subordinate communities of Villafranca, Tarazona, Tarragona, Montblanc, and Cervera. The Jews of Santa Coloma belonged to the latter.

43 Régné nos. 2694 and 2699.

that Jewish lenders could, or would, act excessively against their Christian debtors.

Anti-Jewish legislation did tend to correspond with increased tensions between Christians and Jews generally in Europe. While at times quite extreme, polemics in Catalonia were not tied to significant acts of persecution concerning lending or debt. Jeremy Cohen notes the final goal of scholastic mendicants concerning anti-Jewish preaching: "The Spanish Dominican school of Raymond de Peñaforte masterfully developed the charges of heresy against the Jews and their Talmud into an ideology that called for the elimination, by conversion, of all European Jewry." David Nirenberg's study of the types of violence experienced by Jews in fourteenth-century Iberia found that specific tensions over debt were not central to this violence.[44] Whatever the corresponding elements of persecution in Catalonia, regular economic interaction continued in this period. Catalan legislation did not forbid all lending at interest, but created fair limits for such activity. Accusations and complaints about Jewish creditors did not create prohibitions against their work, but did provide the mechanism by which the count-kings raised revenue through fines and exemption payments.[45] For people within the medieval Crown of Aragon, lending and interest remained important elements of commerce and most recorded credit transactions occurred peacefully within these fair limits.

Jewish and Christian Commercial Credit

Church councils and mendicant sermons may have influenced the attitude of medieval Christians, but did not halt the development of commercial finance. Royal regulation had better success at shaping and profiting from this economic activity, but should not be considered the agent of its development either. The reality of economic exchange utilizing credit originated in the needs of Christian and Jewish businessmen: merchants, artisans, and consumers. The

---

[44] Cohen, *The Friars and the Jews*, 242-243; David Nirenberg, *Communities of Violence: Persecution of Minorities in the Middle Ages* (Princeton: Princeton University Press, 1996). See also R. I. Moore, *The Formation of a Persecuting Society* (Oxford: Blackwell, 1987).

[45] Meyerson, *Jews in an Iberian Frontier Kingdom*, 177-179.

written culture of the Crown of Aragon in which professional notaries—private and public—recorded thousands of commercial transactions provides us with the opportunity to see how these Jewish and Christian businessmen conducted this real economic activity. Unfortunately, the limited number of surviving records in Castile and Portugal restricts a full exploration of Jewish and Christian commercial exchanges in those areas to the same extent. In much of Castile, the maintenance of economic records was dependent on the selections of ecclesiastical archivists, whose choices were driven by a desire to keep records of institutional importance.[46] The professional notarial tradition in Catalonia and later in Mallorca and Valencia, imported during the twelfth and thirteenth centuries from Italy and Southern France, resulted in general economic records being kept in private or communal holdings over the centuries. In conjunction with the extensive record keeping of the count-king's officials, survival of these notarial records provide evidence of thousands of Jewish and Christian credit transactions in the Crown of Aragon.

A close look at one community, the market town of Santa Coloma de Queralt, provides an example of the full potential of commercial credit transactions for both Jews and Christians. Established in the early eleventh century, Santa Coloma was one of the Christian fortifications along the border between Old Catalonia and the Muslim territory that would become New Catalonia as the Christian territorial expansion progressed. Beginning as a settlement next to a small fortification near the hermitage of Santa Maria de Bell-loc,[47] the community grew slowly during the twelfth and early thirteenth centuries. By the last third of the thirteenth century, Santa Coloma de Queralt had become fully integrated into the Catalan economy as a regional market town. Contracts from five notarial registers for the period 1276-1313 provide a sample of commercial debt transactions, revealing over 900 people identified as inhabitants of the town and

---

[46] Teófilo F. Ruiz, "Trading with the 'Other: Economic Exchanges Between Muslims, Jews, and Christians in Late Medieval Northern Castile," in *Medieval Spain: Culture, Conflict and Coexistence. Studies in Honour of Angus MacKay*, ed. Roger Collins and Anthony Goodman (Basingstoke: Palgrave/Macmillan, 2002), 65; Nina Melechen, "Loans, Land, and Jewish-Christian Relations in the Archdiocese of Toledo," in *Iberia and the Mediterranean World of the Middle Ages*, ed. Larry Simon (Leiden: Brill, 1995), 186, 195-198.

[47] Joan Segura i Valls, *Història de Santa Coloma* (Santa Coloma de Queralt: P. Bas y Vich, reprint 1953), 23-27.

district of Santa Coloma. Seventy of these inhabitants were Jewish, six were Muslim, and the remainder Christian.

Drawn from a period of forty years, these 900 people do not represent the entire population of Santa Coloma by any stretch of the imagination, but only those people involved in commercial transactions. Without detailed demographic records, any estimate can only be approximate, but the population of Santa Coloma can be extrapolated from the census figures for Catalonia of 1378 (that is, after the depopulation and limited recovery following the plague). Counting only taxable households rather than all people, the census lists 161 taxable hearths in Santa Coloma (equivalent to 725-800 people), yet the fact that the notarial protocols provide over 900 names of people from the town at the beginning of the century suggests that the total population should be considered significantly higher. A conservative estimate of 300 to 320 households (1,400-1,500 people) is appropriate for Santa Coloma. Thirty households (120-180 people) were Jewish—about 10% of the total population—based upon evidence in a grant from Lady Francesca de Queralt in 1327. Previously, the Jewish proportion of the total population has been overestimated, at upwards of one-third of all inhabitants, based on weak evidence. Yom Tov Assis accepts too easily the claim of Lord Pere VI of Queralt in 1347 that fifty Jewish families had lived in Santa Coloma for generations. The high figure in the claim would have had financial benefit for the lord of Queralt.[48] In addition, Assis underestimates the number of Christians living in Santa Coloma, resulting in a skewed picture of the population of the town. In fact, twenty-five to thirty Jewish families (120-180 people) living in Santa Coloma in the decades around 1300 is both reasonable and supported by the number of Jews active in the notarial documents. Rounding out the population, Muslims were a very small proportion of the 1,500 inhabitants, perhaps fewer than 20. In order to analyze the significance of the credit transactions of Santa Coloma, it is

---

[48] Yom Tov Assis, *The Jews of Santa Coloma de Queralt* (Jerusalem: Magnes Press, 1988), 22-26; Segura i Valls, *Història de Santa Coloma*, 91-92, cites the 1347 claim of fifty Jewish households from a jurisdictional dispute with the crown. Baer, *A History of the Jews in Christian Spain*, vol. 1, 422, n. 8, gives seven Jewish families in Santa Coloma in 1328 and thirty families in 1347.

necessary to keep these population figures in mind, as Christian, Jews and Muslims all participated in the town's commerce.

The market activity of Santa Coloma revolved around the sales of labor-animals, cloth and grain in the period between 1276 and 1313. While many small sales and exchanges of other items most likely occurred, the surviving transactional evidence from the notarial contracts illustrates little of it. Instead the notaries recorded transactions that required debt: arranged as parts of sales or contracted separately as direct loans. In fact, just under 84% of all the contracts recorded in the years 1276-1277, 1287, 1293-1294, 1304-1305, and 1312-1313 were debt transactions. The largest majority were credit-sales and direct loans, as Table 1 demonstrates:

Table 1: Commercial Debt Transactions of Santa Coloma de Queralt[49]

Type / Year	1276-77	1287	1293-94	1304-05	1312-13	Total
Credit-Sales	40	3	293	696	324	1356
Direct Loans	21	12	509	409	483	1434
Other Debts	12	10	235	334	203	794
Total	73	25	1037	1439	1010	3584

As elements of commercial finance, credit-sales and direct loans were closely similar transactions. For all but the stated purpose of the debt, credit-sale and direct loan contracts written in these notarial registers were recorded the same way. A debtor recognized an amount owed to the creditor, set the time at which the amount owed would be repaid, and in most cases provided guarantors for repayment. The notaries then recorded the names of witnesses, normally two, and listed the date of the transaction. At a later time, when repayment had been made and proof provided, the notarial

---

[49] Arxiu Històric de Tarragona, Fondo Notarials, Santa Coloma de Queralt (AHTN), Reg. 8629, 8631, 3804, 3812 and 3821. The group of commercial debt transactions comes from the 4278 total records found in these five notarial protocols (debt contracts made up 83.8% of all the recorded contracts). Only one of these protocols provides records for one full year (for March 25, 1304, to March 24, 1305). The protocol for 1276-77, the earliest surviving, covers four months, while the protocol for 1287 (possibly for the year 1292) is a short fragment of a larger original. The protocols for 1293-94 (nine months) and 1312-1313 (seven months) reflect the maturation of the Santa Coloma marketplace. In Table 1 the category 'other debts' include pledges, deposicione/comanda, debt-consolidations, and debt transfers.

scribes marked the contract with cross-hatching indicating the debt obligation was no longer in force and the transaction was final and complete.

In Santa Coloma, credit-sales and direct loans (37.8 % and 40.0% of all debt contracts respectively) were roughly equal in number and generally concerned an equivalent range of value-owed. In comparison to debts contracted by elites in royal and noble courts, as well as by large-scale businessmen in cities, the debts of Santa Coloma were relatively modest, between 40 to 130 *solidi* in most cases. These were significant amounts to the debtors of Santa Coloma, who were mainly peasant farmers from the surrounding region or artisanal craftsmen from the town itself, financing the basic tools and material needed for their economic livelihood. In comparison, loans in Barcelona were normally of a much higher value. For example, Joan de Banyeres, a Christian merchant of Barcelona, borrowed money eight times in the period 1277-1282 from the family of Azday Solomon, Jews of the city, with the amounts borrowed ranging from 200 to 2,330 *solidi*. Stephen Bensch, studying the urban elite, finds that the average sum of Christian loans made in Barcelona for the period 1221-1290 was between 172 and 245 *solidi*.[50] The debt transactions of Santa Coloma reflect the daily, common economy of a rural peasant society, in which almost all of the debtors were Christian. Among the total 3,548 debt transactions recorded in the Santa Coloma notarial registers, there were only sixty-one Jewish debtors.

The Christian and Jewish creditors of Santa Coloma made choices, along the lines of their religious identities in many cases, about how their lending was reflected in the written records.[51] Contracts involving Christian creditors never indicated an amount of interest owed as a separate entry; instead, their contracts simply listed the total amount owed, for a loan or for goods, and laid out the promised repayment schedule. The large majority of all credit transactions, however, did not separate the interest from the

[50] Elka Klein, *Jews, Christian Society, and Royal Power in Medieval Barcelona* (Ann Arbor: University of Michigan Press, 2006), 185-186; Stephen P. Bensch, *Barcelona and Its Rulers, 1096-1291* (Cambridge: Cambridge University Press, 1995), 284-286.

[51] A detailed discussion of these issues can be found in Gregory B. Milton, "Christian and Jewish Lenders: Religious Identity and the Extension of Credit," *Viator* 37 (2006): 301-18.

principal owed, whether by Jewish or Christian creditors. In fact, only one quarter of direct loans recorded the amount of interest, and they did so at a fixed amount rather than a rate. All but one of these were by Jewish lenders. For example, in February of 1313, Pere and Berenguera Rocha of Pontils contracted a debt of 64 *solidi* of principal and 6 *solidi* of interest that they agreed to pay back to two Jews, Astruc Vidal and Bonjac Abraham, within a period of about eight months.[52] A fixed amount of interest avoided the potential for the interest charged to exceed the principal, and made sense for these short-term loans, assuming most were paid back on time. Only a handful of loans stated the interest owed as a rate, again all by Jewish lenders, in almost all cases at 4 *denarii* per *libra* per month (a rate of 20%), which reflected the limit set by royal legislation in Catalonia. The important conclusion is that the majority of loans with both Christian and Jewish creditors did not indicate the amount of interest owed within the contract, simply providing one total amount owed.

Not all loans, however, were stated in terms of monetary currency, and religious identity played a significant role in currency selection. Wheat-measures were used as the currency of account for 348 loans of Santa Coloma (24.3% of all direct loans) in the same process and form used for monetary currency, and in the same average range of amounts. The primary difference for loans stated in terms of wheat-measures was that the creditors were Christian in 88% of the cases. Christian creditors also lent money in Santa Coloma by 'investing' money and wheat with Jewish partners so that the Jews would create the loans and be recorded as the creditors in the contract. For example, from May 1304 to January 1305, two local Christian nobles, Galcerandus de Tous and Bernat Zanou, provided 1,200 *solidi* and 15 measures of wheat to the Jewish partnership of Jucer Franc, Mosse de Carcasona and their families. Jucer Franc and Mosse de Carcasona were active lenders in Santa Coloma, but the investment by their Christian backers supplied over 70% of all the capital they lent during the period of investment. Through the use of

---

[52] AHTN 3821, f.106. "P. Rocha et eius uxor Bngona., iura, de Pontils debemus vobis Astruch Vidal et Bonjach Abraham judeis Sancte Columbe et vestris xLiiii sol[idi] terni de proprio capitale pro vi sol[idi] lucri illorum racione mutui solvere ad festum omnium sanctorum."

wheat-measures and by acting as hidden partners, Christians could lend without risking the appearance of charging interest. These two approaches to masking the activity of extending credit utilized by Christians corresponded to the very active role Christians played as creditors in sales contracts.[53]

Both Christians and Jews were actively involved in direct lending, but this only reflected about half of all the credit exchanges in the Santa Coloma marketplace. Sales of moveable goods—labor-animals, cloth, and grain—also required the use of credit, with the sellers making loans to their customers. As creditors of sales, Christians were by far the most prevalent lenders in Santa Coloma. Table 2 demonstrates the roles both Jews and Christians played as creditors, and the significant involvement of Christians as creditors for sales. If the only credit transactions in Santa Coloma were direct loans, then it would be acceptable to consider Jews as the dominant financiers of this marketplace. Jews were 70.3% of all creditors of direct loans, yet these loans were only half of the credit transactions of commerce in Santa Coloma.

Table 2: Creditors for All Loans and Credit-Sales in Santa Coloma de Queralt[54]

Creditor	Loans	Sales	Total
Jewish	1103 (70.3% of loan creditors)	26 (1.2% of sale creditors)	1129 (29.5% of all creditors)
Christian	466 (29.7% of loan creditors)	2233 (98.8% of sale creditors)	2699 (70.5% of all creditors)
Total	1569	2259	3828

Other kinds of credit transactions were overwhelming made by Christians, who were 98.8% of creditors for sales. When all these financed commercial exchanges are considered together, Christians were dominant, making up 70.5% of creditors for loans and sales.

[53] Milton, "Christian and Jewish Lenders," 312-316.
[54] AHTN 8629, 8631 3804, 3812 and 3821. Five local Muslims also acted as creditors in Santa Coloma, fifteen times for loans and once for a credit-sale (only 00.4% of all creditors). The number of creditors for both types of contracts exceeds the actual number of loans and sales because of partnerships that result in multiple creditors for some transactions.

248

Jews remained significant and important actors in the finance of commerce in Santa Coloma, making up approximately 10% of the town's population but 29.5% of all creditors. They provided moveable currency which could be used to complete sales, make investments, and pay dues or rent, yet most debtors owed Christian creditors, in amounts which included principal and interest. Christians actively participated in the financing of commerce, yet made choices about the representation of this activity in written contracts which tended to mask the full nature of their financial activity. Monetary lending as part of a sale was relatively safe from accusation of wrongdoing or sin because the profit from the lending was hidden within the sales price of the goods sold, but often when making direct loans, Christians masked the appearance of their activity by utilizing wheat measures and basing repayment options on the market price of the wheat.

The example of the Santa Coloma market transactions suggests that the religious and political rhetoric of medieval Iberia which focused attention on the threat of Jewish lending did not have a basis in economic reality. Rather, this rhetoric reflected concerns about power relations, religious antagonism, and the social consequence of economic development in Iberia from the late twelfth century onward. Mark Meyerson's study of the Jews of Morvedre in the kingdom of Valencia provides corroboration, as he finds that the occasional accusations of oppressive lending and exploitation against Jews in the early 1300s occurred in close conjunction with anti-Jewish sermons made by individual bishops and other high clergy who then attempted to take control of judicial inquiry into the accusations; attempts that challenged royal claims to jurisdiction.[55] Finance in Valencia in the thirteenth and fourteenth centuries, from Jewish and Christian creditors, derived from economic need. The Valencian church attempted to control it, with limited effect. The crown found advantages in regulating it, often by using the existence of anti-usury and anti-Jewish attacks as a rationale to investigate charges against lenders (especially Jews) and enforce collection (primarily from Christians). In the process, the crown gained revenues from

---

[55] Meyerson, *Jews in an Iberian Frontier Kingdom*, 189-194.

fines, fees, and exemption payments, making regulation, instigated by religious rhetoric, a rewarding industry.[56]

In their studies of Barcelona, Stephen Bensch and Elka Klein both find that the financing of commerce by Jews and Christians was much more complex than simply Jewish creditors making loans to Christians debtors. Bensch demonstrates the expansive development of Christian commercial and financial activity during the thirteenth century, as merchant and patrician families strategically managed their economic and political positions in the city.[57] He also notes the increasing proportion of loans made by Jews over the course of the century, rising to 70% of all loans, but argues that the nature of the surviving evidence from Barcelona in this period heavily influenced this proportion. Since full notarial registers do not survive from Barcelona in the thirteenth century, the only evidence of credit activity comes from engrossed charters (individual transactions written out on independent parchments). These charters tended to over-represent Jewish creditors, as the late thirteenth-century legal climate demanded written documentation of Jewish loans more often than Christian.[58] Skewing this emphasis further, Bensch's analysis considers only direct loans in his percentage and not other debt transactions, such as the credit-sales of Santa Coloma, where Christians were much more likely to be the creditors. Christians, therefore, were much more active in the commercial finance of Barcelona than the 70% figure for loans by Jews indicates. In addition, Elka Klein argues that the diversity of economic strategies used by Jewish families in Barcelona, in which lending and credit were significant to some families, especially the "new elite," at certain points in their social progress, were by no means the sole nor the most significant economic activity of life for Barcelonan Jews with the resources to be creditors.[59]

While the evidence for daily economic exchanges in Iberia is much stronger for the territories of the Crown of Aragon, studies by Teofilo Ruiz and Nina Melechen show that Jews and Christians

---

[56] Meyerson, *Jews in an Iberian Frontier Kingdom*, 203-205.

[57] Bensch, *Barcelona and Its Rulers*, 282-304.

[58] Bensch, *Barcelona and Its Rulers*, 284-286; Meyerson, *Jews in an Iberian Frontier Kingdom*, 180.

[59] Klein, *Jews, Christian Society, and Royal Power*, 162-191.

regularly cooperated in credit transactions and property exchanges in other areas of the peninsula. Whether in northern Castile or in the territory of Toledo, these exchanges did not reflect typical economic roles either. Jews extended credit, but not as a monopoly, they acquired and sold property, and at times faced conflicts with Christian partners. Melechen's examination in particular shows how complex, and atypical, conflicts between Jews and Christians over debts could be. In a case from the diocese of Toledo between a Christian debtor, Juan Alfonso of Alcabón, and a Jewish creditor, Abrahem ibn Halegua, the debt began as a cooperative activity, not a loan nor a transaction involving interest or profit for the Jewish partner. Instead, Juan Alfonso owed Abrahem ibn Halegua as his guarantor—a fact Juan Alfonso attempted to dispute—for an earlier debt that Abrahem had paid when Juan Alfonso failed to do so. The original debt involved a sale of cloth, on credit, from a Christian seller.[60] Melechen's exploration of the claims and arbitration of this conflict demonstrates the manner in which the polemical rhetoric of anti-Jewish lending could be utilized in a conflict, without reflecting the real source of the legal claims at issue. She concludes that Juan Alfonso used his original partnership with his Jewish guarantor as a way to create a long-term loan. This was perhaps not the original intention, but in the end Juan Alfonso used a multitude of claims and accusations in order to evade immediate payment for the amount of debt Abrahem covered for him, eventually paying that amount—without additional interest or penalty—after six years of delay. In any case, the limited Castilian evidence of common credit transactions corresponds to the patterns illustrated by the sources from the Crown of Aragon.

Conclusion

Commercial finance in medieval Iberia was a vibrant part of a developing economy, and both Jews and Christians were important agents of it. Extending credit through direct loans, credit-sales, and investments, creditors from both religious groups navigated around and through the canonical and royal legislation which attempted to

---

[60] Nina Melechen, "Loans, Land, and Jewish-Christian Relations," 185-215.

regulate their activity, without ever stopping their use of financial mechanisms. The eventual decline in Jewish lending in Iberia had little to do with the Church or State acting directly against it, and more to do with general changes in politics and culture. Nina Melechen notes that Enrique II Trastámara (r. 1369-1379) called on anti-Jewish popular feeling as a means of attacking his royal rival and half-brother, Pedro I (r.1350-1369) during the Castilian Civil War in the 1350s and 1360s, eventually reducing royal protection of Jewish communities after he took power.[61] Mark Meyerson argues that by this time, Jewish subsidies within the Crown of Aragon declined in value after decades of substantial payments, reflecting lower returns from loans and creating a reduced economic influence on royal policy concerning Jewish lending. Popular anti-Jewish attitudes may have played a role, but the business of Jewish credit in Valencia declined primarily because of a new, Christian controlled loan mechanism—a type of bond called the *censal*—whose sale and resale could be manipulated in more stable and creative ways for financial investment.[62]

In other contexts, some have argued that the marketplace served as a neutral space for Jewish-Christian intellectual interaction, but this neutrality must be understood to extend to the economic reality of Jewish-Christian trade and finance as well.[63] As part of financial commerce, the Jewish lender within the real economy of twelfth- to fourteenth-century Iberia made up a significant, but still minority, proportion of all creditors. Despite the canonical, legal, and cultural legacy which created an anti-Jewish lender stereotype, most debtors in Iberia owed money to Christian creditors. While political and religious polemic became highly influential in Iberian society in the late thirteenth and fourteenth centuries, secular authorities such as the count-kings in the Crown of Aragon skillfully worked the complaints, and potential for complaints, against usury as a means to raise revenue from Jewish communities. In most cases, these complaints did not originate in the economic reality of credit

---

[61] Melechen, "Loans, Land, and Jewish-Christian Relations," 185 and 208.

[62] Meyerson, *Jews in an Iberian Frontier Kingdom*, 205-208.

[63] Thomas F. Glick "'My Master, The Jew': Observations on Interfaith Scholarly Interaction in the Middle Ages," in *Jews, Muslims and Christians in and Around the Crown of Aragon: Essays in Honour of Professor Elena Lourie*, ed. Harvey J. Hames (Boston: Brill, 2004), 160.

transactions themselves; that is, in actual oppressive or exploitive behavior on the part of Jewish lenders. Instead, usually after polemical sermons by prominent clerics, Christian debtors took the opportunity to make complaints as a strategy to extend loan periods, reduce interest payments, and potentially escape the costs of their business transactions. In Iberia, the rise of anti-Jewish violence during the fourteenth and fifteenth centuries did not originate in real aspects of economic activity. The reverse is more accurate: Jewish lending, and the complaints and accusations against it, came to be associated with already developing political and religious attacks. The anti-Jewish polemics based in religious discourse created anti-Jewish attitudes among the Christian population that allowed space for strategic complaints about Jewish financial activity, despite the fact that the majority of debts in Iberia were owed to Christian creditors. Jewish lenders were important actors within Iberian commerce, but their credit activity must be understood within the complexities of Christian religious, political, and economic society, regardless of the stereotypes that have become its legacy in post-medieval culture.

Works Cited:

Assis, Yom Tov. *The Jews of Santa Coloma de Queralt.* Jerusalem: Magnes Press, 1988.

------. *Jewish Economy in the Medieval Crown of Aragon: 1213-1327: Money and Power.* Leiden: Brill, 1997.

Baer, Yitzhak. *A History of the Jews in Christian Spain.* 2 vols. Philadelphia: Jewish Publication Society, 1961.

Bagby, Albert I. "The Jews in the Cántigas of Alfonso X, El Sabio." *Speculum* 46 (1971): 670-88.

Bensch, Stephen P. *Barcelona and Its Rulers, 1096-1291.* Cambridge: Cambridge University Press, 1995.

Cantera Montenegro, Enrique. "Cristianos y judíos en la Meseta Norte castellana: la fractura del siglo XIII." In *Del pasado judío en los reinos medievales hispánicos: Afinidad y distanciamient. XIII. Curso de Cultura Hispanojudía y Sefardí de la Universidad de Castilla-La Mancha,* edited by Yolanda Moreno Koch and Ricardo Izquierdo Benito, 45-88. Cuenca: Universidad de Castilla La Mancha, 2005.

Cinta Mañé, M. and Gemma Escribà. *The Jews in the Crown of Aragon Regesta of the Cartas Reales in the Archivo de la Corona de Aragón,* 2 vols. *Sources for the History of the Jews in Spain* 4. Jerusalem: Hispania Judaica, 1993.

Cohen, Jeremy. *The Friars and The Jews: The Evolution of Medieval Anti-Judaism.* Ithaca, NY: Cornell University Press, 1982.

Conciliorum Oecumenicorum Decreta, 3rd Ed. Edited by Huberto Jedin. Bologna: Instituto per le Scienze Religiose, 1973.

Cortes de los antiguos reinos de Léon y Castilla, 2 vols. Edited by Don Manuel Colmeiro. Madrid: Real Academia, 1883-4.

Decrees of the Ecumenical Councils, vol. 1. Edited by Norman P. Tanner. Washington, D.C.: Georgetown University Press, 1990.

Gilchrist, John T. *The Church and Economic Activity in the Middle Ages.* New York: Macmillan, 1969.

Glick, Thomas F. "'My Master, The Jew': Observations on Interfaith Scholarly Interaction in the Middle Ages." In *Jews, Muslims and*

Christians in and Around the Crown of Aragon: Essays in Honour of Professor Elena Lourie, edited by Harvey J. Hames, 157-182. Boston: Brill, 2004.

Hunt, Edwin S., and James M. Murray. *A History of Business in Medieval Europe, 1200-1550*. Cambridge: Cambridge University Press, 1999.

Jordan, William C. *The French Monarchy and the Jews: From Philip Augustus to the Last Capetians*. Philadelphia: University of Pennsylvania Press, 1989.

Klein, Elka. *Jews, Christian Society, and Royal Power in Medieval Barcelona*. Ann Arbor, MI: University of Michigan Press, 2006.

Le Goff, Jacques. *Your Money or Your Life*. Trans. Patricia Ranum. New York: Zone, 1998.

Little, Lester. *Religious Poverty and the Profit Economy in Medieval Europe*. Ithaca, NY: Cornell University Press, 1978.

Lopez, Robert S. *The Commercial Revolution of the Middle Ages, 950-1350*. Englewood Cliffs, NJ: Prentice Hall, 1971.

Meislin, Bernard J., and Morris L. Cohen. "Backgrounds of the Biblical Law Against Usury." *Comparative Studies in Society and History* 6:3 (April, 1964): 250-267.

Melechen, Nina. "Loans, Land, and Jewish-Christian Relations in the Archdiocese of Toledo." In *Iberia and the Mediterranean World of the Middle Ages*, edited by Larry Simon, 185-215. Leiden: Brill, 1995.

Meyerson, Mark D. *Jews in an Iberian Frontier Kingdom: Society, Economy and Politics in Morvedre (1248-1391)*. Leiden: Brill, 2004.

Milton, Gregory B. "Christian and Jewish Lenders: Religious Identity and the Extension of Credit." *Viator* 37 (2006): 301-18.

Moore, R. I. *The Formation of a Persecuting Society*. Oxford: Blackwell, 1987.

Nirenberg, David. *Communities of Violence: Persecution of Minorities in the Middle Ages*. Princeton: Princeton University Press, 1996.

The Oxford 'Cantigas de Santa Maria' Database. The Centre for the Study of the 'Cantigas de Santa Maria' of Oxford University. http://csm. mml.ox.ac.uk/

Pirenne, Henri. *Economic and Social History of Medieval Europe.* Translated by I. E. Clegg. London: Kegan Paul and Co., 1936.

Ray, Jonathan. *The Sephardic Frontier: The Reconquista and the Jewish Community in Medieval Iberia.* Ithaca: Cornell University Press, 2006.

Régné, Jean. *History of the Jews in Aragon: Regesta and Documents 1213-1327.* Edited by Yom Tov Assis. Jerusalem: Magnes Press, 1978.

Ruderman, David B. "Champion of Jewish Economic Interest." In *Essential Papers on Judaism and Christianity in Conflict,* 513-535. New York: New York University Press, 1991. Originally published in *The World of a Renaissance Jew: The Life and Thought of Abraham ben Mordecai Farissol,* 85-97. Cincinnati: Hebrew Union College Press, 1981.

Ruiz, Teófilo F. "Trading with the 'Other': Economic Exchanges Between Muslims, Jews, and Christians in Late Medieval Northern Castile." In *Medieval Spain: Culture, Conflict and Coexistence. Studies in Honour of Angus MacKay,* edited by Roger Collins and Anthony Goodman, 63-78. Basingstoke: Palgrave Macmillan, 2002.

Segura i Valls, Joan. *Història de Santa Coloma.* Santa Coloma de Queralt: P. Bas y Vich, reprint 1953.

Shatzmiller, Joseph. *Shylock Reconsidered: Jews, Moneylending and Medieval Society.* Berkeley: University of California Press, 1990.

The Song of The Cid: A Dual-Language Edition With Parallel Text. Trans. Burton Raffel. New York: Penguin Books, 2009.

The Jewish Woman in Medieval Iberia

·· Renée Levine Melammed

Assessing the lives of Jewish women in medieval Iberian culture is not an easy task, and there is no doubt about the fact that their experiences were not identical to those of the men. Iberian Jewish men were poets, merchants, rabbis, physicians, courtiers and tax farmers, but what were their wives and mothers and daughters doing? Few images come to mind when one considers the Iberian Jewish woman, leaving one to wonder how she experienced the Golden Age of poetry and philosophy, the Reconquista, the riots of 1391, the Inquisition, and the Expulsion. While the existing evidence does not provide a complete picture of women's lives, one does discover many independent, savvy, strong and determined women. Some defied their husbands as well as both Christian and Jewish authorities. Others relied upon Jewish law in order to validate their independent lifestyle, while yet others turned to non-Jewish authorities in their quest for justice. Outstanding among them were widows, married women whose husbands blatantly ignored clauses in marital contracts, and judeo-conversas. Only by examining some of these lives can one gain a better understanding of the world of the medieval Iberian Jews, regardless of their gender.

While Jews were already residing in Iberia prior to the Visigothic invasion in the fifth century, next to nothing is known about their lives at that time except what is revealed in a series of rules concerning forced conversions and reversions to Judaism; women are only mentioned tangentially. Prohibitions and punishments were not identical for men and women and the latter are scarcely mentioned in the vast lists of anti-Jewish laws.[1] When the peninsula was later conquered by the Muslims in 711, the lives of Jews were altered, but any immediate repercussions of this transfer of power for women remain a mystery. Islamic rule led to urbanization, to demographic explosion, and enabled the hegemony of the Babylonian Talmud among Andalusi Jews, but there are no records as to how these developments might have affected women's lives. No doubt the lingua franca for all of the Jewish communities gradually became Arabic, but determining the influence of this new cultural and religious milieu on women in particular is next to impossible. For example, it cannot be ascertained if, when or where Jewish women wore veils;[2] it is also a challenge to attempt to assess to what degree the Islamic practice of polygamy affected Jewish women's lives.

Jewish men could more easily take advantage of the opportunity to immerse themselves in the cultural world of the Arabs as it developed in Spain and were able to acquire proficiency in linguistics, grammar, philosophy, philology, astronomy and medicine. The creation of the cultural hub of Córdoba under Umayyad rule (756-1008) resulted in a parallel development, albeit on a more modest level, within the male Jewish world. The resulting creativity on the part of the men, who viewed themselves as the spiritual heirs of the Bible, the Talmud and religious poetry, has been categorized as a golden age, but the role of women during this period is rarely discussed.

---

[1] Jean Juster, "The Legal Condition of the Jews under the Visigothic Kings," *Israel Law Review* 11 (1976): 391-414, here 404 and 408.

[2] There is evidence that Muslim women in various locales in Spain were removing their veils in the fourteenth century. María J. Viguera, "Ashluhu li l'ma'ali: On the Social Status of Andalusi Women," in *The Legacy of Muslim Spain*, ed. Salma Khadra Jayyusi (Leiden: Brill, 1992), 714.

Creativity: Poets and Patrons

What, if anything, were the women creating? Cultural activities in this society required patrons; are there records of female patrons? The male poets were writing secular poems of friendship, love, and panegyrics, as well as religious poems, but are there records of women's poetry? Did any of these scholars educate or train their wives or daughters? While the male Jewish scholars and intellectuals were in contact with and influenced by Muslim intellectuals, did the Muslim women's world have any effect on their Jewish counterparts?

Recent studies have revealed a surprising amount of information concerning the cultural activities of Muslim women, including participation in study circles as well as the development of serious patronage on their part of art and architecture, such as building mosques, tombs, schools, and hospitals.[3] In the Jewish world, wealthy women contributed to the upkeep of synagogues, in particular by supplying oil for lamps, to charity foundations, and to the writing of Torah scrolls. Some of the rabbis discussed whether or not to permit female patronage, as they were concerned about the propriety of accepting their jewels and veils for decorating the Torah.[4] Despite occasional objections, the tradition of female patronage continued: women funded scrolls, crowns, and covers for the Torah and were patrons of goldsmiths, embroiderers, writers and builders.[5] In the thirteenth century, Sara, the widow of David de Cabestany of Perpignan, left instructions in her will to establish two charitable foundations, namely a trust fund for the schooling of poor Jewish boys and a dowry fund for similarly unfortunate Jewish girls.[6] There

---

[3] See, for example, Gavin R. G. Hambly, "Becoming Visible: Medieval Islamic Women in Historiography and History," in *Women in the Medieval Islamic World*, ed. Gavin R. G. Hambly (New York: St. Martin's Press, 1998), 3-27, and D. Fairfield Ruggles, "Women Patrons," in *Medieval Islamic Civilization: An Encyclopedia*, vol. 2, ed. Josef W. Meri (New York: Routledge, 2006), 864.

[4] Eleazar Gutwirth, "*Qilusin:* el mecenazgo femenino medieval," in *La mujer judía*, ed. Yolanda Moreno Koch (Córdoba: Ediciones El Almendro, 2007), 107-128, here 115-119. Rabbis involved in such discussions included Hai Gaon (eleventh century Lucena) and Avraham b. Nathan ha-Yarhi (thirteenth century Lunel).

[5] Gutwirth, "*Qilusin,*" 120-127.

[6] She appointed her son and her brother as executors in 1286 to use the funds from houses she owned to endow these two funds. See Rebecca Winer, *Women, Wealth, and Community in Perpignan, c. 1250-1300: Christians, Jews, and Enslaved Muslims in a Medieval Mediterranean Town* (Aldershot: Ashgate, 2006), 78-79.

is also a fourteenth-century elegy written by the nephew of a female donor in which he stresses the fact that she donated a house in order to expand the current size of the synagogue.[7]

The flowering of poetry, Arabic as well as Hebrew, was a hallmark of the era of Muslim Spain. Whereas male poets were strongly influenced by their Arabic cohorts, can one draw a comparison between Muslim and Jewish women? Extant poetry created by Muslim women is somewhat limited as compared to their male counterparts, but, nevertheless, far from nominal, and they far outnumbered the contemporary Jewish women poets. The social hierarchy of the Muslim world also created a poetic hierarchy: slave girls were known for their *ghazal,* or erotic love songs, whereas freeborn women composed *ritha,*[8] or elegies. The most well-known poets lived in the eighth, eleventh and thirteenth centuries.[9]

In both Muslim and Jewish society, men had a monopoly on the transmission of knowledge and women usually obtained their knowledge from within the ranks of the family. Although available sources regarding Jewish society reveal a paucity of material regarding women poets, there is one extant example of a Jewish poetess living in twelfth-century al-Andalus who displayed considerable talent. There are two Arabic sources, namely the writings of al-Suyuti (d. 1505) and those of al-Maqqari (d. 1632), that record fragments of her poetry; the former adds some biographical information as well.[10] Qasmuna was trained by her father, whose name was Isma'il ibn

---

[7] Samuel b. Yosef b. Sasson wrote this poem for Doña Mira in the 1330s lauding the patroness; Gutwirth, "*Qilusin,*" 128.

[8] See, for example, the article by the late Magda Al-Nowaihi, "Elegy and the Confrontation of Death in Arabic Poetry," in *Transforming Loss into Beauty: Essays on Arabic Literature and Culture in Honor of Magda Al-Nowaihi,* ed. Marlé Hammond and Dana Sajdi (Cairo: The American University in Cairo Press, 2008), 3-20.

[9] Dana Sajdi, "Revisiting Layla al-Akhyaliya's Trespass," *Transforming Loss into Beauty,* 185-227; Tahera Qutbuddin, "Women Poets," in *Medieval Islamic Civilization,* vol. 2, 866; and Teresa Garulo, "Una Poetisa Oriental en al-Andalus: Sara al Halabiyya," *al-Qantara: Revista des Estudios Arabes* 6 (1985): 155-77.

[10] Biographical dictionaries were compiled along with anthologies of poems in order to provide information about the poets appearing in them. This was in keeping with the Muslim custom of preserving biographical information about important learned religious figures. Ángeles Gallego points out that Qasmuna's "biography, however, is missing in the printed editions of this book," "Approaches," 70, n. 23. In the introduction to al-Suyuti's book, he cites six or more volumes of an anthology of women's poems that are not extant; Qutbuddin, "Women Poets," 867.

Bagdalah.[11] The style of poetry in which she engaged belonged to the genre known as *muwwashah*, by no means one of the simpler styles, for it entails frequent changes of strophe, rhyme and meter. The surviving fragments of Qasmuna's poetry reveal a witty, intelligent and highly educated young woman. After her father composed two sophisticated lines, his daughter displayed her own prowess by completing each verse. Her poems are original, polished and gentle; they leave no doubt as to the high level of expertise she had acquired in the Arabic language. There are a number of contemporary scholars who believe that she was none other than the daughter of the great Andalusi courtier Samuel ha-Nagid (993-1055), also known as Ibn Naghela, who indeed is known to have fathered a daughter (who had been thought to have died at a young age). The debates as to the identity of this poet and her father continue until this very day.[12]

As Jewish Iberian intellectuals began to develop the Hebrew language on the basis of the Arabic they had mastered, the quality and nature of their secular poetry followed suit. The Córdoban palace of the great patron of culture, 'Abd al-Rahman III, also housed his advisor and cultural emissary, Hasdai ibn Shaprut, who became an active patron of Hebrew culture and poetry in al-Andalus. Poetry in particular continued to flourish, as exemplified by the works of Dunash ibn Labrat, Solomon ibn Gabirol, Yehuda ha-Levi, Samuel ha-Nagid, and others. The assumption has been that women did not have access to Hebrew, except perhaps to the Hebrew of the prayers (which they may or may not have understood). It was precisely during this period that Saadia Gaon in Babylonia responded to a request by the Iberian Jews to record the liturgy and the accompanying rules regarding prayer for them. No doubt the majority of the women were not literate and certainly not in the holy tongue. Taking into account the fact that "poets came from the circles of the intellectual leadership of rabbis, community leaders, talmudic scholars, Bible

---

[11] Jewish women rarely had biblical names, and even in later periods were given Arabic or vernacular names. See Nina Melechen, "Calling Names: The Identification of Jews in Christian Documents from Medieval Toledo," in *On the Social Origins of Medieval Institutions: Essays in Honor of Joseph F. O'Callaghan*, ed. Donald J. Kagay and Theresa M. Vann (Leiden: Brill, 1998), 22, n. 2.

[12] For a summary of this debate, see Ángeles Gallego, "Approaches," 70-72.

exegetes, moralists, and philosophers,"[13] how could women attain similar expertise and learning, whether in the Muslim or in the Jewish world?

Nevertheless, an unexpected discovery by scholars of the Cairo Geniza forced the experts on medieval Hebrew poetry to re-evaluate these assumptions. There is tangible evidence from the close of the tenth century concerning an incredibly talented Hebrew poet who was married to the pioneering grammarian Dunash ibn Labrat. Between 1947 and 1971, reconstruction of fragments and copies of poems that were found in bits and pieces among the Cairo Geniza collection revealed that ibn Labrat's wife had composed verses that originally were assumed to have been the handiwork of her husband.[14] Once a complete version of the poem under discussion was discovered with the inscription "from her, to Dunash ibn Labrat," the conclusion was inevitable. This eminent poet's wife was a remarkable talent unto herself. When a reply to this poem-letter-lament written by ibn Labrat was later discovered, it contained a confirmation of his wife's status by the poet himself. He refers to her as nothing less than a *maskelet,* a highly educated woman; while the source of her education cannot be ascertained, she has since been acclaimed as the first female Hebrew poet. This nameless wife not only displays a mastery of biblical sources, but of the Arabic form of poetry as well; these are considered to be the "two distinctive marks of the nascent poetic school which her husband pioneered."[15] Be that as it may, Tova Rosen astutely points to the uniqueness of her situation in the world of Jewish poets by referring to "her utter solitude," explaining that while she was the first woman Hebrew poet since biblical times, unfortunately "she is also the only one for

---

[13] Tova Rosen, *Unveiling Eve: Reading Gender in Medieval Hebrew Literature* (Philadelphia: University of Pennsylvania Press, 2003), 5, and her comments about Córdoba in the mid-tenth century, 5-6.

[14] For the complete and fascinating reconstruction of this saga, see Ezra Fleischer, "About Dunash ibn Labrat and his wife and son," *Jerusalem Studies in Hebrew Literature* 5 (1984): 189-202 (Hebrew).

[15] Rosen, *Unveiling Eve,* 1. It is possible that her name was not mentioned because of etiquette; in Arabic poems, the names of women of higher status would not be evoked. Jonathan Decter, "Arabic Poetics and Representations of Women in the Andalusian Hebrew Lament," in *Transforming Loss into Beauty,* 115-141, for details and a discussion of Hebrew laments and panegyrics related to women.

centuries to come."[16] It is generally assumed that the sociological situation of medieval Jewish women, including their education or lack thereof, was a serious barrier to their ability to contribute to the literary field. Were there learned women aside from these two poets? Saenz-Badillos and Targarona declare that as compared to what transpired in the world of Arabic poetry, the amount of Hebrew medieval poetry written by women is nominal.[17]

A look at the Muslim world reveals numerous highly educated Andalusi women between the eighth and fourteenth centuries, among whom were scholars, secretaries, copyists, lexicographers and grammarians.[18] Can one find any Jewish women in similar posts? Were there more than just two women poets? Is this dearth of creativity because women were "excluded from the literary marketplace?"[19] Abraham ibn Daud relates an account from eleventh-century Castile concerning a Jewish woman whose husband became a Karaite while visiting Jerusalem. Upon his return, Abu'l-Taras taught his new "Torah" and after his death, his widow, *al-Muallima* (the female teacher) became "the" authority on Karaism in Castile.[20] Clearly, this woman teacher was learned, most likely even prior to her conversion to Karaism, but additional evidence concerning any other learned Jewish (or Karaite) women in Iberia has not been uncovered.[21] Unfortunately, there are no additional records of women's creativity before, during, or after the so-called "Golden Age" of Spain.

---

[16] Rosen, *Unveiling Eve*, 1-2.

[17] Ángel Sáenz-Badillos and Judit Targarona, "La 'Vos femenina' en las poesía hebrea medieval," in *La Mujer judía*, 181.

[18] Viguera, "On the Social Status," 718.

[19] Rosen, *Unveiling Eve*, 3.

[20] See Abraham ibn Daud, *The Book of Tradition*, trans. Gerson D. Cohen (Philadelphia: JPS, 1967), 94-95, for this twelfth-century deprecatory account regarding this nouveau Karaite couple.

[21] There were women teaching in twelfth century Cairo; see Renée Levine Melammed, "He Said, She Said: A Woman Teacher in Twelfth Century Cairo," *AJS Review* 22 (1997): 19-35.

Participation in the Public Sphere and Inheritances

Women have always engaged in work, both in the domestic and public realms. Jewish men did not encourage the presence of women outside the home, yet there were always independent women who did not conform to societal expectations. The documentation concerning women's activities in the medieval Mediterranean society of the Cairo Geniza makes it clear that although they were living under the rule of Islam, women of all classes were working.[22] Although some modern scholars claim that it may have been difficult for Jewish and Muslim males in Spain "to see women active in public as merchants and property owners,"[23] one can assume that women whose husbands had died or were absent from home, or who had their own assets, were nonetheless to be found working outside the home. In Christian society as well, when the head of the family was away, he was replaced by his wife; some of these husbands might have held public or military roles, which meant that as a result, the women were left to manage the family property, businesses and estates.[24]

More material becomes available concerning women's economic activities during the period of Christian hegemony in the Peninsula (1100-1500). The changes that occurred during the early years of the *Reconquista* appear to have granted greater opportunities to Jewish women as well as to Jewish men. Jewish women were money-lenders, owned property, were involved in trade, handicrafts, spinning, weaving, leather crafting, selling shoes, furs, and foodstuffs, and manufacturing. In Castilian towns seeking to foster local commercial enterprise, religious minorities and women could be found owning shops or stalls in the market and working as peddlers.[25]

---

[22] See S. D. Goitein, "The World of Women," *A Mediterranean Society*, vol. 3 (Berkeley: University of California Press, 1978), 312-359.

[23] Avraham Grossman, *Pious and Rebellious: Jewish Women in Medieval Europe* (Waltham, MA: Brandeis University Press, 2004), 114.

[24] Mercedes Borrero Fernández, "Peasant and Aristocratic Women: Their Role in the Rural Economy of Seville at the End of the Middle Ages," in *Women at Work in Spain from the Middle Ages to Early Modern Times*, ed. Marilyn Stone and Carmen Benito-Vessels (New York: Peter Lang, 1998), 23 and 27.

[25] See Heath Dillard, *Daughters of the Reconquest: Women in Castilian Town Society, 1100-1300* (Cambridge, 1984); Grossman, *Pious and Rebellious*, 111-112; and Teófilo Ruiz,

Hebrew as well as Latin documents from Perpignan reveal that in the second-largest Jewish community in the thirteenth-century Crown of Aragon, Jews of both sexes were engaged in money lending.[26] The most active women were widows, but wives were involved as well, sometimes as the result of financial stress or bankruptcy or when there were no males available to run the family business. Many had their own lending concerns: between 1261 and 1286, there are records of twenty-five money-lending activities by women, fifteen of whom were widows. While women's loans tended to be more modest than those of their male counterparts (and were often granted by women to women), the wealthier women were dealing with loans of substantial sums.[27]

Many widows were named as guardians in order to administer their children's finances, and thus experienced a measure of both legal and economic power.[28] As a result, widows, whether Jewish or Christian, were not inclined to remarry, because it would entail surrendering their economic independence. Many of them had been granted guardianship or co-guardianship of their husband's property and of their children. Consequently, remarriage entailed a serious regression in terms of their newly acquired status and was clearly viewed by them as undesirable; essentially it meant a loss of custody of the children as well as a loss of status in the community. Interestingly enough, Jewish law also made remarriage somewhat undesirable. As long as the widow elected to remain single or did not claim her marriage contract (*ketubbah*), she was clearly entitled to support, and this too served as an incentive not to remarry. Her heirs could not easily force her to act against her will, and thus the advantages of not remarrying spoke for themselves.[29]

"Women, Work and Daily Life in Late Medieval Castile," in *Women at Work*, 112.

[26] As it turns out, there is an abundance of Latin archival sources from medieval Catalonia, which provide information regarding Jewish women as demonstrated by Burns, Klein, and Winer.

[27] Ruiz, "Women, Work and Daily Life," 99-106, for an analysis of money-lending activities of women.

[28] It seems that regarding women's actions, "the registers reflect widespread financial knowledge among women and a sophisticated sense of the realities of doing business in Perpignan." Winer, *Women, Wealth*, 89.

[29] Elka Klein, "The Widow's Portion: Law, Custom and Marital Property among Medieval Catalan Jews," *Viator* 31 (2000): 154.

Needless to say, the widow has always been the outstanding example of a woman whose presence in the public sphere is tolerated because limiting her mobility would mean that she and her children might become a burden on the community. For example, in the 1280s, Regina, the widow of Bonsenyor Jacob de Montpellier, had custody of her children and was an active co-guardian of her husband's assets.[30] She arranged for an impressive dowry for her daughter and after the marriage supported the couple as well, promising to help her son-in-law pay a debt to the king.[31] Women like this were efficient and devoted to the care of their wards. They also knew when to seek and when to accept outside help from their co-guardians, who were often members of their or their husband's families, and thus usually had their best interests at heart.

Women in thirteenth-century Catalonia conducted business by themselves or appointed agents when necessary. Because they controlled property, they felt free to initiate lawsuits or to make petitions to the court in order to protect their interests. Some of these women chose their sons as partners; some sold land pledged by debtors. Often they functioned as their husband's heirs: "the participation of Jewish wives in their husband's transactions was rooted in a legal concern, but was greatly expanded by the force of custom. That custom had internal Jewish roots, but seems to have been reinforced by the parallel practices of Catalan Christian society."[32]

The rabbis were aware of the tendency of husbands to leave some or all of their property to their widows. A thirteenth-century ruling in Toledo that took root elsewhere in Spain diverged considerably from the standard halakhic position. If a woman died during her

[30] Winer wrote that "as guardian a widow realized the most self-determination possible for a woman in this society." *Women, Wealth*, 11. She adds that "Jewish women's financial education and potential as businesswomen served as a contingency if an older widow without grown sons was required to provide for herself, or a young widow to raise her minor children as their financial guardian" (p. 13). See also 108-125.

[31] Winer, *Women, Wealth*, 123-124.

[32] Klein, "The Widow's Portion," 163. She adds: "There were many areas of life in which Jews would have been horrified to take Christian practice as a model, but the management of marital property and inheritance were not among them." See Klein, 147-163, and Elka Klein, "Splitting Heirs: Patterns of Inheritance Among Barcelona's Jews," *Jewish History* 16 (2002): 49-71, for wonderful material and analyses of wills, inheritance and widows in thirteenth-century Aragon.

husband's lifetime and there were children involved, the husband and their common children divided her estate equally; thus the widower only received half of what he would normally have been allotted. If they were childless, he shared her estate with heirs from her father's family, but if her mother was alive and had helped provide her daughter's dowry, she received half.[33] By these means as well as others, such as the granting of gifts before and after marriage, mothers, wives and daughters often found themselves financially stable and able to pursue avenues of employment and profit-making that formerly had been closed to them.

At the same time, wills and bequests often left instructions or guarantees of support for widows while unmarried daughters were often provided with dowries. Some wives were even named as executors of wills while others were given control of family resources.[34] Women of means arranged for their own wills, and often left property or money to other women, both friends and family. The Latinate wills found in fourteenth-century Catalonia contain numerous documents recorded for Jewish women, some of which were versions of Hebrew wills that were intended to provide extra security outside of the community. In 1338, one woman left her sister a tidy sum in order to commission a Torah scroll along with money for dowries for Jewish girls in need. Another left her bed, her bedclothes and furnishings to a synagogue, while yet another left all of her money to her husband provided he did not remarry and remained chaste![35] These testaments illustrate both the philanthropic inclination and the human idiosyncrasies of these widows and wives.

One discovers that Spanish Jewish women functioned in the traditional roles of embroiderers and seamstresses, weavers, midwives, wet-nurses, keeners, and bathers of the deceased, as well as working as physicians,[36] money-lenders and businesswomen. While

---

[33] Grossman, *Pious and Rebellious,* 151.

[34] Klein, "Splitting Heirs," 56, 63.

[35] Robert Burns devoted a chapter to women in *Jews in the Notarial Culture: Latinate Wills in Mediterranean Spain, 1250-1350* (Berkeley: University of California Press, 1996); see esp. 114-116.

[36] See Eliyahu Ashtor, *The Jews of Moslem Spain* (Philadelphia: JPS, 1984), 3: n. 270; Yitzhak Baer, *A History of the Jews in Christian Spain,* vol. 2 (Philadelphia: JPS, 1966), 335; and A. Cardoner Planas, "Seis mujeres hebreas practicando la medicina en el reino de Aragon," *Sefarad* 9 (1949): 442-445.

women in wealthier families rarely needed to support themselves, those in the lower strata of society as well as the aforementioned widows and women with absentee husbands all needed to work in order to survive.

One profession that historically has been an option for women was prostitution; some communities had Jewish bordellos and even provided a stipend for them.[37] It is not surprising to discover that their very presence provoked debate among the rabbis, in particular as to whether or not it was permissible for Jewish men to frequent such houses of ill repute. Some claimed that doing so was a serious transgression because the prostitutes did not observe the purity laws;[38] others felt that meeting the male's sexual needs by means of a prostitute was preferable to engaging in adultery with a married woman.[39] Unfortunately there is no information available concerning the prostitutes themselves.

Mobility and Sexual Mores

Rabbinic literature dealt with many of the pressing problems of Jewish society. Earning one's living, whether as a female prostitute or as a male merchant, could greatly complicate life. Thus, travelling husbands would find themselves extending their absences from home, sometimes for legitimate reasons and sometimes clearly not. A groom might postpone nuptial arrangements until after his return; husbands might take second wives in foreign cities. Some marriage contracts limited these absences to four months. Rabbi Isaac Alfasi in the eleventh century and Rabbi Moses ben Maimon (Maimonides) in the twelfth century were both concerned about extended absences on the part of Jewish husbands. Alfasi urged husbands to work where they resided; if they had to travel, they must first receive their wives' consent. He also was opposed to the taking

---

[37] Simha Assaf, "The 'Anusim' of Spain and Portugal in the Responsa Literature" [Hebrew], Me'assef Zion 5 (1933): 35-36, esp. n.1.

[38] See Grossman, *Pious and Rebellious*, 139, regarding R. Judah of Toledo's ruling that they should be expelled.

[39] Yom Tov Assis, "Sexual Behaviour in Mediaeval Hispano-Jewish Society," in *Jewish History: Essays in Honor of Chimen Abramsky*, ed. Ada Rapoport Albert and Steven J. Zipperstein (London: P. Halban, 1988), 52-53.

of second wives during periods of absence from home.[40] Both made rulings that were intended to discourage husbands from absenting themselves for more than one year.[41] Thus they declared that these husbands were to leave divorce writs in their wives' possession so that they could extricate themselves from the marriage in case their husbands did not return within the agreed-upon period of time.[42] The rabbis were concerned with avoiding cases of abandoned wives, who then entered into a frozen state of halakhic (that is, legal) impotency; they were not advocates for those husbands who sought additional wives while out of town. While the rabbis of Castile and Aragon never issued a ban on polygamy akin to that of the Ashkenazi sage Rabbi Gershom, the majority of them could not be described as advocates.[43]

On the other hand, polygamy was, without a doubt, part and parcel of the Islamic lifestyle, and Jewish men were clearly influenced by this phenomenon. Although Iberian Jews were not subject to the rulings of the Ashkenazi rabbis, once Christian rule was solidified throughout most of the Peninsula, the Jews had to accept monogamy as the new norm out of respect for the crown and its laws. There was, however, a means of circumvention by which the Jewish male

[40] This is a case of a storekeeper from Jaen who married and then went to eastern Spain for ten years, leaving his wife as a "chained" wife. When she learned of his whereabouts, she demanded that he be fined, and Alfasi supported her demand. See *Responsa of R. Isaac ben Jacob Alfasi*, ed. Wolf Leiter (Pittsburgh: Mekhon ha-Rambam, 1954; reprint of 1st ed., Leghorn, 1781), sign 120, 83-84. Yom Tov Assis refers to this decision in "Sexual Behaviour," 55, n. 61.

[41] See *Responsa of R. Isaac ben Jacob Alfasi*, sign 118, 831.

[42] See *R. Moses b. Maimon Responsa*, vol. 2, ed. Jehoshua Blau (Jerusalem: Rubin Mass, 1986) 2, sign 347, 624. Maimonides' ruling is interesting because he is concerned with additional problems which might arise when women marry men from outside communities, whose marital status might be uncertain. He demanded that these men provide proof that they were not already married; otherwise they had to take an oath on the Pentateuch to this effect or send their other wives a bill of divorce. At any rate, a groom who wanted to travel, even if his wife agreed to this, had to give her a bill of divorce to be used in the future, according to whatever compromise they made regarding the longevity of the stay, namely, a year or two but no more than three. This ruling as well as Alfasi's came to my attention in the Hebrew edition of Grossman (Jerusalem, 2003), 130, n. 47 and 141, n. 80.

[43] Assis discusses this in his "The 'Ordinance of Rabbenu Gershom' and Polygamous Marriages in Spain," *Zion* 46 (1981): 257 (Hebrew). He writes that while "the Jewish communities north of the Pyrenees affirmed monogamy, among the Jews of Islam polygyny was widely practised. Spanish Jews wavered between the two trends, which coexisted with various clashes until the expulsion." Assis, "Sexual Behaviour," 30.

could offer payment to the king in order to receive papers attesting to the legitimacy of any progeny from his second wife.[44] Clearly, this was possible only for the wealthy, and desirable, for example, if the first wife remained childless and the husband was not interested in divorcing her. The eminent Rabbi Hasdai Crescas found himself in this position after his only son was murdered in the riots of 1391 in Barcelona. Crescas, the chief rabbi of Aragon, received permission from the crown to take a second wife because his first was older and no longer of childbearing age; otherwise he would be left without a male heir.[45] It seems that while the rabbis of Castile were somewhat more outspoken than those of the Crown of Aragon in objecting to polygamy, they never actually issued an edict on the matter.

Under Muslim rule, Jewish fathers often included a monogamy clause in their daughter's *ketubah* in order to prevent the groom from taking a second wife or a maidservant against his wife's wishes.[46] A couple from the Aragonese capital of Saragossa had this very clause in their *ketubah*, but the husband promptly ignored it, gallivanting off to live with a concubine. His wife, however, did not stand by idly, but rather had the authorities imprison her husband, although when he appealed to a Christian judge for a ruling in 1383, he was granted permission to cohabit with his concubine. His wife, Durona, was outraged by this decision and brought the case to the king, who ultimately supported her.[47]

Jewish men consorted with concubines of all three faiths; while under Christian rule, some of them even opted to marry their Muslim concubines after first converting them to Judaism.[48] There were

---

[44] See Renée Levine Melammed, "Medieval and Early Modern Sephardi Women," in *Jewish Women in Historical Perspective*, ed. Judith Baskin (Detroit: Wayne State University Press, 1998), 131, and Assis, "The Ordinance," 253.

[45] See Fritz Baer, *Die Juden im Christlichen Spanien (Aragon and Navarre)* (Berlin: Akademie Verlag, 1929), 711, no. 452. Permission was granted on May 18, 1393.

[46] For a history and explanation of this clause, see Mordechai Akiva Friedman, *Jewish Polygyny in the Middle Ages: New Documents from the Cairo Geniza*, (Jerusalem: The Bialik Institute, 1986), 28-46 (Hebrew).

[47] See Asunción Blasco Martínez, "Mujeres Judías Aragoneses: Entre El Amor, El Desamor, La Rebeldía y La Frustración (Siglos XIV-XV)," in *El Prezente: Studies in Sephardic Culture Gender and Identity*, ed. Tamar Alexander et al. (Beer Sheva: Ben Gurion, 2010), 3: 34.

[48] Assis states that "the phenomenon must be explained as part of the general sexual permissiveness of mediaeval Spain," and that the number of Muslim concubines consorting

also Jewish concubines consorting with Christian men.[49] Contact between men and women of the three religions occurred at each of the different levels of society. Wealthy Jews might encounter non-Jews of the opposite sex in the courts and at social functions, while poor Muslim women might be sold to Jewish men as maidservants.

The following fascinating story reflects the tensions that can arise as the result of crossing these sexual boundaries. An upper class Christian woman from Provence converted to Judaism in the second half of the eleventh century. Because she married a Jew, albeit of the upper class as well, her brothers were outraged and vindictive; thus the couple fled the enraged siblings and headed southward to Castile. This convert and her family had the misfortune of choosing to reside in a small town named Muño near Burgos, where they eventually became victims of anti-Jewish violence. At this time, her husband was murdered and two of their children were taken into captivity. This anonymous woman, now a Jewish widow, was given letters of reference by the Jewish community intended to help her obtain sufficient funds to redeem her children. She somehow managed to rebuild her life and even remarry, but years later, her brothers were still hot on her trail and eventually located her in Najera. There they succeeded in having her arrested, imprisoned and handed a death sentence. At the last minute, she was miraculously saved by Jews who managed to bribe the Christian prison officials and to smuggle her out of her cell in the middle of the night. This woman most likely moved to Cairo, since these documents were found in the Cairo Geniza. Her choice of a Muslim country was logical, for the Fatimid rulers of Egypt were not interested or threatened by a convert who moved from one *dhimmi* group to another. Her saga reveals, among other things, the consistent support of the Jewish community for widows and orphans, and for Jews taken into captivity as well as the complications that can result from interfaith sexual liaisons.[50]

---

with Jewish men in the thirteenth century upset the rabbis. See "Sexual Behaviour," 36-37. In 1281, the community of Toledo issued a ban against this phenomenon, 39.

[49] Assis, "Sexual Behaviour," 40. He claims that "sexual behavior among the Jews was much influenced by the standards which prevailed in the society at large," 51.

[50] This fascinating story was reconstructed by two scholars on the basis of two documents found in the Cairo Geniza. See Edna Engel, "The Wandering of a Provençal Proselyte: A Puzzle of Three Genizah Fragments," *Sefunot* 7 (1999): 13-21 (Hebrew), and Yosef Yahalom,

The Jewish community was equally disgruntled when Jewish women had sexual relations with non-Jewish men. For instance, in fourteenth-century Saragossa, a Jewish woman had been consorting with a Muslim, and Jewish officials requested that the government punish her by disfiguring her face and exiling her.[51] Another woman who married a Christian was murdered by her brothers in 1311 because she was pregnant.[52] Although less common, examples can nonetheless be found of Jewish women involved with Christian lovers. These women presumably sought and even encountered love and protection outside of the Jewish community.

If these women became pregnant, as in the aforementioned case, the status of the children was a delicate issue. Even when the partners were of the same faith, life could become complicated. One Jewish woman lived as a concubine with a Jewish man in Huesca, but eventually left him. She succeeded in finding a husband, a feat admirable unto itself, yet prior to the wedding ceremony, some qualms were expressed whether or not the marriage could be performed. Thus in the second half of the fourteenth century, Rabbi Isaac b. Sheshet Perfet was asked if the couple should wait three months before marrying in order to ascertain that the bride was not pregnant.[53]

When dealing with Jewish couples, the problem of producing a male heir plagued many a family, especially if the husband passed away before one was born. The deceased's brothers had to choose between opting for a levirate marriage in order to produce an heir or freeing the widow from a forced marriage; in Spain, the tendency was to opt for the former. However, if the brother-in-law was already

"The Muño Letters: The Work of a Village Scribe from Northern Spain," *Sefunot* 7 (1999): 23-33 (Hebrew).

[51] There is disagreement regarding the status of this woman, Oro de Par. David Nirenberg refers to her as having Muslim and Christian lovers; in 1356, "Jewish officials were afraid to ask on their own, the petitioners claimed, because they feared violence from Oro's Christian lovers." *Communities of Violence: Persecution of Minorities in the Middle Ages* (Princeton: Princeton University Press, 1996), 136. Blasco Martínez refers to her as the wife of a Muslim in "Mujeres Judías Aragoneses," 31.

[52] Baer, *Die Juden*, 203, no. 164, item 6.

[53] Meritxell Blasco Orellana and José Ramón Magdalena Nom de Déu, "La Mujer judía en la Corona de Aragón Vista a través de los *Responsa* de Rabí Yishaq bar Sheshet Perfet (segunda mitad del siglo XIV)," in *La mujer judía*, ed. Yolanda Moreno Koch (Córdoba: Ediciones el Almendro, 2007), 18.

married, the prospect of polygamy entered the scene. It seems that Maimonides limited the widow to refusing such an arrangement only if her brother-in-law was deformed; if not, she would be considered a rebellious woman. The thirteenth-century Aragonese scholar Solomon ibn Adret (Rashba) was even less lenient, claiming that she should be forced to marry him. Some women managed to avoid this quandary, for example by quickly arranging a fictitious marriage (followed by a divorce) so that the levirate marriage could not take place. Polygamy and inheritance issues could also complicate the situation, as when two brothers encountered the problem of dealing with their deceased brothers' two childless wives or when a brother marrying his widowed sister-in-law claimed that he now deserved more than the other brothers' share of the inheritance.[54]

The Final Century

The devastation caused by the riots of 1391 was not gender-biased. Numerous women died sanctifying the name of God and others found themselves unexpectedly widowed. In a detailed analysis of the phenomenon of the "killer wife," the term given to a Jewish woman who has buried two husbands and wishes to marry again, the possibility is raised that these pogroms played a role in creating this difficult situation for many young brides.[55] Rabbinic literature contains numerous cases of complications that arose for both Jewish and converted women who left the Peninsula with and without their husbands. While some of these cases were the direct result of 1391, they continued to appear throughout the fifteenth and sixteenth centuries in various locales.[56] Different rabbis came to different conclusions, but attempts were generally made to enable

---

[54] Blasco Orellana and Nom de Déu, "La Mujer," 17-18; Ribash dealt with these issues.

[55] Avraham Grossman, "From the Heritage of Spanish Jewry: The Treatment of the 'Killer Wife' in the Middle Ages," *Tarbiz* 50 (1998): 540-541 (Hebrew). Grossman shows how the rationalist rabbi Maimonides vehemently objected to this term, which he attributed to popular superstitions, 559; he also notes the prevalence of child-brides, often poor orphaned girls, whose older husbands died, leaving them as young widows, and questions whether these early marriages are the result of living alongside Muslims, 539-40.

[56] Assaf, "The Marranos," 19-60; B. Netanyahu, "The Marranos According to the Hebrew Sources of the 15th and Early 16th Centuries," *Proceedings of the American Academy for Jewish Research* 31 (1963): 81-164; and B. Netanyahu, *The Marranos of Spain from the Late*

these women to return to or to continue living as professing Jews. For example, the responsa of the aforementioned Rabbi Perfet reveal the case of a conversa from Mallorca who was married in a church ceremony to a converso from Aragon just after 1391. A few months later, this woman, now pregnant, and her husband decided to relocate to North Africa, but the husband fled and abandoned her.[57] Another case from 1393 deals with dowries that were promised by Jewish families in Mallorca but could not be provided once they fled to North Africa because their property was either confiscated or abandoned; this responsum also refers to some men who abandoned their wives and children in Mallorca.[58]

Returning to the women who remained in Spain, evidence points in opposing directions, both regarding their socioeconomic status and regarding the social and religious barriers between Christian, Jew and converso. On one hand, the post-1391 Jewish communities were striving to repair the enormous physical and psychological damage that had resulted from the attacks as well as to resurrect themselves, their leadership, and their institutions. On the other hand, reports can be found from the fifteenth century that allude to the excessive wealth of the upper class and include details regarding the wives of the Jewish aristocrats. In 1415, Rabbi Alami criticized the elders of the community for becoming insolent men whose wives and daughters displayed pearls and other precious stones, for they "dressed like princesses and great ladies."[59] In 1432, Rabbi Abraham Benveniste of Soria published an edict dealing with women's dress that was later adopted by Jews in both Castile and the Crown of Aragon.[60] It describes "the women's apparel and the jewels of rich materials; jewels of gold and silver and *aljofar* (seed pearls). They legislate against clothing of gold, *azeituni* (Chinese silk), gauze, silk,

---

Fourteenth to the Early Sixteenth Centuries According to the Hebrew Sources (New York: American Academy for Jewish Research, 1966).

[57] Blasco Orellana and Nom de Déu, "La mujer judía," 16. This rabbi, known as the Ribash, had also left Spain after 1391 and eventually moved to Algeria.

[58] Blasco Orellana and Nom de Déu, "La mujer judía," 16-17.

[59] Baer, *A History*, vol. 2, 242. Letters like these supported Baer's critical view of the Jewish aristocracy, which, in his opinion, was to blame for the demise of Spanish Jewry.

[60] See Moisés Orfali, "Del lujo y de las leyes suntuarias: Ordenanzas sobre la vestimenta femenina en su contexto social y halájico," *La Mujer judía*, ed. Yolanda Moreno Koch (Córdoba: Ediciones El Almendro, 2007), 179.

camel hair, gold buckles." Nevertheless, in certain cases, women were exempt from these sumptuary laws, namely during the first year of marriage in order for them to remain attractive to their husbands and on special occasions including celebrations, when receiving a Lord or a Lady, or at the king's coronation.[61] Some of the rabbis felt that the women's clothing was too ornate and that such conspicuous consumption might incite the Christians; thus it was preferable to be more discreet.[62] It seems that despite the setbacks created by the riots of 1391, the upper class managed to continue maintaining its lofty lifestyle, a matter that concerned the rabbinic leaders as well as the Christian rulers.[63] Needless to say, by 1492, this perceived problem would be solved, albeit unintentionally.

While the rabbis and government attempted to restrain the wealthy courtier class, this was not the experience of the remainder of the community. As intimated above, the riots of 1391 tore the community apart, and its members found themselves in an unprecedented situation. Many former neighbors, friends, family members and even rabbinical leaders were now converted Catholics; those who regretted their decision could not turn back and live openly as Jews as long as they remained in Spain. Those who miraculously survived or avoided the riots needed to concentrate on rebuilding their own lives. However, this was easier said than done, precisely because every Jew had been affected by the forced conversions, either directly or indirectly. Thus, following the devastations of 1391, it was next to impossible for Iberian Jews to refuse the request of a converso neighbor or relative. These requests ranged from providing kosher meat, wine or matzoh to slaughtering animals according to Jewish law for them to teaching and instructing them in matters of Jewish practice. In 1470, the conversa Teresa Acre asked her sister-in-law to teach her a Jewish prayer; five years later she paid a Jewish

---

[61] Eleazar Gutwirth, "A Song and Dance: Transcultural Practices of Daily Life in Medieval Spain," in *Jews, Muslims and Christians In and Around the Crown of Aragon*, ed. Harvey J. Hames (Leiden: Brill, 2004), 227.

[62] Orfali, "Del lujo," 171.

[63] Orfali claims that especially in Castile, the government began to limit the Jewish women as to specific colors and the number of rings and jewels that could be worn, etc. Orfali, "Del lujo," 179.

woman for private lessons in her home because she was anxious to learn to read.[64]

Once the Inquisition was established in 1478 and began to function in 1481, contact between the Jews and conversos became far more dangerous than before but continued nevertheless. In the early 1480s, a Jew named Ferdinand Trujillo served as the spiritual leader for Judaizing conversos from Ciudad Real who were residing in the village of Palma. While he was there, a bride was encouraged to perform a ritual bath prior to her wedding while Trujillo attempted to perform the marriage ceremony with the traditional wine and blessings.[65]

The establishment of the Inquisition clearly put a damper on open relations between members of the two communities, and the Expulsion effectively ended whatever might have remained. It should be noted that the Edict of Expulsion clearly stated that the Jews had to leave Spain because they were a negative influence on the New Christians, teaching them and supplying them with Jewish foods as well as instructing them in almost every aspect of Jewish observance. The crown insisted that the Spanish New Christians, the majority of whom were descendants of the forced converts of the previous century, would never make a serious transition to the Catholic world as long as the Jews were present in Spain.

Inquisition documents support this contention,[66] for they contain numerous examples of contact between Jews and conversos over the course of the fifteenth century.[67] In 1492, Blanca of Atienza was accused of having given charity to Jews for thirty years. Catalina,

---

[64] This is unusual, since the literacy rate of Jewish women in Spain was not high. Nevertheless, in her confession of 1485, both of these attempts to gain an education were described in Legajo 131, número 5 (1493-94) in the archives of the Archivo Histórico Nacional in Madrid.

[65] Constanza de Bonilla was marrying a converso who was not as enthusiastic as she about engaging in Jewish ceremonies. This incident appears in leg. 143, n° 11 (1483-84), the trial of María Díaz, also of Ciudad Real. This Jew was referred to as "rabbi of the conversos"; he later converted and provided detailed testimony about judaizing activity to the Inquisition. See Haim Beinart, *Records of the Trials of the Spanish Inquisition*, vol. 1 (Jerusalem: Israel Academy of Sciences and Humanities, 1974), 53.

[66] Renée Levine Melammed, *Heretics or Daughters of Israel* (New York: Oxford University Press, 1999), 16-30, for descriptions of contact between conversas and members of the Jewish community prior to the Expulsion.

[67] One different set of documents will be included here, which contains interesting information about judaizing as well as about contact between the conversas and the Jews.

also from Atienza, confessed to having eaten matzoh and Jewish fruits, of having attended their weddings and danced at them while taking refreshments and drinking Jewish wine.[68] As it turns out, many of the conversas in this community were attending Jewish weddings and dancing with Jewish women at these celebrations. Catalina confessed in 1504 to having eaten meat at Jewish weddings, dancing, eating fruit, drinking kosher wine, and giving milk to a Jewish woman.[69]

Guiomar of Atienza confessed in 1492 that she had eaten matzoh and "Jewish fruit" once, and had gone to Jewish weddings where she sang, danced and ate. She also fed some Jews whom her husband had taken prisoner, and had fed a Jewish tax collector employed by the duke (of Sigüenza or Atienza); this same Jew sent her a bowl of Sabbath stew and even erected a booth in her home during the Jewish festival of Sukkot. Another conversa confessed to entering a Jew's booth and eating fruit there.[70] Juana, the wife of Martín Sánchez, explained how, among other things, she had provided light for Jews on the Sabbath, serving as a Sabbath gentile rather than as a crypto-Jew. This is interesting because while the Judaizers had been baptized and were clearly Catholics, they preferred to send their servants to Jewish homes to aid them on the Sabbath rather than to abrogate the Sabbath themselves. In 1504, Juana confessed that she had prepared food for the Sabbath, given alms to her Jewish neighbor, and when Passover ended, sent bread to the Jews to eat, again functioning as a non-Jew. Leonor de Hedo also mentioned supplying Jews with bread at the end of Passover as well as attending and dancing at their weddings. The women in this district seemed to have had very close relationships with one another, for many a conversa attended a Jewish wedding, as well as aiding their Jewish friends by supplying them with bread at the end of the Passover festival. In 1492, the wife of Luís Sánchez confessed to having attended a circumcision where

---

[68] Carlos Carrete Parrondo and Mª Fuencisla García Casar, *Fontes Iudaeorum Regni Castellae, VII: El Tribunal de la Inquisición de Sigüenza, 1492-1505* (Salamanca: Universidad Pontificia de Salamanca, 1997), 45 and 46. It is unclear as to what is meant by "Jewish fruits."

[69] Carrete Parrondo and García Casar, *Fontes Iudaeorum Regni Castellae*, 46.

[70] This was the wife of Martín of Atienza; Carrete Parrondo and García Casar, *Fontes Iudaeorum Regni Castellae*, 94.

she sat at the Jewish family's table and joined them in a repast; on another occasion, she ate fish and spinach together with them. As one can clearly see from the above anecdotes, the social and religious barriers between these two groups were often non-existent.

Leonor of Atienza served as a wet nurse, clearly replacing a Jewish mother in her maternal role, and Francisca of Berlanga also confessed in 1504 to serving as a wet nurse. Sancho's wife María of Atienza confessed to entering a synagogue one day and lighting the lamp there as instructed by the Jews; she also ate matzoh and drank kosher wine.[71] These conversas were sharing food, drink and life events with Jews as well as helping them as wet nurses or by lighting fires for them on the Sabbath in their homes and synagogues.

Elsewhere, María López of Berlanga was paying a Jew on Friday afternoons to prepare Sabbath stews for her.[72] In 1492, Isabel of Cuenca referred to her "friend the Jewess" who sent her a special stew on the Sabbath. She, in turn, sent her servant to help her friend on the Sabbath; the servant was the Sabbath gentile in this case and not the conversa, whose husband was unaware of her activities.[73] Likewise did Juana Sánchez engage in clandestine contact with Jews. This storekeeper sold fish and oil to a Jewish woman, sometimes giving her extra oil for lighting the synagogue lamps. When Juana's husband Alonso discovered what she had been doing, he became infuriated, so she simply proceeded to conceal future activities from him. In addition, she gave wax candles to a Jewish relative for use in the Sigüenza synagogue, again hiding her actions from her husband. When she fasted on Yom Kippur and her husband learned about it, he once again became extremely angry. It seems that her aforementioned Jewish relative was not well off, for she provided her with a skirt, headdresses and other clothes, as well as wheat.[74] Again, there is ample evidence that the women were supporting one another, regardless of the fact that they now technically belonged to

---

[71] Carrete Parrondo and García Casar, *Fontes Iudaeorum Regni Castellae*, 55, 84, 56 and 57.

[72] Carrete Parrondo and García Casar, *Fontes Iudaeorum Regni Castellae*, 94.

[73] "En esta çibdad tenía vna amiga judía, la cual judía me mandó vn día de vn viernes vn asadura; y vn criado que tengo, pasando vn sábado por la judía, le llamó aquella judía para que le hiziese lunbre," Carrete Parrondo and García Casar, *Fontes Iudaeorum Regni Castellae*, 7: 179.

[74] The husband, Alonso Sanchez of Medina, was a scribe. See Carrete Parrondo and García Casar, *Fontes Iudaeorum Regni Castellae*, 197, for details.

two different religious groups. Their familial and social ties had not been broken; they celebrated together, aided one another when in distress, and supported one another.

Although some of these documents were recorded after the Expulsion, they clearly refer to pre-1492 activities that occurred while Jewish women were still residing on the Peninsula. Needless to say, life changed for the conversos as well as for the Jews in 1492. The Inquisition and the Crown assumed that the Judaizing heresy would slowly but surely be extirpated, but did not take into account that the Expulsion was essentially creating a new group of conversos and conversas. The conversions that took place during the spring and summer of 1492 were technically voluntary, but not because these Jews had "seen the light"; those who could not bear to leave their homes were not exactly anxious to become Catholics. The Inquisition learned that it now had to confront this new generation of New Christians who were Judaizing. Post-1492 conversa activity is characterized by the messianic movement led by twelve-year-old Inés of Herrera at the turn of the century, a movement that attracted numerous followers and quickly spread throughout Extremadura. The large number of older women who had converted in 1492 who joined this movement, only to face trials and certain death, speaks for itself.[75] These women were anxious to return to their ancestral religion, for their conversions had been half-hearted.

Attempting to assess the means by which Hispano-Jewish women dealt with this trauma is no easy task. There are, however, a few clues as to their mindset that point to their preference to emigrate rather than convert. As one historian has noted, "Conversion implied a far more violent break with the past and presented difficulties of adjustment and adaptation more daunting than those faced by their husbands."[76] One Jew from Huesca left Aragon with his family because his mother insisted upon it, only to return later with his wife and children once his mother had passed away.[77] Among the heads of family who opted to go north to the small Iberian kingdom

---

[75] For a discussion of the messianic turmoil and an analysis of the women's roles, see Levine Melammed, *Heretics*, 45-72.

[76] Mark D. Meyerson, "Aragonese and Catalan Jewish Converts at the Time of the Expulsion," *Jewish History* 6 (1992): 139.

[77] Meyerson, "Aragonese and Catalan Jewish Converts," 135.

of Navarre in 1492, some were hoping that they would eventually succeed in convincing their wives to convert to Catholicism. One of them told an official that he expected to be converting along with his family, if not now, then later.[78] Women seemed far more reluctant to convert than men. Some men converted without their wives, while others objected to their wives' reluctance to abandon Judaism. Even after the Expulsion, petitions were being presented to the Crown for permission to return by men whose wives had prevented them from converting or had caused the couples to part ways.[79]

The world of Spanish Jewish women was constantly changing, for it reflected their experiences in and with the surrounding society. While tied to their roles as mothers and wives, they were subject to the influences and mores of the ruling religions. These women maneuvered to the best of their abilities, often taking advantage of the offerings and developments around them. A few entered the world of patronage and poetry; others were active in the economic realm. Some crossed religious and sexual borders and others contended with rabbinic rulings within their own communities. The women in medieval Iberia dealt with the influences of two religions, some of which offered them new options and some of which complicated their lives. In the long run, they were not left with many choices: to convert or to abandon their homeland but not their religion. Those conversas who were steadfast in their ties to Judaism were joined by a new wave of converts in 1492. At the same time, many Jewish women chose not to convert but rather to leave the world that had been part and parcel of the lives of their ancestors from time immemorial.

---

[78] Meyerson, "Aragonese and Catalan Jewish Converts," 137.

[79] "The demonstrated reluctance of Jewish women to abandon Judaism in 1492 must have been rooted in their acute sense of responsibility for perpetuating Jewish traditions through socializing their children in them," Meyerson, "Aragonese and Catalan Jewish Converts," 138. See also Luís Suárez Fernández, *Documentos acerca de la Expulsión de los Judíos* (Valladolid: Consejo Superior de Investigaciones Científicas, 1964), 468-69, dated September 7, 1492, and 506-507, dated February 14, 1493.

Works Cited:

Al-Nowaihi, Magda. "Elegy and the Confrontation of Death in Arabic Poetry." In *Transforming Loss into Beauty: Essays on Arabic Literature and Culture in Honor of Magda Al-Nowaihi*, edited by Marlé Hammond and Dana Sajdi, 3-20. Cairo: The American University in Cairo Press, 2008.

Alfasi, Isaac ben Jacob. *Responsa of R. Isaac ben Jacob Alfasi.* Edited by Wolf Leiter. Pittsburgh: Mekhon ha-Rambam, 1954; reprint of 1st ed., Leghorn, 1781.

Ángeles Gallego, María. "Approaches to the Study of Muslim and Jewish Women in Medieval Iberian Peninsula: The Poetess Qasmuna bat Isma`il." *Miscelánea de Estudios Árabes y Hebraicos* 48 (1999): 63-75.

Ashtor, Eliyahu. *The Jews of Moslem Spain, 3 vols.* Philadelphia: Jewish Publication Society, 1984.

Assaf, Simha. "The 'Anusim' of Spain and Portugal in the Responsa Literature" [In Hebrew]. *Me'assef Zion* 5 (1933): 19-60.

Assis, Yom Tov. "Sexual Behaviour in Mediaeval Hispano-Jewish Society." In *Jewish History: Essays in Honor of Chimen Abramsky*, edited by Ada Rapoport Albert and Steven J. Zipperstein, 25-59. London: P. Halban, 1988.

------. "The 'Ordinance of Rabbenu Gershom' and Polygamous Marriages in Spain" [In Hebrew]. Zion 46 (1981): 251-77.

Baer, Yitzhak (Fritz). *Die Juden im Christlichen Spanien* (Aragon and Navarre). Berlin: Akademie Verlag, 1929.

------. *A History of the Jews in Christian Spain*, 2 vols. Philadelphia: Jewish Publication Society, 1966.

Beinart, Haim. *Records of the Trials of the Spanish Inquisition*, vol. 1. Jerusalem: Israel Academy of Sciences and Humanities, 1974.

Blasco Martínez, Asunción. "Mujeres Judías Aragoneses: Entre El Amor, El Desamor, La Rebeldía y La Frustración (Siglos XIV-XV)." In *El Prezente: Studies in Sephardic Culture Gender and Identity*, edited by Tamar Alexander et al., 27-44. Beer Sheva: Ben Gurion University, 2010.

Blasco Orellana, Meritxell and José Ramón Magdalena Nom de Déu. "La Mujer judía en la Corona de Aragón Vista a través de los *Responsa* de Rabí Yishaq bar Sheshet Perfet (segunda mitad del siglo XIV)." In *La mujer judía*, edited by Yolanda Moreno Koch, 11-30. Córdoba: Ediciones el Almendro, 2007.

Cardoner Planas, A. "Seis mujeres hebreas practicando la medicina en el reino de Aragon." *Sefarad* 9 (1949): 441-445.

Carrete Parrondo, Carlos and Mª Fuencisla García Casar. *Fontes Iudaeorum Regni Castellae, VII: El Tribunal de la Inquisición de Sigüenza, 1492-1505*. Salamanca: Universidad Pontificia de Salamanca, 1997.

Borrero Fernández, Mercedes. "Peasant and Aristocratic Women: Their Role in the Rural Economy of Seville at the End of the Middle Ages." In *Women at Work in Spain from the Middle Ages to Early Modern Times*, edited by Marilyn Stone and Carmen Benito-Vessels, 11-31. New York: Peter Lang, 1998.

Burns, Robert I. *Jews in the Notarial Culture: Latinate Wills in Mediterranean Spain, 1250-1350*. Berkeley: University of California Press, 1996.

Decter, Jonathan. "Arabic Poetics and Representations of Women in the Andalusian Hebrew Lament." In *Transforming Loss into Beauty: Essays on Arabic Literature and Culture in Honor of Magda Al-Nowaihi*, edited by Marlé Hammond and Dana Sajdi, 115-141. Cairo: The American University in Cairo Press, 2008.

Dillard, Heath. *Daughters of the Reconquest: Women in Castilian Town Society, 1100-1300*. Cambridge: Cambridge University Press, 1984.

Engel, Edna. "The Wandering of a Provençal Proselyte: A Puzzle of Three Genizah Fragments" [In Hebrew]. *Sefunot* 7 (1999): 13-21.

Fleischer, Ezra. "About Dunash ben Labrat and his wife and son" [In Hebrew]. *Jerusalem Studies in Hebrew Literature* 5 (1984): 189-202.

Friedman, Mordechai Akiva. *Jewish Polygyny in the Middle Ages: New Documents from the Cairo Geniza* [In Hebrew]. Jerusalem: The Bialik Institute, 1986.

Garulo, Teresa. "Una Poetisa Oriental en al-Andalus: Sara al Halabiyya." *al-Qantara: Revista des Estudios Arabes* 6 (1985): 155-77.

Goitein, S. D. *A Mediterranean Society*, vol. 3. Berkeley: University of California Press, 1978.

Grossman, Avraham. "From the Heritage of Spanish Jewry: The Treatment of the 'Killer Wife' in the Middle Ages [In Hebrew]." *Tarbiz* 50 (1998): 531-561.

------. *Pious and Rebellious: Jewish Women in Medieval Europe*. Waltham, MA: Brandeis University Press, 2004.

Gutwirth, Eleazar. "A Song and Dance: Transcultural Practices of Daily Life in Medieval Spain". In *Jews, Muslims and Christians In and Around the Crown of Aragon*, edited by Harvey J. Hames, 207-227. Leiden: Brill, 2004.

------. "*Qilusin:* el mecenazgo femenino medieval." In *La mujer judía*, edited by Yolanda Moreno Koch, 107-128. Córdoba: Ediciones El Almendro, 2007.

Hambly, Gavin R. G. "Becoming Visible: Medieval Islamic Women in Historiography and History." In *Women in the Medieval Islamic World*, edited by Gavin R. G. Hambly, 3-27. New York: St. Martin's Press, 1998.

Ibn Daud, Abraham. *The Book of Tradition*, trans. Gerson D. Cohen. Philadelphia: Jewish Publication Society, 1967.

Juster, Jean. "The Legal Condition of the Jews under the Visigothic Kings." *Israel Law Review* 11:3 (1976): 391-414.

Elka Klein. "The Widow's Portion: Law, Custom and Marital Property among Medieval Catalan Jews." *Viator* 31 (2000): 147-163.

------. "Splitting heirs: Patterns of inheritance among Barcelona's Jews." *Jewish History* 16 (2002): 49-71.

Maimon, Moses ben. *R. Moses b. Maimon Responsa*, vol. 2. Edited by Jehoshua Blau. Jerusalem: Rubin Mass, 1986.

Melammed, Renée Levine. "He Said, She Said: A Woman Teacher in Twelfth Century Cairo." *AJS Review* 22 (1997): 19-35.

------. "Medieval and Early Modern Sephardi Women." In *Jewish Women in Historical Perspective*, edited by Judith Baskin, 115-134. Wayne State University Press, 1998.

------. *Heretics or Daughters of Israel.* New York: Oxford University Press, 1999.

Melechen, Nina. "Calling Names: The Identification of Jews in Christian Documents from Medieval Toledo." In *On the Social Origins of Medieval Institutions: Essays in Honor of Joseph F. O'Callaghan,* edited by. Donald J. Kagay and Theresa M. Vann, 21-34. Leiden: Brill, 1998.

Meyerson, Mark D. "Aragonese and Catalan Jewish Converts at the Time of the Expulsion." *Jewish History* 6 (1992): 131-149.

Netanyahu, Benzion. "The Marranos According to the Hebrew Sources of the 15th and Early 16th Centuries." *Proceedings of the American Academy for Jewish Research* 31 (1963): 81-164.

------. *The Marranos of Spain from the Late Fourteenth to the Early Sixteenth Centuries According to the Hebrew Sources.* New York: American Academy for Jewish Research, 1966.

Nirenberg, David. *Communities of Violence: Persecution of Minorities in the Middle* Ages. Princeton: Princeton University Press, 1996.

Orfali, Moisés. "Del lujo y de las leyes suntuarias: Ordenanzas sobre la vestimenta femenina en su contexto social y halájico." In *La mujer judía,* edited by Yolanda Moreno Koch, 161-179. Córdoba: Ediciones El Almendro, 2007.

Qutbuddin, Tahera. "Women Poets," in *Medieval Islamic Civilization: An Encyclopedia,* vol. 2, edited by Josef W. Meri, 865-867. New York: Routledge, 2006.

Rosen, Tova. *Unveiling Eve: Reading Gender in Medieval Hebrew Literature.* Philadelphia: University of Pennsylvania Press, 2003.

Ruggles, D. Fairfield. "Women Patrons," in *Medieval Islamic Civilization: An Encyclopedia,* vol. 2, edited by Josef W. Meri, 863-865. New York: Routledge, 2006.

Ruiz, Teófilo. "Women, Work and Daily Life in Late Medieval Castile." In *Women at Work in Spain from the Middle Ages to Early Modern Times,* edited by Marilyn Stone and Carmen Benito-Vessels, 101-120. New York: Peter Lang, 1998.

Sáenz-Badillos, Ángel and Judit Targarona. "La voz femenina' en la poesía hebrea medieval." In *La mujer judía,* edited by Yolanda Moreno Koch, 101-120. Córdoba: Ediciones El Almendro, 2007.

Sajdi, Dana. "Revisiting Layla al-Akhyaliya's Trespass." In *Transforming Loss into Beauty: Essays on Arabic Literature and Culture in Honor of Magda Al-Nowaihi*, edited by Marlé Hammond and Dana Sajdi, 185-227. Cairo: The American University in Cairo Press, 2008.

Suárez Fernández, Luís. *Documentos acerca de la Expulsión de los Judíos*. Valladolid: Consejo Superior de Investigaciones Científicas, 1964.

Viguera, María J. "Ashluhu li l'ma'ali: On the Social Status of Andalusi Women." In *The Legacy of Muslim Spain*, edited by Salma Khadra Jayyusi, 709-724. Leiden: Brill, 1992.

Winer, Rebecca. *Women, Wealth, and Community in Perpignan, c. 1250-1300: Christians, Jews, and Enslaved Muslims in a Medieval Mediterranean Town*. Aldershot, England: Ashgate, 2006.

Yahalom, Yosef. "The Muño Letters: The Work of a Village Scribe from Northern Spain" [In Hebrew]. *Sefunot* 7 (1999): 23-33.

Jews as Masters of Secrets in Late Thirteenth-Century Castile

....   Hartley Lachter

Kabbalah is undoubtedly one of the most important intellectual developments of medieval Iberian Jewry. This type of Jewish discourse began in the 1180's in southern France, and reached a peak of creative activity during the late thirteenth century in Castile with the composition of a large number of kabbalistic texts, especially the grouping of writings that eventually came to be known as the *Sefer ha-Zohar*, or Book of Splendor.[1] It was also during this period that the voluminous writings of Moses de Leon, Joseph Gikatilla, Joseph of Hamadan, David ben Yehudah ha-Hasid, and Isaac ibn Sahula, as well as many anonymous kabbalistic texts, were composed and began to circulate. A prominent feature of medieval Kabbalah is the presentation of these traditions as an "esoteric" or secret doctrine

---

[1] On the question of the coherence of the *Sefer ha-Zohar* as a book, see Daniel Abrams, *Kabbalistic Manuscripts and Textual Theory* (Los Angeles: Cherub Press, 2010), ch. 4.

stemming from revelation.[2] Such claims to esoteric knowledge constitute an important strategy employed by kabbalists for establishing the authority of kabbalistic texts and ideas.[3]

Castilian Kabbalah can be regarded as a comprehensive re-imagining of the rabbinic Jewish tradition based on the notion that the most fundamental registers of meaning associated with traditional Jewish texts and religious practices are esoteric or secret matters pertaining to the mysteries of the divine, and accessible only to Jews through a concealed chain of transmission. By situating secret knowledge of divine matters at the center of Judaism, kabbalists sought to enhance the cultural capital associated with Kabbalah, which in turn served to promote the authority of the kabbalists as an important and distinct group of Jewish intellectuals who served as guardians and purveyors of Jewish wisdom. In this chapter we will consider some of the ways that the discourse of secrecy in kabbalistic texts reflects the unique social, intellectual and political climate of late thirteenth-century Castile, creating a context in which the propagation of an esoteric reading of Judaism was able to succeed. The flourishing of Kabbalah in the thirteenth century further demonstrates how Jewish identity on the Iberian peninsula was contested, fluid and local, entailing a number of overlapping and competing conceptions of what Judaism means, and who is empowered with the authority to articulate that meaning.

---

[2] A full assessment of the role of esotericism in medieval Kabbalah, including the controversies surrounding the role of kabbalistic disclosure in the Catalonian context in the mid-thirteenth century, lies beyond the scope of this chapter. On esotericism in medieval Kabbalah, see, for example, Elliot Wolfson, "Beyond the Spoken Word: Oral Tradition and Written Transmission in Medieval Jewish Mysticism," in *Transmitting Jewish Traditions: Orality, Textuality and Cultural Diffusion*, ed. Y. Elman and I. Gershoni (New Haven, CT: Yale University Press, 2000), 166-224; Idel, "Secrecy, Bina and Derisha," in *Secrecy and Concealment: Studies in the History of Mediterranean and Near Eastern Religions*, ed. Hans G. Kippenberg and Guy G. Stroumsa (Leiden: Brill, 1995), 311-343. On esotericism in medieval Jewish thought, see Moshe Halbertal, *Concealment and Revelation: Esotericism in Jewish Thought and its Philosophical Implications* (Princeton: Princeton University Press, 2007); Dov Schwartz, *Contradiction and Concealment in Medieval Jewish Thought* (Jerusalem: Bar-Ilan University Press, 2002).

[3] See Daniel C. Matt, "'New-Ancient Words': The Aura of Secrecy in the Zohar," in *Gershom Scholem's* Major Trends in Jewish Mysticism *50 Years After*, ed. Peter Schäfer and Joseph Dan (Tubingen: Mohr Siebeck, 1993), 181-207; Eitan Fishbane, "Authority, Tradition, and the Creation of Meaning in Medieval Kabbalah," *Journal of the American Academy of Religion* 72, 1 (2004): 59-95.

Kabbalah and Secret Knowledge

Within a relatively short period of time, Kabbalah became a dominant paradigm for the conceptualization of Judaism. In the first half of the thirteenth century in the regions of Provence and Catalonia, there was a fair degree of controversy surrounding the production of kabbalistic literature. Isaac the Blind, an important kabbalist from Provence, protested in a letter sent to Nahmanides against the practices of some kabbalists in Spain who elaborated both orally and in writing on matters relating to Kabbalah. R. Isaac claimed with regard to himself, "I am of an entirely different habit, since my fathers were indeed the most distinguished in the land and public masters of the Torah but never did a word [relating to mystical lore] escape their lips."[4] As Kabbalah migrated west through Spain throughout the thirteenth century, there was an increasing tendency to speak more publicly about at least the *existence* of an esoteric Jewish tradition, though much of the content of that tradition was often withheld. Nahmanides was one of the most important authorities whose integration of allusions to kabbalistic matters into his public writings, especially his commentary on the Torah, played a key role in strengthening the broader acceptance of Kabbalah and the notion of an esoteric core to the Jewish tradition. While Nahmanides was forthcoming regarding the existence of a Jewish esoteric tradition, he was fairly reticent with regard to the specific details. Nahmanides asserts in the introduction to his commentary on the Torah that the meaning of the kabbalistic hints and allusions he has placed in the text cannot be comprehended through human reason, but only through a tradition received "from the mouth of a wise kabbalist to the ear of an understanding kabbalist."[5]

---

[4] Cited from Gershom Scholem, *Origins of the Kabbalah*, Allan Arkush, trans. (Princeton: Princeton University Press, 1987), 394. For a discussion of this letter and the controversies surrounding the beginnings of Kabbalah in Spain during the first half of the thirteenth century, see 393-406; Daniel Abrams, *Kabbalistic Manuscripts and Textual Theory*, 441-442; Moshe Idel, "Nahmanides: Kabbalah, Halakha, and Spiritual Leadership," in *Jewish Mystical Leaders and Leadership in the 13th Century*, ed. M. Idel and M. Ostow (Northvale: Jason Aronson Press, 1998), 27-38; Yehiel Goldberg, "Spiritual Leadership and the Popularization of Kabbalah in Medieval Spain," *Journal for the Study of Sephardic and Mizrahi Jewry* (2009): 2-59, at 7-14.

[5] *Peirush al ha-torah le-rabeinu moshe ben nahman*, ed. Charles Chavel (Jerusalem: Mosad Harav Kook, 1984), 7. There is a sizable body of scholarship on the subject of kabbalah and

Late thirteenth-century Castile, especially during the last three decades of the century, saw the development of a very different ethos with regard to disseminating esoteric discourse. Moshe Idel has referred to this creative moment as a "window of opportunities,"[6] during which many creative modes of kabbalistic literature were composed and circulated. While Castilian kabbalists still accepted the notion of the existence of some secrets that cannot be fully divulged, they defined the boundaries of what can be put down in writing much more capaciously. Many of the kabbalistic texts written during this period are detailed expositions designed to make the reader aware of the kabbalistic meaning of all aspects of scripture and religious praxis. The question that I wish to explore is not the extent to which this literature is innovative or conservative—a dichotomy that Elliot Wolfson has demonstrated is not easily demarcated in texts from this period.[7] Rather, I wish to consider the function of the claim to esoteric knowledge in the advancement of the kabbalistic understanding of Judaism. The fact that this kind of kabbalistic literature was so compelling to so many late thirteenth- and early fourteenth-century Iberian Jews, especially in the region of Castile, is an important indicator of the degree to which the idea of the Jewish sage as a *ba'al sod*, or master of secrets, and the presentation of Judaism as a *torat ha-sod*, or esoteric teaching, spoke to the aspirations of Jews in that particular context.

The content of the esoteric tradition articulated in these kabbalistic texts addresses the mysteries of the Godhead, represented

---

esotericism in Nahmanides' corpus. See, for example, Moshe Idel, "We Have No Kabbalistic Tradition on This," in *Rabbi Moses Nahmanides (RAMBAN): Explorations in his Religious and Literary Virtuosity*, ed. I. Twersky (Cambridge, MA: Harvard University Press, 1983), 51-74; Idel, "Nahmanides: Kabbalah, Halakha, and Spiritual Leadership," 15-96; Elliot Wolfson, "By Way of Truth: Aspects of Nahmanides Kabbalistic Hermeneutic," *AJS Review* 14, 2 (1989): 103-178; Daniel Abrams, *Kabbalistic Manuscripts and Textual Theory*, ch.3; Moshe Halbertal, *By Way of Truth: Nahmanides and the Creation of Tradition*, (Jerusalem: Shalom Hartman Institute, 2006) (Hebrew).

[6] See Moshe Idel, "The Kabbalah's 'Window of Opportunities', 1270–1290," in *Meah Sheharim: Studies in Medieval Jewish Spiritual Life in Memory of Isadore Twersky*, ed. Ezra Fleisher, Gerald Blidstein, Carmi Horowitz, and Bernard Septimus (Jerusalem: Magnes Press, 2001), 173-208; Idel, "Kabbalah and Elites in Thirteenth-Century Spain," *Mediterranean Historical Review*, 9 (1994): 5–19.

[7] See, for example, Elliot Wolfson, "The Anonymous Chapters of the Elderly Master of Secrets: New Evidence for the Early Activity of the Zoharic Circle," *Kabbalah* 19 (2009): 143-278, especially 166-172.

by the symbolic system of the ten *sefirot,* or ten luminous emanations of the divine, and the relationship of these mysteries to the details of Jewish texts and practices. While there are significant differences between individual kabbalists and different kabbalistic schools of thought, a consistent theme that emerges from the diversity of voices in these texts is the notion that Jews, through the study of Jewish lore and the practice of Jewish law, play a central role in maintaining the very being of the fabric of the cosmos, as well as the harmony within the divine realm. In a forceful assertion of Jewish triumphalism, kabbalists imagine a world in which Jews, through the practice of Judaism, maintain the connection of the universe to God. By establishing a harmonious interlocking of the ten *sefirot* with one another and with the divine essence, Jews are able, through the practice of commandments and the study of the secret layers of meaning concealed within the Torah, to serve as the conduits between the supernal and terrestrial realms. Jews thereby constitute the key element uniting the cosmic and divine realities, bringing divine overflow or *shefa* into the world, which sustains the cosmos and propagates blessing for all peoples. In a typical articulation of the kabbalistic understanding of the place of Jews and Judaism in the world, David ben Yehuda ha-Hasid, an important kabbalist from late thirteenth-century Castile, asserts:

> Happy are Israel, more than all other people, for the Holy One, blessed be He, desires them and is jealous of them and is glorified by them, for the world was only created for their sake, in order that they might occupy themselves with the Torah to unite this with that. And Israel below in this world is the sustenance of all, and the sustenance of all other peoples. When is this? When they perform the will of their Lord.[8]

The notion of a secret Jewish triumph operative in this text is one that assigns Jews a central role in the cosmic-divine relationship, and regards Jewish practice as the key to sustaining not only Jews, but other peoples as well. Jewish esoteric discourse thus incorporated a significant polemical element, in which Jews were imagined as masters of secrets whose power and knowledge places them in a

---

[8] *The Book of Mirrors: Sefer Mar'ot ha-Zove'ot,* ed. Daniel C. Matt (Chico, CA: Scholars Press, 1982), 191.

position of superiority vis-à-vis other peoples. As David ben Yehuda ha-Hasid succinctly puts it, "Happy are the righteous in this world and the world to come, for the Holy One, blessed be he, revealed secrets to them that have not been revealed to any other people. Thus it is written, 'he did not do so for any other nation' (Ps. 147:20)."[9]

Joseph Gikatilla, a prolific author of kabbalistic texts in late thirteenth-century Castile, made a similar point when he argued that the superiority of Judaism is that it contains an esoteric dimension— something the religions of other nations lack, in his estimation. Judaism is, in Gikatilla's eyes, the most authoritative and stable tradition upon which to rely regarding ultimate knowledge concerning divine matters, since "they [the religions of the other nations] do not contain the concealed and revealed (*nistar ve-nigleh*), and they lack the [combination of] outward and the hidden (*galui u-muflah*). They are not designed [to reveal] any other [hidden] meaning. Of themselves they cease and perish... 'They shall be trampled under foot' (Isa. 28:3)."[10] Or, as Moses de Leon states in his introduction to *Or Zarua*, one of his earliest kabbalistic treatises, "I have discovered in the secret of the paths of wisdom that God, may He be blessed, and the secret of His truth, cannot be comprehended by knowledge... However, we can attain a measure of His truth through the secret of the paths of the Torah... From it we can understand the secret of His concealed hidden dwelling, and ascend the gradations of the ladder."[11] By asserting that the "wisdom of God" cannot be attained through reason, and by claiming that access to such privileged knowledge can be acquired only through an exclusively Jewish chain of esoteric speculation, kabbalists placed the most desirable and powerful forms of knowledge not only within the text of the Torah, but specifically within the secret layers of meaning associated with the Torah that are known exclusively to the masters of the Kabbalah.[12]

---

[9] *The Book of Mirrors*, 193.

[10] Joseph Gikatilla, *Ginat Egoz* (Jerusalem: Yeshivat ha-Hayyim ve-ha-Shalom, 1989), 6.

[11] Alexander Altmann, "Sefer Or Zarua le-R. Moshe de Leon," *Kovetz al Yad* 9 (19) (1980): 219-293, at 246.

[12] On the paradox within Kabbalah of revealing the secret in a concealed way, see Wolfson, "Occultation of the Feminine and the Body of Secrecy in Medieval Kabbalah," in *Luminal Darkness* (Oxford: Oxford University Press, 2007), 258–94; Wolfson, *Abulafia—Kabbalist and Prophet: Hermeneutics, Theosophy, Theurgy* (Los Angeles: Cherub Press, 2000), 38–93;

The composition and circulation of kabbalistic texts thus entailed a power gesture that constituted a strategy for re-imagining sources of Jewish legitimacy and authority based on claims to esoteric knowledge. The late thirteenth-century Castilian context presented Jews with a number of challenges in the form of Christian anti-Jewish polemics, as well as the spread of rationalism, nominalism[13] and other intellectual currents that were regarded by some Jews as threats to traditional Jewish authority and the continuing relevance of Jewish religious praxis. At the same time, this moment presented Jews with a number of opportunities. The broader cultural climate during this period witnessed an increased interest in esotericism, or secret forms of knowledge associated with a *prisca theologia* often originating in ancient revelation and accessible exclusively through a chain of oral or written transmission. In the dynamic, cosmopolitan environment engendered by King Alfonso X of Castile,[14] philosophical compositions competed for influence with a parallel dissemination of esoteric forms of knowledge, understood to be secret traditions from antiquity, such as Hermetic,[15] Neo-Platonic and Neo-Pythagorean[16]

Wolfson, "Murmuring Secrets: Eroticism and Esotericisn in Medieval Kabbalah," in *Hidden Intercourse: Eros and Sexuality in the History of Western Esotericism*, ed. W. J. Hanegraaff and J. J. Kripal (Leiden: Brill, 2008), 65-110.

[13] See Kocku von Stuckrad, *Locations of Knowledge in Medieval and Early Modern Europe: Esoteric Discourse and Western Identities* (Leiden: Brill, 2010), 99-103.

[14] See, for example, Robert Burns, *Emperor of Culture: Alfonso X of Castile and his Thirteenth-Century Renaissance* (Philadelphia: University of Pennsylvania Press, 1990); H. Salvador Martinez, *Alfonso X, the Learned*, Odile Cisneros, trans. (Leiden: Brill, 2010).

[15] On Hermetic themes in Alfonso el Sabio's *General Estoria*, see Charles Fraker, *The Scope of History: Studies in the Historiography of Alfonso el Sabio* (Ann Arbor: University of Michigan Press, 1996), 190-202; Fraker, "Hermes Trismegistus in *General Estoria*," in *Medieval Iberia: Changing Societies and Cultures in Contact and Transition*, ed. Ivy Corfis and R. Harris-Northall (Woodbridge: Tamesis, 2007), 87-98. On Jewish interest in Hermetic ideas, see Moshe Idel, "Hermeticism and Kabbalah," in *Hermetism from Late Antiquity to Humanism: La tradizione ermetica dal mondo tardo-antico all'Umanesimo*, ed. P. Lucentini, I. Parri and V. Perrone Compagni (Turnhout: Brepolis, 2003), 385–428; Idel, "Hermeticism and Judaism," in *Hermeticism and the Rennaisance*, ed. I. Merkel and A. G. Debus (Washington: Folger Books, 1988), 59–76; Fabrizio Lelli, "Hermes among the Jews: *Hermetica* as *Hebraica* from Antiquity to the Renaissance," *Magic, Ritual, and Witchcraft* 2 (2007): 111–35.

[16] See Moshe Idel, "Johannes Reuchlin: Kabbalah, Pythagorean Philosophy and Modern Scholarship," *Studia Judaica* 16 (2008): 30-55, here 2 n.6; Elke Morlok, *Rabbi Joseph Gikatilla's Hermeneutics* (Tubingen: Mohr Siebeck, 2011), especially 77-83, 153-160, 222-228; Tzvi Langermann, "Studies in Medieval Hebrew Pythagoreanism," *Micrologus* 9 (2001): 219-236.

texts. We find evidence of the participation of Jews in the circulation of these esoteric ideas through their interest in texts such as
Sefer ha-Levanah,[17] or "The Book of the Moon"; the Arabic *Ghayat
al-Hakim*, or "The Goal of the Wise," translated in Alfonso's court
as the *Picatrix*, and known in medieval Jewish circles as the *Tahlit
he-Haham*,[18] as well as the hermetic pseudo-epigraphy transmitted
in the name of Aristotle in Latin as the *Secretum Secretorum*, and in
Hebrew as the *Sod ha-Sodot* or 'Secret of Secrets'.[19] It hardly seems a
coincidence that the historical moment in which classical Kabbalah
underwent its most intensive and creative period of productivity
took place during the Alfonsine renaissance,[20] in which, alongside
rational science, esoteric forms of discourse were accorded legitimacy and prestige. The increased interest in esoteric speculation
during this period presented an opportunity for kabbalists. I would
like to suggest that the propagation of kabbalistic discourse among
Jews in late thirteenth-century Castile was informed by the general
advance of interest in esoteric forms of knowledge in the broader
cultural context. Situating the proliferation of kabbalistic discourse
in this way contributes to our understanding of how Kabbalah, for
both those who produced it and those who chose to value and preserve it, was able to re-conceptualize Jewish identity based on claims
regarding an exclusively Jewish chain of esoteric wisdom.

Kabbalistic Mysteries vs. Rational Truth

The relationship between Kabbalah and philosophy during this
period is complex. On the one hand, kabbalists took serious issue
especially with Aristotelian trends that placed the highest value on

[17] Fabrizio Lelli, "Le versioni ebraiche di un testo ermetico : il "Sefer ha-levanah," *Henoch* 12 (1990): 147-164; *The Book of the Moon*, ed. A. W. Greenup (London: [s.n.], 1912) (Hebrew).

[18] Moshe Idel, "Magical and Neoplatonic Interpretations of Kabbalah in the Renaissance," *Jewish Thought in the Sixteenth Century*, ed. Bernard Dov Cooperman (Cambridge, MA: Harvard University Press, 1983), 186-242, at 192-193; Idel, "Some Images of Maimonides in Jewish Mysticism," *Studie Judaica* 17 (2009): 36-63, at 48-49.

[19] Moses Gaster, *The Hebrew Version of Secretum Secretorum: A Medieval Treatise Ascribed to Aristotle* (London: Journal of the Royal Asiatic Society, 1907–8).

[20] On this issue see Moshe Idel, "On European Cultural Renaissances and Jewish Mysticism," *Kabbalah* 13 (2005): 43-78, at 58–61; Elke Morlok, *Rabbi Joseph Gikatilla's Hermeneutics*, 5-14; Iris Fleix, *Theurgy, Magic and Mysticism in the Kabbalah of R. Joseph of Shushan ha-Birah* (Hebrew University Ph.D. Dissertation, 2005), 11-13.

rationally derived knowledge. Most kabbalists were emphatic that the mysteries of the divine and the relationship between the God and the cosmos cannot be garnered through the use of human reason alone. Only through an *esoteric* revelation can such knowledge be acquired, the kabbalists argued, since the mysteries of the divine are matters that transcend the boundaries of the mind. Many Jewish philosophers, most famously Maimonides, also associated philosophical truths with secret teachings within Judaism, especially those connected to the mysteries of creation (*ma'aseh bereishit*) and the chariot vision of the prophet Ezekial (*ma'aseh merkavah*) mentioned in Mishnah.[21] The key difference between the philosophers and the kabbalists regarding the content of these secret traditions is that the philosophical secrets can be derived rationally, while the kabbalistic secrets can only be accessed through an esoteric and uniquely Jewish, tradition.[22] On the other hand, kabblalists did not deny all legitimacy to rational scientific knowledge. Instead, they tended to adopt a position in which the scope and meaning of rational knowledge was limited by a more capacious esoteric tradition that reveals mysteries that would otherwise be inaccessible to the human mind. By configuring the esoteric tradition in relation to philosophical knowledge in this way, the kabbalists advanced a conception of Jewish wisdom that encompassed all forms of *exoteric* knowledge, while at the same time preserving an elite form of *esoteric* wisdom accessible only through a Jewish revelatory tradition. Philosophical knowledge, when accorded a secondary and subordinate status to Kabbalah, was not inherently problematic for most kabbalists. Rational knowledge only poses a serious threat for them when it is valued more highly than, or even to the exclusion of, esoteric knowledge.

In a discussion found in Gikatilla's *Hassagot al ha-Moreh*, a critical gloss on Maimonides' *Guide of the Perplexed*, he asserts that "the Torah of God, may he be blessed, possesses inner and outer attributes, for the wise man and for the fool... and when one attains the inner matters [of the Torah], then one enters the divine palace and beholds the true faces. This is why all foreign wisdoms are called

---

[21] *Hagiga*, 2:1.

[22] See Yossef Schwartz, "The Esoteric and Inter-religious Aspects of the Relation Philosophy/Kabbalah in Late Medieval and Early Modern Europe," *Studia Judaica* 16 (2008): 126-143, at 129.

'external' (*hitzonot*), for they do not possess the truth of the internal faces. All of them are in accordance with the conventional knowledge of a people, and nothing more."[23] Gikatilla goes on to note that the secret faces of the Torah are included in the multiplicity of readings that were transmitted to Moses and passed on in secret oral tradition, which is the reason why "there is no wisdom or knowledge in the world that is not alluded to in the Torah, be it through a letter, word, vocalization, or some other manner—hear this and understand it."[24] Foreign knowledge, including of course Aristotelian philosophy, is not simply negated by the secret knowledge of the Jewish tradition, but rather subsumed within the all-encompassing esoteric doctrine revealed at Sinai. Gikatilla goes on to describe the nature of one who has mastered this secret tradition with a commentary on *Proverbs* 5:15, "Drink water from your own cistern, running water from your own well," arguing that one must not fabricate one's own Torah from one's own mind, but rather "one must receive the Torah from his teachers in order that he should be able to base his wisdom upon the foundation of the divine wisdom. After one has received [this knowledge] and the secrets of the Torah have been transmitted to him, if he is a wise man who understands on his own, he transforms himself into a well flowing with the matters he has received."[25] The secrets of the Torah were, for Gikatilla, the unique inheritance of the Jewish people that granted them superiority over all other forms of knowledge. By knowing the secrets of the Torah, Jewish masters of esoteric knowledge control all forms of wisdom, both Jewish and non-Jewish, as well as a uniquely Jewish esoteric tradition that entails the ultimate truth of all forms of knowledge. Moreover, the "wise man" in this case is not simply a conduit relating the content of the tradition by rote, but rather a master of secrets who brings forth new innovations based on the esoteric wisdom he has received. Gikatilla's presentation of secret wisdom in this passage accords well with Elliot Wolfson's discussions of the kabbalistic "hermeneutic of esoteric disclosure" in which "mysteries may be transmitted orally

---

[23] Gikatilla, "Hassagot al-ha-Moreh," in Isaac Abravanel, *Ketavim al Mahshevet Yisrael* (Jerusalem: [s.n.], 1967) vol. 3, 20v.

[24] Gikatilla, "Hassagot," 20v.

[25] Gikatilla, "Hassagot," 21r.

from master to disciple, but their elucidation is dependent on the exegetical prowess of the recipient."[26]

In a similar vein, Moses de Leon laments the tendency among some Jews who are drawn to philosophical speculation to rely exclusively on rational knowledge, so much so that they reject non-rational forms of knowledge as both absurd and outside of the confines of true Torah knowledge:

> There are men from the people of our Torah who hold fast to the words of the philosophers, since such men rely exclusively upon the matters of their own thought, and believe that such a path is verily the path of truth, and they think that all of the words of our Torah are contained in that very path [of the intellect]. Anything that would depart from this path is regarded by such men as though it forces them from the path of life, and they refuse to accept it... However, the Torah, which all people of the world accept, says, "But as the heavens are high above the earth, so are my words above your words [*sic*] and my thoughts above your thoughts."[27] How can our knowledge and thought possibly grasp that which transcends it, namely, the perfect thought and knowledge of the Creator, blessed be He... And is the Torah not the thought of the Holy One, Blessed be He, and his perfected knowledge?... No man can grasp His thought and knowledge, may He be exalted. Therefore, it was necessary for Moses to receive through tradition (*kabbalah*) the interpretation of the Torah... All of the Torah is the knowledge of God, may He be blessed, and it does not contain a single story or event that does not pertain to a matter upon which the entire world depends, and which contains the secret of His name, may He be exalted, which is the secret of the Tetragrammaton.[28]

De Leon's response to the Jewish rationalists of his day is to argue that the Torah reflects the knowledge of God, and therefore must entail matters that transcend the capacity of the human mind. The only way to gain true insight into the meaning of the Torah is by reading it in light of a parallel tradition, or "*kabbalah*," deriving

---

[26] Elliot Wolfson, "The Anonymous Chapters of the Elderly Master of Secrets," 160. Wolfson has advanced this conception of kabbalistic esotericism in a number of studies. See, for example, Wolfson, "Beyond the Spoken Word," 166-224; Wolfson, "By Way of Truth: Aspects of Nahmanides Kabbalistic Hermeneutic," *AJS Review* 14 (1989): 103-178.

[27] Based on Isa. 54:16

[28] *Sefer ha-Mishqal: Text and Study*, ed. J. Wijnhoven (Ph.D. dissertation, Brandeis University, 1964), 48-49.

from revelation at Sinai and passed on from Moses to subsequent generations of Jews. De Leon reflects in this comment the general tendency among medieval kabbalists to regard the origin of kabbalistic wisdom as an oral tradition revealed to Moses, similar to the Rabbinic notion of the Oral Torah, in which Moses received a separate legal tradition in terms of which the written legal ordinances of the Torah are to be enacted. By making recourse to this familiar source of authority, kabbalists like Moses de Leon sought to advance a different kind of Oral Torah—one that focuses on theosophical mysteries "upon which the entire world depends," and which reveals the mysteries of God's name through an exclusive Jewish tradition rather than a universal operation of the human intellect. The political implication of this formulation of kabbalistic secrecy is clear: by asserting that Kabbalah relates mysteries inaccessible to the human mind, kabbalists tried to establish a domain of ultimate knowledge that was uniquely Jewish and not subject to rational analysis and debate.

While kabbalah entailed a form of knowledge that transcends the intellect, it was not necessarily in direct confrontation with philosophy in every case. As long as philosophical ideas are subordinated to the claims of kabbalisitc esoteric knowledge, kabbalists are happy to incorporate philosophical ideas and terminology into their discourse.[29] In an anonymous commentary on the ten *sefirot* dating to late thirteenth-century Castile preserved in a manuscript in the Bodleian library, we find a very telling combination of kabbalistic and philosophical ideas. Near the beginning of the composition, the author establishes the esoteric nature of the doctrine he is seeking to explicate for his readers. All of the *sefirot* are regarded as "secret" matters, but the first sefirah, *Keter*, is particularly concealed, so much so that the author asserts, "there is no path by which to enter into it… except for the pure and holy wise men, those who were designated by name,[30] for they fear the Holy One, Blessed be He, and know His name. Blessed be the One who has chosen them and their words, for

---

[29] See Elliot Wolfson, "Beneath the Wings of the Great Eagle: Maimonides and Thirteenth Century Kabbalah," in *Moses Maimonides (1138–1204)—His Religious, Scientific, and Philosophical Wirkensgeschichte in Different Cultural Contexts*, eds. Görge K. Hasselhoff and Otfried Fraisse (Wurzburg: Ergon, 2004), 209–237.

[30] Playing on Num. 1:17, Ezra 8:20 and elsewhere.

they know the truth."[31] As we find reiterated frequently in kabbalistic texts composed during this period, the unique knowledge associated with kabbalah is not accessible through rational speculation. Rather, this particular esoteric knowledge, associated with the divine Name, is accessible only to a privileged Jewish elite who possess the requisite piety and are privy to an esoteric chain of transmission. Nonetheless, in a comment near the very end of the composition, the author reflects generally on the nature of relationship between the Divine and the ten *sefirot*, arguing that

> God, who is the Cause of Causes (*'illat ha 'illot ve-sibat ha-sibot*), He controls the *sefirot* and that which emanates forth from Him, may He be blessed, and they are the instruments of His workmanship, and his essence (*'atzmuto*) is concealed within them, and He is within them and bound to them like the flame is bound to the wick and cleaves to it, for these matters are alluded to in the depths of the Kabbalah, for all ten of the gradations are encompassed and bound within Him.[32]

Here again we encounter the assertion that the mysteries of the Godhead are accessible only through a Jewish esoteric tradition, but it is important to note that the author incorporates the philosophical notion of the Cause of Causes. The core claim of this passage centers around the paradoxical linkage of the ten *sefirot* with the infinite divine essence, and the philosophical terminology is appropriated in a manner that leaves one with the impression that the conception of the deity as the "Cause of Causes" is to be understood in a manner compatible with a kabbalistic theosophy in which God's essence is concealed within the ten *sefirot* and bound to them. The philosophical position was, of course, distinctly *in*compatible with this theosophy. However, if the author's goal was to give priority to an esoteric, rather than a rationalist, conception of Judaism, the passage cited above can be understood as a coherent move in advancing that position. Philosophical ideas and terminology were not regarded as threatening per se, as long as they were accorded meaning within the esoteric theosophical system of the Kabbalah.

---

[31] Bodleian Ms. 1565 (Opp. Add. 4 to 4), 110v.
[32] Bodleian Ms. 1565, 117v.

In the introduction to another anonymous commentary on the ten *sefirot* recently published by Michal Oron,[33] we find an intriguing discussion of the relationship between Jewish esoteric wisdom and other forms of knowledge. According to this anonymous kabbalist, the Torah encompasses all forms of instruction,[34] including moral instruction regarding proper conduct, and "wisdom" or instruction concerning truth. Wisdom, according to this text, entails two forms: the revealed and the concealed. The revealed wisdom itself contains two domains: one addressing natural earthly phenomena, the other addressing astronomical speculation. Regarding these exoteric forms of knowledge, the text argues that "in pursuit of this, the [gentile] sages resort to their minds and intellect/ this is the wisdom of the philosophers."[35] Similarly to de Leon's argument in *Sefer ha-Mishqal* cited above, philosophical knowledge is defined primarily as a product of reason, rendering it inferior since it is constrained by the limits of the human mind.

Esoteric knowledge, on the other hand, is accorded a superior position: "The concealed [form of wisdom] is the wisdom of Kabbalah (*hokhmat ha-kabbalah*)... transcending above the intellect/ thus it is not perceptible to the eyes of the men of this generation/ and their knowledge cannot penetrate it..."[36] This special knowledge associated with Kabbalah is, once again, defined as both of a higher order and more exclusive precisely because it is inaccessible to the rational mind. It is for this reason that "the men of this generation," a reference that could imply both Jewish Aristotelian philosophers and members of the non-Jewish intelligentsia, are unable to acquire this special form of knowledge, i.e., "their mind cannot penetrate it," and they have no other source of truth upon which to rely.

Kabbalistic knowledge is further divided into two more domains, the first of which is described as relating to the knowledge of the magical operation of divine names, biblical texts and *nomina barbara* derived from a tradition, "from one man to another (*ish mi-pi ish*)"

---

[33] *Sefer ha-Shem Attributed to R. Moses de Leon*, ed. Michal Oron (Los Angeles: Cherub Press, 2010).

[34] See also the discussion in Oron, *Sefer ha-Shem*, 78, regarding the all-encompassing nature of the Torah.

[35] *Sefer ha-Shem*, 51.

[36] *Sefer ha-Shem*, 51-52.

since Moses.[37] The second domain of "concealed" or kabbalistic knowledge entails,

> the Wisdom of the Kabbalah concerning knowledge of God... knowledge of His precious names/ mentioned in the holy books/ concerning the knowledge of the ten *sefirot* and knowledge of the mysteries/ which are alluded to and concealed and hidden/ which are sealed in the mysteries of the Torah/ and in the words of the prophets and those who speak in the holy spirit, "[the Lord] among them as in Sinai in holiness,"[38] and the words of the wise men and their secrets according to their schools of thought/ also giving sense to the secret of the small and great letters and their crowns/ and the names written with punctuation according to their kinds/ also their combinations and permutations according to their principles/ and the secret of defective and plene spellings...[39]

Since the "Kabbalah concerning knowledge of God" is the main subject matter of the book, it seems fair to say that for the author of this treatise, such knowledge represents the highest attainable form of wisdom. Like other kabbalists, the anonymous author relates the secrets of this form of Kabbalah to the divine name, the symbolic system of the ten *sefirot*, and the inner meaning of scripture, including the secret meanings associated with scribal practices for the composition of Torah scrolls, and the orthographic anomalies of words found throughout the Hebrew Bible.[40] The author also makes an intriguing reference to "the words of the wise men and their secrets according to their schools of thought," a reference one can reasonably surmise refers to post-rabbinic texts written by kabbalists. The knowledge of the Kabbalah was thus a secret doctrine that not only related to mysteries of the Godhead, but also served as a hermeneutical key for reading the concealed essence of traditional Jewish texts. One who has acquired this tool can, like other kabbalists, perceive the esoteric truth of Judaism from within its exoteric concealment.

---

[37] *Sefer ha-Shem*, 52.

[38] Ps. 68:18.

[39] *Sefer ha-Shem*, 52.

[40] Such scribal and orthographic matters were a matter of interest, as well as a degree of concern, for medieval Jewish authorities. See B. Barry Levy, *Fixing God's Torah: The Accuracy of the Hebrew Bible Text in Jewish Law* (Oxford: Oxford University Press, 2001).

It is at this point that the discussion turns to address the "*ba'alei ha-peshat*" or exegetes who seek to render scripture literally "in the manner that it occurs to them according to their own mind."[41] The anonymous author of *Sefer ha-Shem* was in many respects just as bothered by the literal rendering of scripture as he was by philosophical speculation, since both entail a reliance on the human intellect for determining the ultimate meaning of revelation. According to *Sefer ha-Shem*, such matters can only be known "by way of truth," and not through the rational operations of the human mind,

> for these things are known to those who have knowledge of Kabbbalah, and not through speculation and supposition, as Solomon says, peace be upon him, "She [wisdom] does not chart a path of life,"[42] "does not chart (*pen tifales*)"meaning, in the scale (*peles*) of the balance of speculation and demonstration, as it says, "the path of life is perfect joy in your presence,"[43] and he who is wise will see the truth of this verse with the eyes of his heart.[44]

The author's critical assessment of Jewish biblical exegetes who interpret scripture according to its literal sense, an approach made famous in the commentary of R. Solomon Isaac of Troyes, also known as Rashi, is significant for understanding the intellectual and political strategy at play in the advancement of kabbalistic esotericism. One could understand the conflict with philosophical speculation as a conflict over Jewish vs. non-Jewish intellectual traditions. By objecting to the well established Jewish practice of interpreting scripture literally through a "rational" analysis of the meaning of the text, we can see that our author was not simply privileging "foreign" over the "indigenous" forms of knowledge. More specifically, the intent of the anonymous author of this text, in keeping with that of many other kabbalists, was to privilege a Jewish *esoteric tradition* over *rationally* derived forms of truth or exegetical approaches, be they Jewish or non-Jewish in origin.

---

[41] *Sefer ha-Shem*, 52.

[42] Prov. 5:6.

[43] Ps. 16:11.

[44] *Sefer ha-Shem*, 53.

Towards the end of the prefatory comments, the author of *Sefer ha-Shem* states his intent concerning the composition of the book, indicating that he wrote it to create a guide to help those who are beginners in the wisdom of Kabbalah, as a service "to all of Israel, according to their capacity."[45] He notes that there are many texts addressing the matters put forth in this treatise, but they are confusing and scattered. The author therefore states, "I saw fit to set forth a disquisition to enlighten/ the eyes of one who is beginning to learn Kabbalah."[46] Or, as he informs his reader a few pages later,

> when you understand and comprehend all of the words that we have said in this disquisition, you will be able to understand a number of concealed mysteries in the holy writings, as well as in the words of the wise men... This disquisition is sufficient to set straight every beginner in this wisdom, to guide him and caution him and strengthen him, so that he will not confuse his intellect when he hears analogies (*devar mitokh devar*[47]) in the words of this wisdom.[48]

These passages reaffirm the sentiment expressed earlier regarding the intention of this book to serve as a guide for understanding Judaism in terms of an esoteric kabbalistic tradition. They also introduce another important element of this kabbalist's agenda, namely, the instruction of the uninitiated in the wisdom of the Kabbalah. Far from being a discourse reserved for the elite, this author describes his enterprise as one intended to spread broadly among his coreligionists the notion that Judaism contains, at its core, an esoteric tradition, as well as to relate something of the content of that tradition so that more Jews will be made aware of the mysteries alluded to in Jewish texts.[49] The author returns to this point towards the end of the book, where he describes his project of delineating

---

[45] *Sefer ha-Shem*, 54.

[46] *Sefer ha-Shem*, 54.

[47] This language is similar to a passage adduced by Wolfson from MS Oxford Bodleian 2396, fol. 3b, where the "enlightened" refers to those "who comprehend the secret from within the secret [*sod mi-tokh sod*]," "The Anonymous Chapters," 183 n. 196. In texts such as these, Wolfson is quite right to point out that "Kabbalah is, first and foremost, an exegetical enterprise of deciphering the mysteries of Torah, but in such a way that the mysteries remain occluded." Wolfson, "The Anonymous Chapters," 179.

[48] *Sefer ha-Shem*, 58.

[49] On this issue of popularizing trends in thirteenth-century kabbalah, see Goldberg, "Spiritual Leadership and the Popularization of Kabbalah," Harvey Hames, *The Art of*

the relationships between the cognomens of the divine names and the ten *sefirot* as one designed "to expand a bit wider the apertures of the lattice, the chapter headings, matters to which it is permissible to allude, in order to open an opening for 'he whose spirit is moved'[50] to learn this wisdom and to understand, according to their capacity, the holy books, the mysteries alluded to in the mysteries of the Torah and the books of the wise men."[51]

Conclusion

Late thirteenth-century Castile was a creative, even revolutionary moment in Jewish religious and intellectual history. Castilian Kabbalah was, of course, not created whole cloth during the closing decades of the thirteenth century. Kabbalistic texts like those examined above bear the strong imprint of the kabbalists who came before them. These writings also reflect the many other texts from the long history of Rabbinic Judaism that bear an affinity to various themes and ideas in kabbalistic literature. The primary contribution of kabbalists in the late thirteenth-century Castilian setting was their bold assembling and reformulation of kabbalistic materials in order to put forth a comprehensive, and in many cases highly detailed, reinterpretation of the meaning of Judaism. As Jonathan Ray has demonstrated, the frontier conditions prevailing in late thirteenth-century Castile created a dynamic and fluid environment in which Jews were able to exploit opportunities for economic and social advancement within Castilian society that were in many cases analogous to those available to Christians. While the open society and the many options it accorded to the Jews of the frontier eventually did see a decline, it came at the end of a period in which Jews were able to explore social, political and intellectual avenues less accessible to their coreligionists in the more established communities further east.[52] While it might be tempting to regard the

---

Conversion (Leiden: Brill, 2000); Hames, "Exotericism and Esotericism in Thirteenth Century Kabbalah," *Esoterica* 6 (2004): 102–12.

[50] Based on Ex. 35:21.

[51] *Sefer ha-Shem*, 195.

[52] See Jonathan Ray, *The Sephardic Frontier: The Reconquista and the Jewish Community in Medieval Iberia* (Ithaca: Cornell University Press, 2006).

kabbalistic re-reading of Judaism in terms of esotericism as a kind of Jewish retreat, and a sign that Jews during this period were cloistered in an insular, self-referential world, an analysis of this phenomenon with an eye towards the social and intellectual context leads to a different conclusion. Rather than regard Kabbalah as the product of isolated Rabbinic Jews, it may be more accurate to understand the proliferation of kabbalistic literature in late thirteenth-century Castile as an indicator of the degree to which Jews were full participants in the intellectual conversations of their historical moment. By shifting the emphasis of Rabbinic Judaism towards an esotericism that bore striking affinities to other esoteric trends current in their milieu, kabbalists were imagining Judaism in a way that was consonant with the cultural logic of their day. In this way we can see the transformative development of Kabbalah during this particular time and place as yet another indicator of the ways in which Jewish identities in the frontier context of Castile were, as Ray puts it, "as much a product of the prevailing historical processes and social dynamics of the age as they were of the discrete traditions of the Jewish community."[53] It should come as no surprise that the augmentation of a kabbalistic field of discourse within medieval Judaism is generated in a context in which there were many social and political options open to Jews, and when avenues for intellectual engagement across religious and cultural boundaries were many. As Kocku von Stuckrad has noted, "[r]eligious identities are shaped through communicative processes. They are not found but negotiated."[54] The emergence of a prominent esotericism in the formulation of Judaism in this context is thus best understood not as a singular and internal Jewish retrieval of arcana, but rather a move within a context of multiple competing options, since "[l]ike identities, traditions are negotiated in a complex process of cultural exchange."[55] The Jewish identity negotiated by kabbalists in Castile during the late thirteenth century reveals a rich and complex environment, echoing a conversation that transformed Judaism through an engaged encounter with a unique and cosmopolitan Iberian society.

---

[53] Jonathan Ray, "Beyond Tolerance and Persecution: Reassessing Our Approach to Medieval Convivencia," *Jewish Social Studies* 11 (2005): 1-18, at 12.

[54] *Locations of Knowledge*, 16.

[55] *Locations of Knowledge*, 41.

Works Cited:

Abrams, Daniel. *Kabbalistic Manuscripts and Textual Theory.* Los Angeles: Cherub Press, 2010.

Altmann, Alexander. "Sefer Or Zarua le-R. Moshe de Leon." *Kovetz al Yad* 9 (19) (1980): 219-93.

Bodleian Ms. 1565 (Opp. Add. 4 to 4), 110a-117b.

Burns, Robert. *Emperor of Culture: Alfonso X of Castile and his Thirteenth-Century Renaissance.* Philadelphia: University of Pennsylvania Press, 1990.

David ben Yehuda he-Hasid. *The Book of Mirrors: Sefer Mar'ot ha-Zove'ot.* Edited by Daniel C. Matt. Chico, CA: Scholars Press, 1982.

Felix, Iris. *Theurgy, Magic and Mysticism in the Kabbalah of R. Joseph of Shushan ha-Birah.* Ph.D. dissertation, Hebrew University, 2005.

Fraker, Charles. *The Scope of History: Studies in the Historiography of Alfonso el Sabio.* Ann Arbor: University of Michigan Press, 1996.

------. "Hermes Trismegistus in *General Estoria.*" In *Medieval Iberia: Changing Societies and Cultures in Contact and Transition,* edited by I. Corfis and R. Harris-Northall, 87-98. Woodbridge: Tamesis, 2007.

Fishbane, Eitan. "Authority, Tradition, and the Creation of Meaning in Medieval Kabbalah." *Journal of the American Academy of Religion* 72 (2004): 59-95.

Gaster, Moses. *The Hebrew Version of Secretum Secretorum: A Medieval Treatise Ascribed to Aristotle.* London: Journal of the Royal Asiatic Society, 1907–8.

Gikatilla, Joseph. "Hassagot al-ha-Moreh." In Isaac Abravanel, *Ketavim al Mahshevet Yisrael,* vol. 3, 19a-31b. Jerusalem: [s. n.], 1967.

------. *Ginat Egoz.* Jerusalem: Yeshivat ha-Hayyim ve-ha-Shalom, 1989.

Goldberg, Yehiel. "Spiritual Leadership and the Popularization of Kabbalah in Medieval Spain." *Journal for the Study of Sephardic and Mizrahi Jewry* (2009): 2-59.

Greenup, A. W., ed. *The Book of the Moon.* London: [s. n.], 1912.

Halbertal, Moshe. *Concealment and Revelation: Esotericism in Jewish Thought and its Philosophical Implications*. Princeton: Princeton University Press, 2007.

Idel, Moshe. "Magical and Neoplatonic Interpretations of Kabbalah in the Renaissance." In *Jewish Thought in the Sixteenth Century*, edited by Bernard Dov Cooperman, 186-242. Cambridge, MA: Harvard University Press, 1983.

------. "We Have No Kabbalistic Tradition on This." In *Rabbi Moses Nahmanides (RAMBAN): Explorations in his Religious and Literary Virtuosity*, edited by Isadore Twersky, 51-74. Cambridge, MA: Harvard University Press, 1983.

------. "Hermeticism and Judaism." In *Hermeticism and the Rennaisance*, edited by I. Merkel and A. G. Debus, 59-76. Washington: Folger Books, 1988.

------. "Kabbalah and Elites in Thirteenth Century Spain." *Mediterranean Historical Review* 9 (1994): 5–19.

------. "Secrecy, Bina and Derisha." In *Secrecy and Concealment: Studies in the History of Mediterranean and Near Eastern Religions*, edited by Hans G. Kippenberg and Guy G. Stroumsa, 311-343. Leiden: Brill, 1995.

------. "Nahmanides: Kabbalah, Halakha, and Spiritual Leadership." In *Jewish Mystical Leaders and Leadership in the 13th Century*, edited by M. Idel and M. Ostow, 15-96. Northvale, NJ: Jason Aronson Press, 1998.

------. "The Kabbalah's 'Window of Opportunities', 1270–1290." In *Meah Shearim: Studies in Medieval Jewish Spiritual Life in Memory of Isadore Twersky*, edited by Ezra Fleisher, Gerald Blidstein, Carmi Horowitz, and Bernard Septimus, 173-208. Jerusalem: Magnes Press, 2001.

------. "Hermeticism and Kabbalah." In *Hermetism from Late Antiquity to Humanism: La tradizione ermetica dal mondo tardo-antico all'Umanesimo*, edited by P. Lucentini, I. Parri, and V. Perrone Compagni, 385–428. Turnhout: Brepolis, 2003.

------. "On European Cultural Renaissances and Jewish Mysticism." *Kabbalah* 13 (2005): 43-78.

------. "Johannes Reuchlin: Kabbalah, Pythagorean Philosophy and Modern Scholarship." *Studia Judaica* 16 (2008): 30-55.

------. "Some Images of Maimonides in Jewish Mysticism." *Studia Judaica* 17 (2009): 36-63.

Langermann, Tzvi. "Studies in Medieval Hebrew Pythagoreanism." *Micrologus* 9 (2001): 219-236.

Lelli, Fabrizio. "Le versioni ebraiche di un testo ermetico: il 'Sefer ha-levanah." *Henoch* 12 (1990): 147-164.

------. "Hermes among the Jews: *Hermetica* as *Hebraica* from Antiquity to the Renaissance." *Magic, Ritual, and Witchcraft* 2 (2007): 111–35.

Levy, B. Barry. *Fixing God's Torah: The Accuracy of the Hebrew Bible Text in Jewish Law.* Oxford: Oxford University Press, 2001.

Martínez, H. Salvador. *Alfonso X, the Learned.* Translated by Odile Cisneros. Leiden: Brill, 2010.

Matt, Daniel. "'New-Ancient Words': The Aura of Secrecy in the Zohar." In *Gershom Scholem's* Major Trends in Jewish Mysticism *50 Years After,* edited by Peter Schäfer and Joseph Dan, 181-207. Tubingen: Mohr Siebeck, 1993.

Morlok, Elke. *Rabbi Joseph Gikatilla's Hermeneutics.* Tubingen: Mohr Siebeck, 2011.

Nahman, Moses ben. *Perush al ha-torah le-rabeinu moshe ben nahman,* edited by Charles Chavel. Jerusalem: Mosad Harav Kook, 1984.

Oron, Michal, ed. *Sefer ha-Shem Attributed to R. Moses de Leon.* Los Angeles: Cherub Press, 2010.

Ray, Jonathan. "Beyond Tolerance and Persecution: Reassessing Our Approach to Medieval Convivencia." *Jewish Social Studies* 11 (2005): 1-18.

------. *The Sephardic Frontier: The Reconquista and the Jewish Community in Medieval Iberia.* Ithaca: Cornell University Press, 2006.

Scholem, Gershom. *Origins of the Kabalah.* Translated by Allan Arkush. Princeton: Princeton University Press, 1987.

Schwartz, Dov. *Contradiction and Concealment in Medieval Jewish Thought.* Jerusalem: Bar-Ilan University Press, 2002.

Schwartz, Yossef. "The Esoteric and Interreligious Aspects of the Relation Philosophy/Kabbalah in Late Medieval and Early Modern Europe." *Studia Judaica* 16 (2008): 126-143.

Von Stuckrad, Kocku. *Locations of Knowledge in Medieval and Early Modern Europe: Esoteric Discourse and Western Identities.* Leiden: Brill, 2010.

Wijnhoven, Jochanan H. A. *"Sefer ha-Mishqal*: Text and Study." Ph.D. dissertation, Brandeis University, 1964.

Wolfson, Elliot. "By Way of Truth: Aspects of Nahmanides Kabbalistic Hermeneutic." *AJS Review* 14 (1989): 103-178.

------. "Beyond the Spoken Word: Oral Tradition and Written Transmission in Medieval Jewish Mysticism." In *Transmitting Jewish Traditions: Orality, Textuality and Cultural Diffusion,* edited by Y. Elman and I. Gershoni, 166-224. New Haven, CT: Yale University Press, 2000.

------. *Abraham Abulafia – Kabbalist and Prophet: Hermeneutics, Theosophy, Theurgy.* Los Angeles: Cherub Press, 2000.

------. "Beneath the Wings of the Great Eagle: Maimonides and Thirteenth Century Kabbalah." In *Moses Maimonides (1138–1204 – His Religious, Scientific, and Philosophical Wirkensgeschichte in Different Cultural Contexts,* edited by Görge K. Hasselhoff and Otfried Fraisse, 209–237. Wurzburg: Ergon, 2004.

------. "Occultation of the Feminine and the Body of Secrecy in Medieval Kabbalah." In *Luminal Darkness,* 258–94. Oxford: Oxford University Press, 2007.

------. "Murmuring Secrets: Eroticism and Esotericisn in Medieval Kabbalah." In *Hidden Intercourse: Eros and Sexuality in the History of Western Esotericism,* edited by W. J. Hanegraaff and J. J. Kripal, 65-110. Leiden: Brill, 2008.

------. "The Anonymous Chapters of the Elderly Master of Secrets: New Evidence for the Early Activity of the Zoharic Circle." *Kabbalah* 19 (2009): 143-278.

Hasdai Crescas: Portrait of a Leader at a Time of Crisis

.... Ram Ben-Shalom

There were various kinds of Jewish leaders in medieval Spain. There were spiritual leaders, who focused on developing Judaism's religious heritage, whether in the field of Jewish law (Halakha), philosophy, science, or Kabbalah, and there were social leaders, who concentrated primarily on public life, both within the Jewish communities and at the royal court. The public life of a Jewish minority residing among a Christian majority also compelled Jewish spiritual leaders to address the challenge of Christianity and its claim to religious "truth." In some cases, personal, spiritual activity combined with public leadership, leaving a lasting impression on Spanish Jewry. In times of crisis and persecution in particular, like the devastating events of 1391, the Jews of Spain needed exceptional leaders, capable on the one hand of rebuilding communal life and on the other hand of re-establishing relations with the Christian majority. Such leaders were also called upon to cultivate their spiritual views from within, to re-evaluate the Jewish position in matters of Halakha, philosophy, and messianism, and to try to stop the aggressive missionary pressure exerted upon the Jews by the Church and its various representatives. Hasdai Crescas was one of

309

those spiritual and intellectual leaders who did not act in isolation from the world around them, and whose public activities within the Jewish community and at the royal court were influenced by the burning religious, philosophical and political questions of the day. His long and varied career offers some insight into the world of Jewish leadership during this critical period of instability and crisis, as well as the opportunity to examine his particular model of religious leadership for medieval Iberian Jewry.

A few years after the death of Hasdai ben Abraham Crescas (c. 1340-1412), in the days that followed the great Tortosa Disputation (1413-1414), the Saragossan poet Solomon Reuben Bonafed lamented the condition of the generation, which he compared to a flock without a shepherd:

> Woe to the shepherdless flock whose tenders are prey to the wolf and the bear!
> Ask ye of Hasdai in his heavenly seat, to whom has he put his children in trust?
> The prince of his age was he, he died and this was its death blow! But though Hasdai is dead, his goodness is not.
> And his light is gone out, but the light of his book burneth yet to guide his disciples.[1]

Hasdai Crescas is portrayed in Bonafed's poem as the prince of his generation, whose passing left a void that was not easily filled. Despite the desperate situation, Bonafed adds that Crescas' bereft "children" may look to his writings and spiritual thought for protection against the vicissitudes of the age. In another elegiac poem, Solomon ben Meshulam de Piera of Saragossa also considers Crescas the greatest of his generation, the "glory of our crowning glory" [pe'er gulat gulotenu], and reiterates the motif of Iberian Jewry being "like a flock without a shepherd his faithful remain." The following is a brief excerpt from de Piera's lengthy lament:

---

[1] See Aharon Kaminka, "Poems and Epigrams by R. Solomon b. R. Reuben Bonafed," *Hazofeh Quartalis Hebraica* 12 (1928): 38, VIII (Hebrew). The translation cited here is from Yitzhak Baer, *A History of the Jews in Christian Spain*, trans. Louis Schoffman (Philadelphia: The Jewish Publication Society, 2001), vol. 2, 217f. The phrase "prey to the wolf" [ze'ev yitraf] is based on Gen. 49:27.

Rabbi master of an age, in whom the dispersed
of the faith gained knowledge and waxed stronger,
Rabbi whose opinions were loved by the
righteous and the pure, and whom haters of truth despised,
Rabbi of great fame and ample qualities
to pervade the wanting of heart and they were filled,
Hasdai, whose kindness and virtue so pleasant
sufficed for the world,
From the fragrance of his goodness he nourished
the stinking of ignorance and they became sweet-smelling.
From the speech of his lips complainers learned
instruction, and spoke pure and pleasant words.
And advisers imitated his counsels,
and at the sound of his words put a spoon to their mouths.[2]

Crescas is described as a moral teacher, who guided his people honestly and wisely, but who also knew how to be forceful and to teach his opponents a lesson, when necessary. The poem describes a leader who combines wisdom and political strength with moral and religious leadership. What was it about Crescas that made him the greatest of his generation? What qualities did he possess that engendered the great sense of loss experienced by the members of his generation at his passing? And what led Bonafed to believe that his teachings could provide comfort in times of adversity?

Hasdai was a member of the Crescas family—longstanding leaders of the Jewish community of Barcelona. In his youth, he studied with the spiritual leader and Halakhist Rabbi Nissim ben Reuben Gerondi (c. 1310-1375). As early as 1367, together with another student of Rabbi Nissim, Isaac bar Sheshet Perfet, he played an active role in the leadership of the Barcelona community. Years later, he, his teacher Gerondi, his friend Perfet, and a number of other Jewish leaders were imprisoned. Yitzhak Baer dates the episode to 1367, in the wake of a host-desecration libel against the community at Barcelona, while Abraham Hershman postulates a later date (1370 or 1371) and associates the arrest with Jewish informers, whereas

---

[2] Simon Bernstein, ed., *Divan of Solomon b. Meshulam da Piera* (New York: Alim, 1942), no. 94, 90f (Hebrew).

the host-desecration libel originated with the Christian masses.[3] Regarding those days, Perfet wrote:

> Nearly five months ago, there arose wicked men amongst us, who falsely accused our great Rabbi Nissim, God preserve him, and six notables from the community, including Don Hasdai (God preserve him), myself and my brother (God bless him), and turned us over to the authorities. We are still under bond, though we are blameless. May God repay them according to the work of their hands (Lam. 3:64).[4]

Perfet's words appear to support Hershman's view. The prisoners were released on bond, and life in Barcelona returned to normal, after they were found innocent.

Crescas was one of a number of Jewish scholars who maintained ties to the ruling class of Jewish society, some of whom even played active roles at court. Simon ben Zemah Duran describes a meeting of such scholars, including Hasdai Crescas, Sheshet Perfet and Jonah Desmaestre, head of the academy at Mallorca, at the wedding of a certain Don Todros, in Teruel.[5] In 1370, the circle of scholars in Barcelona, headed by Nissim Gerondi and including Perfet and Crescas, took part in a poetry competition between the poets of the Jewish community of Barcelona and those of the community of Gerona. The competition was a kind of literary game, comprising both metered verse and rhymed prose, seasoned with taunts against the rivals from the neighboring city. The participation of Barcelona's foremost scholars and communal leaders in an inter-community competition of this kind attests to the importance ascribed to poetry in general, and to the significant role of poetry in Jewish intellectual and spiritual life.[6]

Hasdai Crescas served, for some twenty years, as one of the leaders of the Barcelona community (*secretario* and rabbinical court judge). Following Gerondi's death and Perfet's departure

---

[3] A. M. Hershman, *Rabbi Isaac Bar Sheshet Perfet and His Times* (New York: The Jewish Theological Seminary of America, 1943), 161.

[4] Isaac Bar Sheshet, *Responsa of R. Isaac b. Sheshet* (Jerusalem, 1975), sect. 376, 107 (Hebrew).

[5] *Responsa of R. Simon b. Zemah* (Lemberg, 1851), 3, 30, 6b (Hebrew).

[6] Haim Schirmann, *The History of Hebrew Poetry in Christian Spain and Southern France*, ed. Ezra Fleischer (Jerusalem: Magnes Press, 1996/7), 572f (Hebrew).

for Saragossa (and then Valencia), Crescas became the city's preeminent scholar, and his home a meeting place for Torah sages.[7] On one occasion, in 1381, Crescas and other rabbis signed a ruling against Moses Hanoch, found guilty of informing on members of the community. They sentenced him to exile from Catalonia for a period of twelve years. Hanoch, an influential courtier in the service of the queen, managed to gain the upper hand. Upon the queen's request, the king of Aragon wrote a letter to the leaders of the community of Barcelona, asserting Hanoch's innocence and demanding that they revoke his excommunication. The king later removed Hanoch from the legal jurisdiction of the Jewish community, placing him under the jurisdiction of the royal bailiff.

Jewish communal leaders in Christian Iberia scrupulously enforced moral and religious discipline and defended the community's members against informers. Iberian kings often accorded the communities far-reaching privileges for the purpose of eradicating informers in their midst, even when the information provided by such informers might have been useful to the state and to Christian society. The community generally paid a fee to the royal treasury for the legal right to execute informers. The community's judges were not averse to issuing capital sentences, which were carried out by the royal bailiff, contingent upon circumstances and the political influence brought to bear on a given case.[8]

Hasdai Crescas ascribed great importance to the legal authority of the community to try informers. The precedent in Barcelona, in which this legal authority was revoked, influenced his future position on the matter and strengthened his own judicial status in Aragon. In light, however, of the extremist tendencies that developed in the 1380s, whereby the communities sought to strengthen their criminal jurisdiction, he concluded (as did the crown, apparently) that such far-reaching authority should not be entrusted to each and every community and to the limited outlook of local leaders. In 1390, Queen Violante (wife of Juan I) thus appointed Hasdai Crescas supreme judge in matters pertaining to informers in the Jewish communities.

---

[7] Shalom Rosenberg, "The 'Arba'ah Turim of Rabbi Abraham b. R. Judah, disciple of Hasdai Crescas," *Jerusalem Studies in Jewish Thought* 3 (1983/4): 525-621 (Hebrew).

[8] See Baer, *History*, vol. 1, 231-234; vol. 2, 64-71.

He alone was granted the right to impose punishments of all kinds, including capital punishment, upon Jewish offenders.

By this time, Crescas was already active in Saragossa, having been invited a year earlier by the leaders of that community to serve as their rabbi. The legal authority he possessed was unprecedented. Never before had a rabbi, scholar or Jewish courtier in any of the Iberian kingdoms been given exclusive jurisdiction over capital punishment. His appointment as the supreme judge of the Jews of the Crown of Aragon was the only attempt to create a single, central and permanent institution for all of the Jewish communities of the kingdom, since the assembly of the communities at Barcelona, in 1354, and the enactment of the Barcelona ordinances (*takkanot*)—an attempt that failed.[9] The communities generally acted independently, on the basis of the political and juridical privileges they were accorded. At times of crisis, libels or excessive monetary demands by the crown, the representatives of the various communities would gather for purposes of consultation and advocacy at court, but no supra-communal organization was ever established in the Crown of Aragon.

The royal edict that granted unprecedented power to a single supreme judge, and thereby gave the community of Saragossa authority over all of the other communities, reflected a broader attempt to concentrate authority. The process of centralization was not merely imposed from without, but also represented a trend with the communities themselves. These may have begun to sense the instability of their political situation (a year before the massacres), leading them to petition the royal house to help strengthen Jewish leadership. The communities' receptiveness to this effort at centralization was probably heightened by the unique figure of Hasdai Crescas, capable—by virtue of the moral and social authority he enjoyed—of imposing his will on Jewish society. Crescas' writ of appointment attests to his high standing and political power both at court and within the Jewish communities. The document describes Crescas as surpassing all of the Jews of the kingdom "not only in knowledge of the laws of Moses [Halakha], but in power of reasoning

---

[9] Baer, *History*, vol. 2, 124-28.

[philosophy]."[10] These two facets, briefly alluded to in the Christian document, in fact highlight two of Crescas' greatest attributes: eminent Halakhist and influential philosopher who forged new paths in Jewish thought.

After 1391: The Rescue and Reconstruction Efforts of Hasdai Crescas in Aragon

The poets Solomon Bonafed and Solomon de Piera both lament Crescas' death at a time of great crisis, following the terrible persecutions in Castile and Aragon in 1391 in which many Jewish communities were depopulated, new communities of *conversos* arose, and the general status and wellbeing of the Jews in Christian Iberia was greatly reduced. During the persecutions themselves and in their aftermath, Hasdai Crescas was personally responsible for most of the efforts to rescue and rebuild the Jewish communities of the Crown of Aragon. In August 1391, while the massacres were still going on, Crescas departed with one of the highest-ranking diplomats, Francesco d'Aranda, on a royal mission to collect funds to provide for the needs of the Jews. During the course of this journey, the two men were urgently recalled to Saragossa by the queen, "because their absence is very harmful and dangerous in view of the constant reports that reach us daily from our *aljamas* [communities], which are threatened with complete ruin and extermination."[11] The funds collected by d'Aranda and Crescas were intended to pay the wages of the king's troops sent to defend the Jews, to cover the travel expenses of the royal couple, and probably to defray the cost of a diplomatic mission to the papal court in Avignon as well.

Some five months after the outbreak of the violence, Crescas wrote a letter to the Jewish community of Avignon in which he describes, in a convincing and touching manner, the chain of events, the actions of the Jews and the various ways in which they had sought to defend themselves. He highlights the example set by the descendants of Rabbi Asher ben Yehiel and their families and

---

[10] Baer, *History*, vol. 1, 84.
[11] Baer, *History*, vol. 1, 114.

students in Toledo, who chose martyrdom, as opposed to many Jews who preferred conversion because "they were unable to stand up for their lives." His letter shows, however, that the behavior of the rabbis of Toledo, of Ashkenazi origin, was not unusual. Among those martyred was Crescas' own son ("my only son; a bridegroom, an innocent lamb whom I have offered for a burnt-offering ... And I take comfort in the goodness of his share and the pleasantness of his fate"), the rabbis of Gerona, and many others in Barcelona ("of whom many slaughtered themselves and some threw themselves from the tower ... and some went out and sanctified the name [of God] in the street"), Seville, Valencia, Mallorca and elsewhere.[12]

Jewish martyrdom in 1391 was thus, according to Crescas, a common occurrence in Iberia, alongside mass conversion. From his letter, we learn that some of the Jews of Barcelona—in a manner resembling that of the "Ashkanazi pattern of martyrdom"—committed suicide using knives or swords and by throwing themselves from the fortress tower, while others chose to leave the fortress walls to be killed (apparently in battle) by the rioters. This phenomenon is corroborated by Christian sources attesting to Jewish suicides and the killing of those who refused to convert.[13]

The letter to the Jews of Avignon was apparently part of Crescas' efforts to stop the riots and rebuild the communities. It is reasonable to presume that he wished to keep the Jews of Avignon abreast of events in Spain, that they might seek help from Pope Clement VII (1378-1394), who resided at Avignon, asking him to issue a papal bull to stop the violence, or at least not to intervene on the side of the rioters. The government of Aragon also appealed to the pope, beginning in late July 1391, and Queen Violante described the events in Valencia to him, requesting that he not issue orders in favor of the rioters, and that he not act on the matter of the riots until hearing the opinion of the king. Crescas' letter to the Jewish community of

---

[12] The excerpts from Crescas' letter are taken from Solomon ibn Verga, *Scepter of Judah*, ed. M. Wiener (Hannover, 1856), 128-130 (Hebrew). On the martyrdom of Crescas' son, see Marc Saperstein, "A Sermon on the Akeda from the Generation of the Expulsion and its Implications for 1391," in *Exile and Diaspora. Studies in the History of the Jewish People Presented to Professor Haim Beinart*, ed. Aharon Mirski et al. (Jerusalem: Ben Zvi Institute, 1991), 111-113.

[13] See Ram Ben-Shalom, "Kiddush hashem and Jewish Martyrology in Aragon and Castile, in the year 5151 (1391): Between Spain and Ashkenaz," *Tarbiz* 70 (2001): 279-300 (Hebrew).

Avignon was sent in October. At the end of his letter, he writes as follows:

> We [who are alive] here today, in all the cities of Aragon; there is no breach and no outcry, the Lord having been merciful to us, has left a small remnant in all of these places. After strenuous efforts and great dispersal of our possessions, we have nothing left but our bodies.

Crescas appears to believe that the calm achieved in the cities and the abatement of the riots were the result of his fundraising journey with d'Aranda, and the various payments "dispersed" on behalf of the royal house.

In the years that followed, Hasdai Crescas invested his efforts in rebuilding the Jewish communities of the Crown of Aragon. Many communities were completely destroyed, and the efforts of the royal house to reestablish them encountered resistance from the Christian bourgeoisie in those cities. In Barcelona, for example, the king issued an edict to formally abolish the Jewish community (September 1392). Three weeks later, however, a new royal edict ordered the reestablishment of the community, albeit not in the Jewish quarter, the walls of which had since been demolished by the municipal council in order to settle Christians there, but in another area, where the Jewish quarter and synagogue would eventually be rebuilt. The old Jewish cemetery on the "Hill of the Jews" (Montis Judayci, Montjuich) was returned to the Jews. These efforts would appear to have failed, for in May 1393 the king and queen wrote to Crescas that they were determined to reestablish the Jewish communities in Barcelona and Valencia. They authorized him to choose sixty families from the communities of the kingdom, and to compel them to settle in these places. The necessary funds for their resettlement, for the purchase of homes and the construction of protective walls around them, were to be collected from all of the Jewish communities of the kingdom, as they saw fit.

In November 1394, Crescas was urgently summoned to Barcelona by the queen, apparently to resolve the serious difficulties that had arisen concerning the new community and its relationship with the city's inhabitants. A year later, however, the Jews of Barcelona informed the king that the Christians of the city wished to demolish their synagogue. The king asked the queen to intercede, but in that year, all of the Jews left the city. Nevertheless, Crescas attempted, in 1396, to act "regardless of hardships, expense and personal danger," to re-establish the community and redeem its cemetery on the "Hill of the Jews."[14]

Of his fundraising efforts on behalf of the community in Barcelona and the redemption of the cemetery at Montjuich, we may learn from a letter of response received by Crescas from the Jews of Montalbán. The letter was written by the community scribe, Yom Tov b. Hannah, in the name of the community's leaders:

> [Response] to the great Rabbi En Hasdai Crescas of blessed memory, who sent letters to the community, requesting assistance for the redemption of the "house of the living" [viz. cemetery] called Montjuich de Barcelona. As follows:
>
> Crown of beauty of Israel, our honor and our eminence, may the Lord your God accept you in all that you do, and send forth your help from the Sanctuary and Zion. You who dwell in the shelter of the Most High. Father, we have indeed seen your pure intentions for the sake of Heaven, as we find in the chapter "All Holy Scriptures,"[15] which are written with the finger of God. And how shall we glorify and praise your great name, for he is good [to do so]. We have therefore chosen silence which is as consent, and unto you, our lord, the grace of God. How lovely to speak your praises before a great company. We have pledged and offered as we are able, ten gold florins about ten thousand by weight. The needs of your people are great and they are without means, and if [our pledge] is insignificant in relation to your intimated [request], we bow and prostrate ourselves and ask your honor, O lord, to extend your grace upon us, like a father upon his children, to wait until the coming New Year, for we are unable at this time to grant your monetary request in full, for the people in the fields have gone out to gather,[16] and at that time we will strive to bring our money before your honor, and not in full weight [Genesis, 43, 21] as when Pharoah sent [to carry it].[17] The entire people is in distress. May He who hears the needy be gracious to you at your cry, and do you good in the end, to your wise heart's desire and to that of your sons and servants who seek the welfare of your perfect Torah,

---

[14] Baer, *History*, vol 2, 110-130, citation in 126.

[15] See BT, *Šabbat* 16a. The author thus implies that Crescas acted as one who rescues Holy Scripture from a fire.

[16] See Exodus 16:27. This is an image of a group of transgressors of the law.

[17] Gen. 46:5; Exod. 4:21; Exod. 9:7.

trustees [*ne'emanei*] of the community of Montalbán, anon. [*ploni*] and anon.

> In closing:
> The soul of every living creature is the light of God. With charity he is mighty
> to save those who are without strength -
> Our lord and master, Rabbi Hasdai, who abides in the shadow of the Almighty.[18]

The scribe or editor of this collection of letters begins with a description of the circumstances in which the letter was sent. He writes that it is a response to a letter that Hasdai Crescas had sent to the community, requesting financial assistance for the redemption of Barcelona's Jewish cemetery at Montjuich. The trustees of Montalbán apologize to Crescas for failing to provide the sum requested, sending instead ten gold florins. They ask Crescas to wait until the coming New Year, at which time they will add a further sum. The trustees do not explain the precise reasons for their failure to raise the necessary amount. Between the lines however, we discover that the disintegration of the community following the withdrawal of the forced converts (*anusim*), shook the existing order, and apparently entailed economic difficulties as well. We must remember that those wealthy Jews who converted to Christianity in 1391 ceased paying their communal tax, with serious financial consequences for the community. Furthermore, it was generally the wealthy that paid the bulk of the taxes imposed on the Jewish communities.[19] This letter attests to difficulties within the surviving Jewish communities and their inability to raise the necessary funds, as well as to Hasdai Crescas' difficulties—due to dwindling resources—in rebuilding the communities that had suffered fatal blows. Crescas' leadership is reflected here both in his ability to impose responsibility on the shoulders of each and every community for the overall condition of the Jews of Aragon, and in his capacity to recognize the increasing needs and difficulties experienced by the individual communities as a result of the violent crisis that also gave rise to the *anusim*. The

---

[18] MS Oxford, Bodleian, Mich. 155 (formerly 809) [Neubauer 1984], f. 270a-b.

[19] David Romano, "Prorrata de contribuyentes judíos de Jaca en 1377," *Sefarad* 42 (1982): 22.

reply written by the scribe of Montalbán, Yom Tov b. Hannah, is indicative of the delicate balance Crescas needed to maintain in order to rehabilitate Aragonese Jewry.

Nevertheless, Crescas' efforts to rebuild the communities of Barcelona and Valencia were unsuccessful. In 1396, the local authorities in Valencia sought an edict from the king expelling all of the Jews and granting the city the privilege that a Jewish quarter would never again be established within its precincts. Only a handful of Jews remained. In 1401, King Martin I (1395-1410) forbade the establishment of a Jewish community in Barcelona. At that time, Crescas was probably already working on a secret and possibly daring plan, associated with the neighboring kingdom of Navarre, in which the Jews had been relatively unaffected by the riots. During the course of that year, he visited Navarre a number of times, and met with King Carlos III (1387-1425) to discuss a number of matters, presumably related to the Jews of Spain as a whole. The reasons for his various missions were not noted in official records, from which Yom Tov Assis deduces that the issues discussed were of mutual interest to Carlos III and Crescas, and that secrecy was required. The king was willing to defray all of Crescas' expenses for a number of months, in his travels throughout Navarre and Aragon, and Crescas was clearly enthusiastic about the plan. Assis therefore presumes that Crescas was attempting to arrange for the organized immigration of Aragonese Jewry, in whole or in part, to the kingdom of Navarre, then considered the safest place for Jews in all of Western Europe. In the end, there was no significant Jewish immigration from Aragon to Navarre. Apparently, the Jews of Aragon preferred to rebuild their old communities. It is also reasonable to assume that Navarre lacked the financial means to absorb large numbers of Aragonese Jews, and that the king preferred Jewish immigrants of a certain socio-economic class. Some ten years later, however, in 1411, Jewish immigrants from Aragon paid King Carlos III a large sum of money for permission to settle in Tudela. According to the relevant document, the Jewish settlers arrived in Navarre in the wake of violent riots that had broken out following the death of the king of Aragon (Martin I, d. 1410). Their choice of Navarre as a haven, and the willingness of Carlos III to open the gates of the kingdom to them, attests to the concrete aspects of Crescas' immigration plan, developed years earlier.[20]

In short, we can say that in his plans and actions to rehabilitate the Jewish communities of Aragon, Crescas tried to explore a number of different avenues. On the one hand was the need to rebuild the communities that had survived; on the other, the need to raise money from the surviving communities to rebuild those that had been destroyed and could be rebuilt through (voluntary or forced) resettlement. While he was unsuccessful in Barcelona, in the case of Mallorca the community was reestablished through resettlement (until its disbanding in 1432, due to a blood libel trial). At the same time, Crescas prepared a plan for immigration to Navarre, whether he intended it as a general plan for all of the Jews of Aragon, or as a partial solution for certain groups or communities. It is possible that, unlike the king of Navarre, who sought the immediate immigration of some of the Jews, Crescas viewed the plan as a contingency, in case of future persecution.

Hasdai Crescas and the Messianic Idea

Spanish Jewry under Christianity was not characterized by frequent outbursts of messianism. Nevertheless, periods of persecution and crisis were fertile ground for the creation of messianic ferment. In general, the rabbinical and political leadership treated would-be messiahs with suspicion and disdain. The latent presence of the messianic idea, however, was an immanent need of national and religious life that many important thinkers nurtured, developed and engaged in continuously.[21]

Like other such events in the course of Jewish history, the catastrophe of 1391 produced messianic ferment, a movement in which Hasdai Crescas also became engaged. According to Yitzhak

---

[20] Yom Tov Assis, "The Project of R. Hasdai Crescas for the Rehabilitation of the Jewish Communities following the Decrees of 5151 (1391)," in *Proceedings of the Tenth World Congress of Jewish Studies* (Jerusalem, 1989) div. B, vol.1, 145-148 (Hebrew); Baer, *History*, vol. 2, 126; Yitzhak Baer, *Die Juden im Christlichen Spanien: Urkunden und Regesten* (Berlin: Akademie Verlag, 1929), vol. 1, 999-1001.

[21] See Gerson D. Cohen, "Messianic Postures of Ashkenazim and Sephardim Prior to Sabbethai Zevi," in *Studies in the Variety of Rabbinic Cultures*, ed. Gerson D. Cohen (Philadelphia: Jewish Publication Society, 1991), 271-297.

Baer, there were those in Crescas' circle who effected messianic calculations, establishing 1391 as the year of the coming of the messiah. Evidence of this can be found in the writings of a Jewish apostate from Toledo by the name of Maestre Juan the Elder who, in 1416, noted a number of eschatological predictions that had proven false, including those of Rabbi Isaac (Çag) Abendino. Baer identifies Abendino as the father-in-law of Don Alazar Golluf, who was apparently the one who invited Crescas to move from Barcelona to Saragossa. Abendino determined that the messiah would come in the year 1391, based on the numerological exegesis of the verse "For the vision is yet for the appointed time" (Habakkuk 2:3; 'od ḥazon = the Hebrew year [5]151 =1391). It would thus appear that individuals close to Crescas in Saragossa engaged in messianic speculation.[22]

We have no evidence of Crescas' own views in these matters. A number of messianic works disseminated in Spain in the form of letters, and which mixed reality with legend, asserted that Hasdai Crescas looked favorably on the wonders and revelations of a prophet by the name of Moses, who had appeared in the vicinity of the city of Burgos in Castile.[23] The apostate Joshua Halorki (Jeronimo de Santa Fe) believed the rumors to be true, declaring that:

> in our day Rabbi Hasdai Crescas has announced a report and preached to congregations in the synagogues that the messiah was born in Cisneros, in the Kingdom of Castile (a small village in the Province of Palencia).[24]

Further testimony regarding Crescas' homiletic-messianic activities, accompanied by the dissemination of writings, appears in another letter sent at that time by an unknown writer:

> And so as to strengthen weak hands and feeble knees, our teacher [apparently Hasdai Crescas], may God preserve him, explained that these calamities shall serve as a preliminary to the coming of the messiah, after the manner of labor pains, which are a preparation for and a preliminary to birth. Then made they a proclamation in the camp of the Hebrews and sent forth books on eagles' wings, that

---

[22] Baer, *History*, vol. 2, 159f.

[23] See Aaron Zeev Eshkoli, *Jewish Messianic Movements* (Jerusalem: Mossad Bialik, 1987), 244-251 (Hebrew).

[24] Baer, *History*, vol. 2, 160f.

the appearance of our salvation was nigh ... and that all the people would perceive the thundering voice. This one writes about the Lord's messiah that He shall surely come by Passover time, and that one says, behold, he stands already at our walls, tomorrow he shall perform among us wonders and propitious signs, and our enemies shall clothe themselves in disgrace and recoil under disaster before the wrath of the Lord of Hosts; another declares that if the Feast of Tabernacles should arrive and there is yet no messiah, then surely it is God's will to have us die and to harden our heart from His fear; but before he has done talking yet another comes and says, it is rumored that a prophet has risen in Israel who has seen a vision of the Almighty; unto us is born a child who perceives the future and discloses dark secrets ... the years wherein we have seen evil shall be no more: lo, this presages good, this proclaims salvation.

See, O see, you who are exalted above every officer, whether these people among those who calculate the end [of days] sin greatly in their souls, and whether it is so nigh that it will provoke the damage and loss that our rabbis of blessed memory predicted, beyond other great and immense damages too numerous to count and not worthy of mention, for which I fear and tremble at the many things that are incessantly proclaimed at the gates, and dread the fury of the enemy, when it becomes known. I have spoken these things and truth today to the glory of your greatness, and have sent your honored highness copies of letters that have come to us here in this matter, that you might arise to reprove, with equity, the chirpers and mutterers in what is beyond them and hidden from them, and [that you might] on account of your rebuking them, and the healthy and good thoughts to which you will wisely resort, remove from the heart of the masses that have heard these things and believed in them ... though their hearts remain steadfast, trusting in the Lord God of Israel who chose Jerusalem, for he will send a redeemer to Zion, though he tarry, he will surely come and will not delay."[25]

Did Hasdai Crescas lend credence to these prophecies, contrary to the cautious approach taken by Rabbi Solomon ben Adret with regard to popular prophecy and messianism in 1295?[26] According to Yitzhak Baer, the answer is yes, indicating a failure in leadership and a departure from the traditional position of the Jewish leadership in Spain. Baer may have given too much weight, however, to Halorki's testimony, which in fact reflects the false rumors spread in the name

---

[25] Baer, *Urkunden und Regesten*, vol.1, 456a, 719f. The translation of the first paragraph is taken from Baer, *History*, vol. 2, 161.

[26] On the messiah of Avila, see Baer, *History*, vol. 1, 278-281.

of Crescas rather than his authentic position. The author of the above letter was convinced that Crescas himself did not encourage active expressions of messianism and that his approach remained within the normative framework of expectation for the coming of the messiah, while expressing skepticism with regard to active expressions of messianism. Was the conviction of the author of the letter regarding Crescas' position based upon direct knowledge of Crescas' approach? Or is Halorki's testimony correct?

Bonastruc Desmaestre's Hebrew account of the Tortosa Disputation, preserved in Solomon ibn Verga's *Scepter of Judah*, may shed further light on this question. To counter the Talmudic passages cited by Joshua Halorki to demonstrate that the messiah had already been born at the time of the destruction of the Temple, Don Vidal ben Benveniste, i.e. Joseph Vidal b. Lavi, replies:

> The *mestre* [Nahmanides, in the Barcelona Disputation] explained that this does not mean that [the messiah] had actually been born. And even if it was said that he had actually been born, there is no contradiction, because it is possible that he was born on that day and lives in Paradise. And Maimonides has written that the messiah was not born on the day of the destruction, but that the meaning was that from that day forward, in every generation, a man is born who is worthy of being the messiah, if only Israel are worthy, and he who said these things meant to arouse the hearts [of the people] to repentance, and to explain that the [advent of the] messiah is not contingent upon a fixed time, as was the Babylonian exile. And so explained Don Hasdai.[27]

According to Vidal ben Benveniste, Hasdai Crescas espoused the Maimonidean messianic model, whereby one worthy of being the messiah is born in every generation, but that the actualization of his messianic mission depends upon the moral-religious preparedness of that generation, rather than upon a fixed time, in keeping with a preordained divine plan as for example in the case of the Babylonian exile, following the destruction of the First Temple. However, this view, cited in Desmaestre's text, is nowhere to be found in Maimonides' writings. It is reasonable to assume that this or a similar

---

[27] Ibn Verga, *Scepter*, Fortieth [catastrophe], 103.

approach was, in fact, devised by Hasdai Crescas, who appears in the text as having adopted Maimonides' opinion.

If this view was indeed developed by Crescas in Saragossa, it may offer some explanation of Halorki's testimony at Tortosa that Crescas had asserted in a homily at the synagogue that the messiah had already been born. Crescas apparently made a clear distinction between the event of the birth of the messiah *in potentia* and the actualization of messianic potential, contingent upon the actions of that generation.[28] Crescas' approach lays responsibility for redemption upon the Jews themselves, whom he exhorted to take practical action in the form of repentance and socio-spiritual revival—contrary to those who advocated waiting in petrified idleness for the messiah to descend miraculously from heaven, to redeem the people in a single act.

Crescas' interpretation of the messianic idea, as represented by Vidal ben Benveniste, may serve to reinforce the assumption that the anonymous author of the letter cited above was, in fact, quite familiar with Crescas' views on the matter. It was a realistic approach, focused on practical moral revival, rather than supernatural messianic fantasies. The anonymous author's appeal to Crescas to take action against such messianic ferment would thus have been a realistic request, probably based on precise knowledge of his views, circulating alongside the false rumors. Nor does the chapter on the messiah (written in 1405) in Crescas' *Light of the Lord* (completed in 1410) support Baer's theory that he was receptive to popular messianic speculation. In this chapter, Crescas explicitly rejects the path of eschatological calculation.[29] Calculations of the kind made

---

[28] Maimonides, *Mishneh Torah, Laws of Kings*, ch. 11. Maimonides, as a matter of fact, makes verification of the realization of the messianic idea contingent upon the actions of the messiah himself, who must prove his authenticity to the members of his generation by building the Temple and returning the people to its land. See Aviezer Ravitzky, "'To the Utmost of Human Capacity': Maimonides on the Days of the Messiah," in *Perspectives on Maimonides*, ed. J. Kramer (Oxford: Oxford University Press, 1991), 221-256; David Berger, "Some Ironic Consequences of Maimonides' Rationalistic Messianism," in *Maimonidean Studies*, ed. Arthur Hyman (New York: Yeshiva University, 1991), vol. 2, 1-8 (Hebrew).

[29] Hasdai Crescas, *Light of the Lord*, (Ferrara, 1554/5 [facsimile]), Third Treatise, Eighth Principle, ch.2 (Hebrew): "And indeed talk of the limits of the time of his coming is a waste of effort, whether because the time is not specified in Scripture ... or because of what our Rabbis of blessed memory said: May the souls of those who calculate the end expire." On Crescas' messianic views, see W. Z. Harvey's recently published *Rabbi Hasdai Crescas* (Jerusalem: Zalman Shazar Center, 2010), 151-161 (Hebrew).

by Rabbi Isaac Abendino would thus not have been to his liking, and are unlikely to have emerged from the circle of his close associates and disciples.

We may therefore presume that, in the aftermath of 1391, Crescas continued to uphold the traditional, realistic approach of generations of Hispano-Jewish leaders toward expressions of practical messianism. It is possible, in light of pressing circumstances and especially the need to raise the broken spirits of Aragonese Jewry, that Crescas chose to depart from the longstanding position of absolute rejection, walking a fine line between approval of active messianism and turning the suffering of his generation into a political tool for regeneration and rebirth by intensifying immediate hopes for redemption. His cautious ambivalence was distorted and his name used, by others, to spread and afford greater credibility to active messianic rumors. Although he rejected active messianism, Crescas may have been loath to put an end to such rumors if he felt that they might provide some moral support for the rehabilitation of Iberian Jewry. This, despite the danger pointed out by the anonymous author of the above letter, who feared that Christian discovery of such a messianic movement could result in renewed violence against Jews.

Hasdai Crescas the Halakhist

Hasdai Crescas was a Halakhic decisor in many of the public affairs of Spanish Jewry. Few of his Halakhic rulings have survived, however, and his collected responsa were never published, as were the responsa of other rabbis of his time, such as Sheshet Perfet and Simon ben Zemah Duran. He may have been prevented from doing so as a result of his arduous duties at court, or perhaps his disciples took a greater interest in other aspects of his work, in the fields of philosophy, polemics, homiletics or ethics. It is also possible that the new environment encountered by the refugees of 1391 in North Africa favored Halakhists and encouraged them to consolidate their Halakhic works, contrary to the experience of those who remained in Spain. Crescas did not manage to leave behind a coherent Halakhic work, capable of serving as a guide for future generations. There can be no doubt, however, that he sought to leave his mark in this area as well.

According to Crescas' original plan, his philosophical work *Light of the Lord* was meant to be the first part of a larger work (*Lamp of the Lord*) on the divine precepts. His ambitious plan resembled that of Maimonides' *Mishneh Torah* [Repetition of the Law], the first part of which, *The Book of Knowledge*, is a philosophical work in its own right on the subject of Jewish faith and precepts. Crescas' work was intended to replace *Mishneh Torah*. In the introduction to *Light of the Lord*, Crescas criticizes Maimonides' Halakhic method, and especially the fact that he failed to note the disputes of the past and the process whereby Halakha was determined, as well as the lack of Talmudic references for his rulings.[30] Crescas claimed, in light of the differences of opinion between Maimonides and other great Halakhists, that members of his generation were plagued by confusion and doubt. He also argued that Maimonides did not seek to present the principles and reasons behind the precepts, and therefore conveyed only partial knowledge of them. Crescas believed that observance of the precepts without studying and understanding the Halakhic process lacks true religious meaning. He thus expressed his desire that:

> a work be composed, including the precepts of the Torah, their reasons, according to their material subjects, describing their boundaries and rules, and then elucidating them in a meticulous fashion, and citing the places in the Talmud wherefrom they derive, noting as well, the debates of the *geonim* and the rabbis, and contemporary [Achronim, lit. "last ones"] approbation.[31]

Crescas began his Halakhic opus with the Introduction to *Light of the Lord*, in which he offers a "doctrine of principles," or precepts of faith, as well as an explanation of his methodology in classifying and arranging these precepts, and the philosophical meaning of each principle. Crescas completed *Light of the Lord* in 1410, close to his death, and was thus unable to complete his Halakhic project. In another of Crescas' works, his *Sermon on the Passover* (undated),

---

[30] Similar criticism was leveled against Maimonides in his own time, by Rabbi Abraham ben David of Posquières and others.

[31] Crescas, *Light of the Lord*, Introduction.

Aviezer Ravitzky discovered a more detailed expression of his Halakhic approach, as would have been applied to his comprehensive project. The *Sermon on the Passover* indeed includes Talmudic references and closely follows the Talmudic sources, as well as the order and reasoning of the redactor of the Mishnah. Unlike Maimonides in the *Mishneh Torah*, Crescas does not attempt to create an order of his own; like Maimonides, he derives unequivocal rulings from the Talmudic debates.[32]

Other aspects of Crescas' Halakhic and hermeneutic activities can be gleaned from the comments and responsa of Sheshet Perfet, as well as the small number of Crescas' own responsa that have survived, mainly in the works of his students, Joseph Albo, Zerahyah Halevi and Matityahu Hayitzhari. From the responsa of Sheshet Perfet we learn that Crescas was involved in a number of affairs in which Perfet was also asked to offer an opinion.[33] On one of these occasions, Perfet (in Saragossa) sought to ascertain Crescas' view (in Barcelona), regarding a matter that had been brought before him. He did not reveal his own opinion to Crescas, but discovered that they were in agreement.[34] While Crescas was still in Barcelona and Nissim Gerondi was still alive, he was asked questions in matters of Halakha by the Jews of Mallorca,[35] and other communities, such as that of Tudela, in neighboring Navarre.[36] In Saragossa as well, he was asked to intervene as a well-known external arbitrator in events that shook the Jewish communities of Navarre.[37] A number of Crescas' responsa have been preserved in their entirety. One of these attests to the fact that his fame as an important Halakhist extended beyond the borders of Spain, and that he answered questions sent to him from Italy. At the end of his detailed reply (in a matter concerning the validity of a bill of divorce, written in Ancona, in 1400), he writes as follows:

---

[32] Aviezer Ravitzky, *Crescas' Sermon on the Passover and Studies in his Philosophy* (Jerusalem, 1988), 111-126 (Hebrew).

[33] E.g. Bar Sheshet, *Responsa of R. Isaac b. Sheshet*, resp. 372, p. 206; resp. 380, 218; resp. 395, 246.

[34] Bar Sheshet, *Responsa of R. Isaac b. Sheshet*, resp. 447, 139.

[35] Bar Sheshet, *Responsa of R. Isaac b. Sheshet*, resp. 374, 209; resp. 376, 212.

[36] Bar Sheshet, *Responsa of R. Isaac b. Sheshet*, resp. 372, 206.

[37] Z. (H.) Graetz, *History of the Jews*, trans. S. P. Rabinowitz (Warsaw, 1897/8), vol. 4, 407 (Hebrew).

> I have made my reply extremely brief, relying upon your understanding, due to my many duties on behalf of the holy community of Saragossa, which have led me to this village of *Lamunya* [La Almunia], where I am without books ... [So] says Hasdai.[38]

This passage attests to the fact that Crescas' duties as political leader had brought him to the village of La Almunia de Doña Godina, some fifty kilometers from Saragossa, where he was without access to his personal library. He notes this fact in his reply, in order to apologize for the brevity of his responsum (but also as a kind of rhetorical device). We thus learn that, as a Halakhist, he felt a duty to attend to the needs of the entire Jewish world, and that the fact that he was not at home, in Saragossa, did not prevent him from addressing as best he could the needs of communities in other lands.

The dispute of 1386/7 regarding the rabbinate in France also reached Spain, and Hasdai Crescas was asked by the rabbi of Paris, Yohanan ben Matityahu Treves, to rule on the standing of rabbinical ordination.[39] In this affair, Isaiah Astruc, rabbi of Savoy, attempted to impose the Ashkenazi mode of ordination on the Jews of France. He demanded that all rites pertaining to marriage and divorce in particular, and rabbinical functions in general, be entrusted to authorized rabbis only, and that he have exclusive authority over rabbinical appointment. In his attempt to carry out these reforms in France, Astruc enjoyed the support of his Ashkenazi teacher, Rabbi Meir Halevi. In his letter to Sheshet Perfet on the matter, Hasdai Crescas wrote:

> You behold with your eyes, O master, all that is done in the name of MaHaRaM [Rabbi Meir] Halevi, and how he has attempted to take authority from [Rabbi] Yohanan [Treves], and give it to his rival, Rabbi Isaiah [Astruc]. And were it not for the fact that, when I was there, both pledged to abide by all that I should decide between them, I would have written strongly in support of the truth. However, I am writing by means of a responsum to those communities, and I have also written to them both specifically with a messenger sent to me by Rabbi Isaiah regarding a bride for our brother Don Astruc Saporta. I said that I would try, if I could,

---

[38] Bar Sheshet, *New Responsa of R. Isaac b. Sheshet*, (Jerusalem, 1960), resp. 27, 8 (Hebrew).
[39] See Israel Jacob Yuval, *Sages in Their Generation: The Spiritual Leadership of the Jews of Germany in the Late Middle Ages* (Jerusalem: Magnes, 1998/9), 322-350 (Hebrew).

to put out this great fire, and to bring order to that community. And you too, our great sage, you must be jealous for the Lord of Hosts, that they might know that there are judges in the land.[40]

Crescas went to Paris, perhaps on a mission on behalf of the royal court, but there is no doubt that while he was there he tried to impose his authority on the parties to the dispute, both of whom promised that they would abide by any decision he might make on the matter. All of the Spanish rabbis involved in the dispute, including Crescas, favored maintaining the independence of French Jewry in the face of the attempted Ashkenazi reform.[41]

In the new reality created after 1391, the Jews of Christian Iberia had to contend with a wide range of social, religious and economic problems. On the one hand, the rabbis were repeatedly asked to resolve Halakhic issues pertaining to relations with the *anusim* and *conversos*.[42] On the other hand, they were called upon to address Halakhic problems within the communities themselves, arising from the circumstances of some of the deaths during the course of the riots. For example, a clear definition of the religious status of the victims was required, indirectly raising the question of whether most, if not all, should be considered martyrs. We find clear expression of this in responsa concerning the case of a *katlanit* (a "deadly woman," viz. a woman who has lost two husbands and seeks to marry a third time). According to Halakha, such a woman may not be permitted to marry a third time, for fear that her ill fortune may have been the cause of the deaths of her previous husbands, and so as not to endanger the life of her third, intended husband. The view of some Spanish rabbis was that such a woman may be allowed to remarry if the death of one of her husbands could be attributed not to personal fate, but to the general fate of the community (e.g. during the plague). Sheshet Perfet, despite a number of concerns raised by Simon ben Zemah Duran, ruled that those killed in the riots of 1391 were martyrs, and

---

[40] Bar Sheshet, *Responsa of R. Isaac b. Sheshet*, resp. 269, 74.

[41] Bar Sheshet, *Responsa of R. Isaac b. Sheshet*, resp. 258-262, 146-152.

[42] See Benzion Netanyahu, *The Marranos of Spain, From the Late Fourteenth to the Early Sixteenth Century According to Contemporary Hebrew Sources* (Ithaca, NY: Cornell University Press, 1999); Moises L. Orfali, *Los conversos españoles en la literatura rabínica: problemas jurídicos y opinions legales durante los siglos XII-XIV* (Salamanca: Universidad Pontificia, 1982).

that their deaths could, therefore, not be attributed to the "cause of fortune" (i.e. the wife's ill fortune), but rather to the special merit and virtue they possessed that afforded them such a death. Crescas' disciple, Joseph Albo,[43] also considered the victims of 1391 martyrs whose deaths were a matter of general fate and therefore legally distinct from private deaths. Albo cites a ruling by Crescas himself that women whose husbands were killed in the riots may marry a third time:

> And furthermore, my teacher, Rabbi ibn Hasdai, peace be upon him, would say that not only is the wife of one killed at a time of persecution—that is death decreed upon the whole [community]—permitted to marry a third time, but even [the wife of] one who suffers an individual martyr's death may marry a third time. And he determined this from the fact that it is written "he fell from a palm tree and died," and not he ascended to the roof and cast himself down and died.[44] *For death by choice is not considered caused by fortune* [the ill fortune of the woman that resulted in the deaths of her two husbands], nor is the "fountain" [conjugal relations with the "deadly woman"] the cause, *for choice is in the hands of the man, and this is the essence of our Torah* ... My teacher, of blessed memory, also said that heaven forfend that we say of those martyred in sanctification of God's name that their death is brought about by fortune or by the "fountain." But I have not seen fit to rule this way in practice.[45]

This Halakhic innovation of Crescas' is not grounded in the sources, but stems from the reality of the catastrophe of 1391. The ruling was later opposed by many Spanish Halakhists, including Samuel Lemas Hazarfati.[46] Crescas raises an interesting philosophical

---

[43] See the responsum of Rabbi Joseph Albo to the rabbinical judges of Teruel, in J. Buksbaum, "Responsa of the Sages of Spain in the Matter of a *Kaṭlanit*," *Moriah* 6-7 (1977): 5-7. See also *Responsa of R. Simon b. Zemah*, vol. 3, 14, 4a.

[44] Crescas' distinction that the Rabbis did not say "he ascended to the roof and cast himself down and died," but rather gave the example of a man who fell from a tree, refers to discussions in the Babylonian Talmud: *Yevamot* 64b; *Ta'anit* 29a; *Ketubot* 103b. I wonder, however, whether he was not also alluding to the fate of some of the Jews of Barcelona (and perhaps his son among them), who jumped from the tower to their heroic deaths, as noted in his letter cited above.

[45] *Responsa of Rabbi Joseph Albo*, 7 (emphasis added by me). Aware that leading Halakhists had, in the past, ruled otherwise, Albo underscored the right of later decisors to innovate.

[46] See Israel M. Ta-Shma, "On Knowledge of the State of Torah Study in Spain in the 15th Century," in *Jews and Conversos at the Time of the Expulsion*, ed. Yom Tov Assis and Yosef

point regarding the question of fate versus the free choice of the martyr. He stressed the personal desire of the martyr, and choice that depends entirely on the individual, rather than on fate. He did not hesitate to draw practical legal conclusions from this philosophical inquiry. It would appear that Crescas' self-perception, as the political and religious leader of Aragonese Jewry in the generation following 1391, instilled in him the need to innovate in Halakha, in order to provide immediate solutions in a new reality.

Hasdai Crescas the Philosopher

As a philosopher, Hasdai Crescas was a link in the chain of Jewish philosophers stretching from Babylonia (at the time of the geonim), to Muslim al-Andalus, to Maimonides and the Maimonidean schools in Provence and Christian Iberia. In many ways, however, Crescas is considered an outstanding and unusual philosopher, seen by some as the last of the original Jewish philosophers of the Middle Ages. His philosophical work, *Light of the Lord*, is extremely succinct, and remarkably rich despite its brevity. Crescas possessed broad philosophical knowledge. His arguments are rooted in Greek philosophy and its Muslim and Jewish interpretations, on the one hand, and in contemporary Christian scholasticism, and particularly the school of John Duns Scotus (1266-1308) and his students, on the other.[47]

Crescas' importance and originality lay in the innovative critique he developed of Aristotelian philosophy, then the dominant school of thought. It is the detachment of medieval science from Aristotelian physics that enabled the scientific breakthroughs of the Renaissance and beyond, leading to remarkable achievements. In this sense, Crescas' philosophy is a gateway to a new era, although his work—unlike that of Maimonides, for example—failed to produce a school of thought and a body of students capable of consolidating and developing his ideas. In the case of Crescas, many of his students

---

Kaplan (Jerusalem, Magnes, 1999), 59-60 (Hebrew).

[47] Shlomo Pines, *Between Jewish and Gentile Thought* (Jerusalem, 1976/7), 178-262 (Hebrew); Zeev Harvey, "Hasdai Crescas and Bernat Metge on the Soul," *Jerusalem Studies in Jewish Thought* 5 (1985/6): 141-154 (Hebrew). Scholasticism is a method of theological study based on the principles of logic.

even opposed his far-reaching views, or were simply unprepared for such a radical shift in Jewish thought.

Crescas questioned the Aristotelian concepts of space and time. Contrary to Aristotle, he posited that space is infinite, and that time measures duration or, in other words, time measures both motion and rest. These were revolutionary ideas that paved the way for a new kind of physics. In the end however, Crescas employs his great and profound interest in physics to theological ends. That is why he fails to develop his groundbreaking ideas into a new physical method, and relies not on experimentation—like the new physics that began to develop in the Renaissnce—but purely on speculation, like the medieval Scholastics.

Light of the Lord engages in polemics with *The Book of Knowledge*, the first part of Maimonides' monumental *Mishneh Torah*. Like *The Book of Knowledge*, dedicated to the dogmatic exposition of beliefs and precepts, *Light of the Lord* proposes a method of "principles of faith." However, it differs from the former both in approach and in content. Crescas questioned Maimonides' method of presenting the letter of each law without noting the Halakhic process it entails. In other words, he does not question Maimonides' rulings per se, but rather the manner in which they are presented. He believes that observance of the precepts alone, without studying the processes that determine their limits, lacks true religious significance. This is also the source of the literary difference between the two works. In *The Book of Knowledge*, Maimonides offers a summary of basic Jewish theology that every Jew should know. He considered deeper understanding of such matters the exclusive province of advanced readers, capable of understanding his philosophical work, *Guide of the Perplexed*. Crescas, on the other hand, begins with an explanation of his own "doctrine of principles," followed by a discussion of the views held by earlier scholars on each of the principles, thereby providing readers with a more complete understanding of them.

Rabbi Saadia Gaon was the first Jewish philosopher in the Middle Ages to present Jewish beliefs in a systematic fashion. It was not until Maimonides, however, in the twelfth century, that an organized and exhaustive exposition of Jewish dogma was created, detailing the specific beliefs that every Jew is obligated to espouse. Over the course of the subsequent two centuries, the subject was largely ignored. The fifteenth century, however, witnessed renewed interest in the principles of faith among Jewish thinkers in Christian Iberia.

Menachem Kellner has sought to determine why so little attention was devoted to the subject of religious dogma in the two centuries stretching from Maimonides to Hasdai Crescas. According to Kellner, in the Middle Ages, the vast majority of Jewish thinkers did not serve as rabbis or leaders in their respective communities. The situation was reversed completely in the fifteenth century.[48] As a matter of personal-religious rather than general-philosophical inquiry, dogma was of little interest to thirteenth- and fourteenth-century scholars, who aspired to purely intellectual goals, to "comprehension of the intelligibles." The persecution of 1391, the development of converso society, and the missionary pressure exerted by the institutions of the Spanish Church also changed the intellectual agenda of the Jewish leadership in Spain. Alongside efforts to strengthen Jewish faith against the pressure of the Church, communal leaders were urgently called upon—in light of the problem of the *anusim*—to address the question of "who is a Jew." Rabbis and communal leaders began to write theological works in response to the challenges of the day, and many, like Crescas, also composed polemical works against Christianity. The need to address the principles of Jewish faith arose from the claims of the Church, presented in manifestly dogmatic form. Since the Jews were compelled to adopt the rules of intellectual discourse established by the Church, it became necessary to define Jewish dogma for apologetic purposes. The establishment of such tenets of Judaism also helped to reframe the question of "who is a Jew," in accordance with the new circumstances presented by the *anusim*.

Crescas' discussion of the principles of the Torah begins with the rejection of Maimonides' assertion that belief in God is the foremost of all the precepts in the Torah. Crescas does not deny the fact that a Jew must believe in God. On the contrary, he considers belief in the existence of God a basic tenet that every person of religious faith must embrace. If however, the existence of God is the basic premise

---

[48] Menachem Kellner, *Dogma in Medieval Jewish Thought* (Oxford: Oxford University Press, 1986), 108-139.

of the entire Torah, it cannot, at the same time, be one of its precepts. It is therefore inconceivable, in Crescas' opinion, that there should be a precept commanding belief in God, which would result in an endless vicious circle.

Maimonides, on the other hand, ruled in the *Mishneh Torah* that every Jew is commanded to know that God exists. To that end, he must (according to the *Guide of the Perplexed*) understand Aristotle's twenty-six propositions of physics and metaphysics, which he lists there. Zeev Harvey explains that, according to Maimonides, as Crescas understood him, "in order to be a good Jew, one must be a good Aristotelian."[49] Crescas rejects this. While Maimonides sought to prove the unity of Torah (Halakha) and philosophy, Crescas sought to separate religion and philosophy, in order to establish the autonomy of religion, independent of philosophy.

Crescas believed that Maimonidean Aristotelianism had driven adherents away from the original meaning of Scripture and the correct intent of the precepts. In other words, according to Crescas, the spiritual trends—whether philosophical or even Kabbalistic at times—actually distanced believers from the plain meaning of Holy Scripture. Crescas' primary goal was to restore the authority of both the Written and the Oral Law (Tanakh and Talmud), through direct textual understanding and the affirmation of a way of life based on Halakha, as the only path to true divine service. In other words, he tried to effect a return to what he saw as the beliefs of the prophets and the sages.[50]

In *Light of the Lord*, Crescas gives intellectual expression to his views on the theurgic properties inherent in each and every biblical precept. He explains the effect of the precepts in theurgic terms, asserting that just as certain medicinal compounds may lose their efficacy when mixed with other compounds, so sin may hinder the positive effect of the precepts. Crescas associated religious acts with the conceptions of astral magic and theurgic properties prevalent

[49] See Warren Zeev Harvey, "Hasdai Crescas' Critique of the Theory of the Acquired Intellect" (PhD diss., Columbia University, 1973), 25.

[50] See J. Guttmann, *Philosophies of Judaism: A History of Jewish Philosophy from Biblical Times to Franz Rosenzweig*, trans. D. W. Silverman. (New York: Schocken, 1973), 224-241; E. Schweid, preface to *Light of the Lord*, 3-69; Kellner, *Dogma in Medieval Jewish Thought*. On Crescas' attitude toward the Kabbalah, see Warren Zeev Harvey, "Kabbalistic Elements in Crescas' Light of the Lord," *Jerusalem Studies in Jewish Thought* 2 (1982/3): 75-109.

among Neoplatonists. Just as the precepts bestow abundant good upon those who observe them, although inexplicable in Aristotelian terms, so magical actions based on astral or divine influence can be efficacious.[51] Crescas' acceptance of the principles of astral magic does not mean that he accepted other philosophical ideas commonly held in these circles, some of which were rightly condemned as "Averroistic."[52]

Crescas' philosophical approach, ostensibly abstract and speculative, was not detached from the spiritual concerns of his generation. One of the causes of conversion among the Jews of Spain was Averroism—based on the philosophy of Aristotle, as interpreted by the Muslim scholar Ibn Rushd (1126-1198), translated into Latin, and disseminated throughout Western Europe.[53] Aristotelianism in its extreme Averroistic form was seen by many, including Crescas, as a threat to Jewish social cohesion. Some of its views (there is no Providence; the world is governed by eternal natural laws; man's purpose in life is not observance of the precepts but the attainment of consciousness alone; the suffering of the Jewish people in the diaspora has no value) were considered products of radical interpretation of Aristotelian principles. Crescas would appear to have had such groups of Averroists in mind when he wrote: "There have arisen today, servants who break away [from their master], who have turned heresy into the words of the living God, disfiguring that which is consecrated [to God], and the words of the Rabbi [Maimonides]."[54] Although Crescas also criticized Maimonides, finding numerous errors in his work, he believed these errors were made in good faith. The philosophical method of those who purported to be disciples of Maimonides, he defined as heresy that interprets the precepts contrary to their original intention. By means

---

[51] See Dov Schwartz, *Amulets, Properties and Rationalism in Medieval Jewish Thought. Issues and Sources* (Ramat Gan: Bar Ilan University, 2003/4), 131-133 (Hebrew). See also Harvey, "Kabbalistic Elements," 77.

[52] Averroes is the Latin name of the Muslim philosopher Ibn Rushd. According to its opponents among Spanish Jews, Averroism contributed to religious nihilism and to the undermining of simple religious faith.

[53] See Dov Schwartz, *Yashan be-Kankan Hadash: The Philosophy of a Fourteenth Century Jewish Neoplatonic Circle* (Jerusalem: Ben Zvi, 1992) (Hebrew) and Ram Ben-Shalom's critique of Schwartz' book, in *Zion* 64 (1999): 235-242.

[54] Crescas, *Light of the Lord*, Introduction.

of his method of exegesis, which focused on the plain meaning of the text and interpretation of Aristotelian criticism, Crescas sought to restore the Torah to its "original" meaning and glory: belief in the Torah and the precepts, reward and punishment, ancestral merit, the right to the Land of Israel, preservation of the Jewish nation, and assurance of its future destiny.[55]

Crescas' opposition to Averroism and his attempt to undermine its philosophical foundations were particularly important at a time of mass conversions, and in light of the large communities of *anusim* that arose alongside the existing Jewish communities of Iberia. Jews influenced by Averroism (often including heretical popular beliefs, with no direct philosophical bearing) may have been more likely to convert to Christianity, since their intimate bond to the religion of their forefathers was weakened, and their philosophical tendencies could also be realized as Christians. Crescas' philosophy can thus be explained as a tenacious struggle against those who employed incorrect exegetical methods and, in so doing, tended toward conversion.

It is interesting to note that *Light of the Lord* was not intended only for Jews, but also for the recent converts of 1391. As Crescas himself attests, some of the views expressed in *Light of the Lord* are the product of the intellectual discussions of a group of scholars, as opposed to the ideas of a lone thinker, conceived, written and published precisely as envisaged by their author.[56] *Light of the Lord* was composed over many years and in various periods, and displays earlier and later strata. Crescas changed his views over time, and re-edited parts of the book that had already been completed. One of the theories advanced by modern scholarship is that the persecution of 1391 led Crescas to consult with his fellow scholars and re-edit the work—a task he completed in 1410—in light of events of the day: persecution and the rise of a large community of *anusim*.[57] The Florence Manuscript of *Light of the Lord* is the oldest and most reliable of the extant manuscripts. In this manuscript, we find

---

[55] Baer, *History*, vol. 2, 165.

[56] Crescas, *Light of the Lord*, Introduction: "and this indeed by great inquiry and study with the most eminent of [my] friends."

[57] Nathan Ophir, "A New Reading of R. Hasdai Crescas' *Light of the Lord* and the Problem of the *Anusim*," *Proceedings of the Eleventh World Congress of Jewish Studies* (Jerusalem, 1993), div. C, vol. 2, 41-47 (Hebrew).

corrections made by Crescas himself, in his final years, "with the help and concurrence of friends." These corrections include the following: a moderation of Crescas' deterministic approach, a sixth tenet of faith (divine power), the particular providence enjoyed by the Jews, and three additional chapters.

One of Crescas' innovations, appearing in the margins of MS Florence, pertains to the Talmudic principle that "the Torah exempts one who is compelled [anus]," upon which he expands, stating that it is what is in the heart that counts rather than the compelled actions of the anus. His interpretation of the Talmudic maxim "thoughts of sin are worse than sin" would also appear to have been directed at the anusim: Thought is perceived as will, and the willful thought of sin is indeed worse than and, in a sense, more significant than the action of sin. This approach ascribes greater weight to inner service, which may, at times, substitute for the external action of precept-observance.

Another innovation that appears in this manuscript concerns the biblical prohibition against idolatry. In this passage, Crescas summarizes the beliefs that one must accept or be considered an apostate, including belief in the resurrection of the dead and the immortality of the soul. On the rejection of idolatry, which other authorities have numbered among such cardinal beliefs, Crescas wrote in this late redaction: "We have not included the rejection of idolatry in this category, as others have done, for it is not a matter of knowledge, but a precept." The circumstances of the anusim, compelled to worship other gods against their will, may have led Crescas to diminish the importance of rejecting idolatry, affording it the status of one of the precepts, rather than a tenet of faith that marks those who fail to uphold it as apostates.

A further innovation concerns the essence of sin. According to Crescas' deterministic view, even sin flows from the Divine Cause. Every human action is determined by deterministic causality, and therefore, even the righteous must sin at times, against their will. Within this deterministic framework, however, Crescas developed the idea of "feeling of compulsion and constraint" [hergesh 'ones ve-hekhre'ah], whereby even as one is compelled to sin, he is obliged to want to believe in his heart and to rejoice in serving God. Crescas attaches great significance to the commandment to rejoice (on festivals), thereby enabling anusim to fulfill, in their hearts, a central component of divine service.

A special section in *Light of the Lord* (at the end of the Third Treatise) can also be seen as a manifesto for the religious guidance of the *anusim*. In this section, Crescas emphasizes three main points: the importance of "intention of the heart" in prayer, repentance as an "essential belief" and the observance of the festivals and holy days. With regard to prayer, Crescas asserts that even one who is unworthy may, through the intention of his heart in prayer, be heard by God and obtain his desire. This is true for non-Jews as well, who may obtain what they desire, if they pray to the God of Israel. This message would clearly have helped to assuage the guilt felt by the *anusim*, as a result of their conversion, and the sense of helplessness that marked their religious state. By means of true devotional intention, Crescas assured them, they could—despite their own feelings of unworthiness, as non-Jews (Christians)—find a path to God.

In the matter of repentance, Crescas affirms that the gates of repentance are never closed, if the sinner truly feels the weight of his sin and wishes to return to God. Holy days, such as the Day of Atonement, enable men to free themselves from astral determinism and subject themselves to the influence of particular Providence. The *anusim* were thus able to follow the path of repentance based on internal intention without engaging in visible external actions, focusing their spiritual efforts on Jewish festivals and holy days such as the Day of Atonement. This section in *Light of the Lord* can thus be considered a kind of guide to internal, concealed religious service for *anusim*, allowing them to maintain their connection to Judaism under circumstances that precluded observance of the Jewish religious precepts.[58]

---

[58] Ophir, "A New Reading."

Hasdai Crescas the Polemicist

The years following 1391 witnessed an intensification of theological polemics between Jews and Christians. The appearance of the *conversos* as a distinct social unit alongside Jews and Christians further exacerbated religious debate. Within *converso* society, the boundaries between Judaism and Christianity became blurred, facilitating passage from the Jewish to the Christian community. In the past, Jews who had converted to Christianity were constrained to leave their social milieu—the immediate circle of family and the broader circle of community. Henceforth, it was possible to convert and remain in the same house, neighbourhood, family and social circle. There was even a community of *anusim*, with institutions paralleling, in part, those of the Jewish community.[59]

Under these new circumstances, Jewish leaders acted to stem the tide of conversion as well as to maintain ties between the *anusim* and Judaism, in the hope that the previous state of affairs might, one day, be restored. Hasdai Crescas conducted this policy and was one of its architects. In this context, he also engaged in religious debate, and wrote two polemical works in Catalan, the literary language of the Crown of Aragon. The first, *The Refutation of the Christian Principles* (c. 1397), is known only from the Hebrew translation by Joseph ben Shem Tov ibn Shem Tov (1451). The second, no longer extant—primarily because it was never translated into Hebrew—included proofs from the prophets.[60]

In the introduction to *The Refutation of the Christian Principles*, Crescas declares that in every disputed matter between Judaism and Christianity, he will first note those things that the two religions have in common. He will then explain the differences, and refute the Christian premises. He addresses ten Christian dogmas rejected by Judaism: 1. Adam's sin and punishment; 2. redemption from "original" sin; 3. the Trinity; 4. incarnation; 5. the virgin birth; 6. transubstantiation; 7. baptism; 8. the coming of the messiah; 9. the

---

[59] Ram Ben-Shalom, "The Social Context of Apostasy among Fifteenth-Century Spanish Jewry: Dynamics of a New Religious Borderland," in *Rethinking European Jewish History*, ed. Jeremy Cohen and Moshe Rosman (Oxford: Littman Library, 2009), 173-198.

[60] Ibn Shem Tov's remarks, in Daniel Lasker, trans. and ed., *The Refutation of the Christian Principles by Hasdai Crescas* (Albany: State University of New York, 1992), 84.

New Torah [Testament]; and 10. demons.[61] On each of these topics, he refutes Christian beliefs, primarily with philosophical arguments, and tries to show that they stand in contradiction to logic. For example, he points out the contradiction between the Christian belief, shared by Judaism, that God is necessary, perfect and non-composed, and the doctrine of the Trinity, espoused by Christianity alone. Crescas' criticism of Christian dogma is based on the premise (held by both Christianity and Judaism, according to Crescas) that "faith will not force the intellect to believe something which leads to contradiction," i.e. that religion cannot teach absurd doctrines, contrary to logic. In other words, God is not omnipotent in the sense of being able to do the impossible. The intellect must distinguish between true and false religion, by revealing those beliefs that run counter to logic. This position reflects the ideology of Jewish polemicists in late medieval Spain that was influenced by the philosophical school of Ibn Rushd (Averroes; 1126-1198).[62]

Western European Jewish polemical literature was generally written in Hebrew, since it was intended for Jews. Why then did Crescas choose to write his polemical works in Catalan? The answer to this question depends, first and foremost, on the answer to another question: for whom were these works intended? Crescas begins his *Refutation* with the following words:

> Princes and nobles pleaded with me to compose a treatise in which I would present the doubts and refutations which the followers of the Torah of Moses, peace be upon him, can offer against the Christian belief; and that, by evaluating the positions of each side, I should intend by means [of composing this treatise] the worship of the Creator, may He be blessed, by establishing the truth in the ancient dispute between the Christians and the Hebrews. Since this goal is worthwhile in and of itself, and since I had to fulfill their desire (even though I am unworthy), I saw fit in this treatise to prepare and carefully compose that which they commanded me.[63]

Heinrich Graetz, and others in his footsteps, claimed that *The Refutation of the Christian Principles* was intended for a Christian

---

[61] Crescas, *Refutation*, 23f.

[62] Lasker, preface to Crescas, *Refutation*, 5f.

[63] Crescas, *Refutation*, 23.

readership. The princes and nobles who implored Crescas to write a polemical work would thus have been members of the Christian nobility of Aragon, and that is why he chose to write in Catalan. Benzion Netanyahu, on the other hand, argues that Crescas' reference was, in all probability, to Jewish courtiers, rather than to Christian nobles. Attempts to ascertain the identity of these "princes and nobles" may be pointless, however, since the initiative to write the work was, after all, Crescas'. The reference to princes and nobles may thus have been no more than a rhetorical topos, whereby the author attributes the initiative to write a given work to others, rather than to himself.[64] This theory is further supported by Crescas' rhetorical statement that he must satisfy the princes' request despite his unworthiness.

The purpose of the *Refutation*, according to Crescas, was the systematic exposition of arguments for rejecting the Christian faith. Graetz believed that the Christian nobles wished to know what prevents the Jews from converting, and perhaps sought the systematic refutation of Jewish polemical arguments. According to Netanyahu, Jewish courtiers, perturbed by the mass conversions, sought a work addressed to the *anusim* who, by that time, hardly read in Hebrew, which is why Crescas wrote in the vernacular. Netanyahu even sees this as evidence of the extent of voluntary conversion among the *anusim*—if, as he supposes, they no longer read Hebrew works, only six years after the persecution of 1391.[65] I find it hard to accept Netanyahu's assertion regarding the reading habits of the *anusim* in 1397 and the extent of their conversion, on the basis of Crescas' choice to write a book for them in Catalan. The reading habits of the *anusim* six years after their conversion were probably the same as they were in 1391. As previously, the educated among them continued to read philosophical and scientific literature in Hebrew. Those who did not read Hebrew prior to their conversion, however, would have found the work more accessible in the vernacular. There

---

[64] This is not true of all cases, but is evident in a number of polemical works. According to the mores of the time, the very desire to write a book might have been perceived as arrogance. See, e.g., Joseph Kimhi and David Kimhi, *The Book of the Covenant and Other Writings*, ed. Frank Talmage (Jerusalem: Bialik Institute, 1973/4), 21, (Hebrew); R. Isaac Pulgar, *The Support of the Faith*, ed. J. Levinger (Tel Aviv, 1983/4), 30 (Hebrew).

[65] Graetz, *History of the Jews*, vol. 4, 187; Netanyahu, *The Marranos of Spain*, 87.

is thus no reason to reject Netanyahu's view that the book was intended for the *anusim*.

Hasdai Crescas, contrary to Netanyahu's theory, had no need of other Jewish courtiers to urge him to write polemical works for *anusim*. Such works were part of his program for the rehabilitation of Iberian Jewry, including the *anusim*, whom he considered an integral part of the Jewish people. Crescas perhaps presumed that *anusim* might be deterred from openly possessing Hebrew books, and particularly polemical works against Christianity. A number of years earlier, King Juan I promulgated the first edicts (1393) intended to isolate the *anusim* from the Jews, citing various areas of life (e.g. habitation, prayers, meals) in which social and religious separation was to be pursued.[66] A book in Catalan found in the homes of *anusim* would have aroused less suspicion, affording them greater opportunity to read polemical works. Even though a book written in the vernacular would have made it easier for Christians to determine its content, Crescas probably felt that a work in Catalan would reach a wider readership among the *anusim*. This view is supported by the creation, in the first half of the fifteenth century, of a body of translated literature for the use of the *anusim* in Castile: Maimonides' *Guide of the Perplexed* was translated into Castilian (probably completed at Seville, in 1432) in *anusim* circles, which were also probably responsible for the Castilian translation of Judah Halevi's *Kuzari*.[67] Crescas' writings in Catalan also mirror similar trends in the wider Iberian society at that time, including the translation of Latin texts into the vernacular, and original writing in the Romance languages. This trend greatly increased the number of readers in general, and even led to the development of a genre of vernacular anti-Jewish polemical literature.[68]

Crescas' active interest in polemics is also evident in his request to Profiat Duran of Perpignan to write a polemical work. Duran, already an important polemicist, had previously published his

---

[66] Baer, *History*, vol. 2, 125.

[67] Baer, *History*, vol. 2, 486, n.8.

[68] An interesting example of this is the polemical *tratado* of the apostate Maestre Juan *el viejo* [the Elder] of Toledo. See Eleazar Gutwirth, "Maestre Juan el Viejo and his Tratado (Madrid MS)," *Proceedings of the Ninth World Congress of Jewish Studies* (Jerusalem, 1986), div. B, 129-134.

famous letter *Be Not Like Your Fathers* (in 1394 or 1395). Crescas' request is described as follows in the work that resulted from it, *Disgrace of the Gentiles*:

> Glory of rabbis and crown of believers [Hasdai Crescas], your eminence asked me to impart to you what I have discovered regarding the false messiah and his disciples or apostles in general, and if they intended to destroy the divine Torah in whole or in part, as continuously proclaimed by those who believed in him and follow him, and what was their intention in that belief, and on what grounds have the speakers [theologians] of that nation who came after them built their belief and opinion, in what they claim of their own words and of the words of the true prophets of blessed memory and the divine Torah.
>
> Your intention, glory of rabbis, [was] to open the gate, if it is possible to [respond] according to your own words, for this is the true and compelling answer in such matters. And although [not] one of the earlier possessors of the truth saw fit to proclaim and reveal the truth, also because they did not wish to waste their time in such a fashion, you, glory of rabbis, have witnessed the days of evil and wrath poured out upon the exile of Jerusalem that is in Spain, and the many who burst forth and seek deep to hide their counsel, to cast up a mound against the wall of the divine Torah, to make it as a lodge in a cucumber garden, as a besieged and breached city. And you, glory of rabbis, wish to restore the fallen and ruined tabernacle, although the leprosy of apostasy flourishes on the brows of the people, and all the people are at strife, the staff of wickedness has blossomed and arrogance flowered. I have therefore sought to do your will, effacing my own, and I shall write a little of what you desire, in the knowledge that you, in the broadness of your heart and the height of your intellect, will add incisive words [of your own].[69]

This passage would seem to imply that Duran wrote a short work for Crescas, that he might add to. *Disgrace of the Gentiles* is, however, an extensive, methodical, precise and detailed work, which leaves little room for additions. Here too, scholars would appear to have fallen into the trap of rhetoric. Such words of praise and courtesy are to be expected in a book dedicated to an important philosopher such

---

[69] Profiat Duran, *Disgrace of the Gentiles*, in *The Polemical Writings of Profiat Duran*, ed. Frank Talmage (Jerusalem: Zalman Shazar Center, 1980/1), 3 (Hebrew). Frank Talmage, "The Polemical Writings of Profiat Duran," in *Apples of Gold in Settings of Silver: Studies in Medieval Jewish Exegesis and Polemics*, ed. Frank Talmage and Barry Dov Walfish (Toronto: Pontifical Institute, 1999), 281-287.

as Hasdai Crescas, but they need not be taken literally. As Daniel Lasker has shown,[70] the polemical works of Duran and Crescas are quite different from one another. Duran addresses Christian beliefs through criticism of the New Testament, whereas Crescas employs philosophical analysis. Crescas' other, non-extant polemical work was also not based on the New Testament, but included proofs from the prophets.

It would thus appear that Hasdai Crescas' invitation to Profiat Duran was part of a wider polemical program, encompassing most of the themes and methods of Jewish-Christian polemics: ("old") disputation of Scripture (Crescas' work on prophetic proofs), philosophical disputation (Duran's *Be Not Like Your Fathers* and Crescas' *Refutation of the Christian Principles*), and criticism of the New Testament (*Disgrace of the Gentiles*). Crescas himself, like Duran, also engaged in public disputation with the greatest Christian theologians.[71]

The need for these polemical works became apparent in the years that followed. As we have seen, Crescas' view regarding the birth of the messiah was raised during the Tortosa Disputation.[72] The Hebrew translator of *The Refutation of the Christian Principle*, Joseph ibn Shem Tov, also attested to the importance of Crescas' book:

> At the beginning of my commentary, I mentioned six ways in which our righteous predecessors polemicized against the spokesmen of this nation. In the fifth one, I mentioned what was done by Rabbi Hasdai, of blessed memory, in a treatise, small in quantity but great in quality and eminence, which he composed in the vernacular. Because of its brevity and depth, its benefit has escaped the members of our nation. In addition, its language is strange for those who have not been accustomed to study science except in our holy language, and, therefore, its contents have remained like the words of a book that is sealed ... Since, however ... men of science have been lost... They were not able to derive from it the secrets of existence and the divine mysteries, because of the brevity of his language and his excessive use

---

[70] Lasker, *Refutation*, preface, 6f.

[71] As asserted by Crescas' student, Zerahyah Halevi. See Ravitzky, *Sermon on the Passover*, 112. See: R. Ben-Shalom, "Between Official and Private Dispute: The Case of Christian Spain and Provence in the Late Middle Ages," *AJS Review* 27 (2003): 23-71, esp. 46, 55-56.

[72] Ibn Verga, *Scepter*, 103.

of indirect allusion ...And [my students] have requested that I return to the labor of translation, [this time] not merely to transpose the language but to translate its contents, and to add a complementary commentary ... I begin to do this...I will try with all my might to preserve its intention, clearly explaining its secrets and hints, expanding the discussion of each principle so that the benefits spread to all its environs.[73]

By the mid-fifteenth century, religious polemics continued to be at the heart of Jewish-Christian discourse in Spain. Ibn Shem Tov sought to preserve the achievements of the polemical efforts of the late fourteenth century, particularly those of Profiat Duran and Hasdai Crescas. To this end, he translated into Hebrew a Catalan book that had probably been written primarily for the *anusim*. In doing so, he thereby restored this work to the wider Jewish public, most of which did not read in the vernacular or in Latin.[74] Ibn Shem Tov also decided to add necessary explanations and comments to works written in a philosophical vein, since their understanding required a level of philosophical knowledge that readers did not always possess. Ibn Shem Tov's efforts attest to the fact that two generations after Hasdai Crescas, there was still a real need for the polemical works produced by Crescas and Duran. Crescas' polemical program was intended, first and foremost, to rehabilitate Iberian Jewry in the wake of the catastrophe of 1391. However, it subsequently had an impact on Jewish-Christian discourse throughout the fifteenth century, leaving a powerful and lasting impression of the figure of Hasdai Crescas in the collective memory of Spanish Jews.

Conclusion

At the beginning of the chapter, we asked what it was about Crescas that lent him the aura of the "greatest of his generation"; what engendered the great sense of loss experienced by his contemporaries

---

[73] Ibn Shem Tov, Introduction, in Crescas, *Refutation*, 19-21.

[74] We know that letters written in the Romance languages were exchanged by Jews in the years 1300-1492. These were written, however, by a small number of Jewish leaders, who addressed such letters in the vernacular to royalty or nobility. See E. Gutwirth, "Medieval Romance Epistolarity: The Case of the Iberian Jews," *Neophilologus* 84 (2000): 207-224.

at his passing; and why did they believe that his teachings could provide comfort in times of adversity? Crescas' multifaceted personality and wide range of pursuits offer only a partial answer. Of particular note were his abilities as a political leader during Iberian Jewry's darkest hour following the destruction of 1391. Crescas' policy was rooted in a realistic political agenda aimed at preserving the communities that had survived this catastrophe, and attempting to rebuild those that had been destroyed, through assertive tax collection. He also sought to preserve national hopes and aspirations for the glorious messianic future awaiting the Jewish people without giving rise to the active outburst of a full-blown messianic movement. He thus managed to walk a fine line between reality and utopia, consolidating the present through concrete action, while regrouping and strengthening the collective spirit of Iberian Jewry through the dissemination of messianic hopes.

Crescas enjoyed the trust and support of all of the various social strata and spiritual streams within the Jewish community, as well as the confidence of the royal house, which saw him as an authoritative Jewish leader capable of aiding in the concentration of royal power and authority in Aragon. At the same time, Crescas also developed a critical approach to Christianity and the New Testament that contrasted with earlier Jewish polemical works, which had been primarily defensive and apologetic. His work as a polemicist helped to stem the tide of Jews joining the ranks of the *conversos*. In his profound intellectual endeavors, Crescas sought not only to engage in theoretical inquiry, but also to address the urgent needs of his generation. His philosophical and Halakhic thought not only provided solutions to the problems of the day, but also predicted social, political and cultural developments that would arise over the course of the fifteenth century. In all of this, Crescas contributed immensely to the rehabilitation, growth, and development of Iberian Jewry, until the expulsion a century later.

Works Cited:

Assis, Yom Tov. "The Project of R. Hasdai Crescas for the Rehabilitation of the Jewish Communities following the Decrees of 5151 (1391)," *Proceedings of the Tenth World Congress of Jewish Studies*, div. B, vol.1, 145-148. Jerusalem: World Union of Jewish Studies, 1989. (Hebrew)

Baer, Fritz. *Die Juden im Christlichen Spanien: Urkunden und Regesten*, vol. 1. Berlin: Akademie Verlag, 1929.

Baer, Yitzhak. *A History of the Jews in Christian Spain*. Translated by L. Schoffman. Philadelphia: The Jewish Publication Society, 2001.

Bar Sheshet, Isaac. *New Responsa of R. Isaac b. Sheshet*. Jerusalem, 1960. (Hebrew)

------. *Responsa of R. Isaac b. Sheshet*. Jerusalem, 1975. (Hebrew)

Ben-Shalom, Ram. "Review of Schwartz, Dov. *Yashan be-Kankan Hadash: The Philosophy of a Fourteenth Century Jewish Neoplatonic Circle*. (Jerusalem: Ben-Zvi Institute and Bialik Institute, 1992)," *Zion* 64 (1999): 235-242. (Hebrew)

------. "Kiddush ha-Shem and Jewish Martyrology in Aragon and Castile, in the year 5151 (1391): Between Spain and Ashkenaz." *Tarbiz* 70 (2001): 279-300. (Hebrew)

------. "Between Official and Private Dispute: The Case of Christian Spain and Provence in the Late Middle Ages," *AJS Review* 27 (2003): 23-71.

------. "The Social Context of Apostasy among Fifteenth-Century Spanish Jewry: Dynamics of a New Religious Borderland." In *Rethinking European Jewish History*, edited by Jeremy Cohen and Moshe Rosman. Oxford and Portland, Oregon: The Littman Library of Jewish Civilization, 2009. Pp. 173-198

Berger, David. "Some Ironic Consequences of Maimonides' Rationalistic Messianism." In *Maimonidean Studies*, edited by A. Hyman, vol. 2, 1-8. New York: Yeshiva University, 1991. (Hebrew)

Bernstein, Shimeon. ed., *Divan of Solomon b. Meshulam de Piera*. New York: Alim, 1942. (Hebrew)

Buksbaum, Joseph. "Responsa of the Sages of Spain in the Matter of a
    Ḳaṭlanit." *Moriah* 6-7 (1977): 2-11.

Cohen, Gershon David. "Messianic Postures of Ashkenazim and
    Sephardim Prior to Sabbethai Zevi." In *Studies in the Variety
    of Rabbinic Cultures,* edited by Gerson D. Cohen, 271-297.
    Philadelphia: Jewish Publication Society, 1991.

Crescas, Hasdai. *Light of the Lord.* (Ferrara, 1555 (Hebrew). Jerusalem:
    Makor, facsimile.

Duran, Profiat. *Disgrace of the Gentiles.* In *The Polemical Writings of
    Profiat Duran.* Edited by Frank Talmage. Jerusalem: The Zalman
    Shazar Center and The Dinur Center, 1981. (Hebrew)

Duran, Simon ben Zemah. *Responsa of R. Simon b. Zemah* . Lemberg: Uri
    Zeev Salat, 1851. (Hebrew)

Eshkoli, Aaron Zeev. *Jewish Messianic Movements.* Jerusalem: Bialik
    Institute, 1987. (Hebrew)

Graetz, Zevi (H.). *History of the Jews,* vol. 4. Translated by S. P.
    Rabinowitz. Warsaw: Ahisepher, 1897/8. (Hebrew)

Guttmann, Julius. *Philosophies of Judaism: A History of Jewish Philosophy
    from Biblical Times to Franz Rosenzweig.* Translated by D. W.
    Silverman. New York: Schocken, 1973.

Gutwirth, Eleazar. "Maestre Juan el Viejo and his Tratado (Madrid MS)."
    Proceedings of the Ninth World Congress of Jewish Studies, div. B,
    129-134. Jerusalem, 1986.

------. "Medieval Romance Epistolarity: The Case of the Iberian Jews."
    Neophilologus 84 (2000): 207-224.

Harvey, Warren Zeev. "Hasdai Crescas' Critique of the Theory of the
    Acquired Intellect." Ph.D. diss., Columbia University, 1973.

------. "Kabbalistic Elements in Crescas' Light of the Lord," *Jerusalem
    Studies in Jewish Thought* 2 (1982/3): 75-109.

------. "Hasdai Crescas and Bernat Metge on the Soul." *Jerusalem Studies
    in Jewish Thought* 5 (1985/6): 141-154. (Hebrew)

------. *Rabbi Hasdai Crescas.* Jerusalem: The Zalman Shazar Center, 2010.
    (Hebrew)

Hershman, Abraham M. *Rabbi Isaac Bar Sheshet Perfet and His Times.* New York: The Jewish Theological Seminary of America, 1943.

Ibn Verga, Solomon. *Scepter of Judah.* Edited by M. Wiener. Hannover: K. Rimpler, 1856. (Hebrew)

Kaminka, Aharon. "Poems and Epigrams by R. Solomon b. R. Reuben Bonafed." *Hazofeh Quartalis Hebraica* 12 (1928): 33-42. (Hebrew)

Kellner, Menachem. *Dogma in Medieval Jewish Thought.* Oxford: Oxford University Press, 1986.

Kimhi, Joseph and David Kimhi. *The Book of the Covenant and Other Writings.* Edited by F. Talmage. Jerusalem: Bialik Institute, 1974. (Hebrew)

Lasker, Daniel, trans. and ed., *The Refutation of the Christian Principles by Hasdai Crescas.* Albany: State University of New York, 1992.

Maimonides, *Mišneh Torah.* Edited by Zvi H. Preisler. Jerusalem: Ketuvim, 1985.

MS Oxford, Bodleian, Mich. 155 (formerly 809) [Neubauer 1984].

Netanyahu, Benzion. *The Marranos of Spain, From the Late Fourteenth to the Early Sixteenth Century According to Contemporary Hebrew Sources.* Ithaca, NY: Cornell University Press, 1999.

Ophir, Nathan. "A New Reading in R. Hasdai Crescas' *Light of the Lord* and the Problem of the *Anusim." Proceedings of the Eleventh World Congress of Jewish Studies,* div. C, vol. 2, 41-47. Jerusalem, 1993. (Hebrew)

Orfali, Levi Moisés. *Los conversos españoles en la literature rabínica: problemas jurídicos y opinions legales durante los siglos XII-XIV.* Salamanca: Universidad Pontificia, 1982.

Pines, Solomon. *Between Jewish and Gentile Thought.* Jerusalem: Mossad Bialik, 1976/7. (Hebrew)

Pulgar, Isaac. *The Support of the Faith.* Edited by Jacob Levinger. Tel Aviv: The Chaim Rosenberg School of Jewish Studies, Tel Aviv University, 1983/4. (Hebrew)

Ravitzky, Aviezer. *Crescas' Sermon on the Passover and Studies in his Philosophy.* Jerusalem: The Israel Academy of Sciences and Humanities, 1988. (Hebrew)

------. "'To the Utmost of Human Capacity': Maimonides on the Days of the Messiah." In *Perspectives on Maimonides*, edited by J. Kramer, 221-256. Oxford: Oxford University Press, 1991.

Romano, David. "Prorrata de contribuyentes judíos de Jaca en 1377." *Sefarad* 42 (1982): 3-39.

Rosenberg, Shalom. "The *Arba'ah Turim* of Rabbi Abraham b. R. Judah, disciple of Hasdai Crescas." *Jerusalem Studies in Jewish Thought* 3 (1983/4): 525-621. (Hebrew)

Saperstein, Mark. "A Sermon on the Akeda from the Generation of the Expulsion and its Implications for 1391." In *Exile and Diaspora: Studies in the History of the Jewish People Presented to Professor Haim Beinart*, edited by Aharon Mirski et al., 103-124. Jerusalem: Ben-Zvi Institute, 1991.

Schirmann, Haim. *The History of Hebrew Poetry in Christian Spain and Southern France*. Edited by Ezra Fleischer. Jerusalem: The Magnes Press, The Hebrew University, Ben-Zvi Institute, 1997. (Hebrew)

Schwartz, Dov. *Yashan be-Kankan Hadash: The Philosophy of a Fourteenth Century Jewish Neoplatonic Circle*. Jerusalem: Ben-Zvi Institute and Bialik Institute, 1992. (Hebrew)

------. *Amulets, Properties and Rationalism in Medieval Jewish Thought: Issues and Sources*. Ramat Gan: Bar-Ilan University, 2004. (Hebrew)

Schweid, Eliezer. Preface to *Light of the Lord by Hasdai Crescas* [Ferrara 1555]. Jerusalem: Makor, 1971.

Ta-Shma, Israel Moshe. "On Knowledge of the State of Torah Study in Spain in the 15th Century." In *Jews and Conversos at the Time of the Expulsion*, edited by Yom Tov Assis and Yoseph Kaplan, 47-62. Jerusalem: Magnes, 1999. (Hebrew)

Talmage, Frank. "The Polemical Writings of Profiat Duran." In *Apples of Gold in Settings of Silver: Studies in Medieval Jewish Exegesis and Polemics*, edited by F. Talmage and B. D. Walfish, 281-287. Toronto: Pontifical Institute of Mediaeval Studies, 1999.

Yuval, Israel Jacob. *Scholars in Their Time: The Religious Leadership of German Jewry in the Late Middle Ages*. Jerusalem: Magnes, 1988. (Hebrew)

Sephardic Intellectuals: Challenges and Creativity (1391 - 1492)

.... Eric Lawee

Medieval Spanish Jewry's closing chapter began with riots in 1391 that left tens of thousands of Jews dead or forcibly converted to Christianity and ended with the community's total expulsion in 1492. The century in between, marked as it was by further bouts of persecution and other forms of upheaval, seems a poor candidate for a scholarly revival. In the event, however, Sephardic scholarship's final phase saw a slow but steady recovery of learning after 1391, the eventual restoration of a reasonably vibrant intellectual sphere, and the production of novel achievements in various disciplines and genres by an impressive cadre of diverse thinkers and writers. In short, late medieval Hispano-Jewish intellectuals created afresh on the basis of deep erudition, at times prolifically, under trying historical circumstances. That they stand in the shadow of their more famous Sephardic forerunners should not detract from their scholarly and literary attainments—attainments that set the stage for the flourishing of ongoing Jewish education and new intellectual creativity in the far-flung Sephardic diaspora after 1492.

1391-1492: Gloom-Filled Parenthesis?

Late medieval Sephardic scholarship unfolded against a challenging and at times catastrophic set of circumstances. The 1391 riots destroyed scores of Jewish communities and effected a massive depletion in Jewish ranks by creating a novel sub-group within Spanish society, the "new Christians" or *conversos*. Comprising forcibly baptized Jews and their descendants (and, eventually, the more voluntary converts of later decades and their descendants), this group evoked increasing hostility over time and, in some quarters, a "virulent phobia"[1] that persisted long after the last Jew left Spanish soil. As for Spanish Jewry's surviving remnant, it suffered additional setbacks, like the great public missionizing "Disputation of Tortosa" that dragged on under the auspices of the Avignonese pope, Benedict XIII, in 1413-14 and the roughly contemporaneous conversionary campaign conducted by the fiery Dominican, Vincent Ferrer. As more Jews embraced the cross, many Christians celebrated what they deemed miraculous events heralding messianic times.[2]

It would seem that Spanish Jewry's situation stabilized somewhat, politically and economically, after the bitter adversities of the fifteenth century's opening decades; yet new signs of precariousness also appeared. One was growth in the volume and severity of anti-Jewish literature, which included portrayals of Jews as a monster race in collusion with the Antichrist and his allies, most notably the Turks, whose 1453 capture of Constantinople struck terror across Christian Europe.[3] With rumors rife of New Christian cryptojudaizing,

---

[1] David L. Graizbord, *Souls in Dispute: Converso Identities in Iberia and the Jewish Diaspora, 1580–1700* (Philadelphia: University of Pennsylvania Press, 2004), 2. Note: bibliography hereinafter favors English entries and makes no claim to comprehensivity.

[2] Frank Talmage, "Trauma at Tortosa: The Testimony of Abraham Rimoch," *Mediaeval Studies* 47 (1985): 379–81; Eleazar Gutwirth, "Towards Expulsion: 1391–1492," in *Spain and the Jews: The Sephardi Experience 1492 and After*, ed. Elie Kedourie (London: Thames and Hudson, 1992), 55. For the "Christian hatred and fanaticism" that Ferrer bestirred, see Yitzhak Baer, *A History of the Jews in Christian Spain*, trans. Louis Schoffman, with an introduction by Benjamin Gampel, 2 vols. (Philadelphia: Jewish Publication Society, 1992), 2:166.

[3] Moshe Lazar, "Rabbí Moses Arragel as Servant of Two Masters: A Call for Tolerance in a Century of Turmoil," in *Encuentros and Desencuentros: Spanish Jewish Cultural Interaction Throughout History*, ed. Carlos Carrete Parrondo, et. al. (Tel Aviv: University Publishing Projects, 2000), 432, 437.

Isabella of Castile and Ferdinand of Aragon established the Spanish Inquisition in the early 1480s in their recently conjoined kingdoms. Though directed against *conversos*, this institution inevitably cast a hostile spotlight on professing Jews. Blaming the *conversos'* alleged failure to integrate into Christian society on their interaction with these Jews, Spain's monarchs ordered the departure of all Jews from their territories by the summer of 1492.[4]

In light of the foregoing, it occasions little surprise that the last century of medieval Jewish life on Spanish soil is often painted in dark colors, with an especially vivid portrayal along these lines appearing in the most influential account of the Sephardic experience ever written, Yitzhak Baer's *A History of the Jews in Christian Spain*.[5] By contrast, a few recent scholars argue that Spanish Jewry's closing century should be seen, on the whole, as an era of "remarkable resurgence"—nay a "renaissance," if only in socioeconomic terms.[6]

But if 1391-1492 was not simply a "gloom-filled parenthesis,"[7] what of the domains of education, intellectual life, and literary achievement to which "renaissance" labels are usually affixed? The common view of the last century of Sephardic intellectual history is of a period of nearly thorough-going mediocrity, if not a "complete breakdown and virtual collapse of the high level of Jewish learning which had characterized Spanish Jewry from the earliest days."[8] But is this perception accurate? To address this question, we must recapture the arc of Hispano-Jewish intellectual-literary endeavor from its beginnings, the better to appreciate scholarly continuities, diminutions, and novelties in the post-1391 period.

---

[4] Edward Peters, "Jewish History and Gentile Memory: The Expulsion of 1492," *Jewish History* 9 (1995): 9–34.

[5] For orientation in Baer's masterpiece, see Gampel's introduction to the edition of it cited above. For its ongoing influence, see, e.g., Jane S. Gerber, *The Jews of Spain: A History of the Sephardic Experience* (New York: The Free Press, 1992), 115–44, which covers 1391-1492 in a chapter entitled "Path to Expulsion: The Decline and Destruction of Spanish Jewry."

[6] Most notably Mark D. Meyerson, *A Jewish Renaissance in Fifteenth-Century Spain* (Princeton: Princeton University Press, 2004) (who, it should be noted, builds his case on the basis of the experience of a single Jewish community).

[7] Meyerson, *A Jewish Renaissance*, 3.

[8] Norman Roth, *Conversos, Inquisition, and the Expulsion of the Jews from Spain* (Madison: University of Wisconsin Press, 1995), 13.

A Tale of Two Renaissances

The achievements of the most famous representatives of Sephardic learning and literature can be seen in terms of two nearly successive phases of "accelerated" creativity of the sort typical of "renaissance" eras.[9] Beginning in the later tenth century, scholars and writers in Muslim Spain, or al-Andalus, began to articulate the dazzlingly diverse and sophisticated culture that has come to be called the Jewish "golden age" in medieval Iberia.[10] Forged out of an intense scholarly dialogue and disputation with trends abroad in larger Islamic culture, this century and a half of intellectual achievement boasted trailblazing advances in Hebrew poetry, both religious and secular, linguistics, biblical scholarship and theology.[11] Its foremost representative, Moses Maimonides (1138-1204), set forth a rationalist reconfiguration of Judaism that spurred intense scholarly debate throughout the Middle Ages and beyond, not to mention some of medieval Judaism's most vituperative intra- and intercommunal disputes.[12] Its most characteristic feature, however, was the poetry sponsored by a class of Jewish courtiers (some scholars and poets themselves) who cultivated a courtier culture that mirrored the tendencies and tastes of the Muslim courts at which they worked.[13]

Andalusian Jewry suffered a sudden demise in the mid-twelfth century when a fierce North African Berber tribe arrived in al-Andalus to counter an intense and growing Christian threat to

[9] Moshe Idel, "Jewish Philosophy and Kabbalah in Spain," in *Sephardic and Mizrahi Jewry: From the Golden Age of Spain to Modern Times*, ed. Zohar Zion (New York: New York University Press, 2005), 120–21.

[10] This usage endures despite growing awareness of problems that attend this designation, not to mention its growing politicization. See Mark R. Cohen, *Under Crescent and Cross: The Jews in the Middle Ages* (Princeton: Princeton University Press, 1994), 3–14.

[11] Raymond Scheindlin, "Merchants and Intellectuals, Rabbis and Poets: Judeo-Arabic Culture in the Golden Age of Islam," in *Cultures of the Jews: A New History*, ed. David Biale (New York: Schocken, 2002), 313–86.

[12] For controversy over Maimonideanism, see Bernard Septimus, *Hispano-Jewish Culture in Transition: The Career and Controversies of Ramah* (Cambridge, MA: Harvard University Press, 1982).

[13] For courtier culture (and its critics), see Bezalel Safran, "Bahya Ibn Paquda's Attitude Toward the Courtier Class," in *Studies in Medieval Jewish History and Literature*, ed. Isadore Twersky (Cambridge, MA: Harvard University Press, 1979), 154–69.

Islam's Iberian citadels. The Almohads offered Jews a choice between death, apostasy, or escape. While some, like the family of the then-young Moses ben Maimon (Maimonides), sought asylum elsewhere in the "abode of Islam," most headed north to the steadily expanding domain of Iberian Christendom, with the scholars among them arriving with a large body of mainly Judeo-Arabic writings in hand. Once translated into Hebrew, these works, and some of the conflicting intellectual ideals that they embodied, won a fresh lease on life in Jewish communities along Christendom's Mediterranean littoral where, however, they developed along new lines.

The second era of Hispano-Jewish intellectual efflorescence evolved on the Christian side of the Iberian Peninsula against the backdrop of the Christian military successes that transformed Jewish life along the ever-shifting *Reconquista* frontier.[14] Its main feature was the absorption, adaptation, and further development of mystical (kabbalistic) teachings that had come to Spain from southern France at the turn of the twelfth century. Unfolding in several stages, Spanish Kabbalah won the allegiance of important segments of Sephardic Jewry's intellectual elite. It reached its zenith in the later thirteenth century in Castile with the appearance of writings that became the core of theosophical-theurgic Kabbalah's canonical text, *Sefer Ha-Zohar* (The Book of Splendor).[15]

A less heralded but no less monumental dimension of creativity during this second period of accelerated intellectual activity were the many talmudic commentaries, rabbinic responsa, and legal codes produced by a succession of towering rabbinic scholars that constitute one of the foremost accomplishments of medieval Sephardic literature, quantitatively and qualitatively. The feats of fastidious talmudic exegesis and acute halakhic analysis performed by such figures as the mid-thirteenth-century talmudist, biblical commentator, and kabbalist Moses ben Nahman (Nahmanides); his cousin Jonah Gerondi, and members of Nahmanides' school active through the first three quarters of the fourteenth century (like

---

[14] Jonathan Ray, *The Sephardic Frontier: The Reconquista and the Jewish Community in Medieval Iberia* (Ithaca, N.Y.: Cornell University Press, 2006).

[15] Moshe Idel, "The Kabbalah's 'Window of Opportunities,' 1270–1290," in *Me'ah She'arim: Studies in Medieval Jewish Spiritual Life in Memory of Isadore Twersky*, ed. Ezra Fleischer, et. al. (Jerusalem: Magnes Press, 2001), 171–208 (English section).

Solomon ben Adret, Yom Tov ben Abraham of Seville, and Nissim Gerondi) go unregistered in standard accounts of the period.[16]

Though the dynamism of Sephardic learning largely dissipated in the course of the dire fourteenth century (not least due to the violence, famines, and plagues that increasingly encircled Spain's Jews in the second half of the century), some large-scale achievements and noteworthy innovations appeared. For example, the first half of the century saw the appearance of the most important Jewish legal code of the later Middle Ages, 'Arba'ah Turim ("The Four Rows"), composed by Jacob ben Asher, an Ashkenazic immigrant to Spain. Far less influential, but significant in its own way, was the composition of a series of commentaries on the *Commentary on the Torah* of Abraham ibn Ezra, capstone of the Andalusi-Jewish exegetical tradition. This Spanish development stood at the center of a larger fourteenth-century "Ibn Ezra Renaissance."[17]

Rationalism and Its Discontents

With some salient background in hand, we begin our survey of Sephardic scholarship in the century after 1391 with a topic that bedeviled many a medieval scholar, Jewish or otherwise: the relationship between religion and reason, or faith and science.

From the twelfth century on, Jewish reflections on the fraught question of the relationship between Jewish revelation and the Greco-Arabic philosophic tradition took their point of departure from the far-reaching but in some ways enigmatic legacy of Maimonides. Discord over philosophy first entered Europe's Jewish communities by way of a skirmish over Maimonidean eschatology initiated in Maimonides' lifetime by the Castilian talmudist, Meir

---

[16] Yisrael M. Ta-Shma, "Halakhah, Kabbalah, and Philosophy in Christian Spain (A Critique of *A History of the Jews in Christian Spain*)," *The Hebrew Law Annual* 18/19 (1992–94): 479–95 (Hebrew).

[17] Alexander Altmann, "Moses Narboni's 'Epistle on *Shi'ur Qoma*," in *Jewish Medieval and Renaissance Studies*, ed. Alexander Altmann (Cambridge, MA: Harvard University Press, 1967), 241. For the phenomenon in detail, see Uriel Simon, "Interpreting the Interpreter: Supercommentaries on Ibn Ezra's Commentaries," in *Rabbi Abraham Ibn Ezra: Studies in the Writings of a Twelfth-Century Polymath*, ed. Isadore Twersky and Jay M. Harris (Cambridge, MA: Harvard University Center for Jewish Studies, 1993), 86–128.

Halevi Abulafia. Subsequently, Spanish figures assumed pivotal roles in major disputes over Maimonideanism in the 1230s and over philosophy's religious acceptability in the early 1300s. Concern with philosophy's ostensibly corrosive effects only intensified with the unprecedented mass defections from Judaism around the turn of the fifteenth century. Meanwhile, Ibero-Jewish thinkers continued to ruminate on conundrums that the controversies left in abeyance, with many finding in favor of Greco-Arabic philosophy's basic incompatibility with fundaments of Judaism and its generally subversive effect.[18]

One who decried a range of lapses that he deemed the ultimate cause of Sephardic Jews' recent travails was Solomon Alami, an early fifteenth-century moralist. Among others, Alami excoriated those who read the Torah through the distorting lens of "Greek constructs" as well as the self-styled savants who seemingly held that "Aristotle's [rational] inquiry confers upon us a greater benefit than did Moses with his Torah." He also decried rich courtiers who kept Jewish sages on meager rations while evincing no desire to dedicate their children to the "service of the Torah."[19] Given the heavy losses and dislocation suffered by Spanish Jews in the wake of the calamity of 1391, some of these censures may seem somewhat unjust. There could have been few surpluses to sustain scholars, certainly not on the scale of their Christian counterparts. At any rate, when Castile's Jewish leadership convened in Valladolid in 1432 and issued a series of communal statutes, the first problem addressed was the need to support Jewish learning from the elementary level through the advanced rabbinic academies (*yeshivot*).[20]

Of course, moralists tend to overstate the flaws of their flocks, the better to flay them, so Alami's self-criticisms, and especially his contrasting praises of Christian religio-cultural virtues like

[18] See the overview in Eric Lawee, "'The Good We Accept and the Bad We Do Not': Aspects of Isaac Abarbanel's Stance Towards Maimonides," in *Be'erot Yitzhak: Studies in Memory of Isadore Twersky*, ed. Jay Harris (Cambridge, MA: Harvard University Center for Jewish Studies, 2005), 119–60.

[19] Solomon Alami, *'Iggeret Musar* (Epistle of Admonition), ed. A. M. Haberman (Jerusalem: Mossad HaRav Kook, 1946), 41, 48. For a loose English rendering, see Nahum N. Glatzer, *Faith and Knowledge: The Jew in the Medieval World* (Boston: Beacon Press, 1963), 121–23.
20 Baer, *A History*, 2:261–62.

attentiveness at sermons, invite suspicions of hyperbole.[21] Yet many of his denunciations, including the ones focused on philosophy's deleterious impact, echo in later Ibero-Jewish writings. In the mid-fifteenth century, Hayyim ibn Musa complained of preachers who quoted philosophic sources in sermons while leaving the Torah on the reading stand "like a dejected woman . . . without paying her further heed." Joseph Yavetz, himself a preacher, writing after 1492, condemned a long litany of intellectual and religious impairments, with philosophy's corrosive influence topping his list.[22]

To be sure, not all agreed that Sephardic Jewry's embrace of "profane sciences" was a cause of spiritual enfeeblement. Solomon Alami's contemporary, Leon Joseph, a scholar and physician in Perpignan (then part of the Spanish Crown of Aragon), deplored the fact that scientific study was repressed in the Jewish community, a policy he saw as posing a grave threat to Judaism's religious viability. That Leon converted to Christianity at the very end of his life could only have confirmed Alami's worst fears.[23]

Offering a trenchant response to the questions that swirled amidst the conflicting claims on the role of science in Jewish life was Hasdai Crescas, father of one of the murdered during the 1391 riots, who devoted great energy in their aftermath to the rehabilitation of Aragon's decimated communities. If the two decades after 1391 were understandably bereft of much by way of outstanding scholarly achievement, philosophic or otherwise, Crescas' 'Or 'Adonai, a tome

---

[21] Eleazar Gutwirth, "Italy or Spain? The Theme of Jewish Eloquence in *Shevet Yehudah*," in *Daniel Karpi Jubilee Volume* (Tel Aviv: Tel Aviv University, 1996), 53, suggests there is no reason to accept Alami's "absurd statement" implying that all Jews slept or talked through sermons while Christians sat in respectful silence. At the same time, we must heed the observation that a moralist's effectiveness in adducing laudatory examples from a rival community depends upon arousing in his audience "an acceptance of verisimilitude." (Marc Saperstein, "Christians and Jews—Some Positive Images," *Harvard Theological Review* 79 [1986]: 241-42)

[22] *Sefer magen va-romah, ve-'igeret li-veno*, facsimile edition of Adolf Posnanski's manuscript (Jerusalem, 1969), 117-18, translated in Marc Saperstein, "Sermons as Evidence for the Popularization of Philosophy in Fifteenth-Century Spain," in *"Your Voice Like a Ram's Horn": Themes and Texts in Traditional Jewish Preaching* (Cincinnati: Hebrew Union College Press, 1996), 386; Gedaliyah Nigal, "The Opinions of R. Joseph Yawetz on Philosophy, Torah and Commandments," *Eshel Beer Sheva* 1 (1976): 258–87 (Hebrew).

[23] Luis García-Ballester, Lola Ferre, and Eduard Feliu, "Jewish Appreciation of Fourteenth-Century Scholastic Medicine," *Osiris 6 (2nd Series), Renaissance Medical Learning: Evolution of a Tradition*, ed. Michael R. McVaugh and Nancy G. Siraisi (1990): 93–101.

long in the making that appeared in 1410, not long before his death, resoundingly punctured the silence. In it, Crescas offered a bold critique of Aristotelianism and an original alternative to Maimonides' intellectualist Judaism that unquestionably marked a major contribution to Jewish thought.[24] While Crescas' anti-Aristotelian critique served the theological aim of overturning the foundations upon which Maimonidean thought largely rested, it yielded no search for scientific alternatives. Still, in ways that startle, it anticipated aspects of a great break between modern and premodern thought that was as yet centuries away. Due to his possible influence on such diverse later thinkers as Pico della Mirandola in the Renaissance and Spinoza in the Enlightenment, Crescas has even been seen as a turning point in the history of science, though the possibility that some of his ideas trace to new physical theories being developed by Christians at the University of Paris must be borne in mind.[25] If parts of his theology, like his deterministic understanding of human free will, were roundly rejected by later Sephardic scholars,[26] his thought's cogency and originality remain.

Despite Crescas' attempt to demolish pillars of Jewish rationalism, anti-philosophic sentiment did not dominate the fifteenth-century Sephardic intellectual scene.[27] Indeed, philosophic learning was pursued and Maimonidean studies (and in many cases strong Maimonidean allegiances) persisted through 1492. Consider that all four commentaries in the still-standard printed edition of

---

[24] An overview is Daniel J. Lasker, "Chasdai Crescas," in *History of Jewish Philosophy*, ed. Daniel H. Frank and Oliver Leaman (London: Routledge, 1997), 399–414. For Crescas' critique of Maimonides, see, e.g., Warren Zeev Harvey, "Crescas versus Maimonides on Knowledge and Pleasure," in *A Straight Path: Studies in Medieval Philosophy and Culture: Essays in Honor of Arthur Hyman*, ed. Ruth Link-Salinger, et al. (Washington, D.C.: Catholic University of America Press, 1988), 111–23. The classic study of his anti-Aristotelian assault is Harry A. Wolfson, *Crescas' Critique of Aristotle* (Cambridge, MA: Harvard University Press, 1929).

[25] Warren Zeev Harvey, *Physics and Metaphysics in Hasdai Crescas* (Amsterdam: J.C. Gieben, 1998), 23; James T. Robinson, "Hasdai Crescas and Anti-Aristotelianism," in *The Cambridge Companion to Medieval Jewish Philosophy*, ed. Daniel H Frank and Oliver Leaman (Cambridge: Cambridge University Press, 2003), 392, 407.

[26] Lasker, "Chasdai Crescas," 345; Seymour Feldman, "A Debate Concerning Determinism in Late Medieval Jewish Philosophy," *Proceedings of the American Academy for Jewish Research* 51 (1984): 15–54.

[27] Ari Ackerman, "Jewish Philosophy and the Jewish-Christian Debate," in *The Cambridge Companion to Medieval Jewish Philosophy*, 376.

Maimonides' theological *magnum opus, The Guide of the Perplexed,* bear a post-1391 Sephardic stamp. Characterizing the three by playing on the "four sons" motif of the Passover Haggadah, the seventeenth-century polymath Joseph Solomon Delmedigo likened the work of Asher Crescas to that of the "simple" son; Shem Tov ben Joseph to the "wise" son, and Profiat Duran to the "one who does not ask" questions explicitly but who nevertheless "answers well, with brevity and perspicuity," making him "prince of the [*Guide*] commentators."²⁸ As for the fourth commentary in the standard edition, by Isaac Abarbanel (or Abravanel), though it only reached its final form in Italy after 1492, its theological moorings, interpretive approach and, it would seem, initial literary expression, reflect Abarbanel's five and a half Iberian decades, including a Spanish sojourn from 1483 to 1492.²⁹

Whole chapters in fifteenth-century Sephardic Maimonidean interpretation await exploration. Unpublished commentaries by Shem Tov's father, Joseph, on *Guide,* I, 68 and by Joseph's brother, Isaac, on the whole of the *Guide's* lengthy first part serve as cases in point, but even Spanish *Guide* commentaries long in print remain largely *terra incognita.* This neglect is regrettable, since these works open a window on competing Sephardic spiritual stances prior to 1492 and on the most poignant religio-cultural concerns of the era, including ruminations over the Jewish legal requirement to relinquish one's life rather than submit to Christian conversionary pressure.³⁰

To sample the full range of late medieval Sephardic dialogue with Maimonides, one must look beyond formal *Guide* commentaries to a diversity of at times recalcitrant literary media. Writing on the

---

²⁸ *Ha-sofeh me-eres hagar* 4 (1915): 127, translated in Ephraim Fischoff, "The Life and Works of Profiat Duran Efodi with Especial Reference to the Commentary on the Moreh," Ph. D. diss., Cincinnati, Hebrew Union College, 1929, 64 (as cited in Maud Natasha Kozodoy, "A Study of the Life and Works of Profiat Duran," Ph. D. diss., New York, The Jewish Theological Seminary of America, 2006, 152 n. 1). Delmedigo's candidate for the fourth "wicked" son, Moses Narboni, though of southern French origin, composed important works, including his *Guide* commentary in Spain.

²⁹ See my "The Good We Accept," especially 123-25.

³⁰ Bernard Septimus, "Narboni and Shem Tov on Martyrdom," in *Studies in Medieval Jewish History and Literature II,* ed. Isadore Twersky (Cambridge, MA: Harvard University Press, 1984), 447–55.

eve of the expulsion, Abraham Shalom parried scholarly criticisms of Maimonides made by Crescas and others in a commentary on non-legal rabbinic dicta, *Neveh Shalom* (*Abode of Peace*). His contemporary, Abraham Bibago, defended Maimonides from the remonstrations of self-proclaimed "pious ones" in his tract on Jewish dogma, *Derekh 'Emunah* (*Way of Faith*). Isaac Abarbanel variously built on and refuted Maimonidean teachings on miracles, prophetology, and political theory in biblical commentaries written after his arrival in Spain in early 1480s, an engagement with Maimonidean thought that continued and, if anything, intensified, in Italy after 1492.[31] Others from the generation of the expulsion, having taken refuge in Ottoman lands, similarly pursued the Sephardic tradition of ruminating on reason's role in the well lived religious life.[32]

As three generations of scholars from the Ibn Shem Tov clan illustrate, the late medieval Sephardic colloquy on Maimonides could be a family affair that ran the gamut in both substance and tone. Shem Tov ibn Shem Tov, who reached his age of majority around 1391, championed kabbalistic answers to the religious questions that exercised him. While his *Sefer 'Emunot* (*Book of Beliefs*) had no discernible influence in Spain through 1492, with its appeal only coming several decades later,[33] its full-throated assault on philosophy and its foremost Jewish hero, Maimonides, certainly reverberated in the minds of his intellectually oriented sons. The older son, Joseph, retained elements of his father's critique of Maimonidean intellectualism, arguing philosophy's ultimate subordination to

---

[31] Herbert Davidson, *The Philosophy of Abraham Shalom: A Fifteenth-Century Exposition and Defense of Maimonides* (Berkeley: University of California Press, 1964); Joseph Hacker, "The Role of Abraham Bibago in the Polemic on the Place of Philosophy in Jewish Life in Spain in the Fifteenth Century," *Proceedings of the Fifth World Congress of Jewish Studies*, III (Jerusalem, 1972), 156-58 (Hebrew); Lawee, "The Good We Accept."

[32] Joseph Hacker, "The Intellectual Activity of the Jews of the Ottoman Empire During the Sixteenth and Seventeenth Centuries," in *Jewish Thought in the Seventeenth Century*, ed. Isadore Twersky and Bernard Septimus (Cambridge, MA: Harvard University Press, 1987), 116–20.

[33] Moshe Idel, "Man as the 'Possible' Entity in Some Jewish and Renaissance Sources," in *Hebraica Veritas?: Christian Hebraists and the Study of Judaism in Early Modern Europe*, ed. Allison P. Coudert and Jeffrey S. Shoulson (Philadelphia: University of Pennsylvania Press, 2004), 38.

faith.[34] At the same time, he paid rational religion its due in ways reminiscent of the synthesis between faith and reason effected by the great thirteenth-century Christian thinker, Thomas Aquinas. The younger son, Isaac, swore fealty to Maimonides, but only after recasting his ideas in traditionalist fifteenth-century Sephardic molds. As for Shem Tov ben Joseph, his reliance on the radically philosophic fourteenth-century *Guide* interpreter, Moses Narboni, indicates that he entertained (while not always accepting) a more Aristotelian understanding of Maimonides' ideas.[35] By contrast, Narboni served as the principal nemesis to Shem Tov's uncle, Isaac, in his *Guide* commentary.

If we seek to fill out the diverse curiosities and aptitudes represented by the last two generations of Ibn Shem Tovs, we would note Isaac's commentaries on Arabic philosophic and theological writings, mainly those of Averroes; Joseph's biblical and rabbinic commentaries, authorship of the first Hebrew preaching manual (*'En Ha-Qore; Eye of the Reader*) and first full-length Hebrew commentary on Aristotle's *Ethics*, and his theological tome *Kevod 'Elohim* (Glory of the Lord), which fashioned a Jewish view of ultimate human happiness in the course of a running dialogue with Aristotle's account; and Shem Tov ben Joseph's homilies on the Torah, commentary on the Mishnaic tractate *'Avot*, and numerous philosophical writings.[36] If we then recall the anti-philosophic kabbalism of the family patriarch, these figures born of a single family handsomely identify the highly diverse hues of late medieval Sephardic thought. They also buttress the view that post-1391 Sephardic scholarship was not nearly as senescent as is usually

---

[34] Jean-Pierre Rothschild, "Le dessein philosophique de Joseph Ibn Shem Tob (*flor.* 1442–1455)," *Revue des Études juives* 162 (2003): 97–122.

[35] Maurice R. Hayoun, *Moshe Narboni* (Tubingen: TCB Mohr, 1986), 91–98. (For an example of Shem Tov's reliance on Moses that illustrates his tendency to recast his predecessor's radical ideas in more conservative terms, see the article by Septimus cited above, n.30).

[36] For Joseph's preaching manual, see Marc Saperstein, *Jewish Preaching 1200–1800: An Anthology* (New Haven: Yale University Press, 1989), 68, 387–92. For his engagement with the *Ethics* and theology, see Hava Tirosh-Samuelson, *Happiness in Premodern Judaism: Virtue, Knowledge, and Well-Being* (Cincinnati: Hebrew Union College Press, 2003), 397–411; Ruth Birnbaum, *An Exposition of Joseph Ibn Shem Tov's Kevod Elohim (The Glory of God), a Fifteenth-Century Philosophical Work on the Summum Bonum of Man and the True Happiness* (Lewiston, N.Y.: E. Mellen Press, 2001).

claimed. In particular, Joseph ibn Shem Tov emerges as a figure of broad erudition and an intellectually innovating spirit that puts one in mind of figures from earlier, more celebrated, eras of Sephardic learning. Add to this his role as physician and auditor of accounts at the Castilian courts of John II and Henry IV and he fits snugly into that celebrated Sephardic type mentioned earlier, the scholar-courtier seeking to make his way amid court intrigue and political manipulations while pursuing contemplation. In Joseph's case, he also attempted to steer a course within a diversity of intellectual streams in response to ideas and texts (like Aristotle's Ethics) ascendant in Gentile society.[37]

Crisis and Creativity: Two Case Studies

Exemplifying, amidst the desolate shadows of 1391, a characteristic Sephardic fusion of broad learning and significant literary accomplishment were two figures associated with Hasdai Crescas. One was Profiat Duran, whose Hebrew name was Isaac ben Moses Halevi but who wrote under the *nom de plume* "Efodi," while the other was Joseph Albo, one of several defenders of Judaism at the Disputation of Tortosa.

Duran wrestled with the spiritual implications of the forced conversions imposed on so many Spanish Jews, and for good reason. From 1391 until (it appears) the end of his life some two and a half decades later, he lived as a forcibly baptized Jew bearing the Christian name Honoratus de Bonafide. Under such circumstances, time-honored religious issues, such as the relative importance of intention versus deed in religious life, took on a dreadful salience. Other scholars in Crescas' orbit, like Mattathias Yizhari and Zerahiyah Halevi, explored them as well, lending additional elements of vibrancy to a post-1391 religio-intellectual landscape often seen as utterly desolate.[38]

---

[37] On the larger trend, see A. R. D. Pagden, "The Diffusion of Aristotle's Moral Philosophy in Spain, CA. 1400 - CA. 1600," *Traditio* 31 (1975): 287–313.

[38] For their soteriology, see Eric Lawee, "The Path to Felicity: Teachings and Tensions in *'Even Shetiyyah* of Abraham Ben Judah, Disciple of Hasdai Crescas," *Mediaeval Studies* 59 (1997): 183–223 and bibliography cited there.

The scope of Duran's corpus is impressive. It spans philosophy with a Maimonidean bent (his *Guide* commentary has already been mentioned); anti-Christian polemic; astronomy, historical chronicle, biblical interpretation, and grammar. In the introduction to his grammatical work *Ma'aseh 'Efod* (Work of the Efod), Duran advanced a "biblicist" vision of Jewish spirituality that viewed engagement with scripture at any level as meritorious and engagement with it at the highest level as supreme.[39] In so doing, he challenged the main understandings of the path to salvation propounded by Jewish thinkers in later medieval times, which variously held Talmud study or philosophic speculation or engagement with kabbalistic ideas to be the instrument through which ultimate bliss was attained.

While some of Duran's works represent conventional engagements with earlier strata of medieval Jewish tradition, others reflect new turns in southern Mediterranean Jewish culture. One is his precocious if largely tacit utilization of Christian sources, both ancient and medieval, including scholastic ones. It presages a major trend in pre-1492 Sephardic thought and literature.[40] Another is his lost "Memoir of Persecutions," a chronicle later used by several historically attuned post-expulsion Sephardic writers, that reflects a burgeoning Sephardic interest in history, and augurs the explosion of Sephardic historiography after 1492.[41] Attention has also been

---

[39] Frank Talmage, "Keep Your Sons from Scripture: The Bible in Medieval Jewish Scholarship and Spirituality," in *Understanding Scripture: Explorations of Jewish and Christian Traditions of Interpretation*, ed. Clemens Thoma and Michael Wyschogrod (New York: Paulist Press, 1987), 89-93.

[40] On this trend, see below. For Duran, see, e.g., Irene E. Zwiep, "Jewish Scholarship and Christian Tradition in Late-Medieval Catalonia: Profiat Duran on the Art of Memory," in *Hebrew Scholarship and the Medieval World*, ed. Nicholas de Lange (New York: Cambridge University Press, 2001), 224–39.

[41] Frank Talmage, "The Polemical Writings of Profiat Duran," in *Apples of Gold in Settings of Silver: Studies in Medieval Jewish Exegesis and Polemics*, ed. Barry Dov Walfish (Toronto: Pontifical Institute of Mediaeval Studies, 1999), 283. On the larger phenomenon, see Ram Ben-Shalom, *Facing Christian Culture: Historical Consciousness and Images of the Past among the Jews of Spain and Southern France during the Middle Ages* (Jerusalem: Ben-Zvi Institute / The Hebrew University of Jerusalem, 2006) (Hebrew). For post-1492 historiography, see Yosef Hayim Yerushalmi, *Zakhor: Jewish History and Jewish Memory* (New York: Schocken, 1982), 57–69.

drawn to novel "realistic" elements that Duran infiltrated into his Bible exegesis.[42]

Finally, Duran at times anticipated post-medieval habits of mind, most notably the distinctive sort of historical thinking prized by Renaissance humanists, who left an ever greater impress on Iberian scholarship over the course of the fifteenth century.[43] He brilliantly displayed a well-honed capacity for such thinking that combined awareness of evidence with appreciation of temporal perspective, interest in causation, and an ability to examine the past on its own terms, in an anti-Christian tract *Kelimmat ha-Goyim* (*Shame of the Gentiles*). Joined with his historical learning, Duran's powers of philological, chronological, and textual criticism and sense of anachronism allowed him to advance trenchant arguments about ways in which the Christianity of his day diverged from the original version of the religion established by Jesus and his disciples. Duran traced Christianity's evolution over time, and Jesus' and his disciples' own early misconceptions of the Judaism into which they were born, with the aim of highlighting what he took to be the welter of confusion and falsification, witting or otherwise, that undermined the medieval Church's insistence on the inviolability of such beliefs as the trinity and incarnation and such core institutions as the papacy and clerical celibacy.[44] Here was a breakthrough in Jewish approaches to Christianity that showed a profound awareness of Christian sources, including the New Testament, and that reflected not only Duran's outstanding qualities as a thinker and author but also the famously characteristic "cultural breadth and sophistication of Spanish Jewry."[45] Innovations such as these, invariably heralded when they appear in earlier periods of Sephardic history, too often

[42] Eleazar Gutwirth, "Duran on Ahitophel: The Practice of Jewish History in Late Medieval Spain," *Jewish History* 4 (1989): 59.

[43] Jeremy N. H. Lawrance, "Humanism in the Iberian Peninsula," in *The Impact of Humanism on Western Europe*, ed. Anthony Goodman and Angus MacKay (London: Longman, 1990), 220–58.

[44] Eleazar Gutwirth, "History and Apologetics in XVth Century Hispano-Jewish Thought," *Helmantica* 35 (1984): 234–38; Talmage, "The Polemical Writings," 291-97.

[45] Drawing on formulations regarding Duran's portrait of Jesus found in David Berger, "On the Uses of History in Medieval Jewish Polemic Against Christianity: The Quest for the Historical Jesus," in *Jewish History and Jewish Memory: Essays in Honor of Yosef Hayim Yerushalmi*, eds. Elisheva Carlebach, John M. Efron, and David N. Myers (Hanover: Brandeis University Press, 1998), 30.

go unheeded when appearing during the period of ostensible intellectual breakdown after 1391.

Like Duran, Joseph Albo has not been given his due. Often depicted as a supreme exemplar of the superficial epigone said to prevail in late medieval Sepharad,[46] Albo's legacy is only slowly coming to be seen in a far more auspicious light. Deferring until our conclusion discussion of the stress on originality or lack thereof found in many adverse judgments of Albo, we may note the manner in which his *Sefer Ha-'Iqqarim* (*Book of Roots*) makes a soft-spoken case for inquiry into religious faith in a manner that reflects "delicacy and courage."[47] Then too, Albo's writing style, long seen as obliviously contradictory, now commends itself (at least to some) as a continuation of the sort of carefully crafted esoteric discourse cultivated by Maimonides.[48] Albo's status as an important legal theorist who explored basic concepts in the history of western thought like "natural law" (a term he introduced into Jewish literature)[49] is secure. Though it has perhaps been held against him, it might be noted also that Albo's work was popular from the moment it appeared, apparently responding to the deepest concerns of fifteenth-century Spanish Jews. It offers further evidence, then, of Sephardic thought's adroitness as it at once tackled the crises occasioned by the 1391 catastrophe while continuing to address issues that had occupied Sephardic theologians from the Andalusian period on.

---

[46] Isaac Husik, *A History of Mediaeval Jewish Philosophy* (New York: Macmillan, 1916), 406; Julius Guttmann, *Philosophies of Judaism: The History of Jewish Philosophy from Biblical Times to Franz Rosenzweig*, trans. David W. Silverman (New York: Schocken, 1973), 275, 281. (The former deems Albo's philosophizing "of little importance"; the latter speaks of his "cleverness rather than profundity".)

[47] Ralph Lerner, *Maimonides' Empire of Light: Popular Enlightenment in an Age of Belief* (Chicago: University of Chicago Press, 2000), 95.

[48] A classic study is Leo Strauss, *Persecution and the Art of Writing* (Westport, CT: Greenwood Press, 1973). For Albo, see Dov Schwartz, *Contradiction and Concealment in Medieval Jewish Thought* (Ramat Gan: Bar-Ilan University, 2002), 182–217 (Hebrew); Dror Ehrlich, *The Thought of R. Joseph Albo: Esoteric Writing in the Late Middle Ages* (Ramat-Gan: Bar-Ilan University Press, 2009) (Hebrew).

[49] Dror Ehrlich, "A Reassessment of Natural Law in Rabbi Joseph Albo's 'Book of Principles,'" *Hebraic Political Studies* 1 (2006): 413–39 and the literature cited there.

Encountering Christian Culture

Among other things, Duran and Albo played a role in responding to Spanish Christendom's increasingly successful conversionary campaigns and the missionizing arguments put in their service,[50] with Duran contributing two major entries to a genre cultivated by Sephardic scholars in the fifteenth century as never before: anti-Christian polemic. In addition to *Kelimmat ha-Goyim*, discussed above, he wrote an ironic broadside entitled *'Al Tehi Ka-'Avotekha* (*Be Not Like Your Fathers*). In it, he lampooned Christian "mysteries sublime" that overpowered "this humble brain of mine."[51]

Other Sephardic savants also insisted on Christianity's alleged irrationality. Hasdai Crescas authored two anti-Christian works in Catalan. In one, translated into Hebrew under the title *Bittul 'Iqqarei Ha-Nosrim* (*Refutation of the Christian Principles*), he deployed logical-philosophical principles to subvert such Christian doctrines as original sin, trinity, incarnation, and the virgin birth.[52] Entering the polemical fray around mid-century, Hayyim ibn Musa, while assaying mainly exegetical apologies in his *Magen va-Romah* (*Shield and Sword*), reprised the claim of Judaism's superior rationality. To a Christian interlocutor's charge that Jews possessed only a single work of theology, Maimonides' *Guide*, whereas Christians had innumerable such tracts, Ibn Musa rejoined that Jews could suffice with a single *page* of theology upon which would appear Maimonides' "thirteen principles of faith." By contrast, the stacks of

[50] Daniel J. Lasker, "The Impact of Christianity on Late Iberian Jewish Philosophy," in *Iberia and Beyond: Hispanic Jews Between Cultures*, ed. Bernard Dov Cooperman (Newark: University of Delaware Press, 1998), 178–82.

[51] Frank Talmage, *The Polemical Writings of Profiat Duran* (Jerusalem: Zalman Shazar, 1981), 73 (Hebrew), cited according to Talmage's rather free translation in "The Francesc de Sant Jordi-Solomon Bonafed Letters," in *Studies in Medieval Jewish History and Literature*, ed. Isadore Twersky (Cambridge, MA: Harvard University Press, 1979), 341. For a fuller English version of Duran's work, see Franz Kobler, *Letters of Jews Through the Ages: From Biblical Times to the Middle of the Eighteenth Century*, 2 vols. (London: Ararat Publishing Society, 1952), 1:276–82. For the work's literary character, see Maud Kozodoy, "The Hebrew Bible as Weapon of Faith in Late Medieval Iberia: Irony, Satire, and Scriptural Allusion in Profiat Duran's *Al Tehi ka-Avotekha*," *Jewish Studies Quarterly* 18 (2011): 185-201.

[52] *The Refutation of the Christian Principles*, trans. with an introduction and notes by Daniel J. Lasker (Albany: State University of New York, 1992). The title is of the Hebrew translation made in the mid-fifteenth century by Joseph Ibn Shem Tov, this being the only version of the work to have survived.

Latin tomes reflected the futile Christian effort to defend irrational beliefs that nobody raised in the Torah, "which is far removed from these beliefs," could accept.[53]

The context for the surge in post-1391 polemics was grim.[54] In his polemical work, 'Even Bohan (Touchstone), begun before 1391 and completed in 1405, Shem Tov ben Shaprut of Tudela bemoaned the "turbulent times" as manifested in the "desertion of Judaism by many Jews," some of whom persecuted their former coreligionists "by encouraging Christians to debate with them." In his Hebrew translation of Crescas' Refutation, Joseph ibn Shem Tov spoke of the "rigor of exile," with enemies "crushing us every day . . . saying: 'Our fathers inherited naught but lies.'"[55] Even allowing for literary tropes common to the genre, such passages impart the oppressive reality many late medieval Sephardim perceived as they gazed out at Spanish Christendom.

Yet detaching ourselves from their dolorous circumstances, we can appreciate post-1391 polemics as works of the mind and then concur with Robert Chazan's rejection of the criticism that medieval polemics are invariably "intellectually sterile and vapid."[56] Indeed, in their ensemble, the fifteenth-century Sephardic polemics rose to new creative heights, not least in their use of argumentative techniques reliant on a mastery of philosophic ideas and New Testament and later Christian literature.[57] In Crescas and Duran, Sepharad laid

---

[53] Magen va-romah, 133. The passage is cited in Daniel J. Lasker, Jewish Philosophical Polemics Against Christianity in the Middle Ages, 2nd ed. (Oxford: The Littman Library of Jewish Civilization, 2007), 27.

[54] Though the existence of private interfaith wrangles taking place in a relatively tolerant atmosphere should be noted. See Ram Ben-Shalom, "Between Official and Private Dispute: The Case of Christian Spain and Provence in the Late Middle Ages," AJS Review 27 (2003): 23–71 (29–35, 57–61, 68–69 for Sephardic participants in such relatively cordial exchanges).

[55] Libby Garshowitz, "Shem Tov Ben Isaac Ibn Shaprut's Gospel of Matthew," in Jewish History 6 (The Frank Talmage Memorial Volume), ed. Barry Walfish, 2 vols. (Haifa: Haifa University Press, 1992), 297 (311 n. 3 for the work's onset before 1391 and completion in 1405); Refutation (above, n. 52), 19.

[56] Robert Chazan, Fashioning Jewish Identity in Medieval Western Christendom (New York: Cambridge University Press, 2004), 18.

[57] Duran's familiarity with Christian sources has already been mentioned. Another example is Shem Tov Ibn Shaprut's recording of a Hebrew version of the Gospel of Matthew, the first complete one found in Hebrew literature. See Garshowitz, "ShemṬov Ben Isaac," 297-310.

claim to the best philosophical anti-Christian polemicists Judaism ever produced.

Fifteenth-century Spain saw the Jewish heyday of another genre spurred in some measure by the pressure emanating from Christian society: works of dogmatic theology. Not long before 1391, the presiding rabbinic presence in Aragon, Nissim Gerondi, gave renewed attention to questions left in abeyance since Maimonides' inauguration of Jewish creed-formulation two centuries earlier, and Hasdai Crescas and Simon ben Zemah Duran of Mallorca (by then resident in Algiers) pursued the subject with systematic gusto, followed especially by Albo, Bibago, and Abarbanel.[58] Some have seen this surge in dogmatic theology as an endeavor executed by scholars with little innate interest in the subject who felt compelled to engage in it due to the post-1391 historical crisis; yet stated as such this view is untenable. As noted, the seeds of the dogmatic turn were planted by Nissim Gerondi before 1391. More to the point, there is no evidence that the rabbis who invested vast amounts of intellectual energy in the project of dogmatic theology saw it as an imposition. It would be foolish to deny the salience of historical circumstance in explaining the sudden stress on creed. At the same time, there is no evidence to suggest that the new catechisms of the fifteenth century were ever used to, say, decide the religious status of *conversos*. These studies clearly transcend the issue of mass conversion and Christian polemic, important as both factors may have been in stimulating them. Even if modern sensibilities recoil from such exercises, they should not be allowed to obscure the profound intellectual dimensions of an undertaking in which ideas interlace with historical contingencies and polemical exigencies in complex ways.

If late medieval Spanish Christendom posed powerful challenges to Jews, it also modeled religious mores that some rabbis deemed worthy of emulation. Seeking to buttress his biblicist spiritual ideal, Profiat Duran, lamenting what he took to be Jewish neglect of Bible and biblically-based prayer, invoked, without naming names, "a great

---

[58] Menachem Kellner, *Dogma in Medieval Jewish Thought: From Maimonides to Abravanel* (Oxford: Oxford University Press, 1986). I have excluded Simon ben Zemah and figures like him who fled or voluntarily departed Spain after 1391 from consideration in this article, even though their thought and writings fall largely or wholly within a Sephardic framework.

sage of the Romans" whose dream led him to shun philosophic texts in favor of single-minded devotion to holy writ. The allusion here is to Jerome's epistle to Eustochium, commonly known as "Jerome's dream."[59] Joseph ibn Shem Tov, now surveying contemporary Christian society, observed, in his previously mentioned preaching manual, that "a gentile may preach against kings and nobles proclaiming their sins for all to hear but in our own nation no one will raise his tongue against any Jew whatsoever, and certainly not if the man is wealthy."[60] Joseph Yavetz hailed various Christian virtues:

> If you open your eyes, you will envy the nations; for you will see them practicing the rational commandments—doing justice and loving mercy—more than we in our sins. Their nobles pride themselves on the commandment of charity . . . and their scholars are gracious to one another.

After conflating earlier expressions of self-criticism made by Alami and Ibn Shem Tov and commending Christian solicitude for preachers, he concluded: "With us, it is the opposite: the preacher is rebuked and humiliated and the parishioners tell him: 'You who would rebuke the people, did you not do this abominable sin [yourself]?'"[61]

In the more strictly intellectual sphere, post-1391 Sephardic thinkers increasingly adapted and adopted ideas and methods known to them from Christian literature, if not always with full disclosure. Among the greater and lesser to do so were Crescas, Duran, Albo, Meir Alguades, Joseph ibn Shem Tov and his son Shem Tov, Abraham Bibago, Barukh ibn Ya'ish, Abraham Shalom, Eli Habillo, and Isaac Abarbanel.

In particular, some of these thinkers sought to renew Judaism on the basis of adaptations of Christian scholasticism, especially as imparted by Thomas Aquinas. Not long after scholasticism's belated arrival in Christian Spain, a small circle of scholars attested

---

[59] Eleazar Gutwirth, "Actitudes judias hacia los Cristianos en la España del siglo XV: ideario de los traductores del Latin," in *Actas del II Congreso International Encuentro de las Tres Culturas* (Toledo: Ayuntamiento de Toledo, 1985), 191–92.

[60] Saperstein, *Jewish Preaching*, 392.

[61] *Hasdei 'Adonai (Mercies of God)* (Jerusalem, 1934), 36-37.

Jewish interest in scholastic methods and teachings.[62] One result was a translation movement that saw Sephardic scholars rendering Latin theological and philosophical works into Hebrew. If, at the turn of the fifteenth century, such scholars might acquire what they called "the language of the Christians" for the purpose of attacking Christianity, they now found Latin to be a gateway to enhancement of their own spiritual quest. As part of this effort, they created a new Hebrew critical vocabulary capable of imparting scholastic ideas. As one key translator, Eli Habillo, explained, he "deemed it necessary to create new expressions which are not found in our literary language; in other cases, I have used existing expressions, but with meanings different from the usual ones."[63] Working on the eve of the expulsion, Eli and his ilk displayed an intellectual openness similar to the one that propelled so many creations during earlier periods of Sephardic intellectual revival. It is an openness remarkable for appearing when one might have assumed a deepening sense of persecution by bearers of the cross could only have generated a stance of religious and intellectual isolationism, if not outright Jewish hostility, towards all that might emanate from the Christian world.

Of course, Jewish assimilation of Christian ideas and attraction to Christian institutions of higher learning entailed risks. While documents about converts at the time of the expulsion reveal little of their intellectual proclivities, the stated desire of three to pursue "the study of letters" suggests that the prospect of entering the world of Christian learning though conversion held appeal.[64]

Beyond summoning (alleged) Christian solicitude for preachers as a model, pre-expulsion rabbis sought to emulate these preachers' most popular techniques. Striking testimony is forthcoming from the outstanding Jewish preacher of the day, Isaac Arama, a victim of the expulsion whose 'Aqedat Yishaq (Binding of Isaac) contains

---

[62] For the rise of Hispano-Christian scholasticism, see Luis M. Girón-Negrón, *Alfonso de la Torre's Visión Deleytable: Philosophical Rationalism and the Religious Imagination in 15th Century Spain* (Leiden: Brill, 2001), 4–11. For Jewish developments, see Mauro Zonta, *Hebrew Scholasticism in the Fifteenth Century: A History and Source Book* (Dordrecht: Springer, 2006).

[63] Zonta, *Hebrew Scholasticism*, 181.

[64] See Mark D. Meyerson, "Aragonese and Catalan Jewish Converts at the Time of the Expulsion," in *Jewish History* 6 (*The Frank Talmage Memorial Volume*), ed. Barry Walfish, 2 vols. (Haifa: Haifa U niversity Press, 1992), 2:141.

elaborately reworked versions of his sermons delivered in Spain that inspired Jewish preachers for centuries. What merits attention in the current context is the degree to which Arama's procedure self-consciously mimicked those of his Christian counterparts. "For some time now," he explained, apparently though not unquestionably alluding to the phenomenon of forced Jewish attendance at Christian sermons, "calls have gone out . . . summoning the people to hear their [the Christians'] learned discourses. . . . Among those who came were Jews. They heard the preachers and found them impressive. Their appetites were whetted for similar fare." Thus, Arama divided each of his sermons into two parts: an investigation (*derishah*) of particular subjects in the Torah such as the soul, prophecy, or repentance, and a commentary (*perishah*) according to scripture's plain sense. The aim was to "regale" his coreligionists with "gems" in the manner of the Christian preachers who searched "enthusiastically for religious and ethical content" in expounding scripture, unlike the Jewish interpreters, who remained content to explain "the grammatical forms of words and the simple meaning of the [scriptural] stories and commandments."[65] As in earlier epochs, most notably the "golden age," interreligious competition had spurred magnificent scholarly and literary exploits, so it was until the last Jewish preacher left Spanish soil.

Rabbinic Studies: Old Patterns, New Departures

And what of rabbis in their roles not as preachers but talmudists? The first half of the fifteenth century saw, in this sphere, mostly sporadic results. Hasdai Crescas, a legal decisor of the first rank, failed to realize his ambition to write a code in conjunction with 'Or 'Adonai to rival Maimonides' great compendium of Jewish law. Yet his contemporary, Joseph ben David Habiba, wrote extensively (and perhaps comprehensively) on the first classic of Sephardic halakhic literature, the code of the eleventh-century Andalusian scholar, Isaac Alfasi.[66] Foreshadowing what fifteenth-century Sephardic talmudists

---

[65] Saperstein, *Jewish Preaching*, 393.
[66] See the entry of Yehoshua Horowitz on "Ḥabiba, Joseph," in *Encyclopaedia Judaica*, ed. Michael Berenbaum and Fred Skolnik, 2nd ed. (Detroit: Macmillan Reference USA, 2007), 8:177.

would consider among their prize achievements, a methodological treatise that applied Aristotelian logic to the classical talmudic rules of biblical interpretation (the "thirteen hermeneutic principles") may also have its origins in early fifteenth-century Spain.[67] Non-legal segments of the great rabbinic corpora were not neglected. Witness the commentary on the Mishnaic tractate 'Avot composed by Hasdai Crescas' student, Mattathias Yizhari, which may have forged a novel approach to the genre so beloved by late medieval Iberian savants by reading rabbinic words with the hypercritical care usually reserved for scripture.[68]

The most influential developments in rabbinic studies stemmed from ideas of a towering but elusive figure, the mid-fifteenth-century talmudist Isaac Canpanton, whose *Darkhei ha-Talmud* (*The Ways of the Talmud*) set down principles of Sephardic "*iyyun*" ("speculation").[69] Modern scholars trace the principles of Talmud study articulated in his interpretive theory largely to medieval traditions of Aristotelian logic and linguistic philosophy. In ushering canons of logic into the precincts of the rabbinic academy, Canpanton, in addition to forging a precisely calibrated tool of textual analysis, implicitly bridged the gap between teachings on the highest human perfection propounded by representatives of Sephardic Jewry's "philosophic wing," with their intellectualist thrust, and the exclusive focus on Talmud-study characteristic of higher Jewish education in medieval times. A scholar engaged in such study could now be considered to be actualizing his rational potential, thereby attaining intellectual perfection and eternal "union of his perfected

---

[67] Aviram Ravitsky, "On the Date of *Sha'are Sedek*, Attributed to Gersonides," (Hebrew), *Tarbiz* 68 (1999): 401–10.

[68] Shem Tov ben Joseph's commentary on this same Mishnaic tractate written around the time of the expulsion was mentioned earlier. Yizhari is credited with the interpretive breakthrough that found expression in later Iberian 'Avot commentaries by Joseph Hayyun, Isaac Abarbanel, and others in Gidon Garber Rothstein, *Writing Midrash Avot: The Change that Three Fifteenth Century Exegetes Introduced to Avot Interpretation, Its Impact and Origins*, Ph D. diss., Harvard University, Cambridge, MA, 2003.

[69] The best English account is Daniel Boyarin, "Moslem, Christian, and Jewish Cultural Interaction in Sefardic Talmudic Interpretation," *Review of Rabbinic Judaism* 5 (2002): 1–33. A recent jargon-laden post-modern study that renders Canpanton's tome's outlines in English is Sergey Dolgopolski, *What is Talmud?: The Art of Disagreement* (New York: Fordham University Press, 2009).

intellect with God."[70] The Canpantonian approach remained coin of the realm in academies established by Sephardic exiles for centuries. Here, then, is a major late medieval Sephardic advancement that, for all its influence, still remains largely occluded from view.[71]

Beyond striving for a sovereign grasp of Talmud, inhabitants of some rabbinic academies displayed continuity with the Sephardic past by encompassing meta-halakhic and secular disciplines. Some of these may even have been incorporated into an enlarged *yeshiva* curriculum. There is, for instance, some evidence (if slight and after the fact) that in Castilian academies kabbalistic learning was cultivated, albeit not for purposes of originating new mystical ideas.[72] And while Isaac Arama's complaint that philosophy had become the "foundation of our *yeshivot*" sounds polemical, it is, given the proclivities of *yeshiva*-heads like Canpanton and his student Isaac Aboab, conceivable that philosophy also figured in an amplified rabbinic curriculum.[73]

Having spoken about the rabbinic academies, a word is in order about their apparently felicitous state in the later fifteenth century. A pre-1492 Sephardic refugee scholar living in north Africa, Judah Khalatz, casually described pre-1492 Castile as a "land of rabbinic academies and students."[74] Joseph Yavetz averred that "since ancient times" Spain had never been "so full of rabbinic academies and students as it was at the time of the expulsion."[75]

---

[70] Hava Tirosh-Rothschild, "Jewish Philosophy on the Eve of Modernity," in *History of Jewish Philosophy*, 503.

[71] An appreciation of fifteenth-century Sephardic rabbinic learning could only grow if the erudition in Catalo-Aragonese schools as reflected in dozens of forgotten scholars who carried on a more traditional Ashkenazic-based approach to rabbinic study were brought into the light of history. See Yisrael M. Ta-Shma, "Rabbinic Literature in the Middle Ages," in *The Oxford Handbook of Jewish Studies*, ed. Martin Goodman (Oxford: Oxford University Press, 2002), 236.

[72] Joseph Hacker, "On the Intellectual Character and Self-Perception of Spanish Jewry in the Late Fifteenth Century," *Sefunot* New Series 2 (1983): 47-59 (Hebrew).

[73] Marc Saperstein, "The Social and Cultural Context: Thirteenth to Fifteenth Centuries," in *History of Jewish Philosophy*, 305–6.

[74] *Mesiaḥ 'Ilmim*, ed. Moshe Philip (Petah Tikvah: N.p., 2001), 31.

[75] *'Or Ha-Ḥayyim (The Light of Life)* (Lublin, 1912), 8; cited in Abraham Gross, "Centers of Study and Yeshivot in Spain," in *Moreshet Sepharad: The Sephardi Legacy*, ed. Haim Beinart (Jerusalem: Magnes, 1992),1:407

Biblical Interpretation, Homiletics, Book Culture

As the author of a commentary on the most influential work of Jewish scriptural exegesis ever composed, the twelfth-century Torah Commentary of Solomon ben Isaac (Rashi), Judah Khalatz affords a convenient entrée into the world of post-1391 Sephardic biblical scholarship. A focus of Sephardic education and scholarly endeavor from Andalusian times,[76] such scholarship exhibited familiar patterns admixed with new departures in the century prior to 1492. Bible study's great accoutrement, grammar, found its chief exponent in Profiat Duran, who completed his aforementioned *Ma'aseh 'Efod* a dozen years after his conversion. Beyond acuity in treating traditional problems of Hebrew grammar, this work explored subjects rare for the genre, including music, phonology, and the nature of language.[77]

Outstanding among novelties in the sphere of biblical interpretation proper was the famous romance *Biblia de Alba*, commissioned by Don Luys de Guzman, Grand Master of the military Order of Calatrava, in 1422. It was produced under the direction of Moses Arragel, a rabbi from Guadalajara, who worked with a team of Christian collaborators.[78] On the Hebrew side, in addition to the already mentioned sermons of Arama, which largely offered biblical commentary, there was the first full-length biblical commentaries of Isaac Abarbanel, who interpreted most of the Former Prophets while living in Spain in the decade before 1492. In these, Abarbanel displayed a variety of novel humanist skills and sensibilities, especially when addressing long-standing bafflements surrounding the authorship of biblical books or conundrums about the relationship between the Former Prophets and books of Chronicles. Here, in Spanish Jewry's waning days, a transition from medieval to Renaissance biblical scholarship was inaugurated that put Jewish exegesis on a modern path.[79]

---

[76] Nahum M. Sarna, "Hebrew and Bible Studies in Medieval Spain," in *The Sephardi Heritage: Essays on the History and Cultural Contribution of the Jews in Spain and Portugal*, ed. Richard D. Barnett (London: Vallentine, Mitchell, 1971), 323–66.

[77] Talmage, "The Polemical Writings," 282.

[78] Sonia Fellous, "Cultural Hybridity, Cultural Subversion: Text and Image in the *Alba Bible*, 1422–33," *Exemplaria* 12 (2000): 205–29.

[79] Eric Lawee, *Isaac Abarbanel's Stance Toward Tradition: Defense, Dissent, and Dialogue* (Albany: SUNY Press, 2001), 169–202. For a sample in English, see Eric Lawee, "Don Isaac

Another post-1391 innovation in Sephardic biblical interpretation that foreshadowed things to come was the composition of formal commentaries on Rashi's *Commentary on the Torah* (supercommentaries). As noted, fourteenth-century Spain propelled a spurt of commentaries on Abraham ibn Ezra's exposition of the Torah that concluded in the fifteenth century. Now a parallel Sephardic enterprise centering on Rashi's ever more canonical commentary took flight. An early entry issued from the pen of an anonymous colleague of Profiat Duran. Sometime around the mid-fifteenth century, Isaac Aboab, then a young man, contributed a similar work as, eventually, did his fellow *yeshiva*-heads, Isaac de Leon and Jacob Kenizal. In some of the half dozen or more Sephardic Rashi commentaries, analyses in the Canpantonian mode appear, providing further evidence of this method's catalyzing effect on late medieval Sephardic literature. The Sephardic style of extremely fastidious interpretation of Rashi's words became the template for the more famous works of Rashi supercommentary written by Ashkenazic scholars in early modern times.[80]

The art of Sephardic homiletics also waxed in the century before 1492. Beyond Arama's matchless entry in the genre (as discussed below), the post-1391 period produced other extensive collections like those by Mattathias Yizhari, Shem Tov ben Joseph, and the leading rabbinic figure in Spanish Jewry's last generation, Isaac Aboab.[81] Sermons during the period favored increasingly intricate and involved homiletical designs, but beyond their substance and structure, they can be analyzed in light of their socio-religious function, especially in their role as a bridge between elite and popular culture.[82] Such analysis suggests the need to revise standard assumptions about Spanish preachers' imposition of philosophically oriented homilies on a resistant public in ways that corroded

---

Abarbanel: Who Wrote the Books of the Bible?" *Tradition* 30 (1996): 65–73.

[80] See Eric Lawee, "The Reception of Rashi's *Commentary on the Torah* in Spain: The Case of Adam's Mating with the Animals," *Jewish Quarterly Review* 97 (2007): 33–66; Eric Lawee, "From Sefarad to Ashkenaz: A Case Study in the Rashi Supercommentary Tradition," *AJS Review* 30 (2006): 393–425.

[81] For Aboab, see Marc Saperstein, "A Spanish Rabbi on Repentence: Isaac Aboab's Manuscript Sermon for *Shabbat Shuvah*," in *"Your Voice Like a Ram's Horn*," 293–366. For Mattathias and Shem Tov, see Marc Saperstein, *Jewish Preaching*, 156–66, 180–98.

[82] Saperstein, "Sermons," 75.

religious faith. Though complaints along these lines appear,[83] such assumptions fail to appreciate sufficiently that preachers, though occasionally out of step with their parishoners' tastes, can never ignore them completely.[84]

Sephardic manuscript and book culture attest to an additional element of vitality in Sephardic religious and intellectual life on the eve of the expulsion. While Hispano-Jewish manuscript illumination never reclaimed the heights achieved in the fourteenth century, schools of Hebrew manuscript illumination did have a presence in fifteenth-century Castile.[85] Meanwhile, printing, a medium that Jews embraced with a sense of mission and even as a divinely wrought dispensation,[86] came to Jewish Spain almost immediately after its initial appearance in Italy, with Hebrew presses opening in no less than five Spanish cities. The most printed writings during the brief period of Spanish Hebrew mechanical reproduction were biblical texts and Rashi's *Commentary on the Torah*.[87] When the edict of expulsion was issued, the scriptorium was fast giving way to the typographic shop as the primary vehicle for the reproduction of Hebrew liturgical and scholarly texts. Little wonder that the first known printers in the Ottoman Empire (Jewish or otherwise) were David and Samuel Nahmias, who either arrived in Constantinople as part of the 1492 exodus or just prior to the expulsion, where they printed Jacob ben Asher's *'Arba'ah Turim* in 1493.

---

[83] Above, n.22, for Hayyim ibn Musa's critique along these lines.

[84] Bernard Septimus, "Yitzhaq Arama and Aristotle's *Ethics*," in *Jews and Conversos at the Time of the Expulsion*, ed. Yom Tov Assis and Yosef Kaplan (Jerusalem: Merkaz Zalman Shazar, 1999), 7.

[85] Katrin Kogman-Appel, *Jewish Book Art Between Islam and Christianity: The Decoration of Hebrew Bibles in Medieval Spain*, trans. Judith Davidson (Leiden: Brill, 2004), 14.

[86] Menahem Schmelzer, "Hebrew Manuscripts and Printed Books Among the Sephardim Before and After the Expulsion," in *Crisis and Creativity in the Sephardic World 1391-1648*, ed. Benjamin R. Gampel (New York: Columbia University Press, 1997), 359, 382 n. 20.

[87] A.K. Offenberg, *A Choice of Corals: Facets of Fifteenth-Century Hebrew Printing* (Nieuwkoop: De Graaf Publishers, 1992), 135–37; Schmelzer, "Hebrew Manuscripts," 259.

Between Decline and Shifting Emphases

As some areas of inquiry and literary activity flourished, others, including ones for which Sephardic writers had long been renowned, suffered a sharp if not terminal decline. As elegies written to commemorate the 1391 riots indicate, poetry remained as a genre on the cultural scene,[88] but late medieval Sephardic poets were no match for the versatility, profundity, and rhetorical brilliance of Samuel the Prince, Solomon ibn Gabirol, Judah Halevi, Todros Abulafia, and the many other great earlier medieval singers of Sepharad.

Considerable atrophy also occurred in the sphere of kabbalistic thought and literature. Shem Tov ibn Shem Tov's admission that he could find no master to instruct him in Kabbalah says all that needs to be said about the state of affairs at the beginning of the fifteenth century,[89] though Shem Tov's sons and others of their rough intellectual complexion (Crescas, Albo, and Abarbanel among them) drew selectively on kabbalistic ideas and sought to measure the nature and thickness of the boundaries separating philosophy from Kabbalah. The seminal contributions of Nahmanides, Abraham Abulafia, and the authors of the *Zohar* were not to be repeated. Still, a modest mystical revival led by the anonymous kabbalistic author of *Sefer Ha-Meshiv* (*Book of the Responding [Angel]*) took place around the 1470s. This kabbalist excoriated both philosophy and Christianity while effecting a sharp messianic turn in Spanish Kabbalah. The existence of a few active kabbalists on the eve of the expulsion is attested by their appearance in Italy in the decade prior to and after 1492.[90]

---

[88] Wout Van Bekkum, "O Seville! Ah Castille! Spanish-Hebrew Dirges from the Fifteenth Century," in *Hebrew Scholarship and the Medieval World*, ed. Nicholas de Lange (Cambridge: Cambridge University Press, 2001), 156–70; Raymond P. Scheindlin, "Secular Hebrew Poetry in Fifteenth-Century Spain," in *Crisis and Creativity*, 25–37. David Wacks, "Toward a History of Hispano-Hebrew Literature in its Romance Context," *eHumanista* 14 (2010): 196-98.

[89] Moshe Idel, "Jewish Mysticism in Spain: Some Cultural Observations," *Revista espacio, tiempo y forma, Serie III, Historia Medieval* 7 (1994): 311. For a recently discovered kabbalistic work from the period, see Boaz Huss, "On the Status of Kabbalah in Spain after the Riots of 1391: The Book 'Poke'ah 'Ivrim,'" *Pe'amim* 56 (1993): 20-32 (Hebrew).

[90] Moshe Idel, "The Attitude to Christianity in *Sefer Ha-Meshiv*," *Immanuel* 12 (1981): 77–95; Moshe Idel, "Magic and Kabbalah in the 'Book of the Responding Entity,'" in *The Solomon Goldman Lectures* (Spertus Institute of Jewish Studies Press, 1993), 6:125–38;

If poetry and Kabbalah waned while other areas of intellectual endeavor and literary expression waxed, such shifts may suggest that "Sephardic Jewish culture in the fifteenth century did not deteriorate as much as it exhibited a change in its emphases."[91] Why, then, has its reputation for mediocrity been so hard to shake?

For one thing, a significant body of relevant "data" for reconstructing Hispano-Jewish scholarship during its concluding phase remains in manuscript, gathering dust. The publication in recent years of some of the many Rashi supercommentaries written by post-1391 Sephardic scholars furnishes an example of a hitherto overlooked corpus that bespeaks an (admittedly modest) intellectual innovation. Fifteenth-century Sephardic talmudic commentaries and related works lie similarly forlorn, awaiting their scholarly redeemers. To give another example, until Joseph ibn Shem Tov's massive commentary on Aristotle's *Ethics* is analyzed, any understanding of fifteenth-century Hispano-Jewish engagement with this key constituent of the Aristotelian corpus will be fundamentally lacking.[92]

In addition, many late medieval Sephardic writers whose writings have appeared in print expressed themselves through literary media (ornate homiletical tomes, involved exegetical tracts, studies in dogma) that do not warm the hearts of too many modern scholars. Isaac Arama's homiletically brilliant and philosophically astute but theologically dense and stylistically imposing sermons exemplify the sort of splendid late medieval Sephardic production that constitutes hard reading, explaining why their author's considerable intellectual stature and homiletical genius is barely appreciated.[93]

Also contributing to the cool reception accorded to much late medieval Sephardic high culture is a point alluded to above: the period lacks for the sort of epoch-making breakthroughs that appear in such exceptional abundance in earlier phases of Sephardic

Moshe Idel, "Encounters Between Spanish and Italian Kabbalists in the Generation of the Expulsion," in *Crisis and Creativity*, 199–209.

[91] Benjamin R. Gampel, "A Letter to a Wayward Teacher: The Transformations of Sephardic Culture in Christian Iberia," in *Cultures of the Jews: A New History*, ed. David Biale (New York: Schocken, 2002), 431.

[92] Septimus, "Yitzhaq Arama and Aristotle's *Ethics*," 13* n. 48.

[93] Septimus, "Yitzhaq Arama and Aristotle's *Ethics*," 5* n. 16.

intellectual life. About this emphasis on originality or lack thereof in late medieval Sephardic intellectual history a few things should be said. One is that the period did not lack for real and in some cases highly consequential innovations, as our survey has showed. Another is that it is worth asking how much originality should govern evaluations of the intellectual achievements of premodern societies in general and of late medieval Sepharad in particular. Apt in this regard is the observation of one of medieval Jewish thought's foremost twentieth-century students, Leo Strauss, who stated that though "Spinoza was more original in the present day sense of the term than was Maimonides," Maimonides remained nevertheless the "deeper thinker."[94] The many forms and formats in which originality can appear must also be borne in mind. Rashi supercommentaries, beyond reflecting a new genre, show that original ideas, unconventional adaptations, and exegetical nuances are sometimes expressed in what might seem a derivative if not wholly obsequious genre, a commentary on a commentary. Finally, ascriptions of intellectual originality carry little meaning outside the context in which they are made. Though fifteenth-century Sephardic thought is often depicted as a "conservative" reaction to Jewish Aristotelianism, in rejecting many theological structures inherited from the fourteenth century, and certainly in turning to scholastic models, the conservative Sephardic thinkers of the period forged genuinely new intellectual paths.[95]

Beyond lacunae in the historical record, the challenge of working with admittedly challenging media, and modern scholarly exuberance for novel crossing-points in intellectual history of the sort late medieval Sepharad can claim only in modest number, another factor that presumably informs the dim view taken of fifteenth-century Hispano-Jewish scholarship is the almost irresistible urge to contrast it with the exploits of earlier phases of the Hispano-Jewish legacy. Recall, in a claim cited above, the pairing of the supposed "complete breakdown and virtual collapse" in learning in later medieval times with the observation that such learning

---

[94] Leo Strauss, "On A Forgotten Kind of Writing," in *What is Political Philosophy* (Chicago: The University of Chicago Press, 1959), 230.

[95] *The Jewish Philosophy Reader*, ed. Daniel H. Frank, Oliver Leaman, and Charles H. Manekin (London: Routledge, 2000), 264.

"characterized Spanish Jewry from the earliest days." To be sure, if Maimonides, Nahmanides, and the *Zohar* are made the benchmarks of significant intellectual achievement, late medieval Sephardic scholarship will pale by comparison (as will Jewish scholarship from well-nigh any time or place).

Other points of reference, like its Muslim counterpart, may help to see late medieval Sephardic scholarship in a different light. Hispano-Muslim scholarship of the period also evolved in a context of great upheaval and communal distress. Though jurists in the Islamic west required Muslims in lands where they were a subordinate religious minority to emigrate to places of majority Muslim rule,[96] most Spanish Muslims eschewed the demand for a wholesale exodus. The Muslim elite, however, departed Christian Spain in large numbers, leaving the Ibero-Muslim (*mudejar*) community almost completely decapitated, politically and intellectually.[97] By contrast, though Spanish Jewry emerged from the catastrophe of 1391 badly fractured, and with greatly diminished intellectual resources, its scholars restored many areas of learning and developed several important new ones while engaging in serious scholarly introspection and at times offering trenchant criticisms of larger trends in their intellectual and broader communities.

While a comprehensive synthesis of late medieval Sephardic learning and literature remains to be written, our charting of focal points has highlighted a number of important achievements that have been underestimated or missed almost entirely. Despite elements of atrophy in areas for which Sephardic intellectuals had long been famed, like poetry and mysticism, fifteenth-century Sephardic scholars, in aggregate, achieved their fair share of fruitful syntheses and forward-looking discoveries. These figures carried on lively (and at times highly recriminatory) debates about many of the issues that had riveted their more celebrated Sephardic forerunners. Like their predecessors, they pondered carefully the need to balance traditional Jewish studies centered especially on Talmud with the

---

[96] L.P. Harvey, *Islamic Spain, 1250 to 1500* (Chicago: University of Chicago Press, 1990), 197.

[97] Bernard F. Reilly, *The Medieval Spains* (Cambridge: Cambridge University Press, 1993), 197; Kathryn A. Miller, *Guardians of Islam: Religious Authority and Muslim Communities of Late Medieval Spain* (New York: Columbia University Press, 2008).

cultivation of a variety of meta-legal disciplines. And like them, they creatively straddled the line separating "parochial" Jewish pursuits from intellectual endeavors shared with their larger gentile (Christian) milieu. Despite the oppressive post-1391 circumstances and the disappearance of major centers of learning and the forced exile or willing departure of major scholarly colleagues, many Sephardic intellectuals remained curious, energetic, and open to the world while addressing the religio-cultural difficulties that their beleaguered community faced. In so doing, they set the stage for the possibility of a thriving continuation of Sephardic intellectual life after 1492.

In addressing the issue of Sephardic cultural resilience after calamity, we enter a sensitive space where efforts to rethink medieval Jewish life in overly sanguine ways can evoke strong reactions, up to and including "nausea" and "shock."[98] So it is with medieval Spain's famed *convivencia*, in which some seem too determined to find a "culture of tolerance"[99] even as the phenomenon also took in elements of intense rivalry, up to and including massacres, forced conversions, and expulsions. Finding much to admire in the intellectual attainments of late medieval Sephardic scholars need not embroil us in such understandably charged debates—though properly fine-tuned by future research, this essay's more auspicious claims about late medieval Sephardic intellectual life should be entered into ongoing discussions of medieval Jewish experience under the cross in general. For now, it is enough to conclude that the varied and often deft achievements of some fifteenth-century Sephardic scholars can command our respect, even if they do not in their ensemble quite rise to the level of a third renaissance in Sephardic intellectual history.

---

[98] See Jonathan Elukin, *Living Together, Living Apart: Rethinking Jewish-Christian Relations in the Middle Ages* (Princeton, NJ: Princeton University Press, 2007), and the highly critical review of David Nirenberg, "Hope's Mistakes," *The New Republic* vol. 238, no. 4, Feb. 13 (2008), 46-50.

[99] Maria Rosa Menocal, *The Ornament of the World: How Muslims, Jews and Christians Created a Culture of Tolerance in Medieval Spain* (Boston: Little, Brown and Company, 2002).

Works Cited:

Ackerman, Ari. "Jewish Philosophy and the Jewish-Christian Debate." In *The Cambridge Companion to Medieval Jewish Philosophy*, edited by Daniel H. Frank and Oliver Leaman, 371–90. Cambridge: Cambridge University Press, 2003.

Alami, Solomon. *'Iggeret Musar*. Edited by A. M. Haberman. Jerusalem: Mossad HaRav Kook, 1946.

Altmann, Alexander. "Moses Narboni's 'Epistle on *Shi'ur Qoma'.*" In *Jewish Medieval and Renaissance Studies*, edited by Alexander Altmann, 225–88. Cambridge, MA: Harvard University Press, 1967.

Baer, Yitzhak. *A History of the Jews in Christian Spain*. 2 vols. Philadelphia: Jewish Publication Society, 1961–66.

Ben-Shalom, Ram. "Between Official and Private Dispute: The Case of Christian Spain and Provence in the Late Middle Ages." *AJS Review* 27 (2003): 23–71.

------. *Facing Christian Culture: Historical Consciousness and Images of the Past among the Jews of Spain and Southern France during the Middle Ages* (Hebrew). Jerusalem: Ben-Zvi Institute / The Hebrew University of Jerusalem, 2006.

Berger, David. "On the Uses of History in Medieval Jewish Polemic Against Christianity: The Quest for the Historical Jesus." In *Jewish History and Jewish Memory: Essays in Honor of Yosef Hayim Yerushalmi*, edited by Elisheva Carlebach, John M. Efron, and David N. Myers, 25–39. Hanover: Brandeis University Press, 1998.

Birnbaum, Ruth. *An Exposition of Joseph Ibn Shem Tov's Kevod Elohim (The Glory of God), a Fifteenth-Century Philosophical Work on the Summum Bonum of Man and the True Happiness*. Lewiston, NY: E. Mellen Press, 2001.

Boyarin, Daniel. "Moslem, Christian, and Jewish Cultural Interaction in Sefardic Talmudic Interpretation." *Review of Rabbinic Judaism* 5 (2002): 1–33.

Chazan, Robert. *Fashioning Jewish Identity in Medieval Western Christendom*. New York: Cambridge University Press, 2004.

Cohen, Mark R. *Under Crescent and Cross: The Jews in the Middle Ages.* Princeton: Princeton University Press, 1994.

Crescas, Hasdai. *The Refutation of the Christian Principles.* Trans. with an introduction and notes by Daniel J. Lasker. Albany: State University of New York, 1992.

Davidson, Herbert. *The Philosophy of Abraham Shalom: A Fifteenth-Century Exposition and Defense of Maimonides.* Berkeley: University of California Press, 1964.

Dolgopolski, Sergey. *What is Talmud?: The Art of Disagreement.* New York: Fordham University Press, 2009.

Ehrlich, Dror. "A Reassessment of Natural Law in Rabbi Joseph Albo's 'Book of Principles.'" *Hebraic Political Studies* 1 (2006): 413–39.

------. *The Thought of R. Joseph Albo: Esoteric Writing in the Late Middle Ages.* Ramat Gan: Bar-Ilan University Press, 2009. (Hebrew):

Elukin, Jonathan. *Living Together, Living Apart: Rethinking Jewish-Christian Relations in the Middle Ages.* Princeton, N.J.: Princeton University Press, 2007.

Feldman, Seymour. "A Debate Concerning Determinism in Late Medieval Jewish Philosophy." *Proceedings of the American Academy for Jewish Research* 51 (1984): 15–54.

Fellous, Sonia. "Cultural Hybridity, Cultural Subversion: Text and Image in the *Alba Bible*, 1422–33." *Exemplaria* 12 (2000): 205–29.

Fischoff, Ephraim "The Life and Works of Profiat Duran Efodi with Especial Reference to the Commentary on the Moreh," Ph. D. diss., Cincinatti, Hebrew Union College, 1929.

Gampel, Benjamin R. "A Letter to a Wayward Teacher: The Transformations of Sephardic Culture in Christian Iberia." In *Cultures of the Jews: A New History*, edited by David Biale, 389–447. New York: Schocken, 2002.

García-Ballester, Luis, Lola Ferre, and Eduard Feliu. "Jewish Appreciation of Fourteenth-Century Scholastic Medicine." Michael R. McVaugh, and Nancy G. Siraisi, eds., *Osiris, 2nd Series, Renaissance Medical Learning: Evolution of a Tradition* 6 (1990): 85–117.

Garshowitz, Libby. "Shem Tov Ben Isaac Ibn Shaprut's Gospel of Matthew." In *The Frank Talmage Memorial Volume*, edited by Barry Walfish. 2 vols., 1:297–322. Haifa: Haifa University Press, 1992.

Gerber, Jane S. *The Jews of Spain: A History of the Sephardic Experience.* New York: The Free Press, 1992.

Girón-Negrón, Luis M. *Alfonso de la Torre's Visión Deleytable: Philosophical Rationalism and the Religious Imagination in 15ᵗʰ Century Spain.* Leiden: Brill, 2001.

Glatzer, Nahum N. *Faith and Knowledge: The Jew in the Medieval World.* Boston: Beacon Press, 1963.

Graizbord, David L. *Souls in Dispute: Converso Identities in Iberia and the Jewish Diaspora, 1580–1700.* Philadelphia: University of Pennsylvania Press, 2004.

Gross, Abraham. "Centers of Study and Yeshivot in Spain." In *Moreshet Sepharad: The Sephardi Legacy*, edited by Haim Beinart. 2 vols.,1: 399–410. Jerusalem: Magnes, 1992.

Guttmann, Julius. *Philosophies of Judaism: The History of Jewish Philosophy from Biblical Times to Franz Rosenzweig.* Translated by David W. Silverman. New York: Schocken, 1973.

Gutwirth, Eleazar. "History and Apologetics in XVth Century Hispano-Jewish Thought." *Helmantica* 35 (1984): 231–42.

------. "Actitudes judias hacia los Cristianos en la España del siglo XV: ideario de los traductores del Latin." In *Actas del II Congreso International Encuentro de las Tres Culturas*, 189–96. Toledo: Ayuntamiento de Toledo, 1985.

------. "Duran on Ahitophel: The Practice of Jewish History in Late Medieval Spain." *Jewish History* 4 (1989): 59–74.

------. "Towards Expulsion: 1391–1492." In *Spain and the Jews: The Sephardi Experience 1492 and After*, edited by Elie Kedourie, 51–73. London: Thames and Hudson, 1992.

------. "Italy or Spain? The Theme of Jewish Eloquence in *Shevet Yehudah*." In *Daniel Karpi Jubilee Volume*, 35–67. Tel Aviv: Tel Aviv University, Faculty of the Humanities, 1996.

Hacker, Joseph. "The Role of Abraham Bibago in the Polemic on the Place of Philosophy in Jewish Life in Spain in the Fifteenth Century." *Proceedings of the Fifth World Congress of Jewish Studies*, III (Jerusalem, 1972), 156-58. (Hebrew)

------. "On the Intellectual Character and Self-Perception of Spanish Jewry in the Late Fifteenth-Century." *Sefunot* New Series 2 (1983): 47-59. (Hebrew)

------. "The Intellectual Activity of the Jews of the Ottoman Empire During the Sixteenth and Seventeenth Centuries." In *Jewish Thought in the Seventeenth Century*, edited by Isadore Twersky and Bernard Septimus, 95–135. Cambridge, MA: Harvard University Press, 1987.

Harvey, L.P. *Islamic Spain, 1250 to 1500*. Chicago: University of Chicago Press, 1990.

Harvey, Warren Zeev. "Crescas versus Maimonides on Knowledge and Pleasure." In *A Straight Path: Studies in Medieval Philosophy and Culture: Essays in Honor of Arthur Hyman*, edited by Ruth Link-Salinger, et al., 111–23. Washington, D.C.: Catholic University of America Press, 1988.

------. *Physics and Metaphysics in Hasdai Crescas*. Amsterdam: J.C. Gieben, 1998.

Hayoun, Maurice R. *Moshe Narboni*. Tubingen: TCB Mohr, 1986.

Husik, Isaac. *A History of Mediaeval Jewish Philosophy*. New York: Macmillan, 1916.

Huss, Boaz. "On the Status of Kabbalah in Spain after the Riots of 1391: The Book 'Poke'aḥ 'Ivrim." *Pe'amim* 56 (1993): 20-32. (Hebrew)

Ibn Musa, Hayyim. *Sefer magen va-romaḥ, ve-'igeret li-veno*. Facsimile edition of Adolf Posnanski's manuscript, with introduction by Joseph Hacker. Jerusalem, 1969.

Idel, Moshe. "The Attitude to Christianity in *Sefer Ha-Meshiv*." *Immanuel* 12 (1981): 77–95.

------. "Jewish Mysticism in Spain: Some Cultural Observations." *Revista espacio, tiempo y forma, Serie III, Historia Medieval* 7 (1994): 289–314.

------. "Encounters Between Spanish and Italian Kabbalists in the Generation of the Expulsion." In *Crisis and Creativity in the Sephardic World 1391–1648*, edited by Benjamin R. Gampel, 189–222. New York: Columbia University Press, 1997.

------. "The Kabbalah's 'Window of Opportunities,' 1270–1290." In *Me'ah She'arim: Studies in Medieval Jewish Spiritual Life in Memory of Isadore Twersky*, edited by Ezra Fleischer, et. al., 171–208 (English section). Jerusalem: Magnes Press, 2001.

------. "Magic and Kabbalah in the 'Book of the Responding Entity.'" In *The Solomon Goldman Lectures*, M. Gruber, 6:125–38. Chicago: Spertus Institute of Jewish Studies Press, 2003.

------. "Man as the 'Possible' Entity in Some Jewish and Renaissance Sources." In *Hebraica Veritas?: Christian Hebraists and the Study of Judaism in Early Modern Europe*, edited by Allison P. Coudert and Jeffrey S. Shoulson, 33–48. Philadelphia: University of Pennsylvania Press, 2004.

------. "Jewish Philosophy and Kabbalah in Spain." In *Sephardic and Mizrahi Jewry: From the Golden Age of Spain to Modern Times*, edited by Zohar Zion, 120–42. New York: New York University Press, 2005.

The Jewish Philosophy Reader. Edited by Daniel H. Frank, Oliver Leaman, and Charles H. Manekin. London: Routledge, 2000.

Kellner, Menachem. *Dogma in Medieval Jewish Thought: From Maimonides to Abravanel*. Oxford: Oxford University Press, 1986.

Khalatz, Judah. *Mesiaḥ 'ilmim*. Edited by Moshe Philip. Petah Tikvah: N.p., 2001.

Kobler, Franz. *Letters of Jews Through the Ages: From Biblical Times to the Middle of the Eighteenth Century*. 2 vols. London: Ararat Publishing Society, 1952.

Kogman-Appel, Katrin. *Jewish Book Art Between Islam and Christianity: The Decoration of Hebrew Bibles in Medieval Spain*. Translated by Judith Davidson. Leiden: Brill, 2004.

Kozodoy, Maud Natasha. "A Study of the Life and Works of Profiat Duran." Ph. D. diss., New York: The Jewish Theological Seminary of America, 2006.

------. "The Hebrew Bible as Weapon of Faith in Late Medieval Iberia: Irony, Satire, and Scriptural Allusion in Profiat Duran's *Al Tehi ka-Avotekha*," *Jewish Studies Quarterly* 18 (2011): 185-201.

Lasker, Daniel J. "Chasdai Crescas." In *History of Jewish Philosophy*, edited by Daniel H. Frank and Oliver Leaman, 399–414. London: Routledge, 1997.

------. "The Impact of Christianity on Late Iberian Jewish Philosophy." In *Iberia and Beyond: Hispanic Jews Between Cultures*, edited by Bernard Dov Cooperman, 175–90. Newark: University of Delaware Press, 1998.

------. *Jewish Philosophical Polemics Against Christianity in the Middle Ages*, 2nd ed. Oxford: The Littman Library of Jewish Civilization, 2007.

Lawee, Eric. "Don Isaac Abarbanel: Who Wrote the Books of the Bible?" *Tradition* 30 (1996): 65–73.

------. "The Path to Felicity: Teachings and Tensions in *'Even Shetiyyah* of Abraham Ben Judah, Disciple of Hasdai Crescas." *Mediaeval Studies* 59 (1997): 183–223.

------. *Isaac Abarbanel's Stance Toward Tradition: Defense, Dissent, and Dialogue*. Albany: SUNY Press, 2001.

------. "'The Good We Accept and the Bad We Do Not': Aspects of Isaac Abarbanel's Stance Towards Maimonides." In *Be'erot Yitzhak: Studies in Memory of Isadore Twersky*, edited by Jay Harris, 119–60. Cambridge, MA: Harvard University Center for Jewish Studies, 2005.

------. "From Sefarad to Ashkenaz: A Case Study in the Rashi Supercommentary Tradition." *AJS Review* 30 (2006): 393–425.

------. "The Reception of Rashi's *Commentary on the Torah* in Spain: The Case of Adam's Mating with the Animals." *Jewish Quarterly Review* 97 (2007): 33–66.

Lawrance, Jeremy N. H. "Humanism in the Iberian Peninsula." In *The Impact of Humanism on Western Europe*, edited by Anthony Goodman and Angus MacKay, 220–58. London: Longman, 1990.

Lazar, Moshe. "Rabbí Moses Arragel as Servant of Two Masters: A Call for Tolerance in a Century of Turmoil." In *Encuentros and Desencuentros: Spanish Jewish Cultural Interaction Throughout*

History, edited by Carlos Carrete Parrondo, et. al, 431–78. Tel Aviv: University Publishing Projects, 2000.

Lerner, Ralph. *Maimonides' Empire of Light: Popular Enlightenment in an Age of Belief.* Chicago: University of Chicago Press, 2000.

Menocal, Maria Rosa. *The Ornament of the World: How Muslims, Jews and Christians Created a Culture of Tolerance in Medieval Spain.* Boston: Little, Brown and Company, 2002.

Meyerson, Mark D. *A Jewish Renaissance in Fifteenth-Century Spain.* Princeton: Princeton University Press, 2004.

Miller, Kathryn A. *Guardians of Islam: Religious Authority and Muslim Communities of Late Medieval Spain.* New York: Columbia University Press, 2008.

Nigal, Gedaliyah. "The Opinions of R. Joseph Yawetz on Philosophy, Torah and Commandments." *Eshel Beer Sheva* 1 (1976): 258–87. (Hebrew)

Nirenberg, David. "Hope's Mistakes." *The New Republic* 238, no. 4, Feb. 13 (2008): 46-50.

Offenberg, A. K. *A Choice of Corals: Facets of Fifteenth-Century Hebrew Printing.* Nieuwkoop: De Graaf Publishers, 1992.

Pagden, A. R. D. "The Diffusion of Aristotle's Moral Philosophy in Spain, CA. 1400 - CA. 1600." *Traditio* 31 (1975): 287–313.

Peters, Edward. "Jewish History and Gentile Memory: The Expulsion of 1492." *Jewish History* 9 (1995): 9–34.

Ravitsky, Aviram. "On the Date of *Sha'are Sedek*, Attributed to Gersonides." *Tarbiz* 68 (1999): 401–10. (Hebrew)

Ray, Jonathan. *The Sephardic Frontier: The Reconquista and the Jewish Community in Medieval Iberia.* Ithaca, NY: Cornell University Press, 2006.

Reilly, Bernard F. *The Medieval Spains.* Cambridge: Cambridge University Press, 1993.

Robinson, James T. "Hasdai Crescas and Anti-Aristotelianism." In *The Cambridge Companion to Medieval Jewish Philosophy*, edited by Daniel H Frank and Oliver Leaman, 391–413. Cambridge: Cambridge University Press, 2003.

Roth, Norman. *Conversos, Inquisition, and the Expulsion of the Jews from Spain*. Madison: University of Wisconsin Press, 1995.

Rothschild, Jean-Pierre. "Le dessein philosophique de Joseph ibn Shem Tob (*flor.* 1442–1455)." *Revue des Études juives* 162 (2003): 97–122.

Rothstein, Gidon. *Writing Midrash Avot: The Change that Three Fifteenth Century Exegetes Introduced to Avot Interpretation, Its Impact and Origins*. Ph. diss., Harvard University, Cambridge, MA, 2003.

Safran, Bezalel. "Bahya Ibn Paquda's Attitude Toward the Courtier Class." In *Studies in Medieval Jewish History and Literature*, edited by Isadore Twersky, 154–69. Cambridge, MA: Harvard University Press, 1979.

Saperstein, Marc. "Christians and Jews—Some Positive Images." *Harvard Theological Review* 79 (1986): 241-42.

------. *Jewish Preaching 1200–1800: An Anthology*. New Haven: Yale University Press, 1989.

------. "Sermons as Evidence for the Popularization of Philosophy in Fifteenth-Century Spain." In *"Your Voice Like a Ram's Horn": Themes and Texts in Traditional Jewish Preaching*, 75–87. Cincinnati: Hebrew Union College Press, 1996.

------. "A Spanish Rabbi on Repentence: Isaac Aboab's Manuscript Sermon for *Shabbat Shuvah*." In *"Your Voice Like a Ram's Horn": Themes and Texts in Traditional Jewish Preaching*, 293–366. Cincinnati: Hebrew Union College Press, 1996.

------. "The Social and Cultural Context: Thirteenth to Fifteenth Centuries." In *History of Jewish Philosophy*, edited by Daniel H. Frank and Oliver Leaman. Routledge History of World Philosophies 2, 294–330. London: Routledge, 1997.

Sarna, Nahum M. "Hebrew and Bible Studies in Medieval Spain." In *The Sephardi Heritage: Essays on the History and Cultural Contribution of the Jews in Spain and Portugal*, edited by Richard D. Barnett, 323–66. London: Vallentine, Mitchell, 1971.

Scheindlin, Raymond P. "Secular Hebrew Poetry in Fifteenth-Century Spain." In *Crisis and Creativity in the Sephardic World 1391–1648*, edited by Benjamin R. Gampel, 25–37. New York: Columbia University Press, 1997.

Scheindlin, Raymond. "Merchants and Intellectuals, Rabbis and Poets: Judeo-Arabic Culture in the Golden Age of Islam." In *Cultures of the Jews: A New History*, edited by David Biale, 313–86. New York: Schocken, 2002.

Schwartz, Dov. *Contradiction and Concealment in Medieval Jewish Thought*. Ramat Gan: Bar-Ilan University, 2002. (Hebrew)

Schmelzer, Menahem. "Hebrew Manuscripts and Printed Books Among the Sephardim Before and After the Expulsion." In *Crisis and Creativity in the Sephardic World 1391–1648*, edited by Benjamin R. Gampel, 257–66. New York: Columbia University Press, 1997.

Septimus, Bernard. *Hispano-Jewish Culture in Transition: The Career and Controversies of Ramah*. Cambridge, MA: Harvard University Press, 1982.

------. "Narboni and Shem Tov on Martyrdom." In *Studies in Medieval Jewish History and Literature II*, edited by Isadore Twersky, 447–55. Cambridge, MA: Harvard University Press, 1984.

------. "Yitzhaq Arama and Aristotle's *Ethics*." In *Jews and Conversos at the Time of the Expulsion*, edited by Yom Tov Assis and Yosef Kaplan, 1–24 (English section). Jerusalem: Merkaz Zalman Shazar, 1999.

Simon, Uriel. "Interpreting the Interpreter: Supercommentaries on Ibn Ezra's Commentaries." In *Rabbi Abraham Ibn Ezra: Studies in the Writings of a Twelfth-Century Polymath*, edited by Isadore Twersky and Jay M. Harris, 86–128. Cambridge, MA: Harvard University Center for Jewish Studies, 1993.

Strauss, Leo. *Persecution and the Art of Writing*. Westport,CT: Greenwood Press, 1973.

Talmage, Frank Ephraim. *Kitvei Pulmus le-Profet Duran*. Jerusalem: Zalman Shazar, 1981.

------. "The Polemical Writings of Profiat Duran." In *Apples of Gold in Settings of Silver: Studies in Medieval Jewish Exegesis and Polemics*, edited by Barry Dov Walfish. Toronto: Pontifical Institute of Mediaeval Studies, 1999.

Talmage, Frank. "The Francesc de Sant Jordi-Solomon Bonafed Letters." In *Studies in Medieval Jewish History and Literature*, edited by

Isadore Twersky, 337–64. Cambridge, MA: Harvard University Press, 1979.

------. "Trauma at Tortosa: The Testimony of Abraham Rimoch." *Mediaeval Studies* 47 (1985): 379–411.

------. "Keep Your Sons from Scripture: The Bible in Medieval Jewish Scholarship and Spirituality." In *Understanding Scripture: Explorations of Jewish and Christian Traditions of Interpretation*, edited by Clemens Thoma and Michael Wyschogrod, 81–101. New York: Paulist Press, 1987.

Ta-Shma, Yisrael M. "Halakhah, Kabbalah, and Philosophy in Christian Spain (A Critique of *A History of the Jews in Christian Spain*)." *The Hebrew Law Annual* 18/19 (1992–94): 479–95. (Hebrew)

------. "Rabbinic Literature in the Middle Ages." In *The Oxford Handbook of Jewish Studies*, edited by Martin Goodman, 219–40. Oxford: Oxford University Press, 2002.

Tirosh-Rothschild, Hava. "Jewish Philosophy on the Eve of Modernity." In *History of Jewish Philosophy*, edited by Daniel H. Frank and Oliver Leaman. Routledge History of World Philosophies 2, 399–414. London: Routledge, 1997.

Tirosh-Samuelson, Hava. *Happiness in Premodern Judaism: Virtue, Knowledge, and Well-Being*. Cincinnati: Hebrew Union College Press, 2003.

Van Bekkum, Wout. "O Seville! Ah Castille! Spanish-Hebrew Dirges from the Fifteenth Century." In *Hebrew Scholarship and the Medieval World*, edited by Nicholas de Lange, 156–70. New York: Cambridge University Press, 2001.

Wacks, David. "Toward a History of Hispano-Hebrew Literature in its Romance Context," *eHumanista* 14 (2010): 196-98.

Wolfson, Harry A. *Crescas' Critique of Aristotle*. Cambridge, MA: Harvard University Press, 1929.

Yavetz, Joseph. *Hasdei 'Adonai*. Jerusalem: n.p., 1934.

Yerushalmi, Yosef Hayim. *Zakhor: Jewish History and Jewish Memory*. New York: Schocken, 1982.

Zonta, Mauro. *Hebrew Scholasticism in the Fifteenth Century: A History and Source Book*. Dordrecht: Springer, 2006.

Zwiep, Irene E. "Jewish Scholarship and Christian Tradition in Late-Medieval Catalonia: Profiat Duran on the Art of Memory." In *Hebrew Scholarship and the Medieval World*, edited by Nicholas de Lange, 224-39. New York: Cambridge University Press, 2001.

From Al-Andalus to North Africa: The Lineage and Scholarly Genealogy of a Jewish Family[1]

.... Esperanza Alfonso

The Gavisons: A Foundational Story

Abraham b. Meʾir Abi Zimra, of blessed memory [said]: Upon the bitter deportation that took place in Sepharad, about two hundred souls left the city of Granada and arrived in Tlemecen. It was in Granada that a family by the name of Gavison lived. The hand of God rested upon them so that they all died martyrs' deaths and not a single one of them converted, as was the case in all other families. The origin of their exile had been the city of Seville, [as they were counted among] the exiles of 1391.[2] From Seville they arrived in Granada, where neither they nor other [Jewish] families were left in peace, so that all their family, boys and girls, the young and the elderly, died

---

[1] This article has been written within the framework of the project: "Inteleg: Intellectual and Material Legacies of Late Medieval Sephardic Judaism: An Interdisciplinary Approach," funded by the ERC.

[2] Following convention, the date is indicated by means of a Biblical verse which illustrates the events taking place that year, in this case Nahum 1:2: "The Lord is a passionate avenging God," for 1391.

martyrs' deaths. Not even one of them converted. As for these two brothers, wise men, the most prominent among the noble Israelites, an amazing miracle was granted to them and they survived, and came with us to the lands of the Ishmaelites. Their names are Rabbi Jacob and Rabbi Abraham, sons of Rabbi Joseph Gavison.[3]

This passage can be found at the end of 'Omer ha-shikhehah ("The Forgotten Sheaf"), a singularly atypical commentary on the Book of Proverbs written in Algeria by several generations of a Jewish family by the name of Gavison (or Gavishon).[4] Abraham, the author, son of Rabbi Jacob Gavison the Elder, who is mentioned in the passage, seems to have completed a first version of the book by 1574.[5] The commentary is known to have gone through several revisions thereafter and to have been supplemented by additions made by subsequent generations of the family. The text therefore expanded as the family itself grew; it was later forgotten for years, only to be "discovered" by one of the first author's descendants, also called Abraham. It was finally published in Leghorn in 1748.[6] As it has come down to us, 'Omer ha-shikhehah consists of 139 four-

---

[3] Abraham Gavison and Jacob Gavison, 'Omer ha-shikhehah, Livorno: Be-bet u-vi-defus Abraham b. Refa'el Mildolah, 1748; reprint with introduction and notes by René S. Sirat (Jerusalem: Hotsa'at Kedem, 1973), 138a.

[4] This book has remained relatively marginal to modern scholarship. In 1964 René Samuel Sirat wrote an MA thesis ('Omer hašikḥāh: Commentaire sur le livre des Proverbes d'Abraham Gabišon, Mémoire de diplôme d'études supériéures [Strasbourg, 1964]) and a year later a PhD thesis in which he studied the Gavisons' contribution to exegesis and linguistics (Abraham and Jacob Gabišon: Exégètes et linguistes, étude philosophique et linguistique d' 'O.Š, Thèse de doctorat de recherches (Strasbourg, 1965). In the 1960s and 1970s, Sirat also authored a handful of articles on the topic. See "La comparaison linguistique entre l'hébreu, l'araméen et l'arabe chez les auteurs du 'Omer hašikḥāh ('O. Š.)," REJ 124 (1965): 397–407; "'Omer ha-šiḳḥa et la famille Gabišon," WCJS 4, no. 2 (1968): 65–67; and "La vie des juifs en Alger au XVIe siècle d'aprés 'Omer hašikḥāh: Commentaire sur les proverbes d'A. Gabišon," in Mélanges André Neher (Paris: Maisonneuve, 1975), 317–29. See also below, note 21.

[5] This is the date given by Abraham Gavison, the main author, at the beginning of the book (1a). However, Moses Gavison, who was to prepare the book for publication about a century later, indicates that it was written in 1565 (118c). See Sirat's introduction to his reprint of the book: Gavison, 'Omer ha-shikhehah, 17. According to Sirat, Moses was wrong. As for Jacob Gavison's additions, they can be considered a second version of the book. See Sirat's comments in Gavison, 'Omer ha-shikhehah, 18.

[6] It was common for seventeenth-century Maghribi Jewish authors to print their works in Livorno. See Francesca Bregoli, "Hebrew Printing and Communication Networks between Livorno and North Africa, 1740–1789," Report of the Oxford Centre for Hebrew and Jewish Studies: Academic Year 2007–2008 (Oxford: The Centre, 2008), 51–60.

columned pages, and is divided into two sections. Section 1 (1–118c) opens with two prologues by wise men of Algeria who were contemporaries of either the author or the editor.[7] These prologues are followed by the author's own prologue and the commentary proper. The latter, which comprises the main body of the book, includes substantial quotations drawn from previous commentators and is interspersed with popular Arabic proverbs, linguistic and grammatical remarks, lengthy quotations from didactic Hebrew and Arabic narrative works, and a number of historical digressions. Section 2 (118c–139b) gathers together an assortment of disparate materials written by various members of three generations of the family, such as letters, poems for a variety of occasions, a selection of Arabic proverbs with translations, historical passages, and the like.[8]

The passage quoted above, by the poet Rabbi Abraham b. Meir Abi Zimra, a contemporary of Rabbi Abraham Gavison,[9] the author of 'Omer ha-shikhehah, is the last in a list of a few similar and often identical biographical passages describing the Gavisons' origins and extolling their virtues and achievements as a family and as individuals.[10] In this passage, Abi Zimra reports that the family had left Seville for Granada after the riots that ravaged the city in 1391.[11] Having lived through further unrest in Granada for over a century, some members of the Gavison family, whose possible activities in that city are not mentioned and remain unknown, are said to have eventually escaped martyrdom and left for North Africa after the

---

[7] The first prologue was written by four Algerian rabbis in 1747. The ensuing prologues were authored by Simon b. Zemah Duran and Solomon b. Zemah Duran, Mas'ud Ezra, Mandil Abi Zimrah, and an unidentified Western sage. The pages in these prologues are not numbered.

[8] There were precedents for the inclusion of poetic stanzas into a Biblical commentary. A case in point is that of Joseph ben Judah ben 'Aknīn (d. c. 1220) in his commentary on the Song of Songs. See Abraham S. Halkin, "Ibn 'Aknīn's Commentary on the Song of Songs," in *Alexander Marx Jubilee Volume on the Occasion of His Seventieth Birthday*, ed. Saul Lieberman (New York: The Jewish Theological Seminary of America, 1950), 406.

[9] Rabbi Abraham b. Me'ir Abi Zimra, from Malaga, was acquainted with Abraham Gavison, the author. The Abi Zimra family is also said to have left Granada for North Africa in 1492.

[10] In addition to Abraham b. Me'ir Abi Zimra, see the introduction opening the book, the introduction written by Simon b. Zemah Duran, and the author's prologue.

[11] Sirat ("'Omer ha-šikha et la famille Gabišon,") notes that the same origin is mentioned in a letter Jacob Gavison sent to Chayim Kafusi. See Adolf Neubauer, *Mediaeval Jewish Chronicles and Chronological Dates* (Amsterdam: Philo, 1970), 129. The account in this letter is almost identical to Abi Zimra's.

Christian takeover of Granada in 1492. Abi Zimra focuses on three of the family members who lived in that city: Joseph Gavison, a first known common ancestor and the man portrayed as a sort of founding figure of the lineage, who probably died before 1492, and his sons, Jacob and Abraham, the two Gavisons who were miraculously spared and fled to North Africa. As for their relatives, they are all reported to have lost their lives as a result of their refusal to convert after the arrival of the Christians in Granada. Expanding on the idea of martyrdom, other passages in the book describe the lost family members as "a perfect sacrifice, a burnt offering to the heavens."[12]

The scant secondary literature on *'Omer ha-shikhehah* has tried to make sense of this and other biographical and autobiographical accounts, as well as some other passages containing historical information scattered throughout the commentary. Most often taking these accounts at face value, scholarly literature has used them as source material in an effort to shed light on Jewish life in the transition from al-Andalus to North Africa, as well as on the conditions of Jewish life in Algiers well into the seventeenth century.[13]

Admittedly, the biographical and autobiographical remarks that feature in *'Omer ha-shikhehah* are strikingly similar to those found in any number of other autobiographical and biographical passages inserted in the writings of various sorts produced in the aftermath of the expulsions from the Hispanic kingdoms. Most of these reports, however, were not written by Jews from the Kingdom of Granada, but by deportees from Castile and Portugal,[14] a significant fact that

---

[12] See prologue by the wise men from Algiers (not numbered).

[13] For a similar use of poetry as a source for historical information on Jewish communities in North Africa, see Shalom bar-Asher, "La poésie liturgique juive nord-africaine comme source historique," in *Présence juive au Maghrib*, ed. Nicole S. Serfaty and Joseph Tedghi (Saint Denis: Editions Bouchene, 2004), 401–10.

[14] Sirat compares all these passages with passages in Chronicles, travel books and secondary literature on sixteenth- and seventeenth-century Jews. Recent scholarship has closely scrutinised similar descriptions in works by deportees from Castile and Portugal, such as Judah b. Solomon Kalas, Isaac b. Farax, Joseph Garçon, Shem Tov b. Samuel b. Gamil, and Abraham Saba, as well as works written by the descendants of these deportees in North Africa and beyond, all of whom reported the hardships of their exile and most of whom described their suffering at the hands of Christians and Muslims alike. See, for example, Michal Oron, "Autobiographical Elements in the Writings of Kabbalists from the Generation of the Expulsion," *Mediterranean Historical Review* 6 (1991): 102–11, and Javier Castaño, "Traumas individuales en un mundo trastornado: El éxodo de R. Yĕhudah Ya'aqob Chayyat (1492–1496)," in *Movimientos migratorios y expulsiones en la diáspora occidental:*

should be taken into consideration when reading the narrative on the family in the Gavisons' work.

However, instead of understanding Abi Zimra's text as a factual account attesting the accuracy of the historical details provided, one can alternatively read it as the symbolic expression of their experience. From this perspective, it is clear that none of the elements in the narrative on the family's origin and history appear to be accidental. On the contrary, the family's origin in Seville, their departure from that city in 1391, the martyrdom of most of the family members against the background of forced mass conversion in Granada in 1492, the miraculous survival of the two brothers and their journey to North Africa that same year, as well as the inferred association between the dates 1391 and 1492, all come across as elements charged with highly symbolic meaning.

When the symbolic meaning of the text is taken into account, the similarities between Abi Zimra's narrative and other accounts by Castilian and Portuguese Jewish deportees and their descendants become even more meaningful, as the generic similarities between these narratives seem to be the result of deliberate design. Thus, it does not seem to be by accident that Abi Zimra's account follows a lengthy historical narrative in which Moses Gavison[15] recalls the public martyrdom of Israel b. Joseph al-Naqawa in Toledo in 1391.[16] In Moses' account, Judah b. Asher, son of the renowned Talmudist Asher ben Yehiel (d. 1327) is also said to have met martyrdom with Israel al-Naqawa.[17] The impression left is that Ibn Abi Zimra's narrative mirrors that of Moses.

Likewise, rhetoric appears to serve a similar end and to suggest similar associations. Hence, metaphors of sacrifice as a "burnt

---

Terceros encuentros judaicos de Tudela; 14–17 de julio de 1998, ed. Fermín Miranda García (Pamplona: Universidad Pública de Navarra, 2000), 55–67.

[15] Moses Gavison (d. 1698) produced an edition of the book which was never published.

[16] Israel b. Joseph al-Naqawa (d. 1391) studied with Asher b. Yehiel and his son Jacob Ba'al ha-Turim in Toledo. On a Hebrew elegy reporting the events, see Cecil Roth, "Hebrew Elegy on Martyrs of Toledo," *JQR* 39 (1948–1949): 123–50. The elegy does not say that al-Naqawa was burned. Ephraim, son of Israel al-Naqawa, escaped to North Africa.

[17] Judah b. Asher (1270–1349) was the fourth son of Asher b. Jehiel, the German Talmudist who settled in Toledo. From historical records it is known that Judah b. Asher died in 1349. Moses Gavison probably mistakes him for his nephew, Asher b. Yehiel's grandson, also called Judah. See Roth, "Hebrew Elegy," 128.

offering to the heavens" seem to relate to the riots against the Jewish communities in Castile in 1391 only anachronistically. So too do forced mass conversion and experiences of martyrdom remain linked in the collective imagery to life in the Iberian Christian kingdoms in the late fifteenth century and not to the historical experience of Jews from the Kingdom of Granada. Similarities may and have been explained as reflecting the common experience of fifteenth-century deportees from the Iberian Peninsula, but they could also be read as embodying the collective multiple experiences of various groups of deportees in a single narrative. This is a point to which I will turn later.

An Intellectual Self-Portrayal

The foundational story of the Gavisons as retold by Abi Zimra in 'Omer ha-shikhehah is inextricably tied up with numerous other passages where the Gavisons fabricate their intellectual genealogy, as they identify and credit the intellectual models of whom they feel themselves to be the inheritors. The construction of this intellectual genealogy is embedded in the Gavisons' cultural practice—that is, in the nature of the work they write, the sources they draw on, and the materials their commentary gathers—and, what is even more relevant, in their explicit identification with scholars from previous centuries and specific literary genres.

A quick perusal of the book leads to the conclusion that the Gavisons drew from an extensive array of materials both in Arabic and in Hebrew in the commentary to Proverbs and in the appendix to their work. Looking first at the commentary proper,[18] it becomes evident that two thirteenth-century Provençal authors stand at the base of their exegetical program—Menachem ha-Me'iri (d. ca. 1310) and Levi ben Gerson (a.k.a. Gersonides, d. 1344). Citations from

---

[18] After the Expulsion from the Peninsula, homiletics and exegesis dominated intellectual life in the destinations of the deportees. In "The Intellectual Activity of the Jews of the Ottoman Empire during the Sixteenth and Seventeenth Centuries" (*Jewish Thought in the Seventeenth Century*, ed. Isadore Twersky and Bernard Septimus [Cambridge, MA: Harvard University Press, 1987], 95–135) Joseph Hacker explains that the obligations and roles of the scholars dictated their intellectual and literary pursuits. In addition to the Torah, the most popular books were the five scrolls, Job, Proverbs, Psalms, Daniel and Abot.

ha-Me'iri's and Gersonides' works, which are identified and quoted verbatim, represent about a third of the book. Next in importance are selections from *Qav we-naqi* by David ibn Yahya, who is known to have left Portugal for Italy in 1498. Among the remaining exegetical sources to which the Gavisons are indebted, the most prominent are Rashi (d. 1105), who is represented by about forty quotations, many of them indirect, and only three from Proverbs; Isaac Arama (a fifteenth-century exegete who settled in Aragon), with over twenty quotations; Maimonides (d. 1204) with twelve, and the Provençal writer Yedaya ha-Penini (d. 1340) with ten.[19] Regarding their use of Biblical commentaries, the Gavisons' work does not significantly depart from previous and contemporary sources. They go back to a wide variety of Ashkenazi, Provençal and Sephardic authors, most of whom enjoyed universal esteem by their time, with a predilection for those of an ethical, moralistic nature, mostly in the Aristotelian-Maimonidean tradition, as well as for those in the homiletic and midrashic style.

Biblical commentaries aside, their work draws from an assortment of other materials, most prominently historiographical and medical treatises, often written by Arabo-Muslim authors. Proverbs and poems are also used to contribute to the interpretation and/or illustration of specific Biblical passages. Both kinds of materials—poems and proverbs, either written or collected by the Gavisons—are also found in the final appendix. Among the poets they quote, three eleventh- and twelfth-century Andalusi Jewish authors—Solomon ibn Gabirol, Moses ibn Ezra and Judah Halevi—are extensively and equally well represented; the thirteenth-century Abraham Bedersi from Provence, Todros Halevi Abulafia (d.1306) from Castile,[20] and Meshullam b. Solomon de Piera (d. after 1206) from Aragon, are also mentioned, if only in passing.[21] Moreover,

---

[19] We also find seven quotations from Sa'adia's *Tafsir*. Quotations are not verbatim, which makes Sirat believe that the Gavisons did not have Sa'adia's works before them.

[20] It is known that in 1275 Todros accompanied Alfonso X on his trip to Beaucaire. Todros remained with Queen Violante in Perpignan, where he met Abraham Bedersi. The latter wrote several poems to him and his companion, Abū l-Hasan Sa'ul.

[21] The most important Jewish poets in sixteenth-century North Africa came from Malaga (conquered in 1487) and Granada. Prominent among them were: Sa'adia b. Maimon b. Danan (Granada), Abraham b. Solomon Halevi Bukrat (Malaga), Abraham b. Me'ir ibn Abi Zimra (Granada) and his son Isaac b. Abi Zimra, known as Mandil.

and this is most striking, references and direct quotations of Arabic poems proliferate throughout the book. In this regard, 'Omer ha-shikheḥah provides, in truth, a unique and privileged source for the study of sixteenth- and seventeenth-century North African Hebrew poetics, since it includes poems not only by the Gavisons themselves, but by many of their contemporaries.[22]

In the prologues introducing the book and throughout the commentary itself, one often comes across passages that explicitly and selectively associate the Gavisons with some particular cultural practices to the exclusion of others, and with past authors whose legacy the Gavisons claim for themselves as their direct and rightful inheritors.

In one of the prologues to the book, to cite one example, Solomon ben Zemah Duran, who neatly summarises the book's program, pinpoints two elements of great significance: 'Omer ha-shikheḥah, he acknowledges, gathers together many previous commentaries on the Book of Proverbs, which, he remarks, the Gavisons would have received directly from their teachers, the rabbis of Castile, as well as an assortment of poems by Arabs, "to be found sweet by those who understand them and whose translation [into Hebrew] would reveal to those who do not know [Arabic] that they had actually been taken from the Biblical book of Proverbs."[23] The book is therefore said to include all materials pertinent to the topic, received directly from a generally recognized intellectual elite in exegetical matters, that of the rabbis of Castile.[24] Prominent among these Castilian

---

[22] For sixteenth- and seventeenth-North African Hebrew poetry in general, and for the use of 'Omer ha-shikheḥah as a source to reconstruct this period's poetics in particular, see Ephraim Chazan, "From Spain to its Diaspora: The Poetic Heritage in its Transformations," Peʿamim 26 (1986): 46–51 (Hebrew), and "From Spain to North-Africa: Hebrew Poetry in Transition," Peʿamim 59 (1994): 52–64 (Hebrew); see also Joseph Tobi, "Hebrew Poetry in the East after the Spanish Expulsion," Peʿamim 26 (1986): 29–44 (Hebrew), and "Spanish Hebrew Poetry among the Sixteenth-Century Sephardic Jews in Morocco," in "From the Treasures of Spain: Studies on Hebrew Poetry in Spain and its Influence," ed. Judith Dishon and Shmuel Refael, special issue, Criticism and Interpretation: Journal for Interdisciplinary Studies in Literature and Culture 39 (2006): 191–204.

[23] Prologue by Solomon b. Zemah Duran (pages not numbered).

[24] On learning and scholarship in fifteenth-century Castile, see Abraham Gross, "A Sketch of the History of Yeshivot in Castile in the Fifteenth Century," Peʿamim 31 (1987): 3–20 (Hebrew). Gross remarks that sources written immediately after the Expulsion describe Castile as a land of yeshivot. In the introduction to his supracommentary on Rashi, for example, Judah b. Solomon Kalas reports of having left Castile, which he describes as "a

rabbis and frequently quoted in *'Omer ha-shikhehah* are Asher ben Yehiel (d. 1328)[25] and his sons, grandson, and students, as well as Isaac Canpanton (d. 1483) and his students.[26] Indeed, there are many times in the course of their explanations when the Gavisons pride themselves on having received the interpretation of a particular verse directly from the student of a Castilian rabbi. Such is the case, for example, when Abraham Gavison claims to have heard a specific interpretation of Proverbs 27:15 from his teacher Solomon Kalaṣ,[27] who in turn is said to have learned it from the Castilian rabbi Isaac de León.[28] These intellectual genealogies place them emphatically last in what they represent as a list of authorities in exegetical matters.

Credit to the rabbis of Castile is consistent with a few passages in the book describing in further detail the curriculum laid out by the Gavisons, passages which are all made in reference to the culture of the Jews in the Northern Christian kingdoms (thirteenth to fifteenth centuries). For example, in commenting on three verses from Proverbs regarding the effects of honey on the human body Jacob notes that Proverbs 24:13 ("Eat honey, my son, as it is good") is written with regard to those who study the Bible, the Mishnah, the Talmud, *aggadot* (homiletic texts) and *posequim* (legal decisions), since there is no limitation to their study; on the other hand, Proverbs 25:16 ("If you find honey, eat just enough; too much of it and you will vomit") refers to those who learn philosophy, [Maimonides'] *Guide of the Perplexed* and logic. "While speculating on metaphysics is worthwhile and praiseworthy," he notes, "these sciences only served

---

land of academies," and of having reached Islamic lands, "which are lacking in academies and [where the practice of] reading [was not widespread]."

[25] On Asher b. Yehiel, see above, notes 15 and 16.

[26] Isaac Canpanton led a *yeshivah* in Zamora. Isaac Aboab, Isaac de Leon, Shem Tov ibn Shem Tov and, probably, Isaac Arama, are counted among his students.

[27] See Gavison, *'Omer ha-shikhehah*, 98d. Similarly, Abraham Gavison reports having heard a specific explanation of Proverbs 11:24 from his teacher Judah Kalas. Commenting on the following verse he refers to Rashi and again points to the wise men of Castile as Rashi's source (33 c). When commenting on Proverbs 20:12, Jacob Gavison mentions Jacob Bireb and Jacob Qino, both from Castile, and remarks that the famous halakhist Joseph Caro had been Bireb's student in Castile (68 c).

[28] A student of Rabbi Isaac Canpanton, and a friend of Isaac Aboab, Isaac de Leon (d. 1486 or 1490) was a Castilian rabbi and kabbalist. See David, Abraham, "Leon, Isaac de," *EJ*, ed. Michael Berenbaum and Fred Skolnik, 2nd ed. (Detroit: Macmillan Reference USA, 2007): vol. 12, 644-64, *Gale Virtual Reference Library*, accessed 30 April, 2010.

Maimonides in their capacity as cooks and bakers, that is they were servants attending the most honourable and highest lady, our Sacred Torah, and he only used them to sharpen his intellect."[29] Finally, Proverbs 25:27 ("It is not good to eat too much honey") hints at those concerned with Kabbalah and *Zohar*.[30]

A similar tripartite curriculum, well grounded in traditional knowledge and incorporating philosophy and Kabbalah, can be found in Jacob's comments on Proverbs 30:2–3. Here, as on Proverbs 24:13–27, the author remarks that philosophy is limited, and claims that no one can understand "the science of God's works," i.e. metaphysical matters, on the basis of his own intellect or knowledge (*da'at*) and at the expense of the mystical tradition (*qabbalah*), as Aristotle and Plato had attempted to do.

The authors put forth an apology and defence of traditional religious sources, philosophy and, to a lesser extent, Kabbalah. Not only the study of Torah, but also the study of Mishnah, Talmud and other rabbinic sources is consistently advocated throughout.[31] A moderate support for philosophy also becomes apparent, so that the importance of Maimonides' work and its compatibility with traditional and mystical study is often endorsed. Respect for the central figure of Maimonides had evidently run in the family's blood since at least the times of Jacob Gavison the Elder, who was one of the two brothers reported to have fled to North Africa and was said to have written *Derekh ha-sekhel* ("The Way of Wisdom"), a work in support of Maimonides which has not survived.[32] The passages cited previously are part of a long-standing and ongoing debate on the merits and demerits of philosophy, its value for the individual and its place within the broader educational program and scholarly curriculum. This debate dates back to the medieval controversies

---

[29] Jacob is obviously echoing Maimonides' own words in his letter to Rabbi Jonathan of Lunel, where he conceives of the Torah as a legitimate wife and the sciences as foreign lovers. See *Letters and Essays of Moses Maimonides*, ed. Isaac Shailat (Jerusalem: Maliyot Press of Yeshivat Birkat Moshe Maaleh Adumim, 1987): vol. 2, 502.

[30] Gavison, *'Omer ha-shikhehah*, 86 a.

[31] See below, note 37.

[32] See, for example, Gavison, *'Omer ha-shikhehah*, 88 b and 131b.

regarding the works of Maimonides in the Hispanic Christian kingdoms and Provence.[33]

In addition and arguably in parallel to the exegetical material that the Gavisons pride themselves on having received from the intellectual elite of Castile, and also in parallel to the integrating Sephardic curriculum they put forth, the book includes an assortment of Hebrew poems. These poems are written by classical Jewish authors from Sepharad and Provence, and by the Gavisons themselves and their contemporaries, and are introduced on an ad hoc basis to illustrate specific Biblical passages throughout the commentary and in the form of an anthology at the end of it.[34] Both in the introduction and, most notably, in the final appendix, the authors of the prologues opening the book and the Gavisons themselves extol poetry's nature and virtues. Poetry is described as first among the sciences on account of its being an art of the rational soul[35] and having being divinely inspired.[36] Even highly erotic poetry is to be praised and embraced as part of a much treasured legacy.[37]

The Gavisons' persistent defence of the legitimacy of poetry as a cultural practice makes clear that poetry must have had its detractors. Such a defence suggests the existence of opposition to

---

[33] On the reception of Maimonides' works, see Ángel Sáenz-Badillos, "Late Medieval Jewish Writers on Maimonides," and Menachem Kellner, "Maimonides' Disputed Legacy," in *Traditions of Maimonideanism*, ed. Carlos Fraenkel, 223–44 and 245–76 respectively; Maud Kozodoy, "No Perpetual Enemies: Maimonideanism at the Beginning of the Fifteenth Century," in *The Cultures of Maimonideanism: New Approaches to the History of Jewish Thought*, ed. James T. Robinson (Leiden: Brill, 2009), 149–70; and, more akin to the present study, Eric Lawee, "Maimonides in the Eastern Mediterranean: The Case of Rashi's Resisting Readers," in *Maimonides after 800 Years: Essays on Maimonides and his Influence*, ed. Jay M. Harris (Cambridge, MA: Harvard University Press, 2007), 183–206.

[34] For the use of *'Omer ha-shikhehah* as a repository of sixteenth- and seventeenth-century Jewish poetry in North Africa, see above, note 22.

[35] Discussions on the place of poetry within the hierarchies of knowledge are commonly found in a variety of (Arabic, Latin/Romance and Hebrew) sources throughout the Middle Ages. When considered among the sciences, the status assigned to poetry tended to be low. Drawing from Aristotle, medieval Jewish, Christian, and Islamic authors accorded poetry the lowest cognitive power among the logical sciences. By the late twelfth- and early thirteenth-century, and apparently under the influence of Plato's philosophy, the esteem for poetry had decreased even further. It is true, however, that thirteenth-century scholars who were influenced by the Aristotelian concept of politics as the highest science did recognize poetry's capacity for moving one to moral action.

[36] On the status of poetry, see also Gavison, *'Omer ha-shikhehah*, 121 a-b, 125 c, and 128d.

[37] Gavison, *'Omer ha-shikhehah*, 131c-d.

poetry within certain circles in the Gavisons' milieu. The following lines, quoting the words of an unidentified wise man, underscore this opposition. The sage exhorts a friend, saying:

> My friend, you have to know that the science [*hokhmah*] of poetry is lofty and important, as it is an art [*mal'ekhet*] of the rational soul, which is the uttermost precious and important. Even when nowadays the Ishmaelites are more successful and excel at it, poetry is also a Jewish art, and a divine art established between the altar and the atrium. Moreover, Solomon, blessed be he, wrote one thousand and five poems (1 Kings 4.32), and his father wrote the most beautiful song of Israel (Psalms).... Besides, it is only enjoyed by rational men..., rather than those whose minds are unrefined and whose mouths are heavy, those whose tongues are uncircumcised. The man who does not cultivate it is limited, he hates it and hates those who master it, and slanders it, and insults it, saying that only those who know very little of the Bible and Talmud do practice it.[38]

The alleged supremacy of the Arabs in poetry was arguably a source of unease among contemporaries of the Gavisons, who recriminated poets for their poor command of, or disregard for, the Bible and Talmud. Immune to these criticisms, the Gavisons conceived of poetry as a gift only granted to men of sensitive souls. They justified its practice as Jewish, argued that Solomon also wrote poetry, and denied that poets neglected the study of the Bible and Talmud.[39] Poetry, even explicitly sensual love poetry, did not preclude, in their view, the mastery of traditional Jewish sources.[40]

None of these arguments comes as a surprise, given that similar discussions on the merits and shortcomings of poetry proliferated throughout the Middle Ages and the Renaissance, all using related apologetic strategies. Andalusi Jewish advocates of poetry had already acknowledged the Arabs' superiority, yet repeatedly justified

---

[38] Gavison, '*Omer ha-shikhehah*, 126 a-b.

[39] See also Gavison, '*Omer ha-shikhehah*, 129 d, where Jacob's son Abraham explains that the poems he writes on the high status of poetry are intended to silence those who criticize his neglect of Mishnah and Talmud. Similarly, Jacob Gavison makes the lofty status of Talmud manifest and quotes Ibn Danan's poems on the six orders of the Mishnah. See 122 ff.

[40] Abraham, son of Jacob Gavison, who hesitates to write a *qerovah* on "the matters of the body," nevertheless vindicates love poetry by recalling that the Song of Songs represents a precedent of such a practice within the Jewish tradition, and by claiming that Sa'adia ibn Danan and Abraham [Abi Zimra?], who wrote such poems, were free from being morally suspect. See Gavison, '*Omer ha-shikhehah*, 131 d.

its practice among the Jews. They described the poets as prophets,[41] turned to the Bible in search of precedents, and denied the alleged opposition and incompatibility between poetry and religious studies.[42] These arguments appear time and again, not only in Andalusi sources but in Hebrew sources from the Christian Kingdoms, Provence and Italy. Some of them, such as the identification between poets and prophets and the divine inspiration of poetry, are also well known in contemporary Christian sources. This is not to say that discussions on the value of poetry and its place within the curriculum are purely a matter of convention. Indeed, the type of sources these discussions are made part of and the cultural milieu in which they are produced are always to be taken into consideration, as arguments changed over time and served different purposes. Suffice it to note in this regard, and by way of example, the different use of the *topos* of the

---

[41] On the *topos* of "poet as prophet" see Dan Pagis, "The Poet as Prophet in Medieval Hebrew Literature," in *Poetry and Prophecy: The Beginnings of a Literary Tradition*, ed. James L. Kugel (Ithaca, NY: Cornell University Press, 1990), 140–50.

[42] In *The Compunctious Poet: Cultural Ambiguity and Hebrew Poetry in Muslim Spain* (Baltimore: Johns Hopkins University Press, 1991), Ross Brann examines the ways in which medieval scholars adapted Aristotelian positions to their theoretical views and their social and historical circumstances. On the attitude towards poetry among Andalusi Jewish authors, see also Esperanza Alfonso, *Islamic Culture through Jewish Eyes: Al-Andalus from the 10th to the 12th Century* (London: Routledge, 2007), Chapter Two. The idea that the attitude towards poetry in al-Andalus was overly positive in contradistinction to the negative attitude toward poetry in Christian Spain is an over-simplification. While the thirteenth century witnessed a transformation of the attitude towards poetry, the ensuing centuries cannot be considered a period of neglect and decay of poetry. In "From Logic to Ethics: A Redefinition of Poetry in the Thirteenth Century" (in "Al-Andalus and its Legacies," ed. Esperanza Alfonso and Ross Brann, special issue, *Comparative Literature Studies* 45, no. 2 [2008]: 165–81), Aurora Salvatierra examines the changing conception of poetry in the thirteenth century. According to her, while in the Aristotelian system poetry was considered to be within the realm of knowledge, as providing some access to knowledge, however limited, Aristotle's medieval readers placed it within the realm of act, emphasizing its educational and moral character. Fourteenth- and fifteenth-century remarks on poetry among Sephardic Jewish authors are all produced against the background of this dual manner of considering poetry as within the realm of knowledge or of act. Far from having a generally negative attitude towards poetry, as it is often argued, some medieval Jewish poets turned it into the only valid instrument left to convey truth. On this use of poetry as a vehicle for truth, see Arturo Prats, "The Representation of *Conversos* in Bonafed's *Dīwān*," in *Medieval Jewish Identities: Al-Andalus and Beyond*, ed. Carmen Caballero-Navas and Esperanza Alfonso (New York: Palgrave Macmillan, forthcoming). From Prats' analysis of the fifteenth-century poet from Aragon, Solomon Bonafed, it becomes clear that, in Bonafed's view, poetry not only spoke truth but became the only sphere of discourse able to guarantee Judaism and a Jewish identity.

poet as prophet. By the eleventh century, when the association between poet and prophet was already widespread and had become a commonplace, the celebrated Andalusi poet and philosopher Solomon ibn Gabirol invoked this *topos* in the introduction to his *'Anaq*, a long didactic poem on the Hebrew language. Against such a background, and modeling himself on the prophet Jeremiah, Ibn Gabirol claims to have received in a dream a divine commandment to rescue the Hebrew language. By describing the state of decay of Hebrew, and his role as restorer of the language, he is graced with a quasi-prophetic aura which makes his poem seem all the more admirable. In sum, the *topos* serves his self-praise.[43]

In the fifteenth century, the Aragonese poet Solomon ibn Bonafed presented his poetry as a repository of truth and a transmitter of knowledge. At a time of massive conversion in Aragon, when most of the poet's friends had converted or were about to convert, Bonafed identified poetry with prophecy and turned it into a valuable instrument to make converts return to Judaism.[44] In Ibn Gabirol's poem, God's advice to Jeremiah only serves to highlight the poet's role as prophet of the neglected language. In contrast, Bonafed used the convention of the poet as prophet to claim that Biblical prophecy was poetry, and, by the same token, attributed a prophetic sacred power to his own poetry. It is worth noting that in both cases the prophetic character of poet and poetry remained linked to the Hebrew language, as was the case with previous authors.

If we now turn to the Gavisons, it becomes apparent that they invoked the poet-as-prophet *topos* to justify their use of *both* Hebrew and Arabic poetry within a Biblical commentary. It is clear that in their work the idea of prophecy did not remain fundamentally linked to the Hebrew language. Likewise, they did not identify themselves as prophets, as Ibn Gabirol had, nor did they present their poetry as prophecy. They gave poetry the highest status among the sciences, took it as a product of the rational soul, and considered prophecy to be the highest type of knowledge, adducing as proof the poets' technical skills and virtuosity.[45]

---

[43] Alfonso, *Islamic Culture*, 15–17. See also Pagis, "The Poet as Prophet," 146–47.

[44] See Arturo Prats, "La representación de los conversos" (forthcoming).

[45] Gavison, *'Omer ha-shikhehah*, 125 c.

In spite of the differences that might have been introduced, the Gavisons' championing of poetry clearly echoes passages written by Andalusi Jewish poets from the so-called Golden Age. Moreover, the Gavisons themselves explicitly claim to do nothing but follow their Andalusi predecessors, using here the term "Sephardic" as an equivalent to "Andalusi" in reference to Jews living in the Iberian Peninsula under Islamic rule.[46] Hence, Abraham, son of Jacob Gavison, states:

> When I saw that my forefather, the wise Rabbi Abraham Gavison, had acquired the science of poetry, which is the lily among all the sciences, and [having seen] that all my teachers and rabbis from Sepharad who had come before us had all followed its path, had delighted themselves with its practice, and had tasted its sweetness and its honeycomb, and also that my forefather [Jacob Gavison] and his father had largely acquired it, I told myself: In spite of my poor knowledge and intelligence I will also take the path that they followed, as this is what my soul has chosen.[47]

The central role of poetry in the Gavisons' ethos is also made evident in a section where Jacob Gavison laments the death of his son, Abraham, whose poems and exegetical remarks are included in the appendix to *'Omer ha-shikhehah*. According to his father, Abraham died a young bachelor with no children. In spite of his youth, he knew by heart the twenty-four books of the Bible, and was proficient in the exegesis of Biblical words, and all matters pertaining to the prosody and grammar of Biblical Hebrew. Knowledge of the Bible, a background in exegesis, and mastery of the auxiliary sciences required for its study, namely grammar, were at the heart of Abraham's educational program. In addition to this background, he was a skillful poet who wrote beautiful *bakkashot* (petition poems), and a translator of Arabic poems into Hebrew. He mastered—his father adds—Hebrew and Arabic scripts and wrote a book of

---

[46] While the Gavisons call this model "Sephardic," it is obvious that the label only corresponded to the Jewish culture produced in the Hispanic kingdoms in homiletical and exegetical terms. The Gavisons do not refer to Provence as separate from Sepharad, and generally refer to Provençal authors as Sephardic. Likewise, when they refer to the Sephardic scholars, they usually point to Andalusi Jewish authors. They single out Jewish scholars from Christian lands by saying "the rabbis of Castile," and similarly *"rabbotenu ha-lo'azim."*

[47] Gavison, *'Omer ha-shikhehah*, 128 d.

medicine in Arabic characters. His soft voice, handsome face and generosity were qualities that only added to the picture of a young man who epitomized the ideal of a well-rounded Jewish intellectual in his father's eyes.[48]

Jacob's description of his son's skills certainly echo similar well known courses of study as they appear in elegies, poems of praise, ethical wills, and other writings in previous centuries. Jacob ibn Gavison's praise of his son Abraham is particularly reminiscent of Judah ibn Tibbon's admonition to his son Samuel,[49] and Joseph b. Judah ibn 'Aknin's remarks on the proper course of studies in his *Maqālah fī ṭibb al-nufūs* ("Hygiene of the Souls" / *Marpe' ha-nefashot* in Hebrew).[50] Both works were also written on the periphery of al-Andalus at the twilight of the Andalusi period. In all three descriptions of the proper intellectual curriculum for Jews, Hebrew poetry is central to the course of studies and becomes emblematic of it.

Jacob Gavison's descriptions of his son's skills and these courses of studies all called for cultural practice in both Arabic and Hebrew. Likewise, both Abraham Gavison on Proverbs 5:20 and Jacob Gavison in the opening paragraphs to the appendix argue for and endorse such a bilingual model. They point out the proximity between Hebrew, Aramaic, and Arabic; they describe Arabic as "a somewhat corrupted Hebrew"; and they quote a list of authorities— from Talmudic sages to Maimonides—in their support.[51] Hence, Abraham reports that he has counted hundreds of Arabic words of Hebrew origin, some of them, such as *yad, regel, ro'sh, 'enayim, te'enim, 'anavim, rimmonim*, etc. showing no corruption, while others had been slightly corrupted.[52] As was the case with regard to their advocacy of poetry, while the Gavisons described this practice as belonging to Sephardic culture in general terms, it is clear that they were actually referring to Andalusi culture, since they

---

[48] Gavison, *'Omer ha-shikhehah*, 127 d.

[49] See Israel Abrahams, *Hebrew Ethical Wills* (Philadelphia: The Jewish Publication Society of America, 1954), 51–93.

[50] See Hirsch Edelmann, ed., *Divre ḥefeṣ: "Acceptable Words" or Extracts from Various Unprinted Works of Eminent Hebrew Authors* (London: A. P. Shaw, 1953), 23ff.

[51] On comparative linguistics in the Gavisons' work, see Sirat, "La comparaison linguistique." Sirat also addresses in his study the passages I mention further on.

[52] Gavison, *'Omer ha-shikhehah*, 15 b.

make it stand in vivid contrast to that of *rabbotenu ha-lo'azim*, i.e. Jewish scholars from Christian lands. Among them, the Gavisons do not single out an exegete from the Iberian Christian kingdoms, but significantly they do point to the celebrated eleventh-century Ashkenazi commentator Rashi. While both Abraham and Jacob say they are pleasantly surprised by Rashi's reference to Arabic in some passages of his commentary on the Torah (e.g. on Genesis 25:20), they confess to be shocked by his ignorance of this language in many other passages (e.g. Exodus 10:15, and Daniel 6:16). They draw not only from written sources to argue for the importance of Arabic as an exegetical tool, but from their own immediate experiences. A case in point in this regard is Jacob's explanation of the Aramaic word "bal" in Daniel 6:15 ([The king] *was determined* to save Daniel [*we 'al Dani'el sam bal le-shezavutah*]). "Being quite inferior to Rashi"—the author remarks—"I can only be astonished when he admits to ignoring the meaning of the word 'bal.' Even more so when [among us] even a three-year-old knows that the Arabic word 'bal,'[53] means knowledge (*da'at*) and intellect (*sekhel*), as teachers address their students saying *rud ba'alek*, that is 'pay attention.'"[54] Moreover, the register that Jacob uses to shed light on a Biblical verse is not classical Arabic but a contemporary dialect. This use of North African dialects and popular culture in Hebrew exegetical works is quite atypical and certainly worth noting.

Anticipating criticism from, arguably, the Castilian rabbis who had also settled in Algeria and who frowned on the inclusion of Arabic poems in a Biblical commentary, Jacob adds further support to his father's argument in favor of such a practice:

> Who is for us higher than Maimonides?—he wondered—Well, it happens that he explained the *mishnayyot* in Arabic [in a book] called *Al-Siraj*, which means *Ha-Ner* ("The Lamp"),[55] until the rabbis, namely Rabbi al-Harizi and Shemu'el ibn Tibbon, came and translated it into our holy language. [Maimonides] also wrote the

---

[53] Sirat already remarked that this interpretation is mistakenly attributed to Rashi. The Gavisons are actually quoting Abraham ibn Ezra.

[54] Gavison, *'Omer ha-shikhehah*, 119 c. Jacob also uses specific examples drawn from personal experience to interpret by means of an Arabic word various other Biblical passages (Jeremiah 31:20, Isaiah 14:23; 9:8; 25:11; Judges 3:22; Exodus 1:14; 5:18).

[55] It refers to the Commentary on the Mishnah.

Guide of the Perplexed in Arabic and gave it the title *Dalālat al-Ḥā'irīn*, until the abovementioned rabbis came and translated it as it is generally acknowledged and known. And it happened that some of these rabbis were not proficient in both languages and shortened and added to [the book's] intended meaning, to the point of sparking off the infamous controversy on his books between communities, while the *later sages* who succeeded them went to the very depths of its meaning and attributed the shortcomings to the translator, as the Rav, Gaon Rabbi Meshullam noted in a long poem [...].[56] Also, the pious Rabbi Bahya ibn Paqudah wrote *The Book of the Duties of the Heart* in Arabic and Rabbi Judah ibn Tibbon translated it into our sacred language. Its title in Arabic was *Farā'iḍ al-qulūb* and *Sefer hovot ha-levavot* in Hebrew [...] Likewise, Rabbi Moses ibn Ezra wrote a book full of treasures in Arabic under the title *Kitāb al-muḥāḍara wa-l-mudhākara*, which means *Moshav ha-khoḥmah we-zikhronah* ("Book of Discussion and Remembrance") [...]. The wise Abraham Bedersi, father of Rabbi Yedaya Penini, author of *Contemplation of the World*, was a renowned poet, considered a saint, and in his time lived Rabbi Todros Halevi, the author of *'Oṣar ha-kavod* ("Treasury of Glory") and [it is known that] they exchanged sweet and delicious poems written in the holy spirit, that is in the holy language [and it is known] that they translated Arabic poems. Rabbi Bedersi wrote to [Rabbi Todros Halevi] as follows:

> You have defeated us with sweet poems,
> Which translate Arabic poems.
> For this reason we will abandon poetry and will remain silent,
> And as light does we will follow the Arabs.[57]

This scholarly genealogy, which was in all likelihood deployed in anticipation of the Castilian rabbis' objections to the use of Arabic poetry in a Jewish Biblical commentary, is particularly relevant to the issue under discussion here. Addressing the Castilian rabbis, Jacob Gavison offers a list of precedents for the family's use of Arabic by Jewish authors, among them two poets. He presents Maimonides, Bahya ibn Paqudah, Moses ibn Ezra, Abraham Bedersi and Todros Halevi as the Gavisons' intellectual and scholarly forerunners. Throughout the list, it is to be noted, special care is placed on

---

[56] This is Meshullam ben Solomon de Piera (d. 1260). On this poem, see Hayyim Schirmann, *Ha-Shirah ha-ivrit bi-Sefarad u-ve-Provens* (Jerusalem: Bialik; Tel Aviv: Dvir, 1954–60), 2, 295–318.

[57] Gavison, *'Omer ha-shikheḥah*, 119 b.

giving precise reference to all works quoted in the original and in translation, as if original and translation were equally valuable and neither could exist without the other. This scholarly genealogy sheds light in particular on the Gavisons' portrayals of themselves. They knew Arabic, they wrote poetry, and even more significantly, they considered themselves qualified translators.

As has been noted, in their prologues to the book, Solomon ben Zemah Duran and Abraham b. Jacob Gavison had already remarked that, in addition to its collection of previous commentaries on Proverbs, *'Omer ha-shikhehah* featured poems in their original Arabic (to be enjoyed by Arabic-speaking readers) and in translation (for those ignorant of Arabic to see that they drew on the Biblical Book of Proverbs). The book is thus interspersed with a bilingual edition of short poems. Most of these poems are of an ethical nature,[58] as Abraham remarks when quoting the following *azharah* (admonitory poem):

> Abraham [son of Jacob] said: I found a very good poem, which pleased me much as it was a lofty azharah: אכב״ץ צותך אן נטקת כליל / ואל תפת פי אל נהר קבל אל מקאל // ואחרץ אל חייאט אן יכון וראה/סארק / אל סמע ועיין אל מקאל[59]. And translated it into our holy language [as follows]: "Behold not to speak at night / and behold from people at day. // Behold the wall, as someone beneath could steal words said in a whisper.[60]

It is not only poetry that the Gavisons include in this bilingual edition, but also proverbs. Furthermore, in addition to quotations or anthologies of poems and proverbs in bilingual versions, at times the Gavisons will point out that a given poem or a proverb is a translation from Arabic, although they omit to transcribe the original source.[61]

---

[58] On the emphasis on the ethical value of poetry, see above, note 35.

[59] A few mistakes are observable in the Hebrew transliteration. The correct version in Arabic script is as follows: احفظ صوتك ان نطقت بليل/والتفت في النهار قبل المقال//واحرص الحياط ان يكون وراءه/سارق السمع وعين المقال .

[60] Gavison, *'Omer ha-shikhehah*, 134 b. See also 130 c. The original Judeo-Arabic and the Hebrew translation do not match exactly.

[61] This is precisely what happens with a long poem by Al-Ghazzālī, whose original is not quoted. See Gavison, *'Omer ha-shikhehah*, 135 a.

The Gavisons go so far as to assert that some texts within the Hebrew Bible, sections of the Book of Proverbs included, had been translated from foreign languages into Hebrew. When commenting on Proverbs 26:28, Jacob Gavison, who gives an example from the Book of Job, adds:

> The works of the Sages arguing that Moses translated the Book of Job from a [foreign] language to our holy language are well known. In my view, the source language from which it was translated was the language of Paras, that is Turkish,[62] as in this language the subject comes before the attribute, and the object precedes the verb, and the Book of Job is mostly written in such a manner.[63]

Likewise, commenting on the term *he'etiqu* (translated or copied) in Proverbs 25:1 ("These too are proverbs of Solomon, which the men of King Hezekiah of Judah translated/copied") the author remarks:

> This *ha'ataqa* (translation/copy)[64] might refer to an oral account which they [the men of King Hezekiah] had translated from a foreign language into our sacred language as Solomon agreed with some sages from among the gentiles and with their kings, such as Pythagoras the Egyptian, in whose books the forefathers claimed they had read that, having lived in the times of King Solomon, he had gone to meet him, and had seen there [at Solomon's court] the Levites singing, and had taken from them the science of music

---

[62] This comparison with Turkish only makes sense if we remember that Algeria became an autonomous province of the Ottoman Empire in 1544.

[63] Gavison, *'Omer ha-shikhehah*, 95 c. For the traditional attribution of the book of Job to Moses see TB, *Baba Batra*, 14b. From the time of Abraham ibn Ezra it was also held that Job had been translated from another language, perhaps Arabic or Aramaic. See Abraham ibn Ezra on Job 2:11.

[64] Differences in interpretation are prompted by the uncertain meaning of the root '-t-q, which is here interpreted as "translate" (from one language to another) as opposed to "writing or collecting" as in other sources. For this second interpretation, see, for example, the words of the fifteenth-century Castilian exegete Moses Arragel: "E es la razón que todos los ensienplos fasta aquí dichos eran dichos de Salamon, letra por letra; pero estos que de aquí adelante fueron escriptos, trasladados de otros libros que fizo Salamon e tomados e cogidos dellos por ellos; por ende dixo que los trasladaron e coligieron de sus mismos libros de Salamon, e por ende dixo que trasladaron que, otra mente, pues que la lengua toda era vna e avn a sazon non era canbiada la lengua ebrayca por ninguna otra lengua, non auia por que decir trasladaron." See *Biblia: Antiguo Testamento, traducida del hebreo al castellano por Rabi Mose Arragel, publicada por el Duque de Berwick y de Alba* (N.p.: Imprenta Artística, 1929), 793.

and had seen marvellous things.[65] All this is mentioned in question number eighty three of *Derekh ha-sekhel* ("Way of Wisdom"), a book written by Abraham Gavison the Elder, of blessed memory, on the Queen of Sheba and Solomon's answers to her riddles, as it is said that Solomon used to speak with her in her language, and not in Hebrew. This was also what happened with Lemuel and Agur ben Yaqeh and Iti'el, as this is the only time their names are mentioned among the sages of Solomon, and among their kings, neither in the Book of Kings nor in Chronicles.[66] According to the plain meaning of the text, these were pagan sages who came to Solomon to listen to him and learn from his wisdom. Solomon necessarily had to speak to them in a language they could understand. This is the reason why these verses [in Proverbs] are more profound than the previous ones, which were not translated [from a foreign language] [...]. According to the exegetes, however, it would not have been an oral account translated from a given language into another, as the term *ha'ataqah* would mean *ketivah* (writing). They [the men of Hezekiah] must have gathered these Proverbs so that they were together, as there is only one author.[67]

When commenting on Proverbs 30:1, he further argues:

It means that all these [proverbs] were also translated by the men of Hezekiah, King of Judah, as had they not been translated, they would have been included with those Proverbs which are not translations. Were these words interpreted according to the plain meaning of the text, these names would not be found mentioned either in the Book of Kings or in Chronicles, so that it is likely that these were *ḥakhame ha-ummot* ("Gentile sages") who came to study under him [Solomon]. And these proverbs must have also been translated by the men of Hezekiah from a foreign language into ours.

The fact that Solomon mastered several languages, that the Hebrew Bible and more precisely the Book of Proverbs included texts translated from other languages, and that the most distinguished

---

[65] On Pythagoras in Renaissance Jewish sources, see the sources quoted in Moshe Idel, "Johannes Reuchlin: Kabbalah, Pythagorean Philosophy and Modern Scholarship," *Studia Judaica* 16 (2008): 31, no. 6.

[66] Rabbinic sources (TB, *Abot*, Chapter 5) maintain that six names were given to Solomon: Jedidiah, Qohelet, Agur, Yaqeh, Iti'el, and Lemuel. The Gavisons are drawing from another tradition, which dates back at least as far as Sa'adia Gaon, according to which Agur and Lemuel are the names of other authors whose sayings were appended to the Book of Proverbs.

[67] The idea that the Saying of Agur had been translated from another language into Hebrew was known but had not been generally accepted. See above, note 64.

Jewish scholars in Sepharad (meaning al-Andalus) and Provence had originally written their books in Arabic before other celebrated scholars had translated them into Hebrew all legitimize the Gavisons' decision to include in their work poems and proverbs in Arabic, either as individual samples or in short collections, and to translate them into Hebrew. Theirs, they implicitly argue, is a practice sanctioned by the Bible, and commonly known to those they consider classical authors within the Jewish classical pantheon. They were doing nothing, the Gavisons contend, but continuing a long-established legitimate tradition.

Their valorisation of Arabic, their advocacy of secular studies, and their vindication of poetry are all elements that help to fashion a cultural model replicating that upheld by tenth- to twelfth-century Andalusi Jewish intellectuals, and by Jewish writers wishing to transfer the Andalusi model to the Christian kingdoms. The Gavisons duplicate the Andalusi model at a surprisingly late date in a North African setting. In the Gavisons' intellectual self-portrayal and in their sense of belonging to the Andalusi tradition we hear an echo of the arguments employed centuries earlier by several generations of Andalusi intellectuals, those that Ross Brann has called "Arabized Jews"[68]—grammarians such as Dunash ibn Labrat and Yonah ibn Janah, who advocated comparative linguistics; poets such as Samuel ha-Nagid and Moses ibn Ezra, who described themselves as prophets and were conversant with Arabic poetics; and a long list of exegetes, thinkers and scientists who felt compelled to prove that their scientific training did not conflict with or undermine their religious commitment.[69] It is here, in this explicit identification with the Andalusi model (a model they generally describe as Sephardic) where the family's past comes to the fore, and al-Andalus, fifteenth-century Granada, and sixteenth- and seventeenth-century Algeria become part of one and the same ethos in the minds of the Gavisons.

---

[68] Ross Brann, "The Arabized Jews," in *The Cambridge History of Arabic Literature: Al Andalus*, ed. María Rosa Menocal, Raymond P. Scheindlin and Michael Sells (Cambridge: Cambridge University Press, 2000), 435–54.

[69] Similarly, in his commentary on the Song of Songs (see above, note 8) Joseph ben Judah ibn 'Aknīn had also defended himself against those who attacked him for bringing up examples from the Arabic language and poetic stanzas in his work.

In saying this I do not intend to claim any sort of continuity between tenth- and twelfth-century al-Andalus and sixteenth- and seventeenth-century Algeria. On the contrary, I believe we should proceed with great caution in this respect, particularly as our knowledge of the connection between Jewish culture in the early Andalusi period and fifteenth-century Granada is extremely deficient and our information on fifteenth-century Jewish culture in Naṣrid Granada remarkably scant. In this regard, the chains of tradition and intellectual genealogies the Gavisons associate themselves with should not be seen as confirmation of continuity with tradition but actually as reflecting the construction of continuities and the existence of breaks in the collective consciousness of sixteenth- and seventeenth-century North African Jews. In the same vein, I am not trying to draw a dividing line between Jewish culture in Arabic and Romance speaking lands. In spite of what has sometimes been argued, poetry was valued and continued to be praised in the Iberian Christian kingdoms. Moreover, late medieval Jewish poets from the Iberian Christian kingdoms such as Meshullam de Piera and Solomon Bonafed had turned the Andalusi Jewish poets into classics within the Jewish tradition and had posited themselves as their direct and true inheritors.[70] The fact that the Gavisons do not quote Jewish poets from the Iberian Christian kingdoms does not necessarily mean that such poets were unknown to them.[71] The culture of the Iberian Jews, however, was not Arabic but Hebrew, and the model the Gavisons look for is a model both in Arabic and in Hebrew.

---

[70] The continuity between Hebrew poetry produced in al-Andalus and the Iberian Christian kingdom is equally debatable. Arturo Prats has recently argued that the claim made by fifteenth-century Aragonese poets, such as Bonafed, to be the legitimate, direct inheritors of the Andalusi classical poets is to be understood in the context of contemporary Christian poets' search for the classics. See Prats, "The Representation of *Conversos*."

[71] In an article on the topic of eloquence in fifteenth-century Spain, Eleazar Gutwirth points out the links between Granada and the Christian northern kingdoms, highlighting the fact that Saʿadia ibn Danan copied for himself books written in Christian Spain. Likewise, Gutwirth refers to fifteenth-century editors who printed their books in the Christian kingdoms and sent them to Granada. See his "Italy or Spain? The Theme of Jewish Eloquence in *Shevet Yehudah*," in *Daniel Carpi Jubilee Volume: A Collection of Studies in the History of the Jewish People Presented to Daniel Carpi upon his 70th Birthday by his Colleagues and Students*, ed. Daniel Carpi, et al. (Tel Aviv: Tel Aviv University: Lester and Sally Entin Faculty of Humanities / The Hayim Rosenberg School of Jewish Studies, 1996), 61.

Arabic poetry was not unknown among Andalusi Jewish poets, and yet it is common knowledge that they had a clear preference for Hebrew as the language of poetry.[72] The Gavisons highlight one of these precedents, namely those poems exchanged between Abraham Bedersi and Todros Halevi Abulafia, to justify a more generalized, systematic citation of Arabic poems (either alongside or without their Hebrew translation). One has to wonder whether their emphasis on the sweetness of the original language, their choice of Arabic as a valid language for poetry, and their appreciation of popular culture might be showing, rather than a reminiscence of Andalusi poetics, a certain appreciation for the sweetness of original languages as well as the increasing esteem given to rhetoric, the importance accorded to vernacular languages[73] and an interest in popular culture—all of which were ideas that came to the fore in the early fifteenth century as ideals of humanism and the burgeoning Renaissance.

Various passages throughout the commentary reveal the Gavisons' struggle not only to avoid the tensions between the exegetical tradition they associate with the rabbis of Castile, on the one hand, and the model based on bilingualism, poetry and secular matters which represents al-Andalus, on the other, but to claim superiority in both. Interestingly, when singling out a cultural Other, they point to an Ashkenazi—Rashi—whose opinions they respected and often subscribed to, but whom they represented as the epitome of the Jewish intellectual born in "the lands of the idolaters."

Competing Groups in Seventeenth-Century Algeria

The Gavison scholarly genealogy is thoroughly consistent with the foundational story of the Gavison family embedded in their Biblical commentary, and it is likely that both narratives are written for the same purpose. The Gavisons' origin as a family, as well as the story of the two surviving brothers singled out for their wisdom and piety and

---

[72] On Jewish poets writing Arabic poems, see Ross Brann, "Reflexiones sobre el árabe y la identidad literaria de los judíos de al-Andalus," in *Judíos y musulmanes en al-Andalus y el Magreb: Contactos intelectuales*, ed. Maribel Fierro (Madrid: Casa de Velázquez, 2002), 13–28.

[73] The Gavisons not only vindicate Arabic but use the Algerian dialect for comparative linguistics.

described as inheritors to a highly exclusive Andalusi Jewish lineage in their journey from Granada to North Africa, acquires collective overtones and a clearly symbolic dimension. Their story is conceived of as two rites of passage, namely from Seville to Granada in 1391 and then from Granada to North Africa in 1492, and is presented in terms that are meaningful to deportees from other locations within the Iberian Peninsula. The narrative is not only a story of suffering and redemption, of resistance, heroism and survival, but also one of transmission and legitimacy. Concurrently, the fact that they embrace the Andalusi Jewish model as something belonging exclusively to them is also intended to enable them to claim their supremacy in the context of sixteenth- and seventeenth-century Algeria in the face of a competing and reputable cultural tradition—that of the rabbis from Castile. An emphasis on maintaining both languages—Arabic and Hebrew—and claims of mastery in translation entitled the Gavisons to regard themselves as the rightful transmitters of Arabic culture (both Islamic and Jewish) in the face of a competing group which vied for cultural supremacy but originated from Romance-speaking lands and retained Spanish as a language of prestige and communication in their newly acquired land.

Works Cited:

Abrahams, Israel. *Hebrew Ethical Wills.* Philadelphia: The Jewish Publication of America, 1954.

Alfonso, Esperanza. *Islamic Culture through Jewish Eyes: Al-Andalus from the 10th to the 12th Century.* London: Routledge, 2008.

Angel, Marc. "Gavison Family." *Encyclopedia of Jews in the Islamic World*, edited by Norman A. Stillman. Leiden: Brill Online. http://brillonline.nl/subscriber/entry?entry=ejiw_COM-0008360. Accessed 12 May, 2010.

Arragel, Moses. *Biblia: Antiguo Testamento, traducida del hebreo al castellano por Rabi Mose Arragel, publicada por el Duque de Berwick y de Alba.* N.p.: Imprenta Artística, 1929.

Benayahu, Me'ir. "The Sermons of R. Yosef b. Meir Garson as a Source for the History of the Expulsion from Spain and the Sephardi Diaspora." *Michael* 7 (1981): 42–205. (Hebrew)

Bar-Asher, Shalom. "La poésie liturgique juive nord-africaine comme source historique." In *Présence juive au Maghrib: Hommage à Haïm Zafrani*, edited by Nicole S. Serfaty and Joseph Tedghi, 401–10. Saint Denis: Editions Bouchene, 2004.

Berlin, Adele. *Biblical Poetry through Medieval Jewish Eyes.* Bloomington, IN: Indiana University Press, 1991.

Brann, Ross. *The Compunctious Poet: Cultural Ambiguity and Hebrew Poetry in Muslim Spain.* Baltimore: Johns Hopkins University Press, 1991.

------. "The Arabized Jews." In *The Cambridge History of Arabic Literature: Al Andalus*, edited by María Rosa Menocal, Raymond P. Scheindlin and Michael Sells, 435– 54. Cambridge: Cambridge University Press, 2000.

------. "Reflexiones sobre el árabe y la identidad literaria de los judíos de al-Andalus." In *Judíos y musulmanes en al-Andalus y el Magreb: Contactos intelectuales*, edited by Maribel Fierro, 13–28. Madrid: Casa de Velázquez, 2002.

Bregoli, Francesca. "Hebrew Printing and Communication Networks between Livorno and North Africa, 1740–1789." *Report of the*

Oxford Centre for Hebrew and Jewish Studies: Academic Year 2007–2008, 51–60. Oxford: The Centre, 2008.

Bregman, Dvora. "Their Rose in Our Garden: Romance Elements in Hebrew Italian Poetry." In *Renewing the Past, Reconfiguring Jewish Culture: From Al-Andalus to the Haskalah*, edited by Ross Brann and Adam Sutcliffe, 50-58. Philadelphia: University of Pennsylvania Press, 2004.

Castaño, Javier. "Traumas individuales en un mundo trastornado: El éxodo de R. Yĕhudah Yaʻaqob Ḥayyaṭ (1492–1496)." In *Movimientos migratorios y expulsiones en la diáspora occidental: Terceros encuentros judaicos de Tudela; 14–17 de julio de 1998*, edited by Fermín Miranda García, 55–67. Pamplona: Universidad Pública de Navarra, 2000.

Cohen, Moshe. "Saʻadya Ibn Danan: Un linguiste et poète contemporain de l'expulsion d'Espagne." In *Présence juive au Maghrib: Hommage à Haïm Zafrani*, edited by S. Serfaty and Joseph Tedghi, 313–26. Saint Denis: Bouchère, 2004.

Edelmann, Hirsch, ed. *Divre ḥefes: "Acceptable Words" or Extracts from Various Unprinted Works of Eminent Hebrew Authors.* London: A. P. Shaw, 1953.

Fenton, Paul B. "L'arabe dans Rachi et Rachi en arabe." In *Héritages de Rachi*, 2nd ed., edited by René-Samuel Sirat, 261-70. Paris: Éditions de l'éclat, 2008.

Fraenkel, Carlos, ed. *Traditions of Maimonideanism.* Leiden: Brill, 2009.

Gavison, Abraham and Jacob Gavison. *ʻOmer ha-shikheḥah.* Livorno: Be-bet u-vi-defus Abraham b. Refaʼel Mildolah, 1748. Reprinted with introduction and notes by René S. Sirat. Jerusalem: Hotsaʻat Kedem, 1973.

Gross, Abraham. "A Sketch of the History of Yeshivot in Castile in the Fifteenth Century." *Peʻamim* 31 (1987): 3–20. (Hebrew)

Gutwirth, Eleazar. "Écrire l'expulsion." In *1492: L'expulsion des juifs d'Espagne*, edited by R. Goetschel, 25-35. Paris: Maisonneuve et Larose, 1995.

------. "Italy or Spain?: The Theme of Jewish Eloquence in *Shevet Yehudah*." In *Daniel Carpi Jubilee Volume: A Collection of Studies in the History of the Jewish People Presented to Daniel Carpi upon his 70th Birthday by his Colleagues and Students*, edited by Daniel Carpi et al., 35–67. Tel Aviv University: Lester and Sally Entin Faculty of Humanities / The Hayim Rosenberg School of Jewish Studies, 1996.

Hacker, Joseph. "On the Intellectual Character and Self-Perception of Spanish Jewry in the Late Fifteenth Century." *Sefunot*, n.s., 2 (1983): 21–95. (Hebrew)

------. "The Intellectual Activity of the Jews of the Ottoman Empire during the Sixteenth and Seventeenth Centuries." In *Jewish Thought in the Seventeenth Century*, edited by Isadore Twersky and Bernard Septimus, 95–135. Cambridge, MA: Harvard University Press, 1987.

------. "Pride and Depression: Polarity of the Spiritual and Social Experience of the Iberian Exiles in the Ottoman Empire." In *Culture and Society in Medieval Jewry: Studies Dedicated to the Memory of Haim Hillel Ben Sasson*, edited by Menahem Ben Sassoon, Robert Bonfil and Joseph R. Hacker, 2–68. Jerusalem: The Historical Society of Israel / The Zalman Shazar Center, 1989. (Hebrew)

Halkin, Abraham S. "Ibn 'Aknīn's Commentary on the Song of Songs." In *Alexander Marx Jubilee Volume on the Occasion of His Seventieth Birthday*, edited by Saul Lieberman, 389–424. New York: The Jewish Theological Seminary of America, 1950.

------. "The Medieval Jewish Attitude Toward Hebrew." In *Biblical and Other Studies*, edited by Alexander Altmann, 233–48. Cambridge, MA: Harvard University Press, 1963.

Ḥazan, Ephraim. *La Poesie hébraïque en Afrique du Nord.* Jerusalem: Magnes / Hebrew University, 1985.

------. "From Spain to its Diaspora: The Poetic Heritage in its Transformations." *Pe'amim* 26 (1986): 46–51.

------. "From Spain to North-Africa: Hebrew Poetry in Transition." *Pe'amim* 59 (1994): 52–64. (Hebrew)

Idel, Moshe. "Johannes Reuchlin: Kabbalah, Pythagorean Philosophy and Modern Scholarship." *Studia Judaica* 16 (2008): 30–55.

Kellner, Menachem. "Maimonides' Disputed Legacy." In *Traditions of Maimonideanism*, edited by Carlos Fraenkel, 245–76. Leiden: Brill, 2009.

Kozodoy, Maud. "No Perpetual Enemies: Maimonideanism at the Beginning of the Fifteenth Century." In *The Cultures of Maimonideanism: New Approaches to the History of Jewish Thought*, edited by James T. Robinson, 149–70. Leiden: Brill, 2009.

Lawee, Eric. "Maimonides in the Eastern Mediterranean: The Case of Rashi's Resisting Readers." In *Maimonides after 800 Years: Essays on Maimonides and His Influence*, edited by Jay M. Harris, 183–206. Cambridge, MA: Harvard University Press, 2007.

Lesley, Arthur M. "A Survey of Medieval Hebrew Rhetoric." In *Approaches to Judaism in Medieval Times*, edited by David R. Blumenthal, 107–33. Chico, CA: Scholars Press, 1984-85.

Lida de Malkiel, María Rosa. "La métrica de la Biblia: Un motivo de Josefo y Jerónimo en la Métrica de la Biblia." In *Estudios hispánicos: Homenaje a Archer M. Huntington*, 335–59. Wellesley, MA, 1952.

Maimonides, Moses. *Letters and Essays of Moses Maimonides.* A critical edition of the Hebrew and Arabic letters (including response on beliefs and attitudes) based on all extant manuscripts, translated and annotated, with introductions and cross-references by Isaac Shailat. 2 vols. Jerusalem: Maliyot Press of Yeshivat Birkat Mose Maaleh Adumim, 1987.

Neubauer, Adolf. *Mediaeval Jewish Chronicles and Chronological Dates.* Amsterdam: Philo, 1970.

Oron, Michal. "Autobiographical Elements in the Writings of Kabbalists from the Generation of the Expulsion." *Mediterranean Historical Review* 6 (1991): 102–11.

Pagis, Dan. "The Poet as Prophet in Medieval Hebrew Literature." In *Poetry and Prophecy: The Beginnings of a Literary Tradition*, edited by James L. Kugel, 140–50. Ithaca: Cornell University Press, 1990.

Prats, Arturo. "The Representation of *Conversos* in Bonafed's *Dīwān*." In *Medieval Jewish Identities: Al-Andalus and Beyond*, edited by Carmen Caballero-Navas and Esperanza Alfonso. New York: Palgrave Macmillan, forthcoming.

Roth, Cecil. "Hebrew Elegy on Martyrs of Toledo." *Jewish Quarterly Review* 39 (1948–1949): 123–50.

Rozen, Minna. "Collective Memories and Group Boundaries: The Judeo-Spanish Diaspora between the Lands of Christendom and the World of Islam." In *Michael: On the History of Jews in the Diaspora*. Vol. 14, edited by Minna Rozen et al., 35–52. Tel Aviv: Diaspora Research Institute, 1997.

Sáenz-Badillos, Ángel. "Šelomoh Bonafed, último gran poeta de Sefarad, y la poesía hebrea." *eHumanista* 2 (2002): 1–22.

------. "Shem Tob ibn Falaquera sobre la lengua hebrea." *Anuario de Estudios Mirandeses* 25 (2005): 161–79.

------. "Late Medieval Jewish Writers on Maimonides." In Fraenkel, *Traditions of Maimonideanism*, edited by Carlos Fraenkel, 223–44. Leiden: Brill, 2009.

------. "Defining Borders: Early Fifteenth-Century Jews from the Crown of Aragon in Search of their Identity." In *Medieval Jewish Identities: Al-Andalus and Beyond*, edited by Carmen Caballero-Navas and Esperanza Alfonso. New York: Palgrave Macmillan, forthcoming.

Salvatierra Ossorio, Aurora. "From Logic to Ethics: A Redefinition of Poetry in the Thirteenth Century." In "Al-Andalus and its Legacies," edited by Esperanza Alfonso and Ross Brann. Special issue, *Comparative Literature Studies* 45, no. 2 (2008): 165–81.

Scheindlin, Raymond P. "Secular Poetry in Fifteenth-Century Spain." In *Crisis and Creativity in the Sephardic World 1391–1648*, edited by Benjamin R. Gampel, 25–37. New York: Columbia University Press, 1997.

Schirmann, Hayyim. *Ha-shirah ha-'ivrit bi-Sefarad u-we-Provence*. 2 vols. Jerusalem: Bialik; Tel Aviv: Dvir, 1954–60.

------. "Gavison (or Gavishon)." *Encyclopedia Judaica* 7, 397.

Sirat, René Samuel. *'Omer hašikḥāh: Commentaire sur le livre des Proverbes d'Abraham Gabišon*, Mémoire de diplôme d'études supérieures. Strasbourg, 1964.

------. *Abraham and Jacob Gabišon: Exégètes et linguistes, étude philosophique et linguistique d' 'O.Š.* Thèse de doctorat de recherches. Strasbourg, 1965.

------. "La comparaison linguistique entre l'hébreu, l'araméen et l'arabe chez les auteurs du *'Omer hašikḥāh ('O. Š.)." Revue des études juives* 124 (1965): 397–407.

------. "'Omer ha-šiḵha et la famille Gabišon." *WCJS* 4, no. 2 (1968): 65–67.

------. "La vie des juifs en Alger au XVIe siècle d'aprés *'Omer hašikḥāh*: Commentaire sur les proverbes d'A. Gabišon." In *Mélanges André Neher*, 317–29. Paris: Maisonneuve, 1975.

Tobi, Yosef. "Hebrew Poetry in the East after the Spanish Expulsion." *Peʿamim* 26 (1986): 29–44. (Hebrew)

------. *Proximity and Distance: Medieval Hebrew Poetry and Arabic Poetry.* Leiden: Brill, 2004.

------. "Spanish Hebrew Poetry among the Sixteenth-Century Sephardic Jews in Morocco." In "From the Treasures of Spain: Studies on Hebrew Poetry in Spain and its Influence," edited by Judith Dishon and Shmuel Refael. Special issue, *Criticism and Interpretation: Journal for Interdisciplinary Studies in Literature and Culture* 39 (2006): 191–204. (Hebrew)

Contributors

Esperanza Alfonso (PhD 1998 in Hebrew Studies, Universidad Complutense, Madrid) is a research fellow at the CCHS-CSIC, in Madrid. She is the author of *Islamic Culture through Jewish Eyes: Al-Andalus from the Tenth to the Twelfth Century* (London: Routledge, 2008), has edited "Patronage in Islamic Societies," special issue, *Al-Qantara* 29.2 (2008), and co-edited (with Ross Brann) "Al-Andalus and Its Legacies," special issue, *Comparative Literature Studies* 45.2 (2008), and (with Carmen-Caballero-Navas) *Late Medieval Jewish Identities: Iberia and Beyond* (New York: Palgrave, 2010). She is currently working on the project: "INTELEG: Intellectual and Material Legacies of Late Medieval Sephardic Judaism; An Interdisciplinary Approach" funded by the ERC.

Yom Tov Assis is professor of medieval history at the Hebrew University of Jerusalem, specializing in the history of the Jews in Iberia, Provence and in the Sephardi Diaspora. He has published many books and numerous articles in a variety of languages, and is the editor of *Hispania Judaica Bulletin*. He is the head of two research centers at the Hebrew University, and the Academic Chair of the Ben Zvi Institute for the Study of Oriental Jewry. Professor Assis has also served as visiting professor at a number of universities, including University College, London, the Sorbonne, Paris, UCLA, Yale, Case Western Reserve University, the University of Sydney, and Shandong University in China.

Ram Ben-Shalom is a senior lecturer in the Department of History, Philosophy, and Judaic Studies at the Open University of Israel, and a specialist in the history of Jewish-Christian relations and the history of the Jews in Spain and Southern France during the Middle Ages. His book *Facing Christian Culture. Historical Consciousness and Images of the Past among the Jews of Spain and Southern France during the Middle Ages* (Hebrew), (*Medieval Jews and the Christian*

Past: Jewish Jewish Historical Consciousness in Spain and Southern France, Littman Library, 2013) won the Samuel Toledano prize in 2007.

Jonathan P. Decter is an associate professor and the Edmond J. Safra Professor of Sephardic Studies at Brandeis University. His first book, *Iberian Jewish Literature: Between al-Andalus and Christian Europe* (Indiana University Press), was awarded the Salo W. Baron Prize for best first book in Jewish Studies, 2007. His research interests include Jews in the Islamic world, Iberian Jewry, medieval Hebrew, and Judeo-Arabic literature.

Jane Gerber is professor of history, director of the Institute for Sephardic Studies, and interim Jack F. Skirball Director of the Center for Jewish Studies at the Graduate Center of the City University of New York. She is author and editor of five books, including *The Jews of Spain*, which won the National Jewish Book Award in Sephardic Studies in 1993. She is the recipient of numerous honors and awards including for excellence in teaching. She is past president of the Association for Jewish Studies and serves on the editorial board of the Cambridge History of Judaism series, Cambridge University Press. Her forthcoming books are *The Jewish Diaspora in the Caribbean* and *Cities of Splendor in the Shaping of Sephardic Jewry* (Littman Library).

Mariano Gómez Aranda is a tenured scientist at the CCHS (CSIC, Madrid). His research focuses on medieval Jewish exegesis and science with particular attention to the connection between Jews and Arabs in the Iberian Peninsula. His most recent articles include "The Connection Between Muslims and Jews in the Field of Science in the Middle Ages," *Encounters of the Children of Abraham from Ancient to Modern Times* (Leiden: Brill, 2010: 231-251) and "Jacob's Blessings in Medieval Jewish Exegesis," *Rewritten Biblical Figures* (Turku, Finland-Indiana, USA: Åbo Akademi University-

Einsebrauns, 2010: 235-258). He has also published *Dos comentarios de Abraham ibn Ezra al libro de Ester* (Madrid: CSIC, 2007) and *El comentario de Abraham ibn Ezra al libro de Job* (Madrid: CSIC, 2004). He is a professor of cultural studies at New York University in Madrid and at Middlebury College in Vermont, USA.

Maud Kozodoy is Mellon Post-Doctoral Fellow in Medieval Jewish History at Brown University. Her research focuses on the intersection between science and literature, Jewish-Christian polemics, and mnemonics. Her "Medieval Hebrew Medical Poetry: Uses and Contexts" is forthcoming in *Aleph: Historical Studies in Science and Judaism*. Her current project is a monograph on the late-fourteenth-century *converso* Profiat Duran.

Hartley Lachter is an associate professor of Religion Studies and director of Jewish Studies at Muhlenberg College in Allentown, PA. His recent work includes "Kabbalah, Philosophy, and the Jewish Christian Debate: Reconsidering the Early Works of Joseph Gikatilla," *Journal for Jewish Thought and Philosophy*, 16:1 (2008), and "Spreading Secrets: Kabbalah and Esotericism in Isaac ibn Sahula's Meshal ha-Kadmoni," *JQR*, 100:1 (2010). He is currently working on a book manuscript entitled *Kabbalistic Revolution: Re-imagining Judaism in Medieval Spain*.

Eric Lawee is a professor in the Department of Humanities at York University in Toronto, where he mainly teaches Jewish studies. His book *Isaac Abarbanel's Stance Toward Tradition: Defense, Dissent, and Dialogue* won a Canadian Jewish Book Award in Biblical and Rabbinic Scholarship and was a Finalist for a National Jewish Book Award (USA) in the area of Scholarship.

Renée Levine Melammed is a professor of Jewish history at the Schechter Institute in Jerusalem. She has published numerous articles dealing with women in Jewish history as well as the conversos of Spain and the Inquisition. Her major publications include *Heretics or Daughters of Israel: The Crypto-Jewish Women of Castile* (Oxford University Press, 1999); *A Question of Identity: Iberian Conversos in Historical Perspective* (Oxford University Press, 2004); and *An Ode to Salonika: The Ladino Verses of Bouena Sarfatty* (Indiana University Press, 2012).

Vivian B. Mann is director of the Masters Program in Jewish Art at the Graduate School of the Jewish Theological Seminary, and curator emerita of the Jewish Museum, New York. She is the author of numerous articles on medieval art and Jewish art. Her latest book, *Uneasy Communion: Jews, Christians and Altarpieces in Medieval Spain*, was published in 2010. In 2009, she was elected to the American Academy of Jewish Research, the oldest professional organization of Judaica scholars in North America, and in 2010 she was honored by her colleagues with a *Festschrift, Images: A Journal of Jewish Art and Visual Culture*.

Gregory B. Milton specializes in the social and economic history of the Middle Ages, and has writen about the market and community in the Catalan town of Santa Coloma de Queralt. Dr. Milton completed his Ph.D. at the University of California, Los Angeles, in 2004 and has taught at the U.S. Naval Academy, Marquette University, and the University of South Florida, Tampa, where he is currently an assistant professor of history.

Jonathan Ray is the Samuel Eig Associate Professor of Jewish Studies in the Theology Department at Georgetown University. He is author of *The Sephardic Frontier: The Reconquista and the Jewish Community in Medieval Iberia* (Cornell University Press), which was awarded the John Nicholas Brown Prize from the Medieval Academy in 2010. He is currently completing a book on the formation of the Sephardic Diaspora.

Index

Series JEWS IN SPACE AND TIME

NEW DIRECTIONS IN ANGLO-JEWISH HISTORY

Edited by Geoffrey ALDERMAN

July 2010
208 pages
Cloth 978-1-936235-13-1
$65.00 / £44.25
Electronic 978-1-61811-055-8
$45.50/ £27.75

The past two decades have witnessed a remarkable renaissance in the academic study of the history of the Jews in Great Britain and of their impact upon British history. In this volume, Professor Geoff rey Alderman presents essays that refl ect the richness of this renaissance, penned by a new generation of British and American scholars who are uninhibited by the considerations of communal image and public obligation that once exercised a powerful infl uence on Anglo-Jewish historiography. History does not have lessons, says Alderman, but it may provide signposts, and he adds that in the case of the essays presented here, "I believe there is one signpost that we would all do well to ponder: in multicultural Britain hard-working immigrants may be welcome, or they may be feared—or both. They are destined to remain not quite British, and, for better or worse, they are destined to bequeath this otherness to the generations that follow them."

Geoffrey Alderman studied history at the University of Oxford, where he completed his DPhil in 1969. Currently Michael Gross Professor of Politics & Contemporary History at the University of Buckingham, he is the acknowledged authority on the history of the Jews in modern Britain. In 2006 Oxford conferred on him the degree of Doctor of Letters in respect of his work in this field.

"This excellent collection is the advance guard of the second wave of scholarly research into the Jewish experience in Britain since the predominance of gifted amateurs ended in the 1980s. It is multi-disciplinary, wide-ranging, conceptually sophisticated, full of irony and frequently witty. There are no apologetics here. With these mainly young scholars, who hail from a variety of backgrounds, British Jewish history has reached maturity. The results are fascinating: sometimes shocking, but always illuminating."
—David Cesarani, research professor in history at Royal Holloway, University of London

"All the texts [in this book] carry insights which remain relevant in an age of globalization, when migration continues apace and other immigrants and refugees continue to confront that mixture of "dream and nightmare" such uprooting invariably entails."
— Colin Holmes, Emeritus Professor of History, University of Sheffield

GERMAN JEWRY BETWEEN HOPE AND DESPAIR, 1871-1933

Edited by Nils ROEMER

June 2012
400 pages
Cloth 978-1-934843-87-1
$59.00 / £40.25
Electronic 978-1-61811-049-7
$59.00 / £40.25

German Jewry between Hope and Despair,1871-1933, provides important interpretations of this tumultuous and conflict-ridden period and invites readers to partake in the ongoing debate over modern Jewish identities and cultures. Marked at the outset by emancipation and the emergence of modern anti-Semitism, the period witnessed a profound transformation of Jewish social, political, and religious life culminating in the renaissance of Jewish cultures on the eve of the Holocaust. This textbook unites studies that inform our understanding of this historical epoch to this day as well as significant historical revisions. Amongst the many contributions are texts by Michael Brenner, Willi Goetschel, Marion Kaplan, George L. Mosse, Peter Pulzer, and Till van Rahden.

Nils Roemer (PhD Columbia University) is an associate professor of Jewish studies at the University of Texas at Dallas. His recent publications include *"The City of Worms in Modern Jewish Traveling Cultures of Remembrance"* (2005) and *Jewish Scholarship and Culture in the Nineteenth Century Germany* (2005).

CANADA'S JEWS

In Time, Space and Spirit

Edited by Ira ROBINSON

August 2012
250 pages
Cloth 978-1-934843-86-4
$70.00 / £47.50
Electronic 978-1-61811-027-5
$70.00 / £47.50

Canada is home to one of the world's largest and most culturally creative Jewish communities, one of the few in the Diaspora that continues to grow demographically. With its ability to mirror trends found in Jewish communities elsewhere (particularly the United States) while simultaneously functioning as a distinct society, Canada's Jewish community holds great interest for scholars, exercising a measurable influence on the culture and politics of World Jewry. Consisting of a series of essays written by experts in their respective fields, Canada's Jews is a topical encyclopedia, covering a wide variety of topics, from history and religion to the intellectual and cultural contributions of Canada's Jews.

Ira Robinson (PhD Harvard University) is professor of Judaic studies in the Department of Religion of Concordia University, Montreal, Quebec, and serves as the president of the Canadian Society for Jewish Studies. His recent books include: *Rabbis and Their Community: Studies in the Eastern European Orthodox Rabbinate in Montreal, 1896-1930* (2007) and *Translating a Tradition: Studies in American Jewish History* (2009).